Anniversaries
AND Holidays

FIFTH EDITION

Anniversaries AND Holidays

BERNARD TRAWICKY

AMERICAN LIBRARY ASSOCIATION
Chicago and London
2000

While extensive effort has gone into ensuring the reliability of information appearing in this book, the publisher makes no warranty, express or implied, on the accuracy or reliability of the information, and does not assume and hereby disclaims any liability to any person for any loss or damage caused by errors or omissions in this publication.

Project manager, Cynthia Fostle

Cover by Design Solutions

Text design by Dianne M. Rooney

Composition by the dotted i using Berkeley and Copperplate typefaces and QuarkXpress 4.04 for Macintosh

Printed on 50-pound natural offset, a pH-neutral stock, and bound in Holliston Roxite C by Sheridan Books

The paper used in this publication meets the minimum requirements of American National Standard for Information Sciences—Permanence of Paper for Printed Library Materials, ANSI Z39.48-1992. ∞

Library of Congress Cataloging-in-Publication Data

Trawicky, Bernard.
    Anniversaries and holidays / Bernard Trawicky. — 5th ed.
      p.   cm.
    Rev. and updated ed. of: Anniversaries and holidays / by Ruth W. Gregory. 4th ed. c1983.
    Includes bibliographical references (p.   ) and index.
    ISBN 0-8389-0695-8 (alk.paper)
    1. Holidays. 2. Anniversaries. 3. Fasts and feasts. 4. Holidays—Bibliography. 5. Anniversaries—Bibliography. 6. Fasts and feasts—bibliography. I. Gregory, Ruth W. (Ruth Wilhelme), 1910- Anniversaries and holidays. II. Title.
    GT3930.T73   2000
    394.26—dc21   99-056166

Printed in the United States of America.

04   03   02   01   00   5   4   3   2   1

CONTENTS

PREFACE

This volume of *Anniversaries and Holidays* is the fifth edition of a book of days originated in 1928 by the late Mary Emogene Hazeltine, former director of the Library School of the University of Wisconsin. The second edition, again by Hazeltine, was published in 1944. Ruth W. Gregory, also a librarian, compiled the third edition in 1975, and the fourth edition in 1983. The fourth edition is superb, and much of it has been retained in the fifth edition.

It is both inspiring and humbling to realize that *Anniversaries and Holidays* was begun a century ago, by librarians in my own city of Madison. My predecessors were engaged in the same enterprise as I, were refreshed by the same views of lakes, trees, and houses, and were absorbed in similar fascinations with celebration, commemoration, and time. I'm sure they were good company and fascinating conversationalists.

Like its predecessors, the fifth edition provides a discriminating and trustworthy collection of the most important holidays, events, and anniversaries in the United States and the world. It also includes more entries, more precise dating of holidays and anniversaries, deeper explanations of the significance of events, and essays on commonly used calendar systems.

The fifth edition aims to satisfy the general reader. It will also be of aid to community and academic reference librarians; those wanting information about particular holidays and anniversaries; teachers wanting information on a region's, country's, or culture's holidays and calendar systems; students with school projects; professors and university students; independent scholars; researchers; international travelers; business professionals; those seeking more celebration or ritual in their lives; and calendar makers. Although most users will be Americans, and observances of the United States still predominate in this edition, the needs of international audiences have been kept in mind.

The fifth edition includes 3,085 entries for specific events: 2,996 in part 1 and 99 in part 2. The fourth edition contained 2,637 entries; 1,945 of these have been retained in the fifth edition, and all but 72 have been refined.

ORGANIZATION OF THE FIFTH EDITION

This edition of *Anniversaries and Holidays* is divided into four parts:

- Calendar of Fixed Days, a day-by-day list of civic and religious events in the Gregorian calendar

- On Calendars, essays on various calendar systems and calendars of non-Gregorian events

- Resources Related to Anniversaries and Holidays

- Index

Part 1, the Calendar of Fixed Days, is arranged by the months and days of our Gregorian year. Each day's events are further arranged by the three categories of holy days and feast days, holidays and civic days, and anniversaries and special events days. Not every day of the year includes all three categories.

Entries in the category of holy days and feast days are arranged alphabetically by the name of the event or revered person. Many purely local celebrations containing a religious component are listed as special events days.

The category of holidays and civic days comprises not only national official public holidays, observed by an entire country, but also local official public holidays that are observed by a region or city, and days that are not public holidays but are observed by public institutions or schools (such as a U.S. state's Admission Day). Entries are arranged first by country of observance and then by the name of the holiday. International or multinational holidays precede country-specific holidays.

Anniversaries and special events days are arranged first by the kind of event and then by key word or surname. Anniversaries, birthdays, and death days precede other events.

Within each month are events that do not occur on the same day each year. Most of these *movable* events (such as Labor Day in the United States and Canada, on the first Monday in September) are listed at the end of their respective months and are arranged in the same three categories.

However, some events are based on historical anniversaries and are listed on that date, even though their date of observance varies. (For instance, Martin Luther King Day appears at January 15, Dr. King's actual birthday, even though the official observance is on the third Monday in January.) The abbreviation *ca.* (circa) before the date of an entry indicates that the event is observed at a time near that date.

Christian feast days are in most cases listed at their modern (post–1972) dates for universal or purely Western feasts. Orthodox feast days are usually listed on their Gregorian dates (their dates in the Greek Orthodox Church).

The dates of anniversaries for the period 1582–1922 are in either the Gregorian or Julian calendars, without specifying which. Note that in dating the year of an event, I pretend that in all centuries, and in all places, New Year's Day fell on January 1.

Part 2, On Calendars, includes events based on non-Gregorian calendars. It contains an overview of calendar systems and discussions of the Gregorian calendar and its antecedents, the Christian liturgical calendar, the Jewish calendar, the Islamic calendar, and the Chinese calendar. The discussion of each calendar system is accompanied by a list of principal holidays with their exact dates within the system.

Note that in China, Japan, and South Korea, many traditional events are now also observed in the Gregorian calendar on dates parallel to their lunar calendar dates. Thus, the birthday of Confucius, on the lunar date of the ninth month, twenty-eighth day, is also observed on September 28.

Part 3, Resources Related to Anniversaries and Holidays, is an annotated bibliography of books and other materials pertaining to calendars, anniversaries, and holidays. The fifth edition offers a new and particularly valuable element—Web sites about calendar- and event-related topics. The compilation of resources in part 3 carries out one of the original purposes of *Anniversaries and Holidays* by providing suggestions for reading for enjoyment or for information about a holiday or about people or events associated with a particular day. It includes resources for all age groups, chosen for quality and usefulness. Serious researchers will especially appreciate the author's list of references at the end of part 3.

Anniversaries and Holidays concludes with an index that is the key to the date of a feast, a holiday, an anniversary of the birth or death of a notable person, or a special event in either parts 1 or 2. The prime index entries for holidays are the unique or specific names, such as April Fools' Day or Sun Pageant Day. Feast days are entered alphabetically under the names of saints. People are entered under their commonly known names and events under their popular or official names. Official public holidays are listed by country. The index entries refer readers to dates for events that occur on fixed days and to page numbers for movable days and for topics or events in parts 2 and 3.

I invite anyone wishing more information on holidays, anniversaries, or calendar systems to contact me. I shall surely be engrossed in this subject for many years to come. I also implore anyone detecting errors (typographical, factual, or conceptual) to alert me. Ditto for anyone with suggestions for new entries. There will be an ongoing collection of errors and additions that will be addressed in the sixth edition. This work depends on collegial cooperation.

I may be reached at my home address (2330 Willard Ave., Madison, WI 53704, USA), or through the Returned Peace Corps Volunteers of Wisconsin (P.O. Box 1012, Madison, WI 53701, USA).

Acknowledgments

Composing this book has been an engrossing occupation for more than 6 years, and many people have helped me along the way. It is a pleasure to recall them here.

First, I am grateful to my friends in the Returned Peace Corps Volunteers (RPCV) of Wisconsin, of which I am a member (PC/Nepal, group 17, 1968–70). Our group has produced an annual *International Calendar* since 1988, and I've been the text editor since 1990. Part of my job is to seek out holidays, festivals, and anniversaries around the world and to master the underlying calendar systems so I can compute holiday dates well in advance. The expertise acquired in that endeavor prepared me to compose this book.

My work on the *International Calendar* has subsidized contact with a wide range of sources and the acquisition of books, and the gift of a complementary calendar to people who helped me acquire trustworthy, and often primary, data often stimulated further helpfulness.

All in all, the *International Calendar* and *Anniversaries and Holidays, Fifth Edition* have been complementary spurs, keeping me diligent and benefiting both enterprises.

My fellow RPCVs in Wisconsin have listened to my speeches and rantings with courtesy, interest, or informed interjection. Others have written to offer new holidays or to correct errors. I am grateful to them all, and their friendship sustains me. Furthermore, the calendar is good karma: I suspect that everyone who has worked on it has noticed some improvement in his or her life.

I am grateful to Ruth Gregory, who composed the third and fourth editions of *Anniversaries and Holidays*. The latter provided the skeleton for the present book. Gregory's entries display discrimination in fields where I'm a tyro, especially music and art. I also admire the composers of the earliest incarnations of this book.

I am immensely grateful to my companion, Sharon Lewandowski (PC/Philippines, 1977–79), who has supported me in many ways before and during this project. She's the love of my life, and I'm a better person because of her. She has given me time and silence. She understands me, has helped me nightly in refining my understanding of what I study, is amused by my obsessions, and has been the catalyst for various entries. When asked, she studies my prose and improves it. I aspire to be so successful that she can retire and devote her talents to improving the world; it would only be fair. Sharon has been the most essential person in the creation of this book.

I thank my good friend Don Sauer (PC/Afghanistan). For a year he let me appear in his apartment each morning to use his computer, while he went off to work for a bureaucracy. And he was delighted, each afternoon, to talk with me about my discoveries. Then he gave me his computer when he returned to Afghanistan, his second home.

I thank the American Library Association's editors, notably Herbert Bloom, who accepted my initial proposal and thrashed out the projected content; Patrick Hogan, who shepherded the book to completion; and Cynthia Fostle, Mary Cavanagh, Patricia Stahl, and Regina Wells, who edited my manuscript, to its betterment.

ACKNOWLEDGMENTS

My mother and father, true to their natures, have given me consistent and proud support, with enduring good wishes, intelligent criticism of my manuscript, and the gift of a new computer.

I'm grateful to my past: for having been an Eagle Scout; for having received a superb education at the hands of Jesuits, who confirmed in me a habit of lifelong learning; for having spent my junior year of college studying fairy tales in Tübingen, Germany; for having served in the Peace Corps, as an agriculture extension agent in Nepal; for having devoted so many self-employed years to restoring houses and their furnishings, which developed my faculties and gave me at least 6 hours daily for reading; and for having lived since 1972 on the near east side of Madison, Wisconsin, the sweetest city in the Midwest.

I am grateful to my colleagues for their attentive help: Phoenix, a fellow calendar maker in Ukiah, California; Michael Erlewine and his Tibetan-calendar colleagues at KTD Dharma Goods, in Big Rapids, Michigan; Bill Chase, the creator of *Chase's Annual Events*, and his successors, Mary Eley and Sandy Whitely; Michael Belanger, Associate Editor, *Merriam-Webster's Collegiate Dictionary*; the editors of *Special Days and Weeks for Planning the School Calendar* (Educational Research Service; Arlington, Virginia); the Bollandists, in Brussels, Belgium, who are the ultimate authority on Christian saints; the editorial department of the *Encyclopaedia Britannica*; Mark Thiel of the University of Wisconsin–Milwaukee; J. C. Eade, author of *Southeast Asian Ephemeris: Solar and Planetary Positions,* A.D. *638–2000,* and other works; Edward M. Reingold, coauthor of *Calendrical Calculations;* and Devendra Trivedi, author of the annual *Palani Panchang: Trivedi's American Panchang.*

I am grateful to the many people serving in embassies and official tourism organizations who helped me far beyond their job descriptions. Almost every country's U.S. embassy, U.N. mission, or official tourism bureau has helped me. I especially thank those persons representing Australia, the Baltic countries, Belgium, Bhutan, Brazil, many Caribbean countries, the Central Asian countries of the former USSR, Costa Rica, El Salvador, Eritrea, Ethiopia, the French West Indies, Germany, Guatemala, Honduras, India, Iran, Ireland, Japan, Malta, Mongolia, Namibia, Nepal, New Zealand, Nicaragua, Niger, the Order of Malta, Panama, Poland, the Scandinavian countries, Slovenia, South Korea, Spain, Sweden, Taiwan, and the United Kingdom.

Two series of traveler's books are especially helpful, and I salute them: the *Insight Guides* series, and the *Lonely Planet* series.

Several long-dead authors of books on the Hindu calendar have helped me greatly, and I revere them: Dewan Bahadur Pillai, author of *An Indian Ephemeris, 1800–2000,* and *Indian Chronology;* and Robert Sewell and Shankara Balkrishna Dikshit, authors of *The Indian Calendar.*

I also have high regard for the calendrical work of Julius Caesar, Dionysius Exiguus, and Pope Gregory XIII, though surely they are by now oblivious to my praise.

INTRODUCTION

A calendar is a device for reckoning the beginning, length, and divisions of a year and for locating a holiday or any other particular day. It is taken for granted as one of the essential tools of daily life. It seems simple, but a calendar is actually an ingenious and complicated system for reckoning and recording time. And it is a rare person who understands how his or her own culture's calendar works.

For Westerners, the major problem in determining a holiday's date is that there are three basic types of calendars in use in the twentieth century: the solar, the lunar, and the lunisolar. There are cultural or religious variations among these calendar types because each is designed to satisfy particular cultural needs.

Most solar calendars are based on the seasonal, or *tropical,* year—the time it takes the earth to go once around the sun. A typical solar calendar is based on the time from one spring equinox to the next, when the sun rises due east and the daylight is 12 hours long. The tropical year is a period of 365.2422 days, commonly divided into 12 months of unequal lengths. To compensate for the almost quarter-day differential between the exact astronomical year and the 365-day common year, it is necessary to introduce a leap year of 366 days every fourth year. The Gregorian calendar, used by Western nations for public and private purposes and by other nations for civil or commercial purposes, is a solar calendar. (*See* the essays on calendar systems and the Gregorian calendar in part 2.)

A lunar calendar represents a year composed of 12 months determined by complete cycles of the moon. In the Islamic calendar, the only significant modern example of a purely lunar calendar, each month represents the time required for the moon to wax and wane from a new moon to a full moon and back again to a new moon. (*See* the essay on the Islamic calendar in part 2.)

At the new moon, the moon is almost directly between the sun and the earth and is thus invisible. At the full moon, it is almost directly opposite the sun and the earth and is fully illuminated. (Eclipses occur when these bodies are in direct alignment.) The average time from one new moon to the next is slightly more than 29½ days, but the exact length varies from month to month. Twelve lunar months average approximately 354 days. Thus, an event dated in a lunar calendar will each year occur 10 or 11 days earlier in the Gregorian calendar than it did the previous year; this is the case with the Islamic calendar.

A lunisolar calendar strives to reckon time by both the moon and the sun and to reconcile their motions. This is a tough problem: The moon's motion is complex from month to month and over time, and the sun's motion is all but constant annually but is variable within a year. Lunar months do not divide evenly into a solar year.

Lunisolar calendars are well illustrated by the Jewish calendar, in which the months are reckoned by the moon and the years by the sun. In the Jewish calendar, a month is reckoned as the time from one new moon to the next. However, the year's length is constrained within tight limits, so in some years there are 13 months instead of 12, to keep the lunar months in accord with the solar year. The extra month is called an *intercalary month*; it is inserted 7 times in 19 years. (*See* the essay on the Jewish calendar in part 2.) By such adjustments, a lunisolar calendar's festivals are confined to the proper season of the year.

The Hindu calendar is a variant of the lunisolar calendar. Its solar year is *sidereal* rather than tropical: It measures the time it takes the sun to return to the same position relative to the stars, rather than the time it takes to return to the spring equinox. A sidereal year is approximately 20 minutes longer than a tropical year, so the starting point of the Hindu year will each year occur slightly later in the Gregorian calendar than it did the previous year.

Some calendars lie beyond the bounds of these definitions. Some Native American calendars, for instance, reckon by planetary and stellar motions. The Balinese Wuku calendar of 210 days is purely additive and ignores both sun and moon.

Time, astronomy, and calendrical notation are of immense antiquity. Calendars are an assertion that time is patterned, and that events recur predictably. Paleolithic Cro-Magnon people were scrupulously recording the behavior of the moon more than 12,000 years ago. The neolithic builders of England's Stonehenge were probably forecasting eclipses. And from the beginnings of agriculture, knowing the length of the year and being able to predict the recurrence of planting times were critical survival skills.

The Sumerians of the Fertile Crescent are credited with the creation of one of the first surviving lunar calendars, and the Egyptians with the first known solar calendar.

In 46 B.C., Julius Caesar established the Julian calendar. It became the calendar of the Roman Empire and was refined at the Council of Nicaea in A.D. 325 to serve as the official calendar of the Christian Church. It became the universal calendar of the early Western world and is still used by the Orthodox and other Eastern Christian Churches.

There were two inaccuracies in the Julian calendar, the more important being that the year was too long by approximately 3 days in 4 centuries. Over time, the Julian calendar drifted out of step with the seasons, and festivals were occurring later than they should. Consequently, in 1582, Pope Gregory XIII promulgated a revised calendar and decreed that the day following Thursday, October 4, 1582, was to be Friday, October 15, 1582, thus advancing all dates in the calendar by 10 days. The Gregorian calendar came to be known as the New Style calendar, and the Julian calendar as the Old Style calendar (abbreviated N.S. and O.S.).

The Gregorian calendar was not immediately adopted by all nations of the Western world. The Roman Catholic countries adopted it in 1582, but the Protestant nations and principalities of Europe adopted it gradually. This led to generations of confusion in the recording of births, deaths, and historic dates, and still bedevils historians.

The United Kingdom and the British Empire, including the American colonies, did not adopt the Gregorian calendar until 1752. In that year, New Year's Day in England, hitherto on March 25, occurred on January 1; and Wednesday, September 2, was followed by Thursday, September 14—an extra 11 days. Thus, most of America's Revolutionary War personalities were born under one calendar and died under another. Russia and its territories (including Poland) did not adopt the Gregorian calendar until 1918, nor was it fully adopted in China until 1930.

It was not until after World War II that the Gregorian calendar took a dominant position among world calendars, and its widespread use has facilitated world trade and intergovernmental relations. However, it has not replaced the lunar and lunisolar calendars for religious and cultural date calculations.

Many nations use both the Gregorian calendar and their own time-honored calendars, and holidays are tied to local or national time-measurement customs.

HOLIDAYS IN HISTORY

Holidays, festivals, and other acts of leisure are features of all human cultures. They allow people to rise above the workaday world, to savor the cyclic nature of time, and to briefly enter eternity.

Centuries ago, the word *holiday* was written as *holy day*, signifying, and limited to, a religious commemoration. In the course of history, the meaning of *holiday* broadened to encompass civic and secular as well as religious observance. It even came to be used to designate a vacation period, days of individual freedom from routine obligations. In the strictest sense, holidays are days set aside by nations, or groups within nations, for religious, civil, or secular observances on a universal or optional free-day basis.

A compilation of holidays provides an insight into life situations that humankind has considered important enough to cherish with carefully preserved customs and continued recognition. Holidays evolved as a human response to the mysteries of nature, the awareness of a supreme deity, respect for the dead, hero worship, the growth of a tribal or national spirit, and unusual events.

The mysteries of the changing seasons inspired the most ancient celebrations, especially at the equinoxes and solstices. Each culture celebrated its New Year's Day, which affirms the cyclical aspect of earthly time. The favorite celebration period was the spring equinox, which gave rise to spring festivals that are observed even today. Gratitude for a good growing season was, and still is, expressed with harvest festivals and thanksgiving days. Though most Westerners are unaware of it, the spring equinox and Easter are the pivot point of both the Gregorian and Julian calendars.

The veneration of nature by early societies merged with their worship of deities, at least in terms of the calendar. Many early religious festivals coincided with seasonal observances. However, religious holy days and festivals came to be a visible affirmation of the beliefs and traditions of all faiths. Many of the holidays observed throughout the modern world are related to religious practices. For instance, Christmas Day is a public holiday in about 145 nations, and Good Friday is a public holiday in about 90. Each community in the Roman Catholic countries of Europe and Latin America has its own special saint's day, which is usually a local holiday. In the Islamic nations, almost all holidays are religious.

Holiday festivals honoring the dead are an ancient and universal custom. Days of tributes to ancestors have evolved into the festivals of the modern nations of the Far East. Mexico's Day of the Dead is also notable. Every country in the contemporary world has some kind of memorial day as a separate observance, combined with a religious festival, or centered around commemoration of a single individual.

Each nation celebrates civic holidays commemorating significant events in its history, such as Independence Day or National Day.

The United Nations has added important days to the world calendar. These include Human Rights Day, World Literacy Day, World Health Day, and others that affirm universal human goals. Most United Nations days are observed as special events days; some are holidays among the newer nations.

Special events days are not holidays in the usual sense. They are days of recognition or commemoration of events that have significance in the history of a nation, an organization, a profession, or a technological development. Some, such as Moon Day, the day when humans first landed on the moon, occur only once in history, but others have become holidays in some parts of the world. An example is Arbor Day, which has its counterpart in the tree-planting days in various

African nations where restoration is not only essential, but also a matter of national pride.

Anniversaries and holidays have varied life spans. Some, like Christmas, are part of the fabric of life. Others, such as civic holidays, are vulnerable to changes in government and may be wiped off the calendar or completely altered in purpose. Still others diminish in interest. A particular holiday will last only as long as people want it to. This may be for a decade or for thousands of years.

ABBREVIATIONS AND CONVENTIONS

A.D.	*anno Domini,* in the year of the Lord
A.H.	*anno Hegirae,* in the year of Muhammad's Hegira
A.M.	before noon; *anno mundi,* in the year of the world
B.C.	before Christ
ca.	circa (when used before numbers or dates)
e.g.	for instance (*exempli gratia*)
Jan., Feb., etc.	abbreviations of month names
Jan. 1 or 14	Old Style date with New Style conversion
L.1 2	1st lunar month, 2nd day
N.S.	New Style (Gregorian calendar date)
Orth.	Orthodox (Greek, Russian, etc.)
O.S.	Old Style (Julian calendar date)
P.M.	after noon
R.C.	Roman Catholic
SS.	Saints
St.	Saint
U.K.	United Kingdom (Great Britain)
U.S.	United States
USSR	Soviet Union
U.T.	Universal time

PART ONE

CALENDAR OF FIXED DAYS

January

January, the first month in the Gregorian calendar, begins with the most popular civil day of the entire year. All but a few countries celebrate New Year's Day as a public holiday.

The name *January* was derived from the Latin *Januarius mensis,* "the month of Janus." In the old Roman year, it was a festival month honoring Janus, the god of gates and doorways. Janus is depicted on coins and works of sculpture as a deity with 2 faces: one looking into the past, the other into the future. Janus is associated in mythology with new beginnings for all human enterprises. January, consequently, is one of the most appropriately named months of the year.

January has 31 days and 2 official flowers. The chief flower is the carnation, and the alternative is the snowdrop. The January birthstone is the garnet.

HOLY DAYS AND FEAST DAYS

1

Orthodox Feast of St. Basil the Great (329–Jan. 1, 379). Cappadocian scholar, monk, and archbishop. Assured the victory of Orthodoxy over Arianism, and founded Eastern monasticism. One of the giants of Christianity; a doctor of the church and patron saint of Eastern monks. Orth.: Jan. 1 or 14.

1

Feast of the Circumcision. Commemorates the initiation of Jesus into Jewish society as a symbol of the believer's initiation into Christian life. In the Catholic Church, now replaced by the feast of Mary, Mother of God. Orth.: Jan. 1 or 14.

1

Feast of Mary, Mother of God; official public holiday in Vatican City. Honors Mary's divine mater-

nity, on the octave of Christmas. Replaces the feast of the Circumcision.

1

World Peace Day in the Catholic Church; official public holiday in Vatican City. Observed in Receife, Brazil, as Universal Brotherhood Day; local official public holiday.

HOLIDAYS AND CIVIC DAYS

1

New Year's Day, the 1st day of the 1st month in the Gregorian calendar. An official public holiday in almost all nations of the world and in all states and territories of the U.S.

1

Liberation Day in Cuba; official public holiday. Also called Revolution Day or the Day of National Celebration. Commemorates both the attainment of independence from Spain on Jan. 1, 1899, and the overthrow of the dictator Fulgencio Batista y Zaldívar, who fled to Miami on Jan. 1, 1959.

1

Independence Day in Haiti; official public holiday. Commemorates the declaration of independence by Jean-Jacques Dessalines from France on Jan. 1, 1804.

1

Founding of the independent Slovak Republic; official public holiday. Commemorates the anniversary of the peaceful separation on Jan. 1, 1993, of the Czech and Slovak Republics.

1

Independence Day in Sudan; official public holiday. Celebrates independence attained from Egypt and the U.K. on Jan. 1, 1956.

1

Foundation Days in Taiwan; official public holiday. Commemorates the founding of the Republic of China on Jan. 1, 1912; most people celebrate on Jan. 2, also.

1

Colonial Flag Day in the U.S. Anniversary of the official formation of the Continental Army under George Washington on Jan. 1, 1776, and of the raising of the first flag of the united colonies, known as the Grand Union flag. The site of the first raising is marked by a memorial tower and observatory in Somerville, Mass.

1

Emancipation Day in the U.S. Anniversary of the Emancipation Proclamation of Jan. 1, 1863, by President Abraham Lincoln, which declared free all slaves in the rebelling states. Commemorated by various organizations and in schools. The abolition of slavery throughout the U.S. was made public law with the ratification of the 13th Amendment on Dec. 6, 1865.

ANNIVERSARIES AND SPECIAL EVENTS DAYS

1

Anniversary of the opening of the immigration station on Ellis Island in upper New York Bay on Jan. 1, 1892. Before its closing on Nov. 12, 1954, 20 million immigrants passed through its halls. The main building is now the Ellis Island Museum of Immigration.

1

Anniversary of the signing of the Treaty of Union by the U.K. and Ireland on Jan. 1, 1801, producing the United Kingdom of Great Britain and Ireland, now called the United Kingdom of Great Britain and Northern Ireland.

1

Birthday of William Henry Harrison Beadle (Jan. 1, 1838–Nov. 13, 1915). American educator, superintendent of public schools in the Dakota Territory. Represents S.Dak. in Statuary Hall.

1

Birthday of Baron Pierre de Coubertin (Jan. 1, 1863–Sept. 2, 1937). French educator who on Nov. 25, 1892, proposed a modern revival of the ancient Olympic Games.

1

Birthday of Sir James George Frazer (Jan. 1, 1854–May 7, 1941). Scottish anthropologist famous for his classic work on sacred kingship, *The Golden Bough,* especially the 12-volume 3rd edition (1911–15).

1

Birthday of J. (John) Edgar Hoover (Jan. 1, 1895–May 2, 1972). Director of the Federal Bureau of Investigation, 1924–72.

1

Birthday of Paul Revere (Jan. 1, 1735–May 10, 1818). American patriot and craftsman of Boston, whose famous ride on Apr. 18, 1775, placed him among the immortals of the American Revolution.

1

Birthday of Betsy Ross (born Elizabeth Griscom; Jan. 1, 1752–Jan. 30, 1836). American colonial woman of Philadelphia, an official flag maker for the Pennsylvania navy, who is reputed to have made the first American flag in 1776, under Washington's direction.

1

Birthday of Manuel Roxas y Acuña (Jan. 1, 1892–Apr. 15, 1948). Philippine statesman and first president of the Philippines.

1

Birthday of Anthony Wayne (Jan. 1, 1745–Dec. 15, 1796). American Revolutionary War officer whose brilliant action in storming an almost impregnable fort at Stony Point, N.Y. (on July 16, 1779), lifted the hearts of his countrymen; known as Mad Anthony for his audacious style of battle.

1

Birthday of Ulrich Zwingli (Jan. 1, 1484–Oct. 11, 1531). Swiss humanist, author, preacher, and politician. With John Calvin, a leader of the Protestant Reformation in Switzerland.

1

First-Foot Day; in the early hours of Jan. 1. An old New Year's custom, still surviving in Scotland and in Britain generally. If the First-Foot, or Lucky Bird, traditionally a dark-haired man, is the first person in the year to cross a house's threshold with his good wishes and symbolic gifts of coal and salt, the house will have good fortune in the coming year. (*See also* Hogmanay, Dec. 31.)

1

Mobile Carnival in Mobile, Ala. Elaborate New Year's celebration that originated in 1831.

1

Mummers Day parade in Philadelphia. Dates from 1876; characterized by unusual costuming, string bands, clowns, mummers, and other performers.

1

Polar Swim Day in Canada and the northern U.S. In "a rite of lunacy," swimmers plunge into frigid waters to welcome the New Year. Began in Vancouver in 1920. American Polar Bear Clubs thrive in the Great Lakes area and on the Atlantic coast.

1

Tournament of Roses in Pasadena, Calif. Held on New Year's Day since 1890; with flower-decorated floats forming processions that are hours (and miles) long. The climax of the day is the Rose Bowl football game, first held in 1902. The Rose Bowl preceded other bowl games by three decades.

HOLIDAYS AND CIVIC DAYS

2

The day after New Year's Day is an official public holiday in a number of countries, including Dominica, Liechtenstein, Mauritius, Romania, Russia, Seychelles, South Korea, and Scotland.

2

Forefathers Day in Haiti; official public holiday. Also called Ancestry Day. Honors the nation's founders and heroes.

2

Berchtoldstag in Switzerland; official public holiday in many cantons. Honors the 12th-century Duke Berchtold V, who founded the city of Berne ("bear") with a promise to name it for the first animal killed in a hunt. Now mainly a children's holiday, with neighborhood parties involving games using nuts saved since autumn.

2

Ratification Day in Ga. On Jan. 2, 1788, Ga.'s legislature unanimously voted to ratify the Constitution, and Ga. entered the Union as the 4th state.

ANNIVERSARIES AND SPECIAL EVENTS DAYS

2

Birthday of Count Folke Bernadotte (Jan. 2, 1895–Sept. 17, 1948). Swedish soldier and statesman who headed the Swedish Red Cross during World War II and saved 20,000 persons from the Nazi death camps. United Nations mediator in Palestine (May 20–Sept. 17, 1948), where he was assassinated by Israeli terrorists.

2

Birthday of James Wolfe (Jan. 2, 1727–Sept. 13, 1759). English general who led his troops to victory on the Plains of Abraham, in the Battle of Quebec, the most important battle of the French and Indian War. Wolfe was killed at the hour of victory, but the battle decided the war, and as a result, control of Canada was transferred from France to Britain.

HOLY DAYS AND FEAST DAYS

3

Feast of St. Geneviève (ca. 422–500). French nun who cared for the people of Paris and protected them from invaders; patron saint of Paris and of secretaries, actors, and lawyers. Orth.: Jan. 3 or 13.

HOLIDAYS AND CIVIC DAYS

3

Anniversary of the 1966 Upheaval in Burkina Faso; official public holiday. Commemorates the change in government leadership on Jan. 3, 1966, following general strikes and street demonstrations protesting waste and corruption in government.

3

Alaska Admission Day. Anniversary of Alaska's admission as the 49th state on Jan. 3, 1959.

3

Day on which the U.S. Congress officially begins its year's business, at noon, as prescribed by the 20th Amendment, "unless they by law appoint a different day."

ANNIVERSARIES AND SPECIAL EVENTS DAYS

3

Birthday of J. R. R. (John Ronald Reuel) Tolkien (Jan. 3, 1892–Sept. 2, 1973). Oxford professor of Old English and philology, author of *The Hobbit* and *The Lord of the Rings;* honored by Tolkien societies and student groups.

HOLY DAYS AND FEAST DAYS

4

Feast of Elizabeth Ann Bayley Seton (Aug. 28, 1774–Jan. 4, 1821). First American-born saint.

Founder of the Sisters of Charity and pioneer leader of the American Catholic school system.

HOLIDAYS AND CIVIC DAYS

4

Independence Day in Myanmar (Burma); official public holiday. Commemorates the attainment of independence from the U.K. on Jan. 4, 1948, when the nation achieved full sovereignty and simultaneously left the British Commonwealth.

4

Admission Day in Utah. Anniversary of Utah's admission as the 45th state on Jan. 4, 1896.

ANNIVERSARIES AND SPECIAL EVENTS DAYS

4

Birthday of Louis Braille (Jan. 4, 1809–Jan. 6, 1852). Blind French educator of blind people; originated the Braille system of printing and writing.

4

Birthday of Jacob Grimm (Jan. 4, 1785–Sept. 20, 1863). German philologist and mythologist who, with his brother, Wilhelm Carl Grimm (Feb. 24, 1786–Dec. 16, 1859), published the famous *Grimm's Fairy Tales.*

4

Birthday of Sir Isaac Newton (Jan. 4, 1643–Mar. 31, 1727). English physicist, mathematician, and metrologist; leader in the 17th-century scientific revolution; discoverer of the law of gravity.

4

Birthday of Benjamin Rush (Jan. 4, 1746–Apr. 19, 1813). American physician and medical pioneer, called the Father of Psychiatry; signer of the Declaration of Independence. Rush University in Chicago is named for him.

CA. 4

Perihelion; varies between Jan. 1 and Jan. 4. At this time the earth is closest to the sun. (*See also* Aphelion, July 4.)

CA. 4

Quadratid meteor showers; Jan. 1–5, main day Jan. 4. Visible toward the east at midnight. Blue, with silver trails.

HOLY DAYS AND FEAST DAYS

5

Feast of John Nepomucene Neumann (Mar. 28, 1811–Jan. 5, 1860). Bohemian-born American Re-

demptorist priest renowned for holiness, pastoral work, and preaching. The first American male saint.

HOLIDAYS AND CIVIC DAYS

5

George W. Norris Day in Nebr.; day of special school observance. Honors George William Norris (July 11, 1861–Sept. 2, 1944), U.S. senator from Nebr. (1912–43) who was instrumental in the establishment of the Tennessee Valley Authority; the first TVA dam was named in his honor. Author of the 20th Amendment, known as the Lame Duck Amendment, which provided for inauguration of a newly elected president on Jan. 20 instead of on Mar. 4.

ANNIVERSARIES AND SPECIAL EVENTS DAYS

5

Birthday of Stephen Decatur (Jan. 5, 1779–Mar. 22, 1820). American naval officer who is remembered for his toast "Our country! . . . may she always be in the right; but our country, right or wrong."

5

Birthday of Zebulon Montgomery Pike (Jan. 5, 1779–Apr. 27, 1813). American general who commanded an early exploring expedition into the West. Pikes Peak, one of the highest summits in the Rocky Mountains, is named in his honor.

5

Death anniversary of George Washington Carver (ca. 1864–Jan. 5, 1943). African American chemist, noted for his research in the industrial uses of vegetable crops, who greatly benefited agriculture in the South; founder of the Carver Foundation for Research at the Tuskegee Institute.

5

Bird Day. Anniversary of the incorporation of the National Association of Audubon Societies on Jan. 5, 1905, with the purpose of protecting bird life. Bird Day is frequently observed with Arbor Day, on varying dates in the various states.

5

Epiphany Eve. Also called Twelfth Night. Traditional end of the Christmas season in many countries. In places where Epiphany, or Three Kings Day, is celebrated, Twelfth Night is a time of merrymaking.

5

La Befana in Italy, especially in Florence and Venice. On Epiphany Eve (Jan. 5), the *Befana*, a good witch with a broom and a gift basket, gives presents to children, who may also light fires. ("Bad" children get charcoal-shaped sweets.) With fairs and parades on Jan. 6 (or Jan. 5–6). In lore, the *Befana* was too busy cleaning house to join the Three Kings in giving gifts to the Christ child.

HOLY DAYS AND FEAST DAYS

6

Feast of Epiphany. Also called Three Kings Day or the Baptism of the Lord. Commemorates the manifestation of the divinity of Christ (the Theophany) in his birth, his baptism by John the Baptist, and, in the West, the adoration of the Magi. The second-oldest Christian feast, after Easter. Orth.: Jan. 6 or 19.

6

Christmas in Armenia and among Armenian Christians worldwide; official public holiday in Armenia, and in Cyprus for Armenian Christians. Uniquely, celebrated on the feast of Epiphany.

CA. 6

Feast of Our Lord of a Good Ending (*Nosso Senhor do Bonfim*) in Salvador, Brazil; at the Bonfim cathedral, sacred to the *orixá* Oxalá, and the holiest place in Condomblé (a syncretic religion). Ritual washing of the steps *(lavagem)*, Thursday before Jan. 6; high feast day, Jan. 6; a parade, 3rd Sunday in Jan.; a festival for Our Lady of the Valley *(Ribeira)*, the next day; and a festival for St. Lazarus *(Omulu)*, 4th Sunday in Jan.

HOLIDAYS AND CIVIC DAYS

6

Admission Day in N.Mex. Anniversary of N.Mex.'s admission as the 47th state on Jan. 6, 1912.

6

Sam Rayburn Day in Tex.; a day of special school observance. Honors Samuel Taliaferro Rayburn (Jan. 6, 1882–Nov. 16, 1961), Democratic Speaker of the House of Representatives, 1940–61 (with two Republican interruptions); congressman, 1913–61.

ANNIVERSARIES AND SPECIAL EVENTS DAYS

6

"Birthday" of Sherlock Holmes, fictional detective in the works of Sir Arthur Conan Doyle. Cele-brated on or near this date by the Baker Street Irregulars (a society of Holmes enthusiasts) and other aficionados.

6

Birthday of Carl Sandburg (Jan. 6, 1878–July 22, 1967). American poet, historian, folklorist, and biographer of Abraham Lincoln.

6

Blessing of the Waters in Orthodox countries (Jan. 6 or 19); held on Epiphany (*Theophania*). In Greece, for example, in Piraeus and Crete, the seas are blessed, and boys dive for a cross thrown into the waves. In Turkey, the Bosporus is blessed.

6

Crown of St. Stephen Day. Anniversary of the Jan. 6, 1978, return to Hungary of the famous crown of Stephen I, a gift of Pope Sylvester II; it had been secured at Fort Knox since World War II.

6

Kings Day in Spain, including the Canary Islands; official public holiday. Also called Three Kings Day. The year's main gift-giving occasion. Towns often have a Three Kings parade (sometimes on the eve), with camels and floats. Then people exchange presents over family dinners at home. In the Canaries, this is a bigger holiday than New Year's Day.

6

Maroon Day in Jamaica. Also called the Maroon Festival. Commemorates and invokes the 1738 Treaty of Cudjoe between Maroons (ex-slaves of the expelled Spanish colonists) and Great Britain, which recognized free Maroon territory in the mountains; no Jamaican government has ever fulfilled the treaty. Held annually since 1738.

CA. 6

Three Kings Festival (*La Fête des Rois*) in the French West Indies; on a Sunday near Jan. 6. Celebrated with wining and dining at home and in hotels, culminating in the serving of the traditional cake called *galette des rois*. The 1st weekend after New Year's Day also marks the start of the preparatory season for Carnaval: every town works on its costumes and floats, and there are special preparatory events each weekend until Lent begins.

HOLY DAYS AND FEAST DAYS

7

Christmas Day among Orthodox and other Christians using the Julian calendar exclusively, notably in the Russian and the Coptic Orthodox Churches (Dec. 25 O.S., Jan. 7 N.S.).

In Ukraine, *Koliada,* an ancient winter solstice rite celebrated at Christmas. On Christmas Eve (Jan. 6) is the Holy Supper (*Sviata Vecheria),* with special meals followed by carols to welcome Christ's birth.

In Ethiopia, called *Genna;* on Jan. 7 in most years; official public holiday. At dawn, all gather in churches to watch ancient ceremonial dances. Then they feast at home and give presents to the children. In the afternoon, men play *genna,* an extremely intense game resembling field hockey.

7

Feast of St. Raymond of Peñafort (1175–Jan. 6, 1275). Spanish Dominican famed for his preaching and for codifying papal decrees that became the cornerstone of canon law until the revision of 1917. Patron saint of medical record librarians.

HOLIDAYS AND CIVIC DAYS

7

Seven Herbs Festival (*Nanakusa Matsuri*) in Japan; official public holiday. End of the New Year season; all decorations are taken down, and a traditional 7-herb rice dish is served.

ANNIVERSARIES AND SPECIAL EVENTS DAYS

7

Anniversary of the first international airmail flight and the first crossing of the English Channel by balloon. On Jan. 7, 1785, the French balloonist Jean-Pierre-François Blanchard and the American physician John Jeffries delivered mail on their historic balloon flight from Dover, England, to Forêt de Felmores, France.

7

Birthday of Millard Fillmore (Jan. 7, 1800–Mar. 8, 1874). N.Y. lawyer and congressman; 13th president of the U.S. (1850–53; Whig; had been elected vice president and on President Zachary Taylor's death filled the balance of his term). During his presidency, his stance on slavery pleased neither faction, and he was not renominated; in 1856, ran unsuccessfully on the Know-Nothing ticket. Some use his birthday as the justification for parties. Buried at Buffalo, N.Y.

7

Birthday of Jacques-Étienne Montgolfier (Jan. 7, 1745–Aug. 2, 1799). French merchant and inventor; balloon experimenter who made the first successful balloon flight with his brother Joseph-Michel on June 5, 1783.

7

St. Distaff's Day, the day when housewives resume normal work after the celebration (and heavy work) of the Christmas season. A tongue-in-cheek medieval fabrication that became widely observed, at least in England.

HOLIDAYS AND CIVIC DAYS

8

Battle of New Orleans Day; official public holiday in Louisiana. Also called Old Hickory's Day or Jackson Day. Anniversary of the battle in the War of 1812, on Jan. 8, 1815; General Andrew Jackson won decisively (but the war had already ended). Widely celebrated before the Civil War.

ANNIVERSARIES AND SPECIAL EVENTS DAYS

8

Anniversary of the founding of the African National Congress on Jan. 8, 1912, dedicated to racial equality and an end to white minority rule in South Africa.

8

Anniversary of the first State of the Union Message, delivered by George Washington on Jan. 8, 1790.

8

Birthday of Jacob Collamer (Jan. 8, 1791–Nov. 9, 1865). Senator from Vt. and postmaster general, 1849–50. Represents Vt. in Statuary Hall.

8

Birthday of Alfred Russell Wallace (Jan. 8, 1823–Nov. 7, 1913). English naturalist who worked in Borneo; formulated, independently of Charles Darwin, the theory of natural selection. The two presented their findings in a joint paper before the Linnean Society in 1858.

8

Death anniversary of Charles Alexander Eastman (1858–Jan. 8, 1939). Native American (Sioux) physician, author, and ombudsman who worked for better U.S. government policies toward Native Americans; helped organize the Boy Scouts of America and the Camp Fire Girls.

8

Death anniversary of Marco Polo (ca. 1254–Jan. 8, 1324). Italian merchant-adventurer of Venice, famous for his travel to and life in China, in the service of Kublai Khan.

8

Elvis Presley Day in Memphis, Tenn. Anniversary of the birthday of Elvis Aaron Presley (Jan. 8, 1935–Aug. 16, 1977), American rock-and-roll singer of enormous popular influence. The anniversaries of his birth and death are celebrated at Graceland, his Memphis home.

8

Women's Day in Greece. Also called Midwife's Day. A rare day off work for women, and a de facto official public holiday. Women while away the day in cafés, and men do the chores and mind the children.

HOLIDAYS AND CIVIC DAYS

9

Ratification Day in Conn. On Jan. 9, 1788, Conn. ratified the Constitution and became the 5th state.

ANNIVERSARIES AND SPECIAL EVENTS DAYS

9

Birthday of Carrie Lane Chapman Catt (Jan. 9, 1859–Mar. 9, 1947). American suffrage reformer, a moving force behind the adoption of the 19th Amendment to the U.S. Constitution and founder in 1919 of the National League of Women Voters. Elected to the National Women's Hall of Fame.

9

Birthday of Richard Milhous Nixon (Jan. 9, 1913– Apr. 22, 1994). Calif. congressman and senator; vice president under Eisenhower; 37th president of the U.S. (1969–74; Republican). Presided over the latter portion of the Vietnam War; permitted détente with China. Resigned the presidency in disgrace, under threat of impeachment following the Watergate scandal. Buried in Yorba Linda, Calif.

9

Birthday of John Broadus Watson (Jan. 9, 1878– Sept. 25, 1958). American psychologist and founder of the behaviorist school of psychology in the U.S.

9

Death anniversary of Caroline Lucretia Herschel (1750–Jan. 9, 1848). German-born English astronomer who received a gold medal from the Royal Astronomical Society in 1828 for her discoveries of 8 comets and many nebulae.

CA. 9

Black Nazarene fiesta in Quiapo, Metro Manila, Philippines; Jan. 1–9. Cultural events, fireworks, and parades honor the patron saint of the district; culmination is a procession of the statue on the afternoon of Jan. 9. Manila's largest religious procession.

ANNIVERSARIES AND SPECIAL EVENTS DAYS

10

Anniversary of the founding of the League of Nations on Jan. 10, 1920, in a worldwide movement toward peace and cooperation among nations. The League was dissolved on Jan. 18, 1946.

10

Anniversary of the first session of the General Assembly of the United Nations, held on Jan. 10, 1946, in London; on the 26th anniversary of the founding of the unsuccessful League of Nations.

HOLIDAYS AND CIVIC DAYS

CA. 11

National Unity Day (*Prithvi Jayanti*) in Nepal; official public holiday. Honors the birthday of Prithvi Naryan Shah (1723–75), Nepali general and statesman who conquered and united numerous principalities to form Nepal.

ANNIVERSARIES AND SPECIAL EVENTS DAYS

11

Birthday of Chaim Nachman Bialik (Jan. 11, 1873– July 4, 1934). Russian Jewish poet, famous for his poetry in Hebrew.

11

Birthday of Ezra Cornell (Jan. 11, 1807–Dec. 9, 1874). American capitalist and philanthropist who established and endowed Cornell University. His birthday is observed as Founder's Day at Cornell.

11

Birthday of Alexander Hamilton (Jan. 11, 1755–July 12, 1804). A founding father of the U.S., coauthor of the *Federalist Papers,* and first secretary of the treasury; died from injuries suffered in a duel with Aaron Burr. Elected to the Hall of Fame for Great Americans.

11

Birthday of William James (Jan. 11, 1842–Aug. 26, 1910). American psychologist and philosopher; author of *Pragmatism.*

11

Birthday of Aldo Leopold (Jan. 11, 1887–Apr. 21, 1948). American naturalist, forester, and ecologist, whose most influential book is *A Sand County Almanac* (1949).

11

Birthday of John Alexander Macdonald (Jan. 11, 1815–June 6, 1891). Canadian statesman and first prime minister (1867–73; 1878–91).

11

Hostos Day in Puerto Rico. Birthday of Eugenio María de Hostos y Bonilla (Jan. 11, 1839–Aug. 11, 1903), Puerto Rican philosopher, scholar, prolific author, and outstanding patriot.

HOLIDAYS AND CIVIC DAYS

12

Zanzibar Revolution Day in Tanzania; official public holiday. Zanzibar (with Pemba) attained independence from the U.K. on Dec. 10, 1963, and the ruling sultan was overthrown on Jan. 12, 1964.

ANNIVERSARIES AND SPECIAL EVENTS DAYS

12

Anniversary of the election on Jan. 12, 1932, of Hattie Caraway of Ark. as the first woman senator in the U.S.

12

Birthday of Edmund Burke (ca. Jan. 12, 1729–July 9, 1797). British orator, politician, and philosopher.

12

Birthday of Jack (John Griffith) London (Jan. 12, 1876–Nov. 22, 1916). American novelist and writer, especially of the sea and of the Far North.

12

Birthday of Johann Heinrich Pestalozzi (Jan. 12, 1746–Feb. 17, 1827). Swiss educational reformer whose beliefs and system laid the foundations for elementary education.

12

Birthday of John Singer Sargent (Jan. 12, 1856–Apr. 15, 1925). Distinguished American portraitist and muralist. A series of Sargent's decorative panels was executed for the Boston Public Library.

12

Birthday of John Winthrop (Jan. 12, 1588–Mar. 26, 1649). American colonial leader; first governor of the Massachusetts Bay Colony.

HOLIDAYS AND CIVIC DAYS

13

Liberation Day in Togo; official public holiday. A new constitution went into effect on Jan. 13, 1980, and the Third Togolese Republic was proclaimed.

ANNIVERSARIES AND SPECIAL EVENTS DAYS

13

Anniversary of the founding of the National Geographic Society on Jan. 13, 1888, in Washington, D.C. The organization became the largest nonprofit scientific and educational institution in the world, in large part because of the popularity of its magazine, *National Geographic.*

13

Anniversary of the world's first radio broadcast on Jan. 13, 1910, by the radio pioneer Lee De Forest in New York City, who transmitted the singing of Enrico Caruso.

13

Anniversary of the founding of public radio station WHA in Madison, Wis. "The oldest station in the nation" began operation in 1917 as station 9XM, and received the call letters WHA on Jan. 13, 1922. It still flourishes as a public radio station under the aegis of the University of Wisconsin.

13

Death anniversary of Edmund Spenser (1552–Jan. 13, 1599). English poet laureate (1591–99), best known for *The Faerie Queen.*

13

Death anniversary of Suger (1081–Jan. 13, 1151). French abbot and adviser to kings, responsible for the creation and development of the Gothic style of architecture, and instrumental in fusing popular devotion to the shrine of St. Denis (patron saint of France) and the institution of the French monarchy.

13

St. Knut's Day in Sweden (*Tjugondag Knut,* "The 20th Day of Knut") and *Tyvendedagen* ("20th Day") in Norway. Traditional end of the Christmas season, when the Christmas tree is dismantled at a final Christmas party.

13

Stephen Foster Memorial Day. Death anniversary of Stephen Collins Foster (July 4, 1826–Jan. 13, 1864), American composer and writer of songs reflecting the sentiments of pre–Civil War America, such as "Oh! Susannah," "Camptown Races," and "Swanee River." Elected to the Hall of Fame for Great Americans.

HOLIDAYS AND CIVIC DAYS

CA. 14

Makara (or *Magh*) *Sankranti* in India; official public holiday in Sri Lanka. Called *Thai Pongal* among Tamils. Honors the sun deity. A day for ritual bathing (especially in the sacred Ganges). In Sri Lanka and south India, *Thai Pongal* is a merry harvest festival when a special meal of sweetened rice (*pongal*) is ritually eaten.

14

Ratification Day. Anniversary of the Jan. 14, 1784, ratification of the Treaty of Paris, thus officially ending the Revolutionary War and establishing the United States of America as a sovereign nation; by the Continental Congress, at the Md. State House, where the ratification is honored annually with special ceremonies.

ANNIVERSARIES AND SPECIAL EVENTS DAYS

14

Birthday of Benedict Arnold (Jan. 14, 1741–June 14, 1801). Brilliant Revolutionary War general who in 1779 switched to the Loyalist side, possibly out of patriotism, but whose name is an epithet for *traitor.*

14

Birthday of Matthew Fontaine Maury (Jan. 14, 1806–Feb. 1, 1873). American hydrographer and naval officer; the first to completely describe the Gulf Stream and to chart specific routes for Atlantic crossings. Elected to the Hall of Fame for Great Americans.

14

Birthday of Albert Schweitzer (Jan. 14, 1875–Sept. 4, 1965). French theologian, medical missionary in Gabon, musician, and author. Received the 1952 Nobel Peace Prize for his work toward the brotherhood of nations.

HOLIDAYS AND CIVIC DAYS

15

Adults' Day in Japan; official public holiday. Also called Coming of Age Day (*Seijin-no-Hi*). Honors young men and women who have become 20 years old and are thus full citizens. Honorees visit a shrine in special kimonos; parents, friends, and teachers wish them good luck.

CA. 15

Martin Luther King Day; federal official public holiday on the 3rd Monday in Jan. since 1986. Anniversary of the birth of Dr. Martin Luther King Jr. (Jan. 15, 1929–Apr. 4, 1968). African American clergyman, champion of civil rights, proponent of nonviolence, author, and recipient of the 1964 Nobel Peace Prize.

ANNIVERSARIES AND SPECIAL EVENTS DAYS

15

Anniversary of the opening of the British Museum, in London, on Jan. 15, 1759. The foundation of the museum's collection comprised the books, manuscripts, coins, and antiquities bequeathed by the physician and naturalist Sir Hans Sloane.

15

Baptismal day of Molière (Jean-Baptiste Poquelin; baptized Jan. 15, 1622–Feb. 17, 1673). French dramatist recognized as the greatest French writer of comedy. His finest work is considered to be *Le Misanthrope.*

15

Birthday of Sonya Kovalevski (Jan. 15, 1850–Feb. 10, 1891). Russian mathematician who pioneered in a field that was hostile to women; received the Prix Bordin of the Paris Academy for her achievements.

15

Birthday of Gamal Abdel Nasser (Jan. 15, 1918–Sept. 28, 1970). Egyptian army officer, leader in a coup that overthrew King Farouk, and subsequently prime minister (1954–56) and president (1956–70).

15

Birthday of Edward Teller (Jan. 15, 1908–). Hungarian-born American physicist, crucial to the development of the hydrogen bomb.

15

Death anniversary of Mathew B. Brady (ca. 1823–Jan. 15, 1896). American photographer who made the first photographic war records on the battlefields of the Civil War.

HOLIDAYS AND CIVIC DAYS

16

National Day of Peace in El Salvador; official public holiday. Anniversary of the official end of the civil war in El Salvador with the signing of a peace treaty on Jan. 16, 1992; ended 12 years of war between the armed forces and both leftist insurgents and the civilian population.

16

John Chilembwe Day in Malawi; official public holiday. Honors an early martyr for independence who led an uprising against the British in 1915; died ca. Jan. 16, 1915.

ANNIVERSARIES AND SPECIAL EVENTS DAYS

16

Birthday of Robert Service (Jan. 16, 1874–Sept. 11, 1958). English-born Canadian poet of the Northwest, famous for "The Ballad of Sam McGee."

16

Prohibition Day. Anniversary of the beginning of Prohibition on Jan. 16, 1920, when the 18th Amendment to the Constitution of the U.S. became law and the sale of alcoholic beverages became illegal. Repealed by the 21st Amendment.

16

Religious Freedom Day. Anniversary of the statute adopted by the Va. legislature on Jan. 16, 1786, that guaranteed religious freedom and tolerance in the state. The statute had been drafted by Thomas Jefferson and introduced by James Madison, and became the model for the 1st Amendment to the U.S. Constitution.

HOLY DAYS AND FEAST DAYS

17

Feast of St. Antony (251–Jan. 17, 356). Egyptian hermit and founder of a desert community of ascetics; considered the founder of Christian monasticism. Animals are blessed on his feast day in Spain and Mexico. Orth.: Jan. 17 or 30.

ANNIVERSARIES AND SPECIAL EVENTS DAYS

17

Anniversary of President Dwight D. Eisenhower's farewell address (Jan. 17, 1961), in which he said, "In the councils of government, we must guard against the acquisition of unwarranted influence, whether sought or unsought, by the military-industrial complex. The potential of the disastrous rise of misplaced power exists and will persist."

17

Birthday of Benjamin Franklin (Jan. 17, 1706–Apr. 17, 1790). American printer, statesman, inventor, and diplomat; America's first world citizen. Elected to the Hall of Fame for Great Americans. International Printing Week, Sunday–Saturday, is the week including Jan. 17, and Printing Ink Day is the Tuesday. Schools in some states start Thrift Week on Franklin's birthday.

17

Birthday of David Lloyd George (Jan. 17, 1863–Mar. 26, 1945). British statesman, one of the leading figures in 20th-century British history.

17

Death anniversary of Skanderbeg (George Kastrioti; 1405–Jan. 17, 1468). Albanian national hero; repulsed 13 Turkish invasions, 1444–66, thereby becoming the hero of Europe.

17

Battle of Cowpens Day. Anniversary of the Revolutionary War battle of Jan. 17, 1781, near Spartansburg, S.C., that thwarted the plans of British General Charles Cornwallis to move into the middle of the Carolinas.

17

Nautilus Day. Anniversary of the launching of the U.S. submarine *Nautilus*, the world's first atomic-powered vessel, on Jan. 17, 1955.

HOLIDAYS AND CIVIC DAYS

18

Foundation Day in Lima, Peru; local official public holiday. Celebrates the founding of the city by Francisco Pizarro on Jan. 18, 1535; festivities last a week.

ANNIVERSARIES AND SPECIAL EVENTS DAYS

18

Birthday of Rubén Dario (Jan. 18, 1867–Feb. 6, 1916). Nicaraguan poet and short-story writer recognized as one of the outstanding poets of Latin America.

18

Birthday of Peter Mark Roget (Jan. 18, 1779–Sept. 12, 1869). English physician and medical author, but famous for his *Thesaurus of English Words and Phrases.*

18

Birthday of Daniel Webster (Jan. 18, 1782–Oct. 24, 1852). American statesman, Mass. lawyer, and orator. Elected to the Hall of Fame for Great Americans.

18

Pooh Day. Anniversary of the birth of Alan Alexander Milne (Jan. 18, 1882–Jan. 31, 1956), English poet and playwright best known for his verse and stories for children, notably *Winnie-the-Pooh.*

18

Santa Prisca Day in Taxco, Mexico. Honors the local patron saint. Climax of one of Latin America's most colorful festivals; features a dance of the Moors and Christians.

HOLY DAYS AND FEAST DAYS

19

Epiphany in churches using the Julian calendar exclusively: *see* Jan. 6.

19

Feast of St. Canute (died July 19, ca. 1086). King of Denmark and supporter of the clergy and missionaries; the country's patron saint.

19

Timket (Epiphany) in the Coptic and Ethiopian Orthodox Churches; on Jan. 20 in some years; official public holiday in Ethiopia and Eritrea. The greatest festival of the Ethiopian year. On the eve are dramatic processions, a late-night Mass, and all-night picnics. On *Timket,* water is blessed and sprinkled on the people in symbolic baptism, followed by more processions. The festival lasts through Jan. 20 (or 21), a feast of St. Michael the Archangel, the most popular saint. Everyone parties, and horsemen play *gugs,* a form of martial horsemanship.

HOLIDAYS AND CIVIC DAYS

19

Name day of Archbishop Makarios III (Mikhail Khristodolou Mouskos; Aug. 13, 1913–Aug. 3, 1977); official public holiday in Cyprus for Greek Cypriots. Honors the man who had led the movement for unification with Greece and at independence served as the first president of Cyprus.

ANNIVERSARIES AND SPECIAL EVENTS DAYS

19

Anniversary of the founding of the American Civil Liberties Union (ACLU) on Jan. 19, 1920, by Roger Baldwin.

19

Birthday of Robert Edward Lee (Jan. 19, 1807–Oct. 12, 1870). American soldier and educator; commander of the Army of Northern Va. in the Civil War and the greatest military leader of the Confederacy; subsequently, president of the institution known today as Washington and Lee University. Elected to the Hall of Fame for Great Americans, and represents Va. in Statuary Hall.

19

Birthday of Edgar Allan Poe (Jan. 19, 1809–Oct. 7, 1849). American poet, short-story writer, magazine editor, and critic; of great influence on poetry and fiction. Elected to the Hall of Fame for Great Americans. Edgar Allan Poe Awards are presented annually by the Mystery Writers Association.

19

Birthday of James Watt (Jan. 19, 1736–Aug. 25, 1819). Scottish engineer and inventor who developed a separate condensing vessel for the steam engine. The watt and kilowatt units of power are named in his honor.

HOLY DAYS AND FEAST DAYS

20

Feast of St. Sebastian (died ca. 288). By legend, a soldier martyred by arrows. Patron saint of archers, athletes, and soldiers, and of Rio de Janeiro, Brazil; invoked against plague. Orth.: Dec. 18 or 31.

HOLIDAYS AND CIVIC DAYS

20

Day of the Martyrs in Azerbaijan; official public holiday. Commemorates the many Azeri civilians killed by Soviet troops on Jan. 20, 1990, in a futile Soviet attempt to stave off independence.

20

Foundation Day in Rio de Janeiro, Brazil; local official public holiday. Founded by the French, Jan. 20, 1555.

20

Heroes' Day in Cape Verde and in Guinea-Bissau; official public holiday in both. Honors both countries' courageous and sacrificial citizens, especially Amilcar Cabral, assassinated on this day in 1973.

20

Presidential Inauguration Day in the U.S.; in years following presidential elections (thus, in 2001, 2005, etc.). The ceremony occurs in Washington, D.C.; at noontime, the chief justice of the Supreme Court administers the oath of office to the president-elect; there follows an inauguration parade, with lavish inaugural balls in the evening.

ANNIVERSARIES AND SPECIAL EVENTS DAYS

20

Birthday of André-Marie Ampère (Jan. 20, 1775–June 10, 1836). French physicist, mathematician, and discoverer of Ampère's law.

20

Birthday of Euclides (Rodrigues Pimenta) da Cunha (Jan. 20, 1866–Aug. 15, 1909). Brazilian engineer, soldier, and journalist who wrote the epic *Os Sertões* (1902), translated as *Rebellion in the Backlands*, describing the war of Brazil against the city of Canudos.

20

Birthday of Federico Fellini (Jan. 20, 1920–Oct. 31, 1993). Italian cinematographer, noted for his films *La Dolce Vita* and *8½*.

20

Birthday of Johannes Vilhelm Jensen (Jan. 20, 1873–Nov. 25, 1950). Danish novelist and lyric poet whose series of epic novels describing the northern peoples from the Ice Age to the 15th century brought him the 1944 Nobel Prize in literature.

20

Birthday of Janis Joplin (Jan. 19, 1943–Oct. 4, 1970). Husky-voiced rock superstar whose hits included "Me and Bobby McGee," "Mercedes Benz," "Piece of My Heart," and "Cry Baby."

20

Birthday of King Sebastian (Sebastião) of Portugal (Jan. 20, 1554–Aug. 4, 1578). Adulated ruler of Portugal, himself fanatically religious; died on crusade against the Moroccans. Thereafter, popularly regarded as a future savior who would deliver his people from Spanish rule (in Portugal) and later from miscellaneous ills (in Brazil).

20

Birthday of Wolfe Tone (Jan. 20, 1763–Nov. 19, 1798). Irish republican and rebel; led the Society of United Irishmen, joining Protestants and Catholics; led a military force from France to Ireland during the insurrection of 1798; executed.

HOLY DAYS AND FEAST DAYS

21

Feast of St. Agnes (died ca. 304). Roman virgin and martyr; symbol of virginal innocence. Patron saint of chastity, young girls, and Girl Scouts. On this day the Pope blesses two lambs whose wool is used to make circular bands called *pallia*, which he sends to his archbishops. Orth.: Jan. 21 or Feb. 3.

HOLIDAYS AND CIVIC DAYS

21

Errol Barrow Day in Barbados; official public holiday. Honors Errol Barrow (Jan. 21, 1920–June 1, 1987), who led Barbados peacefully into independence and died in office as prime minister.

ANNIVERSARIES AND SPECIAL EVENTS DAYS

21

Anniversary of the founding of Kiwanis International; the first Kiwanis Club was chartered on Jan. 21, 1915, in Detroit, Mich.

21

Birthday of Ethan Allen (Jan. 21, 1738–Feb. 12, 1789). American Revolutionary War commander, organizer of the Green Mountain Boys. Represents Vt. in Statuary Hall.

21

Birthday of Roger Nash Baldwin (Jan. 21, 1884–Aug. 26, 1981). Founder of the American Civil Liberties Union (ACLU), the country's unofficial defender of its civil liberties.

21

Birthday of John Charles Frémont (Jan. 21, 1813–July 13, 1890). American surveyor and army officer who made official expeditions into the West; frequently called the Pathfinder.

21

Birthday of Thomas Jonathan "Stonewall" Jackson (Jan. 21, 1824–May 10, 1863). American, born in Clarksburg, Va. (later W.Va.). Confederate general, famous in the Civil War for his strategy and tactics, especially with cavalry. His death was a grave loss for the Confederacy. Elected to the Hall of Fame for Great Americans.

HOLIDAYS AND CIVIC DAYS

CA. 22

Wellington Day in Wellington Province, New Zealand; provincial anniversary day and official public holiday on the Monday nearest Jan. 22. Commemorates the founding of the city, now the capital, on Jan. 22, 1840.

22

St. Vincent and the Grenadines Day in St. Vincent and the Grenadines; official public holiday. Also called Discovery Day. Commemorates the sighting by Columbus on Jan. 22, 1498 (St. Vincent of Saragossa's Day). St. Vincent is the island's patron saint. Also on this day is the Diamond Dairy Road Relay.

22

Ukrainian Day in Ukraine. Commemorates the Jan. 22, 1918, proclamation of the Ukrainian National Republic.

ANNIVERSARIES AND SPECIAL EVENTS DAYS

22

Anniversary of the *Roe* v. *Wade* decision by the U.S. Supreme Court on Jan. 22, 1973. The decision struck down state laws prohibiting abortion in the first 6 months of pregnancy.

22

Birthday of Francis Bacon (Jan. 22, 1561–Apr. 9, 1626). English essayist, philosopher, and jurist who developed the inductive method of inquiry.

22

Birthday of Lord Byron (George Gordon Byron; Jan. 22, 1788–Apr. 19, 1824). English Romantic poet famous for his *Childe Harold.*

22

Birthday of D. W. (David Wark) Griffith (Jan. 22, 1875–July 23, 1948). Pioneer director-producer of American motion pictures; made *Birth of a Nation* (1915).

22

Birthday of August Strindberg (Jan. 22, 1849–May 14, 1912). Swedish playwright and novelist who wrote plays of social criticism and the conflict between the sexes; best known for *Miss Julie.*

22

Birthday of Beatrice Potter Webb (Jan. 22, 1858–Apr. 30, 1943). English economist who collaborated with her husband, Sidney Webb, on many works on economics.

22

Death anniversary of Molly Pitcher (born Mary Ludwig; ca. 1759–Jan. 22, 1833). Heroine of the American Revolution who earned her nickname as a water carrier at the Battle of Monmouth (June 28, 1778). By legend, she became a replacement gunner when her husband, John Hays, was wounded; called Sergeant Molly after Washington issued her a warrant as a noncommissioned officer.

HOLY DAYS AND FEAST DAYS

23

Feast of St. Ildephonsus (607–Jan. 23, 667). Spanish monk devoted to the Virgin Mary; considered a doctor of the church in the Spanish church. The cathedral in Toledo, Spain, where he experienced an apparition of the Virgin is a major pilgrimage center. In the San Ildefonso pueblo in N.Mex., this day is celebrated with the buffalo dance and other dances combining Native American religious rites and Christian ceremonies.

ANNIVERSARIES AND SPECIAL EVENTS DAYS

23

Anniversary of the day in 1907 when Charles Curtis (Jan. 25, 1860–Feb. 8, 1936) of Kans., a Kaw Indian, became the first Native American U.S. senator; he was later vice president under Hoover, 1929–32.

23

Birthday of John Hancock (Jan. 23, 1737–Oct. 8, 1793). American Revolutionary patriot, first signer of the Declaration of Independence. His name has become synonymous with *signature,* because of his deliberately bold signing of the Declaration. Today is called National Handwriting Day, to encourage more legible handwriting.

23

Birthday of Stendhal (Marie-Henri Beyle; Jan. 23, 1783–Mar. 23, 1842). French novelist who wrote *The Red and the Black* and *The Charterhouse of Parma.*

23

Anti–Poll Tax Day. Anniversary of the 1964 ratification of the 24th Amendment to the U.S. Constitution, forbidding the collection of a poll tax as a requirement for voting in national elections.

HOLY DAYS AND FEAST DAYS

24

Feast of St. Francis de Sales (Aug. 21, 1567–Dec. 28, 1622). French Jesuit leader of the Counter-Reformation, noted for his intellect and wisdom. Doctor of the church. Patron saint of authors, journalists, and the Catholic press.

ANNIVERSARIES AND SPECIAL EVENTS DAYS

24

Birthday of Edith Newbold Wharton (Jan. 24, 1862–Aug. 11, 1937). American novelist, notable for *Ethan Frome* and *The Age of Innocence;* Pulitzer Prize winner in 1921 and 1935. The first woman granted an honorary degree from Yale University.

24

Alacitas ("Fair") in La Paz, Bolivia. A festival of abundance, dating from Inca times, and dedicated to Ekeko, the household god of agricultural abundance.

24

California Gold Rush Day. Anniversary of the accidental discovery of gold in northern Calif. on Jan. 24, 1848, provoking the Gold Rush.

HOLIDAYS AND CIVIC DAYS

25

Foundation Day in São Paulo, Brazil; local official public holiday. The city was founded on Jan. 25, 1554.

ANNIVERSARIES AND SPECIAL EVENTS DAYS

25

Birthday of Anne of Brittany (Jan. 25, 1477–Jan. 9, 1514). Noblewoman of intelligence, vivacity, charm, and high education, who married Charles VIII of France in the interests of her people and earned their undying gratitude (and developed a loving marriage). Every Breton town remembers her.

25

Birthday of Robert Boyle (Jan. 25, 1627–Dec. 30, 1691). Irish physicist and chemist who set forth the famous Boyle's law.

25

Birthday of Tom (Antonio Carlos) Jobim (Jan. 25, 1927–Dec. 8, 1994). Brazilian songwriter and composer. A major figure in bossa nova music. Created, with the poet and lyricist Vinícius de Moraes, the famous song "The Girl from Ipanema."

25

Birthday of Virginia Woolf (born Adeline Virginia Stephen; Jan. 25, 1882–Mar. 28, 1941, by suicide). English novelist, essayist, and critic; women's rights activist; wrote *To the Lighthouse, Mrs. Dalloway, Orlando,* and *A Room of One's Own.*

25

Burns Night. Anniversary of the birth of Robert Burns (Jan. 25, 1759–July 21, 1796), Scotland's national poet; a champion of the common man, a scorner of hypocrisy, a romantic; transmitter of "Auld Lang Syne." Scots and others all over the world gather to honor him at the Burns Supper, with special menus, programs, and toasts.

HOLIDAYS AND CIVIC DAYS

26

Australia Day in Australia; official public holiday. Commemorates the landing of Captain Arthur

Phillip and his company of British convicts on Jan. 26, 1788. Observed since 1817; official public holiday since 1838.

26

Duarte Day in the Dominican Republic; official public holiday. Honors Juan Pablo Duarte (Jan. 26, 1814–July 15, 1876), leader in the fight for independence from Haiti, and in the subsequent republic.

26

Republic Day in India; official public holiday. Commemorates the proclamation of the republic and attainment of full independence from the U.K. on Jan. 26, 1950. A day of civic grandeur, with an enormous parade in New Delhi.

26

Admission Day in Mich. Anniversary of Mich.'s admission as the 26th state on Jan. 26, 1837.

ANNIVERSARIES AND SPECIAL EVENTS DAYS

26

Birthday of Roy Chapman Andrews (Jan. 26, 1884–Mar. 11, 1960). American naturalist, explorer, and author; famous for finding dinosaur eggs, new geological formations, and the remains of baluchithere, a very large, extinct, rhinoceros-like mammal.

26

Birthday of Douglas MacArthur (Jan. 26, 1880–Apr. 5, 1964). American general, supreme commander of Allied forces in the Southwest Pacific in World War II, military governor of Japan following the surrender, and influential commander during the Korean War until removed by President Truman for insubordination (Apr. 11, 1951).

HOLY DAYS AND FEAST DAYS

27

Feast of Angela Merici (Mar. 21, ca. 1470–Jan. 27, 1540). Founder of the Ursuline Order in 1535, the first teaching order of nuns in the Catholic Church.

ANNIVERSARIES AND SPECIAL EVENTS DAYS

27

Anniversary of the liberation of the Auschwitz concentration camp by Russian forces on Jan. 27, 1945.

27

Anniversary of the lifting of the siege of Leningrad. The people of the Soviet Union's second-largest city were besieged and decimated by German forces from Sept. 4, 1941, to Jan. 27, 1944.

27

Anniversary of the ending of the Vietnam War; on Jan. 27, 1973, the U.S., North Vietnam, South Vietnam, and the Viet Cong signed a peace treaty in Paris, to take effect on Jan. 28.

27

Birthday of Lewis Carroll (Charles Lutwidge Dodgson; Jan. 27, 1832–Jan. 14, 1898). English mathematician and author of the classic *Alice's Adventures in Wonderland*.

27

Birthday of Wolfgang Amadeus Mozart (Jan. 27, 1756–Dec. 5, 1791). Austrian concert pianist and world-renowned composer. In appreciation of his work, Mozart's birthday is celebrated by musical societies in all nations.

27

Birthday of Hyman George Rickover (Jan. 27, 1900–July 9, 1986). Russian-born American naval admiral, called the Father of the Nuclear Navy; supervised the development of nuclear-powered submarines such as the *Nautilus*.

HOLY DAYS AND FEAST DAYS

28

Death anniversary and feast of the Blessed Charlemagne (Apr. 2, ca. 742–Jan. 28, 814; ruled 800–814). Frankish king and greatest of the Carolingian dynasty, crowned Emperor of the West on Dec. 25, 800, by Pope Leo III. Presided over the remarkable Carolingian Renaissance in western Europe. In French colleges, this is St. Charlemagne's Day, when he is honored at a speechmaking, champagne-drinking breakfast.

28

Feast of St. Thomas Aquinas (ca. 1225–Mar. 7, 1274). Italian Dominican priest; professor and theologian at the University of Paris. Prolific writer, noted for the *Summa theologiae*. The most impressive and influential intellect of the medieval church. Doctor of the church, called the Angelic Doctor. Patron saint of all academic institutions.

HOLIDAYS AND CIVIC DAYS

28

Feast of St. Devota (Sainte-Dévote; died 303) in Monaco; official public holiday. Corsican martyr; patron saint of Monaco and Corsica. A boat is ceremoniously burned on the eve.

ANNIVERSARIES AND SPECIAL EVENTS DAYS

28

Anniversary of the explosion of the U.S. space shuttle *Challenger* on Jan. 28, 1986, killing all 7 aboard. Observed in Ill. schools as Christa McAuliffe Day, in commemoration of space exploration. Christa McAuliffe (born Sharon Christa Corrigan; Sept. 2, 1948–Jan. 28, 1986), a N.H. schoolteacher, would have been the first ordinary citizen in space.

28

Birthday of Charles George Gordon (Jan. 28, 1833–Jan. 26, 1885). British soldier and military hero known as Gordon Pasha, Gordon of Khartoum, or Chinese Gordon.

28

Birthday of José Julian Martí y Perez (Jan. 28, 1853–May 19, 1895). Cuban poet and independence hero against the Spanish.

28

Birthday of Sir Henry Morton Stanley (born John Rowlands; Jan. 28, 1841–May 10, 1904). Anglo-American explorer remembered for his fulfillment of the mission to find the explorer David Livingstone.

28

Death anniversary of Sir Francis Drake (ca. 1540–Jan. 28, 1596). English navigator, the first Englishman to circumnavigate the globe (1577–80), and the admiral who defeated the Spanish armada; the most renowned seaman of the Elizabethan Age.

HOLIDAYS AND CIVIC DAYS

29

Auckland Day in Auckland, New Zealand; provincial anniversary day and official public holiday on nearest Monday. Commemorates the founding of the city on Jan. 29, 1841.

29

Kansas Day. Commemorates the admission of Kans. as the 34th state on Jan. 29, 1861. Has been a special day of celebration for Kans. Republicans since 1892 and is a popular day for political meetings.

ANNIVERSARIES AND SPECIAL EVENTS DAYS

29

Anniversary of the institution by Queen Victoria of the Victoria Cross, the most coveted of all British orders, on Jan. 29, 1856, to reward individual acts of bravery.

29

Birthday of Anton Pavlovich Chekhov (Jan. 29, 1860–ca. July 14, 1904). Russian dramatist and short-story writer whose works realistically explore the frustrations of the rural upper and middle classes of his time. His 4 most influential plays were *The Seagull, Uncle Vanya, The Three Sisters,* and *The Cherry Orchard.*

29

Birthday of William McKinley (Jan. 29, 1843–Sept. 14, 1901). Ohio lawyer; Civil War officer; congressman and governor of Ohio; 25th president of the U.S. (1897–1901; Republican). Died by assassination (shot by an anarchist, Sept. 6, 1901). His administration was dominated by financial issues (tariffs, the gold standard), and he presided over the Spanish-American War. Buried in Canton, Ohio. On McKinley Day (the last Saturday in Jan.), a William McKinley banquet is held annually in Canton, his hometown.

29

Birthday of Thomas Paine (Jan. 29, 1737–June 8, 1809). American Revolutionary propagandist and author of *Common Sense, The Rights of Man,* and *The Age of Reason.* This day is called Common Sense Day in his honor, to encourage people to use good sense in appreciating and protecting the rights of all people. Thomas Paine Day, on the Sunday nearest Jan. 29, is celebrated by the Huguenot–Thomas Paine Historical Society with annual meetings.

29

Birthday of Emanuel Swedenborg (Jan. 29, 1688–Mar. 29, 1772). Swedish scientist, inventor, author, mystic, and religious leader.

16

HOLY DAYS AND FEAST DAYS

30

St. Charles Day in the Church of England. Honors Charles I (Charles Stuart), king of Great Britain (Nov. 19, 1600–Jan. 30, 1649; ruled 1624–49); beheaded by Order of Parliament under Oliver Cromwell, and then widely pronounced a martyr; the only post-Reformation Anglican saint. The Society of Charles the Martyr holds services on the scaffold site in the courtyard of the Royal United Services Museum. Additionally, on or near Feb. 2, services are held at the Church of St. Martin-in-the-Fields and in Trafalgar Square in London.

30

Synaxis of the Three Hierarchs, the saints Basil the Great, Gregory the Theologian, and John Chrysostom. All three men are fathers of the church; they are highly revered in the Orthodox Church and symbolize Orthodoxy. Each also has his own feast. Orth.: Jan. 30 or Feb. 12.

HOLIDAYS AND CIVIC DAYS

30

The King's Birthday in Jordan; official public holiday. Honors King Abdullah II (Jan. 30, 1962– , ruled June 9, 1999–); son of the late King Hussein.

ANNIVERSARIES AND SPECIAL EVENTS DAYS

30

Birthday of Franklin Delano Roosevelt (Jan. 30, 1882–Apr. 12, 1945). Lawyer; governor of N.Y.; statesman; assistant secretary of the navy under President Woodrow Wilson; 32nd president of the U.S. (1933–45; Democrat); died in office. The only president to serve more than 2 terms. Vigorously worked to end America's Great Depression. Stoutly resisted the growth of fascism in Europe and was crucially involved in the Allied victory in World War II. One of the most important presidents in American history, on a par with Washington and Lincoln. Buried in Hyde Park, N.Y., where his house and library are under the jurisdiction of the federal government.

30

Woman Peerage Day in the U.K. Anniversary of the passage of a bill by the House of Lords on Jan. 30, 1958, and by the House of Commons on Feb. 13, 1958, establishing lifetime peerages for both men and women, thus admitting women into the House of Lords for the first time in its history.

HOLY DAYS AND FEAST DAYS

31

Feast of St. John Bosco (Don Bosco; 1815–Jan. 31, 1888). Italian priest who worked with neglected boys and girls; founded the Society of St. Francis de Sales (the Salesians) and the Daughters of Our Lady, Help of Christians. Patron saint of editors. In 1883, he predicted the creation of the city of Brasília, Brazil, and is a cult figure there.

ANNIVERSARIES AND SPECIAL EVENTS DAYS

31

Anniversary of the first successful launching of a U.S. satellite; *Explorer I* was launched on Jan. 31, 1958, and discovered the Van Allen radiation belt.

31

Birthday of Irving Langmuir (Jan. 31, 1881–Aug. 16, 1957). American chemist who is credited with the development of the basic scientific principles and discoveries that have been applied in the atomic age. Received the 1932 Nobel Prize in chemistry.

31

Birthday of Thomas Merton (Jan. 31, 1915–Dec. 10, 1968). American Trappist monk and author; his first major work was *The Seven Storey Mountain*.

31

Birthday of Robert Morris (Jan. 31, 1734–May 8, 1806). American merchant, financier of the American Revolution, and signer of the Declaration of Independence.

31

Birthday of Anna Pavlova (Jan. 31, 1881–Jan. 23, 1931). Russian ballerina, perhaps the greatest dancer of all time, famed for her role in *Giselle* and for "The Dying Swan."

31

Birthday of Jackie (Jack Roosevelt) Robinson (Jan. 31, 1919–Oct. 24, 1972). First African American athlete to play in major-league baseball (Brooklyn Dodgers, 1947–56). Recipient of the Spingarn Medal. Elected to the Baseball Hall of Fame. Robinson broke baseball's color barrier on Apr. 15, 1947, in a game between the Boston Braves and the Brooklyn Dodgers, who won 5–3.

31

Birthday of Franz Peter Schubert (Jan. 31, 1797–
Nov. 19, 1828). Austrian composer, famous for
The Unfinished Symphony and for such songs as
"Who Is Sylvia?"

MOVABLE DAYS IN JANUARY

HOLY DAYS AND FEAST DAYS

IROQUOIS MID-WINTER CEREMONY; 8
days, beginning on the 5th night after the moment
of the 1st new moon in Jan. A ceremony of thankfulness to the creator for the past year's favors and
of hope for blessings in the coming year. At this
time the Pleiades are at their highest in the night
sky and nighttime travel is well-lit by the moon.

ANNIVERSARIES AND
SPECIAL EVENTS DAYS

WORLD RELIGION DAY; 3rd Sunday in Jan. A
day of meditation and prayer sponsored since
1950 by the Baha'i National Spiritual Assembly in
the U.S. to promote unity among the peoples of
the world through demonstrating the truth in the
concept of oneness in all revealed religion.

MT. CAMEROUN RACE IN CAMEROON; usu-
ally the last Sunday in Jan. Africa's most demanding footrace, up and down the mountain.

BON SOO WINTER CARNIVAL IN SAULT
STE. MARIE, CANADA; 10 days, beginning
last Friday in Jan. One of Canada's largest winter
carnivals.

SUNRISE FESTIVAL IN INUVIK, CANADA; on
the night preceding the year's first sunrise. A night
of fireworks, bonfires, and refreshments while
awaiting the first sunrise after 6 weeks of night.

ATI-ATIHAN FESTIVAL IN KALIBO, PHILIP-
PINES; 3rd Saturday–Sunday in Jan. The Philippines' most famous and ardent fiesta, with
columns of musicians and dancers, and enthusiastic street dancing. Celebrates the 1212 arrival of
Bornean religious refugees fleeing Muslim conquerors; the aboriginal Ati granted coastal lands.
The festival began as a harvest peace festival of
gratitude to Ati benefactors. Later, it was combined with gratitude to the child Jesus, who had
been invoked in repelling a Muslim invasion.

MEITLISUNNTIG IN THE SEETAL DIS-
TRICT, ARGAU, SWITZERLAND; 2nd Sunday
in Jan. A festival featuring a military procession of
girls reenacting the role of women in the Villmer-
gen War of 1712.

DICING FOR THE MAID'S MONEY DAY IN
GUILDFORD, ENGLAND; last Thursday in Jan.
A ceremony to fulfill the terms of a 17th-century
will providing for the casting of dice by 2 maidser-
vants for the interest from a trust; amount is about
12 pounds; was intended as dowry money.

UP-HELLY-AA AT LERWICK IN SCOT-
LAND'S SHETLAND ISLANDS; last Tuesday
in Jan. A spectacular Viking midwinter fire ceremony, with the burning of a longship. The whole
town participates, and tourists are unwelcome.

NATIONAL SCHOOL NURSE DAY IN THE
U.S.; 4th Wednesday in Jan.

ST. PAUL WINTER CARNIVAL IN ST. PAUL,
MINN.; 10 days, beginning last Friday in Jan. A
festival celebrating winter, with sleigh and cutter
parades, ice capades, frolics, and sports, high-
lighted by events centered around Boreas, King of
the Winds; the Queen of the Snows; and the
king's enemy, Vulcanus. Since 1886; Minn.'s largest
attraction.

February

February, the 2nd month of the Gregorian calendar, gets its name from *Februa* through the verb *februare,* meaning "to purify." It is the shortest month, with 28 days, except in leap years, when it has 29. In ancient Rome, it was the month of purification, with special ceremonies of repentance held on the 15th. In modern times, for many Christians it is a period of preparation for Easter. It is frequently the month of Mardi Gras and other pre-Lenten carnivals. In the U.S., February is sometimes called Presidents' Month because of the observance of the birthdays of 2 great American presidents, Washington and Lincoln. It is also African American History Month and American History Month.

The flowers for February are the violet and the primrose. The birthstone is the amethyst.

HOLY DAYS AND FEAST DAYS

1
Feast of St. Brigid (ca. 450–Feb. 1, 528). Irish abbess and friend of St. Patrick; founder of the double monastery (of monks and nuns) at Kildare; a woman of great influence famous for learning, art, spirituality, and hospitality. Patron saint of Irish nuns, of dairy workers, and of Ireland, Wales, Australia, and New Zealand.

HOLIDAYS AND CIVIC DAYS

1
National Freedom Day in the U.S. Anniversary of the signing by President Lincoln on Feb. 1, 1865, of the 13th Amendment to the Constitution, which abolished slavery, effective Dec. 18, 1865. A presidential proclamation of 1949 established the perpetuity of this observance.

ANNIVERSARIES AND SPECIAL EVENTS DAYS

1
Birthday of (William) Clark Gable (Feb. 1, 1901–Nov. 16, 1960). American film actor; the premier leading man after the introduction of talking films; famous for his 1939 role as Rhett Butler in *Gone with the Wind.*

1
Birthday of Victor Herbert (Feb. 1, 1859–May 26, 1924). American composer and conductor whose operettas *Babes in Toyland, Naughty Marietta,* and others are a part of the musical heritage of the U.S.

1
Birthday of Langston Hughes (Feb. 1, 1902–May 22, 1967). African American poet; innovator in the interpretation of the African American experience. Known also for his anthologies *The Poetry of the Negro* and *The Book of Negro Folklore,* compiled with Arna Bontemps.

CA. 1
Bean-Throwing Ceremony (*Setsubun,* "Parting of the Season") in Japan; Feb. 1–3, depending on locality. Marks the beginning of spring, when evil spirits are exorcised. In the evening, roasted beans are thrown into dark corners to banish demons.

1
Festival of Our Lady of Charity (*Virgen de la Caridad*) in Mira, Ecuador. Observed with fireworks, dances, ball games, and rodeos.

HOLY DAYS AND FEAST DAYS

2
Candlemas. Traditional feast of the Purification of the Blessed Virgin Mary among Catholics and Protestants; but in the Catholic Church since 1970, replaced on this day by the Presentation of the Lord in the Temple. Traditionally, liturgical

candles were blessed on this day. As *Candelaria*, this feast is widely celebrated in Latin countries, particularly in Brazil and Andean South America.

2

Feast of the Presentation of the Lord in the Temple. Occurs 40 days after Jesus' birth, following ancient Jewish practice. In the Eastern Churches, dates from before the 4th century. In the Catholic Church, replaces the traditional Purification of the Blessed Virgin Mary, or Candlemas. The Episcopalian Church uses both names. Orth. Feb. 2 or 15.

2

Iemanjá Day in the syncretic religion of Condomblé, in Salvador, Brazil. Honors Iemanjá, Queen of the Waters; fishers send her gaily decorated gift boats, loaded with presents, accompanied by Condomblé music. (Elsewhere in Brazil, celebrated on Jan. 1, Aug. 15, Dec. 8, or Dec. 13.)

ANNIVERSARIES AND SPECIAL EVENTS DAYS

2

Anniversary of the signing of the Treaty of Guadalupe Hidalgo, ending the Mexican-American War, on Feb. 2, 1848; ceded territory that later became Tex., N.Mex., Ariz., and Calif. to the U.S.

2

Birthday of James Joyce (Feb. 2, 1882–Jan. 13, 1941). Irish novelist and poet; his *Ulysses* and *Finnegan's Wake* are considered masterpieces.

2

Birthday of Damding Sukhbaatar (Feb. 2, 1893–Feb. 22, 1923, poisoned). Revered Mongolian independence hero; brilliant general and minister of war who drove out the Manchus, allowing Mongolia to proclaim its independence.

2

Death anniversary of Giovanni Palestrina (ca. 1525–Feb. 2, 1594). Italian composer celebrated for his masses and other sacred music.

2

Groundhog Day in the U.S. According to folklore, if the groundhog, or woodchuck, emerges from his burrow on this day and sees his shadow, winter will last another 6 weeks. Punxsutawney, Pa., is the center of this observance, said to have been introduced by early German settlers.

2

Robinson Crusoe Day. Anniversary of the rescue of a Scot, Alexander Selkirk, from an uninhabited island on Feb. 2, 1709, an event that inspired Daniel Defoe in his writing of *Robinson Crusoe*.

HOLY DAYS AND FEAST DAYS

3

Feast of St. Ansgar (ca. 801–Feb. 3, 865). Missionary to Scandinavia, called the Apostle to the North.

3

Feast of St. Blaise (died ca. 316). Bishop and martyr of Sebastea, Armenia. Invoked for illness of the throat; patron saint of Paraguay (called Blas in Latin America). Orth.: Feb. 11 or 24.

HOLIDAYS AND CIVIC DAYS

3

Heroes' Day in Mozambique; official public holiday. Honors all heroic citizens, particularly Eduardo Chivambo Mondlane, the first president of the independence organization FRELIMO; assassinated on Feb. 3, 1969.

3

Anniversary of the founding of the Vietnamese Communist Party on Feb. 3, 1930; official public holiday in Vietnam.

ANNIVERSARIES AND SPECIAL EVENTS DAYS

3

Anniversary of the ratification, on Feb. 3, 1870, of the 15th Amendment to the U.S. Constitution, whereby no citizen may be denied the right to vote on account of race, color, or previous condition of servitude.

3

Anniversary of the ratification, on Feb. 3, 1913, of the 16th Amendment to the U.S. Constitution, whereby Congress is granted the power to levy taxes on income.

3

Birthday of Elizabeth Blackwell (Feb. 3, 1821–May 31, 1910). First woman physician in the U.S., founder of the New York Infirmary for Women and Children, and lecturer on hygiene and preventive medicine. An American Women's Medical Association Award for distinguished service is presented in her honor.

3

Birthday of Sidney Lanier (Feb. 3, 1842–Sept. 7, 1881). American poet, musician, and critic. Elected to the Hall of Fame for Great Americans.

3

Birthday of Felix Mendelssohn-Bartholdy (Feb. 3, 1809–Nov. 4, 1847). German romantic composer famous for piano and violin concertos, oratorios, and chamber music.

3

Birthday of Alexander Mieklejohn (Feb. 3, 1872–Sept. 16, 1964). British-born American educator; head of the University of Wisconsin's Experimental College (1927–32), the inspiration for all of America's experimental colleges. In later life, he was a prominent scholar and defender of the 1st Amendment's freedom of speech.

3

Birthday of Norman Rockwell (Feb. 3, 1894–Nov. 8, 1978). American artist and illustrator, noted for his cover art for the *Saturday Evening Post*.

3

Birthday of Gertrude Stein (Feb. 3, 1874–July 27, 1946). American expatriate author whose *Making of Americans* led to a heated literary controversy over style and meaning. *The Autobiography of Alice B. Toklas* is actually Gertrude Stein's autobiography.

3

Death anniversary of Charles Hardin "Buddy" Holly (Sept. 7, 1936–Feb. 3, 1959). American musician, composer, and band leader; very innovative and influential, a pioneer of rock and roll. Died in a plane crash with two other musicians, on "the day the music died."

3

Gutenberg Day. Death anniversary of Johannes Gutenberg (ca. 1390–Feb. 3, 1468). German inventor of movable type; publisher of the Gutenberg Bible, "the finest example of printer's art ever known."

CA. 3

Li Chhun ("Spring Is Here") in the Chinese calendar. Traditional beginning of spring; an important date in the farming year.

HOLIDAYS AND CIVIC DAYS

4

Beginning of the Armed Struggle Day in Angola; official public holiday. Commemorates the beginning of the war of independence against the Portuguese in 1961.

4

National Day in Sri Lanka; official public holiday. Commemorates independence attained from the U.K. on Feb. 4, 1948. Ceylon changed its name to Sri Lanka in 1972.

ANNIVERSARIES AND SPECIAL EVENTS DAYS

4

Anniversary of the incorporation by Congressional Charter of what is now the American Academy of Arts and Letters on Feb. 4, 1913, with the objective of fostering literature, music, and the fine arts in the U.S. Election to the Academy, or to receive one of its awards, is considered the highest formal recognition of artistic merit in the U.S. Awards and honors are conferred at an annual ceremony, usually the 3rd Wednesday in May.

4

Anniversary of the founding of the United Service Organizations (U.S.O.) on Feb. 4, 1941, to serve the social, educational, religious, and welfare needs of the U.S. armed forces. The anniversary is observed annually at service centers.

4

Birthday of Mark Hopkins (Feb. 4, 1802–June 17, 1887). American educator and moral philosopher who served as president of Williams College. Elected to the Hall of Fame for Great Americans.

4

Birthday of Tadeusz Andrzej Bonawentura Kościuszko (Feb. 4, 1746–Oct. 15, 1817). Polish patriot and revolutionary leader, and soldier for the American Revolution. Today is Kościuszko Day, celebrated by Polish-Americans.

4

Birthday of Charles Augustus Lindberg (Feb. 4, 1902–Aug. 26, 1974). American aviator known as the Lone Eagle for his pioneering solo flight across the Atlantic, New York to Paris, on May 20–21, 1927; the first American private citizen to become a public hero.

4

Death anniversary of Miguel Covarrubias (1904–Feb. 4, 1957). Mexican painter, illustrator, and author; noted for *The Island of Bali* and *The Eagle*.

4

Death anniversary of the 47 *Ronin,* in Japan. On Feb. 4, 1702, 47 *ronin* (masterless samurai) committed ritual suicide after avenging the death of their master, and thereby became models of selfless loyalty. They are honored at the Yasukini shrine in Tokyo.

4

Torture Abolition Day. Anniversary of the signing by 20 countries of the United Nations "Convention against Torture" on Feb. 4, 1985; adopted on Dec. 10, 1984, by the U.N. General Assembly. The U.S. signed but never ratified the convention.

HOLY DAYS AND FEAST DAYS

5

Feast of St. Agatha (ca. 3rd century). Sicilian martyr, the patron saint of Malta and San Marino, and of nurses, bell founders, jewelers, and firefighters; invoked against fire in homes. Orth.: Feb. 5 or 18.

HOLIDAYS AND CIVIC DAYS

5

Unity Day in Burundi; official public holiday. Established in 1992 to encourage an end to strife between Hutus and Tutsis.

5

Constitution Day in Mexico; official public holiday. Commemorates the anniversary of the constitutions of 1857 and 1917.

5

Anniversary of the Liberation of the Republic, and St. Agatha's Day, in San Marino; official public holiday. Celebrates the restoration of the republic's independence on Feb. 5, 1740, following an occupation by the Papal States. St. Agatha is San Marino's patron saint.

ANNIVERSARIES AND SPECIAL EVENTS DAYS

5

Birthday of Dwight Lyman Moody (Feb. 5, 1837–Dec. 22, 1899). American evangelist who built the first YMCA building in America in Chicago; conducted revivals all over the world with Ira Sankey, organist; and founded the Chicago Bible Institute, now known as the Moody Bible Institute.

5

Birthday of Robert Peel (Feb. 5, 1788–July 2, 1850). English prime minister, orator, and advocate of liberal reforms. British police became known as "bobbies" (and the Irish as "peelers") as a result of his interest in public safety and criminal-investigation reforms.

5

Birthday of Adlai Ewing Stevenson (Feb. 5, 1900–July 14, 1965). American lawyer; governor of Ill.; unsuccessful candidate for president, 1952 and 1956; U.S. representative to the United Nations.

5

Death anniversary of Hazrat Inayat Khan (July 5, 1882–Feb. 5, 1927). Indian musician and Sufi missionary; founder and leader of the Sufi Order of the West. Succeeded by his son, Pir Vilayat Inayat Khan, born June 19, 1916.

5

Roger Williams Day. Observed by American Baptists to celebrate the arrival from England of Roger Williams, their American founder, on the North American continent on Feb. 5, 1631. Williams represents R.I. in Statuary Hall.

5

Runeberg's Day in Finland. Commemorates the national poet, Johan Ludvig Runeberg (Feb. 5, 1804–May 6, 1887).

5

Weatherman's Day. Anniversary of the birth of John Jeffries (Feb. 5, 1744–Sept. 16, 1819), a Boston physician and America's first weatherman, who for many years kept continuous meteorological records.

HOLY DAYS AND FEAST DAYS

6

Feast of St. Dorothy (died 303). Martyr, perhaps apocryphal. Patron saint of gardeners and brides.

HOLIDAYS AND CIVIC DAYS

6

Waitangi Day in New Zealand; official public holiday. Also called New Zealand Day. Commemorates the signing of the Feb. 6, 1840, Treaty of Waitangi for peaceful coexistence between the Maori and the Europeans, which opened the islands to settlement under the British Crown.

6

Anniversary of the accession of Elizabeth II to the British throne on Feb. 6, 1952, at the death on that day of her father, George VI; commemorated annually by royal salutes fired by the Queen's Troops of the Royal Horse Artillery, one shot for each year of her reign. Her formal coronation was on June 2, 1953.

6
Anniversary of Mass.'s ratification of the U.S. Constitution on Feb. 6, 1788, making it the 6th state.

ANNIVERSARIES AND SPECIAL EVENTS DAYS

6
Anniversary of the defeat of Palmares and the death of its leader, Ganga Zumba, in Brazil. The autonomous republic of Palmares, consisting of up to 10 communities inhabited by escaped African slaves, flourished in the interior of Alagoas State, 1630–94. Palmares became a scandal to the Portuguese, and they launched 6 expeditions against it, 1680–86; the last succeeded, and on Feb. 6, 1686, the republic fell and its leader was killed.

6
Anniversary of the ratification of the 20th Amendment to the U.S. Constitution on Feb. 6, 1933, transferring the date of presidential inaugurations from Mar. 4 to Jan. 20, and setting Jan. 3 as the official annual opening date for Congress.

6
Birthday of Henry Irving (Feb. 6, 1838–Oct. 13, 1905). English actor-manager who made his reputation in the role of Hamlet. Knighted in 1895, the first actor to receive this honor; buried in Westminster Abbey.

6
Birthday of Károly Kisfaludy (Feb. 6, 1788–Nov. 21, 1830). Hungarian romantic poet and dramatist who inspired his countrymen to voice their national cultural heritage.

6
Birthday of Ronald Wilson Reagan (Feb. 6, 1911–). Film actor; governor of Calif. (1967–75); 40th president of the U.S. (1981–89; Republican).

6
Birthday of George Herman "Babe" Ruth (Feb. 6, 1895–Aug. 16, 1948). American baseball player with the New York Yankees; a left-handed pitcher, he hit 714 home runs in 22 major-league seasons and played in 10 World Series. Last major-league game played Sept. 24, 1934; his home-run record

was not exceeded until 1974, by Henry Aaron of the Atlanta Braves.

6
Bob Marley Day in Jamaica. Anniversary of the birth of Robert Nesta Marley (Feb. 6, 1945–May 11, 1981), Jamaican musician, Rastafarian, and national hero.

HOLIDAYS AND CIVIC DAYS

7
Independence Day in Grenada; official public holiday. Commemorates independence attained from the U.K. on Feb. 7, 1974.

ANNIVERSARIES AND SPECIAL EVENTS DAYS

7
Birthday of John Deere (Feb. 7, 1804–May 17, 1886). American inventor and manufacturer of the steel plow.

7
Birthday of Charles Dickens (Feb. 7, 1812–June 9, 1870). First-magnitude English novelist; wrote *Oliver Twist, David Copperfield,* and *A Tale of Two Cities.* Buried in Westminster Abbey.

7
Birthday of (Harry) Sinclair Lewis (Feb. 7, 1885–Jan. 10, 1951). American writer best known for his novels satirizing small-town life in the Midwest, including *Main Street, Babbitt,* and *Elmer Gantry.* First American to receive the Nobel Prize in literature (1930).

7
Birthday of Sir James Augustus Henry Murray (Feb. 7, 1837–July 26, 1915). Scottish philologist and lexicographer whose lifework was as editor in chief of the 10-volume *New English Dictionary on Historical Principles* (Feb. 1, 1884–Apr. 19, 1928), now known as the *Oxford English Dictionary.*

7
Birthday of Laura Ingalls Wilder (Feb. 7, 1867–Feb. 10, 1957). American author of the Little House stories. First recipient of the Wilder Medal Award, named in her honor to recognize an author or illustrator whose books, published in the U.S., have made an important contribution to children's literature. Additionally, De Smet, S.Dak., hosts a summer pageant in her honor.

HOLY DAYS AND FEAST DAYS

8

Feast of St. Jerome Emiliani (1481–Feb. 8, 1537). Italian soldier, mayor, and priest; founder of the Clerks Regular of Somascha, devoted to the care of orphans and abandoned children, whose patron saint he is.

HOLIDAYS AND CIVIC DAYS

8

Prešeren Day in Slovenia; official public holiday. Also called Culture Day. Honors France Prešeren (Dec. 3, 1800–Feb. 8, 1849), Slovenia's national poet, the first to demonstrate the full literary potential of Slovene; wrote *A Wreath of Sonnets* and provided the national anthem.

ANNIVERSARIES AND SPECIAL EVENTS DAYS

8

Birthday of William Tecumseh Sherman (Feb. 8, 1820–Feb. 14, 1891). American general remembered as the leader of the Union march through Ga. during the Civil War and famous for the phrase "War is hell." Elected to the Hall of Fame for Great Americans.

8

Birthday of Jules Verne (Feb. 8, 1828–Mar. 24, 1905). French novelist famous for *Twenty Thousand Leagues under the Sea;* his writing stimulated the development of science fiction.

8

Boy Scouts Day in the U.S. Anniversary of the incorporation of the Boy Scouts of America on Feb. 8, 1910, by William Boyce, inspired by Sir Robert Baden-Powell and the British Boy Scouts. Boy Scout Week is the week containing Feb. 8, beginning with Boy Scout Sunday and ending with Boy Scout Sabbath. Feb. is Boy Scout Month.

8

Sun Pageant Day in Narvik, Norway. Celebrates the return of the sun after its winter absence.

HOLY DAYS AND FEAST DAYS

9

Feast of St. Maron (died 410). Syrian founder of the Maronite Church, a church of the Antiochene rite in communion with the Roman Catholic Church since the 12th century. Called Feast of St. Maroun in Lebanon, where it is an official public

holiday honoring the country's patron saint. Orth.: Feb. 14 or 27.

ANNIVERSARIES AND SPECIAL EVENTS DAYS

9

Anniversary of the proclamation of the Confederate States of America on Feb. 9, 1861. Jefferson Davis became the provisional president on Feb. 18, 1861.

9

Birthday of Brendan Behan (Feb. 9, 1923–Mar. 20, 1964). Irish playwright and poet known for his ribaldry and satire; his works included *The Quare Fellow, The Hostage,* and the autobiographical *Borstal Boy.*

9

Birthday of Mrs. Patrick Campbell (Feb. 9, 1865–Apr. 9, 1940). English actress and great friend of George Bernard Shaw, who wrote *Pygmalion* as a vehicle for her talents.

9

Birthday of William Henry Harrison (Feb. 9, 1773–Apr. 4, 1841). Ohio lawyer, general, and military hero; first governor of Indiana Territory; superintendent of Indian affairs; congressman, senator; 9th president of the U.S. (1841; died after 32 days in office; Whig). Son of Benjamin Harrison, signer of the Declaration of Independence. Buried at North Bend, Ohio.

9

Birthday of Amy Lowell (Feb. 9, 1874–May 12, 1925). American poet, biographer, and critic; a leader among the imagist poets; author of a monumental life of Keats. Sister of Percival Lowell.

9

Birthday of Samuel Jones Tilden (Feb. 9, 1814–Aug. 4, 1886). American politician and philanthropist whose will established the Tilden Foundation, one of the integral components of the New York Public Library.

HOLY DAYS AND FEAST DAYS

10

Feast of St. Paul's Shipwreck; official public holiday in Malta. Paul was shipwrecked off the coast of Malta in A.D. 60, at which time he introduced Christianity there; St. Paul is a patron saint of Malta.

10

Birthday of Charles Lamb (Feb. 10, 1775–Dec. 27, 1834). English essayist and critic of great range, from *Last Essays of Elia* to *Tales from Shakespeare.*

10

Birthday of Boris Leonidovich Pasternak (Feb. 10, 1890–May 30, 1960). Russian poet, novelist, and translator who was awarded the 1958 Nobel Prize in literature but was forced to refuse it because of political opposition; wrote *Doctor Zhivago.*

10

Birthday of William Allen White (Feb. 10, 1868–May 30, 1944). American journalist, author, editor of the *Emporia* (Kans.) *Gazette,* and Pulitzer Prize winner; known as the Sage of Emporia. The William Allen White Children's Book Award is given annually for a children's book chosen by Kans. schoolchildren.

10

Plimsoll Day. Anniversary of the birth of Samuel Plimsoll (Feb. 10, 1824–June 3, 1898), English coal merchant, politician, social reformer, and "the sailor's friend"; instrumental in reforming Britain's shipping regulations in favor of sailors' safety.

HOLY DAYS AND FEAST DAYS

11

Feast of Our Lady of Lourdes. Commemorates the apparition of the Virgin Mary, under the aspect of the Immaculate Conception, to Bernadette Soubirous at Lourdes, France; 18 apparitions reported between Feb. 11 and July 16, 1858. The site became a world pilgrimage center famous for healing. In the Philippines, there is a spectacular fete with rites, long processions, and a fiesta; Our Lady of Lourdes is also beloved in Brazil.

11

Feast of St. Caedmon (died ca. 680). English lay brother at Whitby Monastery; first to compose sacred verse in Anglo-Saxon; considered the Father of English Sacred Poetry.

HOLIDAYS AND CIVIC DAYS

11

Youth Day in Cameroon; official public holiday. Dedicated to children and young people.

11

Victory Day of the Revolution in Iran; official public holiday. Commemorates the success of the Islamic revolution of 1979 and the return to Iran of the exiled Ayatollah Ruhollah Khomeini. He returned on Jan. 31, and the government of Shah Mohammad Reza Pahlavi fell on Feb. 10–11. Each year, the period from Jan. 31 through Feb. 11 is marked by public celebration, especially in Tehran, with the climax on Feb. 11, the "Dawn of God" *(Yaum Allah).*

11

National Foundation Day *(Kenkoku Kinen-no-Hi)* in Japan; official public holiday. Commemorates the founding of the Japanese empire on the official date of Feb. 11, 660 B.C., when Emperor Jimmu ascended the throne.

11

Anniversary of the Lateranensi (or Lateran) Pacts, treaties concluded on Feb. 11, 1929, between the Italian government of Benito Mussolini and the Vatican; among other settlements, the treaties established the sovereignty of the Vatican City State, the smallest independent country in the world.

11

Anniversary of the release of Nelson Mandela from a South African prison on Feb. 11, 1990, after he had served more than 27 years for resisting the government's policy of apartheid. He and Frederik W. de Klerk were jointly awarded the 1993 Nobel Peace Prize. Mandela was subsequently elected president of South Africa (1994–99).

11

Birthday of Thomas Alva Edison (Feb. 11, 1847–Oct. 18, 1931). American inventor who took out more than a thousand patents. His best-known inventions are the phonograph and the incandescent lamp. Elected to the Hall of Fame for Great Americans. The Thomas Alva Edison Foundation presents 4 awards annually in his honor: for the best science books for children and for youth and for books that contribute to character development and to an understanding of American history.

11

Birthday of Josiah Willard Gibbs (Feb. 11, 1839–Apr. 28, 1903). American physicist and chemist. Elected to the Hall of Fame for Great Americans.

11

White Shirt Day in Flint, Mich.; has been observed by local proclamation. Anniversary of the United Auto Workers–General Motors agreement (Feb. 11, 1937) following 44 days of sit-down strikes at Flint's auto plants. Blue-collar workers wear white shirts on this day as a symbol of dignity won.

HOLIDAYS AND CIVIC DAYS

12

Union Day in Myanmar (Burma); official public holiday. Celebrates the formation of the Union of Burma on Feb. 12, 1947, when Aung San concluded a satisfactory agreement with Burma's ethnic minorities. On this day the country's flag, which has been carried by runners to each of the state capitals, is returned to Rangoon.

ANNIVERSARIES AND SPECIAL EVENTS DAYS

12

Anniversary of the arrival at the headwaters of the Amazon River; called *Día del Oriente* in Ecuador. An expedition left Quito on Christmas Day, 1539; after reaching the Amazon headwaters on Feb. 12, 1541, Francisco de Orellana and his fellow explorers floated downstream and entered the Atlantic in Aug. 1541.

12

Anniversary of the inception of the National Association for the Advancement of Colored People (NAACP) on Feb. 12, 1909, when W. E. B. Du Bois and other notable persons issued the call for its formation; following a conference (May 31–June 1, 1909), the NAACP was formally created. The NAACP has awarded the Spingarn Medal annually since 1914 for the highest achievement by an African American.

12

Birthday of Peter Cooper (Feb. 12, 1791–Apr. 4, 1883). American industrialist and civic leader whose name lives on in the Cooper Union for the Advancement of Science and Art, which he founded and endowed. Elected to the Hall of Fame for Great Americans.

12

Birthday of Charles Robert Darwin (Feb. 12, 1809–Apr. 19, 1882). English biologist whose theory of evolution by natural selection came to be known as Darwinism. His most noted work is *On the Origin of Species by Means of Natural Selection; or the Preservation of Favored Races in the Struggle for Life*. The theory of natural selection was simultaneously and independently propounded by the English naturalist Alfred Wallace, working in Borneo, and the two presented their findings in a joint paper before the Linnean Society in 1858.

12

Birthday of Abraham Lincoln (Feb. 12, 1809–Apr. 15, 1865). Fought in the Black Hawk War; Ill. lawyer, congressman, and debater; opposed the Mexican War; 16th president of the U.S. (1861–65; Republican), assassinated in office. Called the Great Emancipator. Elected to the Hall of Fame for Great Americans. Ran for president on an anti-slavery platform; in response to his election, S.C. promptly seceded (Dec. 20, 1860), followed by 10 other states. Was president throughout the Civil War; died 6 days after Lee's surrender. Remembered are his Emancipation Proclamation, his Gettysburg Address, and his proclamation of the last Thursday in Nov. as Thanksgiving Day. Buried in Oak Ridge Cemetery, Springfield, Ill. Formerly, Lincoln's birthday was widely celebrated as an official public holiday on Feb. 12; now it is commonly observed as an official public holiday with Washington's birthday on the 3rd Monday of Feb., often called Presidents' Day.

12

Birthday of Cotton Mather (Feb. 12, 1663–Feb. 13, 1728). American colonial minister, man of letters, and author of the most important literary work produced in the colonies, the *Magnalia Christi Americana,* an ecclesiastical history of New England.

12

First Horse Day Festival (*Hatsu-uma Matsuri*) in Kyoto, Japan, and at other Inari shrines elsewhere. Dedicated to Fushimi Inari Taisha, the Shinto god of crops. Procession to the shrine by thousands of celebrants; observed since the 9th century.

12

Georgia Day in Ga. Also called Oglethorpe Day. Commemorates the landing of General James Edward Oglethorpe at Savannah on Feb. 12, 1733, and the founding of the state. Major celebrations occur in Savannah with the ringing of bells, processions, an Oglethorpe banquet, and displays of historic memorabilia.

ANNIVERSARIES AND SPECIAL EVENTS DAYS

13

Anniversary of the premier issue of the first magazine published in America, Andrew Bradford's *The American Mercury,* dated Feb. 13, 1741; Benjamin Franklin's *General Magazine* began publication 3 days later.

13

Anniversary of the establishment of the American Society of Composers, Authors and Publishers (ASCAP) on Feb. 13, 1914.

13

Anniversary of the firebombing of Dresden, Germany, on the night of Feb. 13–14, 1945, during the last months of World War II; 2,400 Allied bombers conducted an incendiary raid that consumed the city and its inhabitants in a firestorm.

13

Birthday of Georges Simenon (Feb. 13, 1903–Sept. 1989). Belgian-born author of detective novels; published more than 300 works.

HOLY DAYS AND FEAST DAYS

14

Feast of SS. Cyril and Methodius. Cyril (ca. 827–Feb. 14, 869) and Methodius (ca. 826–Apr. 6, 884) were Greek brothers, the former a professor, the latter a governor, and both monks. As successful missionaries to the Slavs, they invented the glagolithic script for scriptural translation and devised a liturgy, marking the beginning of Slavic literature and the first use of "noncanonical" vernacular language in liturgy. Called Apostles to the Slavs and, more recently, patron saints of Europe. Orth.: May 11 or 24.

14

Feast of St. Valentine (died Feb. 14, ca. 289). Roman priest and physician; martyred. Patron saint of lovers, and invoked against epilepsy, plague, and fainting diseases. Orth.: Feb. 14 or 27.

HOLIDAYS AND CIVIC DAYS

14

Admission Day in Ariz. Ariz. was admitted to the Union on Feb. 14, 1912, as the 48th state.

14

Statehood Day in Oreg. Oreg. was admitted to the Union on Feb. 14, 1859, as the 33rd state.

ANNIVERSARIES AND SPECIAL EVENTS DAYS

14

Birthday of Richard Allen (Feb. 14, 1760–Mar. 26, 1831). American clergyman, founder, and first bishop of the African Methodist Episcopal Church; the first African American to be regularly ordained in the Methodist Church.

14

Birthday of Anna Howard Shaw (Feb. 14, 1847–July 2, 1919). American suffrage leader, physician, and minister; the first woman ordained in the Methodist Church.

14

Selma March Day. Anniversary of the key day in the historic 160-mile civil rights march from Selma to Montgomery, Ala., led by Martin Luther King Jr. in 1965. The march, marked by its opponents' violence, influenced the passage of the New Voting Rights Act, signed on Aug. 6, 1965.

CA. 14

Trifon Zarezan in Bulgaria; all of 1st half of Feb., with Feb. 14 the main day. A Dionysian wine fest, millennia old. Vines are pruned and sprinkled with wine, with ritual songs and dances; a Vine King is chosen, crowned with vine twigs, and treated with respect—a fertile harvest depends on his happiness.

14

Valentine's Day. A day to send ornate and sometimes anonymous messages of affection to sweethearts or to those loved from a distance. The custom of exchanging Valentines stems from a medieval belief that birds begin to pair on this day.

ANNIVERSARIES AND SPECIAL EVENTS DAYS

15

Birthday of John Barrymore (born John Blythe; Feb. 15, 1882–May 29, 1942). Member of a famous American acting family. Played both Shakespearean stage roles and romantic film leads. Films include *Dr. Jekyll and Mr. Hyde* and *Grand Hotel.*

15

Birthday of Galileo Galilei (Feb. 15, 1564–Jan. 8, 1642). Italian astronomer, mathematician, and physicist; considered to be the founder of the experimental method.

15

Birthday of Cyrus Hall McCormick (Feb. 15, 1809–
May 13, 1884). American inventor of the mechanical reaper, industrialist, and philanthropist.

15

Birthday of Charles Lewis Tiffany (Feb. 15, 1812–
Feb. 18, 1902). American jeweler famous for the high quality of his work. His son Lewis Comfort Tiffany (Feb. 18, 1848–Jan. 17, 1933) did remarkable work with iridescent glass.

15

Birthday of Alfred North Whitehead (Feb. 15, 1861–Dec. 30, 1947). English mathematician and philosopher. His most distinguished work is *Principia Mathematica,* which he wrote with Bertrand Russell.

15

Maine Memorial Day. Also called Battleship Day or Spanish-American War Memorial Day. Anniversary of the explosion in Havana harbor of the American battleship *Maine* on Feb. 15, 1898. "Remember the *Maine!*" was used to whip up public opinion; war was declared with Spain on Apr. 25, 1898.

15

Menéndez Day in St. Augustine, Fla. Observed to honor the birthday of the city's founder, Pedro Menéndez de Avilés (Feb. 15, 1519–Sept. 17, 1574) of Spain. In a traditional ceremony, a wreath is laid before his statue.

15

Susan B. Anthony Day. Anniversary of the birth of Susan Brownell Anthony (Feb. 15, 1820–Mar. 13, 1906), American abolitionist; pioneer crusader for women's rights, temperance, and African American suffrage; author and lecturer. Elected to the Hall of Fame for Great Americans. Honored with the 1979 Susan B. Anthony dollar; the first woman to have her likeness on American coinage.

HOLY DAYS AND FEAST DAYS

16

Feast of St. Gilbert of Sempringham (ca. 1083–
Feb. 4, 1189). English monk; founder of the Gilbertines, the only monastic order founded in medieval England.

HOLIDAYS AND CIVIC DAYS

16

Independence Day in Lithuania; official public holiday. Commemorates the 1918 declaration of independence from Russia. (Lithuania again declared independence, from the USSR, on Mar. 11, 1990. The USSR recognized the independence of all 3 Baltic nations [Lithuania, Latvia, and Estonia] on Sept. 6, 1991.)

ANNIVERSARIES AND SPECIAL EVENTS DAYS

16

Birthday of Henry Brooks Adams (Feb. 16, 1838–
Mar. 27, 1918). American historian and philosopher; best known for *Mont-Saint-Michel and Chartres* and *The Education of Henry Adams;* recipient of the Pulitzer Prize.

16

Birthday of Charles Taze Russell (Feb. 16, 1852–
Oct. 31, 1916). American founder of the International Bible Students Association, which became the Jehovah's Witnesses.

ANNIVERSARIES AND SPECIAL EVENTS DAYS

17

Birthday of Dorothy Canfield Fisher (Feb. 17, 1879–Nov. 9, 1958). American novelist of stories dealing with Vt. life; a member of the book-selection committee of the Book-of-the-Month Club (1926–51). A Dorothy Canfield Fisher Library Award has been established by the Book-of-the-Month Club as a memorial, with funds to be used by small libraries for the purchase of books.

17

Birthday of René Théophile Laënnec (Feb. 17, 1781–Aug. 13, 1826). French physician who invented the stethoscope; called the Father of Chest Medicine.

17

Death anniversary of Giordano Bruno (born Filippo Bruno; 1548–Feb. 17, 1600). Italian philosopher, mathematician, astronomer, and occultist; rejected earth-centered cosmology and argued for the multiplicity of worlds and an infinite universe; burned at the stake for heresy by the Roman Inquisition.

17

Death anniversary of Geronimo (Goyathlay, "One Who Yawns"; June 1829–Feb. 17, 1909). Leader of the Chiricahua Apache of Ariz. who, in desperation, rose up with a small band against federal expropriation of reservation lands in the territory.

After immense effort by 5,000 soldiers, he surrendered for the last time on Sept. 4, 1886, in Mexico, and was thereafter confined at Fort Sill, Okla., where he dictated his autobiography.

CA. 17

Holetown Festival in Barbados; week containing Feb. 17. Commemorates the landing of the first settlers on Feb. 17, 1627.

17

National PTA Founders' Day in the U.S. Anniversary of the founding of the National Congress of Parents and Teachers in Washington, D.C., on Feb. 17, 1897, by Phoebe Apperson Hearst and Alice McLellan Birney.

HOLY DAYS AND FEAST DAYS

18

Feast of Fra Angelico (born Guido di Pietro, also called John of Faesulis; ca. 1400–Feb. 18, 1455). Florentine Dominican; notable painter of the early Renaissance.

HOLIDAYS AND CIVIC DAYS

18

Independence Day in The Gambia; official public holiday. Celebrates the attainment of independence from the U.K., within the British Commonwealth, on Feb. 18, 1965. The Gambia became a republic on Apr. 24, 1970.

ANNIVERSARIES AND SPECIAL EVENTS DAYS

18

Anniversary of the 1963 eruption of Mt. Agung in Bali, Indonesia. Following many disturbing omens, President Sukarno compelled the priests of Mt. Agung, the island's sacred center, to perform the *Eka Dasa Rudra* ceremony prematurely. (The ceremony is properly celebrated only once every 100 years.) The mountain erupted, sparing only the temple. There followed a coup attempt and 1965's horror of 100,000 murders in Bali alone. The ceremony was later performed in 1979, at its proper time, with no rumbles from the mountain.

18

Birthday of Shalom Aleichem (born Sholem Rabinowitz; Feb. 18, 1859–May 13, 1916). Jewish-American author (born in Ukraine), a master of the short story; known as the Yiddish Mark Twain.

18

Birthday of Nikos Kazantzakis (Feb. 18, 1883–Oct. 26, 1957). Greek (Cretan) author and statesman; wrote *Zorba the Greek* and much else.

18

Birthday of George Peabody (Feb. 18, 1795–Nov. 4, 1869). American merchant, financier, and philanthropist. Elected to the Hall of Fame for Great Americans.

18

Birthday of Alessandro Volta (Feb. 18, 1745–Mar. 5, 1827). Italian physicist and pioneer in the science of electricity; inventor of the electric battery.

HOLIDAYS AND CIVIC DAYS

CA. 19

Democracy Day (*Rashtriya Prajatantra Divas*) in Nepal; official public holiday. Celebrates the Feb. 18, 1951, overthrow of the Ranas by the grandfather of the present king; on this day democracy was royally proclaimed. The day was dropped as an official public holiday in 1992 and later reinstated by popular demand.

ANNIVERSARIES AND SPECIAL EVENTS DAYS

19

Birthday of Nicolaus Copernicus (Mikolaj Kopernik, or Niklas Koppernigk; Feb. 19, 1473–May 24, 1543). Polish physician, scientist, and astronomer. Considered the founder of modern astronomy, for his Copernican system of a sun-centered solar system. His *De Revolutionibus Orbium Coelestium* was of profound influence.

19

Birthday of Sven Anders Hedin (Feb. 19, 1865–Nov. 26, 1952). Swedish scientist and explorer whose explorations in central and eastern Asia determined the source of the Indus and the continuity of the trans-Himalayan range.

ANNIVERSARIES AND SPECIAL EVENTS DAYS

20

Death anniversary of Klas Pontus Arnoldson (Oct. 27, 1844–Feb. 20, 1916). Swedish author, founder of the Swedish Society for Peace and Arbitration; corecipient of the 1908 Nobel Peace Prize.

20

Death anniversary of Frederick Douglass (ca. Feb. 1817–Feb. 20, 1895). American escaped slave; leader in the abolition movement and first African American to hold high rank in the U.S. government, as a consultant to President Lincoln and as U.S. minister to Haiti.

20

John Glenn Day. Commemorates the first orbit of the earth by a U.S. astronaut; John Herschel Glenn Jr. (July 18, 1921–) orbited on Feb. 20, 1962.

HOLIDAYS AND CIVIC DAYS

21

Ekushey Day in Bangladesh; official public holiday. Also called Shaheed ("Martyr") Day. A national day of mourning, commemorating the students of the Language Movement killed in 1952, as early martyrs for independence from West Pakistan.

ANNIVERSARIES AND SPECIAL EVENTS DAYS

21

Anniversary of the publication of the premier issue of *New Yorker* magazine, dated Feb. 21, 1925.

21

Anniversary of the dedication on Feb. 21, 1885, of the Washington Monument in Washington, D.C.; designed by Robert Mills. The cornerstone had been laid on July 4, 1848.

21

Birthday of Wystan Hugh Auden (Feb. 21, 1907–Sept. 27, 1973). English-born American poet known as a "poet's poet." Awarded the 1984 Pulitzer Prize for his long philosophical poem *The Age of Anxiety.*

21

Birthday of Otto Hermann Kahn (Feb. 21, 1867–Mar. 29, 1934). American banker and philanthropist who organized the Metropolitan Opera Company in 1907.

21

Birthday of Alice Freeman Palmer (Feb. 21, 1855–Dec. 6, 1902). Pioneer American educator. Elected to the Hall of Fame for Great Americans.

21

Death anniversary of Malcolm X (born Malcolm Little; May 19, 1925–Feb. 21, 1965). Militant African American civil rights leader; wrote *The Autobiography of Malcolm X* (1965), a book of widespread interest and influence; activist and leader in the Nation of Islam; broke with its founder, Elijah Muhammad, and in 1964 formed the rival Organization of Afro-American Unity, which favored brotherhood rather than separation; assassinated at an OAAU meeting in New York City.

ANNIVERSARIES AND SPECIAL EVENTS DAYS

22

Birthday of Sir Robert Stephenson Smyth Baden-Powell (Feb. 22, 1857–Jan. 8, 1941). British major general, founder of the Boy Scouts and, with his sister, Agnes Baden-Powell (1858–1945), of the Girl Guides. Girl Guides Thinking Day is observed on this day by Girl Guides in the U.K. and the British Commonwealth.

22

Birthday of Eric Gill (Feb. 22, 1882–Nov. 17, 1940). Prolific English sculptor, engraver, typographer, author, and illustrator.

22

Birthday of James Russell Lowell (Feb. 22, 1819–Aug. 12, 1891). American poet, essayist, and diplomat. Remembered for *The Vision of Sir Launfal.* Elected to the Hall of Fame for Great Americans.

22

Birthday of Edna St. Vincent Millay (Feb. 22, 1892–Oct. 19, 1950). American poet. She received the Pulitzer Prize for *The Harp Weaver* and wrote the libretto for *The King's Henchmen,* an opera composed by Deems Taylor.

22

Birthday of Arthur Schopenhauer (Feb. 22, 1788–Sept. 21, 1860). German philosopher and author; wrote *The World as Will and Idea.*

22

Birthday of George Washington (Feb. 22, 1732–Dec. 14, 1799). English ancestry; Va. planter; surveyor; Va. militia colonel; member of the House of Burgesses; commander in chief of the Continental Army (from June 15, 1775) during the Revolutionary War; first president of the U.S. (1789–97; Federalist; inaugurated Apr. 30, 1789). Elected to the Hall of Fame for Great Americans. Washington was the person most essential to the success of the Revolution and the subsequent durable establishment of the U.S.; he was truly the Father of

His Country. Buried at Mount Vernon, Va. Since 1971, the date of Washington's Birthday as a federal official public holiday has been transferred to the 3rd Monday in Feb.

22

Cat Day in Japan. Celebrated in Tokyo with a Cat Day Festival, where cats win prizes for the most endearingly unique behavior.

HOLY DAYS AND FEAST DAYS

23

Feast of St. Polycarp (ca. 66–Feb. 23, ca. 155). Disciple of St. John the Evangelist and bishop of Smyrna. Probably the most influential Christian in Roman Asia during the 2nd century; an important ecclesiastical writer and martyr. Orth.: Feb. 23 or Mar. 8.

HOLIDAYS AND CIVIC DAYS

23

National Day in Brunei; official public holiday. Celebrates independence attained from the U.K. on Feb. 23, 1984.

23

Republic Day in Guyana; official public holiday. Commemorates Guyana's establishment as a republic within the British Commonwealth on Feb. 23, 1970. It had attained independence from the U.K. on May 26, 1966.

ANNIVERSARIES AND SPECIAL EVENTS DAYS

23

Baptismal day of Jean-Baptiste Le Moyne, Sieur de Bienville (baptized Feb. 23, 1680–Mar. 7, 1767). French-Canadian explorer and colonizer; founder of New Orleans in 1718.

23

Birthday of W. E. B. (William Edward Burghardt) Du Bois (Feb. 23, 1868–Aug. 27, 1963). American sociologist, educator, and author; awarded the 1920 Spingarn Medal for leadership in securing opportunities for African Americans. A founder of the NAACP.

23

Birthday of George Frideric Handel (Feb. 23, 1685–Apr. 20, 1759). German-born English composer, master of baroque music, famous for oratorios and operas. Handel's *Messiah* (1742) is sung around the world during the Christmas season.

23

Birthday of Samuel Pepys (Feb. 23, 1633–May 26, 1703). English writer famous for the most frequently quoted diary in the English language.

23

Birthday of Emma Willard (Feb. 23, 1787–Apr. 15, 1870). Pioneer American educator whose primary concern was the education of girls and young women. Elected to the Hall of Fame for Great Americans.

23

Death anniversary of César Augusto Sandino (1893–Feb. 23, 1934). Nicaraguan guerrilla leader, statesman, and mystic, who led resistance against American occupation of the country, 1926–33; assassinated by the agents of Anastasio Somoza. He inspired the U.S. Good Neighbor Policy of Franklin Roosevelt's administration and the Sandinista revolution of 1979.

23

Iwo Jima Day. Anniversary of the raising of the American flag atop Mt. Suribachi on Iwo Jima by U.S. marines on Feb. 23, 1945, after the World War II battle; immortalized by Joseph Rosenthal's photograph and in the Marine War Memorial monument in Arlington, Va.

HOLY DAYS AND FEAST DAYS

24

Traditional feast of St. Matthias (1st century). Disciple chosen to take the place of Judas Iscariot, who betrayed Jesus. Orth.: Aug. 9 or 22.

HOLIDAYS AND CIVIC DAYS

24

National Day in Estonia; official public holiday. Commemorates independence declared from Russia on Feb. 24, 1918. No public celebrations, but flags are everywhere.

24

Flag Day in Mexico. Also called Independence Proclamation Day. Anniversary of the proclamation of Iturbide's Plan of Iguala (Feb. 24, 1821), projecting independence from Spain.

ANNIVERSARIES AND SPECIAL EVENTS DAYS

24

Anniversary of the European revolutions of 1848, republican revolts against the monarchies of

Europe. The process began in Sicily in Jan. 1848, erupted in France on Feb. 24, and thereafter spread through Germany, Italy, and the Austrian Empire. Though harshly suppressed, the revolts later resulted in universal suffrage and freedom of the press and of assembly.

24

Anniversary of the founding of Hadassah on Feb. 24, 1912, to foster Jewish education in the U.S. and nursing services in Israel.

24

Anniversary of *Marbury* v. *Madison,* in which, on Feb. 24, 1803, the U.S. Supreme Court for the first time overturned a U.S. law.

24

Birthday of Winslow Homer (Feb. 24, 1836–Sept. 29, 1910). American landscape and seascape painter elected to the National Academy of Design in 1865.

24

Death anniversary of (René) Auguste Chouteau (baptized Sept. 7, 1749–Feb. 24, 1829). American fur trader, cofounder of the city of St. Louis, Mo., on Feb. 15, 1764.

HOLIDAYS AND CIVIC DAYS

25

National Day in Kuwait; official public holiday. Commemorates the 1978 accession of King Shaykh Sir 'abdallah Al-Salim al-Sabah.

25

George Rogers Clark Day in Ind.; official commemorative day. Honors Clark for his contributions in the Revolutionary War and in establishing the first permanent American settlement in the Northwest Territory.

ANNIVERSARIES AND SPECIAL EVENTS DAYS

25

Birthday of Anthony Burgess (Feb. 25, 1917–Nov. 25, 1993). Prolific English author, famous for the novel *A Clockwork Orange.*

25

Birthday of Enrico Caruso (Feb. 25, 1873–Aug. 2, 1921). Italian operatic tenor of legendary voice and fame.

25

Birthday of Benedetto Croce (Feb. 25, 1866–Nov. 20, 1952). Italian humanist, historian, and editor;

the foremost Italian philosopher of the first half of the 20th century.

25

Birthday of Millicent Fenwick (Feb. 25, 1910–Sept. 16, 1992). American congresswoman from N.J., noted for her active support for the Helsinki Accords and for civil rights, peace in Vietnam, aid for poor people, and the reduction of military programs; also for her sense of humor.

25

Birthday of Charles Lang Freer (Feb. 25, 1856–Sept. 25, 1919). American art collector who specialized in Chinese and Japanese painting and Oriental pottery. His collections were presented to the nation, and he endowed the Freer Gallery in Washington, D.C., to house them.

25

Birthday of Carlo Goldoni (Feb. 25, 1707–Feb. 6, 1793). Italian author; founder of Italian realistic comedy.

25

Birthday of Pierre-Auguste Renoir (Feb. 25, 1841–Dec. 17, 1919). A leader and founder of the French Impressionist school who experimented with many subjects and painting styles in the course of his lifetime.

25

Birthday of José Francisco de San Martín (Feb. 25, 1778–Aug. 17, 1850). Latin American general, liberator of Chile from Spanish control, and leader in the wars of independence in Argentina and Peru. Honored in Chile for moral grandeur, military genius, and statesmanship.

HOLIDAYS AND CIVIC DAYS

26

Liberation Day in Kuwait; official public holiday. Commemorates the liberation of Kuwait City from Iraqi forces on Feb. 26, 1991, during the Gulf War.

26

People Power Day in the Philippines, especially Manila. Also called *Fiesta da EDSA.* Anniversary of the popular nonviolent overthrow of President Ferdinand Marcos, Feb. 22–26, 1986. On Feb. 22–25, perhaps 2 million people stood as protectors between rebellious soldiers and pro-Marcos forces; no blood was shed. Marcos was discredited, and fled on Feb. 26. As part of the commemoratory celebrations, Manila holds the monthlong Silayan Arts Festival.

ANNIVERSARIES AND SPECIAL EVENTS DAYS

26

Birthday of William Frederick "Buffalo Bill" Cody (Feb. 26, 1846–Jan. 10, 1917). American frontiersman and buffalo hunter, and later an internationally known showman of Wild West acts.

26

Birthday of Honoré Daumier (Feb. 26, 1808–Feb. 11, 1879). French painter and caricaturist famous for his satirical and comic lithographs.

26

Birthday of Victor Hugo (Feb. 26, 1802–May 22, 1885). French novelist and dramatist known universally for his novel *Les Misérables.*

26

Birthday of Levi Strauss (Feb. 26, 1829–ca. Sept. 26, 1902). Bavarian-born American inventor of denim blue jeans for miners in Calif.'s Gold Rush.

CA. 26

Ayyam-i-Ha, the intercalary days in the Baha'i calendar, 4 in common years and 5 in Gregorian leap years, which adjust the 19-month calendar to the solar year; the intercalary days extend from Feb. 26 to Mar. 1 and are observed as days of hospitality, charity, gift giving, and rejoicing.

HOLIDAYS AND CIVIC DAYS

27

Independence Day in the Dominican Republic; official public holiday. Commemorates the Feb. 27, 1844, start of the final struggle for independence from Haiti, by Juan Pablo Duarte and others. At this time also is *Carnaval,* notable for a parade along Santo Domingo's Malecón on Feb. 27.

27

Patriotism and National Unity Day in Ecuador. Commemorates the Battle of Tarqui in 1829, against the Spanish; features student oaths to the flag and civic events.

ANNIVERSARIES AND SPECIAL EVENTS DAYS

27

Birthday of Henry Wadsworth Longfellow (Feb. 27, 1807–Mar. 24, 1882). American poet famed for *Evangeline* and *The Song of Hiawatha.* Elected to the Hall of Fame for Great Americans.

27

Birthday of Rudolf Steiner (Feb. 27, 1861–Mar. 30, 1925). Austrian scientist, editor of Goethe's works, and founder of anthroposophy.

27

Independence Day in the Western Sahara. On Feb. 27, 1976, the Western Sahara declared its independence from all other countries, including Spain, Algeria, and particularly Morocco, which occupies the country.

HOLIDAYS AND CIVIC DAYS

28

Andalusia Day in the Andalusia region of Spain; regional official public holiday.

28

Memorial for the February 28 Incident, or Two-Twenty-Eight, in Taiwan; official public holiday. Instituted in 1997 to apologize to and commemorate the many thousands of native Taiwanese killed on Feb. 28, 1947, and subsequently, following the transfer of the island from Japanese to Nationalist control.

ANNIVERSARIES AND SPECIAL EVENTS DAYS

28

Birthday of Charles Blondin (born Jean-François Gravelet; Feb. 28, 1824–Feb. 19, 1897). French acrobat and aerialist; famous for his tightrope walks across Niagara Falls on June 30, 1859, and on subsequent occasions.

28

Birthday of Mary Lyon (Feb. 28, 1797–Mar. 5, 1849). Pioneer educator; founder and first principal of Mt. Holyoke Seminary, which later became Mt. Holyoke College. Elected to the Hall of Fame for Great Americans.

28

Birthday of Michel Eyquem de Montaigne (Feb. 28, 1533–Sept. 13, 1592). French essayist who coined the term "essay" to describe the literary form he so successfully executed.

28

Birthday of Louis Joseph de Montcalm de Saint-Véran (Feb. 28, 1712–Sept. 14, 1759). French general, mortally wounded in battle with General James Wolfe on the Plains of Abraham near Quebec, in the French and Indian War (1754–63).

28

Birthday of Sir John Tenniel (Feb. 28, 1820–Feb. 25, 1914). English cartoonist and illustrator remembered as the illustrator of Lewis Carroll's *Alice's Adventures in Wonderland*.

28

Kalevala Day in Finland. Parades and ceremonies commemorating Finland's national epic; Dr. Elias Lönnrot (Apr. 9, 1802–Feb. 10, 1835) transcribed 20,000 verses from the memories of his compatriots; his book's preface was dated Feb. 28, 1835.

ANNIVERSARIES AND SPECIAL EVENTS DAYS

29

Birthday of Ann Lee (Feb. 29, 1736–Sept. 8, 1784). English founder of the Shakers (United Society of Believers in Christ's Second Appearing), a celibate and musical religious sect of subtle influence on American culture. The Shakers were founded in 1772 and moved to America in 1774.

29

Birthday of Gioacchino Antonio Rossini (Feb. 29, 1792–Nov. 13, 1868). Italian composer famous for the operas *The Barber of Seville* and *William Tell* and for the sacred composition *Stabat Mater*.

29

Leap Year Day. Extra day added in leap years, those whose number is divisible by 4 (such as A.D. 2000, 2004), except in centurial years not divisible by 400 (A.D. 1900 was not a leap year; A.D. 2000 is). Also called Bachelors Day, when by tradition women could propose marriage to men, who paid a forfeit on refusal.

MOVABLE DAYS IN FEBRUARY

AFRICAN AMERICAN HISTORY MONTH IN THE U.S. Widely observed in schools. Launched in 1926 by Dr. Carter G. Woodson and others. Originally for a week; monthlong since 1976. (Feb. contains Abraham Lincoln's birthday and Frederick Douglass's death anniversary; hence the choice.)

AMERICAN HISTORY MONTH IN THE U.S. Sponsored by the Daughters of the American Revolution and widely observed in schools, especially in Mass., Maine, and Tenn. (Feb. is the birth month of Washington and Lincoln; hence the choice.)

HOLIDAYS AND CIVIC DAYS

PRESIDENTS' DAY IN THE U.S.; 3rd Monday in Feb.; federal official public holiday, and official public holiday in most states. A holiday observing in combination the birthdays of George Washington (Feb. 22) and Abraham Lincoln (Feb. 12), and of all U.S. presidents generally.

ANNIVERSARIES AND SPECIAL EVENTS DAYS

HOBART REGATTA DAY IN TASMANIA, AUSTRALIA. Celebrated with several days of aquatic carnivals and sailing races.

QUEBEC WINTER CARNIVAL (CARNAVAL DE QUÉBEC) IN QUEBEC CITY, CANADA; 11 days, beginning the 1st Thursday in Feb. A world-famous winter carnival; features a notable ice-sculpture contest and a hazardous ice-canoe race on the St. Lawrence River. Began in 1955.

SNOW FESTIVAL (YUKI MATSURI) IN SAPPORO, JAPAN; about 5 days, in early Feb. World-famous snow and ice sculptures. Originated in 1949, when schoolchildren built 6 enormous snowmen.

GREAT SAMI WINTER FAIR (JOKKMOKKS MARKNAD) IN JOKKMOKK, SWEDEN; 3 days, beginning the 1st Thursday in Feb. An occasion for the Sami (Lapps) to meet, stock up on winter supplies, and hold a folk festival; held since the early 15th century.

BROTHERHOOD SUNDAY IN THE U.S.; the Sunday of Brotherhood/Sisterhood Week, the 3rd full week in Feb. Sponsored by the National Conference of Christians and Jews, to stimulate mutual knowledge and tolerance among all faiths and a reaffirmation of human kinship.

GASPARILLA PIRATE FESTIVAL IN TAMPA, FLA.; ideally, on the 1st Saturday in Feb. An intense celebration evoking the quasi-historical 19th-century Spanish pirate Jose Gaspar, his buccaneers, and their 3-masted sloop. Gaspar's pirate ship lands in Tampa, with welcoming ceremonies (the Pirate Invasion), followed by an extensive Pirate Parade, followed by a street festival with much music late into the night. Celebrated since 1904.

ILLUMINATED NIGHT PARADE (KREWE OF SANT' YAGO ILLUMINATED NIGHT PARADE) IN TAMPA, FLA.; ideally, on the Saturday following the Gasparilla Pirate Festival. Daylong street festival (Fiesta Day) celebrating Tampa's diverse cultural heritage, followed by the spectacular Illuminated Night Parade, led by the krewe of the Knights of Sant' Yago (Santiago), with floats and krewes from all over the Southeast.

CHARRO DAYS IN BROWNSVILLE, TEX., AND MATAMOROS, MEXICO, IMMEDIATELY ACROSS THE RIO GRANDE; 4 days, beginning the last Thursday in Feb. A border fiesta that evokes that superb horseman, the *charro*; features the costumes of the Spanish dons and other Mexican equestrian outfits, parades, costume dances in the streets, cultural exhibits, and brilliant balls.

BIRKEBEINER CROSS-COUNTRY SKI RACE IN HAYWARD, WIS.; main day, last Saturday in Feb. The largest and most famous cross-country ski race in the U.S.

March

March, the 3rd month of the year, was named for Mars, the Roman god of war. In the days of the Julian calendar, March included New Year's Day. New Year's was then March 25 and was the day on which annual leases for homes and farms were signed, a time schedule that has continued in many parts of the world, even though New Year's Day was moved to January with the adoption of the Gregorian calendar.

March was called the "loud month" or "the stormy month" by the early Britons. It is the month of the vernal equinox, the official beginning of spring. The young people in the canton of Grisons in Switzerland are among the first to respond to the season, by wearing herders' costumes with wide belts from which are hung countless cowbells to "ring out the winter."

The most popular March day is the 17th, St. Patrick's Day. It is a major holiday in Ireland, but it is celebrated in New York City, too, with the "wearing of the green" by all nationalities joining in a spectacular St. Patrick's Day parade, a tradition that began in 1762.

The flower for the month is the jonquil or daffodil, and the birthstones are the bloodstone and the aquamarine.

March is Women's History Month and Red Cross Month.

HOLY DAYS AND FEAST DAYS

1
Feast of St. David (Dewi; 6th century). Welsh monk and by tradition the archbishop of Wales; patron saint of Wales. Buried in St. David's Cathedral in Pembrokshire, which became a major pilgrimage center. Traditional death anniversary is Mar. 1, 588.

HOLIDAYS AND CIVIC DAYS

1
Independence Day in Bosnia and Herzegovina; official public holiday. Commemorates the passage of a referendum on sovereignty on Feb. 29, 1992, and the subsequent declaration of independence from the Yugoslav Union.

1
National Heroes' Day in Paraguay; official public holiday. Honors all who have died for the country, especially Mariscal Francisco Solano López (July 24, 1826–Mar. 1, 1870), hero of the War of the Triple Alliance, 1865–70.

1
Independence Movement Day (*Samiljol*) in South Korea; official public holiday. Honors the Mar. 1, 1919, declaration of independence from Japanese colonial rule and the formal beginning of the passive resistance movement. The proclamation, signed by 33 patriots, is read in a ceremony at Pagoda Park in Seoul.

1
State Day in Nebr. Anniversary of Nebr.'s admission as the 37th state on Mar. 1, 1867.

1
Admission Day in Ohio. Anniversary of Ohio's admission as the 17th state on Mar. 1, 1803.

ANNIVERSARIES AND SPECIAL EVENTS DAYS

1
Anniversary of the passage of the U.S. Census Act by Congress on Mar. 1, 1790.

1

Anniversary of the establishment of the Peace Corps by President John F. Kennedy on Mar. 1, 1961, with 3 goals: to provide direct local assistance by Americans to communities in poorer countries; for citizens of those countries to know Americans as colleagues and neighbors; and for returned Peace Corps Volunteers to help inform their fellow Americans about the realities of the rest of the world. Peace Corps Day is observed on the 1st Tuesday in Mar.

1

Anniversary of the establishment of Yellowstone Park on Mar. 1, 1872; the first of the great national parks of the U.S.

1

Birthday of Frédéric Chopin (Mar. 1, 1810–Oct. 17, 1849). Polish pianist and composer of well-known preludes, études, nocturnes, songs, and concertos for piano and orchestra. His romance with the novelist George Sand has been the subject of many books.

1

Birthday of Ralph Ellison (Mar. 1, 1914–Apr. 16, 1994). American teacher and writer; famous for his single novel, *Invisible Man*.

1

Birthday of Dimitri Mitropoulos (Mar. 1, 1896–Nov. 2, 1960). Greek-born American symphony orchestra conductor and composer. Director of the Minneapolis Symphony, the New York Philharmonic Orchestra, and the Metropolitan Opera; known for his interpretation of 20th-century musical works.

1

Birthday of Augustus Saint-Gaudens (Mar. 1, 1848–Aug. 3, 1907). American sculptor whose works include statues of Abraham Lincoln and General Sherman. Elected to the Hall of Fame for Great Americans.

1

Chalanda Marz in the Engadine, Switzerland. Celebrates the coming of spring, by chiming bells. Young people in herders' costumes dance wearing many cowbells on leather belts.

1

Martenitza begins in Bulgaria, and *Martisor* in Romania. A national custom unique to Bulgaria and Romania, inherited from the ancient Thracians; one of the most popular days of the year. In Bulgaria, a red thread is tied around the wrist and worn all month, then hung on a bush. More elaborate rural customs invoke fertility of land and cattle. In Romania, women receive a ribbon and wear it for at least a few days.

1

St. David's Day in Wales. Traditional day of the Welsh, celebrated by Welsh all over the world, wearing either the leek or daffodil (both national emblems). St. David's Day celebrations usually include either a musical program or a dinner with a guest speaker.

1

Whuppity Scoorie Day in Lanark, Scotland. An ancient custom to drive away winter and protect the crops from blighting spirits. As its bells peal, children run around the church 3 times, beating each other with paper balls on strings. Afterward, officials throw them copper coins.

HOLY DAYS AND FEAST DAYS

CA. 2

Nineteen-Day Fast in the Baha'i faith; Mar. 2–20, the entire month of *Ala* ("Loftiness"). Baha'is aged 15 and older fast from sunrise to sundown.

HOLIDAYS AND CIVIC DAYS

2

Aduwa Day in Ethiopia; official public holiday. Also called Commemoration Day. Anniversary of the Ethiopian defeat of Italian forces at the Battle of Aduwa in 1896, which resulted in the recognition of Ethiopia's independence and put heart into anticolonial movements everywhere. Also observed by Rastafarians.

2

Texas Independence Day in Tex.; official public holiday. The anniversary of Tex.'s declaration of independence from Mexico on Mar. 2, 1836, at the convention at Washington-on-the-Brazos. Also on Mar. 2, as special observance days, are Texas Flag Day and Sam Houston Day. Mar. 1–7 is Texas Week.

ANNIVERSARIES AND SPECIAL EVENTS DAYS

2

Birthday of Sam (Samuel) Houston (Mar. 2, 1793–July 26, 1863). American statesman; first president of the republic of Tex. (1836–38, 1841–44), governor of the state of Tex., and regional leader for whom the city of Houston is named. Represents Tex. in Statuary Hall.

2
Birthday of Dr. Seuss (Theodore Seuss Geisel; Mar. 2, 1904–Sept. 24, 1991). American author and illustrator, famous for his children's books, such as *The Cat in the Hat*. Awarded the Pulitzer Prize.

2
Birthday of Bedřich Smetana (Mar. 2, 1824–May 12, 1884). Czech composer and orchestral leader whose opera *The Bartered Bride* has become popular. The Smetana Society in Prague maintains a museum dedicated to his work.

HOLIDAYS AND CIVIC DAYS

3
Liberation Day in Bulgaria; official public holiday. Celebrates independence attained from the Ottoman Empire on Mar. 3, 1878, by the Treaty of San Stefano.

3
Martyr's Day in Malawi; official public holiday. Honors the nation's heroes for independence.

3
Throne Day in Morocco; official public holiday. Commemorates the accession of King Hassan II on Mar. 3, 1961.

3
Admission Day in Fla. Anniversary of Fla.'s admission as the 27th state on Mar. 3, 1845.

ANNIVERSARIES AND SPECIAL EVENTS DAYS

3
Birthday of Alexander Graham Bell (Mar. 3, 1847–Aug. 2, 1922). Scottish-born American physicist and inventor, famous for the invention of the telephone; founder of the Bell Telephone Company. Elected to the Hall of Fame for Great Americans.

3
Birthday of Norman Bethune (Mar. 3, 1890–Nov. 11, 1939). Canadian physician who worked in the front lines in World War I, the Spanish Civil War, and the Chinese Revolution. The only Western man recognized as a hero of the Chinese Revolution.

3
Birthday of William Green (Mar. 3, 1873–Nov. 21, 1952). American labor leader and president of the American Federation of Labor (AFL) from Dec. 19, 1924, until his death.

3
Birthday of George Mortimer Pullman (Mar. 3, 1831–Oct. 19, 1897). American cabinetmaker and inventor; originator of the railroad sleeping car; president of the Pullman Palace Car Company.

3
Dolls' Festival (*Hina Matsuri*) in Japan. Honors little girls and their dolls. Also called the Peach Blossom Festival (*Momo-no-sekku*), since this flower is considered to symbolize the attributes of little girls. Dolls are on display, and the girls are hostesses to their friends and are honored by their families.

3
National Anthem Day in the U.S. On Mar. 3, 1931, "The Star-Spangled Banner" was adopted as the official national anthem. It was written by Francis Scott Key, Sept. 13–14, 1814, during the nightlong British bombardment of Ft. McHenry in Baltimore during the War of 1812 and published in the Sept. 21, 1814, *Baltimore American*.

HOLY DAYS AND FEAST DAYS

4
Feast of St. Casimir (Oct. 3, 1458–Mar. 4, 1484). Of the Polish royal family; remembered as an active and competent ruler, but also holy and just, and loving contemplation. A patron saint of Poland and Lithuania.

HOLIDAYS AND CIVIC DAYS

4
Old Inauguration Day in the U.S. From 1789 to 1933, Mar. 4 was Inauguration Day for the offices of president and vice president of the U.S., as well as for senators and representatives. The 20th Amendment transferred Inauguration Day to Jan. 20 for the president and vice president, and to Jan. 3 for senators and representatives. The first Congress under the Constitution met on Mar. 4, 1789.

4
Mayors' Day in the Chicago school system. Commemorates past mayors of Chicago, particularly Richard J. Daley (May 15, 1902–Dec. 20, 1976) and Harold Washington (Apr. 15, 1922–Nov. 25. 1987).

4

Charter Day in Pa. Anniversary of the granting by Charles II of England of a charter on Mar. 4, 1681, to William Penn, the founder of the state, to satisfy a royal debt of £16,000. The charter was officially proclaimed on Apr. 2, 1681.

4

Admission Day in Vt. Anniversary of Vt.'s admission as the 14th state on Mar. 4, 1791.

Anniversaries and Special Events Days

4

Anniversary of the establishment of the Greenwich Observatory (in greater London) on Mar. 4, 1675. On this date, King Charles II by royal warrant commissioned John Flamsteed his "astronomical observator" (Astronomer Royal); within 2 days, crown property at Greenwich had been designated the site of the royal observatory. The first observations were made on Sept. 16, 1676.

4

Anniversary of Jeannette Rankin's first day in the House. On Mar. 4, 1917, Jeannette Rankin of Mont. became the first woman to serve in the U.S. Congress.

4

Birthday of Prince Henry the Navigator (Henrique, Infante du Portugal; Mar. 4, 1394–Nov. 13, 1460). Portuguese founder and first director of the century-long program of Portuguese research and exploration that discovered the trans-African sea routes to Asia. By-products were Cabral's arrival in Brazil and Columbus's landfall in the Bahamas.

4

Birthday of Count Casimir (Kazimierz) Pulaski (Mar. 4, 1747–ca. Oct. 11, 1779). Polish patriot and revolutionary soldier against Russian dominion, exiled following Poland's partition; a hero of the American Revolution; organizer of a corps of guerrilla cavalry and light infantry known as Pulaski's Legion; mortally wounded in the siege of Savannah. The 1st Monday in Mar. is an official public holiday in Ill. and a day of special school observance in Ind., as is Mar. 4 in Wis. Pulaski Memorial Day is observed in Nebr. schools and elsewhere on his death anniversary, Oct. 11. In New York City, the Pulaski Day parade is on the Sunday nearest Oct. 11.

4

Birthday of Knute Kenneth Rockne (Mar. 4, 1888–Mar. 31, 1931). Norwegian-born American football coach famed for his leadership in the sport and for the development of the "Fighting Irish" and the "Four Horsemen," which are a part of the Notre Dame football legend.

4

Birthday of Johann Rudolf Wyss (Mar. 4, 1782–Mar. 21, 1830). Swiss folklorist and editor of his father's *Swiss Family Robinson,* which has been translated into many languages.

4

Death anniversary of Saladin I (Salah ad-Din Yusuf ibn Ayyub; ca. 1137–Mar. 4, 1193). Kurd; Ayyubid dynasty sultan of Egypt and Syria; the most famous of Muslim heroes: victorious, chivalrous, and generous. Led the Muslim counterattack that recaptured Jerusalem on Oct. 2, 1187, following his overwhelming victory at the Battle of Hattin on July 4, 1187. Thereafter, he frustrated the Third Crusade, which failed to regain Jerusalem.

Holidays and Civic Days

5

Boston Massacre Day; observed annually in Boston. Anniversary of the attack by British troops on a mob of colonial citizens on Mar. 5, 1770, killing 5 (including Crispus Attucks) and wounding 6; the event was widely publicized and strengthened revolutionary sentiment.

5

Crispus Attucks Day; celebrated by name in N.J., as part of Boston Massacre Day in Boston, and as Black American Day in Calif. schools. Death anniversary of the American Revolutionary patriot who led the group whose anti-British defiance precipitated the Boston Massacre; honored as the first African American to die for national independence. Crispus Attucks (ca. 1723–Mar. 5, 1770) was probably an escaped slave and was perhaps part Massachuset; when killed, he had been a whaler for 20 years.

Anniversaries and Special Events Days

5

Birthday of Elisha Harris (Mar. 5, 1824–Jan. 31, 1884). American physician; pioneer in public health and one of the organizers of the American Public Health Association.

5

Birthday of James Merrit Ives (Mar. 5, 1824–Jan. 3, 1895). American lithographer; a partner in the firm of Currier & Ives, publishers of prints showing the historic events, manners, and customs of 19th-century America.

5

Birthday of Howard Pyle (Mar. 5, 1853–Nov. 9, 1911). American illustrator, painter, and author, best known for his children's books.

CA. 5

Waking of Creatures in the Chinese calendar. Also called Festival of the Insects, *Ching Che* (or *Jingzhe*) in Chinese, or *Kyongchip* in Korean. Marks the true beginning of spring, when insects and other creatures awake from their winter dormancy.

HOLIDAYS AND CIVIC DAYS

6

Independence Day in Ghana; official public holiday. Celebrates the attainment of independence from the U.K. on Mar. 6, 1957.

ANNIVERSARIES AND SPECIAL EVENTS DAYS

6

Birthday of José Antonio de Aguirre y Lembe (Mar. 6, 1904–Mar. 22, 1960). The Oct. 7, 1936, election of Aguirre (or Agirre) to lead the Basque people of Spain, held under the sacred, ancient, and still-surviving oak of Guernica, was an event of enormous importance for the Basque people. Aguirre served as president of the Basque Republic throughout the Spanish Civil War and remains a political icon in the Basque region of Spain.

6

Birthday of Elizabeth Barrett Browning (Mar. 6, 1806–June 29, 1861). English poet and wife of the poet Robert Browning. Her best-known work is *Sonnets from the Portuguese.*

6

Birthday of Michelangelo (Michelangelo di Lodovico Buonarroti Simoni; Mar. 6, 1475–Feb. 18, 1564). Italian sculptor, painter, architect, and poet, famous for his statues of David and of Moses, the paintings in the Sistine Chapel, and the famous cupola of St. Peter's Basilica.

6

Birthday of Philip Henry Sheridan (Mar. 6, 1831–Aug. 5, 1888). American soldier who made the famous ride to Cedar Creek and turned a Union defeat into a great victory of the Civil War; known as Little Phil because of his size.

6

Alamo Day in Tex. Commemorates the fall of the Alamo, a Tex. fort besieged by Mexican forces under Santa Anna from Feb. 23 until Mar. 6, 1836, when the last defender was slain. "Remember the Alamo!" became the Texans' battle cry, and General Sam Houston defeated the Mexican army on Apr. 21, ending the war and securing independence for Tex.

6

French Academy Woman's Day. Anniversary of the Mar. 6, 1980, election of the novelist, essayist, and translator Marguerite Yourcenar as the first woman member of the select, more than 3-centuries-old French Academy.

HOLIDAYS AND CIVIC DAYS

7

Birthday of Luther Burbank (Mar. 7, 1849–Apr. 11, 1926), and Arbor Day in Calif. American naturalist and plant breeder who introduced more than 600 varieties of plants to America, many of which form the basis of fruit industries. In Calif., Burbank's birthday is observed as Conservation, Bird, and Arbor Day, especially in schools.

ANNIVERSARIES AND SPECIAL EVENTS DAYS

7

Birthday of Alessandro Manzoni (Mar. 7, 1785–May 22, 1873). Italian novelist and poet whose novel *The Betrothed* is considered a model of Italian prose.

7

Birthday of Tomáš G. Masaryk (Mar. 7, 1850–Sept. 14, 1937). Fervent nationalist and first president of Czechoslovakia (1918–35). Both he and his son Jan are fondly remembered.

7

Birthday of Maurice Joseph Ravel (Mar. 7, 1875–Dec. 28, 1937). French composer whose *Bolero* has been one of the most popular concert selections of the 20th century.

HOLY DAYS AND FEAST DAYS

8

Feast of St. John of God (Mar. 8, 1495–Mar. 8, 1550). Portuguese layman devoted to the care of sick and poor people; patron saint of sick people, nurses, and hospitals, and of book and print sellers.

HOLIDAYS AND CIVIC DAYS

8

International Women's Day. An internationally recognized day to honor working women; has its roots in a Mar. 8, 1857, revolt of American women protesting working conditions in the textile and garment industries. The most widely observed holiday of recent origin; was named and proclaimed at an international conference of women in Helsinki, Finland, in 1910; Clara Zetkin (German; July 5, 1857–June 20, 1933) was cited as the day's initiator. The week containing Mar. 8 is Women's History Week, and March is Women's History Month.

ANNIVERSARIES AND SPECIAL EVENTS DAYS

8

Anniversary of the creation of the Volunteers of America on Mar. 8, 1896, by Ballington Booth and his wife, Maud, at a public rally in New York City. The organization is a spiritual movement of active voluntary service to others, and is both large and effective. National Volunteers of America Week is the Sunday–Sunday that includes Mar. 8.

8

Birthday of Frederick William Goudy (Mar. 8, 1865–May 11, 1947). American printer and type designer; honored by printers' guilds and publishing associations.

8

Birthday of Kenneth Grahame (Mar. 8, 1859–July 6, 1932). English banker, and author of *The Wind in the Willows,* a children's classic dramatized by A. A. Milne as *Toad of Toad Hall,* which has become a popular play for Christmas presentations.

8

Birthday of Oliver Wendell Holmes Jr. (Mar. 8, 1841–Mar. 6, 1935). American jurist and one of the most famous and revered justices of the U.S. Supreme Court; known as the Great Dissenter. Elected to the Hall of Fame for Great Americans.

HOLY DAYS AND FEAST DAYS

9

Feast of St. Catherine of Bologna (born Caterina Vigri; 1413–Mar. 9, 1463). Italian Poor Clares nun and mystic; patron saint of artists.

HOLIDAYS AND CIVIC DAYS

9

Baron Bliss Day in Belize; official public holiday. Honors, on the anniversary of his birth, Sir Henry Edward Ernest Victor Bliss, a yachting Englishman who, in 1926, paused in Belize (then British Honduras) to recover from illness and came to admire the character of the people but died, bequeathing a fortune to Belize; soundly invested, the money has built many schools, clinics, and libraries.

ANNIVERSARIES AND SPECIAL EVENTS DAYS

9

Anniversary of the Battle of Hampton Roads, the U.S. Civil War engagement between the *Monitor* and the *Merrimac* on Mar. 9, 1862.

9

Birthday of Leland Stanford (Mar. 9, 1824–June 21, 1893). American capitalist; politician; president of the Central Pacific railroad and one of the builders of the first transcontinental railroad in the U.S., driver of the Golden Spike. Founder of Stanford University, a memorial to his son.

9

Birthday of Amerigo Vespucci (Mar. 9, 1451–Feb. 22, 1512). Italian navigator, merchant, and explorer of South America; the first to proclaim that here was a new continent, not the Orient. The Americas were named in his honor.

9

Shevchenko Day in Ukraine. Commemorates Ukraine's great national poet, Taras Hryhorovych Shevchenko (Mar. 9, 1814–Mar. 10, 1861).

HOLY DAYS AND FEAST DAYS

10

Feast of St. Macarius of Jerusalem (died ca. Sept. 13, 335). Bishop of Jerusalem; active at the Council of Nicaea. By legend, assisted St. Helena in finding the True Cross. Commissioned by the emperor Constantine to build the basilica over Christ's sepulchre, consecrated in 335.

ANNIVERSARIES AND SPECIAL EVENTS DAYS

10
Anniversary of the arrival of the Salvation Army in the U.S. On Mar. 10, 1880, Commissioner George Scott Railton and 7 women officers landed in New York City to begin its work; it was officially organized in the U.S. on Mar. 28, 1885.

10
Birthday of John McCloskey (Mar. 10, 1810–Oct. 10, 1885). American Roman Catholic prelate; first president of St. John's College (later Fordham University) and the first American cardinal of the Roman Catholic Church.

10
Birthday of Lillian D. Wald (Mar. 10, 1867–Sept. 1, 1940). American sociologist; founder of the Henry Street Settlement and organizer of the first nonsectarian public-health nursing system in the world. Elected to the Hall of Fame for Great Americans.

10
Death anniversary of Harriet Tubman (ca. 1820–Mar. 10, 1913). American escaped slave, abolitionist, and organizer of Underground Railroad escape routes for others; she helped more than 300 slaves reach freedom.

10
Alexander Bell Day. On Mar. 10, 1876, Alexander Graham Bell transmitted the first message by telephone, saying "Mr. Watson, come here, I want you." The first telephone exchange opened on Jan. 28, 1878, in New Haven, Conn.

10
Dance of Those Who Fly (*Voladores*) in Huachinango, Mexico; begins on Mar. 10. Also held in Papantla, Mexico, on Corpus Christi. Ritual performed by Totonac Indians. One man (representing the sun) plays a flute atop a tall pole while 4 others on unwinding ropes revolve 13 times (representing the number of years in an Aztec century). Dangerous and elegant. The date is perhaps New Year's Day in a modern version of the pre-Conquest Aztec calendar.

10
Tibetan Uprising Day. On Mar. 10, 1959, Tibetans revolted against China's occupation of their country (invaded in 1951).

HOLY DAYS AND FEAST DAYS

11
Farvardegan (also *Farvadin* or *Farvardin*) days begin among Zoroastrians, especially the Parsis of India; Mar. 11–20, ending on New Year's Eve, the day before *Nav Roz*. A time to remember the spirits of the dead, who have returned to Ahura Mazda to help fight against evil. All attend ceremonies for the dead on the hills in front of the towers of silence and at shrines in their homes.

HOLIDAYS AND CIVIC DAYS

11
Restoration of Statehood Day in Lithuania; official public holiday. Commemorates the Mar. 11, 1990, declaration of independence from the USSR. The USSR recognized the independence of all 3 Baltic nations on Sept. 6, 1991.

ANNIVERSARIES AND SPECIAL EVENTS DAYS

11
Anniversary of the start of the worldwide Spanish influenza epidemic of 1918. On Mar. 11, 1918, soldiers in Fort Riley, Kans., reported sick, and some died, from what was later diagnosed as a lethal variation of the common flu. The disease was carried to Europe with troops sent to fight in World War I; there it further mutated, spread worldwide, and killed 20 million people, including 548,000 in the U.S.

11
Birthday of Vannevar Bush (Mar. 11, 1890–June 28, 1974). American electrical engineer; developer of the first analog computer.

11
Birthday of Thomas Hastings (Mar. 11, 1860–Oct. 22, 1929). American architect of the firm Carrère & Hastings, designer of the New York Public Library and the Frick mansion, which houses the Frick Collection.

11
Birthday of Torquato Tasso (Mar. 11, 1544–Apr. 25, 1595). Italian epic poet of the late Renaissance whose masterpiece is *Jerusalem Delivered.*

HOLIDAYS AND CIVIC DAYS

12

Moshoeshoe's Day in Lesotho; official public holiday. Honors Moshoeshoe (born Mosesh; 1786–Mar. 12, 1870), founder of the Basotho tribe and of Lesotho, a peaceful refuge from the internecine wars in southern Africa launched by the Zulu leader Shaka.

12

National Day in Mauritius; official public holiday. Celebrates independence attained from the U.K. on Mar. 12, 1968. Mauritius became a republic within the British Commonwealth on Mar. 12, 1992.

12

Arbor Day in Taiwan. Observed on the death anniversary of Sun Yat-sen (Nov. 12, 1866–Mar. 12, 1925).

ANNIVERSARIES AND SPECIAL EVENTS DAYS

12

Anniversary of the formal end of the Peloponnesian War. On Mar. 12, 1996, the mayors of Athens and Sparta, Greece, signed a peace treaty formally ending the war of 431–404 B.C., which rent the ancient Greek world in a fratricidal tragedy.

12

Birthday of Gabriele D'Annunzio (Mar. 12, 1863–Mar. 1, 1938). Italian soldier and the leading Italian author of his time; vigorously promoted Italian patriotism.

12

Birthday of Simon Newcomb (Mar. 12, 1835–July 11, 1909). Canadian-born American scientist; one of the greatest mathematical astronomers. Elected to the Hall of Fame for Great Americans.

12

Girl Scout Day. Anniversary of the founding of the first American troop of Girl Guides, which subsequently became the Girl Scouts of America, on Mar. 12, 1912, by the American youth leader Juliet Low (Oct. 31, 1860–Jan. 17, 1927) in Savannah, Ga. Girl Scout Week includes Mar. 12; Girl Scouts and their leaders celebrate with community projects, parties, plays, and ceremonies.

12

Jane Delano Day. Sponsored by the American Red Cross Nursing Service, to honor its founder and first chairperson on her traditional birthday. Jane Arminda Delano (Mar. 12, 1862?–Apr. 15, 1919) was a dedicated American nurse and teacher, superintendent of the U.S. Army Nurse Corps, and posthumous recipient of the Distinguished Service Medal. Recent discoveries suggest that her true date of birth is Mar. 26, 1858.

12

Water-Drawing Ceremony (*O-Mizutori Matsuri*) in Nara, Japan, at the Todaiji Temple; Mar. 1–15, main day Mar. 12. A famous fire festival, 12 centuries old; solemn, dramatic, and mysterious. On the evening of the 12th, great torches are lit, casting showers of sparks; at midnight, sacred water is drawn from the Wakasa Well and distributed.

ANNIVERSARIES AND SPECIAL EVENTS DAYS

13

Anniversary of the discovery of the planet Uranus on Mar. 13, 1781, by the German-born British astronomer William Herschel.

13

Birthday of Percival Lowell (Mar. 13, 1855–Nov. 12, 1916). American astronomer who laid the groundwork for the discovery of the planet Pluto. The discovery was announced on his birthday, Mar. 13, 1930, by the Lowell Observatory, which he founded.

13

Birthday of Joseph Priestley (Mar. 13, 1733–Feb. 6, 1804). English discoverer of oxygen.

13

Birthday of Helen Candaele St. Aubin (Mar. 13, 1929–Dec. 8, 1992). American baseball player called the Ted Williams of Women's Baseball. Played under the name Helen Callaghan in the Girls Professional Baseball League in the 1940s.

ANNIVERSARIES AND SPECIAL EVENTS DAYS

14

Birthday of Thomas Hart Benton (Mar. 14, 1782–Apr. 10, 1858). American congressman known as

Old Bullion because of his stand on gold and silver currency. Represents Mo. in Statuary Hall.

14

Birthday of Albert Einstein (Mar. 14, 1879–Apr. 18, 1955). German-born Swiss, later American, physicist noted for his theory of relativity. Awarded the Nobel Prize in physics in 1921 for his photoelectric law and work in theoretical physics.

14

Birthday of Casey Jones (born John Luther Jones; Mar. 14, 1864–Apr. 30, 1900). American railroad engineer and folk hero who drove the Cannon Ball express. Killed when his train collided with a freight train and he stayed in the cab to apply the brakes, thus saving his passengers and crew. Immortalized in a ballad originally composed by Wallace Saunders.

14

Birthday of Isadore Gilbert Mudge (Mar. 14, 1875–May 17, 1957). American librarian, author, and bibliographer. Since 1959, a citation has been given annually in her name through the American Library Association to a reference librarian for "a distinguished contribution to reference librarianship."

14

Birthday of Jens Jacob Asmussen Worsaae (Mar. 14, 1821–Aug. 15, 1885). Danish archaeologist and principal founder of prehistoric archaeology.

14

Death anniversary of Sir Thomas Malory (flourished ca. 1470; may have died Mar. 14, 1471). English adventurer and author of the Arthurian romance *Morte d'Arthur.*

HOLIDAYS AND CIVIC DAYS

15

Constitution Day in Belarus; official public holiday. Anniversary of the present constitution, adopted on Mar. 15, 1994.

15

Memorial Day for the 1848 Revolution and War of Independence in Hungary; official public holiday. Anniversary of the 1848 revolution in Hungary, when the country briefly attained internal autonomy from Austria and its modern parliamentary tradition began. The war of 1848–49 ended in defeat by huge Russian and Austrian forces on Aug. 13, 1849. Mar. 15 has been celebrated since 1860, despite any overlords' objections.

15

J. J. Roberts Day in Liberia; official public holiday. Honors Joseph Jenkins Roberts (Mar. 15, 1809–Feb. 24, 1876), the country's first president, elected in 1848.

15

Statehood Day in Maine. Anniversary of Maine's admission as the 23rd state on Mar. 15, 1820. Maine Cultural History Week is the week containing Mar. 15.

ANNIVERSARIES AND SPECIAL EVENTS DAYS

15

Birthday of Lady Augusta Gregory (Mar. 15, 1852–May 22, 1932). Irish playwright and poet; leader in the Irish literary revival and cofounder of the Irish Literary Theater.

15

Birthday of Andrew Jackson (Mar. 15, 1767–June 8, 1845). Revolutionary War veteran (at age 13); frontiersman and soldier; self-taught Tenn. lawyer; congressman and senator; general in the War of 1812, 7th president of the U.S. (1829–37; Democrat), defeating John Quincy Adams. Regarded by Democrats as a founding father of the party, along with Thomas Jefferson. Buried at the Hermitage, near Nashville, Tenn. Elected to the Hall of Fame for Great Americans, and represents Tenn. in Statuary Hall.

15

Buzzard Day in Hinckley, Ohio. Traditional day for the annual return of buzzards (or turkey vultures) from wintering in the Great Smokey Mountains. The Hinckley Buzzard Day Festival is the Sunday following Mar. 15; held since 1958.

15

Ides of March in the Roman calendar, and the anniversary of the assassination of Julius Caesar (Gaius Julius Caesar; traditionally July 12 or 13, 100 B.C.–Mar. 15, 44 B.C.). Roman general, statesman, and writer; proto-emperor during the transition from the Roman Republic to the Empire.

ANNIVERSARIES AND SPECIAL EVENTS DAYS

16

Anniversary of the fall of the Cathar stronghold of Montségur in Languedoc (southern France), in the Albigensian Crusade (launched, 1229). Montségur surrendered on Mar. 16, 1244; on this day 200 Cathars emerged and went singing to the stake, with their treasure saved (whatever it was).

16

Anniversary of the My Lai Massacre. On March 26, 1968, during the Vietnam War, U.S. infantry-men murdered approximately 300 noncombatant villagers at My Lai and Mykhe, Vietnam.

16

Anniversary of the first greeting of the Pilgrims by the Native American Samoset (Abenaki; 1590–1653), on Mar. 16, 1621.

16

Birthday of James Madison (Mar. 16, 1751–June 28, 1836). Va. lawyer; Revolutionary patriot and statesman known as the Father of the Constitution, who helped frame the Bill of Rights and fought the Alien and Sedition Acts; 4th president of the U.S. (1809–17; Democrat Republican); rector of the University of Virginia. President during the War of 1812. A strict constructionist, he resisted the broad Federalist interpretation of the Constitution. Buried at Montpelier, Orange County, Va. Elected to the Hall of Fame for Great Americans.

16

Birthday of René Sully Prudhomme (Mar. 16, 1839–Sept. 7, 1907). French poet and critic; the first recipient of the Nobel Prize in literature (1901).

16

Black Press Day. Anniversary of the Mar. 16, 1827, founding in New York City of *Freedom's Journal*, the first newspaper in the U.S. published by and for African Americans.

16

Founders Day at West Point. Anniversary of the establishment of the U.S. Military Academy at West Point, N.Y., by an Act of Congress on Mar. 16, 1802; observed during March by the Corps of Cadets at West Point on the Thursday before Spring Leave, and by graduates throughout the country at ceremonial dinners.

16

Freedom of Information Day. A day to celebrate and preserve the Bill of Rights, a free press, and public access to government information. Observed on James Madison's birthday, in honor of his ardent and effective concern with those issues.

Since 1989, the annual James Madison Award has customarily been presented on this day by the Coalition on Government Information to persons who protect and promote public access to government information.

16

Goddard Day. Recalls the Mar. 16, 1926, flight of the first liquid-fueled rocket, developed by Robert Goddard, at Auburn, Mass.

16

St. Urho's Day; observed on Mar. 16 or the Saturday nearest Mar. 16. A mock-serious event created in 1956 by Minn. Finns. St. Urho drove the grape-eating grasshoppers out of Finland and is the patron saint of Finnish wine makers. His day intentionally precedes St. Patrick's and is an occasion for midwinter frolics.

HOLY DAYS AND FEAST DAYS

17

Feast of St. Joseph of Arimathea (1st century). Disciple of Jesus who provided the tomb for Jesus' burial. By tradition, he was Jesus' uncle and took him to Britain on a tin-trading trip. After the Crucifixion, Joseph and others settled at Glastonbury in A.D. 63 or 64, erecting the first church in Britain, which became its most sacred spot. Patron saint of tin workers, working travelers, and funeral directors.

17

Feast of St. Patrick (ca. 389–ca. 461). Romano-Briton kidnapped into slavery in Ireland who returned to convert the Irish to Christianity. A man of great sweetness of character, and the first to unequivocally denounce slavery. By tradition, he retired to Glastonbury. The primary patron saint of Ireland. Mar. 17 is Ireland's greatest holy day and holiday. Orth.: Mar. 17 or 30.

HOLIDAYS AND CIVIC DAYS

17

Evacuation Day in Boston and Suffolk County, Mass.; local official public holiday in Suffolk County since 1941. Commemorates the forced withdrawal of British forces from Boston on Mar. 17, 1776, during the Revolutionary War. In Boston, celebrated with St. Patrick's Day.

ANNIVERSARIES AND SPECIAL EVENTS DAYS

17

Anniversary of the foundation of the Irish Republican Brotherhood on Mar. 17, 1858, in the U.S., with the American branch called the Fenians ("Warriors"); founded by James Stephens, who subsequently enlisted American Civil War veterans. Dedicated to the formation of a democratic independent Irish republic; it later evolved into the Irish Republican Army (IRA).

17

Birthday of Nat "King" Cole (Nathaniel Adams Cole; Mar. 17, 1919–Feb. 25, 1965). Notable American musician and singer; the first African American entertainer to host a national television show.

17

Birthday of Kate Greenaway (Mar. 17, 1846–Nov. 6, 1901). English watercolor artist whose drawings of children provided an exemplary model for book illustration.

17

Birthday of Mujibur Rahman (called Sheik Mujib; Mar. 17, 1920–Aug. 15, 1975). Bangladeshi independence leader and cofounder in 1949 of the Awami League; first prime minister of Bangladesh, and later its president; assassinated in a coup d'état.

17

Birthday of Stephen Samuel Wise (Mar. 17, 1874–Apr. 19, 1949). American reform rabbi and Jewish leader; president of the Zionist Organization of America; founder of the Jewish Institute of Religion and instrumental in the founding of the World Jewish Congress.

17

Death anniversary of George Parker, 2nd Earl of Macclesfield (1697–Mar. 17, 1764). Notable English astronomer; president of the Royal Society from 1752 until his death. One of the main authors, with Lord Chesterfield, of the Bill for Regulating the Commencement of the Year, also called the British Calendar Act of 1751.

17

Camp Fire Boys and Girls Founders Day. Commemorates the establishment of the Camp Fire Girls (now the Camp Fire Boys and Girls) on Mar. 17, 1910. The Sunday on or before Mar. 17 is Birthday Sunday, the beginning of Camp Fire Boys and Girls Birthday Week.

17

St. Patrick's Day. Celebrated wherever the Irish live, and many temporary Irishmen spring up for the day. The devout attend Mass, but for most this is a festively secular occasion. In the U.S., there are St. Patrick's Day parades, especially in New York City and Boston. New York's is the most famous, and participation is awesomely large; its recorded history dates from 1762. Boston's parade dates from 1737 and is the oldest in the U.S.; there, St. Patrick's Day and Evacuation Day are combined, giving the day a heightened fervor.

HOLIDAYS AND CIVIC DAYS

18

Anniversary of Mexican Economic Independence, commemorating the nationalization of the country's oil fields on Mar. 18, 1938, under President Lázaro Cárdenas.

ANNIVERSARIES AND SPECIAL EVENTS DAYS

18

Birthday of John Caldwell Calhoun (Mar. 18, 1782–Mar. 31, 1850). American statesman; congressman from S.C.; brilliant exponent of states' rights; vice president of the U.S. (resigned Dec. 28, 1832). Represents S.C. in Statuary Hall.

18

Birthday of (Stephen) Grover Cleveland (Mar. 18, 1837–June 24, 1908). N.Y. lawyer; 22nd and 24th president of the U.S. (1885–89, 1893–97; Democrat). Notably honest administrator; fought Tammany Hall and its ilk; enlarged the Civil Service. Buried at Princeton, N.J. Elected to the Hall of Fame for Great Americans.

18

Birthday of Nikolay Andreyevich Rimsky-Korsakov (Mar. 18, 1844–June 21, 1908). Influential Russian composer and teacher whose best-known works include *Capriccio Espagnol* (1887) and *Scheherazade* (1888). Among his students were Ottorino Respighi and Igor Stravinsky.

18

De Molay Day. Observed each year by the Masonic Order of De Molay in commemoration of the martyrdom at the stake of Jacques De Molay, the last grand master of the Order of Knights Templar, on Mar. 18 or 19, 1314. Almost all Templars in France had been arrested on Oct. 16, 1307, at the order of King Philip the Fair, with the connivance of Pope Clement V. The Knights Templar had been founded in Jerusalem, ca. 1018.

18

Sheelah's Day. Observed in Ireland with shamrocks saved from St. Patrick's Day to honor Sheelah, who may have been St. Patrick's wife or mother. One's shamrock is "drowned" in the evening's last glass of whiskey.

HOLY DAYS AND FEAST DAYS

19

Feast of St. Joseph (1st century); official public holiday in some countries; sometimes celebrated also as Father's Day. Husband of the Virgin Mary; patron saint of Belgium and of the Universal Church, also of workers, carpenters, and social justice.

HOLIDAYS AND CIVIC DAYS

19

National Day of Oil in Iran; official public holiday. Commemorates the anniversary of the nationalization of Iran's oil fields in 1963.

19

St. Joseph's Day in Madrid; official public holiday. Start of the bullfighting season. During the season, there are bullfights on Sundays and important fiestas, and daily during the San Isidro Festival in May and during a week in Sept. The season officially ends on Hispanity Day, Oct. 12.

19

The *Fallas* ("Bonfires") in Valencia, Spain; official public holiday. A festival of medieval origin; originally a day for carpenters to burn their accumulated wood scrap in festive bonfires on the feast of their patron saint, but now a festival (Mar. 12–19) in which colorful images, on display all week, are burned one by one in the evening of the 19th. By midnight, the whole city appears to be aflame.

ANNIVERSARIES AND SPECIAL EVENTS DAYS

19

Anniversary of the Standard Time Act in the U.S. On Mar. 19, 1918, Congress authorized the establishment of standard time zones in the U.S. The railroads had adopted them on Nov. 18, 1883, persuaded by Charles Ferdinand Dowd and others.

19

Birthday of William Jennings Bryan (Mar. 19, 1860–July 26, 1925). American lawyer and political leader, known as the Silver-Tongued Orator, whose career ended shortly after the famous Scopes trial involving the antievolution law. Bryan gave powerful support to women's suffrage and was an ardent "free silver" advocate. Represents Nebr. in Statuary Hall.

19

Birthday of Wyatt Berry Stapp Earp (Mar. 19, 1848–Jan. 13, 1929). Legendary American frontiersman and lawman, famous for his participation in the gunfight at the O.K. Corral.

19

Birthday of David Livingstone (Mar. 19, 1813–May 1, 1873). Scottish doctor, explorer, and medical missionary; discoverer of Victoria Falls; the subject of the famous search by Henry Stanley following reports of his death in Africa.

19

Swallows Day. Day when the swallows traditionally return to the San Juan Capistrano Mission in Calif.; recorded since 1776.

HOLY DAYS AND FEAST DAYS

20

Feast of St. Niklaus von Flüe (1417–Mar. 21, 1487). Switzerland's only outstanding religious figure. After an active and effective political life, spent 20 years in solitary prayer and fasting. His grave is visited by many thousands.

HOLIDAYS AND CIVIC DAYS

20

Independence Day in Tunisia; official public holiday. Commemorates the attainment of independence from France on Mar. 20, 1956. The following day, Mar. 21, is Youth Day, also an official public holiday.

ANNIVERSARIES AND SPECIAL EVENTS DAYS

20

Anniversary of the formation of the Republican Party on Mar. 20, 1854, at Ripon, Wis., led by Alvan Earle Bovay.

20

Birthday of Charles William Eliot (Mar. 20, 1834–Aug. 22, 1926). American educator, president of Harvard (1869–1909), and editor of the famous "five-foot shelf of books," the 50-volume Harvard Classics.

20

Birthday of Henrik Ibsen (Mar. 20, 1828–May 23, 1906). Norwegian playwright, famous for *Peer Gynt* and other plays.

20

Lajos Kossuth Day in Hungary; observed by Hungarians worldwide. Death anniversary of Lajos Kossuth (Sept. 19, 1802–Mar. 20, 1894). Hungarian statesman; leader with Count István Széchenyi in the 1848 revolution against Austria.

HOLY DAYS AND FEAST DAYS

21

Feast of *Naw-Ruz*. Baha'i New Year's Day, the 1st day of the month of *Baha;* a holy day, and Baha'is abstain from work. Observed with prayers and readings from the Baha'i scriptures, consultation on affairs of the faith, and enjoyment of Baha'i music and fellowship.

21

Kordad Sal among Zoroastrians and Parsis. Celebrates the birthday of the founder, Zoroaster (Zarathushtra), the 6th-century Persian prophet who formalized the worship of Ahura Mazda, the Wise Lord.

HOLIDAYS AND CIVIC DAYS

21

Navroz ("New Day") in the Persian calendar; observed on Mar. 21, or on the actual vernal equinox. A celebration of the old New Year's Day and the coming of spring. Observed with picnics; and with religious rituals among Parsis and other Zoroastrians; celebrated with farm fairs and kite flying in Afghanistan and Pakistan, and often with *buzkashi*, an ancient form of polo. Many people take vacations at this time.

21

National Tree Planting Day in Lesotho; official public holiday.

21

Benito Juárez's Birthday in Mexico; official public holiday. Honors Benito Pablo Juárez (Mar. 21, 1806–July 18, 1872), the first Mexican president (1861–65, 1867–72) of Indian descent; known as the Mexican Washington.

21

Independence Day in Namibia; official public holiday. Celebrates attainment of independence from South Africa on Mar. 21, 1990.

ANNIVERSARIES AND SPECIAL EVENTS DAYS

21

Anniversary of the first presentation of the West Point Sylvanus Thayer Award, named for the 5th superintendent of the U.S. Military Academy at West Point, N.Y., on Mar. 21, 1958. This medal, given annually by the Association of Graduates of the United States Military Academy, is bestowed on "the United States citizen whose service and accomplishments in the national interest exemplify devotion to the ideals expressed in the West Point motto—Duty, Honor, Country."

21

Birthday of Johann Sebastian Bach (Mar. 21, 1685–July 28, 1750). German composer and instrumentalist. A master of counterpoint, Bach is considered one of the foremost composers of all time. Among his masterpieces are the *Goldberg Variations* and the *Brandenburg Concertos* as well as numerous religiously inspired works, such as *St. Matthew Passion, B Minor Mass,* and *Christmas Oratorio.*

21

Elimination of Racial Discrimination Day. Initiated by the United Nations in 1966 as a memorial to all victims of racial injustice. Date is the anniversary of the massacre of protesters against racial injustice in Sharpeville, South Africa, on Mar. 21, 1960.

21

Future birthday of Captain James T. Kirk, of the starship *Enterprise* NCC1701. Kirk will be born on Mar. 21, 2228, at Riverside, Iowa, behind what is now the former town barbershop.

CA. 21

Marzenna Day in Poland; Saturday or Sunday nearest Mar. 21. A spring festival, especially for young people, along the Vistula River. With songs, dances, and the placing of a straw effigy of a girl in the river to bring to life the old story of a young man's faith in one god, which stopped the sacrifice of a girl's life to placate the gods of storms and floods.

21

Master Gardener Day. Created in 1992 to honor the Master Gardener programs in many states. Amateurs are given specialized training and after certification assist their extension agents by answering the public's gardening questions. To date, 60,000 Master Gardeners have been certified.

CA. 21

National Agriculture Day, or Ag Day, in the U.S.; on the first day of spring. Established in 1973; frequently announced by presidential proclamation; a tribute to farmers, ranchers, and growers; observed by farm bureaus, marketing associations, and the National Future Farmers of America. National Agriculture Week is the week that includes Ag Day.

CA. 21

The spring, or vernal, equinox occurs on Mar. 20 or 21. On this day the sun crosses the equator, and day and night are everywhere of equal length. (There is another equinox in the autumn; *see* Sept. 23.)

CA. 21

Vernal Equinox Day in the Chinese calendar. Among other events on this day, ancient Confucian rites honoring Korean and Chinese sages are held in South Korea, at the Confucian Shrine at Sungkyunkwan University, north of Seoul. The same ceremony recurs on Autumnal Equinox Day, ca. Sept. 23.

HOLIDAYS AND CIVIC DAYS

22

Emancipation Day in Puerto Rico; official public holiday. Celebrates the end of slavery on Mar. 22, 1873.

ANNIVERSARIES AND SPECIAL EVENTS DAYS

22

Birthday of Randolph Caldecott (Mar. 22, 1846–Feb. 12, 1886). English artist and illustrator for whom the Caldecott Medal is named; the medal is awarded annually to the artist who has illustrated the most distinguished children's picture book published in the preceding year.

22

Birthday of Robert Andrews Millikan (Mar. 22, 1868–Dec. 19, 1953). American physicist; specialist in research on cosmic rays. He received the 1923 Nobel Prize in physics for isolating the electron, and the Presidential Medal of Merit for his work on rockets and jet propulsion during World War II.

22

Birthday of Sir Anthony Van Dyck (Mar. 22, 1599–Dec. 9, 1641). Flemish painter of society portraits. One of his most famous is that of Charles I.

HOLIDAYS AND CIVIC DAYS

23

Pakistan Day in Pakistan; official public holiday. Also called Republic Day. Commemorates the anniversary of the Mar. 23, 1940, adoption by the All-India Muslim League of a resolution by Mohammed Ali Jinnah calling for an independent Muslim state; also commemorates the declaration of the Republic of Pakistan on Mar. 23, 1956.

ANNIVERSARIES AND SPECIAL EVENTS DAYS

23

Birthday of John Bartram (Mar. 23, 1699–Sept. 22, 1777). American naturalist and explorer who founded the first botanical garden in the U.S.; known as the Father of American Botany.

23

Birthday of Sidney Hillman (Mar. 23, 1887–July 10, 1946). American labor leader and union official in whose name the Sidney Hillman Foundation presents an annual award for a book dealing with race relations, civil liberties, trade-union development, or world understanding.

23

Liberty Day. Anniversary of Patrick Henry's Mar. 23, 1775, speech to the Virginia Convention in Richmond, Va., which concluded with the words "Give me liberty or give me death!"; considered by historians to be the masterpiece of American patriotic oratory.

23

World Meteorological Day. Anniversary of the founding of the World Meteorological Organization, a specialized agency of the United Nations, on Mar. 23, 1950, to facilitate an international system of standardizing and coordinating weather observations and data. Observed by meteorological services worldwide.

ANNIVERSARIES AND SPECIAL EVENTS DAYS

24

Birthday of Galen Clark (Mar. 24, 1814–Mar. 24, 1910). American naturalist who discovered the Mariposa Grove of giant sequoia, or redwood, trees in 1857. Mount Clark in Yosemite is named in his honor.

24

Birthday of Andrew William Mellon (Mar. 24, 1855–Aug. 26, 1937). American financier and secretary of the Treasury who gave his art collection to the nation in 1937 for the establishment of the National Gallery of Art.

24

Birthday of William Morris (Mar. 24, 1834–Sept. 23, 1902). English poet; craftsman who designed fine furniture, wallpapers, and tapestries; and translator of Icelandic sagas. The William Morris Society was established in 1955 to revive interest in his ideas and works.

24

Birthday of John Wesley Powell (Mar. 24, 1834–Sept. 23, 1902). American Civil War veteran, geologist, and anthropologist who made a daring exploration of the Colorado and Green Rivers in 1869. Published the first classification of Native American languages and was the first director of the U.S. Bureau of Ethnology; a founder of the U.S. Geological Survey, called the Father of Land Preservation in the West.

24

Death anniversary of John "Longitude" Harrison (Mar. 1693–Mar. 24, 1776). English clock maker; creator of the first marine chronometers sufficiently accurate and reliable to allow navigators to determine precise longitude at sea.

24

Death anniversary of Harun ar-Rashid (ca. 766–Mar. 24, 809). Famous caliph (786–809) of Baghdad who ruled Islam at the height of its power and luxury. Idealized as the caliph in *The Thousand and One Nights*.

HOLY DAYS AND FEAST DAYS

25

Feast of the Annunciation of the Lord. In the Catholic Church, formerly called the Annunciation of the Virgin Mary; in the Eastern Churches, called the Annunciation of the Theotokos ("God Bearer"). Celebrates the Incarnation and Conception of Christ announced by the Archangel Gabriel to Mary. Orth.: Mar. 25 or Apr. 7.

25

Feast of St. Dismas (1st century). The Good Thief of the New Testament, crucified alongside Jesus.

Patron saint of prisoners, persons condemned to death, and funeral directors.

HOLIDAYS AND CIVIC DAYS

25

Independence Day in Greece; official public holiday in Greece and Cyprus. On Sunday, Mar. 25, 1821, at Hóra Sfakíon, Crete, the Greek flag was first raised in revolt against the Ottoman Empire. Independence was attained in 1829.

25

Maryland Day in Md.; official public holiday. Celebrates the landing of the colonists sent to the New World in 1634 by Lord Baltimore under the leadership of his brother, Leonard Calvert.

ANNIVERSARIES AND SPECIAL EVENTS DAYS

25

Anniversary of the Triangle Shirtwaist Fire in 1911 in New York City. The sweatshop's emergency exits had been chained shut by policy; when the building caught fire, 146 workers, mostly young women, died by smoke or fire, or by jumping to their deaths. A scandalous disaster that provoked worker-safety legislation.

25

Birthday of Béla Bartók (Mar. 25, 1881–Sept. 26, 1945). Hungarian composer noted for his use of folk tunes in his concert works; famous for *Hungarian Folk Music,* a standard musical reference work.

25

Birthday of Gutzon Borglum (John Gutzon de la Mothe Borglum; Mar. 25, 1867–Mar. 6, 1941). American sculptor and painter. Best known for his colossal head of Lincoln in the Capitol and for the Mt. Rushmore Memorial figures of Washington, Jefferson, Lincoln, and Theodore Roosevelt, in the Black Hills of S.Dak.

25

Birthday of Arturo Toscanini (Mar. 25, 1867–Jan. 16, 1957). Italian musician considered by critics to be the greatest conductor of the first half of the 20th century.

25

Birthday of William Bell Wait (Mar. 25, 1839–Oct. 25, 1916). American educator and pioneer in the field of education of blind people; devised an embossing machine for printing books for blind people and also a typewriter for their use.

25

Lady Day in Ireland, England, and Wales. Also called Quarter Day. A traditional day to pay rent or change lodgings. Among the Sami (Lapps) of Scandinavia, this day and Easter Sunday are the favored days for weddings.

25

Memorial Day in Latvia. Commemorates the mass deportation of Balts to Siberia in 1949.

25

Old New Year's Day. Mar. 25 was New Year's Day in Great Britain and its colonies until Britain's adoption of the Gregorian calendar in 1752 and had been one of many different New Year's Days used in Europe since the fall of the Roman Empire. Mar. 25 fell on the vernal equinox in the original version of the Julian calendar, and New Year's Day was placed on either Mar. 25 or Jan. 1 during different periods of the Roman Republic.

HOLIDAYS AND CIVIC DAYS

26

Independence Day in Bangladesh; official public holiday. Commemorates the declaration by Bangladesh (then East Pakistan) of independence from West Pakistan on Mar. 26, 1971.

26

Kuhio Day (Prince Jonah Kuhio Kalanianaole Day) in Hawaii; official public holiday. Celebrates the contributions to his people of Hawaii's first delegate to Congress. A day of festivals, parades, and balls depicting Hawaii's history and culture.

ANNIVERSARIES AND SPECIAL EVENTS DAYS

26

Birthday of Nathaniel Bowditch (Mar. 26, 1773–Mar. 16, 1838). American navigator, mathematician, and astronomer famous for *The New American Practical Navigator* and for the discovery of the Bowditch curves, which had important applications for future developments in physics and astronomy.

26

Birthday of Robert Lee Frost (Mar. 26, 1874–Jan. 29, 1963). American Pulitzer Prize–winning poet especially known for his lyric poem "A Boy's Will"

and the narrative poem "North of Boston"; poetry consultant at the Library of Congress.

26

Birthday of Louise Otto (Mar. 26, 1819–Mar. 13, 1895). German author and founder of the feminist movement in Germany.

26

Death anniversary of Sarah Bernhardt (born Henriette Rosine Bernard; ca. Oct. 22, 1844–Mar. 26, 1923). French actress known in theatrical history as the Divine Sarah.

26

Camp David Accord Day. Anniversary of the Mar. 26, 1979, signing of a peace treaty in Jerusalem between Egypt and Israel, represented by Anwar as-Sadat and Menachem Begin; thus ended 30 years of war.

26

The Tichborne Dole at Alresford, England. Annually, the head of the Tichborne family gives a gallon of flour to each adult and half a gallon to each child in the village to fulfill a deathbed promise and to avoid a curse on the house of Tichborne; special permission for allocation was given during World War II.

HOLIDAYS AND CIVIC DAYS

27

Resistance Day in Myanmar (Burma); official public holiday. Also called Armed Forces Day. Commemorates Mar. 27, 1945, when Burma officially joined the Allies in World War II; honors its guerrilla forces, many of whom had fought the Japanese from the beginning of the war.

ANNIVERSARIES AND SPECIAL EVENTS DAYS

27

Anniversary of the condemnation of Meister Eckehart (Johannes Eckehart; ca. 1260–ca. 1327). German Dominican theologian, administrator, writer, and the greatest of German speculative mystics. His writings were posthumously condemned in a papal bull of John XXII dated Mar. 27, 1329.

27

Birthday of Nathaniel Currier (Mar. 27, 1813–Nov. 20, 1888). American publisher and founder of the firm of Currier & Ives, printmakers who recorded American history from 1835 to the end of the century in famous prints that are now collector's items.

27
Birthday of Wilhelm Conrad Röntgen (or Roentgen; Mar. 27, 1845–Feb. 10, 1923). German scientist whose discovery of the X ray made him the first recipient of the Nobel Prize in physics, in 1901.

27
Birthday of Edward Jean Steichen (Mar. 27, 1879–Mar. 25, 1973). World-renowned American photographer and artist; associated for many years with the Museum of Modern Art; creator of such celebrated works as *The Family of Man*. Colleague-mentor of Georgia O'Keeffe.

27
Death anniversary of Constance Lindsay Skinner (died Mar. 27, 1939). American author and editor of the valuable Rivers of America series. The Constance Lindsay Skinner Award is presented annually in her honor by the Woman's National Book Association to an outstanding woman in the book world.

27
Alaska Earthquake Day. Anniversary of the Mar. 27, 1964, earthquake of ruinous consequences.

HOLIDAYS AND CIVIC DAYS

28
British Bases Evacuation Day in Libya; official public holiday. Commemorates the closing of British military installations at Tobruk and El Adem on Mar. 28, 1970.

ANNIVERSARIES AND SPECIAL EVENTS DAYS

28
Birthday of Comenius (born Jan Ámos Komenský; Mar. 28, 1592–Nov. 15, 1670).Czech theologian, humanist, and educational reformer, author of *The World in Pictures* (1654).

28
Birthday of Wade Hampton (Mar. 28, 1818–Apr. 11, 1902). American Confederate general, congressman, and governor of S.C. He represents S.C. in Statuary Hall.

HOLIDAYS AND CIVIC DAYS

29
Boganda Day in the Central African Republic; official public holiday. Commemorates the death on Mar. 29, 1959, of Barthelemy Boganda, the first president.

29
Memorial Day in Madagascar; official public holiday. Also called Commemoration Day. Honors the citizens who lost their lives in the 1947 revolt against French colonialism.

29
Youth Day in Taiwan; official public holiday.

ANNIVERSARIES AND SPECIAL EVENTS DAYS

29
Anniversary of the ratification of the 23rd Amendment to the U.S. Constitution on Mar. 29, 1961, through which residents of the District of Columbia acquired the right to vote in presidential elections.

29
Anniversary of the Sicilian Vespers rebellion, in Sicily, on Easter Monday, Mar. 29, 1282. The most significant rebellion in Sicily's history, both a patriotic uprising and a revolt against feudalism. The ensuing War of the Vespers between the Angevins and Aragonese left Sicily in Spanish hands.

29
Anniversary of the Mar. 29, 1973, withdrawal of American forces from the Vietnamese conflict. Listed in some books as Vietnam Veterans' Day, but in fact not observed by Vietnam veterans at all: they instead observe Memorial Day, Veterans' Day, and July 4.

29
Birthday of John Tyler (Mar. 29, 1790–Jan. 18, 1862). Lawyer; congressman, governor of Va., and senator; elected vice president; succeeded to the presidency on the death of President William Harrison 1 month after the inauguration; 10th president (1841–45; independent Whig). As president, annexed Tex.; favored preemption of government lands by settlers; refused to honor the spoils system. Later, tried to avert civil war, but upon secession joined the Confederacy and was elected to the Confederate congress. Buried in Hollywood Cemetery, Richmond, Va.

29

Birthday of Isaac Mayer Wise (Mar. 29, 1819–Mar. 26, 1900). American rabbi and educator; a principal founder of the Union of American Hebrew Congregations and president of the Hebrew Union College.

ANNIVERSARIES AND SPECIAL EVENTS DAYS

30

Birthday of Clifford Whittingham Beers (Mar. 30, 1876–July 9, 1943). American founder of the mental-hygiene movement; awarded the gold medal "for distinguished services for the benefit of mankind" by the National Institute of Social Sciences.

30

Birthday of Jo Davidson (Mar. 30, 1883–Jan. 2, 1952). American sculptor whose work includes sculptures of many prominent people, including Woodrow Wilson, Anatole France, Walt Whitman, and Robert La Follette.

30

Birthday of Vincent van Gogh (Mar. 30, 1853–July 29, 1890). Dutch painter, lithographer, etcher, and a leader of the Postimpressionist school. His letters to his brother, published under the title *Dear Theo,* are of continuing interest.

30

Birthday of Francisco José de Goya y Lucientes (Mar. 30, 1746–Apr. 16, 1828). A consummately Spanish artist, most famous for his *Disasters of War* series (1810–14), depicting the effects of the Napoleonic invasions.

30

Birthday of Moses Maimonides (born Moses ben Maimon; Mar. 30, 1135–Dec. 13, 1204). Jewish philosopher, jurist, and physician; the foremost intellectual figure of medieval Judaism. Wrote *The Guide of the Perplexed,* a classic of religious philosophy.

30

Birthday of Sean O'Casey (born John Casey; Mar. 30, 1880–Sept. 18, 1964). Irish playwright whose plays, such as *Juno and the Paycock,* depicted the effects of poverty and war on the Irish.

30

Doctors' Day. A day of tribute to the medical profession and to the first use of ether as an anesthetic agent on Mar. 30, 1842, by Dr. Crawford

Long. Observed since 1933; the scarlet carnation is the official flower of Doctors' Day.

HOLIDAYS AND CIVIC DAYS

31

Freedom Day in Malta; official public holiday. Anniversary of the amicable closure of the last British military base in 1974; with commemorative ceremonies at the War Memorial in Floriana, and regatta races in the Grand Harbour.

31

Transfer Day in the U.S. Virgin Islands; official public holiday. Commemorates the transfer of ownership from Denmark to the U.S. on Mar. 31, 1917.

ANNIVERSARIES AND SPECIAL EVENTS DAYS

31

Birthday of René Descartes (Mar. 31, 1596–Feb. 1, 1650). French mathematician and philosopher who made contributions to theories of algebra and geometry and to the field of philosophy of pure reason. Called the Father of Modern Philosophy.

31

Birthday of Edward FitzGerald (Mar. 31, 1809–June 14, 1883). English poet celebrated for his translation of the *Rubáiyát of Omar Khayyám.*

31

Birthday of Arthur Griffith (Mar. 31, 1872–Aug. 12, 1922). Irish patriot and main founder of the independence organization *Sinn Féin* ("We Ourselves"); assassinated.

31

Birthday of Franz Joseph Haydn (Mar. 31, 1732–May 31, 1809). Austrian composer, sometimes called Papa Haydn in recognition of his influence on instrumental music and on the development of the modern symphony.

31

Birthday of Andrew Lang (Mar. 31, 1844–July 20, 1912). Scottish author famous for Homeric translations and studies, fairy tales, children's books, folklore, history, biography, and fiction.

31

Birthday of Robert Ross McBurney (Mar. 31, 1837–Dec. 27, 1898). American YMCA leader and first paid secretary of the YMCA in N.Y. in 1862; responsible for the centralized system of leadership in effect in the YMCA.

31

Death anniversary of John Donne (1572–Mar. 31, 1631). English clergyman, poet of the metaphysical school, and the English language's greatest love poet.

31

Bunsen Burner Day. Honors Robert Wilhelm Bunsen (Mar. 31, 1811–Aug. 16, 1899), German professor of chemistry and inventor of the Bunsen burner.

CA. 31

Oranges and Lemons Day in London; celebrated since 1920 on or near Mar. 31. A religious festival for children, at St. Clement Danes Church; ends with each child receiving an orange and a lemon as the bells ring out the old nursery rhyme "Oranges and lemons, say the bells of St. Clemens."

MOVABLE DAYS IN MARCH

RED CROSS MONTH IN THE U.S. Intended to inform the public about the American Red Cross and its service to the nation's communities. Annually since 1943, by presidential proclamation.

WOMEN'S HISTORY MONTH IN THE U.S.; often by presidential proclamation. A time to celebrate the contributions and achievements of women. Core day is Mar. 8, International Women's Day; the week containing Mar. 8 is Women's History Week.

HOLIDAYS AND CIVIC DAYS

CANBERRA DAY IN THE AUSTRALIAN CAPITAL TERRITORY; 3rd Monday in Mar.; official public holiday. Commemorates the Mar. 12, 1913, founding of Canberra as the Australian capital. Canberra Day concludes the 10-day Canberra Festival, an outdoor community event of great variety.

LABOUR DAY IN TASMANIA AND WESTERN AUSTRALIA (1st Monday in Mar.) and in Victoria (2nd Monday in Mar.); official public holiday.

NATIONAL YOUTH DAY IN FIJI; 2nd Friday in Mar.; official public holiday.

DISCOVERY DAY IN GUAM; 1st Monday in Mar.; official public holiday. Also called Magellan Day. Commemorates the arrival at Guam of Ferdinand Magellan in 1521; features flotillas of pleasure boats and fiestas.

SEWARD'S DAY IN ALASKA; last Monday in Mar.; official public holiday. Commemorates the Mar. 30, 1867, purchase of Alaska from Russia, negotiated by the American statesman William Seward.

TOWN MEETING DAY IN VT.; 1st Tuesday in Mar.; official public holiday. A day when citizens elect town officers, approve local budgets, and deal with other civic issues in daylong public meetings.

ANNIVERSARIES AND SPECIAL EVENTS DAYS

WORLD DAY OF PRAYER; 1st Friday in Mar. Sponsored by Church Women United. Ecumenical, and observed in many countries.

PROCRASTINATION WEEK; actually begins 1st Sunday in Mar., but usually observed a week late.

HOLMENKELLEN DAY IN OSLO, NORWAY; 2nd Sunday in Mar. The main day of a winter festival on Holmenkellen Hill, attracting thousands of skiers and spectators.

CARNAVAL MIAMI IN MIAMI, FLA.; 10 days, beginning 1st Friday in Mar. Celebration of Hispanic culture; Miami's largest event, begun in 1938. Highlight is the Calle Ocho Open House, "the world's longest block party."

YOUTH DAY IN ZAMBIA; official public holiday. During 2nd week in Mar., on a day decided by the cabinet and proclaimed by the president. Dedicated to the interests and activities of young people; focal point is Lusaka's Independence Stadium.

April

The name for April, the 4th month of the year, comes either from *Aprilis,* the Roman derivation of Aphrodite, which is the Greek name for Venus, or from the Latin verb *aperire,* meaning "to open." The month begins with a day and ends with a night that are linked in many lands with age-old customs.

The first day is April Fools' Day, or All Fools' Day, which is a day at one time popular for pranks and harmless practical jokes. The origin of this tradition is not positively known. Records show that it has been going on at least since 1564, when January 1 was reestablished in France as the first day of the year. The change confused many people, but in time it led to the fun of exchanging false greetings for the first day of the year on the old day. A one-time April Fools' prank of the Scots was "hunting the gowk," which sent the victim on false errands; anyone who fell for this prank was called a "gowk," or cuckoo.

The last hours of the month of April are observed as Walpurgis Night in some parts of Europe. It is the custom in Scandinavian countries and in the mountains of Germany to light huge bonfires and hold festive events on the night of April 30 in remembrance of an old folkway that defended people and beasts from witches and demons. In Sweden and Finland, university students start wearing white velvet caps on that night and join together to sing spring songs. In some parts of Switzerland, a bachelor, if he observes old traditions, may plant a pine tree on the last day of April at the home of a woman he admires.

The sweet pea and the daisy are the flowers for April. The gem is the diamond.

HOLIDAYS AND CIVIC DAYS

1
Islamic Republic Day in Iran; official public holiday. Also called National Day. Commemorates Apr. 1, 1979, when the constitution of the new Islamic republic was approved by popular referendum.

ANNIVERSARIES AND SPECIAL EVENTS DAYS

1
Birthday of Edwin Austin Abbey (Apr. 1, 1852–Aug. 1, 1911). American painter and illustrator of editions of Shakespeare and Goldsmith. He painted the *Quest of the Holy Grail* murals in the Boston Public Library.

1
Birthday of William Harvey (Apr. 1, 1578–June 3, 1657). English physician, anatomist, and physiologist known for his discovery of the circulation of the blood.

1
Birthday of Sergey Rachmaninoff (Apr. 1, 1873–Mar. 28, 1943). Russian pianist and composer; last of the leading proponents of the musical tradition of Russian romanticism.

1
Birthday of Edmond Rostand (Apr. 1, 1868–Dec. 2, 1918). French poet and playwright whose best-known drama is *Cyrano de Bergerac.*

1
April Fools' Day, or All Fools' Day, a day of practical jokes and high humor. Apr. 1 has also been established as Intolerance Day to confine intolerance to the most appropriate day of the year, April Fools' Day.

HOLIDAYS AND CIVIC DAYS

2

Florida Day in Fla. Also called Pascua Florida Day. Officially designated as Florida Day in 1953; the governor may proclaim Pascua Florida Week, Mar. 27–Apr. 2, for observance by schools and the citizenry. Ponce de Leon sighted, and may have landed in, Fla. ca. Apr. 2, 1513, naming it Pascua Florida ("Easter Flowering").

ANNIVERSARIES AND SPECIAL EVENTS DAYS

2

Anniversary of the establishment of the U.S. Mint in 1792 in Philadelphia, by the Coinage Act.

2

Birthday of Hans Christian Andersen (Apr. 2, 1805–Aug. 4, 1875). Danish poet and novelist best known for fairy and folk tales. His birthday is International Children's Book Day.

2

Birthday of Frédéric Auguste Bartholdi (Apr. 2, 1834–Oct. 4, 1904). French sculptor whose work includes the Statue of Liberty (*Liberty Enlightening the World*) in New York harbor, presented to the U.S. by the people of France in 1885 and dedicated on Oct. 28, 1886.

2

Birthday of Nicholas Murray Butler (Apr. 2, 1862–Dec. 7, 1947). American educator; president of Columbia University, 1901–45. A champion of international understanding who helped establish the Carnegie Endowment for International Peace; shared the 1931 Nobel Peace Prize with Jane Addams.

2

Birthday of Giacomo Girolamo Casanova de Seingalt (Apr. 2, 1725–June 4, 1798). Italian writer-librarian, social adventurer, rogue, and spy; famous for his brilliant autobiographical *Mémoires* (*The History of My Life*; 12 volumes, 1826–38).

2

Birthday of Émile Zola (Apr. 2, 1840–Sept. 28, 1902). French novelist who founded the school of naturalism in French literature. His belief that life is determined entirely by heredity and environment is illustrated in such novels as *Thérèse Raquin* (1867), *Nana* (1880), and *Germinal* (1885).

2

International Children's Book Day. Anniversary of the birth of Hans Christian Andersen. Observed worldwide to stimulate interest, through the use of books, in the lifestyles, customs, and contributions of people in nations throughout the world. A literary award, the Hans Christian Andersen Prize, is presented biennially at each Congress of the International Board on Books for Young People.

2

Mildred L. Batchelder Award Announcement Day. Established by the Children's Services Division (now the Association for Library Service to Children) of the American Library Association in 1966 to honor its former executive secretary with an annual award to an American publisher of an outstanding children's book originally published in a foreign language in a foreign country.

ANNIVERSARIES AND SPECIAL EVENTS DAYS

3

Anniversary of the beginning of the Pony Express, between Sacramento, Calif., and St. Joseph, Mo., on Apr. 3, 1860; the service ended on Oct. 24, 1861, with the completion of the first transcontinental telegraph.

3

Birthday of John Burroughs (Apr. 3, 1837–Mar. 29, 1921). American essayist and literary naturalist. A Burroughs Medal is presented annually in his memory by the John Burroughs Association for the year's best book in the field of natural history.

3

Birthday of Washington Irving (Apr. 3, 1783–Nov. 28, 1859). American historian, essayist, and storyteller famous for the legends of Rip Van Winkle and Ichabod Crane. Elected to the Hall of Fame for Great Americans.

CA. 3

Kite-Flying (*Takoage*) in Nagasaki, Japan; Apr. 3–29. One of Japan's most famous kite events; includes a kite-fighting contest. Other notable kite-fighting celebrations are held in Hamamatsu, May 1–5, ending on Children's (Boys') Day, and featuring giant kites; and in Shirane on June 5–12.

3

Tweed Day. Anniversary of the birth of William March Tweed (Apr. 3, 1823–Apr. 12, 1878). A day to consider the cost of political corruption, as personified by Boss Tweed, whose Tweed Ring was accused of stealing many millions of dollars from the city of New York. He died in prison. The political cartoonist Thomas Nast was a principal in Tweed's downfall.

HOLY DAYS AND FEAST DAYS

4

Feast of St. Isidore (Isidro) of Seville (ca. 560–Apr. 4, 636). Spanish bishop, educator, and encyclopedist; "the last of the ancient Christian philosophers"; doctor of the church.

HOLIDAYS AND CIVIC DAYS

CA. 4

Ching Ming ("Clear and Bright") in the Chinese calendar; official public holiday in Hong Kong and Macau; important among all Chinese. A day to remember and honor one's dead; families visit and repair graves, offer food, and picnic. Formerly, no fires were lit on this day. In South Korea, observed as *Hanshik* ("Cold Food Day") or Grave Visiting Day.

4

Independence Day in Senegal; official public holiday. Commemorates the Apr. 4, 1960, completion of agreements to give independence to Senegal, the oldest French colony in sub-Saharan Africa.

ANNIVERSARIES AND SPECIAL EVENTS DAYS

4

Anniversary of the foundation of the North Atlantic Treaty Organization (NATO) on Apr. 4, 1949, when delegates from 12 nations met in Washington, D.C., to sign the North Atlantic Treaty.

4

Anniversary of the election of the first woman mayor in the U.S. On Apr. 4, 1887, Susanna Medora Salter was elected mayor of Argonia, Kans.

4

Birthday of Dorothea Lynde Dix (Apr. 4, 1802–July 17, 1887). American social reformer and author; superintendent of women nurses during the Civil War; a pioneer in the establishment or improvement of asylums for mentally ill people.

4

Birthday of Isoroku Yamamoto (Apr. 4, 1884–Apr. 18, 1943). Japanese admiral; Japan's greatest naval strategist and a major figure of World War II.

4

Death anniversary of Martin Luther King Jr. (Jan. 15, 1929–Apr. 4, 1968). Assassinated by James Earl Ray.

HOLIDAYS AND CIVIC DAYS

5

Arbor Day in South Korea; official public holiday. Schoolchildren and adults plant trees in the countryside as part of a national reforestation program.

5

Tomb Sweeping Day in Taiwan; official public holiday. A day to honor ancestors and neaten their tombs; observed on the death anniversary of Chiang Kai-shek (Oct. 31, 1887–Apr. 5, 1975).

ANNIVERSARIES AND SPECIAL EVENTS DAYS

5

Birthday of Joseph Lister (Apr. 5, 1827–Feb. 10, 1912). English physician, founder of aseptic surgery.

5

Birthday of Algernon Charles Swinburne (Apr. 5, 1837–Apr. 10, 1909). English poet famous for his elegies and monographs on Shakespeare.

5

Birthday of Booker Taliaferro Washington (Apr. 5, 1856–Nov. 14, 1915). American educator, author, and lecturer; founder of the Tuskegee Institute (1881). The first African American to be depicted on a postage stamp; elected to the Hall of Fame for Great Americans.

5

Birthday of Elihu Yale (Apr. 5, 1649–July 8, 1721). English philanthropist for whom Yale University is named; son of a founder of New Haven, Conn., and a governor of the East India Company.

HOLIDAYS AND CIVIC DAYS

6

Founders' Day in South Africa; formerly an official public holiday. Also called Van Riebeek Day. Honors the founders of the nation, particularly Jan Van Riebeek, the Dutch East India commander who landed at the Cape of Good Hope on this date in 1652 and established a halfway station (later Cape Town), the first European toehold on the southern tip of Africa.

6

Chakri Day in Thailand; official public holiday. Celebrates the founding in 1782 of the present dynasty by King Rama I (ruled 1782–1809), who founded Bangkok as his capital. People take flowers and incense to the Temple of the Emerald Buddha to pay respect to former kings.

6

California Poppy Day; a day of special school observance in Calif. State statutes urge schools on this day to honor the California Poppy, to give instruction about native plants and the economic and aesthetic value of wildflowers, and to encourage a spirit of protection and responsible use of natural resources.

ANNIVERSARIES AND SPECIAL EVENTS DAYS

6

Anniversary of the founding of the Mormon Church (the Church of Jesus Christ of Latter-Day Saints) on Apr. 6, 1830, by Joseph Smith and Oliver Cowdery, at Fayette, N.Y. The church's annual conference is now held to encompass this date.

6

Anniversary of the first modern Olympic Games, held beginning Apr. 6, 1896, in Athens, Greece, at the Herod Atticus Stadium. Baron Pierre de Coubertin (Jan. 1, 1863–Sept. 2, 1937) was responsible for the Games' revival.

6

Anniversary of the U.S. entry into World War I on Apr. 6, 1917, with a formal declaration of war on the Central Powers.

6

Birthday of Raphael (born Raffaello Sanzio; probably Apr. 6, 1483–Apr. 6, 1520). Italian painter and architect noted for his idealized Madonnas and great frescoes; one of the masters of the Italian High Renaissance style.

6

Death anniversary of William Strickland (1788–Apr. 6, 1854). American architect, the outstanding exponent of the Greek revival in the U.S. He designed the first U.S. customhouse and the marble sarcophagus of Washington at Mt. Vernon.

6

North Pole Day. Anniversary of the Apr. 6, 1909, discovery of the North Pole by Robert E. Peary, Matthew A. Henson, and 4 Inuit guides, Coqueeh, Ootah, Eginwah, and Seegloo. The Peary expedition was declared the authentic first discovery by the National Geographic Society in 1911.

HOLIDAYS AND CIVIC DAYS

7

Women's Day in Mozambique; official public holiday. Honors the women of the nation on the death anniversary of Josina Machel, killed during the struggle for independence. Her husband was the first president, Samora Machel.

7

The Genocide's Remembrance in Rwanda; official public holiday. Memorial to the horrific genocidal massacres of 1994.

ANNIVERSARIES AND SPECIAL EVENTS DAYS

7

Birthday of Walter Camp (Apr. 7, 1859–Mar. 14, 1925). American coach who did more than anyone else to develop the game of football; originator of the All-American selections.

7

Birthday of William Ellery Channing (Apr. 7, 1780–Oct. 2, 1842). American Unitarian clergyman and author who played an influential role in the intellectual life of New England. Elected to the Hall of Fame for Great Americans.

7

Birthday of David Grandison Fairchild (Apr. 7, 1869–Aug. 6, 1954). American botanist and explorer who traveled the globe in search of useful plants for introduction into the U.S. The Fairchild Tropical Garden at Coral Gables, Fla., is named for him.

7

Birthday of Gabriela Mistral (born Lucila Godoy de Alcayaga; Apr. 7, 1889–Jan. 19, 1957). Chilean poet and educator; held important posts in the Chilean educational systems and helped reorganize the rural schools of Mexico. Awarded the 1945 Nobel Prize in literature.

7

Birthday of Ravi Shankar (Apr. 7, 1920–). Indian sitar player and composer; founder of the National Orchestra of India. He and the sarod player Ali Akbar Khan (Apr. 14, 1922–) are famous for their recordings of ragas and other traditional Indian music.

7

Birthday of William Wordsworth (Apr. 7, 1770–Apr. 23, 1850). English poet laureate famous for "I Wandered Lonely as a Cloud" and "Ode: Intimations of Immortality"; the greatest poet of the English romantic movement.

7

Death anniversary of El Greco (Doménikos Theotokópoulos; 1541–Apr. 7, 1614). Masterly Cretan-born painter in Spain, and a notable Renaissance humanist.

7

Death anniversary of Toussaint-Louverture (born François-Dominique Toussaint; ca. 1743–Apr. 7, 1803). Former slave, brilliant general, and admirable ruler who, after bitter warfare, led Saint-Domingue, Hispaniola (Haiti after 1804), to its first independence from France (1795–1801). When Napoleon reconquered Saint-Domingue in 1802, Toussaint-Louverture was captured and taken to France, where he died in prison.

CA. 7

Spring Cherry Blossom Festival in Kamakura, Japan; Apr. 7–14. At the Hachiman Shrine. Each area of Japan celebrates during its local season of flowering; Kamakura's blossoms are especially famous.

7

World Health Day. Anniversary of the founding of the World Health Organization on Apr. 7, 1948.

HOLY DAYS AND FEAST DAYS

8

The Buddha's Birthday (*Hana Matsuri*) in Japan. Celebrated in temples, where statues of Buddha are ladled with hydrangea tea in the Buddha Baptizing Ceremony (*Hana Kambutsue*).

ANNIVERSARIES AND SPECIAL EVENTS DAYS

8

Anniversary of the ratification of the 17th Amendment to the U.S. Constitution on Apr. 8, 1913 (declared by the secretary of state on May 31, 1913), requiring the direct popular election of senators.

HOLY DAYS AND FEAST DAYS

9

Feast of St. Mary Clopas (also called St. Mary Jacoby; 1st century). Mother of the apostle James the Less, and sister of Mary the mother of Jesus. Was present at the Crucifixion and the Tomb. By one tradition, after the Crucifixion she traveled to Provence with Martha and Lazarus; by another, she went to Spain.

HOLIDAYS AND CIVIC DAYS

9

Day of Valor (*Araw ng Kagitingan*) in the Philippines; official public holiday. Anniversary of the 1942 fall of Bataan and Corregidor in the Philippines to the Japanese during World War II and the beginning of Filipino (and U.S.) resistance to Japanese occupation. Ceremonies at Fort Santiago commemorate the heroism of Filipinos and others who fought for the country's liberation.

9

Martyrs' Day in Tunisia; official public holiday. Honors those killed in the 1938 demonstrations for independence from France.

ANNIVERSARIES AND SPECIAL EVENTS DAYS

9

Anniversary of the establishment of the Golf Hall of Fame by the Professional Golfer's Association on Apr. 9, 1941.

9

Birthday of Charles Baudelaire (Apr. 9, 1821–Aug. 31, 1867). French poet and critic whose *Les Fleurs du Mal* was an important influence on French symbolists and modern poets.

9

Birthday of W. C. Fields (born Claude William Dukenfield; Apr. 9, 1879–Dec. 25, 1946). American stage and film actor, expert juggler.

9

Death anniversary of François Rabelais (ca. 1494–ca. Apr. 9, 1553). French writer, famous for *Gargantua* and *Pantagruel*.

9

Appomattox Day. Anniversary of the Apr. 9, 1865, surrender of General Robert E. Lee, commander of the Army of Northern Virginia, to Ulysses S. Grant, commander in chief of the Union Army, at Appomattox Court House, Va.; ended 4 years of conflict between the North and South known as the American Civil War.

9

Budget Day in London. By tradition, a dispatch box of the official papers by the chancellor of the exchequer is displayed to the public on its route from No. 10 Downing Street to the House of Commons.

9

Marian Anderson Day. On Easter Sunday, Apr. 9, 1939, the African American contralto Marian Anderson (Feb. 27, 1897–Apr. 8, 1993) sang an open-air concert on the steps of the Lincoln Memorial in Washington, D.C., after being denied the use of Constitution Hall by the Daughters of the American Revolution. Her inspirational autobiography is titled *My Lord, What a Morning*.

ANNIVERSARIES AND SPECIAL EVENTS DAYS

10

Birthday of Hugo Grotius (Apr. 10, 1583–Aug. 28, 1645). Dutch jurist and statesman; founder of the science of international law.

10

Birthday of Joseph Pulitzer (Apr. 10, 1847–Oct. 29, 1911). American journalist and publisher who, through his will, founded the Columbia University Graduate School for Journalism and the Pulitzer Prizes in journalism, letters, and music. The prizes are announced in early Apr. The first Pulitzer Prizes were awarded on June 4, 1917.

10

Birthday of George Russell (Apr. 10, 1897–July 17, 1935). Irish poet and mystic who wrote under the name Æ.

10

Death anniversary of Emiliano Zapata (probably Aug. 8, 1879–Apr. 10, 1919). Mexican revolutionary reformer and leader in the struggle to oust the dictator Porfirio Díaz; author of the Plan of Ayala (Nov. 25, 1911), and instrumental in the constitution of 1917; assassinated.

10

Commodore Perry Day. Anniversary of the birth of Matthew Calbraith Perry (Apr. 10, 1794–Mar. 4, 1858), American naval officer who reached Tokyo Bay on July 8, 1853, and opened diplomatic and trade relations between Japan and the U.S. The first treaty between the 2 countries was signed on Mar. 31, 1854.

10

Frances Perkins Day. Anniversary of the birth of Frances Perkins (born Fannie Coralie Perkins; Apr. 10, 1880–May 14, 1965), the first woman member of a U.S. presidential cabinet. An appointee of Franklin Roosevelt, Perkins served as secretary of labor from 1933 to 1945.

10

Humane Day. Anniversary of the incorporation of the American Society for the Prevention of Cruelty to Animals (ASPCA) on Apr. 10, 1866.

10

Salvation Army Founder's Day. Commemorates the birth of General William Bramwell Booth (Apr. 10, 1829–Aug. 20, 1912) of England.

HOLY DAYS AND FEAST DAYS

11

Feast of St. Stanislaus (July 26, 1030–Apr. 11, 1079). Polish bishop of Cracow, martyred for denouncing royal injustices. A symbol of Polish nationhood and patron saint of Cracow.

HOLIDAYS AND CIVIC DAYS

11

Juan Santamaría Day in Costa Rica; official public holiday. Also called Battle of Rivas Day. Celebrates the Apr. 11, 1856, Battle of Rivas, a major defeat of William Walker, U.S. invader of Central America.

11

Liberation Day in Uganda; official public holiday. Celebrates the overthrow of the dictatorship of Idi Amin when Tanzanian relief forces captured Kampala on Apr. 11, 1979.

ANNIVERSARIES AND SPECIAL EVENTS DAYS

11

Anniversary of the authorization by the U.S. Congress of the Distinguished Service Medal for the Merchant Marine on Apr. 11, 1942. The first recipient was Edwin Fox Cheney Jr.

11

Birthday of Charles Evans Hughes (Apr. 11, 1862–Aug. 27, 1948). American jurist, statesman, and 11th chief justice of the Supreme Court.

11

Buchenwald Liberation Day. Anniversary of the Apr. 11, 1945, liberation by Allied troops of the

Buchenwald concentration camp (near Weimar, Germany), the oldest (from 1937) and one of the worst. Also commemorated as Holocaust Remembrance Day on Nisan 27 in the Jewish calendar and in the Days of Remembrance at the Holocaust Memorial Museum in Washington, D.C.

ANNIVERSARIES AND SPECIAL EVENTS DAYS

12
Anniversary of the Big Wind. On Apr. 12, 1934, at the Mt. Washington Observatory in N.H., there occurred the strongest natural wind ever recorded on the earth's surface, with gusts at 231 miles per hour.

12
Anniversary of the announcement on Apr. 12, 1955, that the Salk vaccine against polio was "safe, potent, and effective." This and other preventive vaccines all but eradicated infantile paralysis, or poliomyelitis.

12
Birthday of Henry Clay (Apr. 12, 1777–June 29, 1852). American statesman known as the Great Compromiser in the effort to preserve the Union. Elected to the Hall of Fame for Great Americans, and represents Ky. in Statuary Hall.

12
Birthday of Frederick G. Melcher (Apr. 12, 1870–Mar. 9, 1963). American publisher, editor, and a founder of Children's Book Week in 1919. Donor of the Newbery and Caldecott Medals awarded annually for outstanding children's books.

12
Fort Sumter Day. Anniversary of the bombardment of Fort Sumter, in Charleston, S.C., on Apr. 12, 1861; marked the beginning of the American Civil War.

12
Halifax Resolves Day in N.C. Also called Halifax Independence Day. Anniversary of the signing of the Halifax Resolves of Independence adopted in N.C. on Apr. 12, 1776, which were influential in bringing about the adoption of the Declaration of Independence.

12
Space Probe Day. Anniversary of the first manned orbit around the earth, achieved on Apr. 12, 1961, by the Soviet astronaut Yury Gagarin.

12
Space Shuttle Columbia Day. Anniversary of the successful American launching on Apr. 12, 1981, of the world's first reusable spacecraft, a cargo shuttle.

HOLIDAYS AND CIVIC DAYS

CA. 13
New Year's Day in the Indian subcontinent; Apr. 13 or 14; official public holiday in Bangladesh, Nepal, and Sri Lanka. Both a holiday and a holy day among Hindus of north and south India, Buddhists of south India and Sri Lanka, Jains, and Sikhs. Observances are often within the home, or personal, with rituals to begin the year on the right foot.

CA. 13
Traditional New Year's day in Southeast Asia; on Apr. 13, sometimes a day or 2 later; official public holiday, usually for 3 days.

13
Songkran in Thailand; official public holiday, usually for 3 days including Apr. 13. The traditional New Year's Day, formerly the official civil New Year's Day, and still the official religious (Buddhist) New Year's Day. Celebrated with religious ceremonies and public festivals, with a theme of cleansing. Buddha images are washed, and people splash each other.

ANNIVERSARIES AND SPECIAL EVENTS DAYS

13
Anniversary of the dedication of the Jefferson Memorial on the 200th anniversary of Jefferson's birth, Apr. 13, 1943.

13
Birthday of Samuel Beckett (ca. Apr. 13, 1906–Dec. 22, 1989). Irish playwright and novelist who spent much of his life in France and often wrote in French. Noted for *Waiting for Godot;* winner of the 1969 Nobel Prize in literature.

13
Birthday of John Hanson (Apr. 13, 1721–Nov. 22, 1783). Observed in Md. as John Hanson Day. American Revolutionary political leader; first president of the Congress of the Confederation. Represents Md. in Statuary Hall.

13

Birthday of Thomas Jefferson (Apr. 13, 1743–July 4, 1826). Polymath; Va. lawyer; Revolutionary patriot and statesman; 3rd president of the U.S. (1801–09; Democratic Republican). His presidency was notable for its strong allegiance to the consent of the governed, instead of executive control; for the Louisiana Purchase; and for the Lewis and Clark Expedition. Buried at Monticello, Va. Elected to the Hall of Fame for Great Americans. He composed his epitaph: "Here was buried Thomas Jefferson, author of the Declaration of American Independence, of the statute of Virginia for religious freedom, and father of the University of Virginia."

13

Huguenot Day. Anniversary of the signing of the Edict of Nantes by the French king Henry IV on Apr. 13, 1598; observed by the Huguenot Society of America. The edict promulgated limited religious freedom for Huguenots (French Protestants).

CA. 13

Thailand International Kite Festival in Pattaya, Thailand; held at the time of *Songkran*. With kites of all sizes, and notable kite fights.

13

Turtle Release Festival at Phuket, Thailand; on *Songkran*, the traditional Thai New Year's Day. Sea turtles are released at Nai Yang beach for their migratory journey into the sea. Accompanied with religious ceremonies, music and dance, sports, and food.

HOLIDAYS AND CIVIC DAYS

14

Pan American Day in the U.S. and elsewhere; official public holiday in Honduras (as Day of the Americas) and Haiti. Commemorates the first International Conference of American States, held on Apr. 14, 1890, in Washington, D.C.

ANNIVERSARIES AND SPECIAL EVENTS DAYS

14

Anniversary of the promulgation in Sicily of the Carta de Lugo, an organically developed constitution of laws, on Apr. 14, 1392, by Eleanora the Judge (died 1404; ruled 1383–1404). Eleonora, with her noble family, is an icon of Sardinian independence from Spain and Italy, and Sardinians love her. The Carta de Lugo remains a cornerstone of Sardinian national consciousness.

14

Birthday of Anne Mansfield Sullivan (Apr. 14, 1866–Oct. 20, 1936). American educator famous as the teacher and companion of Helen Keller.

ANNIVERSARIES AND SPECIAL EVENTS DAYS

15

Anniversary of the sinking of the *Titanic* on Apr. 15, 1912; the supposedly unsinkable luxury liner struck an iceberg on Apr. 14 and sank within a few hours; more than 1,500 persons died.

15

Birthday of Leonardo da Vinci (Apr. 15, 1452–May 2, 1519). Italian painter, sculptor, scientist, and inventor; one of the greatest minds of all time.

15

Birthday of John Lothrop Motley (Apr. 15, 1814–May 29, 1877). American historian and diplomat; author of *The Rise of the Dutch Republic*. Elected to the Hall of Fame for Great Americans.

15

Birthday of Charles Willson Peale (Apr. 15, 1741–Feb. 22, 1827). American painter famous for his many portraits of George Washington.

15

Death anniversary of Abraham Lincoln, president of the U.S., on Apr. 15, 1865. Lincoln was shot by John Wilkes Booth on Apr. 14 while watching a performance of *Our American Cousin* at Ford's Theater in Washington, D.C.

15

Income Tax Return Day in the U.S. Commonly, income tax returns and payments must be mailed on or before this date. Observed but never celebrated.

HOLY DAYS AND FEAST DAYS

16

Feast of St. Bernadette (born Marie-Bernarde Soubirous; Jan. 7, 1844–Apr. 16, 1879). French peasant girl of Lourdes who experienced repeated visions of the Virgin Mary from Feb. 11 through Mar. 25, 1858; she was directed to build a chapel where a spring had appeared. Lourdes swiftly became one of the great Christian pilgrimage spots.

HOLIDAYS AND CIVIC DAYS

16

De Diego's Birthday in Puerto Rico. Honors the independence patriot José de Diego (Apr. 16, 1866–July 17, 1918).

ANNIVERSARIES AND SPECIAL EVENTS DAYS

16

Anniversary of the Battle of Culloden, near Inverness, Scotland, on Apr. 16, 1746. The Jacobite army (partisans of the Stuarts) of the "Forty-Five Rebellion" was destroyed by English artillery; the last pitched battle on British soil.

16

Birthday of Herbert Baxter Adams (Apr. 16, 1850–July 30, 1901). American historian, founder and first secretary of the American Historical Association, in whose name the association offers an annual award for a book on history.

16

Birthday of Charlie (Sir Charles Spencer) Chaplin (Apr. 16, 1889–Dec. 25, 1977). American-born British film actor and director, especially in silent films; famous for his portrayal of the "little tramp."

16

Birthday of Anatole France (Apr. 16, 1844–Oct. 13, 1924). French novelist, playwright, and critic; received the Nobel Prize in literature in 1921.

16

Birthday of John Millington Synge (Apr. 16, 1871–Mar. 24, 1909). Irish playwright, noted for his *Playboy of the Western World.*

16

Birthday of Wilbur Wright (Apr. 16, 1867–May 30, 1912). American pioneer aviator who, with his brother Orville, invented the airplane. Elected to the Hall of Fame for Great Americans.

16

Queen Margrethe's Birthday in Denmark. A day of special events for children at Amalienberg Palace. Margrethe II was born Apr. 16, 1940.

HOLIDAYS AND CIVIC DAYS

17

Flag Day in American Samoa; official public holiday. Commemorates Apr. 17, 1900, when the 7 high chiefs voluntarily signed the Instrument of Cession at the invitation of President Theodore Roosevelt and the American flag was raised. It also commemorates the establishment of Samoan constitutional government on Apr. 17, 1960. Celebrated with singing, dancing, and parades.

17

Independence Day in Syria. Also called Evacuation Day. Anniversary of the attainment of full independence from France on Apr. 17, 1946, with the withdrawal of the last French military forces.

ANNIVERSARIES AND SPECIAL EVENTS DAYS

17

Birthday of Isak Dinesen (born Christentze Dinesen; subsequently known as Karen Blixen; separated from Baron Blixen-Finecke; Apr. 17, 1885–Sept. 7, 1962). Danish fiction writer, with many stories set in Africa. Her *Out of Africa* was adapted into an Oscar-winning film.

17

Bay of Pigs Day. Anniversary of the Apr. 17, 1961, unsuccessful attempt by Cuban exiles, with the help of the U.S. government, to invade Cuba and overthrow its government.

17

Verrazano Day in N.Y. Commemorates the sighting of New York harbor on Apr. 17, 1524, by the Florentine navigator Giovanni da Verrazano.

HOLIDAYS AND CIVIC DAYS

18

Independence Day in Zimbabwe; official public holiday. Also called Republic Day. Celebrates the end of white minority rule and the formation of the Republic of Zimbabwe (formerly Rhodesia) on Apr. 18, 1980. Celebrated with rallies, parades, dances, singing, and fireworks.

ANNIVERSARIES AND SPECIAL EVENTS DAYS

18

Anniversary of the Constitution Act of 1982 in Canada, which provided Canada with a new constitution, replacing that of the British North America Act of 1867; became effective Apr. 18, 1982.

18

Anniversary of the very destructive and deadly San Francisco earthquake and fire. San Francisco was struck on Apr. 18–19, 1906; magnitude was

8.3 on the Richter scale. Periodically commemorated with special events in Calif.

18

Birthday of Clarence Seward Darrow (Apr. 18, 1857–Mar. 13, 1938). American lawyer associated with the Scopes trial and other dramatic court cases of the early 20th century.

18

Birthday of Richard Harding Davis (Apr. 18, 1864–Apr. 11, 1916). American journalist and editor, one of the first of the roving correspondents.

18

Panama Canal Day. Anniversary of the Apr. 18, 1978, Senate approval of the full transfer of the Panama Canal to Panama by Dec. 31, 1999.

18

Paul Revere Night. Anniversary of the famous ride made by Paul Revere and William Dawes on the night of Apr. 18, 1775, to warn the U.S. patriots of Boston and Concord, Mass., that "the British are coming!"

HOLIDAYS AND CIVIC DAYS

19

The King's Birthday in Swaziland; official public holiday. King Mswati III was born Apr. 19, 1968.

CA. 19

Patriots' Day; official public holiday in Mass. and Maine; 3rd Monday in Apr. Also called Battles of Lexington and Concord Day or Lexington Day. Commemorates the first battle of the Revolutionary War, on Apr. 19, 1775.

19

Landing of the 33 Patriots Day in Uruguay; official public holiday. Commemorates the landing of 33 patriotic exiles on Apr. 19, 1825, to begin the campaign that resulted in the attainment of Uruguay's independence from Brazil in 1828.

19

Independence Day in Venezuela; official public holiday. Anniversary of the formation of the revolutionary junta in 1810, which later proclaimed the colony's independence from Spain.

ANNIVERSARIES AND SPECIAL EVENTS DAYS

19

Anniversary of the Warsaw Ghetto Uprising. On Apr. 19, 1943, Jews herded into the Warsaw Ghetto by the Nazis rose in fierce rebellion, to resist being deported to the Treblinka concentration camp. Resistance was crushed on May 16, 1943.

19

Birthday of Roger Sherman (Apr. 19, 1721–July 23, 1793). American Revolutionary patriot and statesman. The only person to sign all 4 documents of American independence—the Articles of Association, the Declaration of Independence, the Articles of Confederation, and the Constitution. Represents Conn. in Statuary Hall.

19

Death anniversary of Simon Fraser (1776–Apr. 19, 1862). American-born Canadian explorer and fur trader who explored the upper course of the Fraser River in British Columbia.

ANNIVERSARIES AND SPECIAL EVENTS DAYS

20

Birthday of Daniel Chester French (Apr. 20, 1850–Oct. 7, 1931). American sculptor commissioned to create many statues of prominent Americans. His best-known work includes the seated figure of Abraham Lincoln in the Lincoln Memorial in Washington, D.C., and the *Minute Man* at Concord, Mass.

20

Birthday of Adolf Hitler (Apr. 20, 1889–Apr. 30, 1945; ruled 1934–45). Austrian-born German fascist dictator of Germany, overwhelmingly elected *führer* on Aug. 19, 1934. Responsible for World War II in Europe.

HOLY DAYS AND FEAST DAYS

CA. 21

Anniversary of the Declaration of Baha'u'llah in the Baha'i faith, and the start of the 12-day Feast of Ridvan (Apr. 21–May 2). Commemorates the Declaration of Baha'u'llah, made over a 12-day period in 1863, articulating a plan whereby the divergent peoples of the world may live in peace and harmony. The 1st day of Ridvan, the 9th, and the 12th are holy days, and Baha'is abstain from work.

21

Feast of St. Anselm (ca. 1033–Apr. 21, 1109). Italian monk; archbishop of Canterbury. Defender of church rights against English kings, and a doctor of the church. Called the Father of Scholasticism.

HOLIDAYS AND CIVIC DAYS

21

Brasília Day in Brazil. Commemorates the presidential inauguration of Apr. 21, 1960 (on Tiradentes Day), naming Brasília the capital of Brazil, replacing Rio de Janeiro.

21

Tiradentes Day in Brazil; official public holiday on nearest Monday. Honors Joaquim José da Silva Xavier (nicknamed Tiradentes ["Toothpuller"]; 1748–Apr. 21, 1792). Brazilian patriot and revolutionary; a dentist of wide learning and noble character who led the first major revolt for independence from Portugal; executed.

21

Kartini Day in Indonesia. Commemorates the birthday of Raden Ajeng Kartini (Apr. 21, 1879–Sept. 17, 1904), leader in the emancipation of Indonesian women. Her collected *Letters* is a classic. On this day, women throughout Indonesia wear national dress, and the men do all the work; there are parades, lectures, and social activities.

21

Natale di Roma in Rome. Traditional day for observing the founding of Rome in 753 B.C.; celebrated with parades and public speeches.

CA. 21

Observance for fallen Japanese soldiers at the Yasukini shrine in Tokyo; 4 days, beginning Apr. 21. Honors the deified spirits of Japanese soldiers who died in wars.

21

Falkland Islands Day in the Falkland Islands (U.K.); official public holiday. Commemorates the birth of Queen Elizabeth II on April 21, 1926—one of the few places to celebrate on the queen's actual birthday.

21

San Jacinto Day in Tex.; official public holiday. Commemorates the Battle of San Jacinto on Apr. 21, 1836, by which Texans under Sam Houston won independence from Mexico. Texas Conservation and Beautification Week (Apr. 19–26) begins 2 days before San Jacinto Day and ends 2 days after National Wildflower Day (Apr. 24).

ANNIVERSARIES AND SPECIAL EVENTS DAYS

21

Birthday of Alexander Anderson (Apr. 21, 1775–Jan. 17, 1870). American engraver and illustrator who made the first wood engravings completed in the U.S. His best-known work includes engravings for an edition of the plays of Shakespeare.

21

Birthday of Fredrik Bajer (Apr. 21, 1837–Jan. 22, 1922). Danish statesman and author; founder of the Danish Peace Society and the International Peace Bureau; recipient of the 1908 Nobel Peace Prize.

21

Birthday of Charlotte Brontë (Apr. 21, 1816–Mar. 31, 1855). English novelist famous for *Jane Eyre* and other novels interpreting women in conflict with their individual needs and social conditions.

21

Birthday of Elizabeth II (Elizabeth Alexandra Mary, daughter of George VI, House of Windsor; Apr. 21, 1926–). Queen of the U.K., crowned Feb. 6, 1952. Her official birthday is in June.

21

Birthday of Friedrich Froebel (or Fröbel; Apr. 21, 1782–June 21, 1852). German educator; founder of the kindergarten system. His birthday is Kindergarten Day in the U.S.

21

Birthday of John Muir (Apr. 21, 1838–Dec. 24, 1832). Scottish-born American naturalist; influential advocate of forest conservation who discovered the glaciers in the High Sierras. The only stand of redwoods in the National Park System is named the Muir Woods National Monument in his honor. In Calif., John Muir Day is a day of special school observance, when teachers stress the importance of an ecologically sound environment and praise his contributions to the state.

CA. 21

Fiesta San Antonio in San Antonio, Tex.; the 10 days, Fri.–Sun., that include Apr. 21 (San Jacinto Day). Highlights are the Battle of Flowers Parade at the Alamo (a boisterous confetti ritual) and celebrations in the old part of town.

ANNIVERSARIES AND SPECIAL EVENTS DAYS

22

Anniversary of the official first sighting and landing in Brazil on Apr. 22, 1500, of the Portuguese navigator Pedro Álvares Cabral (ca. 1467–1520), while leading a major expedition to India; he landed at Porto Seguro, Bahía State, where Discovery Day is celebrated, usually Apr. 19–22.

22

Birthday of Alphonse Bertillon (Apr. 22, 1853–Feb. 13, 1914). French anthropologist; chief of the department of identification in the prefecture of police in Paris who devised the Bertillon system for identifying criminals.

22

Birthday of Henry Fielding (Apr. 22, 1707–Oct. 8, 1754). English novelist and playwright; founder, with Samuel Richardson, of the English novel; best remembered for *The History of Tom Jones, a Foundling.*

22

Birthday of Immanuel Kant (Apr. 22, 1724–Feb. 12, 1804). German philosopher who influenced such philosophies as Kantianism and idealism; author of *The Critique of Pure Reason.*

22

Birthday of Lenin (born Vladimir Ilich Ulyanov; Apr. 22, 1870–Jan. 21, 1924). Russian revolutionary leader and writer whose ideas and career laid the foundations for Soviet totalitarianism; first head of the Soviet state. In the former USSR, his birthday was an official public holiday, observed with high pomp; now lapsed.

22

Birthday of Julius Sterling Morton (Apr. 22, 1832–Apr. 27, 1902), and formerly Arbor Day in Nebr. American conservationist and politician who started Arbor Day in Nebr. in 1872. Represents Nebr. in Statuary Hall. From 1885 until 1988, Arbor Day in Nebr. was observed on Apr. 22, but it is now the last Friday in Apr.

22

Birthday of (Julius) Robert Oppenheimer (Apr. 22, 1904–Feb. 18, 1967). American theoretical physicist; director of the Los Alamos laboratory (1943–45) during the development of the atomic bomb; later, directed the Institute for Advanced Study at Princeton University. Received the Atomic Energy Commission's Enrico Fermi Award in 1963.

22

Earth Day; observed internationally, particularly in the U.S. First observed on Apr. 22, 1970; its purpose is to emphasize the necessity for the conservation of the natural resources of the world. International Earth Day is celebrated on the vernal equinox but has a much smaller following.

HOLY DAYS AND FEAST DAYS

23

Feast of St. George (died ca. 303). Martyr in Palestine; by legend, a part-Jewish Roman soldier of admirable and lovable character who voluntarily submitted to martyrdom, pausing en route to rescue a princess from a Lebanese dragon. An archetypal protector of the helpless. Patron saint of England, Portugal, Germany, Aragon, Genoa, and Venice, and of the Order of the Garter. His day is the occasion for numerous festivals. Orth.: Apr. 23 or May 6.

HOLIDAYS AND CIVIC DAYS

23

Catalan National Day throughout Catalonia, Spain; unofficial regional holiday. More particularly, this is Book and Lover's Day in Barcelona and Catalonia, a celebration both of St. George, patron saint of Catalonia, and of Cervantes, who died on this day. Celebrated at least since 1714. Men give roses to mothers, wives, and sweethearts, and women give books to men.

23

National Sovereignty Day and Children's Day in Turkey; official public holiday. Also an official public holiday in Cyprus, for Turkish Cypriots. Commemorates the declaration of the republic and the inauguration of the Grand National Assembly on Apr. 23, 1923. Honors youth as the symbol of modern Turkey.

ANNIVERSARIES AND SPECIAL EVENTS DAYS

23

Anniversary of the Battle of Clontarf (1014) in Ireland, and likely death anniversary of Brian Boru, fondly remembered High King of Ireland (941–Apr. 23, 1014; ruled 1002–1014). The battle destroyed Norse power in Ireland.

23

Anniversary of the opening of the Boston Latin School, the first public school in the future U.S., on Apr. 23, 1635; it still operates.

23

Anniversary of the establishment of the Order of the Garter, the oldest and most illustrious of British orders of knighthood, on St. George's Day, Apr. 23, 1348.

23

Birthday of James Buchanan (Apr. 23, 1791–June 1, 1868). Fought in the War of 1812; Pa. lawyer; congressman, President Andrew Jackson's minister to Russia, senator; secretary of state under Polk, favoring annexation of Tex., the Mexican War, and reaching agreement with Britain over Oreg.; 15th president of the U.S. (1857–61; Democrat). The only bachelor president. As president, he favored states' choice on slavery and upheld the Dred Scott decision; he denied the states' right to secede but would not use force to preserve the Union. Buried in Woodward Hill Cemetery, Lancaster, Pa.

23

Birthday of Michel Fokine (Apr. 23, 1889–Aug. 22, 1942). Russian-born American dancer and choreographer; created *The Dying Swan* for Anna Pavlova; a major influence on 20th-century classical ballet repertoire.

23

Birthday of Lester Bowles Pearson (Apr. 23, 1897–Dec. 27, 1972). Prime minister of Canada and ambassador to the U.S.; awarded the 1957 Nobel Peace Prize for his success in averting war at the time of the 1957 Suez crisis.

23

Birthday, and death anniversary, of William Shakespeare (Apr. 23, 1564–Apr. 23, 1616). Traditional date for his birth (was baptized Apr. 26). He is universally acknowledged the world's greatest dramatist and poet. His birthday is a festival day at Stratford-upon-Avon, England, his birthplace, and is observed by Shakespeare societies in many nations.

23

Birthday of James Mallord Turner (Apr. 23, 1775–Dec. 19, 1851). English landscape painter, admired for his unusual use of light and color.

23

Death anniversary of Miguel de Cervantes Saavedra (baptized Oct. 9, 1547–Apr. 23, 1616). Leading Spanish novelist, playwright, and poet famed for *Don Quixote*.

CA. 23

April Fair (*Feria de Abril*) in Seville, Spain; Apr. 18–23. Seville's best festival: everyone dresses in flamboyant Andalusian garb and enjoys wine, food, bullfights, horses, and flamenco; began in 1848 as a livestock fair.

CA. 23

Fiesta of St. George in Alcoy, Spain; Apr. 22–24. Alcoy's patron saint. Features a ritual battle between Christians and Moors, commemorating a Christian victory in 1276. Very elaborate and spectacular, symbolizing the melding of both cultures; held since 1663.

CA. 23

Peppercorn Day in Bermuda. In a formal ceremony, officials pay Freemasons the annual rent of 1 peppercorn for the use of the Old State House in St. George; held on the most suitable day nearest Apr. 23, St. George's Day.

HOLIDAYS AND CIVIC DAYS

24

Armenian Genocide Memorial Day in Armenia; official public holiday. Commonly called Armenian Martyrs' Day, and observed by Armenians worldwide and in the Armenian Apostolic Church. Mourns the genocide of Armenians by the Young Turks of the Ottoman Empire in 1915–16; half of Turkey's Armenians died. The genocide began on Apr. 24, 1915, with the arrest and murder of political and intellectual leaders.

ANNIVERSARIES AND SPECIAL EVENTS DAYS

24

Anniversary of the establishment of the Library of Congress by an Act of Congress on Apr. 24, 1800.

24

Anniversary of the beginning of the Spanish-American War. On Apr. 24, 1898, Spain declared war on the U.S.; on Apr. 25, the U.S. Senate declared war on Spain, retroactive to Apr. 21. Spanish forces surrendered on July 17. The Treaty of Paris formally ended the war on Dec. 10, 1898.

24

Birthday of John Russell Pope (Apr. 24, 1874–Aug. 27, 1937). American architect whose work includes the National Gallery of Art and the Jefferson Memorial.

24

Birthday of Robert Penn Warren (Apr. 24, 1905–Sept. 15, 1989). American poet, novelist, essayist, and critic. America's first official poet laureate, 1986–88.

24

Death anniversary of Daniel Defoe (ca. 1660–Apr. 24, 1731). English pamphleteer, journalist, and novelist; renowned for *Robinson Crusoe* and *Moll Flanders*.

24

Children's Day in Iceland. Children hear a speech in the morning and are entertained with music in the afternoon.

24

Easter Rising Day. Anniversary of the Apr. 24, 1916, insurrection in Dublin on Easter Monday, by Irish patriots rebelling against British rule; led by Padraic Pearse; a failure in the short term but led to the Anglo-Irish Treaty of Dec. 6, 1921, with Partition and limited independence for Ireland. The beginning of the end of the British Empire.

Holy Days and Feast Days

25

Feast of St. Mark (died ca. 74). Evangelist, disciple of Jesus, and writer of the second Gospel. As San Marcos, he is patron saint of Venice, Italy, which claims to have his relics. Coptic Christians consider him the founder of their church. Orth.: Apr. 25 or May 8.

Holidays and Civic Days

25

Anzac Day in Australia and New Zealand, also in Tonga and Western Samoa; official public holiday in each. Since 1920, a memorial day and veterans' observance on the anniversary of the courageous, bloody, and unsuccessful landing of the Australian and New Zealand Army Corps (ANZAC) at Gallipoli, Turkey, in World War I.

25

Sinai Day in Egypt; official public holiday. Also called Liberation of Sinai Day. Commemorates the return of Sinai to Egypt as part of the Israeli-Egyptian Peace Treaty of 1982.

25

Liberation Day in Italy; official public holiday. On Apr. 25, 1943, the Grand Council of Fascism voted to depose Mussolini, Il Duce.

25

Liberty Day in Portugal, including Macau; official public holiday. Anniversary of the popular 1974 coup that led to the downfall of the authoritarian corporatist (fascist) state that had existed for 42 years under the Salazar-Caetano dictatorship. In Lisbon, there's a large parade.

25

National Flag Day in Swaziland; official public holiday. Honors the flag and the responsibilities of citizenship. Swaziland's beautiful flag, which includes a shield and spears, was first hoisted on Apr. 25, 1967, from the King's Residence.

Anniversaries and Special Events Days

25

Birthday of Oliver Cromwell (Apr. 25, 1599–Sept. 3, 1658). English statesman, and general in the Civil War; Lord Protector, 1653–58.

25

Birthday of Charles Ferdinand Dowd (Apr. 25, 1825–Nov. 12, 1904). American educator and proponent of uniform time zones to replace the individual system whereby each city and railroad had its own time system. Dowd's ideas about standard time were adopted by most cities of the U.S. and by railroads on Nov. 18, 1883.

25

Birthday of Ella Fitzgerald (Apr. 25, 1918–June 15, 1996). Very influential American jazz and popular singer.

25

Birthday of Guglielmo Marconi (Apr. 25, 1874–July 20, 1937). Italian electrician who perfected wireless telegraphy (1895) and experimented with shortwaves and ultrashort waves. He was corecipient of the 1909 Nobel Prize in physics.

25

Birthday of Edward R. Murrow (Apr. 25, 1908–Apr. 27, 1965). American journalist, radio and television news broadcaster. One of the world's most influential journalists, from World War II onward.

Holidays and Civic Days

26

Union Day in Tanzania; official public holiday. The national day that honors Apr. 26, 1964, when mainland Tanganyika and the islands of Zanzibar and Pemba joined in one country, soon named Tanzania.

ANNIVERSARIES AND SPECIAL EVENTS DAYS

26
Anniversary of the Apr. 26, 1937, bombing of the ancient and sacred Basque town of Guernica, by the fascists. The most infamous incident of the Spanish Civil War; inspired the painting *Guernica* by Pablo Picasso.

26
Birthday of John James Audubon (Apr. 26, 1785–Jan. 27, 1851). American ornithologist and artist. His book *Birds of America* is recognized as the finest example of ornithological illustration. Elected to the Hall of Fame for Great Americans.

26
Birthday of Esek Hopkins (Apr. 26, 1718–Feb. 26, 1802). American commodore; first commander in chief of the U.S. Navy, during the Revolutionary War.

26
Birthday of Frederick Law Olmsted (Apr. 26, 1822–Aug. 28, 1903). American landscape architect, noted for his design of Central Park in New York City and for planning Yosemite National Park and the Niagara Falls Park project.

26
Birthday of Ludwig Josef Johan Wittgenstein (Apr. 26, 1889–Apr. 29, 1951). Austrian-born English philosopher.

HOLY DAYS AND FEAST DAYS

27
Feast of Our Lady of Montserrat in Spain. Spain's major Marian shrine, on Catalonia's holy mountain; contains a miraculous black wooden statue *(la Morenita)*, by legend the work of St. Luke. The site's monastery has long been a center of national reconciliation.

HOLIDAYS AND CIVIC DAYS

27
Independence Day in Sierra Leone; official public holiday. Celebrates independence attained from the U.K. on Apr. 27, 1961.

27
Insurrection Day in Slovenia; official public holiday. Commemorates the foundation of the Liberation Front on Apr. 27, 1941, to resist Slovenia's occupation by German, Italian, and Hungarian fascists; the first such organized resistance in Europe.

27
Freedom Day in South Africa; official public holiday. Anniversary of the first genuine multiracial general election in South Africa, on Apr. 26–27, 1994. A day of national exultation; the black populace cheerfully endured all foul-ups to finally vote as citizens, a right they had desired all their lives. Nelson Mandela was overwhelmingly elected president, and inaugurated on May 10, 1994.

27
Independence Day in Togo; official public holiday. Independence was attained from France on Apr. 27, 1960.

ANNIVERSARIES AND SPECIAL EVENTS DAYS

27
Anniversary of the end of slavery in all French territory. Effective Apr. 27, 1848, France abolished all slavery in its territory. Various French possessions, especially in the Caribbean, observe Emancipation Day on varying dates, depending on the actual date of local promulgation.

27
Birthday of Edward Gibbon (Apr. 27 1737–Jan. 6, 1794). English historian, famous for his *History of the Decline and Fall of the Roman Empire.*

27
Birthday of Ulysses Simpson Grant (Apr. 27, 1822–July 23, 1885). West Point graduate and officer in the Mexican War; Ill. tanner; officer, then victorious general in chief of the Union forces in the Civil War; 18th president of the U.S. (1869–77; Republican). His administration achieved civil service reform, an amnesty bill, and the 15th Amendment, but these achievements were overshadowed by his appointees' notorious corruption. Buried on Riverside Drive, New York City. Elected to the Hall of Fame for Great Americans.

27
Birthday of Samuel Finley Breese Morse (Apr. 27, 1791–Apr. 2, 1872). American artist and inventor of the electric telegraph and the Morse code.

Elected to the Hall of Fame for Great Americans. The first telegraph message on the first telegraph line, between Washington, D.C., and Baltimore was sent by Morse from the Supreme Court building on May 24, 1844; the message was, "What hath God wrought?"

27
Death anniversary of Ferdinand Magellan (Fernão de Magalhães; ca. 1480–Apr. 27, 1521). Portuguese admiral; set sail to circumnavigate the world on Sept. 20, 1519; killed in the Philippines (by Lapu Lapu); his Basque navigator-colleague, Juan Sebastian de Elcano, led the fleet home.

HOLIDAYS AND CIVIC DAYS

28
Formation of the Islamic State's Victory (*Inqilab-e-Islam*) in Afghanistan; official public holiday. Commemorates the 1992 capture of Kabul by Muslim fundamentalist Mujaheddin forces (Apr. 25) and the installation of a government (Apr. 28), ending the Soviet-supported communist regime (1978–92); Soviet troops had withdrawn on Feb. 15, 1989, after invading in Dec. 1979.

28
Maryland Ratification Day. Md. ratified the U.S. Constitution and thereby entered the Union on Apr. 28, 1788, as the 7th state of the original 13.

ANNIVERSARIES AND SPECIAL EVENTS DAYS

28
Anniversary of the signing of the Rush-Bagot Treaty between the U.S. and Great Britain on Apr. 28–29, 1817. The treaty limited armaments on the Great Lakes and eventually led to the longest unmilitarized border in the world, between the U.S. and Canada.

28
Birthday of James Monroe (Apr. 28, 1758–July 4, 1831). Va. lawyer; Revolutionary soldier; U.S. congressman, senator, and statesman; 5th president of the U.S. (1817–25; Democratic Republican). His administration, dubbed the Era of Good Feeling, eliminated forts on the Canadian border and added Fla. to the Union. Enunciated the Monroe Doctrine; a strong supporter of the Bill of Rights. Buried in Hollywood Cemetery, Richmond, Va. Elected to the Hall of Fame for Great Americans.

28
National Day of Mourning in Canada. A day of mourning for workers killed or injured on the job in Canada.

28
Workers Memorial Day in the U.S. Anniversary of the Occupational Safety and Health Act of Apr. 28, 1989. The day was established by a joint resolution of both houses of Congress in 1989. In some places, observed on the 4th Friday of Apr.

HOLY DAYS AND FEAST DAYS

29
Feast of St. Catherine of Siena (Mar. 25, 1347–Apr. 29, 1380). Italian Dominican; notable mystic; persuaded Pope Gregory XI to return the papacy from Avignon to Rome. Patron saint of Italy, and a doctor of the church.

HOLIDAYS AND CIVIC DAYS

29
Greenery Day (*Hana-to-Midori-no-Hi*) in Japan; official public holiday. Commemorates the birth of Hirohito Michi-no-Miya (Apr. 29, 1901–Jan. 27, 1989), former emperor of Japan and also a noted marine biologist. An official public holiday during his lifetime, and retained though renamed. A day devoted to nature and environmental preservation. Golden Week begins on this day; additional public holidays on May 3, 4, and 5 make this the favorite time to take vacations.

ANNIVERSARIES AND SPECIAL EVENTS DAYS

29
Birthday of Sir Thomas Beecham (Apr. 29, 1879–Mar. 8, 1961). English conductor; founder of the London Philharmonic Orchestra in 1932; champion of the music of Frederick Delius.

29
Birthday of Duke (Edward Kennedy) Ellington (Apr. 29, 1899–May 24, 1974). American jazz musician of enormous influence, creator of more than 1,000 musical pieces.

29

Birthday of Oliver Ellsworth (Apr. 29, 1745–Nov. 26, 1807). American jurist; 3rd chief justice of the Supreme Court (1796–1800); major author of the Federal Judiciary Act of Sept. 24, 1789, establishing the federal court system.

29

Birthday of Lorado Taft (Apr. 29, 1860–Oct. 30, 1936). American sculptor whose notable works include *Black Hawk* at Oregon, Ill., and *Solitude of the Soul* at the Art Institute of Chicago.

HOLY DAYS AND FEAST DAYS

30

Zarthastno Diso among Zoroastrians and Parsis. Commemorates the death of Zoroaster (Zarathustra) in 551 B.C.

HOLIDAYS AND CIVIC DAYS

30

Walpurgisnacht (St. Walpurga's Night) in Germany, Sweden, Finland (official public holiday), and Slovenia. Also called *Valborg* or *Vappu*. Ancient festival to welcome spring and to ward off witches, warlocks, and demons. Celebrated with bonfires and all-night revelry.

30

Queen's Birthday (*Koninginnendag*) in the Netherlands and the Netherlands Antilles. The Dutch monarch's official birthday; it originally honored the beloved Juliana, now Queen Mother (Juliana Louise Emma Marie Wilhelmina; Apr. 30, 1909– ; ruled 1948–80). She abdicated in favor of her also-beloved daughter Beatrix (Jan. 31, 1938–), queen since Apr. 30, 1980. Amsterdam celebrates with a street market, street parties, fireworks, and festivities on Dam Square; the rest of Holland celebrates similarly.

30

Louisiana Admission Day. La. was admitted to the Union on Apr. 30, 1812, as the 18th state.

30

Liberation Day in Vietnam; official public holiday. Celebrates the Apr. 30, 1975, fall of Saigon to communist forces, ending the Vietnam War.

ANNIVERSARIES AND SPECIAL EVENTS DAYS

30

Anniversary of the inauguration of George Washington as president of the U.S. The oath of office was administered in New York City on Apr. 30, 1789, by Robert R. Livingston, chancellor of N.Y.

30

Anniversary of the first national holiday in the U.S.; authorized by an Act of Congress to honor the Apr. 30, 1889, centennial of the inauguration of George Washington.

30

Birthday of Jaroslav Hašek (Apr. 30, 1883–Jan. 3, 1923). Czech author of *The Good Soldier Schweyk* (1921), a novel puncturing the pretensions of militarism.

MOVABLE DAYS IN APRIL

DAYLIGHT SAVING TIME (DST) BEGINS IN THE U.S. AND CANADA at 2 A.M. on the 1st Sunday in Apr.; ends 2 A.M. on the last Sunday in Oct. Clocks are advanced 1 hour ("spring forward, fall back"). States and localities may exempt themselves; Ariz. and parts of Ind. do so. Daylight saving time was first proposed by Benjamin Franklin, in 1784; was temporarily adopted during World War I by the U.K., Germany, U.S., and Australia; and was formally adopted in the U.S. in 1967.

HOLIDAYS AND CIVIC DAYS

FAST AND PRAYER DAY IN LIBERIA; 2nd Friday in Apr.; official public holiday. A day dedicated to prayer, self-examination, and self-discipline.

SECHSELAUTEN ("SIX RINGING FESTIVAL") IN ZURICH, SWITZERLAND; 3rd Sunday–Monday in Apr.; local official public holiday. Datable from the 19th century but may be much older. Celebrates, as a guild holiday, the medieval innovation when the cathedral bells rang at 6 instead of 7 o'clock for the end of the working day. On Sunday, processions of costumed children; on Monday, parades of notables costumed as guildsmen and the burning of Böögg, an effigy of winter. The city's largest and most enduring festival.

NATIONAL ARBOR DAY IN THE U.S., and particularly in Nebr.; last Friday in Apr. An educational day to emphasize the importance of planting and tending trees and shrubs and all plants. Not proposed as the Arbor Day for all states— local conditions dictate the best planting time— but many states have adopted this date. The first Arbor Day was on Apr. 10, 1872, in Nebr., the work of Julius Morton; a million trees were planted on that day in Nebr.

CONFEDERATE MEMORIAL DAY IN 2 U.S. STATES: in Ala., on the 4th Monday in Apr., official public holiday; in Miss., on the last Monday in Apr., official public holiday.

STUDENT GOVERNMENT DAY IN MASS.; 1st Friday in Apr. Intended to provide students with an insight into practical government.

FAST DAY IN N.H.; 4th Monday in Apr. Commemorates the observance of a day of prayer and fasting that began in 1679; for most, it is now a day for outdoor recreation and chores.

ANNIVERSARIES AND SPECIAL EVENTS DAYS

INTERNATIONAL ASTRONOMY DAY; ideally, on the Saturday closest to the 1st quarter moon between mid-April and mid-May. A day sponsored by astronomical organizations and institutions to take astronomy to the people; observed in hundreds of communities, mainly in the U.S.

ARBOR WEEK IN CANADA; last Friday in Apr.–2nd Sunday in May (Mother's Day). A period in which to plant and appreciate trees. Sponsored by the Arbor Day Council of Canada.

GLARUS FESTIVAL IN GLARUS, SWITZERLAND; 1st Thursday in Apr. Honors the defeat of the Austrians by the men of Glarus on Apr. 9, 1388; observed with a pilgrimage procession to Nafels, including a visit to the 11 memorial stones that mark the Austrians' 11 unsuccessful attacks.

NATIONAL COIN WEEK; 3rd full week in Apr. Sponsored by the American Numismatic Association since 1924, to promote the history and lore of numismatics and the hobby of coin collecting.

NATIONAL LIBRARY WEEK; usually the 2nd full week of Apr. Celebrates libraries, librarians, and the pleasures and importance of reading, and invites library use and support. Held annually since 1958; sponsored by the American Library Association; thousands of libraries participate.

TRADITIONAL OPENING DAY FOR MAJOR-LEAGUE BASEBALL; 1st Monday in Apr. Traditionally a home game for the Cincinnati Reds (the oldest team); all other National League teams and all American League teams began play on the following Tuesday. Now, however, the Opening Day schedule is unpredictable, and several different games may occur on that day.

SECRETARIES' DAY IN THE U.S.; Wednesday of last full week in Apr. Also called Professional Secretaries' Day, and the week is Professional Secretaries Week. Honors the skills and contributions of secretaries, office managers, and other linchpins of the office. Began in 1952. In Springfield, Mo., secretaries standing in a cherry picker toss typewriters at a target, competing for accuracy.

TAKE OUR DAUGHTERS TO WORK DAY IN THE U.S.; 4th Thursday in Apr. Began in 1993; overseas observances have been noted. Sponsored by the Ms. Foundation for Women.

NATIONAL CHERRY BLOSSOM FESTIVAL IN WASHINGTON, D.C.; held for 2 full weeks during the blooming of the cherry trees that were presented to the U.S. by Tokyo in 1912 and planted around the Potomac River Tidal Basin; season of blossoming can vary from Mar. 20 to Apr. 15. Climax is the cherry blossom parade on the final day (Saturday). Began in 1948.

TATER DAY IN BENTON, KY.; 1st Monday in Apr. and preceding Saturday–Sunday. Oldest trade day in the U.S., held continuously since 1843. Honors the sweet potato, with a parade, arts and crafts, music, a flea market, many sweet potato dishes, and a beauty contest.

NEW ORLEANS JAZZ FESTIVAL; 10 days, Friday–Sunday, in late Apr. First held in 1968; thousands of musicians, artisans, and cooks entertain the city.

BOSTON MARATHON IN BOSTON; 3rd Monday in Apr., on Patriots' Day. The most famous marathon race in the U.S.; sponsored by the Boston Athletic Association; held since Apr. 19, 1897; begins at noon.

FESTIVAL OF NATIONS IN ST. PAUL, MINN.; last weekend in Apr. or 1st weekend in May. Minn.'s largest ethnic celebration, held since 1932.

NATIONAL WHISTLERS CONVENTION IN LOUISBURG, N.C.; 2nd or 3rd weekend in Apr. The only whistlers' convention in the U.S.; began in 1974. Features contests, demonstrations, a school, and a whistled church service.

VIRGIN ISLANDS CARNIVAL IN THE U.S. VIRGIN ISLANDS, ESPECIALLY ON ST. THOMAS; last 2 weeks in Apr. Features the Children's Carnival Parade (last Friday) and the Grand Carnival Parade (next day). Dates from the time of slavery; revived in 1952. Notable for the spangled *Moko Jumbi* ("Make-Believe Spirit") stilt-walker; with processions, limbo, calypso, steel bands, and water sports.

May

May, the 5th month of the year, may have been named for Maia, the Roman goddess of spring and growth, or for the *Majores,* a branch of the Roman senate. It is a month that is associated with flowers and mild weather in the Northern Hemisphere, but it is a winter month in the Southern Hemisphere.

The first day, called May Day, was once a popular festival honoring Flora, the goddess of flowers. It was a day of maypole dancing and other charming customs, many of which have disappeared with the fast pace of progress in the Western world. Since the latter half of the 20th century, May 1 has been celebrated as a favorite international holiday for workers of all kinds. More than 140 nations of the world celebrate Labor Day on May 1 with parades, speeches, and civic gatherings. In a few European countries, such as Finland, the day is also a special festival for students.

May is the month of Mary for Roman Catholics throughout the world. The Virgin Mary is honored during the entire month with pilgrimages and observances at great cathedrals and at special shrines.

In the U.S., the most popular May observance is Mother's Day.

Japan's Golden Week, a favored vacation time, occurs from April 29 through the first week in May.

The special flowers for the month of May are the hawthorn and the lily of the valley. The birthstone is the emerald.

HOLIDAYS AND CIVIC DAYS

1

International Labor Day; observed in more than 140 countries under various names (Labor Day, Worker's Day, etc.); often an official public holiday; on a Monday in a few countries. In the U.S., observed by labor organizations as Worthy Wage Day. Celebrates the central contribution of workers to the economic life of their nation, and celebrates workers' solidarity. May Day was designated an international Labor Day by the International Socialist Congress of 1889, though it had been observed earlier, partly in commemoration of the Haymarket massacre in the U.S.

1

May Day (or Spring Holiday, etc.); official public holiday under various names in 15 countries, often on a Monday.

1

Law Day in the U.S. Sponsored by the American Bar Association and announced by presidential proclamation since 1958; its aim is to further public knowledge, appreciation, and respect for the ideals of equality and justice under the law; observed by legal societies, schools, and the media. Supplanted the former Loyalty Day, also on May 1. Both events were created in alarm at the importance of International Labor Day.

ANNIVERSARIES AND SPECIAL EVENTS DAYS

1

Anniversary of the official opening of the Empire State Building in New York City on May 1, 1931.

1

Anniversary of the Treaty of Union between the kingdoms of Scotland and of England and Wales. The treaty took effect on May 1, 1707; it incorporated the Scottish parliament into the English parliament at Westminster. The United Kingdom was thereby created, and the foundations of the British Empire were laid.

1

Birthday of Benjamin Henry Latrobe (May 1, 1764–Sept. 3, 1820). American architect who designed the Roman Catholic cathedral in Baltimore, the first cathedral to be constructed in the U.S., and who rebuilt the Capitol after it was burned by the British in 1814.

1

Amtrak Day. Anniversary of the May 1, 1971, beginning of the unified rail passenger system in the U.S.

1

Dewey Day. Honors Admiral George Dewey and the anniversary of the Battle of Manila Bay on May 1, 1898; observed primarily by veterans' organizations.

1

Lei Day in Hawaii. A flower festival, the only fete of its kind; dedicated to the lei (a flower garland) as a symbol of Hawaiian beauty and friendship. Celebrated on May 1 since 1928; statewide and very lavish. On May 2, the leis from all over the islands are reverently placed on the graves of Hawaii's royalty at the Royal Mausoleum.

1

May Day in Europe and elsewhere. Traditional celebration of spring since pre-Christian times. Traditionally observed with dancing around beribboned maypoles, honors to the May Queen, flower festivals, and fertility rituals.

1

Sant'Efisio *sagra* (religious folk festival) in Cagliari, Sardinia (Italy), to honor St. Ephysius (died 303). Patron saint of Cagliari, credited with saving the city from the black death. His statue is carried in triumphant procession to the site of his martyrdom, with costumed attendants, music played on shepherds' pipes, and a vast crowd. The most famous and popular event on Sardinia, and one of the world's best festivals.

1

Start of the Tivoli Gardens season in Copenhagen, Denmark; customarily from May 1 through the 3rd Sunday in Sept. The park is treasured for its beautiful flower displays, music and other performances, and fine food.

1

Unofficial popular feast day of Difunta Correa (the Dead Correa), especially in Vallecito, northwest Argentina. Argentina's strongest popular cult. Truckers especially revere her, and leave offerings of water bottles and automotive parts at her shrines. By legend, Deolinda Correa perished of thirst during the civil wars of the 1940s, but preserved her baby: an archetype of maternal selflessness.

HOLY DAYS AND FEAST DAYS

2

Feast of St. Athanasius (ca. 297–May 2, 373). Bishop of Alexandria; participant in the Council of Nicaea. One of the great doctors of the church and a champion of Orthodoxy. Introduced knowledge of Egyptian monasticism to the West. The Athanasian Creed was later drawn from his writings. Orth.: Jan. 18 or 31, with St. Cyril of Jerusalem.

HOLIDAYS AND CIVIC DAYS

2

Dos de Mayo ("2nd of May") in Madrid; regional official public holiday. Fiesta commemorating the rebellion of Madrid citizens against Napoleon's occupation, on May 2, 1808, memorialized in Goya's painting of the same name. Celebrated with concerts, street theater, and fireworks.

ANNIVERSARIES AND SPECIAL EVENTS DAYS

2

Raskova's Regiments Reunion in Moscow; on May 2 (which is International Labor Day, an official public holiday in Russia). A gathering of women veterans of World War II bomber and fighter crews, recruited by Marina Raskova (aviatrix and national heroine) into 3 all-women regiments.

2

Robert's Rules Day. Anniversary of the birth of Henry M. Robert (May 2, 1837–May 11, 1923). American army general who wrote *Robert's Rules of Order.*

HOLY DAYS AND FEAST DAYS

3

Traditional feast of the Holy Cross. Observed with fervor on the traditional date in many parts of Latin America, notably in Bolivia, Mexico, Peru, and Venezuela.

Bolivia's Holy Cross Festival (*Fiesta de la Crúz),* in Tarija (southern highlands), lasts 15 days, starting May 3. Features music, parades, and drinking, with prayers for agricultural fertility.

3

Feast of Our Lady of Czestochowa in Poland; official public holiday. A national patron saint; proclaimed Queen of Poland in 1656, as national protector and symbol of Polish nationalism and religious liberty. A million Poles visit her shrine and its revered icon on this day, the anniversary of the lifting of the Swedish siege of 1655.

3

Feast of St. James the Less (died ca. 62). One of the 12 Apostles; son of Alphaeus and "brother of the Lord." (Some churches regard these as 2 men.) After the Crucifixion, became the head of the primitive church in Jerusalem. Martyred by stoning. Orth.: Oct. 9 or 22 for James the son of Alphaeus, and Oct. 23 or Nov. 5 for James the brother of the Lord.

3

Feast of St. Philip (1st century). One of the 12 Apostles; shares his feast day with St. James the Less. Orth.: Nov. 14 or 27 and also Oct. 11 or 24.

HOLIDAYS AND CIVIC DAYS

3

Constitution Memorial Day (*Kempo Kinen-bi*) in Japan; official public holiday. Celebrates the establishment on May 3, 1947, of a democracy under parliamentary rule.

3

Constitution Day (*Swieto Trzeciego Majo*) in Poland; official public holiday. Commemorates Poland's first constitution, adopted on May 3, 1791; it was a model for the rest of Europe.

ANNIVERSARIES AND SPECIAL EVENTS DAYS

3

Anniversary of the first broadcast by National Public Radio, the national American noncommercial radio network, on May 3, 1971.

3

Birthday of Niccolò Machiavelli (May 3, 1469–June 21, 1527). Italian political statesman and author whose fame is based on *The Prince* and *The Discourses*.

CA. 3

Holiday Festival (*Dontaku Matsuri* or *Hakata Dontaku*) in Fukuoka, Japan; May 3–5, main day the 3rd. Japan's largest festival, held during Golden Week (Apr. 29–1st week in May); features a long

parade of legendary deities, floats, musicians, and dancers. Originated ca. A.D. 1400 and was once held at New Year's time.

3

Holy Cross Day (*Santa Cruz*) in Mexico. A festive day for Mexican construction workers; a day to place a flower-decorated cross on all structures under construction and to enjoy parties courtesy of the clients.

3

Thatcher Day in the U.K. Anniversary of the election of Margaret Thatcher as Britain's first woman prime minister, on May 3, 1979.

HOLIDAYS AND CIVIC DAYS

4

Rhode Island Independence Day. Civic day commemorating through public meetings, celebrations, and school programs the colony's unilateral Declaration of Independence proclaimed on May 4, 1776, 2 months before the Continental Congress made its declaration. May is Rhode Island Heritage Month.

ANNIVERSARIES AND SPECIAL EVENTS DAYS

4

Anniversary of the Haymarket Riot. On May 4, 1886, Chicago police violently attempted to disperse a large crowd of striking labor unionists in Haymarket Square who were protesting police brutality. The anarchist labor leader August Spies and 3 others were subsequently hanged for alleged complicity.

4

Birthday of Thomas Henry Huxley (May 4, 1825–June 29, 1895). English biologist, educator, and writer; champion of the Darwinian theory of evolution.

4

Birthday of Horace Mann (May 4, 1796–Aug. 2, 1859). American educator and crusading champion of educational reforms; known as the Father of the Public School System. Elected to the Hall of Fame for Great Americans. Horace Mann Day has been a commemorative day in Mass., his home state, since 1975.

4

Ashoka Day. Anniversary of the only precisely dated event in the reign of Ashoka (ruled ca.

265–238 B.C.), of India's Mauryan dynasty; fondly remembered as India's most exemplary, benign, and capable ruler; notable for his sincere conversion to Buddhism. On May 4, 249 B.C., a solar eclipse occurred during the construction or dedication of many Buddhist temples, preceding his solemn visit to the Buddha's birthplace at Lumbini (now in Nepal).

4

Kent Students Memorial Day at Kent, Ohio. Commemorates the memory of 4 students shot dead by the Ohio National Guard during antiwar demonstrations at Kent State University on May 4, 1970, following the American invasion of Cambodia. A candlelight procession and vigil begins at midnight and ends 12 hours later; ceremonies include tributes to students martyred elsewhere.

4

Remembrance Day in the Netherlands, and Memorial Day in Curaçao. A day to honor and grieve for the dead of World War II.

4

Youth Day in China. Commemorates student political demonstrations of May 4, 1919, in Tienanmen Square (Beijing), protesting Western domination.

HOLIDAYS AND CIVIC DAYS

5

Ethiopian Patriots Victory Day in Ethiopia; official public holiday. Anniversary of the 1941 liberation of Addis Ababa in 1941 by British and Ethiopian forces; Ethiopians had resisted Italian occupation since the invasion of 1935.

5

Children's Day (*Kodomo-no-Hi*) in Japan; official public holiday. Before 1948, was Boys' Day (*Tango-no-Sekko*). Families picnic, and carp windsocks fly from houses with boys, symbolizing the strength to swim upstream.

5

Cinco de Mayo ("5th of May") in Mexico; official public holiday. Anniversary of the May 5, 1862, Battle of Puebla, a major victory over French forces attempting to impose the imperial rule of the would-be emperor Maximilian I. Joyfully celebrated by Mexicans everywhere with parades, festivals, dances, and speeches. Olvera Street in Los Angeles has a notable celebration. Puebla, Mexico, reenacts the battle.

5

Liberation Day in the Netherlands; official public holiday for public servants. Celebrates May 5, 1945, when German forces were finally expelled from the country by the Allies; marked by military parades and special concerts.

5

Coronation Day in Thailand; official public holiday. Commemorates the May 5, 1946, coronation of the current king (Bhumibol Adulyadej) and queen. Privately celebrated in the Royal Chapel of the Grand Palace, where high-ranking government officials pay their respects to the king.

ANNIVERSARIES AND SPECIAL EVENTS DAYS

5

Anniversary of the suborbital space flight of Alan Bartlett Shepard Jr. (Nov. 18, 1923–July 21, 1998) on May 5, 1961; the second man and first U.S. astronaut in space.

5

Birthday of Søren Aabye Kierkegaard (May 5, 1813–Nov. 11, 1855). Danish philosopher whose writings influenced existentialism and other modern schools of thought.

5

Birthday of Karl Marx (May 5, 1818–Mar. 14, 1883). German philosopher and socialist, founder of modern communism; author of *Das Kapital* and (with Friedrich Engels) *The Communist Manifesto*.

5

Birthday of Henryk Sienkiewicz (May 5, 1846–Nov. 15, 1916). Polish novelist who wrote a patriotic trilogy dealing with Poland's struggle for freedom in the 17th century. Received the 1905 Nobel Prize in literature.

5

Death anniversary of Napoleon Bonaparte (Aug. 15, 1769–May 5, 1821). Emperor of France, commemorated with a Mass at his tomb in the Invalides in Paris, attended by his descendants and admirers.

5

International Midwifery Day. Also called International Day of the Midwife. Instituted in 1991 to further understanding and appreciation of the role and contributions of midwives.

5

Liberation Day in Denmark. Marks the end on May 5, 1945, of 5 years of German occupation during World War II.

5

Youth Day in South Korea. Families take their children on excursions to parks and playgrounds, which are packed with colorfully dressed children.

ANNIVERSARIES AND SPECIAL EVENTS DAYS

6

Birthday of Sigmund Freud (May 6, 1856–Sept. 23, 1939). Austrian physician and psychoanalyst, considered the Father of Psychoanalysis.

6

Birthday of Rear Admiral Robert Edwin Peary (May 6, 1856–Feb. 20, 1920). American Arctic explorer; the first to reach the North Pole, on Apr. 6, 1909.

6

Birthday of Rudolph Valentino (born Rodolfo Alfonzo Raffaelo Pierre Filibert Guglielmi di Valentina d'Antonguolla; May 6, 1895–Apr. 23, 1926). Romantic idol of the silent film era whose movies included *The Sheik* (1921), *Blood and Sand* (1922), and *Monsieur Beaucaire* (1924).

6

St. George's Day in Orthodox countries using the Julian calendar exclusively, notably in Bulgaria and Ukraine; called St. Yurii in Ukraine. The beginning of the agricultural year. On the eve, blossoming willow twigs decorate the house, pens, and cattle; in the night, sheep are turned out to graze; on the day, ritual bread and foods are eaten, with merry songs, and the fields are blessed.

HOLIDAYS AND CIVIC DAYS

7

Day of the Soldier in El Salvador; official public holiday. Anniversary of the founding of the Legion of Liberty, the forerunner of the country's armed forces, on May 7, 1824. Celebrated mainly by the military.

ANNIVERSARIES AND SPECIAL EVENTS DAYS

7

Anniversary of the organization of the American Medical Association (AMA) on May 7, 1847, in Philadelphia, with Dr. Jonathan Knight as the first president.

7

Anniversary of the end of the Battle of Dien Bien Phu in northern Vietnam, on May 7, 1954, thus ending French colonial rule in Indochina and the first phase of the Vietnam War.

7

Birthday of Johannes Brahms (May 7, 1833–Apr. 3, 1897). German composer, considered one of the foremost musicians of all times; honored by annual music festivals throughout the world.

7

Birthday of Robert Browning (May 7, 1812–Dec. 12, 1889). English poet who climaxed his career with *The Ring and the Book.*

7

Birthday of David Hume (May 7, 1711–Aug. 25, 1776). Scottish philosopher and historian.

7

Birthday of Rabindranath Tagore (May 7, 1861–Aug. 7, 1941). Bengali Hindu poet, philosopher, and artist. Author of *Gitanjali, The Religion of Man,* and other books. Awarded the 1913 Nobel Prize in literature. In Bangladesh, his birthday is observed with songs, dances, and discussions of his works.

7

Birthday of Pyotr Ilich Tchaikovsky (May 7, 1840–Nov. 6, 1893). Russian composer famous for his symphonies, operas, orchestral works, and ballet scores, including the Christmas favorite *The Nutcracker.*

7

Birthday of Tito (born Josip Broz; May 7, 1892–May 4, 1980). Leader (Marshall) of communist Yugoslavia, 1943–80; defied Stalin and the USSR in 1948, thereafter pursuing a policy of nonalignment with either the USSR or the U.S.

7

The Harbor Birthday (*Hafengeburtstag*) in Hamburg, Germany. Festival lasting several days, ending on the 7th, to celebrate Hamburg's establishment as a Free City of the Hanseatic League on May 7, 1189.

7

Lusitania Day. Anniversary of the German attack on, and sinking of, the British passenger liner *Lusitania* on May 7, 1915.

ANNIVERSARIES AND SPECIAL EVENTS DAYS

8

Anniversary of the end of World War II in Western Europe; called V-E (Victory in Europe) Day in the U.S., and Armistice, Liberation, or Victory Day elsewhere. On May 8, 1945, German forces in Western Europe signed an armistice of unconditional surrender, to take effect at 1 minute past midnight, May 9, 1945.

8

Birthday of Jean-Henri Dunant (May 8, 1828–Oct. 30, 1910). Swiss philanthropist, convener of the First Geneva Convention (1864), and founder of the Red Cross Society (1863); corecipient of the first Nobel Peace Prize in 1901. World Red Cross Day is celebrated on his birthday.

8

Birthday of Oscar Hammerstein (May 8, 1846–Aug. 1, 1919). German-born American opera impresario, playwright, and inventor who established the Manhattan Opera House for the presentation of popular musical events.

8

Birthday of Miguel Hidalgo y Costilla (May 8, 1753–July 31, 1811). Roman Catholic priest; organizer of a movement that became a social and economic revolution; known as the Father of Mexican Independence. Hidalgo's 1810 Cry of Delores, given in the village of Delores, summoned Mexicans to seize their independence.

8

Birthday of Harry S. Truman (May 8, 1884–Dec. 26, 1972); official public holiday in Mo. Officer in World War I; Mo. senator; vice president, succeeding on the death of President Roosevelt; 33rd president of the U.S. (1945–53; Democrat). Authorized the use of atomic bombs against Japan; responsible for creating NATO and the Marshall Plan and for articulating the Truman Doctrine; oversaw the Korean War, and fired General Douglas MacArthur for insubordination; also oversaw much social legislation. Devoted his retirement to building the archives in the Truman Library in Independence, Mo., and is buried in its rear courtyard.

8

Death anniversary of Helena Petrovna Blavatsky (Aug. 12, 1831–May 8, 1891). Russian theosophist who founded the Theosophical Society in N.Y. and whose book *Isis Unveiled* became a classic in theosophical literature; today is commemorated by theosophical societies throughout the world.

8

Adbar in Ethiopia. A tree ritual celebrated by the Oromo people. Sacred trees are blessed with blood and butter, followed by joyous feasting.

8

Flag Day in Norway. Celebrates the surrender of German forces in Norway on May 8, 1945.

8

Furry Day in Helston, England; on May 8, but if May 8 is a Sunday or Monday, then on the previous Saturday. Originally celebrated St. Michael's victory over Satan; now a spring festival. From early morning, residents of the town, men in top hats and women in fancy dresses, dance through streets and buildings to the old Furry Dance.

HOLIDAYS AND CIVIC DAYS

9

Liberation Day in the Channel Islands; official public holiday on Jersey and Guernsey. Anniversary of the removal of German occupation forces in 1945. Guernsey celebrates with street fairs and processions.

9

Schuman Day in the European Union; official public holiday for civil servants and other employees. Anniversary of the May 9, 1950, announcement of the Schuman Plan for establishing a single authority for production of coal, iron, and steel (all essential war matériel) in France and Germany. The French statesman Robert Schuman is regarded as the father of what became successively the European Common Market, the European Economic Community, the European Communities, and now the European Union.

9

Victory Day in Russia and other countries of Eastern Europe; official public holiday. Also called the Day of Liberation from Fascism. Celebrates the surrender of German forces in Eastern Europe on May 9, 1945. Russia lost many millions in the "Great Patriotic War"; the day is ardently commemorated there.

ANNIVERSARIES AND SPECIAL EVENTS DAYS

9

Birthday of Sir James Matthew Barrie (May 9, 1843–June 9, 1937). Scottish playwright and novelist with a gift for whimsy; wrote *Peter Pan,* which has provided a celebrated role for generations of famous actresses.

9
Birthday of Belle Boyd (May 9, 1843–June 11, 1900). American actress who was, before her theatrical career, one of the most successful Confederate spies during the Civil War.

9
Birthday of José Ortega y Gasset (May 9, 1883–Oct. 18, 1955). Spanish philosopher and humanist, a leader in Spain's cultural renaissance of the 20th century.

9
Death anniversary of William Bradford (Mar. 1590–May 9, 1657). American Pilgrim father, author of the *History of Plimoth Plantation,* and governor of the Plymouth Colony for 30 years.

9
John Brown Day. Anniversary of the birth of John Brown (May 9, 1800–Dec. 2, 1859), American abolitionist who led an attack on Harpers Ferry on Oct. 16, 1859; convicted of treason and hanged.

9
North Pole Flight Day. Anniversary of the first flight over the North Pole, achieved by Commander Richard E. Byrd of the U.S. Navy and Floyd Bennett on May 9, 1926.

HOLIDAYS AND CIVIC DAYS

10
Mother's Day in Guatemala (official public holiday for mothers) and Mexico.

10
Constitution Day in the Federated States of Micronesia; official public holiday. Commemorates a constitution enacted in 1979, shortly before independence from the U.S.

10
Confederate Memorial Day in N.C. and S.C.; optional official public holiday in S.C.

ANNIVERSARIES AND SPECIAL EVENTS DAYS

10
Birthday of Augustin-Jean Fresnel (May 10, 1788–July 14, 1827). French physicist; developer of the Fresnel lens for lighthouses.

10
Death anniversary of George Vancouver (1758–May 10, 1798). English navigator and explorer; surveyor of western North America. Vancouver Island, Canada, is named in his honor.

10
Adler Planetarium Day. Anniversary of the opening of the Adler Planetarium in Chicago on May 10, 1930, the first public planetarium in the U.S.

10
Burning of the Books Day. Anniversary of the massive burning of proscribed books in public squares in Germany on May 10, 1933, to demonstrate Hitler's intent to curb freedom of the press and freedom of expression of individual thought.

10
Fort Ticonderoga Day. Anniversary of the battle of May 10, 1775, when Ethan Allen and his Green Mountain Boys, assisted by Benedict Arnold, overwhelmed the British at Fort Ticonderoga; the first American victory in the War of Independence.

10
Golden Spike Day. Commemorates the meeting of the Union and Central Pacific Railroads with the driving of a golden spike on May 10, 1869, to symbolize the unification of the East and the West by railroad; observed since 1952 at the Golden Spike Historical Monument at Promontory Summit, Utah.

HOLY DAYS AND FEAST DAYS

11
Feast of St. Mamertius (or Mammertus; died ca. 475), and of the Frost Lords. Learned bishop in Gaul; noted for originating the Rogation Days. Mamertius is one of the 3 Frost Saints in France and of the 3 Severe Lords in Germany, invoked with St. Pancras and St. Servatus for protection of crops from killing frost at this time.

HOLIDAYS AND CIVIC DAYS

11
Admission Day in Minn. Minn. entered the Union on May 11, 1858, as the 32nd state.

ANNIVERSARIES AND SPECIAL EVENTS DAYS

11
Anniversary of the inauguration of Constantinople (formerly Byzantium) as the capital of the

Eastern Roman Empire in A.D. 330 by the emperor Constantine; this was a de facto separation from the West and the beginning of the Eastern Orthodox Byzantine Empire. Constantinople fell to the Ottoman Turks on May 29, 1453.

11

Birthday of Salvador Dalí (May 11, 1904–Jan. 23, 1989). Leading Catalan Spanish surrealist painter.

11

Birthday of Maria Sandoz (May 11, 1901–Mar. 10, 1966). Author of *Old Jules* and other books on the American pioneer period; May 11 was proclaimed Maria Sandoz Day by the Nebr. legislature to honor her birthday and work.

ANNIVERSARIES AND SPECIAL EVENTS DAYS

12

Birthday of Robert Baldwin (May 12, 1804–Dec. 9, 1858). Canadian statesman and exponent of representative government.

12

Birthday of Lincoln Ellsworth (May 12, 1880–May 26, 1951). American engineer and polar explorer who led the first transarctic flights in 1926 and the first transantarctic flights in 1935.

12

Birthday of Jiddu Krishnamurti (May 12, 1895–Feb. 17, 1986). Indian sage and philosopher of wide influence and great sweetness of character.

12

Birthday of Florence Nightingale (May 12, 1820–Aug. 13, 1910). English nurse and the founder of modern nursing; called the Lady with the Lamp during the Crimean War. The first woman to receive the Order of Merit. Her birthday is International Nurses Day.

12

Birthday of Gabriel Dante Rossetti (May 12, 1826–Apr. 9, 1882). English poet and painter who was the most important member of the Pre-Raphaelites.

12

Garland Day in Abbotsbury, England. A survival of old May Day festivities; children carry garlands door to door and receive gifts to welcome May; the garlands are later laid before the War Memorial.

12

International Nurses Day. Honors the dedication and services of the world's nurses; on the birthday of Florence Nightingale. National Nurses Week in the U.S. is always May 6–12. Today is also National Hospital Day in the U.S.; observed on Florence Nightingale's birthday since 1921; especially by hospitals and hospital associations, with special programs honoring her.

12

Limerick Day. Anniversary of the birth of Edward Lear (May 12, 1812–Jan. 29, 1888), English writer of light verse noted for creating the limerick, "the only verse form indigenous to the English language"; his *Book of Nonsense* made limericks popular.

12

Snellman Day in Finland. Honors J. V. Snellman (May 12, 1806–July 4, 1881), journalist, statesman, and leader of the Nationalist movement; ceremonies are held at his statue in Helsinki.

ANNIVERSARIES AND SPECIAL EVENTS DAYS

13

Anniversary of the abolition of slavery and the emancipation of all slaves in Brazil, on May 13, 1888.

13

Birthday of Sir Arthur Seymour Sullivan (May 13, 1842–Nov. 22, 1900). English composer who with William Gilbert created the unique and perennially popular Gilbert and Sullivan operettas.

ANNIVERSARIES AND SPECIAL EVENTS DAYS

14

Baptismal day of Thomas Gainsborough (baptized May 14, 1727–Aug. 2, 1788). English portrait and landscape painter, known for such paintings as *The Blue Boy*.

14

Birthday of Gabriel Daniel Fahrenheit (May 14, 1686–Sept. 16, 1736). German physicist who introduced the use of mercury for thermometers and invented the Fahrenheit temperature scale.

14

Birthday of Robert Owen (May 14, 1771–Nov. 17, 1858). Welsh manufacturer and educator; founder of British socialism and of the utopian colony at New Harmony, Ind.

14

Jamestown Day. Anniversary of the establishment of the first permanent English settlement in America on May 13 (sighting) and 14 (landing), 1607, in Va. Commemorative services are held at the Jamestown site annually on the Saturday nearest May 14, and the Sunday.

CA. 14

Midnight Sun Days in North Cape, Norway; May 14–July 30. Between these dates, at North Cape's latitude, the sun never sets; celebrated with a series of festivals.

HOLY DAYS AND FEAST DAYS

15

Feast of St. Dymphna (died ca. 650). Celtic martyr; patron saint of people with epilepsy and people with mental illness. Particularly honored in Geel, Belgium, where the townspeople take care of mentally or emotionally disturbed people through a "boarding out" system. Pilgrimages are made to her tomb in Geel.

HOLIDAYS AND CIVIC DAYS

15

Independence Day in Paraguay; official public holiday. Celebrates independence attained from Spain and from Buenos Aires on May 15, 1811. This is also Mother's Day.

15

Police Memorial Day in the U.S. Also called Peace Officer Memorial Day; Police Week includes May 15. Established by presidential proclamation in 1963 to commemorate police officers killed in the line of duty. Observed by local police departments, at the Police Hall of Fame and Museum in Miami, and at Congressional Park in Washington, D.C. The date was chosen to complement Law Day (May 1) without stealing its thunder.

ANNIVERSARIES AND SPECIAL EVENTS DAYS

15

Birthday of Lyman Frank Baum (May 15, 1856–May 6, 1919). American newspaperman, writer, and playwright remembered chiefly for a series of books about the imaginary land of Oz; observed by the International Wizard of Oz Clubs.

15

Birthday of Richard Schirrmann (May 15, 1874–Dec. 14, 1961). German schoolteacher and founder of the Youth Hostel movement; opened the first hostel on Aug. 26, 1909, in Germany; the first permanent hostel opened in 1912, in Altena, Germany.

15

Birthday of Norkey Tenzing (May 15, 1914–May 9, 1986). Nepali Sherpa; mountaineer; Edmund Hillary and Tenzing were the first climbers to reach the summit of Mt. Everest.

15

Candle Race (*Corsa dei Ceri*) in Gubbio, Italy. Young bearers carry 3 giant wooden candles to the Basilica of St. Ubaldo of Gubbio, atop Monte Ingino.

15

Cold Sophie in Bavaria, Germany. The local feast day of St. Sophia, believed to be the last day of killing frost.

15

Festivals for St. Isidore the Farmer (1070–May 15, 1130). In Spain, the day is a local official public holiday in Madrid (where he is the patron saint), Estepona, and Nerja. In Dominica, farmers of Grand Bay have a harvest festival in his honor. In villages of Gran Canaria in the Canary Islands, this is a form of rustic May Day, celebrated with festivals.

15

Hollyhock Festival (*Aoi Matsuri*) in Kyoto, Japan. The world's oldest festival, from the 6th century. Features a procession in costumes from the Heian period (794–1185) and combines colorful costumes, elegance, and reverence.

CA. 15

Kanda Myojin Festival in Tokyo; May 14–16. One of Tokyo's major festivals, centered on the Kanda Myojin shrine. Neighborhoods carry portable shrines (*mikoshi*) in garrulous procession.

CA. 15

Rice-Planting (*Hama-Taue*) Festival in Kochi City, Japan; May 15–17. At the Wakamiya Hachiman shrine, the sacred rice paddy is planted, with women ruling the men. Rice in all its aspects is very important in Japan and is honored with many festivals; the first planting is especially solemn and sacred, yet playful, and is often accompanied by the *kagura*, a sacred drama with music.

CA. 15

Tulip Time in Holland, Mich.; 11 days, core days are the Wednesday nearest May 15 and the Thursday–Saturday of the following week. Flower festival and celebration of the town's Dutch roots; celebrated since 1929 with beautiful plantings in Tulip Lanes and parks, and with flower shows, parades, *klompen* dancing, pageants, street scrubbing, musicals, and exhibits at the Netherlands Museum.

HOLY DAYS AND FEAST DAYS

16

Feast of St. Brendan the Navigator (ca. 484–ca. 577). Irish monk; founder of Clonfert and other monasteries, and missionary to England and Scotland. Especially famed for his voyages, described in his *Navigatio*, which gives accurate sailing instructions to North America. A patron saint of sailors.

16

Feast of St. John Nepomucene (1340–Mar. 20, 1393). Bohemian defender of the faith; patron saint of gardeners and principal patron saint of Bohemia and the Czech Republic.

ANNIVERSARIES AND SPECIAL EVENTS DAYS

16

Birthday of Edmund Kirby-Smith (May 16, 1824–Mar. 28, 1893). American soldier and educator; West Point graduate who served with the Confederate Army during the Civil War. Represents Fla. in Statuary Hall.

16

Birthday of Elizabeth Palmer Peabody (May 16, 1804–Jan. 3, 1894). American educator and author; one of the famous Peabody sisters, a pioneer in championing the study of history in public schools, and the founder of the first kindergarten in the U.S. in 1860.

16

Birthday of William Henry Seward (May 16, 1801–Oct. 10, 1872). American statesman; secretary of state under President Lincoln; negotiator of the purchase of Alaska from Russia.

HOLIDAYS AND CIVIC DAYS

17

Constitution Day (*Grunnlovsdag*) in Norway; official public holiday. Also called *Syttende Mai* ("17th of May"), and celebrated as such by Norse-Americans. Commemorates Norway's constitution of May 17, 1814, wherein the Norse rejected the rearrangements following the Napoleonic Wars and (unsuccessfully) asserted independence from both Denmark and Sweden. This promptly became a day of national rejoicing. Celebrated with flags everywhere, and parades of children in national costume, but with no militarism. May, with its several holidays, is Norway's month of patriotism, parties, and long weekends.

ANNIVERSARIES AND SPECIAL EVENTS DAYS

17

Anniversary of the Supreme Court decision in *Brown v. Board of Education* on May 17, 1954; racial segregation in public schools was unanimously ruled unconstitutional, as a violation of the 14th Amendment guaranteeing equal protection of all citizens. The case was argued and won by the distinguished African American lawyer Thurgood Marshall.

17

Bianou ("Death of the Ground") at the Saharan crossroads town of Agadez, northern Niger. Observed by Tuareg nomads, at the traditional start of summer. Begins with drummers, chants, and processions. Government officials take a census and provide medical care.

17

Mut al-Ard ("Death of the Ground") in Morocco. Considered the first day of summer, and a time of potential danger and evil. Various rituals and superstitions are used for protection.

HOLY DAYS AND FEAST DAYS

18

Feast of St. Erik of Sweden (died May 18, 1160). King Erik IX of Sweden (ruled 1150–60); lawgiver and martyr. A patron saint of Sweden, though never formally canonized.

HOLIDAYS AND CIVIC DAYS

18

Flag and University Day in Haiti; official public holiday.

18

Revival and Unity Day in Turkmenistan; official public holiday. Commemorates the 1992 adoption of the Turkmen Constitution.

18

Battle of Las Piedras Day in Uruguay; official public holiday. Commemorates the Battle of Las Piedras, fought for independence from Spain on May 17, 1811.

ANNIVERSARIES AND SPECIAL EVENTS DAYS

18

Birthday of Bertrand Arthur William Russell (3rd Earl Russell; May 18, 1872–Feb. 2, 1970). English logician and philosopher; noted for his work for international peace and nuclear disarmament.

18

Mt. St. Helens Day. Anniversary of the May 18, 1980, eruption of one of the most beautiful mountains in the state of Wash., blowing off almost a cubic mile of its summit and creating major disasters for nature and people. The last major eruption had been in 1857.

HOLY DAYS AND FEAST DAYS

19

Feast of the Blessed Alcuin (ca. 735–May 19, 804). English monk of notable scholarship; appointed by Charlemagne to head the imperial school at Aachen, making it a center of European learning; the moving personality in the Carolingian renaissance.

19

Feast of St. Dunstan (910–988). English Benedictine monk, abbot of Glastonbury, and archbishop of Canterbury. The reviver of monasticism in England and one of the great Anglo-Saxon saints. A notable musician, metalworker, and artisan. Patron saint of goldsmiths, locksmiths, and jewelers.

HOLIDAYS AND CIVIC DAYS

19

Youth and Sports Day in Turkey; official public holiday; also an official public holiday in Cyprus, for Turkish Cypriots. Commemorates the 1919 landing at Samsum by Kemal Ataturk, the beginning of the movement for independence, and the creation of Turkey. Young athletes carry torches to the sites of athletic contests.

19

Birthday of Ho Chi Minh (born Nguyen That Thanh; May 19, 1890–Sept. 2, 1969); official public holiday in Vietnam. Leader in the war for independence from France, and during the Vietnam War; president of North Vietnam (the Democratic Republic of Vietnam), 1945–69; Vietnam's George Washington.

ANNIVERSARIES AND SPECIAL EVENTS DAYS

19

Anniversary of the organization of the Federated Boys' Clubs on May 19, 1906; now known as the Boys & Girls Clubs of America.

19

Pardon of St. Yves (St. Ivo Hèlory of Kermartin, patron saint of lawyers) at Tréguier, France. Attended by lawyers from many countries, who form a robed procession. Ivo is also the patron saint of Breton fishermen and seamen.

HOLIDAYS AND CIVIC DAYS

20

National Day in Cameroon; official public holiday. Also called Reunification Day or Constitution Day. Commemorates the popular choice to unify the 2 previously separate parts under one government with a new constitution on May 20, 1972.

ANNIVERSARIES AND SPECIAL EVENTS DAYS

20

Anniversary of the signing of the Homestead Act of 1862, granting free family farms to U.S. settlers.

20

Birthday of Honoré de Balzac (May 20, 1799–Aug. 18, 1850). French master of realism, whose series of related novels, *La Comédic humaine,* include nearly a hundred richly detailed works examining the complex social, political, and economic forces that shaped all levels of French society.

20

Mecklenburg Day in N.C. Anniversary of the signing of the Mecklenburg Declaration of Independence on May 20, 1775, by citizens of Mecklenburg County, N.C.; a day of special observance in N.C.

20

Weights and Measures Day. Anniversary of the May 20, 1875, signing of a treaty establishing the International Bureau of Weights and Measures.

HOLIDAYS AND CIVIC DAYS

21

Naval Glories Day (*Glorias Navales*) in Chile; official public holiday. Also called Battle of Iquiqie Day. Honors the Chilean navy on the anniversary of the Battle of Iquiqie on May 21, 1879, during the War of the Pacific (1879–83), when Chile seized the nitrate-rich Atacama desert from Peru and Bolivia.

ANNIVERSARIES AND SPECIAL EVENTS DAYS

21

Anniversary of the organization of the American Red Cross on May 21, 1881, by Clara Barton, who became its first president; its official recognition came after years of patient effort.

21

Birthday of Lázaro Cárdenas (May 21, 1895–Oct. 19, 1970). President of Mexico (1934–40); responsible for many reforms and affectionately remembered.

21

Birthday of Glenn Hammond Curtiss (May 21, 1878–July 23, 1930). American aviator and aeronautical inventor who set many pioneer flying records, established the first flying school, and invented the flying boat and the first heavier-than-air craft intended for transatlantic flight.

21

Birthday of Albrech Dürer (May 21, 1471–Apr. 6, 1528). German painter and printmaker; great artist of German Renaissance altarpieces, religious works, and engravings.

21

Birthday of Elizabeth Gurney Fry (May 21, 1780–Oct. 12, 1845). English prison reformer who founded an association to improve conditions for women prisoners at Newgate.

21

Birthday of Alexander Pope (May 21, 1688–May 30, 1744). English poet and essayist known for his *Essay on Man*; outstanding satirist of the English Augustan period.

21

Anasternarides Festival in Macedonia, Greece; also in a few nearby villages in Bulgaria. Notable for its fire-walking. Held on the Orthodox feast day of SS. Constantine and Helena, but much older.

21

Lilies and Roses Day at the Tower of London, England. Commemorates the death of King Henry VI on May 21, 1471; founder in 1441 of Eton College and of King's College, Cambridge. Services are attended by representatives of the 2 colleges carrying lilies and roses for the traditional ceremonial; the flowers are laid in the cell where he was murdered.

21

Lindberg Flight Day. Commemorates the landing of Charles Lindberg in Paris on May 21, 1927, which concluded the first successful nonstop transatlantic flight.

HOLIDAYS AND CIVIC DAYS

22

Emancipation Day in Martinique, French West Indies; official public holiday. Celebrates, with picnics and parties, the end of slavery in French territories in 1848, locally promulgated on May 22, 1848.

22

National Heroes' Day in Sri Lanka; official public holiday. Honors the citizens who died for their country in the insurrection of 1971. Sri Lanka ratified its basic constitution on May 22, 1972.

22

National Maritime Day in the U.S. Also called Merchant Marine Day. A commemorative day, recognizing the contributions of commercial shipping and sailors. First proclaimed by President Franklin Roosevelt in 1933 on the anniversary of the May 22, 1819, departure of the *Savannah* from her home port in Ga., for the world's first transatlantic crossing using steam power. The day is observed especially in Atlantic port cities, with open house at ships and maritime events; the governors of Maine and Mass. issue proclamations.

22

National Day in Yemen; official public holiday. Celebrates the peaceful unification of North and South Yemen on May 22, 1990.

ANNIVERSARIES AND SPECIAL EVENTS DAYS

22

Birthday of Mary Cassatt (May 22, 1844–June 14, 1926). American Impressionist painter; lived in France; friend and pupil of Edgar Degas; noted for her renderings of the human figure and the common gestures of everyday life.

22

Birthday of Sir Arthur Conan Doyle (May 22, 1859–July 7, 1930). British physician and novelist; creator of the fictional detective Sherlock Holmes of Baker Street, London; the day is observed by the Baker Street Irregulars and other Sherlock Holmes societies.

22

Birthday of (Wilhelm) Richard Wagner (May 22, 1813–Feb. 13, 1883). German composer famous for the operas *Tannhäuser, Lohengrin, Parsifal,* and *The Ring of the Nibelungs.*

22

Death anniversary of the Roman emperor Constantine I, the Great (Feb. 27, ca. 288–May 22, 337; ruled 306–37). The first Roman emperor to embrace Christianity officially, and the creator of the conditions for Byzantine and Western medieval civilization.

HOLY DAYS AND FEAST DAYS

23

Anniversary of the Declaration of the Bab in the Baha'i faith. A holy day, and Baha'is abstain from work. Commemorates the Bab's prophecy on May 23, 1844, in Shiraz, Persia, of the coming of a spiritual leader who would inaugurate a new era in religious history. This day is considered the foundation day of both the Babi faith (an outgrowth of Shia Islam) and that of its successor and fulfillment, the Baha'i faith.

HOLIDAYS AND CIVIC DAYS

23

Labor Day in Jamaica; official public holiday.

23

Ratification Day in S.C. On May 23, 1788, S.C. ratified the Constitution, becoming the 8th state of the original 13.

ANNIVERSARIES AND SPECIAL EVENTS DAYS

23

Anniversary of the Defenestration of Prague and the start of the Thirty Years' War. May 23, 1618, marked the official start of the destructive Europewide war between Protestants and Catholics. Peace was concluded with the Peace of Munster of Jan. 30, 1648, between Spain and the liberated Republic of the United Netherlands, and then with the more general Peace of Westphalia of Oct. 24, 1648.

23

Birthday of Margaret (Sarah) Fuller (May 23, 1810–July 19, 1850). American teacher, writer, and critic who is considered the first professional book-review editor, with columns running in the *New York Tribune* beginning in 1844.

23

Birthday of Carolus Linnaeus (born Carl von Linné; May 23, 1707–Jan. 10, 1778). Swedish naturalist who developed new methods of classifying plants; his *Species Plantarum* is the official bible of botanical nomenclature. His home and gardens in Uppsala are maintained as a monument and memorial.

23

Birthday of Friedrich Anton Mesmer (May 23, 1734–Mar. 5, 1815). German physician who used magnetism and hypnotism (mesmerism) to treat disease.

HOLIDAYS AND CIVIC DAYS

24

Anniversary of the Battle of Pichincha in Ecuador; official public holiday. The May 24, 1822, battle marked the final defeat of Spain in Ecuador.

24

Independence Day in Eritrea; official public holiday. On May 24, 1993, Eritrea declared its independence from Ethiopia.

ANNIVERSARIES AND SPECIAL EVENTS DAYS

24

Anniversary of the official opening on May 24, 1883, of the Brooklyn Bridge over the East River in New York City. Begun, 1869.

24

Anniversary of the creation of the Royal Geographical Society on May 24, 1830, in London, by members of the Raleigh Club, as the Geographical Society of London; it was incorporated under its present name in 1859. The Royal Geographical

Society and the National Geographic Society are the world's foremost geographical societies.

24

Anniversary of the first telegraph message on May 24, 1844.

24

Birthday of Jan Christian Smuts (May 24, 1870–Sept. 11, 1950). South African soldier and statesman, originator of the concept of the British Commonwealth of Nations, and a leader in the establishment of the League of Nations and the United Nations.

24

Birthday of Queen Victoria of the U.K. (Alexandrina Victoria; May 24, 1819–Jan. 22, 1901; ruled 1837–1901). Originally called Victoria Day, and thereafter Empire Day, an official public holiday throughout the British Empire from 1903 to 1957; has subsequently been renamed and transferred to other dates a number of times and is no longer an official public holiday. Some formerly British countries still observe one or another of these holidays.

24

Education Day in Bulgaria. Also called the Day of Slavonic Letters, or Enlightenment and Culture Day. Honors Sts. Cyril and Methodius, the men who gave a canonical alphabet to the Slavic nations. Bulgaria has celebrated this day since the mid-19th century; now Russia has begun to.

CA. 24

Festival of the Holy Marys (la Fête des Saintes Maries) in Les Saintes-Maries-de-la-Mer (Provence), France; May 24–25. By legend, Mary Magdalene, Martha Lazarus, the Virgin Mary's sisters Mary Jacoby and Mary Salome, and the servant Sara of Egypt landed in Provence after the Crucifixion. Two overlapping events on May 24–25 commemorate their landing. One is a centuries-old pilgrimage by Provençals in honor of SS. Mary Jacoby and Mary Salome and of Sara. Its main day is May 25. The women's relics are brought from the church and blessed in their symbolic boat, at the sea. The other event, held since the mid-19th century, is a grand pilgrimage by Gypsies from all over Europe to honor their adopted patron, the Egyptian servant Sara, May 24. Sara's statue is draped with new robes; after Mass, there's a horseback procession of the statue to the sea. A time for Gypsies to renew far-flung contacts.

HOLY DAYS AND FEAST DAYS

25

Feast of Bede, the Venerable (ca. 672–May 25, 735). English monk and scholar; his Historia Ecclesiastica, a history of the English church, is a primary document of high quality; the first English historian to date events anno Domini (A.D.). Doctor of the church.

HOLIDAYS AND CIVIC DAYS

25

Africa Day; official public holiday in some African countries. Also called African Freedom Day or O.A.U. Day. Anniversary of the formation of the Organization of African Unity by 30 African leaders on May 25, 1963, in Addis Ababa, Ethiopia, to achieve, among other goals, a better life for the people of Africa. Africa Day celebrates freedom from colonial rule and continental cooperation; a day of sports contests, political rallies, and tribal dances.

25

Revolution of May (Revolución de Mayo) in Argentina; official public holiday. Also called Day of the Nation (Día de la Patria). Honors Argentina's first revolt against Spain and the proclamation of the first independent government, in 1810.

25

Independence Day in Jordan; official public holiday. Commemorates independence attained from the U.K., and a kingdom established, on May 25, 1946.

ANNIVERSARIES AND SPECIAL EVENTS DAYS

25

Birthday of Miles Davis (May 25, 1926–Sept. 28, 1991). Innovative American jazz trumpeter and composer who ushered in the "birth of cool" and continued to experiment with new musical forms throughout his career.

25

Birthday of Ralph Waldo Emerson (May 25, 1803–Apr. 27, 1882). American essayist, poet, philosopher, and lecturer. Elected to the Hall of Fame for Great Americans.

25

Birthday of John Raleigh Mott (May 25, 1865–Jan. 31, 1955). American religious and social worker;

general secretary of the International Committee of the Young Men's Christian Association (YMCA); organizer of the World's Student Christian Federation. Received the Nobel Peace Prize in 1946 with Emily Green Balch.

25
Flitting Day in Scotland. Traditional day to renew one's lease or change lodgings ("sit or flit"). Observed on May 1 in some parts as Term Day.

HOLIDAYS AND CIVIC DAYS

26
Independence Day in the nation of Georgia; official public holiday. Commemorates the May 26, 1918, declaration of independence from Russia. Georgia was absorbed by the USSR in 1922. Georgia declared its independence from the USSR on Apr. 9, 1991. Independence was formally attained with the dissolution of the Soviet Union on Dec. 26, 1991.

ANNIVERSARIES AND SPECIAL EVENTS DAYS

26
Birthday of Isadora Duncan (born Angela Duncan; May 26, 1877–Sept. 14, 1927). American dancer who developed interpretive dancing through adaptation of the classical dances of Greece.

26
Army Abolition Day in Panama. On May 26, 1995, Panama's constitution was amended to abolish the country's armed forces.

26
Dunkirk Day. Anniversary of the May 26–June 3, 1940, evacuation of the bulk of the British Expeditionary Force from Dunkerque on the coast of France to avoid its total annihilation by German forces; the successful cooperation of civilian and naval craft in effecting the evacuation and the return of the force to England was called "a moral triumph in the face of a military catastrophe."

HOLY DAYS AND FEAST DAYS

27
Feast of St. Augustine of Canterbury (died May 26, 604). Roman Benedictine monk and the first archbishop of Canterbury, sent by Pope Gregory the Great to evangelize England; he succeeded in pagan southeast England.

HOLIDAYS AND CIVIC DAYS

27
Emancipation Day in Guadeloupe, French West Indies; official public holiday. Celebrates, with picnics and parties, the end of slavery in French territories in 1848, locally promulgated on May 27, 1848.

ANNIVERSARIES AND SPECIAL EVENTS DAYS

27
Birthday of Sir Francis Beaufort (May 27, 1774–Dec. 11, 1857). English naval officer in the Napoleonic Wars, admiral, surveyor, and hydrographer. Creator of the Beaufort scale of wind velocity (1805). Head of the Admiralty's Hydrographic Office (1829–55) and perfecter of the Admiralty Chart. Some of his own surveys remain definitive.

27
Birthday of Amelia Jenks Bloomer (May 27, 1818–Dec. 30, 1894). American social reformer who fought for temperance and women's rights but is remembered chiefly for her advocacy of "sensible" dress, which she demonstrated by wearing full trousers that came to be known as "bloomers."

27
Birthday of Rachel Louise Carson (May 27, 1907–Apr. 14, 1964). American biologist whose book *Silent Spring* (1962) aroused worldwide concern for the dangers of environmental pollution.

27
Birthday of (Samuel) Dashiell Hammett (May 27, 1894–Jan. 10, 1961). American Pinkerton operative turned author; founder of the "hard-boiled" school of detective fiction; wrote *The Maltese Falcon.*

27
Birthday of James Butler "Wild Bill" Hickok (May 27, 1837–Aug. 2, 1876). Legendary American frontiersman, army scout, marksman, and gambler.

27
Birthday of Julia Ward Howe (May 27, 1819–Oct. 17, 1910). American author, social reformer, author of "The Battle Hymn of the Republic," and first woman member of the American Academy of Arts and Letters.

27

Birthday of Hubert Horatio Humphrey (May 27, 1911–Jan. 13, 1978). U.S. senator from Minn.; co-founder of the Peace Corps; vice president under President Lyndon Johnson.

HOLY DAYS AND FEAST DAYS

28

Feast of St. Bernard of Montjoux (ca. 996–1081). Italian priest and missionary; founded two hospices for travelers in the Alpine passes now called the Great and Little Bernard; patron saint of mountain climbers. Not to be confused with St. Bernard of Menthon.

HOLIDAYS AND CIVIC DAYS

28

Overthrow of the Derg Regime in Ethiopia; official public holiday. Anniversary of the 1991 defeat of the junta that had seized control of the country on Sept. 12, 1974, and dethroned the emperor, Haile Selassie I.

ANNIVERSARIES AND SPECIAL EVENTS DAYS

28

Anniversary of the landing in Fla. on May 28, 1539, of the Spanish explorer Hernando de Soto. Celebrated in Bradenton for a week.

28

Birthday of Louis Agassiz (May 28, 1807–Dec. 14, 1873). Swiss-born American teacher, naturalist, biologist, geologist, and ichthyologist; a prodigious author. Established the Museum of Comparative Zoology at Harvard, the model of all American natural-history museums, and founded the Anderson School of Natural History on Penikese Island, Buzzards Bay, Mass., the forerunner of all marine and lacustrine stations. Elected to the Hall of Fame for Great Americans.

28

Birthday of Joseph-Ignace Guillotin (May 28, 1738–Mar. 26, 1814). French physician; member of the Constituent Assembly who urged the use of the decapitation machine named for him; it was first used on Apr. 25, 1792, to execute a highwayman.

28

Birthday of Jim (James Francis) Thorpe (May 28, 1888–Mar. 28, 1953). Native American (Sauk and Fox) athlete who won gold medals in the decathlon and pentathlon at the 1912 Olympics; one of the most accomplished all-around athletes in history. Apr. 16 is Jim Thorpe Day in Okla., a day of special school observance.

28

Freeing the Insects in Japan. On May 28, insects in tiny bamboo cages are bought and kept as tuneful pets for the summer; in late Aug. or early Sept., they are released to freedom.

HOLY DAYS AND FEAST DAYS

29

Ascension of Baha'u'llah in the Baha'i faith. A holy day, and Baha'is abstain from work. Commemorates the death on May 29, 1892, of Baha'u'llah ("Glory of God"), the great spiritual leader of Baha'i; observed at 3 A.M., the time of his death.

HOLIDAYS AND CIVIC DAYS

29

Ratification Day in R.I. On May 29, 1790, R.I. ratified the Constitution and entered the Union as the last of the original 13 states.

29

Wisconsin Day. Anniversary of Wis.'s admission as the 30th state of the Union on May 29, 1848.

ANNIVERSARIES AND SPECIAL EVENTS DAYS

29

Anniversary of the fall of Constantinople on May 29, 1453, to assault by Ottoman Turks; the formal end of the Byzantine Empire. Constantinople (or Byzantium, the older name; now Istanbul) was named the seat of the Eastern Roman Empire by the emperor Constantine I on May 11, 330.

29

Anniversary of the first successful ascent of Mt. Everest on May 29, 1953; the summit was reached at 11:30 A.M. by Edmund Hillary of New Zealand and the Nepali Sherpa Norkey Tenzing. Mt. Everest is the world's highest mountain (29,028 feet).

29

Birthday of Gilbert Keith Chesterton (May 29, 1874–June 14, 1936). English journalist, novelist, poet, and critic; creator of the fictional priest-detective Father Brown.

29

Birthday of Patrick Henry (May 29, 1736–June 6, 1799). American Revolutionary statesman and orator, famous for his speech of Mar. 23, 1777, for arming the Va. militia.

29

Birthday of Bob Hope (born Leslie Townes Hope; May 29, 1903–). English-born American comedian best known for his commitment to entertaining American military troops stationed abroad.

29

Birthday of John Fitzgerald Kennedy (May 29, 1917–Nov. 22, 1963). World War II hero; Mass. congressman and senator; author; 35th president of the U.S. (1961–63; Democrat); assassinated in Dallas, Tex. His administration captured the popular imagination during the height of American international power. Notable events included the Bay of Pigs operation, the Cuban Missile Crisis, the first major commitment of U.S. troops in Vietnam, the expansion of the space program, much social change, and the founding of the Peace Corps, which celebrates his birthday as Founder's Day. Buried in Arlington National Cemetery.

29

Birthday of Oswald Spengler (May 29, 1880–May 8, 1936). German historian; author of *The Decline of the West*.

29

Oak Apple Day. Also called Royal Oak Day or Nettle Day. Observed in parts of England in honor of King Charles II (May 29, 1630–Feb. 6, 1685; ruled 1660–85) on the anniversary of his restoration to the throne on May 29, 1660. He was saved from his pursuers in the Battle of Worcester (1651) by an oak apple tree. Formerly, wearing an oak leaf on this day was popular, as were maypole ceremonies.

HOLY DAYS AND FEAST DAYS

30

Feast of St. Joan of Arc (Jan. 6, 1412–May 30, 1431, burned at the stake). French peasant girl inspired by visions during the Hundred Years' War (1331–1453) to save Orleans, and all France, from the English by aiding the Dauphin, rousing her countrymen, and leading French troops in battle. Sold to the British and burned at the stake for heresy, witchcraft, and wearing men's attire. The French national heroine and the 2nd patron saint of France, after St. Denis. Honored in France with the *Fête de Jeanne d'Arc,* especially in Rouen and Orleans, with banners, garlands, and portraits of her. New Orleans (U.S.) celebrates on May 9, the anniversary of the 1429 rescue of Orleans, France. Her life is also commemorated on her birthday, or on May 16, the anniversary of the day when she was named a saint (1920).

HOLIDAYS AND CIVIC DAYS

30

Statehood Day in Croatia; official public holiday. Anniversary of the institution of Croatia's parliament on May 30, 1990. Independence was subsequently declared from the Yugoslav Union on June 25, 1991.

ANNIVERSARIES AND SPECIAL EVENTS DAYS

30

Anniversary of the dedication of the Hall of Fame for Great Americans on the campus of New York University, in New York City, on May 30, 1901.

30

Anniversary of the dedication on May 30, 1922, of the Lincoln Memorial, in Washington, D.C.; designed by Henry Bacon and housing the seated Lincoln statue by Daniel Chester French.

30

Birthday of Countee Cullen (May 30, 1903–Jan. 9, 1946). American poet; a leader of the Harlem Renaissance; author of *The Black Christ and Other Poems* and *The Ballad of the Brown Girl.*

HOLY DAYS AND FEAST DAYS

31

Feast of the Visitation. Commemorates the Virgin Mary's visit to her cousin Elizabeth following the Annunciation and before the birth of John the Baptist. The Magnificat, one of the few New Testament canticles, is recited.

HOLIDAYS AND CIVIC DAYS

31

Republic Day in South Africa; formerly an official public holiday. Also called Union Day. On May 31, 1961, the Republic of South Africa was established, severing its ties to the British Commonwealth. Also, on May 31, 1910, the Union of

South Africa was established, uniting the various South African colonies. And May 31, 1902, was the formal ending of the Boer War, which began on Oct. 12, 1899.

ANNIVERSARIES AND SPECIAL EVENTS DAYS

31
Birthday of Walt (Walter) Whitman (May 31, 1819–Mar. 26, 1892). American poet; author of the great elegy "When Lilacs Last in the Dooryard Bloom'd" and the famous *Leaves of Grass.* Known as the Good Gray Poet. Elected to the Hall of Fame for Great Americans.

31
Death anniversary of Tintoretto (born Jacopo Robusti; ca. 1518–May 31, 1594). Italian painter of the late Renaissance, famous for *The Last Supper.*

31
Johnstown Flood Day. Anniversary of the collapse of the Conemaugh Dam and the consequent flooding of Johnstown, Pa., on May 31, 1889, with 2,300 persons killed.

MOVABLE DAYS IN MAY

HOLY DAYS AND FEAST DAYS

MAY FLOWER FESTIVALS (FLORES DE MAYO) IN THE PHILIPPINES; all month, culminating on May 31. With flower festivals, processions, and balls in honor of the Virgin Mary, notably as Our Lady of Namacpacan (May 31).

ROSE FESTIVALS FOR THE VIRGIN MARY IN THE BASQUE AND CATALAN REGIONS OF SPAIN; 1st Sunday in May and other dates in May. Roses are blessed at dawn or dusk, and preserved to scent nighttime dreams. Some places hold joyful rose processions, with songs to the Virgin.

HOLIDAYS AND CIVIC DAYS

MAY DAY IN SOME COUNTRIES; 1st Monday in May; official public holiday. Also called International Labor Day. In the U.K.; recently created official public holiday (ca. 1980), replacing Whitmonday (Pentecost Monday).

LABOUR DAY IN QUEENSLAND AND MAY DAY IN NORTHERN TERRITORY, AUS-TRALIA; 1st Monday in May; official public holiday in both.

DISCOVERY DAY IN THE CAYMAN ISLANDS; 3rd Monday in May; official public holiday. Commemorates Columbus's arrival on May 10, 1503.

RATU SIR LALA SUKUNA DAY IN FIJI; last Monday in May; official public holiday. Honors Ratu Lala Sukuna (Apr. 22, 1888–May 30, 1958), Fiji's greatest modern-day statesman. Of chiefly lineage and extensive education; a highly decorated hero in World War I; thereafter a barrister and statesman, overseeing Fiji's progress toward independence.

SPRING BANK HOLIDAY IN THE U.K.; last Monday in May; official public holiday. A day of sports and picnics, and engagement in old customs such as the Lord Mayor's Parades in Oxford and London; cheese rolling at Cooper's Hill, Gloucestershire; and Morris dancing at Bampton, Oxfordshire.

ARMED FORCES DAY IN THE U.S.; 3rd Saturday in May. By presidential proclamation since 1950, to symbolize the 1947 unification of the various branches under the Department of Defense. Replaced Army Day, on Apr. 6 (which began in 1936). Military bases hold open house.

MEMORIAL DAY IN THE U.S.; last Monday in May; federal official public holiday. A day to honor and grieve for Americans who have died in the country's wars. Proclaimed annually by the president since 1948 as a day of prayer for permanent peace. An official public holiday in all states on this day. Impressive ceremonies include those at the Tomb of the Unknowns at Arlington National Cemetery and at Gettysburg, Pa., where schoolchildren strew flowers on the graves. All over, flags are flown at half-mast.

CONFEDERATE MEMORIAL DAY IN VARIOUS SOUTHERN STATES OF THE U.S., on varying dates (such as May 10 in the Carolinas); official public holiday in some states. Also called Decoration Day. Created, like national Memorial Day, to honor and grieve for the Civil War dead, friend and foe alike, by decorating their graves with flowers. Sometimes combined with Jefferson Davis's Birthday.

ANNIVERSARIES AND SPECIAL EVENTS DAYS

INTERNATIONAL MIGRATORY BIRD DAY; 2nd Saturday in May. Created to educate the public and gain attention regarding migratory birds and the preservation of their habitats in the U.S. and Central America. Began in 1993 in the U.S.; is becoming international.

INTERNATIONAL OPEN HOSTEL DAY; 1st Sunday in May. Youth hostels worldwide hold open house. The Youth Hostel movement began in Germany; the first hostel opened on Aug. 26, 1909. The first hostel in the U.S. was opened on Dec. 27, 1934, in Northfield, Mass., by Monroe and Isabel Smith.

INTERNATIONAL ORCHID AND TEXTILE FESTIVAL IN MEDELLÍN, COLOMBIA; last week in May and 1st week in June. The orchid capital of the world celebrates with corridas, art shows, street dances, and concerts.

OBERAMMERGAU PASSION PLAY (PASSIONSPIELE) IN OBERAMMERGAU, GERMANY; held every 10 years (1990, 2000, etc.), May–Sept. A passion play depicting Christ's agony and passion, produced and performed by a large portion of the whole community, in continuing fulfillment of a communal vow of 1633, made in thanks for relief from the black death.

WOMEN'S POETRY BEE IN HISONIN, KYOTO, JAPAN; 4th Sunday in May. Women in the dress of the Heian period reenact a game wherein they match 100 poems with the authors.

NATIONAL WINDMILL DAY IN THE NETHERLANDS; 2nd Saturday in May. As many windmills as possible (300–950) are set working on this day, as a national display.

BERGEN INTERNATIONAL FESTIVAL IN BERGEN, NORWAY; late May–early June. Norway's major cultural event, emphasizing music; in the hometown of Edvard Grieg, who sponsored the first festival in 1898; the modern version dates from 1952.

ROYAL SHRINE RITE (CHONGMYO TAEJE) IN SEOUL, SOUTH KOREA; 1st Sunday in May. The 27 kings and queens of the Yi dynasty (1392–1910) are honored in a colorful Confucian ceremony at the Chongmyo Royal Ancestral Shrines, by their descendants and the public.

SHEPHERDS' FESTIVAL IN RIPOLI (CATALONIA), SPAIN; 3rd Sunday in May. Shepherds in traditional costume drive in and shear their sheep, sell the wool, and hold a festival. The remnants of a fertility ritual—a wedding is held, either staged or actual. And in nearby Castellar de N'Hug, sheepdog trials are held on the last Sunday in Aug.

MOTHER'S DAY IN SWEDEN; last Monday in May. Festivities resemble a birthday celebration.

CHELSEA FLOWER SHOW IN LONDON; Tuesday–Friday, ending 4th Friday in May. Britain's premier flower show, with huge attendance.

FIRE SERVICE RECOGNITION DAY IN THE U.S. AND CANADA; 2nd Saturday in May. A day for citizens to visit their local fire stations and become acquainted with the firefighters, their equipment, and the services they provide the community.

MOTHER'S DAY IN THE U.S. AND CANADA; 2nd Sunday in May. The first Mother's Day was held in Philadelphia on May 10, 1908, following suggestions made by Julia Ward Howe in 1872 and Anna M. Jarvis in 1907. The day received national recognition on May 9, 1914, when President Wilson issued a proclamation asking American citizens to give a public expression of reverence to mothers. Carnations were made a symbol of the day, pink for a living mother and white in remembrance. Mother's Day is one of the most fervent American customs: long-distance phone use is exceptionally heavy.

NATIONAL DAY OF PRAYER IN THE U.S.; 1st Thursday in May. By presidential proclamation since 1981; began in 1957; until 1981, was in Oct.

TEACHER DAY IN THE U.S.; Tuesday of the 1st full week in May (Teacher Appreciation Week). Also called School Family Day. Sponsored by the National Education Association.

NATIONAL SPELLING BEE FINALS IN WASHINGTON, D.C.; Wednesday–Thursday after Memorial Day. A spelling contest for school-children.

INDIANAPOLIS 500 IN INDIANAPOLIS; Sunday before Memorial Day. The Indy 500 is a 500-mile automobile race, the "greatest spectacle in racing"; began in 1911.

KENTUCKY DERBY DAY IN LOUISVILLE, KY.; 1st Saturday in May. A day of horse racing at Churchill Downs. First held on May 17, 1875, and won by the horse Aristides. The first jewel in the Triple Crown, followed by the Preakness Stakes in Baltimore (2nd Saturday after the Derby), and the Belmont Stakes in New York (5th Saturday after the Derby). The Derby is a 1¼-mile race for 3-year-old Thoroughbreds. Derby Day is the climax of the 10-day Kentucky Derby Festival, featuring a steamboat race, parade, fireworks, concerts, and a ball.

EMMETT KELLY CLOWN FESTIVAL IN HOUSTON, MO.; 1st Friday–Sunday in May. A festival at the start of the circus season, with hundreds of clowns in Kelly's hometown. Saturday is the main day, Emmett Kelly Day, in honor of Emmet Kelly Sr. (Dec. 9, 1899–Mar. 28, 1979), American clown, inventor of Weary Willy the hobo clown, the only original American clown type, and in his lifetime the most famous clown in the world. Festival began in 1988.

WORLD SERIES OF POKER IN LAS VEGAS, NEV.; Monday–Thursday after Mother's Day. At Binion's Horseshoe casino. The game is Texas Hold 'Em; the buy-in is $10,000; the 1st-place prize is $1 million. Follows several weeks of lead-up contests.

PORTLAND ROSE FESTIVAL IN PORT-LAND, OREG.; 25 days, beginning the Thursday after Memorial Day. A world-class festival celebrating Portland's roses; extremely large attendance. Held since June 20, 1907 (its forerunner began in 1888). Features numerous events, notably the queen's coronation (1st Thursday), the rose show (2nd Thursday–Friday), and the grand floral parade (2nd Saturday). Portland has been known as the City of Roses since the early-19th century.

MEMPHIS KEMET JUBILEE IN MEMPHIS, TENN. Formerly the Cotton Makers' Jubilee. Grand Jubilee Parade on 1st Saturday in May. The Jubilee proper lasts about 2 weeks, with related events spanning several months. Began in 1936, to salute workers in the cotton industry, and in reaction to the exclusiveness of the Cotton Carnival. Includes the largest multiracial parade in the U.S., with many high-school bands from Memphis and the Southeast.

MEMPHIS IN MAY INTERNATIONAL FESTIVAL IN MEMPHIS, TENN.; all month, especially on weekends. Salutes a different country each year, with many events and displays intended to educate and entertain Memphians.

OLE TIME FIDDLERS' AND BLUEGRASS FESTIVAL IN UNION GROVE, VA.; Memorial Day weekend. A convention of serious traditional fiddlers and other musicians; audience is limited to 5,000.

June

June, the 6th month in the Gregorian calendar, was named according to legend for Juno, the goddess of women and of marriage. If this is true, it is an appropriate name, since June is a favored month for weddings. Some authorities, however, claim that the month was named for the *Juniores,* the lower branch of the Roman senate, or that it was associated with the consulate of Junius Brutus.

Many traditional events are associated with the month of June. Among the most famous are the great flower festivals of the world. June has long been commencement time, when students graduate from schools and colleges. It is also the month when the British celebrate the official, not the actual, birthday of Queen Elizabeth, scheduled to assure more favorable weather for the public ceremonies. The most ancient of June festivals are those associated with Midsummer Eve, in which bonfires have been added to the merrymaking and festivities from time immemorial.

June is Dairy Month in the U.S.

The special flower for the month of June is the rose, and the gems are the moonstone, the pearl, and the alexandrite.

HOLY DAYS AND FEAST DAYS

1

Pilgrimage season begins (ends Aug. 15) at St. Patrick's Purgatory, on the island of Lough Derg (County Donegal), Ireland. St. Patrick fasted here for 40 days; a pilgrimage center from medieval times, and still extremely popular; exercises last 3 days, with partial fasting; the only modern pilgrimage conducted as in medieval times.

1

Feast of St. Justin Martyr (ca. 100–ca. 165). Greek-born philosopher, martyred in Rome. One of the first Christian apologists. Patron saint of philosophers. Orth.: June 1 or 14.

HOLIDAYS AND CIVIC DAYS

1

Madaraka Day in Kenya; official public holiday. Commemorates the attainment of internal autonomy and self-government on June 1, 1963. *Madaraka* means "autonomy" or "self-rule" in Swahili.

1

Statehood Day in Ky. On June 1, 1792, Ky. was admitted as the 15th state of the Union. Observed with many festivals and ceremonies.

1

Statehood Day in Tenn. Historical day commemorating Tenn.'s admission as the 16th state on June 1, 1796.

1

Independence Day in Western Samoa; official public holiday on June 1–3. Celebrates independence attained from New Zealand on Jan. 1, 1962. Observed in June to avoid the Jan. rains.

ANNIVERSARIES AND SPECIAL EVENTS DAYS

1

Birthday of Carl von Clausewitz (June 1, 1780–Nov. 16, 1831). Prussian general and military theorist, whose *Vom Kriege (On War)* (1833) has been of immense influence on generations of military planners and frontline officers.

1

Birthday of Philip Kearny (June 1, 1814–Sept. 1, 1862). American general; leader of the New Jersey Volunteers in the Civil War. Represents N.J. in Statuary Hall.

1

Birthday of Jacques Marquette (June 1, 1637–May 18, 1675). French Jesuit missionary and explorer of the territory of the Wisconsin, Mississippi, and Illinois Rivers. Represents Wis. in Statuary Hall.

1

Birthday of John Masefield (June 1, 1878–May 12, 1967). English poet; British poet laureate; noted for poems of the sea such as *Salt Water Ballads;* awarded the Order of Merit in 1935.

1

Birthday of Marilyn Monroe (born Norma Jean Mortenson; June 1, 1926–Aug. 5, 1962). American actress and sex symbol of the 1950s. Films include *Gentlemen Prefer Blondes* (1953) and *Some Like It Hot* (1959).

1

Birthday of Brigham Young (June 1, 1801–Aug. 29, 1877). American Mormon leader; president of the Mormon Church; founder of Salt Lake City, Utah.

1

Mint Julep Day at Oxford University, England. Commemorates June 1, 1845, when mint juleps were introduced to New College, Oxford, by William Trapier of S.C.; a festival day that has continued through the years with the use of Trapier's own recipe.

HOLIDAYS AND CIVIC DAYS

2

Coronation Day in Bhutan; official public holiday. Anniversary of the June 2, 1974, formal coronation of the 4th king of Bhutan, Druk Gyalpo Jigme Singye Wangchuck.

2

Republic Day in Italy. Commemorates the proclamation of the republic established by the referendum of June 2, 1946. A majority vote was cast for a republic as opposed to retention of the monarchy.

ANNIVERSARIES AND SPECIAL EVENTS DAYS

2

Birthday of Thomas Hardy (June 2, 1840–Jan. 11, 1928). English novelist and poet; wrote *The Return of the Native.*

ANNIVERSARIES AND SPECIAL EVENTS DAYS

3

Anniversary of the Battle of Midway, June 3–6, 1942. Brilliant American campaign that shattered the Japanese fleet and turned the tide of World War II in the Pacific.

3

Death anniversary of Pope John XXIII (born Angelo Giuseppe Roncalli; Nov. 25, 1881–June 3, 1963; ruled 1958–63). One of the most important of all popes, and greatly loved; inaugurated a new era in the Roman Catholic Church by his openness to change and especially by convening the Second Vatican Council; wrote *Pacem in Terris* and other important encyclicals.

3

Jefferson Davis Day. Anniversary of the birth of Jefferson Davis (June 3, 1808–Dec. 6, 1889), American soldier, senator, and statesman; president of the Confederate States of America (1861–65). Deprived of his citizenship after the Civil War. (President Jimmy Carter posthumously restored it.) Represents Miss. in Statuary Hall. At Arlington National Cemetery in Va., Confederate Memorial Services are held on the Sunday nearest June 3. And in Richmond, Va., the Massing of the Flags is held at the Jefferson Davis Monument. His birthday is observed in some southern states, usually on June 3, and sometimes as Confederate Memorial Day.

HOLIDAYS AND CIVIC DAYS

4

Flag Day in Finland. Also called Mannerheim's Day. Occurs on the birth of Carl Gustav Mannerheim (June 4, 1867–Jan. 27, 1951) and the anniversary of his promotion to general. Mannerheim led Finland's military campaign for independence from Russia and the heroic Winter War against Russia (1940) in World War II; he was also active with the International Red Cross.

4

Imam Khomeini's Memorial Day in Iran; official public holiday. Anniversary of the death of Ayatollah Ruhollah Khomeini (ca. Oct. 15, 1900–June 3, 1989), Iranian Muslim Shiite religious leader who led the Islamic Revolution against the government of the shah, and thereafter headed the strict government of Iran from 1979 until his death.

ANNIVERSARIES AND SPECIAL EVENTS DAYS

4

Birthday of George III, King of England and the U.K. (June 4, 1738–Jan 29, 1820). During his reign, the American Revolution occurred.

4

Chinese Human Rights Day. Anniversary of the Tiananmen Square Massacre of June 4, 1989, in Beijing, China. Student demonstrations for democracy began on Apr. 22. In the early morning of June 4, with 100,000 protesters gathered in the square, Red Army troops and tanks attacked, killing 5,000 and wounding 10,000. Many thousands more were imprisoned.

HOLY DAYS AND FEAST DAYS

5

Feast of St. Boniface (ca. 680–June 5, 754). English missionary to pagan Germany; called the Apostle of Germany.

HOLIDAYS AND CIVIC DAYS

5

Constitution Day in Denmark; official public holiday. Commemorates the constitution signed on June 5, 1849, and the new constitution adopted on June 5, 1953.

5

Fifteenth of Khordad in Iran; official public holiday. Commemorates the deaths of Islamic cleric-scholars in Qom on June 5, 1963, in a clash between the shah's forces and his opponents.

ANNIVERSARIES AND SPECIAL EVENTS DAYS

5

Anniversary of the introduction of the Baha'i religion into the U.S. On June 5, 1894, the first formal classes on Baha'i were held in Chicago, leading to the founding of the Baha'i National Spiritual Assembly in the U.S.

5

Anniversary of the shooting of Senator Robert F. Kennedy, brother of the assassinated President John F. Kennedy, on June 5, 1968, while he was campaigning for the Democratic presidential nomi-

nation in Los Angeles, by Sirhan Sirhan; Kennedy died the next day.

5

Anniversary of the beginning of the Six-Day War, June 5–10, 1967, between Israel and the forces of Egypt, Syria, and Jordan. The Suez Canal was closed until June 5, 1975.

5

Baptismal day of Adam Smith (baptized June 5, 1723–July 17, 1790). Scottish economist and philosopher celebrated for his *Inquiry into the Nature and Causes of the Wealth of Nations*.

5

Birthday of John Couch Adams (June 5, 1819–Jan. 21, 1892). English astronomer who first observed the planet Neptune on Sept. 23, 1846. The Adams Prize, awarded biannually at Cambridge University, commemorates his discovery.

5

Birthday of Jabez Lamar Monroe Curry (June 5, 1825–Feb. 12, 1903). American educator and statesman; president of the Southern Educational Board; founder of grade schools and normal schools throughout the South. Represents Ala. in Statuary Hall.

5

Birthday of Federico García Lorca (June 5, 1898–ca. Aug. 19, 1936). Spain's greatest poet and playwright since the country's golden age; wrote *Gypsy Ballads* and *Blood Wedding*; murdered by the Nationalists during the Spanish Civil War.

5

Birthday of John Maynard Keynes (June 5, 1883–Apr. 21, 1946). English economist of great international influence. A pioneer in the development of modern economics, he contended that government policies could maintain high levels of employment and economic activity.

5

World Environment Day. A day to focus attention on the environment and humanity's place in it; established by resolution at the June 1972 Stockholm Conference on the Human Environment.

HOLY DAYS AND FEAST DAYS

6

Feast of St. Norbert (ca. 1080–June 6, 1134). Prussian nobleman, monk, and itinerant preacher in France. Initiated the institution of lay brothers.

HOLIDAYS AND CIVIC DAYS

6

Memorial Day in South Korea; official public holiday. Honors the victims of war with memorial services at the National Cemetery in Seoul.

6

Anniversary of D Day, June 6, 1944, when the Allies, under the command of General Dwight Eisenhower, began their invasion of Europe by landing in Normandy. A pivotal event of World War II.

ANNIVERSARIES AND SPECIAL EVENTS DAYS

6

Birthday of Pierre Corneille (June 6, 1606–Oct. 1, 1684). French dramatist whose classical verse tragedies, such as *Le Cid,* are frequently revived.

6

Birthday of Nathan Hale (June 6, 1755–Sept. 22, 1776). American soldier, known as the Martyr Spy of the American Revolution; hanged for espionage.

6

Birthday of Thomas Mann (June 6, 1875–Aug. 12, 1955). German novelist famous for *Buddenbrooks,* for 4 novels about the biblical Joseph, and for *The Magic Mountain;* awarded the Nobel Prize in literature in 1929.

6

Birthday of Aleksandr Sergeyevich Pushkin (June 6, 1799–Feb. 10, 1837). Russian poet frequently called the Founder of Russian Literature. Noted for his poetic range; other works include the drama *Boris Godunov* (1831) and the novel *Eugene Onegin* (1833).

CA. 6

Annual Sibelius Festival in Helsinki, Finland; on or near June 6. Honors Finland's greatest composer.

6

YMCA Founding Day. Anniversary of the founding of the Young Men's Christian Association on June 6, 1844, by George Williams of London. The YMCA spread over the globe in the 20th century.

ANNIVERSARIES AND SPECIAL EVENTS DAYS

7

Anniversary of the destruction of Port Royal, Jamaica, by earthquake, on June 7, 1692. Port Royal was a notorious pirate den, called "the wickedest city on earth."

7

Birthday of Susan Elizabeth Blow (June 7, 1843–Mar. 26, 1916). American educator who pioneered in the establishment of public kindergartens and training schools for kindergarten teachers; called the Mother of the Kindergarten in the Public Schools of the U.S.

7

Birthday of Paul Gauguin (June 7, 1848–May 8, 1903). French painter and author who described his life in Tahiti in his *Noa Noa* and *Intimate Journals.*

7

Boone Day. Anniversary of June 7, 1769, when Daniel Boone, the great frontiersman, reportedly first saw the forests and woodlands of present-day Ky.; observed annually by the Kentucky Historical Society.

ANNIVERSARIES AND SPECIAL EVENTS DAYS

8

Birthday of Frank Lloyd Wright (June 8, 1867–Apr. 9, 1959). American architect of enormous influence; famous for the Imperial Hotel in Japan, the Solomon R. Guggenheim Museum in New York City, and other buildings. Wright established the Taliesin Fellowship for experimentation in the arts.

8

Birthday of Marguerite Yourcenar (born Marguerite de Crayencour; June 8, 1903–Dec. 17, 1987). French-American classicist, author, and translator; wrote *Memoirs of Hadrian;* first woman elected to the French Academy (1980).

8

Death anniversary of Muhammad (ca. 570–June 8, 632). Arabian founder and prophet of Islam.

HOLY DAYS AND FEAST DAYS

9

Feast of St. Columba (521–June 9, 597). Irish monk; founder of monasteries in Ireland and Scotland, especially Iona in the Hebrides (ca. 563), which became the greatest monastery in Christendom, sending missionaries throughout Europe. A man of enormous influence. A patron saint of Ireland.

9

Feast of St. Ephraim (4th century). Called the Sweet-Singer, the Melodist. Syrian known for his writings and for the introduction of hymns in public worship; creator of the Nisibeian hymns and canticles. Doctor of the church. Orth.: Jan. 28 or Feb. 10.

HOLIDAYS AND CIVIC DAYS

9

Accession Day in Jordan; official public holiday. Commemorates the accession to the throne of King Abdullah II on June 9, 1999, following the death of his father, King Hussein.

ANNIVERSARIES AND SPECIAL EVENTS DAYS

9

Birthday of the cartoon character Donald Duck (June 9, 1934–). Created by Walt Disney.

9

Birthday of Luis Kutner (June 9, 1908–Mar. 1, 1993). American human rights attorney, responsible for the release of many unjustly confined prisoners; author of the living will; founded World Habeas Corpus; nominated 9 times for the Nobel Peace Prize.

9

Birthday of Carl Nielsen (June 9, 1865–Oct. 3, 1931). Danish composer.

9

Birthday of George Stephenson (June 9, 1781–Aug. 12, 1848). English inventor who perfected the locomotive.

9

Birthday of Sylvanus Thayer (June 9, 1785–Sept. 7, 1872). American soldier, and outstanding Superintendent (1817–33) of the U.S. Military Academy at West Point, N.Y.; transformed the Academy into the nation's first engineering school and was of profound and beneficial influence on education in the 19th-century U.S. Elected to the Hall of Fame for Great Americans as the Father of Technology in the U.S. The West Point Sylvanus Thayer Award is presented annually in his name.

HOLIDAYS AND CIVIC DAYS

10

Day of National Reconciliation in Congo (Congo-Brazzaville); official public holiday. A day to reaffirm the principles of peaceful multiparty democracy. June 10, 1991, was the final day of an official conference by Congo's political groups that formalized this aspiration.

10

Arab Renaissance Day in Jordan; official public holiday. Also called Army Day. Commemorates the Great Arab Revolt of June 10, 1916, which led to independence from the Ottoman Empire.

10

Camões Day; official public holiday in Portugal and in Macau (as Portugal Communities Day). Also called Portugal Day. Anniversary of the death of Portugal's immortal national poet, Luiz Vaz de Camões (or Camoëns; ca. 1524–June 10, 1580); famous for the *Lusiad*. A festal day in Portugal and its territories.

ANNIVERSARIES AND SPECIAL EVENTS DAYS

10

Anniversary of the establishment of Alcoholics Anonymous, founded by William G. Wilson and Dr. Robert Smith in Akron, Ohio, on June 10, 1935.

10

Anniversary of the establishment of the first mint in the future U.S. On June 10, 1652, the silversmith John Hull opened a mint in defiance of British colonial law, and issued coins for 30 years.

10

Anniversary of the Salem Witch Trials in Salem, Mass. Beginning on Jan. 20, 1692, the testimony of a few young girls provoked hysterical fear of witches among the people of Salem. The first execution of a woman accused of witchcraft occurred on June 10, when Bridget Bishop was hanged; 20 people were executed.

10

Anniversary of the declaration of war by Tripoli on June 10, 1801, against the U.S., which refused to pay additional tribute to the Arab corsairs (the Barbary pirates) at Tripoli, Algiers, and Tunis. The 3 cities were defeated in land and sea campaigns, and sued for peace on June 4, 1805.

10

Death anniversary of Alexander the Great (356 B.C.–ca. June 10, 323 B.C.). Alexander III of Macedon, son of Philip. Macedonian king, outstanding general, and effective visionary, who created a short-lived empire of great expanse and enduring subsequent influence.

10

Lidice Day in the Czech Republic. Anniversary of the razing of the village of Lidice and the massacre of its people by the Nazis on June 10, 1942, in revenge for the assassination of Reinhard Heydrich by Czech agents of the Allies. Under the communists, this was a very important day, at least in the press; now Lidice is the venue for the International Children's Exhibition of Fine Arts, on a date linked to June 10, in memory of the village's murdered children.

HOLY DAYS AND FEAST DAYS

11

Feast of St. Barnabas (1st century). Disciple of St. Paul; by tradition the founder of the Cypriot Church. Orth.: Bartholomew and Barnabas, June 11 or 24.

HOLIDAYS AND CIVIC DAYS

11

American Bases Evacuation Day in Libya; official public holiday. Commemorates the closing of U.S. facilities at Wheeling Air Force Base near Tripoli on June 11, 1970.

11

King Kamehameha Day in Hawaii; official public holiday. Celebrates with many festivities the victories and achievements of King Kamehameha I (1758–1819; ruled 1795–1819), who unified the Hawaiian Islands.

ANNIVERSARIES AND SPECIAL EVENTS DAYS

11

Birthday of Jacques-Yves Cousteau (June 11, 1910–June 25, 1997). French marine scientist, explorer, filmmaker, and environmentalist; coinventor of the Aqua-Lung and inventor of other underwater devices.

11

Birthday of Ben Jonson (ca. June 11, 1572–Aug. 6, 1637). English playwright and poet famous for *Valpone* and other important plays of the Elizabethan and Jacobean periods.

11

Birthday of Vince (Vincent Thomas) Lombardi (June 11, 1913–Sept. 3, 1970). American football coach for the Green Bay Packers, 1959–67; a national symbol of single-minded determination to win.

11

Birthday of Jeannette Rankin (June 11, 1880–May 18, 1973). American pacifist, crusader for social and electoral reform, and first woman member of Congress, representing Mont. (1917–19, 1941–43).

HOLIDAYS AND CIVIC DAYS

12

Helsinki Day in Finland. Celebrates the founding of the city in 1550; observed since 1959.

12

Independence Day in the Philippines; official public holiday. Celebrates the June 12, 1898, declaration of independence from Spain and of the first Philippine Republic by Emilio Aguinaldo (1869–1964).

12

Independence Day in Russia; official public holiday. Commemorates the presidential inauguration of Boris Yeltsin on June 12, 1991, and the end of communist totalitarian government.

ANNIVERSARIES AND SPECIAL EVENTS DAYS

12

Anniversary of the volcanic eruption of Mt. Pinatubo, in Luzon, Philippines. Eruptions began June 12, 1991; main activity was June 14–16. Damage was massive, and worldwide weather patterns were extensively disrupted.

12

Birthday of George Herbert Walker Bush (June 12, 1924–). Naval pilot in World War II; oil company executive; Tex. congressman; ambassador; CIA director; vice president; 41st president of the U.S. (1989–93; Republican). His administration continued President Ronald Reagan's policies; it was notable for the Gulf War, following Iraq's invasion of Kuwait.

12

Birthday of Anne Frank (June 12, 1929–ca. Mar. 1945). German-Dutch adolescent of sensitivity and talent whose diary of 2 years of hiding from the Nazis was published under the title *The Diary of a Young Girl*; the exact date of her death in a concentration camp is unknown.

12

Birthday of Charles Kingsley (June 12, 1819–Jan. 23, 1875). English clergyman, novelist, and poet remembered for the novels *Westward Ho!* and *Hereward the Wake*.

HOLY DAYS AND FEAST DAYS

13

Feast of St. Anthony of Padua (1195–June 13, 1231). Lisbon-born Portuguese Franciscan friar; one of the greatest preachers of all time, and much beloved; a doctor of the church. Patron saint of poor people and oppressed people, and invoked for the return of lost articles. In Latin countries, the patron saint of lovers. Unofficial patron saint of Lisbon.

HOLIDAYS AND CIVIC DAYS

13

Malvinas Day in Argentina. Commemorates the Falklands War between Argentina and the U.K. for control of the Falkland Islands (in Argentina, called Las Malvinas), and specifically the final battle for Stanley on June 10–13, 1982.

ANNIVERSARIES AND SPECIAL EVENTS DAYS

13

Birthday of William Butler Yeats (June 13, 1865–Jan. 29, 1939). Irish poet, dramatist, and leader of the Irish literary revival; received the Nobel Prize in literature in 1923.

HOLIDAYS AND CIVIC DAYS

14

Liberation Day in the Falkland Islands; official public holiday. Commemorates June 14, 1982, when British troops liberated Stanley and ended the war between Argentina and the U.K. over possession of the Falkland/Malvinas Islands.

14

Freedom Day in Malawi; official public holiday. Celebrates the free elections of June 14, 1994, and the end of Kamuzu's rule.

14

Flag Day in the U.S. Commemorates the adoption of the Stars and Stripes by the Continental Congress on June 14, 1777, replacing the Grand Union Flag. Flag Day was established in perpetuity by presidential proclamation in 1916; reproclaimed annually since 1941; made official in 1949. Flag Week, Sunday–Saturday, contains June 14. Flag Day is a day for the display of the flag on public buildings and homes, and for special programs.

ANNIVERSARIES AND SPECIAL EVENTS DAYS

14

Anniversary of the first presentation of the Caldecott Medal. Awarded annually to the artist of the most distinguished picture book for children published in the U.S. during the preceding year; first presented on June 14, 1938, to Dorothy P. Lathrop for *Animals of the Bible*. The award is made by the American Library Association at its annual conference in the summer.

14

Anniversary of the founding of the Canadian Library Association, or the Association Canadienne des Bibliothèques, on June 14, 1946.

14

Anniversary of June 14, 1954, the day when the pledge of allegiance to the flag of the U.S. was amended by Congress and approved by President Dwight D. Eisenhower to add the words "under God," so that the last line of the pledge now reads "One Nation under God indivisible, with liberty and justice for all." The original version of the pledge was composed by Francis Bellamy and published in the *Youth's Companion* for Sept. 8, 1892.

14

Birthday of Che Guevara (Ernesto Guevara de la Serna; June 14, 1928–Oct. 1967). Cuban theoretician and tactician of guerrilla warfare, deeply involved in the Cuban revolution that overthrew the Batista regime, and in other guerrilla wars; later killed by the Bolivian military while attempting to stimulate revolution in Bolivia.

14

Birthday of Robert Marion La Follette Sr. (June 14, 1855–June 18, 1925). American statesman, reform leader, presidential candidate for the Progressive Party; exponent of the "Wisconsin Idea." Represents Wis. in Statuary Hall. His birthday is a day of special school observance in Wis.

14

Birthday of Harriet Beecher Stowe (June 14, 1811–July 1, 1896). American novelist and humanitarian; author of *Uncle Tom's Cabin* (1852), the best-selling novel of the 19th-century U.S. Elected to the Hall of Fame for Great Americans.

14

Remembrance Day in Estonia and Latvia. Commemorates the mass deportations of Estonians and Latvians to Siberia in 1941, under Joseph Stalin.

HOLIDAYS AND CIVIC DAYS

15

Valdemar's Day in Denmark. Also called Flag Day. Commemorates the victory of King Valdemar's troops on June 15, 1219, over the Estonians. According to lore, the Danish flag miraculously floated down from heaven on this day. Observed nationwide: flags fly everywhere, and pageants recreate the original events.

15

Arkansas Admission Day. Anniversary of Ark.'s admission to the Union as the 25th state on June 15, 1836.

ANNIVERSARIES AND SPECIAL EVENTS DAYS

15

Anniversary of the Declaration of Rights by Malta in 1802. After the Napoleonic Wars, the Maltese requested that the U.K.'s king become theirs, but they formally denied the U.K. the right to later transfer possession of Malta to any but themselves.

15

Anniversary of Ben Franklin's kite experiment. On June 15, 1752 (traditional date), Benjamin Franklin, flying a special kite in a thunderstorm, proved that lightning is electricity. He subsequently invented the lightning rod.

15

Birthday of Edvard Grieg (June 15, 1843–Sept. 4, 1907). Norwegian composer who established a new musical image for his country; composed the *Peer Gynt* suites and arrangements of songs and Norwegian dances; commemorated annually in the country by Grieg music festivals.

15

Farmer's Day in South Korea. The formal day to transplant rice seedlings. Farmers celebrate with dances and music while they labor through a long day.

15

Magna Carta Day. Anniversary of June 15, 1215, when the English barons forced King John to sign the Magna Carta, at Runnymede; the first charter of English liberties and a central document in the history of human freedom.

15

Native American Citizenship Day. Also called Indian Citizenship Day. Anniversary of the passage of a law by the U.S. Congress on June 15, 1924, recognizing the citizenship of Native Americans.

15

Oregon Treaty Day. Anniversary of the signing of the Oregon Treaty on June 15, 1846, between the U.S. and the U.K., to fix the northwest boundary at the 49th parallel extending to the Pacific.

ANNIVERSARIES AND SPECIAL EVENTS DAYS

16

Bloomsday. A day of appreciation of James Joyce that attracts scholars and admirers to gatherings in Dublin, Ireland; a commemorative day recalling the June 16, 1904, events associated with Leopold Bloom, a major character in Joyce's *Ulysses*.

16

Marie Laveau Day in the U.S. Anniversary of the death on June 16, 1881, of Marie Laveau, aged by varying reports 70–103 years. Laveau was an extraordinary Voodooienne, called the Voodoo Queen of New Orleans.

HOLIDAYS AND CIVIC DAYS

17

National Day in Iceland; official public holiday. Celebrates the declaration of full independence from Denmark on June 17, 1944; the day was chosen to coincide with the birthday of Jón Sigurdsson (June 17, 1811–Dec. 7, 1879), the original leader of the struggle, and a scholar of high repute. In Reykjavik, celebrated with parades, street theater, and music.

17

Bunker Hill Day in Boston and Suffolk County, Mass.; local official public holiday. Commemorates the June 17, 1775, Battle of Bunker Hill (actually fought on Breed's Hill), an early, heroic, heart-lifting victory of the Revolutionary War.

Celebrated in Boston with commemorative services, parades, exhibitions, and dinners.

ANNIVERSARIES AND SPECIAL EVENTS DAYS

17

Birthday of Charles Gounod (June 17, 1818–Oct. 18, 1893). French composer whose Marguerite in the opera *Faust* was the first operatic role for a lyric soprano.

17

Birthday of James Weldon Johnson (June 17, 1871–June 26, 1938). American poet and anthologist; first African American to be admitted to the Fla. bar; a founder and the secretary of the National Association for the Advancement of Colored People; awarded the Spingarn Medal.

17

Birthday of Igor Fyodorovich Stravinsky (June 17, 1882–Apr. 6, 1971). Russian-born American composer of ballets, chamber music, concertos, and orchestral works; his best-known ballets include the *Firebird* and the *Rite of Spring*.

17

Birthday of John Wesley (June 17, 1703–Mar. 2, 1791). English evangelical preacher; founder of Methodism; influential leader in the 18th-century revival movement in North America.

17

Watergate Day in the U.S. Anniversary of the June 17, 1972, break-in at the Democratic Party headquarters in the Watergate complex in Washington, D.C., by operatives of the Nixon administration; they were arrested in the act, leading to revelations of widespread political espionage and other illegalities, and resulting in the resignation of President Richard M. Nixon.

ANNIVERSARIES AND SPECIAL EVENTS DAYS

18

Anniversary of the adoption of the Library Bill of Rights by the Council of the American Library Association on June 18, 1948.

18

Birthday of Henry Clay Folger (June 18, 1857–June 11, 1930). American industrialist; collector of Shakespeareana, bequeathed to the American people and now housed in the Folger Shakespeare Library in Washington, D.C.

18

Evacuation Day in Egypt. Commemorates the 1956 departure of the last of the British occupation troops from their Suez Canal bases.

18

Night of the Droplet in Egypt; on the night of June 17–18. By tradition, on this night, the annual Nile flood begins, with a single droplet of rain; celebrated since pharaonic times.

18

War of 1812 Declaration Day. Anniversary of the June 18, 1812, declaration by Congress of war with Great Britain; a war resulting from Britain's violation of American rights on the high seas, and other causes. The war ended with the Treaty of Ghent, Dec. 24, 1814.

18

Waterloo Day. Anniversary of the Battle of Waterloo, lost by Napoleon in 1815, finally ending the Napoleonic Wars. Napoleon was defeated by the Duke of Wellington (U.K.) and General Gebhard Leberecht von Blücher (Prussia).

HOLIDAYS AND CIVIC DAYS

19

Artigas Day in Uruguay; official public holiday. Honors General José Gervasio Artigas (June 19, 1764–Sept. 23, 1850), the father of Uruguayan independence from Spain, Portugal, Brazil, Argentina, and all other countries.

19

Juneteenth in the U.S.; official public holiday and school holiday in Tex., where it's called Emancipation Day. Commemorates June 19, 1865, when slaves in Tex. were finally told of the Emancipation Proclamation by General Gordon Granger. Long celebrated mainly in African American communities in Tex. and throughout the South, with homecomings, picnics, parades, and baseball games, often on the nearer weekend.

ANNIVERSARIES AND SPECIAL EVENTS DAYS

19

Birthday of John Barrow (June 19, 1764–Nov. 23, 1848). English geographer; chief founder of the Royal Geographical Society in 1830.

19

Birthday of Blaise Pascal (June 19, 1623–Aug. 19, 1662). French philosopher, mathematician, and scientist whose work on the pressure of liquids resulted in Pascal's law. His religious thought, which emphasizes "reasons of the heart," is expressed in his *Pensées*.

HOLIDAYS AND CIVIC DAYS

CA. 20

Flag Day (*Día de la Bandera*) in Argentina; official public holiday. Death anniversary of Manuel Belgrano (June 3, 1770–June 20, 1820), designer of the Argentine flag; the flag was first unfurled ca. 1812. Flag Week, which climaxes on June 20, is held in his hometown, Rosario, where there is a huge monument to the flag.

20

Martyrs' Day in Eritrea; official public holiday. Commemorates the country's martyrs for independence.

20

West Virginia Day; official public holiday. Anniversary of W.Va.'s admission to the Union as the 35th state on June 20, 1863; it seceded from Va. during the Civil War, as an antislave state, but separatism had been a strong sentiment even at the founding of the Union. Marked by ceremonies, and the occasion for various festivals.

ANNIVERSARIES AND SPECIAL EVENTS DAYS

20

Anniversary of the Continental Congress's approval of the Great Seal of the U.S. on June 20, 1782. The project was the work of a committee of Benjamin Franklin, John Adams, and Thomas Jefferson, appointed by the Continental Congress on July 4, 1776, to devise a seal; William Barton designed the obverse, and Charles Thompson designed the reverse. The seal, which adorns the back of the 1-dollar bill, shows an American bald eagle with a ribbon in its mouth bearing the legend *E pluribus unum* ("One out of many") and bearing in its talons the arrows of war and the olive branch of peace; on the reverse is an unfinished pyramid with the eye of Providence above it and the legends *Annuit Cœptis* ("He has favored our undertakings") and *Novus Ordo Seclorum* ("A new order of the ages"). Today is also Bald Eagle Day.

20

Anniversary of the establishment of the Lifesaving Medal of the U.S., awarded by the Treasury Department, authorized by Act of Congress on June 20, 1874. The first award was presented to Lucian M. Clemons, keeper of the U.S. Lifesaving Service Station, on June 19, 1876, for saving the men of the schooner *Consuelo* on May 1, 1875.

20

Birthday of Adam Ferguson (June 20, 1723–Feb. 22, 1816). Scottish philosopher of the "common sense" school, historian, and patriot. The forefather of modern sociology.

HOLY DAYS AND FEAST DAYS

21

Feast of St. Aloysius Gonzaga (Mar. 9, 1568–June 21, 1591). Italian Jesuit priest; teacher of catechism to poor people and provider of aid to plague victims; patron saint of young students and of Catholic youth.

HOLIDAYS AND CIVIC DAYS

21

Admission Day in N.H. On June 21, 1788, N.H. ratified the Constitution and entered the Union as the 9th of the original 13 states.

ANNIVERSARIES AND SPECIAL EVENTS DAYS

21

Birthday of Daniel Carter Beard (June 21, 1850–June 11, 1941). American naturalist, writer, and illustrator; pioneering spirit of the Boy Scouts of America.

21

Birthday of Rockwell Kent (June 21, 1782–Mar. 13, 1971). American painter and illustrator of the American scene; one of the most popular artists of the first half of the 20th century.

CA. 21

The summer solstice in the Northern Hemisphere usually occurs on June 21. On the summer solstice, the sun rises and sets at its northernmost extreme. On this day in the Northern Hemisphere, the period of daylight is at its longest of the year. (There is also a winter solstice; *see* Dec. 22.) In the Southern Hemisphere, the summer solstice occurs ca. Dec. 22, and the winter solstice ca. June 21.

Called *Hsia Chih* in the Chinese calendar and *Doan-Ngu* in Vietnam, where it is regarded as an unhealthy time of epidemics and the God of Death is propitiated.

White Nights in St. Petersburg, Russia, occur ca. June 21–29. The night sky is pearly, even at midnight, and the city's pastel buildings are especially beautiful; celebrated with ballet and folk dancing, also concerts and theater.

HOLY DAYS AND FEAST DAYS

22

Feast of St. Thomas More (Feb. 6, 1478–July 6, 1535). English lawyer, humanist, and statesman, author of *Utopia* (1515–16); martyred under King Henry VIII. Patron saint of lawyers. A medal is presented annually in his name by the Thomas More Association for the most distinguished contribution to Catholic publishing during the year.

HOLIDAYS AND CIVIC DAYS

22

Antifascist Struggle Commemoration Day in Croatia; official public holiday. Anniversary of an uprising against fascist invaders on June 22, 1941.

CA. 22

Organic Act Day in the U.S. Virgin Islands; 3rd Monday in June; official public holiday. Commemorates the Organic Act of June 22, 1936, wherein the U.S. conferred a constitution to the islands, and the Revised Organic Act of June 22, 1954.

ANNIVERSARIES AND SPECIAL EVENTS DAYS

22

Anniversary of the presidential signing of the G.I. Bill of Rights on June 22, 1944, providing extensive benefits to American veterans of World War II, particularly as tuition grants and low-interest home loans.

22

Schoolteacher's Day in El Salvador. Teachers get the day off, but the polite ones appear at their schools, as guests of honor.

HOLIDAYS AND CIVIC DAYS

23

Victory Day in Estonia; official public holiday. Commemorates the Battle of Vonnu (or Vannu) against the Germans, in 1919, during the War of Independence.

23

National Day in Luxembourg; official public holiday. Official birthday of the grand duke, currently Jean (Jan. 5, 1921– ; rule 1964–). Observed in Luxembourg City with major celebrations.

ANNIVERSARIES AND SPECIAL EVENTS DAYS

23

Birthday of Alan Turing (June 23, 1912–June 7, 1954). English mathematician and logician who pioneered in computer theory.

HOLY DAYS AND FEAST DAYS

24

Feast of St. John the Baptist, or the Precursor (1st century). Celebration of the birth of the precursor and baptizer of Jesus the Messiah. Son of Saints Zachary and Elizabeth and cousin of Jesus; ascetic hermit and preacher, the last of the Old Testament prophets; martyred by beheading. The only saint besides the Virgin Mary whose birthday is a Christian feast day. June 24 is a holiday, and often an official public holiday, in many countries. Orth.: June 24 or July 7 (birth); Aug. 29 or Sept. 11 (martyrdom).

HOLIDAYS AND CIVIC DAYS

CA. 24

Discovery Day in Newfoundland, Canada; provincial official public holiday on the Monday nearest June 24. Commemorates the landing on June 24, 1497, of the Italian explorer John Cabot.

24

National Day (*Fête Nationale*) of Quebec, Canada; on St. John's Day; provincial official public holiday. Honors St. John the Baptist, patron saint of Quebec. Formerly called *Fête Jean-Baptiste*. Ardently celebrated.

24

Macau Day in Macau; official public holiday. Commemorates the defeat of the Dutch invasion of 1622 and honors St. John the Baptist.

24

Manila Day (*Araw ng Maynila*) in Manila, Philippines; local official public holiday. Commemorates the capture and founding of the city in June 1571, by Miguel Lopez de Legazpi, who claimed the archipelago for King Philip II of Spain. Celebrated with a parade and cultural and film festivals.

24

Battle of Carabobo Day in Venezuela; official public holiday. Commemorates a victory near Caracas on June 24, 1821, that assured Venezuelan independence from Spain.

ANNIVERSARIES AND SPECIAL EVENTS DAYS

24

Anniversary of the start of the Berlin Airlift on June 24, 1948, when the U.S. began to airlift supplies into Berlin, which was blockaded by the communists. The blockade ended on May 12, 1949.

24

Anniversary of the first "flying saucer" sighting in the U.S., on June 24, 1947, over Mt. Ranier, Wash.; by Kenneth Arnold of Boise, Idaho, while flying his private airplane.

24

Birthday of Henry Ward Beecher (June 24, 1813–Mar. 8, 1887). American Congregationalist clergyman, reformer, lecturer, and author. Elected to the Hall of Fame for Great Americans.

24

Birthday of Ambrose (Gwinnett) Bierce (June 24, 1842–ca. Jan. 1914). American journalist, short story writer, and satirist of savage brilliance, famous for *The Devil's Dictionary*. Disappeared in Mexico during Pancho Villa's insurrection.

24

Birthday of Horatio Herbert Kitchener (June 24, 1850–June 5, 1916). British general (later a field marshall) who avenged the death of General Charles Gordon and became a national hero in 1898; one of the 12 original members of the Order of Merit; a major British military leader in early World War I.

24

Death anniversary of Carlos Gardel (Dec. 10, 1887 or 1890–June 24, 1935). Famous Argentine tango singer, called the Songbird of Buenos Aires (*El Zorzal Criollo*). A powerful cult figure from 1917; many suicides were attributed to grief at his death.

24

Death anniversary of William Smellie (1740–June 24, 1795). Scottish editor of the first edition of the *Encyclopaedia Britannica* (first volume issued Dec. 1768).

24

Bannockburn Day in Scotland. Anniversary of the decisive Battle of Bannockburn (June 24, 1314), when Robert the Bruce (July 11, 1274–June 7, 1329) won independence for Scotland by expelling the English.

24

The Incan solar festival of *Inti Rayami* in Ecuador and Peru; also Cuzco Day in Peru. In Ecuador, the festival begins on June 23 and lasts about 1 week. A surviving Incan festival of the winter solstice, transferred after the Spanish conquest to St. John's Day. Among the Otaveleño Ecuadorians, men in clever and varied costume dance from house to house each night for a week. There are also ritual rock battles. In Peru, the festival is observed on June 24 in Cuzco, at the Sacsayhuamán fortress, in a revived reenactment of the ancient ceremony. Cuzco Day is the climax of Cuzco Week.

24

Midsummer Day in the Northern Hemisphere, and from earliest Christian practice, the feast of St. John the Baptist. By ancient European tradition, the longest day and shortest night of the year, and a celebration of the sun; a time of power, healing, and peril. Bonfires with rituals, originally on heights, are customary on this day's night, or on the preceding eve (June 23). The northern countries retain a deep fondness for this time.

24

St. John's Day in Brazil. St. John's Day (*São João*) and June Festivals (*Festivais Juinos*) are especially celebrated in the northeast. The period lasts all June, with festivals on weekends, on St. Anthony's Day (June 13), and intensely from St. John's Day through St. Peter's Day (June 29). People visit friends or relatives in the countryside, wear rustic garb, dance the *forro*, party around bonfires, and shoot off fireworks. Towns and villages hold festivals in the plazas, and there are church bazaars, neighborhood bonfires, balloons and fireworks, and foods of corn and beef. An amiable combination of American Thanksgiving and the 4th of July, and a favorite vacation time.

24

St. John's Day in Puerto Rico. The island honors its patron saint with a 10-day carnival, especially in San Juan. The eve is celebrated with concerts, street dances, and nightlong beach parties concluding with church services at dawn. At midnight of June

23–24, all walk backwards 3 times into the ocean to renew good luck for the coming year.

HOLIDAYS AND CIVIC DAYS

25

Independence Day in Mozambique; official public holiday. Commemorates the attainment of independence from Portugal on June 25, 1975.

25

National Day in Slovenia; official public holiday. Commemorates Slovenia's formal secession on June 25, 1991, from the Yugoslav Union, and its declaration of separate independence.

25

Virginia's Ratification Day. Va. ratified the U.S. Constitution on June 25, 1788, and entered the Union as the 10th state.

ANNIVERSARIES AND SPECIAL EVENTS DAYS

25

Anniversary of the Battle of the Little Big Horn (Custer's Last Stand, or the Battle of the Greasy Grass) on June 25, 1876; the most famous of Native American–U.S. battles. Lieutenant Colonel George Armstrong Custer (Dec. 5, 1839–June 25, 1876) led 264 soldiers of the 7th Cavalry into a surprise attack on a huge encampment of Native Americans, mainly Sioux, who, led by Sitting Bull and Crazy Horse, exterminated all of them in 2 hours. The day is observed on the Pine Ridge Reservation but with no overt fanfare. And at this time, during Little Big Horn Days in Hardin, Mont., the battle is scrupulously reenacted based on accounts by a Sioux historian, and enlisting Sioux descendants of the defenders. This event began in 1964, later lapsed, and was revived in 1990.

25

Anniversary of the beginning of the Korean War. North Korea invaded South Korea on June 25, 1950. The U.S. entered the conflict on June 27, in response to the U.N. Security Council's appeal to its member nations to aid South Korea. Hostilities ended with an armistice signed on July 27, 1953.

25

Anniversary of the beginning of the civil war in the former Yugoslavia. On June 25, 1991, Croatia and Slovenia declared their independence from the Yugoslav Union, sparking ethnic civil war throughout the formerly communist country.

25

Birthday of Antonio Gaudí y Cornet (June 25, 1852–June 10, 1926). Catalan architect, most famous for Barcelona's cathedral of the Holy Family (El Temple Expiatori de la Sagrada Família).

25

Birthday of George Orwell (Eric Arthur Blair; June 25, 1903–Jan. 21, 1950). English satirist and essayist; author of *Animal Farm* and *1984*.

HOLIDAYS AND CIVIC DAYS

26

Independence Day in Madagascar; official public holiday. Celebrates the attainment of independence from France on June 26, 1960.

ANNIVERSARIES AND SPECIAL EVENTS DAYS

26

Anniversary of the creation of the Order of Merit, a British order designed as a special distinction for eminent men and women, on June 26, 1902. Florence Nightingale is the only woman to have received this honor.

26

Anniversary of the dedication of the St. Lawrence Seaway on June 26, 1959, by President Eisenhower and Queen Elizabeth II. The joint U.S.-Canadian project gave ships unbroken access between the Atlantic and the Great Lakes.

26

Birthday of Bernard Berenson (June 26, 1865–Oct. 6, 1959). American art critic whose *Italian Painters of the Renaissance* was of great influence.

26

Birthday of Pearl Buck (born Pearl Sydenstricker; June 26, 1892–Mar. 6, 1973). American author noted for *The Good Earth* and other novels of life in China; recipient of the Nobel Prize in literature in 1938.

26

Birthday of Abner Doubleday (June 26, 1819–Jan. 26, 1893). American soldier, Civil War general, and reputed inventor of baseball in 1839.

26

Birthday of Lord Kelvin (William Thomson, Baron Kelvin; June 26, 1824–Dec. 17, 1907). British mathematician and physicist; the Kelvin scale of temperature is named in his honor.

26

United Nations Charter Day. Commemorates the signing of the United Nations charter on June 26, 1945, by 50 nations, in San Francisco.

HOLY DAYS AND FEAST DAYS

27

Feast of St. Cyril of Alexandria (ca. 376–444). Egyptian scholar, theologian, and patriarch of Alexandria; doctor of the church. Orth.: Jan. 18 or 31 and June 10 or 23.

27

Feast of St. Ladislaus (Laszlo), King of Hungary (July 29, 1040–July 29, 1095; ruled 1077–95). Monarch noted for his tolerance and for his defense and consolidation of Hungary. A national hero.

HOLIDAYS AND CIVIC DAYS

27

Independence Day in Djibouti; official public holiday. Commemorates the attainment of independence from France on June 27, 1977.

27

Emancipation Day in St. Barthélemy, French West Indies; official public holiday. Celebrates, with picnics and parties, the end of slavery in French territory, locally promulgated on June 27, 1848.

ANNIVERSARIES AND SPECIAL EVENTS DAYS

27

Anniversary of the first presentation on June 27, 1922, of the Newbery Medal, awarded annually since 1922 to the author of the most distinguished contribution to American literature for children published during the preceding year; the first recipient was Hendrik van Loon for *The Story of Mankind*. The award is made by the American Library Association at its annual conference in the summer.

27

Birthday of Emma Goldman (June 27, 1869–May 14, 1940). Lithuanian international anarchist, active in the U.S. from 1890 until her deportation in 1917.

27

Birthday of João Guimarães Rosa (June 27, 1908–Nov. 19, 1967). Brazilian diplomat and author, famous for the novel *Grande Sertão: Veredas* (1956; translated as *The Devil to Pay in the Backlands)*.

27

Birthday of Helen Adams Keller (June 27, 1880–June 1, 1968). The most accomplished deaf and blind woman of the 20th century; author of *The Story of My Life* and other works. Her birth is honored annually by many associations for blind people. Her birthplace, Tuscambia, Ala., holds an annual Helen Keller Festival on the last Friday–Sunday in June, with a variety of entertainment.

27

Birthday of Charles Stewart Parnell (June 27, 1846–Oct. 6, 1891). Irish political leader active in the Home Rule Party, which opposed British control; his fall due to amorous scandal was a major blow to Ireland.

27

Death anniversary of James Smithson (1765–June 27, 1829). English chemist and mineralogist, whose will established the Smithsonian Institution in Washington, D.C.

CA. 27

Gay and Lesbian Pride Day in the U.S.; formal date is the Sunday nearest June 27. Commemorates the Stonewall Riots in Greenwich Village, New York City; riots began on June 27, 1969, when homosexual patrons of the Stonewall Inn refused any longer to be bullied by police; the official birth of the Gay Liberation Movement. New York City's celebration, on the formal date, is largest; San Francisco's is also large; various other cities celebrate on Sundays in June and July.

ANNIVERSARIES AND SPECIAL EVENTS DAYS

28

Birthday of Luigi Pirandello (June 28, 1867–Dec. 10, 1936). Italian dramatist and novelist whose plays have been translated into 39 languages; awarded the Nobel Prize in literature in 1934.

28

Birthday of Jean-Jacques Rousseau (June 28, 1712–July 2, 1778). French philosopher and author of great influence; wrote the celebrated *Confessions* and other works.

28

Birthday of Peter Paul Rubens (June 28, 1577–May 30, 1640). Flemish painter famous for historical and religious scenes and portraits of kings, clergymen, and scholars.

28

Death anniversary of Primož Trubar (ca. June 9, 1508–June 28, 1586). Slovene Catholic priest and convert to Lutheranism; translated the Bible into Slovene, thus demonstrating the language's richness, and engendering Slovene national consciousness. Called the Father of the Slovene Nation.

28

Sarajevo Day. Anniversary of the beginning of World War I with the assassination on June 28, 1914, of Archduke Francis Ferdinand, heir to the Austro-Hungarian throne, in Sarajevo, Bosnia; an act that flamed the tensions that led to world war.

28

Versailles Treaty Day. Anniversary of the signing of the Treaty of Versailles on June 28, 1919, officially ending World War I.

HOLY DAYS AND FEAST DAYS

29

Feast of the SS. Peter and Paul. Commemorates their martyrdoms. Peter, born Simon (1st century), was one of the 12 Apostles and was named their chief by Jesus; after the Crucifixion, was bishop of Rome and the first pope. A patron saint of sailors and fishermen. Paul, born Saul of Tarsus (1st century), was at first a persecutor of Christians but was converted by a vision; was thereafter a great missionary and a prolific writer of epistles. By tradition, Paul and Peter were martyred in Rome on the same day, Paul by beheading and Peter by crucifixion. Worldwide, there are many festivals on June 29. Orth.: June 29 or July 12.

HOLIDAYS AND CIVIC DAYS

29

Republic Day in Seychelles; official public holiday. Celebrates independence attained from the U.K. on June 29, 1976. In 1976, the people celebrated for 3 months.

ANNIVERSARIES AND SPECIAL EVENTS DAYS

29

Birthday of William E. Borah (June 29, 1865–Jan. 19, 1940). American statesman and lawyer, opponent of America's affiliation with the League of Nations. Represents Idaho in Statuary Hall.

29

Birthday of William James Mayo (June 29, 1861–July 28, 1939). American surgeon, specialist in cancer and gallstones, a member of the medical family who developed the world-famous Mayo Clinic.

29

Birthday of Antoine de Saint-Exupéry (June 29, 1900–July 31, 1944). French pioneer airmail aviator, combat pilot, and author of novels based on his experiences; famous for *The Little Prince*. Disappeared while on an aerial reconnaissance mission.

29

Mnarja, Malta's ancient harvest festival; official public holiday. Folkloric celebration at Buskett Gardens, near Rabat; all-night picnic (with traditional rabbit stew) and splendid fireworks on the eve of the feast of SS. Peter and Paul; on the day are horse and donkey races through the streets below Rabat.

HOLY DAYS AND FEAST DAYS

30

Feast of the Blessed Ramon Llull (also spelled Llul, Lull, or Lully; ca. 1232–Sept. 29, 1316). Prolific medieval polymath of Majorca, Spain, of profound influence on Western philosophy and literature. Father of the modern novel (*Blanquerna,* ca. 1284) and a voice for peace between Christendom and Islam.

HOLIDAYS AND CIVIC DAYS

30

Army Day in Guatemala; official public holiday. Formerly called Revolution Day, in honor of the soldiers who revolted on June 30, 1871, for agrarian reform.

30

Revolution Day in Sudan; official public holiday. Commemorates the anniversary of a bloodless 1989 coup led by the current ruler, President General Omar Hassan Ahmad Al-Bashir.

MOVABLE DAYS IN JUNE

JUNE IS DAIRY MONTH IN THE U.S. Sponsored, since 1937, by the American Dairy Association, to honor dairy farmers and subsidiary enterprises, such as cheese making.

HOLIDAYS AND CIVIC DAYS

FOUNDATION DAY IN WESTERN AUSTRALIA; 1st Monday in June; official public holiday. Commemorates the 1838 creation of the colony, later a state.

SEAMAN'S DAY (SJÓMANNADAGUR) IN ICELAND. 1st Sunday in June; local official public holiday. The year's major celebration in many fishing villages, featuring rowing, swimming, and rescue contests; medals are given for the past year's rescues.

HEAD OF STATE'S OFFICIAL BIRTHDAY (YANG DI PERTUAN AGONG) IN MALAYSIA; 1st Saturday in June; official public holiday. Honors the head of state, who rules for 5 years through parliament; sultans of the 9 ruling families elect one of their number as *Agong*. Each sultan's birthday is also a local official public holiday in his state.

QUEEN'S OFFICIAL BIRTHDAY IN THE U.K. AND THE BRITISH COMMONWEALTH; formerly, following inherited custom, on the 2nd Saturday in June; now is ad hoc, on the 1st, 2nd, or 3rd Saturday in June, with the 2nd Saturday in June still the favored date. Elizabeth II was born Apr. 21, 1926, but English Aprils are inclement. On this day, on the Parade Ground in London is Trooping the Colour, when a selected regiment with its flag passes in review and salutes the queen, in Britain's most brilliant military parade.

ANNIVERSARIES AND SPECIAL EVENTS DAYS

WIMBLEDON LAWN TENNIS CHAMPIONSHIPS AT WIMBLEDON, ENGLAND; 14 days, beginning on the Monday 6 weeks before the 1st Monday in Aug. Major international tennis competition; the finals for the men's and women's singles and doubles, and for the mixed doubles, are on the final Saturday and Sunday respectively.

CHILDREN'S DAY IN THE U.S.; traditionally observed on the 2nd Sunday in June or on the last day of the Sunday-school year. Also called Children's Sunday. A day of dedication to children and young people in the church services of many denominations.

FATHER'S DAY IN THE U.S.; 3rd Sunday in June. A day to appreciate one's father. The first Father's Day was held on June 19 (3rd Sunday), 1910, originated by Sonora Louise Smart Dodd and promoted by the Ministerial Association and the YMCA of Spokane, Wash. Officially approved by President Calvin Coolidge (1924); by presidential proclamation since 1966.

RACE UNITY DAY; 2nd Sunday in June. Sponsored by the Baha'i Spiritual Assembly in the U.S. since 1957 to promote concord and mutual understanding among people of all races as the foundation of permanent peace.

CONCRETE CANOE COMPETITION FINALS IN WASHINGTON, D.C.; mid-June. Held annually since 1988 by the student members of the American Society of Civil Engineers; colleges compete to produce the most structurally elegant canoe and a winning team of paddlers, and thereby improve the field of concrete science.

CARNIVAL MEMPHIS IN MEMPHIS, TENN.; the Friday before the 1st Saturday in June. A devolution of the older mid-May Cotton Carnival, which from 1931 to the mid-1970s served to promote cotton and celebrate its contribution to Memphis. Carnival Memphis emphasizes all of Memphis's industries; it has dropped the Cotton Carnival's parade but retains the tradition of private balls and visitations. Krewes participate but with their own balls.

July

July, the 7th month in the Gregorian calendar, was named for Julius Caesar, the Roman who reformed the calendar in 46 B.C.

July is an important month in the U.S. because it was on July 4, 1776, that the Continental Congress, meeting in Philadelphia, adopted the Declaration of Independence. July 4 is now a legal holiday for all Americans. The U.S. Independence Day is also observed by neighboring parts of Canada, in England, Norway, Sweden, Denmark, Guatemala, and the Philippines, and at all American embassies in foreign lands.

July is one of the most important months for the continuance of old customs. For example, Japan observes an ancient festival in July and August called *Bon,* the Festival of Lanterns. At this time the spirits of the dead are thought to revisit earth for a brief time.

The July flowers are the water lily and the larkspur, and the birthstone is the ruby.

HOLIDAYS AND CIVIC DAYS

1
Sir Seretse Khama Day in Botswana; official public holiday. Honors the first president, Sir Seretse Khama (July 1, 1921–July 13, 1980).

1
Fête Nationale in Burundi; official public holiday. Celebrates the attainment of independence from Belgium on July 1, 1962.

1
Canada Day, formerly Dominion Day; official public holiday. Canada's national day. Celebrates the confederation of the provinces of Canada into the Dominion of Canada under the terms of the British North America Act of July 1, 1867. Celebrated with parades, fireworks, and singing of "O Canada," the national anthem.

1
Half-Year Day in Hong Kong, China, and Midyear Day in Thailand; official public holiday in both places.

1
Republic Day in Ghana; official public holiday. On July 1, 1960, Ghana became a republic within the British Commonwealth.

1
Independence Day in Rwanda; official public holiday. Commemorates independence attained from Belgium on July 1, 1962.

1
Liberation Day in Suriname; official public holiday. Celebrates, with festivals and fairs, the July 1, 1863, abolition of slavery in Dutch territory.

1
Territory Day in the British Virgin Islands; official public holiday.

ANNIVERSARIES AND SPECIAL EVENTS DAYS

1
Anniversary of the establishment of the Bureau of Internal Revenue (later the Internal Revenue Service), on July 1, 1862.

1
Anniversary of the reversion of Hong Kong from British to Chinese control, on July 1, 1997. The original lease was signed on June 9, 1898.

1
Anniversary of the establishment of the first zoo in the U.S., at Philadelphia on July 1, 1874.

1

Birthday of Louis Blériot (July 1, 1872–Aug. 2, 1936). French engineer and aviation pioneer; the first to fly an airplane across the English Channel (July 25, 1909).

1

Birthday of George Sand (born Amandine-Aurore-Lucie Dupin; July 1, 1804–June 8, 1876). French novelist, playwright, essayist, and prodigious letter writer. A liberated woman whose unconventional approach to life and literature foreshadowed the women's movement by more than a century.

1

Birthday of Walter White (July 1, 1893–Mar. 21, 1955). American author; longtime secretary of the National Association for the Advancement of Colored People (the NAACP); awarded the Spingarn Medal in 1937 for his fight against lynching.

1

American Stamp Day. Anniversary of the issuance of the first adhesive American postage stamps on July 1, 1847; observed by philatelic societies.

CA. 1

Gathering of the Clans in Pugwash, Canada, on the Friday–Sunday nearest July 1. Highland games and events.

1

Gettysburg Day. Anniversary of the beginning of the 3-day Battle of Gettysburg on July 1, 1863, one of the most decisive conflicts of the American Civil War; observed with annual commemorative services at Gettysburg, Pa.

CA. 1

Tombées de la Nuit ("Nightfall") in Rennes, France; 1st 10 days in July. A citywide street festival of theater, mime, poetry, dance, and song, with international Celtic participation.

ANNIVERSARIES AND SPECIAL EVENTS DAYS

2

Anniversary of the authorization on July 2, 1926, of the Distinguished Flying Cross of the U.S. for "heroism or extraordinary achievement while participating in an aerial flight." The first recipient was Charles Lindbergh, who received the medal on June 11, 1927, for his solo Atlantic flight.

2

Anniversary of the official establishment of the national Statuary Hall in the U.S. Capitol on July 2, 1864, when Congress approved an act authorizing the president to invite each state to furnish 2 statues representing illustrious citizens.

2

Birthday of Thomas Cranmer (July 2, 1489–Mar. 21, 1556). Archbishop of Canterbury and chief author of the *Book of Common Prayer.*

2

Birthday of Thurgood Marshall (July 2, 1908–Jan. 24, 1993). American lawyer; director-counsel of the NAACP; won *Brown v. Board of Education* on May 17, 1954. First African American Supreme Court justice (Oct. 2, 1967–1991).

CA. 2

Corso del Palio ("Race for the Banner") in Siena, Italy; on July 2 and again on Aug. 16 (Madonna del Voto Day)—exact dates may vary. The city's ancient wards compete in a bareback horse race following a day of medieval pageantry and parades.

HOLY DAYS AND FEAST DAYS

3

Feast of St. Thomas (1st century). One of the 12 Apostles, surnamed Didymus (the Twin), best known for doubting Christ's Resurrection. By tradition, he evangelized in India and was martyred there. A patron saint of India and Pakistan; also patron of architects. Orth.: Oct. 6 or 19; also 1st Sunday after Easter.

HOLIDAYS AND CIVIC DAYS

3

Independence Day in Belarus; official public holiday. Anniversary of the July 3, 1944, liberation of the capital, Minsk. (Belarus declared its independence from the USSR on Aug. 25, 1991; independence was formally attained with the dissolution of the Soviet Union on Dec. 26, 1991.)

3

Idaho Admission Day. Commemorates Idaho's admission to the Union on July 3, 1890, as the 43rd state.

3

Emancipation Day in the U.S. Virgin Islands; official public holiday. Also called Freedom Day. Celebrates the anniversary of the July 3, 1848, end of slavery in Danish territory. Also remembered is the 1733 Insurrection, when the islands' slaves first revolted en masse and kept control for 6 months.

3

Anniversary of the first child workers strike. On July 3, 1825, child workers demonstrated in Paterson, N.J., to demand a 66-hour, 6-day work week.

3

Birthday of Franz Kafka (July 3, 1883–June 3, 1924). Czech (Austro-Hungarian) novelist and essayist whose work expresses the frustrations and anxieties of modern life; wrote *The Trial* and *The Castle.*

3

Birthday of Alfred Habdank Skarbek Korzybski (July 3, 1879–Mar. 1, 1950). Polish-born American scientist, author, pioneer in semantics, founder of general semantics. Wrote *Science and Sanity.*

3

Dog Days; usually reckoned as lasting about 40 days, July 3–Aug. 15, but considered by others to last between 30 and 54 days. Regarded as the time of oppressively hot, sultry weather.

HOLIDAYS AND CIVIC DAYS

CA. 4

Caricom Day in the Caribbean. Commemorates the establishment of the Caribbean Community of 10 member states, on July 4, 1973, with goals of a common market, cooperation, and coordination of foreign policy. Observed in Guyana and St. Vincent on the 1st Monday in July.

4

Liberation Day in Rwanda; official public holiday. The anniversary of the July 4, 1994, capture of Kigali, Rwanda, by the rebels' army, following genocidal massacres by the Hutu government.

4

Independence Day, or Fourth of July; official public holiday throughout the U.S. and its territories. The birthday of the U.S. Celebrates the adoption by Congress of the Declaration of Independence on July 4, 1776, and its signing by John Hancock and Charles Thomson. Celebrated with fireworks, picnics, concerts, patriotic speeches, and outdoor events. This holiday is also observed in friendship by neighboring parts of Canada, and in Denmark, Norway, Sweden, England, Guatemala, and the Philippines.

4

Anniversary of the first publication of the anthem "America, the Beautiful" by Katharine Lee Bates on July 4, 1895. She was inspired by the view from Pikes Peak, Colo.

4

Anniversary of the first public singing of the anthem "America" ("My Country, 'Tis of Thee") on July 4, 1831, in the Park Street Church, Boston. Rev. Samuel Francis Smith, a Baptist clergyman, wrote the words and unintentionally chose the melody of "God Save the Queen/King."

4

Birthday of (John) Calvin Coolidge (July 4, 1872–Jan. 5, 1933). Mass. lawyer; governor of Mass.; vice president, succeeding on the death of President Warren G. Harding; 30th president of the U.S. (1923–29; Republican). His administration was frugal and minimalist. Buried in Plymouth, Vt.

4

Birthday of Nathaniel Hawthorne (July 4, 1804–May 19, 1864). American novelist, famous for *The Scarlet Letter.* Elected to the Hall of Fame for Great Americans.

4

Aphelion; varies between July 3 and July 6. At this time, the earth is farthest from the sun. (*See also* Perihelion, Jan. 4.)

4

Garibaldi Day in Italy. Honors Giuseppi Garibaldi (July 4, 1807–June 2, 1882), the most forceful figure in the unification of Italy in the 19th century.

CA. 4

Hopi Artists' Exhibition at Flagstaff, Ariz.; Fourth of July weekend, Saturday–Wednesday. The best of Hopi traditional art and craft is judged and sold. Began in 1930.

HOLIDAYS AND CIVIC DAYS

5

Independence Day, and Youth Day, in Algeria; official public holiday. Commemorates the attainment of independence from France on July 5, 1962. The war of independence began Oct. 31, 1954.

5

Independence Day in Cape Verde; official public holiday. Commemorates the attainment of independence from Portugal on July 5, 1975.

5

National feast day of SS. Cyril and Methodius in the Czech and Slovak Republics; official public holiday. By tradition, the brothers Cyril (ca. 827– Feb. 14, 869) and Methodius (ca. 826–Apr. 6, 884) arrived in the region on July 5, 863.

5

Tynwald Day on the Isle of Man (U.K.); official public holiday. The Tynwald, the Manx parliament, assembles at Ancient Tynwald Hill, the meeting place made by the Vikings. Laws passed during the preceding year are confirmed, and citizens' petitions are heard.

5

Independence Day in Venezuela; official public holiday. Celebrates Venezuela's declaration of independence from Spain at the Congress of Cabildos on July 5, 1811; the first Spanish-American colony to do so.

ANNIVERSARIES AND SPECIAL EVENTS DAYS

5

Anniversary of the founding of the Salvation Army in London, England, by William Booth on July 5, 1865.

5

Birthday of Phineas Taylor Barnum (July 5, 1810– Apr. 7, 1891). American showman; pioneer advertiser; manager of Jenny Lind's concert tour; author.

5

Birthday of Dwight Filley Davis (July 5, 1879– Nov. 28, 1945). American public official; donor in 1900 of the Davis Cup, the most prized team trophy in international tennis.

5

Birthday of Davis Glasgow Farragut (July 5, 1801– Aug. 14, 1870). American naval officer, Civil War hero of the Battles of New Orleans and of Mobile Bay (Aug. 5, 1864). Elected to the Hall of Fame for Great Americans.

5

Birthday of Wanda Louise Landowska (July 5, 1879–Aug. 16, 1959). Polish pianist and harpsi-

chordist responsible for a revival of interest in early musical instruments.

5

Birthday of Cecil John Rhodes (July 5, 1853–Mar. 26, 1902). English colonial statesman; developer of Rhodesia; founder of the coveted Rhodes Scholarships at Oxford University.

HOLIDAYS AND CIVIC DAYS

6

Anniversary of the Comoro Islands' declaration of independence from France on July 6, 1975.

6

Jan Hus Day in the Czech Republic; official public holiday. Jan Hus (ca. 1372–July 6, 1415, burned at the stake), a Czech preacher and philosopher whose teachings inspired the revolutionary Hussite movement to reform the church, is still an inspiring legendary figure.

6

Day of Statehood in Lithuania; official public holiday. Commemorates the 1252 crowning of Mindaugas, who united Lithuania and fought the Teutonic Knights.

6

Republic Day in Malawi; official public holiday. Celebrates independence attained from the U.K. on July 6, 1965.

ANNIVERSARIES AND SPECIAL EVENTS DAYS

6

Anniversary of the establishment of the U.S. Medal of Freedom on July 6, 1945; awarded to civilians for meritorious acts or service against the enemy on or after Dec. 7, 1941.

6

Birthday of the Dalai Lama, Tenzin Gyatso (June 6, 1935–). Tibetan head of the Yellow Hat, or *Gelukpa* ("Virtuous"), sect, the reformed wing of Tibetan Buddhism; installed as the 14th Dalai Lama on Feb. 22, 1940; the spiritual leader of Tibet; also revered by Mongolians. Recipient of the 1989 Nobel Peace Prize. He heads the Tibetan government in exile in Dharamsala, India.

6

Birthday of John Paul Jones (born John Paul; July 6, 1747–July 18, 1792). Scottish-American naval officer of the Revolutionary period and founder of the American navy. Elected to the Hall of Fame for Great Americans.

6

Birthday of Eino Leino (born Armas Eino Leopold Lönnbohm; July 6, 1878–Jan. 10, 1926). Finnish poet, playwright, and novelist who expressed the aspirations of the Finnish people.

HOLIDAYS AND CIVIC DAYS

7

Saba Saba ("Seven-Seven") Day in Tanzania; official public holiday. Also International Trade Fair Day. Marks the anniversary of the formation in 1954 of TANU, the ruling party of the Tanzania mainland. Also called Farmer's Day or Peasants' Day. Officially celebrated in a different region of the country each year with traditional dances, sports, activities, processions, rallies, and fairs.

7

Victory Day in Yemen; official public holiday. Celebrates the July 7, 1994, end of the brief civil war that followed Yemen's unification.

ANNIVERSARIES AND SPECIAL EVENTS DAYS

7

Birthday of Robert A. Heinlein (July 7, 1907–May 8, 1988). Influential American science fiction author.

7

Birthday of Leroy Robert "Satchel" Paige (ca. July 7, 1906–June 8, 1982). African American baseball player with a gift for memorable phrases; a pitcher of extraordinary ability in the Negro Southern Association and the Negro National League during the 1930s and 1940s; in 1948, he became one of the first African Americans to play in the major leagues.

7

Death anniversary of Thomas Hooker (ca. July 7, 1586–July 7, 1647). American colonial clergyman; a founder of Hartford, Conn.; his interpretation of the theory that the people have the right to choose their public officials gave him the name the Father of American Democracy.

CA. 7

Fiesta of San Fermín (*Encierro de San Fermín),* and the Running of the Bulls, in Pamplona, Spain. A wild, weeklong public celebration, with wine, dance, song, and bullfights; the famous running of the bulls begins on July 7, when bulls are loosed in the streets and harried to the stadium; daring males run among them. St. Firminius of Amiens (4th century) is the patron saint of bullfighters.

7

Kupalo in Ukraine; on St. John's Day. Greenery possesses special powers on this day. On the eve, the paporot fern blooms and girls tell each other's fortunes, foreseeing future husbands. Young men leap over bonfires.

ANNIVERSARIES AND SPECIAL EVENTS DAYS

8

Birthday of John Davison Rockefeller Sr. (July 8, 1839–May 23, 1937). American industrialist and philanthropist. Head of the Standard Oil Company; later, a benefactor of the University of Chicago, the Rockefeller Foundation, and other important institutions.

CA. 8

Loyalist Days in Saint John, Canada; often the week including July 8. Reenacts the Loyalists' landing at Market Slip ca. July 8, 1793, following the American Revolutionary War; also features the Great Bay of Fundy Whaler Race.

8

Olive Branch Petition Day. Anniversary of the July 8, 1775, signing, by colonial moderates, of a petition addressed to King George III in an effort to avoid the American Revolutionary War.

HOLY DAYS AND FEAST DAYS

9

Anniversary of the Martyrdom of the Bab in the Baha'i faith. A holy day, and Baha'is abstain from work. Honors the Bab ("The Gate"; born Mirza Ali Mohammed; ca. 1819–July 9, 1850). The founder of the Babi faith and the prophet of the Baha'i faith. This day especially commemorates his martyrdom on July 9, 1850. Observed at noon, the hour of his death.

HOLIDAYS AND CIVIC DAYS

9

Independence Day in Argentina; official public holiday. Celebrates Argentina's formal declaration of independence from Spain on July 9, 1816, in Tucumán (northwest Argentina).

9

Youth Day *(Aïd Chebeb)* in Morocco; official public holiday. The birthday of King Hassan II (July 9, 1929–July 23, 1999; ruled Mar. 3, 1961–July 23, 1999).

ANNIVERSARIES AND SPECIAL EVENTS DAYS

9

Anniversary of the July 9, 1918, authorization of the Distinguished Service Cross of the U.S. Army to honor extraordinary heroism on the part of persons serving the army in any capacity.

9

Birthday of Elias Howe (July 9, 1819–Oct. 3, 1867). American inventor and manufacturer who invented the sewing machine (1846). Elected to the Hall of Fame for Great Americans.

HOLIDAYS AND CIVIC DAYS

10

Independence Day in the Bahamas; official public holiday. Commemorates full independence attained from the U.K. on July 10, 1973.

10

Wyoming Statehood Day. Commemorates Wyo.'s admission to the Union on July 10, 1890, as the 44th state; the first state to grant the vote to women through its original constitution.

ANNIVERSARIES AND SPECIAL EVENTS DAYS

10

Birthday of Mary McLeod Bethune (July 10, 1875–May 18, 1955). American educator, founder of Bethune-Cookman College, and founder and president of the National Council of Negro Women.

10

Birthday of Sir William Blackstone (July 10, 1723–Feb. 14, 1780). English jurist; famous for his influential *Commentaries on the Laws of England* (4 volumes, 1765–69).

10

Birthday of John Calvin (born Jean Chauvin; July 10, 1509–May 27, 1564). Major French-born Protestant theologian and reformer; forced to flee to Switzerland, where he published *Institutes of the Christian Religion.*

10

Birthday of Toyohiko Kagawa (July 10, 1888–Apr. 23, 1960). Japanese social reformer and evangelist, a leader in the Japanese labor movement and in the establishment of cooperatives.

10

Birthday of Marcel Proust (July 10, 1871–Nov. 19, 1922). French author; wrote the multivolume *Remembrance of Things Past.*

10

Birthday of Nikola Tesla (ca. July 9, 1856–Jan. 7, 1943). Croatian-born American electrical engineer, inventor, and visionary; discoverer of the rotating magnetic field; inventor of the complete system of alternating current propagation and delivery; master of lightning.

10

Death anniversary of El Cid (Rodrigo Díaz de Vivar; ca. 1043–July 10, 1099). Castilian Spanish military leader and national hero in the reconquest of Spain from the Moors; eponymous hero of Spain's epic poem.

HOLY DAYS AND FEAST DAYS

11

Feast of St. Benedict of Nursia (ca. 480–Mar. 21, 547). Italian monk; founder of the Benedictine order and of the monastery at Monte Cassino, the birthplace of Western monasticism. Patron saint of Europe.

HOLIDAYS AND CIVIC DAYS

11

Naadam Day in Mongolia; July 11–12; official public holiday; the national day. The Naadam Festival is celebrated in Ulan Bator on these dates, and elsewhere in the week before or after. Celebrated on the anniversary of the Mongolian revolution of July 11, 1921, when independence was attained from the Manchu (Chinese) overlords. Under the communists, the festival was used to glorify the state. Now it is once again a true national day and a traditional summer fair, featuring the "3 manly sports": horse riding, wrestling, and archery.

11

Anthony Wayne Day in Mich. Commemorates July 11, 1796, when Anthony Wayne raised the American flag over Detroit to proclaim that Detroit and the Northwest were now American territory, not British. On this day, a 15-star flag is raised at Wayne State University.

ANNIVERSARIES AND SPECIAL EVENTS DAYS

11
Anniversary of the July 11, 1995, resumption of diplomatic ties between the U.S. and Vietnam, for the first time since the fall of Saigon and the end of the Vietnam War.

11
Birthday of John Quincy Adams (July 11, 1767–Feb. 23, 1848). Son of John Adams (2nd president) and Abigail Adams; educated at Harvard and abroad; Mass. lawyer; senator; minister abroad; helped draft the peace treaty ending the War of 1812; secretary of state under President James Monroe; composed a masterly report on weights and measures, and helped draft the Monroe Doctrine; 6th president of the U.S. (1825–29; Democratic Republican); subsequently defeated by Andrew Jackson. Thereafter served as congressman for 17 years until his death. Buried at Unitarian Church, Braintree, Mass. Elected to the Hall of Fame for Great Americans. He was antislavery and anti-imperialist, opposing the annexation of Tex. and the Mexican War. He helped establish the Smithsonian Institution and was mocked for proposing national astronomical observatories.

11
Birthday of Colin Purdie Kelly (July 11, 1915–Dec. 10, 1941). American army captain and aviator, first U.S. air hero of World War II, posthumously awarded the Distinguished Service Cross.

11
Birthday of George William Norris (July 11, 1861–Sept. 2, 1944). American statesman and congressman from Nebr. who was instrumental in establishing the Tennessee Valley Authority; the first TVA dam was named in his honor. Author of the 20th Amendment, known as the "lame duck" amendment, which provided for inauguration of a newly elected president on Jan. 20 instead of Mar. 4.

11
World Population Day. Anniversary of the Day of the Five Billion, July 11, 1987, when the world's population reached this quantity. A day to focus public attention on the urgency of population issues. In 1999, the world's population reached 6 billion.

HOLIDAYS AND CIVIC DAYS

12
Orangeman's Day in Northern Ireland; official public holiday; also an official public holiday in Newfoundland, Canada (usually on the nearer Monday). Also called Orange Day, the Orange Walk, or The Glorious Twelfth. The height of the Ulster Protestant year. Celebrates the anniversaries of both the Battle of the Boyne (July 1, 1690), won by the British (Protestant) King William III of Orange against the (Catholic) pretender, James II, and the yet more decisive Battle of Aughrim (July 12, 1691), which ended warfare in Ireland by James's partisans. Notable for parading by the Orange Society and others, superb brass bands, and picnics. Belfast's celebration is largest, followed by that of Edinburgh, Scotland.

ANNIVERSARIES AND SPECIAL EVENTS DAYS

12
Anniversary of the authorization of the Medal of Honor by Congress on July 12, 1862, to honor noncommissioned officers and privates who distinguish themselves in actual conflict by gallantry and intrepidity at the risk of life beyond the call of duty. The first award was made to 6 members of a Union army raiding party.

12
Birthday of (Richard) Buckminster Fuller (July 12, 1895–July 1, 1983). American engineer, architect, and seminal inventor of systems and devices such as the geodesic dome. His great-aunt was Margaret Fuller.

12
Birthday of Pablo Neruda (born Neftalí Ricardo Reyes Basoalto; July 12, 1904–Sept. 23, 1973). Chilean poet; awarded the Nobel Prize in literature in 1971.

12
Birthday of Sir William Ostler (July 12, 1849–Dec. 29, 1919). Canadian physician and teacher noted for his research on the circulatory system.

12
Birthday of Henry David Thoreau (July 12, 1817–May 6, 1862). American author and philosopher, famous for *Walden, or Life in the Woods*. Elected to the Hall of Fame for Great Americans.

12

Death anniversary of Desiderius Erasmus (ca. Oct. 28, 1467–July 12, 1536). Dutch author and scholar; humanist, and friend of Thomas More; best known for his *In Praise of Folly* (*Encomium Moriae*).

HOLY DAYS AND FEAST DAYS

13

Feast of Our Lady of Fátima. Commemorates the apparition of the Virgin Mary to 3 peasant children at Fátima, Portugal, in 1917; with 6 appearances between May 13 and Oct. 13. Fátima swiftly became an important Marian shrine. Major pilgrimages by Portuguese and others occur on July 13, May 13, and Oct. 13.

CA. 13

Feast of Lanterns (*Bon,* or *O-Bon*) in Japan; July 13–15 in cities, Aug. 13–15 in rural areas, Aug. 7–16 in Kyoto. A time of communion with the spirits of the dead, when they briefly revisit earth. Celebrated with visits to lantern-lit graves and special dances; observed since A.D. 650.

HOLIDAYS AND CIVIC DAYS

13

Night Watch (*La Retraite aux Flambeaux*) in France. The eve of Bastille Day. At night, Paris lights are darkened, and in the streets are parades of soldiers, patriotic bands, and marchers with torches and lanterns.

ANNIVERSARIES AND SPECIAL EVENTS DAYS

13

Anniversary of the passage of the Northwest Ordinance by the Continental Congress on July 13, 1787. It provided for government of the territory north of the Ohio River and west of N.Y.; prohibited slavery; and guaranteed religious freedom, the right to trial by jury, and support for schools

13

Death anniversary of Bertrand du Guesclin (ca. 1320–July 13, 1380). Brittany's greatest military hero; superb warrior and general of the Hundred Years' War, and Constable of France.

HOLY DAYS AND FEAST DAYS

14

Feast of St. Bonaventure (born Giovanni di Fidanza; 1221–July 15, 1274). Italian Franciscan priest and theologian, colleague of St. Thomas Aquinas and one of the great medieval minds; reformer of the Franciscans; doctor of the church (the Seraphic Doctor). On Fuerteventura, Canary Islands (Spain), he is patron saint, and the festival on this day is the year's most important event.

14

Feast of the Blessed Kateri Tekakwitha (1656–Apr. 17, 1680) in the U.S. Algonquin woman raised among the Mohawks; called the Lily of the Mohawks. By how she lived her brief life, she deeply influenced other Native Americans during her lifetime, and posthumous miracles were attributed to her.

HOLIDAYS AND CIVIC DAYS

14

Bastille Day (*La Fête Nationale*) in France and its possessions; official public holiday. On this day in 1789 the Bastille prison in Paris was stormed by citizens, and its political prisoners were freed; the start of the French Revolution. Enthusiastically celebrated in France, the French West Indies, and French Polynesia. Also observed by French societies all over the world.

ANNIVERSARIES AND SPECIAL EVENTS DAYS

14

Anniversary of the patent of the first tape measure in the U.S., on July 14, 1868.

14

Birthday of Florence Bascom (July 14, 1862–June 18, 1945). American geologist. First woman to receive a degree from Johns Hopkins University and the first woman to receive a doctorate from any American university.

14

Birthday of Gerald Rudolph Ford (July 14, 1913–). Lawyer; naval officer in World War II; Mich. congressman; appointed vice president upon the resignation of Spiro Agnew; succeeded President Richard Nixon when he resigned; 38th president of the U.S. (Aug. 9, 1974–1977; Republican).

14

Birthday of Jules Mazarin (July 14, 1602–Mar. 9, 1661). Neapolitan-born French statesman, first minister to Louis XIV, Roman Catholic cardinal, and founder of the Mazarin Library.

14

Birthday of Sylvia Emmeline Pankhurst (born Sylvia Emmeline Goulden; July 14, 1858–June 14, 1928). English women's suffrage leader who used militant methods of campaigning and was sentenced to prison. She lived to see the passage of the Representation of the People Act on June 9, 1928, which gave full and equal suffrage to women. A memorial statue to her was erected near the Houses of Parliament in London.

14

Birthday of James Abbott McNeill Whistler (July 14, 1834–July 17, 1903). American artist and wit. Elected to the Hall of Fame for Great Americans.

HOLY DAYS AND FEAST DAYS

15

Feast of St. Swithin (died July 2, 862). English bishop. By lore, if it rains on St. Swithin's Day, it will rain for 40 days.

HOLIDAYS AND CIVIC DAYS

15

The Sultan's Birthday in Brunei; official public holiday. Honors Sultan Sir Muda Hassanal Bolkiah Mu'izzadin Wadaulah (July 15, 1946– ; rule Aug. 1, 1968–).

ANNIVERSARIES AND SPECIAL EVENTS DAYS

15

Anniversary of the storming of Jerusalem by the forces of Christendom, on July 15, 1099. The climax of the First Crusade. Jerusalem was recaptured by the Muslims on Oct. 2, 1187.

15

Birthday of Clement Clarke Moore (July 15, 1779–July 10, 1863). American scholar and poet. Best known for the poem *A Visit from Saint Nicholas*.

15

Birthday of Rembrandt (Rembrandt Harmensz van Rijn; July 15, 1606–Oct. 4, 1669). Dutch painter and etcher, foremost member of the Dutch school of painting.

15

Death anniversary of Rosalía de Castro (Feb. 1837–July 15, 1885). The most famous poet of Galicia Province, Spain. Her *Cantares Gallegos* (*Galician Songs,* 1863) is one of the great works of Spanish literature. She identified with the rural poor's tribulations and love of the land.

HOLY DAYS AND FEAST DAYS

16

Feast of Our Lady of Einsiedeln at Einsiedeln, Lake Lucerne, Switzerland; on the Sunday after July 16. A revered pilgrimage site dating from the time of St. Meinrad (died 863); its Black Madonna is much loved.

16

Feast of Our Lady of Mount Carmel. Commemorates the apparition of the Virgin Mary on July 16, 1251, to the English Carmelite St. Simon Stock. An important feast in Spain, the Canary Islands (she's a protector of fishermen), and in Latin America; many girls are named Carmen.

HOLIDAYS AND CIVIC DAYS

16

District of Columbia Day. Anniversary of the establishment on July 16, 1790, of the District of Columbia and the authorization of D.C. as the permanent capital of the U.S.

ANNIVERSARIES AND SPECIAL EVENTS DAYS

16

Anniversary of the first atomic bomb explosion, at Alamogordo Air Base, N.M., on July 16, 1945; at the Trinity test site; overseen by Robert Oppenheimer.

16

Anniversary of the East-West Schism, divorcing the two halves of Christendom. On July 16, 1054, Leo IX's papal bull of excommunication was delivered in Constantinople, anathematizing the patriarch there, who thereupon excommunicated the pope. Reconciliation was finally effected on Dec. 7, 1965, when the mutual excommunications were expunged by Pope Paul VI and the ecumenical patriarch Athenagoras I.

16

Birthday of Sir Joshua Reynolds (July 16, 1723–Feb. 23, 1792). English portrait painter and first president of the Royal Academy.

CA. 16

Gion Festival (*Gion Matsuri*) in Kyoto, Japan; July 16–24, main days July 17 and 24. A very old and important Japanese festival. Honors the brother of the sun goddess, who responded to the petitions of the people and stopped a 10th-century plague; celebrated with ceremonies and processions of huge floats.

16

Muhammad's *Hijrah* ("Hegira"). On the evening preceding July 16, A.D. 622, Muhammad departed Mecca to go to Medina. This event is the starting point of the Islamic calendar, Muharram 1, A.H. 1. (A.H. = anno hegirae). He reached Medina on Sept. 24, A.D. 622.

HOLIDAYS AND CIVIC DAYS

17

King's Birthday in Lesotho; official public holiday. Honors Letsie III, born July 17, 1963.

17

Muñoz Rivera Day in Puerto Rico; official public holiday. Honors Luis Muñoz Rivera (July 17, 1859–Nov. 15, 1916), Puerto Rican independence patriot, statesman, journalist, poet, and first resident commissioner in Washington, D.C.

17

Constitution Day in South Korea; official public holiday. Celebrates the proclamation of the republic's constitution on July 17, 1948, with ceremonies at Seoul's capitol plaza and in all major cities.

ANNIVERSARIES AND SPECIAL EVENTS DAYS

17

Death anniversary of Bartolomé de las Casas (Aug. 1474–July 17, 1566). Spanish Dominican missionary and historian in Mexico; secured laws to protect native peoples from slavery; author of invaluable historical works on Mexico.

17

Czar Nicholas Day. Anniversary of the July 17, 1918, murder of the Russian czar Nicholas II and his family by the Bolsheviks.

17

Grape festival of Agíos Sotiris in Greece; called in Athens and Crete the Réthimnon Wine Festival, or, near Athens, the Daphni Wine Festival. The first grapes are now ready for harvest; a time of fights with eggs, flour, yogurt; was once religious, is now secular. Crete follows this with Music Week.

HOLIDAYS AND CIVIC DAYS

18

Constitution Day (*Jura de la Constitución*) in Uruguay; official public holiday. Commemorates the country's first constitution, of July 18, 1830.

ANNIVERSARIES AND SPECIAL EVENTS DAYS

18

Anniversary of the beginning of the Spanish Civil War, on July 18, 1936, when army officers led by Francisco Franco revolted against the republic; Franco's nationalists defeated the republicans in a war ending on Mar. 28, 1939, leaving more than 600,000 dead. Under the Franco regime, July 18 was an official public holiday.

18

Birthday of Laurence Housman (July 18, 1865–Feb. 20, 1959). English illustrator, author, and playwright remembered particularly for the play *Victoria Regina*.

18

Birthday of Nelson Rolihlahla Mandela (July 18, 1918–). South African lawyer and a leader of the African National Congress. Imprisoned by the South African government, but an enduring and worthy symbol of hope, peace, and unity. Released on Feb. 11, 1990. Subsequently a 1993 Nobel Peace Prize laureate and president of South Africa (inaugurated May 10, 1994).

18

Birthday of William Makepeace Thackeray (July 18, 1811–Dec. 24, 1863). English novelist and satirical humorist famous for *Vanity Fair* and *The History of Henry Esmond*.

18

Railroad Day. Anniversary of the completion of the Grand Trunk line, the first international railroad on the American continent, on July 18, 1853.

Holidays and Civic Days

19

Martyrs' Day in Myanmar (Burma); official public holiday. Commemorates Aung San, the country's founding father, who was assassinated with other leaders on July 19, 1947. Special ceremonies are held at Martyrs Mausoleum, Rangoon.

19

Triumph of the Revolution in Nicaragua; official public holiday. Also called the Day of Joy (*Día de Alegría*), or Liberation Day. Celebrates the July 19, 1979, flight of the dictator Anastasio Somoza Debayle, defeated by the Sandinista National Liberation Front.

Anniversaries and Special Events Days

19

Anniversary of the first women's rights convention, at Seneca Falls, N.Y., on July 19–20, 1848, led by Lucretia Mott and Elizabeth Cady Stanton. The "Declaration of Sentiments and Resolutions," drafted by Stanton, demanded that women "have immediate admission to all the rights and privileges which belong to them as citizens of the United States." Similar conventions were held annually until the Civil War.

19

Baptismal day of Inigo Jones (baptized July 19, 1573–June 21, 1652). English architect whose restoration of St. Paul's Cathedral in London and other buildings revived classical architecture.

19

Birthday of Mary Ann Ball Bickerdyke (July 19, 1817–Nov. 8, 1901). American nurse known as Mother Bickerdyke for her services to the Union armies in the west during the Civil War.

19

Birthday of Edgar Degas (July 19, 1834–Sept. 26, 1917). French Impressionist artist, noted for his paintings of dancers in motion.

19

Birthday of Vladimir Vladimirovich Mayakovsky (July 19, 1893–Apr. 14, 1930). Leading poet of the Russian Revolution and of the early Soviet period.

19

Birthday of Charles Horace Mayo (July 19, 1865–May 26, 1939). American surgeon, specialist in goiters and preventive medicine; cofounder of the Mayo Clinic.

Holy Days and Feast Days

20

Orthodox feast of Elias, or Elijah. Old Testament prophet, revered in the Byzantine rite. Orth.: July 20 or Aug. 2; also June 14 or 27.

Holidays and Civic Days

20

Independence Day in Colombia; official public holiday. Commemorates the declaration of independence from Spain on July 20, 1810.

Anniversaries and Special Events Days

20

Anniversary of the establishment of the Legion of Merit Medal by Act of Congress on July 20, 1942; awarded for meritorious service performed by individuals in the armed services of the U.S. or by citizens of other nations.

20

Birthday of Sir Edmund Percival Hillary (July 20, 1919–). New Zealand mountaineer who, with Norkey Tenzing, first climbed to the summit of Mt. Everest.

20

Birthday of Petrarch (Francesco Petrarca; July 20, 1304–July 18, 1374). Italian lyric poet and scholar. Major figure in the Italian Renaissance.

20

Moon Day. Anniversary of the landing on the moon on July 20, 1969, of the lunar module *Eagle,* manned by the American astronauts Neil Armstrong and Edwin "Buzz" Aldrin Jr., who became the first men to explore the moon's surface. Michael Collins, pilot of *Apollo XI,* remained aloft.

Holy Days and Feast Days

21

Feast of St. Lawrence of Brindisi (born Giulio Cesare de Rossi; July 22, 1559–July 22, 1619). Italian Capuchin priest and scholar; notable administrator and Counter-Reformation preacher; leader in the defense of Hungary against the Turks. Doctor of the church.

HOLIDAYS AND CIVIC DAYS

21

Independence Day, or National Day, in Belgium; official public holiday. Commemorates the July 21, 1831, election of Leopold of Saxe-Coburg as king of Belgium; this day was thereupon declared one of national rejoicing.

21

Schoelcher Day in Guadeloupe and St. Martin, French West Indies; official public holiday. Celebrates the end of slavery and especially honors Victor Schoelcher (July 22 [sic], 1804–Dec. 26, 1893), French journalist and parliamentarian, the principal advocate of abolishing slavery in the French Empire. Emancipation occurred on Apr. 27, 1848. St. Martin celebrates with sailboat and bike races, music, and African dances.

21

Liberation Day in Guam; official public holiday. Commemorates July 21, 1944, when U.S. soldiers and marines freed the island from the Japanese, who had seized it in Dec. 1941.

ANNIVERSARIES AND SPECIAL EVENTS DAYS

21

Anniversary of the dedication of the Women's Hall of Fame on July 21, 1979, at Seneca Falls, N.Y., the birthplace of the women's rights movement.

21

Birthday of Ernest Miller Hemingway (July 21, 1899–July 2, 1961). American novelist, short-story writer, and journalist. His book *The Old Man and the Sea* won the 1953 Pulitzer Prize. He was awarded the Nobel Prize in literature in 1954.

21

Birthday of Paul Julius von Reuter (born Israel Beer Josaphat; July 21, 1816–Feb. 25, 1899). German-born British journalist and founder of Reuter's News Agency, which pioneered in gathering news from all over the world.

HOLY DAYS AND FEAST DAYS

22

Feast of St. Mary Magdalene (1st century). Disciple of Jesus who had 7 devils cast out of her. Was present at the Crucifixion and was the first at the tomb. Traditionally but unjustifiably identified as the unnamed sinner who anointed Jesus' feet. By ancient tradition, after the Crucifixion she went with the evangelist John to Ephesus and died there. Alternatively, by pious legend, she accompanied Martha, Lazarus, and others to Provence, where she is highly revered. Patron saint of Marseilles and Provence.

ANNIVERSARIES AND SPECIAL EVENTS DAYS

22

Birthday of Stephen Vincent Benet (July 22, 1898–Mar. 13, 1943). American poet and novelist who received the Pulitzer Prize in poetry in 1929 for *John Brown's Body* and in 1944 for the posthumously published *Western Star.*

22

Birthday of Emma Lazarus (July 22, 1849–Nov. 19, 1887). American poet and essayist who wrote *The New Colossus,* the closing lines of which are engraved on the Statue of Liberty.

22

Death anniversary of John Dillinger (June 28, 1902–July 22, 1934). American bank robber, murderer, and prison escapee; the first person to be named Public Enemy No. 1 by the FBI. Killed by FBI agents. (His death is disputed.)

22

Rat Catcher's Day. Anniversary of the Pied Piper of Hamelin in Germany. By lore, on July 22, 1376, the people of Hamelin were relieved of a plague of rats by a pied piper but refused to pay him; in revenge, he entranced their children and led them within a mountain.

22

Spooner's Day. A day to remember the English clergyman William Spooner (July 22, 1844–Aug. 29, 1930). Spooner achieved lasting fame for his "spoonerisms"—unintentional transpositions of letters into amusing slips of the tongue.

HOLY DAYS AND FEAST DAYS

23

Feast of St. Anthony Pechersky (or Anthony of the Kiev Caves; 983–1073). Ukrainian monk; founder, with Theodosius Pechersky, of Russian monasticism. R.C.: July 10; Orth.: July 10 or 23.

23

Feast of the Magi: Balthasar, Caspar, and Melchior. By ancient tradition and modern speculation, they were the 3 wise men or kings of the New Testament who brought gifts to the infant Jesus, and were astrologers from Babylonia or Arabia.

23
Feast of St. Bridget (Birgitta) of Sweden (June 14, 1303–ca. July 23, 1373). Swedish mystic and political activist; founder of the Order of the Most Holy Trinity (the Brigetines). Her mystical book *Revelations* was the first major Swedish contribution to European thought. Patron saint of Sweden.

HOLIDAYS AND CIVIC DAYS

23
Revolution Day in Egypt; official public holiday. Commemorates the revolution of July 23, 1952, led by Gamal Abdel Nasser, which overthrew King Farouk (1920–1965; ruled 1936–1952, abdicated) and declared a republic.

ANNIVERSARIES AND SPECIAL EVENTS DAYS

23
Birthday of Raymond Chandler (July 23, 1888–Mar. 26, 1959). English-born American mystery writer of great skill and influence, the successor of Dashiel Hammett; his most famous novel is *The Long Goodbye.*

23
Birthday of Charlotte Saunders Cushman (July 23, 1816–Feb. 17, 1876). American actress known for her portrayal of Lady Macbeth. Elected to the Hall of Fame for Great Americans.

23
Birthday of John Dee (July 13, 1527–Dec. 1608). English mathematician and scientist, metaphysician, magus, and polymath; astrologer to Elizabeth I, tutor to her court, and central figure in the Rosicrucian Enlightenment.

23
Birthday of Haile Selassie (born Lij Tafari; July 23, 1892–Aug. 27, 1975; ruled Nov. 2, 1930–Sept. 12, 1974). Emperor of Ethiopia; deposed by a military coup.

HOLIDAYS AND CIVIC DAYS

24
Pioneer Day in Utah; official public holiday. Celebrates the entry of Brigham Young and the Mormon pioneers into the valley of the Salt Lake in 1847 and the establishment of the first settlement in the area. Celebrated since 1849 on varying dates near July 24.

ANNIVERSARIES AND SPECIAL EVENTS DAYS

24
Anniversary of the conclusion of the Scopes Trial (the "Monkey Trial") on July 24, 1925. John Thomas Scopes (Aug. 3, 1900–Oct. 21, 1970) was convicted of teaching evolution in a Dayton, Tenn., high school and was fined $100 and costs. William Jennings Bryan and Clarence Darrow argued for the prosecution and the defense, respectively.

24
Birthday of Simón Bolívar (July 24, 1783–Dec. 17, 1830). Celebrated especially in Venezuela and Ecuador; official public holiday in Venezuela. Soldier-statesman, principal leader in the independence struggle of Spain's South American colonies; proclaimed the Liberator. Bolivia is named for him.

24
Birthday of John Middleton Clayton (July 24, 1796–Nov. 9, 1856). American statesman, senator from Del., and secretary of state under President Zachary Taylor. Represents Del. in Statuary Hall.

24
Birthday of Amelia Earhart (July 24, 1897–disappeared, July 2, 1937). Famous American aviatrix; first woman to fly the Atlantic as a passenger, June 17–18, 1928; first woman to pilot a plane across the Atlantic, May 20–21, 1932; first woman to win the Distinguished Flying Cross. She and her navigator, Fred Nunn, disappeared in the Pacific, near the international date line, while flying around the world.

HOLY DAYS AND FEAST DAYS

25
Feast of St. Christopher (died ca. 251). The Christ Bearer; patron saint of travelers, particularly motorists.

25
Feast of St. James the Greater (died 42). One of the 12 Apostles, the first Apostle martyred (by beheading, in Jerusalem). By ancient tradition, preached in Spain after the Crucifixion. A patron saint of Spain (as Santiago); his feast is important throughout Latin America. Orth.: Apr. 30 or May 13.

HOLIDAYS AND CIVIC DAYS

25

Guanacaste Day in Costa Rica; official public holiday. Celebrates the 1814 Spanish transfer of Guanacaste from Nicaragua to Costa Rica; a local referendum on July 25, 1825, confirmed the transfer, in a proudly remembered early instance of Costa Rican self-determination.

25

Constitution Day, or Commonwealth Day, in Puerto Rico; official public holiday. Commemorates July 25, 1952, when the constitution of the Commonwealth of Puerto Rico was proclaimed.

25

Republic Day in Tunisia; official public holiday. Commemorates the proclamation of the republic on July 25, 1957.

ANNIVERSARIES AND SPECIAL EVENTS DAYS

25

Birthday of Davidson Black (July 25, 1884–Mar. 15, 1934). Canadian physician and professor of anatomy whose contributions to anthropology in studying protohuman remains and in identifying the Peking man brought him international fame.

25

Birthday of Flora Adams Darling (July 25, 1840– Jan. 6, 1910). American author and founder of patriotic societies, the most important being the Daughters of the American Revolution.

25

Wagner Festival (*Wagner Festspiele*) in Bayreuth, Germany; always July 25–Aug. 28. Wagner's operas are performed daily. Attendance is avid and huge.

HOLY DAYS AND FEAST DAYS

26

Feast of St. Ann (1st century B.C.). Mother of Mary, the mother of Jesus, and wife of St. Joachim. Patron saint of housewives and miners, and of Canada. Especially revered in Brittany, Canada, the Philippines, and Sri Lanka. The pilgrimage to the Basilica of Sainte Anne de Beaupré in Quebec, Canada, is one of the largest in North America. Orth.: July 25 or Aug. 7.

HOLIDAYS AND CIVIC DAYS

CA. 26

Moncada Anniversary, or National Rebellion Day, in Cuba; official public holiday, July 25–27. Commemorates the beginning of the Cuban revolution, with the unsuccessful attack on July 26, 1953, against the Batista government's Moncada garrison, by Fidel Castro and others. This is also the time of Carnaval in Havana and Santiago.

26

Independence Day in Liberia; official public holiday. Celebrates the establishment of the Free and Independent Republic of Liberia on July 26, 1847, following its founding in 1822 by the American Colonization Society as a place to send free African Americans from the U.S., by authority of a charter granted by the U.S. Congress in 1816.

26

Ratification Day in N.Y. On July 26, 1788, N.Y. ratified the U.S. Constitution and entered the Union as the 11th state.

ANNIVERSARIES AND SPECIAL EVENTS DAYS

26

Birthday of Constantino Brumidi (July 26, 1805– Feb. 19, 1880). Italian-American painter whose lifework was the painting of portraits and frescoes for the Capitol in Washington, D.C.

26

Birthday of George Catlin (July 26, 1796–Dec. 23, 1872). American artist who made special studies and portraits of Native Americans. His work is displayed in the Catlin Gallery of the U.S. National Museum and at the American Museum of Natural History in New York City.

26

Birthday of George Clinton (July 26, 1739–Apr. 20, 1812). American Revolutionary War soldier; lawyer; first governor of N.Y.; twice vice president of the U.S. (1805–13). Represents N.Y. in Statuary Hall.

26

Birthday of Serge Koussevitzky (July 26, 1874– June 4, 1951). Russian-American bass player, conductor of the Boston Symphony Orchestra, and founder of the Berkshire Music Center.

26

Birthday of George Bernard Shaw (July 26, 1856–Nov. 2, 1950). Irish-English dramatist, critic, novelist, and pamphleteer. Recipient of the 1925 Nobel Prize in literature; he used the award money to establish an institution for the study of Scandinavian literature in Great Britain. His birthday is observed by Shaw societies throughout the U.S.

26

Death anniversary of Evita Perón (María Eva Duarte de Perón; May 7, 1919–July 26, 1952), of Argentina; wife of President Juan Domingo Perón; the first Argentine feminist; a cult figure of ambiguous reputation. Her epitaph is "Don't cry for me, Argentina. I remain quite near to you."

HOLIDAYS AND CIVIC DAYS

27

Barbosa Day in Puerto Rico; official public holiday. Honors José Celso Barbosa (July 27, 1857–1921), black physician and independence hero.

ANNIVERSARIES AND SPECIAL EVENTS DAYS

27

Birthday of (Joseph-Pierre) Hilaire Belloc (July 27, 1870–July 16, 1953). English journalist, essayist, poet, historian, and man of general literary parts, linked with G. K. Chesterton and G. B. Shaw; his *The Path to Rome* is one of the world's great travel books.

27

Korean War Armistice Day in the U.S. Anniversary of the end of the Korean conflict that began on June 25, 1950, and ended on July 27, 1953.

HOLY DAYS AND FEAST DAYS

28

Russian Orthodox feast of St. Vladimir I of Kiev (ca. 975–1015). King of Russia and convert to Christianity; the Enlightener of Russia; Patron saint of Russia and Ukraine. Orth.: July 15 or 28.

HOLIDAYS AND CIVIC DAYS

28

Independence Day in Peru; official public holiday. Celebrates the declaration of independence from Spain on July 28, 1821.

ANNIVERSARIES AND SPECIAL EVENTS DAYS

28

Birthday of Beatrix Potter (July 28, 1866–Dec. 22, 1943). English author and illustrator, famous for *The Tale of Peter Rabbit.*

28

Death anniversary of John Peter Zenger (1697–July 28, 1746). German-born American printer and journalist tried for seditious libels. His 1735 acquittal is considered the first important victory for freedom of the press in the colonies. The University of Ariz. presents a John Peter Zenger Award.

28

Founder's Day for the Volunteers of America. Honors the birth of Ballington Booth (July 28, 1857–Oct. 5, 1940), who with his wife, Maud, founded the organization on Mar. 8, 1896; he was the son of William Booth, founder of the Salvation Army.

28

Joseph Lee Day. Sponsored by the National Recreational Association to commemorate the death of the Father of the Playground Movement (Mar. 8, 1862–July 28, 1937).

HOLY DAYS AND FEAST DAYS

29

Feast of St. Martha (1st century). Sister of Mary of Bethany and Lazarus, in charge of the household and the archetype of the activist Christian. By tradition, all 3 evangelized Provence following the Crucifixion. Patron saint of cooks, innkeepers, housekeepers, and laundresses.

29

Feast of St. Olaf (995–July 29, 1030; ruled 1016–1029). King of Norway and national hero; noted for unifying and christianizing the country. His shrine became the Cathedral of Trondheim, a major pilgrimage center for all Scandinavia. Patron saint of Norway.

ANNIVERSARIES AND SPECIAL EVENTS DAYS

29

Anniversary of the founding of the International Atomic Agency on July 29, 1957.

29

Anniversary of the defeat of the Spanish Armada at the Battle of Gravelines (July 29, 1588). The frustration of Spain's attempt to invade and conquer England dates from this inconclusive battle; the survivors fled north before a great tempest, and were harried and destroyed piecemeal, mainly by the elements.

29

Birthday of George Bradshaw (July 29, 1801–Sept. 6, 1853). English originator of railway timetables, in 1839; his famous *Bradshaw's Monthly Railway Guide* was first published for Dec. 1841.

29

Birthday of Dag Hammarskjöld (July 29, 1905–Sept. 18, 1961). Swedish economist; 2nd secretary-general of the United Nations; awarded the Nobel Peace Prize posthumously in 1961.

29

Birthday of Benito Mussolini (July 29, 1883–Apr. 28, 1945; ruled 1922–1943). Italian fascist who ruled as prime minister and then as absolute dictator *(Il Duce);* ally of Adolph Hitler during the Spanish Civil War and World War II. Repudiated in 1943; subsequently arrested and executed by his countrymen.

29

Birthday of (Newton) Booth Tarkington (July 29, 1869–May 19, 1946). American author who won the Pulitzer Prize in 1919 for *The Magnificent Ambersons* and in 1922 for *Alice Adams.* Perhaps best known for *Penrod.*

29

Birthday of Alexis de Tocqueville (July 29, 1805–Apr. 16, 1895). French statesman and author of the 4-volume *Democracy in America,* which won the Montyon Prize of the French Academy in 1836.

ANNIVERSARIES AND SPECIAL EVENTS DAYS

30

Anniversary of the publication of the first 10 Penguin paperback books in the U.K. on July 30, 1935. Allen Lane and his brothers founded Penguin Books on Jan. 15, 1935, with the goal of publishing high-quality books at modest prices. They revolutionized the industry.

30

Anniversary of the organization of the WAVES (Women Accepted for Volunteer Emergency Service), the women's reserve unit of the U.S. Naval Reserves, on July 30, 1942.

30

Birthday of Emily Brontë (July 30, 1818–Dec. 19, 1848). English author, famous for her novel *Wuthering Heights.*

30

Birthday of Henry Ford (July 30, 1863–Apr. 7, 1947). American inventor, automobile manufacturer, and philanthropist whose fortune established the Ford Foundation.

30

First Assembly Day. Anniversary of the July 30, 1619, election of the House of Burgesses in Jamestown, Va., the first representative assembly in the New World.

30

Marseillaise Day. "La Marseillaise," the French national anthem, was first sung in Paris on July 30, 1792, by 500 men from Marseilles.

HOLY DAYS AND FEAST DAYS

31

Feast of St. Ignatius Loyola (born Iñigo de Loyola; 1491–July 31, 1556). Spanish Basque, soldier and mystic, author of the *Spiritual Exercises;* founder in 1541 of the Society of Jesus (the Jesuits), Roman Catholic order dedicated to missionary work, education, scholarship, and social justice.

ANNIVERSARIES AND SPECIAL EVENTS DAYS

31

Birthday of John Ericsson (July 31, 1803–Mar. 8, 1889). Swedish-born American inventor of the screw propeller, pioneer in modern naval construction, builder of the warship *Monitor;* memorials to him have been built in the U.S. and in Sweden. In Sweden, today is John Ericsson Day, or Sweden-America Day. In Kyrkviken, Filipstad, wreaths are laid on his grave and a Swedish-American High Mass is celebrated; the battle between the *Monitor* and *Merrimac* is reenacted on Lake Daglösen.

31

Birthday of James Kent (July 31, 1763–Dec. 12, 1847). American lawyer, jurist, and famous legal commentator. Elected to the Hall of Fame for Great Americans.

CA. 31
Basque Festival, or St. Ignatius Loyola Picnic, in Boise, Idaho; Sunday nearest July 31. Held by Boise's Basque community, the country's largest.

MOVABLE DAYS IN JULY
HOLY DAYS AND FEAST DAYS

ZULU FESTIVAL, OR SHEMBE FESTIVAL, IN SOUTH AFRICA, AT EMATABETULU VILLAGE, NEAR INANDA; core day is last Sunday in July; begins July 1. Members of the Nazareth Baptist Church gather for a month of sacred dancing and ritual. A mix of pagan, Old Testament, and Christian elements, codified in 1911 by the sect's founder, Shemba.

YUCHI GREEN CORN DANCE AND FESTIVAL IN KELLEYVILLE, OKLA.; at the full moon of July; lasts several days. The Yuchi nation's major religious ceremony and festival. Visitors are welcome.

HOLIDAYS AND CIVIC DAYS

DARWIN SHOW DAY IN NORTHERN TERRITORY, AUSTRALIA; last Friday in July; official public holiday.

PRESIDENTS' DAY IN BOTSWANA; 3rd Monday in July and the following Tuesday; official public holiday. Honors all the country's presidents, particularly the first, Sir Seretse Khama, reelected 3 times.

CONSTITUTION DAY IN FIJI; 4th Monday in July; official public holiday. Commemorates the new constitution of July 25, 1990, promulgated following the coups of May 14 and Sept. 25, 1987, both aimed at assuring power to indigenous Fijians threatened by immigrant Indians.

HURRICANE SUPPLICATION DAY IN THE U.S. VIRGIN ISLANDS; 4th Monday in July; official public holiday. A day of prayer for safety in the hurricane season.

HEROES' DAY IN ZAMBIA; 1st Monday in July; official public holiday. The next day is Unity Day, also an official public holiday. Honors citizens who died in the struggle for independence. Political rallies stress unity.

ANNIVERSARIES AND SPECIAL EVENTS DAYS

OMMEGANG FESTIVAL IN BRUSSELS, BELGIUM; 1st Thursday in July. Began as a religious procession in the 14th century, honoring the arrival of a miraculous statue of the Virgin; developed into a carnival, re-creating the extravagant state visit of Charles V, Holy Roman Emperor, in 1549. Now features 2,000 participants in historical costumes, in the Grand-Place; historical persons are sometimes represented by their own descendants. Features flag dances, duels of stilt walkers, fire breathers, and tumblers.

JUST FOR LAUGHS (JUSTE POUR RIRE) IN MONTREAL, CANADA; about 12 days, ending the last Sunday in July. Also called the Montreal International Comedy Festival. Comics of all sorts perform.

MERENGUE FESTIVAL IN THE DOMINICAN REPUBLIC, OR MALECÓN IN SANTO DOMINGO; last week of July–1st week of Aug. The merengue is the most popular Dominican dance.

FÊTES DE CORNOUAILLE IN QUIMPER, FRANCE; last week of July. One of Brittany's great festivals, celebrating all aspects of Breton and Celtic culture.

FESTIVAL OF FORT-DE-FRANCE, MARTINIQUE, FRENCH WEST INDIES; 12 days, ending 1st Wednesday in July. A cultural festival of music, dance, and theater; held since 1972.

SHOOTING FESTIVAL (SCHUTZENFESTE) IN HANOVER, GERMANY; 1st full week in July, the preceding Friday–Saturday and the following Sunday, for 10 days total. The largest of many German shooting festivals, more than 450 years old. Thousands of international marksmen compete; complemented by a huge folk festival.

BLACK CROM'S SUNDAY IN IRELAND; last Sunday in July. Popular traditional day for pilgrims to climb the steep holy mountain of Croagh Patrick or Croagh Dubh ("Black Hill") in County

Mayo. Croagh Dubh was a mountain holy to the Celtic god Crom; Patrick consecrated it to Christianity after remaining atop it for 40 days. Also called Reek Sunday.

FEAST OF THE REDEEMER (IL REDENTORE) IN VENICE, ITALY; 3rd Sunday in July. Held in thanks for salvation from a Black Death plague, ca. 1576. On the eve, Venetians float on the lagoon in lantern-lit flower boats for fireworks and all-night feasts; they watch sunrise from the Lido. On Sunday, there's a thanksgiving procession on a bridge of boats to light candles at the votive Church of the Redeemer and to hear Mass; in the evening, the patriarch blesses the city.

RED WAISTCOAT FAIR (COLETTE ENCARNADO) IN VILA FRANCA DE XIRA (NEAR LISBON), PORTUGAL; 5 days, including the weekend of the 1st Sunday in July. A festival of cowboys in red waistcoats, with folk dances, bullfights, and a running of the bulls.

MUSIC ON LAKE SILJAN FESTIVAL, INCLUDING THE BINGSJÖ GATHERING, IN DALARNA PROVINCE, SWEDEN; during the 1st full week of July, with the Gathering on Wednesday. Sweden's premiere folk music and fiddling contest and gathering.

GUARDIAN ANGEL FESTIVAL (SCHUTZENGELFEST) IN APPENZELL, SWITZERLAND; 2nd Sunday in July. At a mountain cave-chapel in the Alpstein mountains. Event dates from 1621; features morning worship followed by a choir of yodelers and parties in nearby villages.

TOBAGO HERITAGE FESTIVAL IN TOBAGO (OF TRINIDAD AND TOBAGO); last 2 weeks in July. With goat and crab races, folk dancing, a reenacted Tobago wedding, and the usual festivities.

FAIR FORTNIGHT IN GLASGOW, SCOTLAND; begins the Saturday after the 2nd Monday in July, lasts 2 weeks. Glasgow's annual holiday and fair, dating from at least 1190.

LLANGOLLEN INTERNATIONAL MUSICAL EISTEDDFOD IN LLANGOLLEN, WALES; for a week in July. Began in 1945; draws competitors from all the world, and includes non-Welsh music.

RAGBRAI IN IOWA; last full week in July. The *Des Moines Register*'s Annual Great Bicycle Ride across Iowa, held since 1973; an event that attracts cyclists of all ages from all parts of the country for the sheer love of the ride. There are no winners or prizes.

SHAKER FESTIVAL IN SOUTH UNION, KY.; starts 2nd Thursday in July, for 10 days. Tells the Shaker story; outdoor drama nightly, traditional meals, craft demonstrations. Shakers made many contributions to American crafts and domestic science, with simple design and clever invention; they gave us the clothespin, long-handled broom, screw propeller, and circular saw.

GRANDFATHER MOUNTAIN HIGHLAND GAMES AND GATHERING OF SCOTTISH CLANS NEAR LINVILLE, N.C.; 2nd Friday–Sunday in July. The largest Scottish event in the U.S.; with Scottish music and dance, sports, and parades.

EAA INTERNATIONAL FLY-IN CONVENTION AND SPORT AVIATION EXHIBITION IN OSHKOSH, WIS.; 7 days, usually starts last Friday in July. Said to be the world's largest and most significant annual aviation event. Sponsored by the Experimental Aviation Association.

FRONTIER DAYS IN CHEYENNE, WYO.; last full week in July, sometimes longer. First held on Sept. 23, 1897, the first Frontier Day anywhere. Re-creates the history and customs of the Old West with pageants, rodeos, ceremonial Native American dances, and old-time vehicle parades.

August

August, the 8th month of the year, was named for the Roman emperor Augustus. In many countries it is a traditional time for music festivals, fairs, exposition bns, and family holidays.

The one religious day in August that is observed around the world is August 15, the feast of the Assumption of Mary, a holy day and a holiday in many Roman Catholic countries. On this day the Italian, Spanish, and Latin American peoples cherish age-old religious processions, often followed by fiestas.

In the Caribbean, on the islands that once were or still are British territory, the period around August 1 is carnival time, exuberantly celebrating both the end of slavery in 1834 and 1838, and the sugarcane harvest.

The flowers for August are the gladiolus and the poppy. The birthstones are the sardonyx and the peridot.

HOLY DAYS AND FEAST DAYS

1
Feast of St. Alfonso Maria de' Liguori (Sept. 21, 1696–Aug. 1, 1787). Italian lawyer and priest; founder of the Congregation of the Most Holy Redeemer (the Redemptorists); doctor of the church. Patron saint of confessors and moralists.

1
Feast of the Holy Maccabees (died ca. 160 B.C.). Honors Eleazar, and also 7 brothers and their mother, all Jews, executed for resisting efforts to Hellenize the Jews; their remains are by tradition in the church of St. Peter in Chains in Rome. Orth.: Aug. 1 or 14.

HOLIDAYS AND CIVIC DAYS

1
Independence Day in Benin; official public holiday. Also called National Day. Commemorates the attainment of independence from France by Benin (then Dahomey) on Aug. 1, 1960.

1
PLA Day in China. Anniversary of the founding of the (Chinese) People's Liberation Army, on Aug. 1, 1927, at the Nanchang Uprising.

1
Swiss Confederation Day; official public holiday. Switzerland's national day. Commemorates the founding of the Swiss Confederation by the 3 Forest Cantons on Aug. 1, 1291. Very enthusiastically celebrated.

1
Emancipation Day in Trinidad and Tobago; official public holiday. Also called Discovery Day; renamed Emancipation Day in 1985, in harmony with other formerly British islands; popularly celebrated under its older name for the presumed date of Columbus's landing, on Aug. 1, 1498. Features a ceremonial drama in which Columbus lands on the beach with his fleet and is blessed.

CA. 1
Summer Festival in the Virgin Islands, British West Indies; climax the 1st Sunday–Wednesday in Aug.; official public holiday. Was originally religious, then a celebration of emancipation and of the sugarcane harvest. 2 weeks of contests, parades, dancing, music. At the climax, all business stops.

1
Colorado Day in Colo. Commemorates Colo.'s admission as the 30th state on Aug. 1, 1876.

ANNIVERSARIES AND SPECIAL EVENTS DAYS

1

Anniversary date of the last diary entry by the German girl Anne Frank, on Aug. 1, 1944. She and her family were captured by the Nazis on Aug. 4, 1944.

CA. 1

Anniversary of the approximate date in 1958 when the famous photograph "A Great Day in Harlem" was taken for *Esquire* magazine. The photographer convened as many notable jazz musicians as possible for a group photograph on the steps of a Harlem brownstone. The photo was published in *Esquire*'s Jan. 1959 issue.

1

Anniversary of the Warsaw Uprising. On Aug. 1, 1944, the Polish Home Army in Warsaw attacked the occupying German army; fighting lasted for 63 days, while the Russian army watched from across the Vistula River; 200,000 Poles died. The fiercest single act of resistance against the Nazis in Occupied Europe. A potent symbol of the Poles' desire for freedom; observance of this day was suppressed while Poland was controlled by the USSR. Now observed annually.

1

Birthday of William Clark (Aug. 1, 1770–Sept. 1, 1838). American soldier and explorer; younger brother of George Rogers Clark; a leader with Meriwether Lewis of the epic Lewis and Clark expedition to the Pacific Northwest, 1804–6. Their joint command was harmonious and complementary; Clark was mapmaker and artist to the expedition. Their expedition opened a route to the Pacific and stimulated the westward expansion of the American nation.

1

Birthday of Richard Henry Dana (Aug. 1, 1815–Jan. 6, 1882). American author, lawyer, and sailor best known for his memoir *Two Years before the Mast.*

1

Birthday of Francis Scott Key (Aug. 1, 1779–Jan. 11, 1843). American lawyer; author of the national anthem "The Star-Spangled Banner."

1

Birthday of Jean-Baptiste Lamarck (born Jean-Baptiste de Monet, Chevalier de Lamarck; Aug. 1, 1744–Dec. 18, 1829). French naturalist who proposed that acquired traits are inherited.

1

Birthday of Andrew Melville (Aug. 1, 1545–1622). Scottish Protestant successor to John Knox.

1

Birthday of Herman Melville (Aug. 1, 1819–Sept. 28, 1891). American author; his novel *Moby Dick* (1851) won him a permanent place in world literature.

1

Birthday of Maria Mitchell (Aug. 1, 1818–June 28, 1889). American astronomer; first woman to be elected to the American Academy of Arts and Sciences. Elected to the Hall of Fame for Great Americans.

1

Doggett's Coat and Badge Race up the River Thames, England. Also called the Waterman's Derby. Originated in 1716 as a tribute to the Company of Watermen of the River Thames; reported to be the world's oldest annual sporting event and the longest rowing race (4.5 miles); now supervised by the Fishmongers' Company.

1

Emancipation Day in present or former British territories. Slavery in the British Empire was officially abolished effective Aug. 1, 1834 and 1838. The end of slavery is exuberantly celebrated in the British parts of the Caribbean, often as an offical public holiday, usually on Aug. 1 or on the 1st Monday in Aug.

1

Lammas Day (*Lunasdal*) in Scotland and parts of Ireland. Ancient harvest festival celebration in honor of Lugh, the Celtic sun god. Lammas was the forerunner of Thanksgiving in the U.S. and the Harvest Festival in Canada. In Scotland and Ireland, Lammas Fairs were once very common on Lammas Day, and August fairs are still common.

CA. 1

Nebuta Festival in Hirosaki and Aomori, Japan; Aug. 1–7. The prefecture's main festival. Features large translucent floats of warriors, birds, and other objects illuminated from within. An extraordinarily merry festival for both cities.

HOLY DAYS AND FEAST DAYS

2

Ethiopian feast of St. Frumentius (or Fremnatos; ca. 300–ca. 380). In Ethiopia he's called *Abuna* ("Our Father") and Salama I, the first patriarch. Introduced Christianity to Ethiopia. Patron saint of Ethiopia.

2

Feast of the Iron Father (*Demir Baba*) in Bulgaria. A Muslim Shiite holiday, but observed on the former date of the Orthodox feast of St. Elijah. The perhaps mythical Muslim patron saint is honored at dawn, at his tomb, revering his shoes, knife, and sand-club.

2

Feast of Our Lady of the Angels in Costa Rica; official public holiday. In honor of Costa Rica's patron saint, a day of pilgrimage to the basilica in Cartago, built at the discovery site of a small black stone statue (the Black Virgin of Cartago, La Negrita), discovered on Aug. 2, 1635, by a girl, Juana Pereira.

HOLIDAYS AND CIVIC DAYS

2

Illenden in Macedonia; official public holiday. Also called Ilija Day, Prophet Elias Day, or National Day. Commemorates the Aug. 2, 1903, uprising of Macedonians against the Ottoman Empire.

ANNIVERSARIES AND SPECIAL EVENTS DAYS

2

Anniversary of the Treblinka Uprising. On Aug. 2, 1943, Jewish prisoners in the Treblinka Nazi concentration camp rose in a planned revolt; many escaped, and a portion survived to bear witness.

2

Birthday of James Arthur Baldwin (Aug. 2, 1924–Nov. 30, 1987). African American author, best known for *Go Tell It on the Mountain* (1953).

2

Birthday of Pierre-Charles L'Enfant (Aug. 2, 1754–June 14, 1825). French-born American army engineer and an officer in the American Revolutionary army; honored as the designer of the plans for the city of Washington, D.C.

2

Birthday of Henry Steel Olcott (Aug. 2, 1832–Feb. 17, 1907). American spiritualist and first president of the Theosophical Society.

2

Harriet Quimby Day. Anniversary of the Aug. 2, 1911, licensing of Harriet Quimby as America's first woman pilot.

HOLIDAYS AND CIVIC DAYS

3

Armed Forces Day in Equatorial Guinea; an important official public holiday.

3

Pidjiguiti Martyrs' Day in Guinea-Bissau; official public holiday. Honors those who died in the struggle for independence.

3

Independence Day in Niger; official public holiday. Celebrates the attainment of independence from France on Aug. 3, 1960.

ANNIVERSARIES AND SPECIAL EVENTS DAYS

3

Anniversary of the departure of Christopher Columbus on Aug. 3, 1492, on his first voyage of exploration. He sailed from Palos, Spain, with about 88 men in 3 ships, the *Pinta*, the *Niña,* and his flagship, the *Santa María.* Observances are held annually on this day in Columbus, Ohio, at its full-size replica of the *Santa María.*

3

Anniversary of the ceding of the Northwest Territory to the U.S. As a condition of a peace treaty between Native Americans and the U.S., signed on Aug. 3, 1795, at Fort Greenville, by General Anthony Wayne and Little Turtle (1752–1812; Miami) and other chiefs, most of Ohio was ceded. The chiefs' authority and the treaty's legality were hotly denied by the Native American populace.

3

Birthday of Rupert Brooke (Aug. 3, 1887–Apr. 23, 1915). English poet killed in World War I. His youth and poetic gifts made him a suitable symbol of that war's Lost Generation.

3

Birthday of Ernie (Ernest Taylor) Pyle (Aug. 3, 1900–Apr. 18, 1945). American journalist and spokesperson for the American soldier; the most famous American war reporter of World War II; died by machine gun fire in the Pacific.

3

Birthday of Lady Isabella Caroline Somerset (Aug. 3, 1851–Mar. 12, 1921). English philanthropist; temperance worker; successor to Frances Willard as president of the Women's Christian Temperance Union; founder of a pioneer farm colony for alcoholic women in 1895, the first such institution in England.

HOLY DAYS AND FEAST DAYS

4

Traditional feast of St. Dominic (born Domingo de Guzmán; (1170–Aug. 6, 1221). Spanish priest; founder, in 1216, of the Order of Preachers (Dominicans). Patron saint of astronomers, the Dominican Republic, and Managua, Nicaragua.

HOLIDAYS AND CIVIC DAYS

4

Revolution Day in Burkina Faso; official public holiday. Commemorates a coup of Aug. 4, 1983, when rebels led by Captain Thomas Sankara seized power and governed until superseded in 1987.

CA. 4

Santo Domingo Fiesta in Managua, Nicaragua; Aug. 1–10; official public holiday on 1st and 10th. St. Dominic is Managua's patron saint. The festival is very important; the whole city goes on holiday for 10 days.

ANNIVERSARIES AND SPECIAL EVENTS DAYS

4

Birthday of Oliver Perry Morton (Aug. 4, 1823–Nov. 1, 1877). Ind.'s Civil War governor who represents his state in Statuary Hall.

4

Birthday of Joseph Justus Scaliger (Aug. 4, 1540–Jan. 21, 1609). French scholar, the Father of Scientific Chronology, inventor of the Julian Period.

4

Birthday of Percy Bysshe Shelley (Aug. 4, 1792–July 8, 1822). English Romantic poet, in whose honor the Poetry Society of America presents the annual Shelley Memorial Award to a living American poet.

4

Coast Guard Day. Anniversary of the establishment on Aug. 4, 1790, of the Revenue Cutter Service, which merged with the Life Saving Service in 1915 to become the U.S. Coast Guard.

4

Nautilus Day. Anniversary of the Aug. 4, 1958, passage of the U.S. atomic-powered submarine *Nautilus* under the North Pole.

HOLY DAYS AND FEAST DAYS

5

Feast of the dedication of the Basilica of St. Mary Major; better known as the feast of Our Lady of the Snows. On Aug. 5, 352, a snowfall in Rome predicted by vision-dreams outlined the shape of her church-to-be. Celebrated, usually with showers of white flower petals, in Rome, Spain, the Canary Islands, the Philippines, Bolivia, and Ecuador.

HOLIDAYS AND CIVIC DAYS

5

Independence Day in Burkina Faso; official public holiday. Commemorates the attainment of independence from France on Aug. 5, 1960.

5

Homeland Thanksgiving Day in Croatia; official public holiday.

ANNIVERSARIES AND SPECIAL EVENTS DAYS

5

Birthday of Mary Ritter Beard (Aug. 5, 1876–Aug. 14, 1958). American historian who in numerous books concentrated on women's roles in society; collaborated with her husband, Charles, in the writing of American history.

5

Birthday of John Eliot (Aug. 5, 1604–May 21, 1690). American clergyman, the Apostle to the Indians; author of a catechism that was the first book printed in a Native American language; his translation of the Bible into the Pequot language, completed in 1663, was the first Bible printed on the American continent.

5

Birthday of (Henri-René-Albert) Guy de Maupassant (Aug. 5, 1850–July 6, 1893). French novelist and one of the great short-story writers of the 19th century.

5

Birthday of Raoul Gustaf Wallenberg (Aug. 5, 1912–ca. July 17, 1947). Swedish architect and humanitarian; saved 100,000 Jews from the Nazi death camps. Arrested by the Soviets on Jan. 17, 1945, and died in prison, perhaps in 1947.

HOLY DAYS AND FEAST DAYS

6

Russian Orthodox feast of St. Boris (died 1015). Russian; patron saint of Moscow. R.C.: July 24; Orth.: July 24 or Aug. 6.

6

Feast of the Transfiguration of the Lord. Commemorates the revelation by Jesus of his divinity as the Messiah to the apostles Peter, James the Greater, and John. Orth.: Aug. 6 or 19.

HOLIDAYS AND CIVIC DAYS

6

Independence Day in Bolivia; official public holiday. Celebrates the declaration of independence from Peru, at the Congress of Chuquisaca on Aug. 6, 1825. Some communities celebrate enthusiastically for a week.

6

Accession Day in Abu Dhabi, United Arab Emirates; official public holiday in Abu Dhabi. Commemorates the accession of Shaikh Zaid ibn Sultan an-Nahayan, ruler of Abu Dhabi and first president of the U.A.E. since 1971.

ANNIVERSARIES AND SPECIAL EVENTS DAYS

6

Anniversary of the discovery of life on Mars. On Aug. 6, 1996, NASA officials unofficially announced that scientists, having analyzed an ancient meteorite found in Antarctica, had concluded that it contained organic molecules pointing to the existence of a primitive form of microscopic life on Mars more than 3 billion years ago.

6

Birthday of Sir Alexander Fleming (Aug. 6, 1881–Mar. 11, 1955). Scottish bacteriologist who discovered penicillin; corecipient of the Nobel Prize in physiology or medicine in 1945.

6

Birthday of Alfred, Lord Tennyson (Aug. 6, 1809–Oct. 6, 1892). Celebrated English poet; poet laureate (1850–92); best-known poems include "The Lady of Shalott" and "The Charge of the Light Brigade."

6

Hiroshima Day. Anniversary of the dropping of the first atomic bomb on Hiroshima, Japan, on Aug. 6 (Japan time), 1945. Hiroshima is now a city dedicated to world peace and the site of the Atomic Bomb Casualty Commission, which is devoted to medical and biological research. Annually on this day are observances to foster world peace; in Hiroshima's Peace Memorial Park there is a moving lantern festival in memory of the dead.

HOLIDAYS AND CIVIC DAYS

7

Battle of Boyacá Day in Colombia; official public holiday. Commemorates the victory of South American insurgents over Spanish forces on Aug. 7, 1819.

7

Independence Day in Côte d'Ivoire; official public holiday; formerly observed on Dec. 7. Independence was attained from France on Dec. 7, 1960; the Ivory Coast officially changed its name to Côte d'Ivoire in Oct. 1985.

ANNIVERSARIES AND SPECIAL EVENTS DAYS

7

Anniversary of the dedication of the International Peace Bridge on Aug. 7, 1927, a cantilever bridge erected between Buffalo, N.Y., and Fort Erie, Canada, honoring the amity that exists between Canada and the U.S.

7

Anniversary of the establishment of the Order of the Purple Heart. U.S. decoration for military merit was created by George Washington on Aug. 7, 1782, for enlisted men and noncommissioned officers. The first recipients were Sergeants Daniel Bissel, Daniel Brown, and Elijah Churchill of the Conn. regiment, who were honored on May 9, 1783. The award was reinstituted on Feb. 22,

1932, the bicentennial of Washington's birth, and recognizes those wounded in action. It is a commemorative day in the states of Mass. and Wash.

7
Anniversary of the founding of the U.S. Lighthouse Service. On Aug. 7, 1789, President George Washington signed legislation creating a lighthouse service and providing for federal construction of lighthouses. The Lighthouse Service was substantially reformed following the Oct. 9, 1852, creation by Congress of the Lighthouse Board.

7
Anniversary of the transmission of the first photograph of Earth taken from space, sent on Aug. 7, 1959, by the U.S. satellite *Explorer VI*. For the first time we could see the Earth whole.

7
Birthday of Ralph Johnson Bunche (Aug. 7, 1904–Dec. 9, 1971). American statesman; a founder and leader of the United Nations. Winner of the 1950 Nobel Peace Prize for the negotiation of an Arab-Israeli truce. The first African American to receive a Nobel Prize.

7
Birthday of Alonso de Ercilla y Zúñiga (Aug. 7, 1533–Nov. 29, 1594). Basque Spanish soldier and poet in Chile; wrote the classic epic poem *La Araucuna,* the first one about America, notable for its scrupulous respect for the Araucuna people of Chile.

7
Birthday of Nathanael Greene (Aug. 7, 1742–June 19, 1786). American Revolutionary War general who represents R.I. in Statuary Hall.

HOLIDAYS AND CIVIC DAYS

8
Farmers' Day in Tanzania; official public holiday. Also called *Nane Nane* ("8–8").

ANNIVERSARIES AND SPECIAL EVENTS DAYS

8
Birthday of Charles Bulfinch (Aug. 8, 1763–Apr. 4, 1844). American architect who introduced the styles of Christopher Wren and Robert Adam into American architecture; the first professional architect in the U.S.

8
Birthday of Matthew A. Henson (Aug. 8, 1866–Mar. 9, 1955). African American explorer, discoverer of the North Pole with his colleague Robert Peary in 1909; awarded the Congressional Medal in 1945 for his contributions to science.

8
Birthday of Ernest Orlando Lawrence (Aug. 8, 1901–Aug. 27, 1958). American physicist, inventor of the cyclotron, recipient of the 1939 Nobel Prize in physics; recipient of the first Sylvanus Thayer Award.

8
Birthday of Henry Fairfield Osborn (Aug. 8, 1857–Nov. 6, 1935). American paleontologist and author who broadened public understanding of paleontology through instructive museum displays.

HOLIDAYS AND CIVIC DAYS

9
National Day in Singapore; official public holiday. Commemorates the Aug. 9, 1965, withdrawal of Singapore from the Federation of Malaysia; celebrated with music, parades, dancing. (Singapore attained independence from the U.K. on Sept. 16, 1963.)

ANNIVERSARIES AND SPECIAL EVENTS DAYS

9
Anniversary of the founding of the Daughters of the American Revolution on Aug. 9, 1890. Membership is limited to women who can prove descent from American Revolutionary times. The DAR's purpose is education, preservation, and patriotic service. It was chartered by Congress on Dec. 2, 1895.

9
Anniversary of the dropping of the 2nd atomic bomb, on Nagasaki, Japan, on Aug. 9, 1945; a moment of silence in memory of the dead is held in Nagasaki's Peace Memorial Park.

9
Anniversary of the resignation of President Richard Nixon. To avoid impeachment for his part in the Watergate affair Nixon resigned on Aug. 9, 1974; the only president of the U.S. to resign his office.

9
Birthday of Dr. William Thomas Green Morton (Aug. 9, 1819–July 15, 1868). American dentist

who received an award from the French Academy of Science in 1852 for the application of the discovery of etherization to surgical operations. Elected to the Hall of Fame for Great Americans.

9
Birthday of Isaak Walton (Aug. 9, 1593–Dec. 15, 1683). English biographer and author famous for *The Compleat Angler.*

9
Death anniversary of Jerry (Jerome John) Garcia (Aug. 1, 1942–Aug. 9, 1995). American musician; leader of The Grateful Dead, a rock band of enormous musical influence, with possibly the longest-lasting following of any rock band.

9
Raising the Maypole (*Meyboom*) in the Grand-Place of Brussels, Belgium. One of Brussels's two major celebrations. The other is the Ommegang Festival in July.

HOLY DAYS AND FEAST DAYS

10
Feast of St. Lawrence (died 258). Roman deacon; martyred by roasting. Patron saint of cooks, protector of vineyards, and invoked against rheumatism and fire. The Saint Lawrence River is named for him. Orth.: Aug. 10 or 23.

HOLIDAYS AND CIVIC DAYS

10
Independence Day in Ecuador; official public holiday. Commemorates the Aug. 10, 1809, declaration of independence from Spain, in Quito, which began Latin America's independence wars. Celebrated with military and school parades, especially in Quito.

10
Missouri Admission Day. Mo. was admitted to the Union as the 24th state on Aug. 10, 1821.

ANNIVERSARIES AND SPECIAL EVENTS DAYS

10
Anniversary of the Pueblo Revolt. On Aug. 10, 1680, Pueblo tribes (Rio Grande, Hopi, and Zuni) with Apache help, and led by the medicine man Popé (a Tewa of San Juan pueblo), successfully revolted against the persecution of Spanish colonists and priests, and remained free for 12 years, until the reconquest of New Mexico by Governor Pedro de Vargas.

10
Anniversary of the establishment of the Smithsonian Institution. On Aug. 10, 1846, President James Polk signed the Act of Congress establishing the Smithsonian in Washington, D.C.

10
Birthday of Camillo Benso di Cavour (Aug. 10, 1810–June 6, 1861). Italian statesman, premier of Italy, major leader in Italian unification.

10
Birthday of Herbert Clark Hoover (Aug. 10, 1874–Oct. 20, 1964). Iowa-born mining engineer; international relief administrator and humanitarian; 31st president of the U.S. (1929–33; Republican). Chairman, Commission for Reorganization of the Executive Branch. Founded the Hoover Library on War, Revolution, and Peace at Stanford University. Buried at West Branch, Iowa. His administration saw the stock market crash and the onset of the Great Depression.

10
Death anniversary of Handsome Lake (ca. 1750–Aug. 10, 1815). Native American (Seneca Iroquois) regenerator of the traditional Iroquois religion (1799–1815), in the form later called the Old Way of Handsome Lake, in response to the cultural despair caused by the destruction of traditional lifeways following the Revolutionary War.

CA. 10
Female Chefs' Festival (*La Fête des Cuisinières*) in Guadeloupe, French West Indies; usually on the Saturday after Aug. 10. Female chefs in creole costume honor their patron saint, St. Lawrence, and flaunt their prowess with a High Mass blessing their samples, a parade of their work, a ceremony, a public banquet, and dancing.

CA. 10
Herbert Hoover Day in Iowa; the Sunday nearest Aug. 10. Honors President Herbert Hoover, especially in his birthplace in West Branch, Iowa; observed with programs by civic organizations in West Branch and throughout the country by the Federated Boys' Clubs of America.

HOLY DAYS AND FEAST DAYS

11
Feast of St. Clare (July 11, 1194–Aug. 11, 1253). Italian friend of St. Francis of Assisi and founder of the Franciscan order of the Poor Clares; responsible with Francis for the growth and development of the Franciscans; patron saint of television.

HOLIDAYS AND CIVIC DAYS

11
Independence Day in Chad; official public holiday. Celebrates independence attained from France on Aug. 11, 1960.

11
Heroes' Day (Aug. 11) and Defense Forces Day (Aug. 12) in Zimbabwe; official public holidays. Honor the nation's civil and military heroes.

ANNIVERSARIES AND SPECIAL EVENTS DAYS

11
Birthday of Joseph H. Hirshhorn (Aug. 11, 1900–Aug. 31, 1981). American financier, uranium mining tycoon, art collector, and founder and donor to the nation of the Hirshhorn Museum and Sculpture Garden in Washington, D.C.

11
Birthday of Gifford Pinchot (Aug. 11, 1865–Oct. 4, 1946). American conservationist; the first professional American forester; first head of the U.S. Forest Service; governor of Pa. (1923–27, 1931–35).

HOLIDAYS AND CIVIC DAYS

12
Queen's Birthday in Thailand; official public holiday. Privately celebrated at the royal palace by Queen Sirikit, who makes offerings to monks and attends religious services.

ANNIVERSARIES AND SPECIAL EVENTS DAYS

12
Birthday of Katherine Lee Bates (Aug. 12, 1859–Mar. 28, 1929). American educator and writer, author of the text for the national hymn "America the Beautiful."

12
Birthday of Cantinflas (born Mario Moreno Reyes; Aug. 12, 1911–Apr. 20, 1993). Mexico's most famous comic actor.

12
Birthday of Robert Mills (Aug. 12, 1781–Mar. 3, 1855). American architect, the first to study exclusively in the U.S.; his most memorable work is the Washington Monument.

12
Perseid Meteor Showers; July 25–Aug. 18, main day Aug. 12. Visible toward the east at midnight.

The richest and most spectacular of all meteor showers.

HOLIDAYS AND CIVIC DAYS

13
Independence Day in the Central African Republic; official public holiday. Commemorates independence attained from France on Aug. 13, 1960.

13
Women's Day in Tunisia; official public holiday. Celebrates the independence of women and recognizes their contributions to the nation, on the anniversary of the Aug. 13, 1956, proclamation of the Persons Status Code, recognizing women as persons in law.

ANNIVERSARIES AND SPECIAL EVENTS DAYS

13
Anniversary of the erection of the Berlin Wall by the East German government on Aug. 13, 1961. The concrete wall sealing the border between East and West Berlin was erected to halt the exodus of people to the West. The Fall of the Berlin Wall occurred on Nov. 9, 1989, when it was opened for free passage; a prelude to the reunification of Germany.

13
Birthday of John Logie Baird (Aug. 13, 1888–June 14, 1946). Scottish inventor known as the Father of Television.

13
Birthday of Annie Oakley (born Phoebe Ann Moses; Aug. 13, 1860–Nov. 3, 1926). American sharpshooter whose personality and exploits are re-created in pageants of the American West.

13
International Lefthanders Day. Promotes the rights of left-handed people and encourages manufacturers to consider their special needs; sponsored by Lefthanders International and celebrated since Friday, Aug. 13, 1982.

13
Lucy Stone Day. Anniversary of the birth of the leading American suffragist and abolitionist (Aug. 13, 1818–Oct. 18, 1893). Known for her insistence on keeping her maiden name after marriage, thus inspiring generations of Lucy Stoners. Honored by many organizations, including the Lucy Stoner League in New York City, a center for studies on the status of women.

13

William Caxton Day. Anniversary of the birth of the first English printer, William Caxton (Aug. 13, ca. 1422–1491). In 1477 he printed the first book in England, *The Mirror of the World*; his birthday is observed by collectors and literary organizations.

HOLY DAYS AND FEAST DAYS

14

Feast of St. Maximilian Kolbe (born Raymond Kolbe; Jan. 7, 1894–Aug. 14, 1941). Polish Franciscan priest who was imprisoned by the Gestapo in the Nazis' Auschwitz concentration camp and volunteered for execution in place of a married man with family.

HOLIDAYS AND CIVIC DAYS

14

Independence Day in Pakistan; official public holiday. Celebrates the attainment of independence from the U.K. on Aug. 14, 1947.

14

Liberty Tree Day. Memorializes the American colonists' challenge to the British governor on Aug. 14, 1765, by hanging two effigies in a Boston elm tree, soon to be known as the Liberty Tree; proclaimed by the governor of Mass.

ANNIVERSARIES AND SPECIAL EVENTS DAYS

14

Atlantic Charter Day. Anniversary of the signing of the Atlantic Charter by Franklin Roosevelt and Winston Churchill on Aug. 14, 1941, in which the signatories outlined the 8 points that were later incorporated in the United Nations declaration.

14

Social Security Day. Anniversary of the passage of the Social Security Act on Aug. 14, 1935.

14

V-J (Victory over Japan) Day. Anniversary of the Aug. 14, 1945, announcement that Japan had surrendered unconditionally to the Allies, thus ending World War II in the Pacific. The official ratification of the surrender occurred on Sept. 2, 1945. The formal peace treaty was signed on Sept. 8, 1951.

HOLY DAYS AND FEAST DAYS

15

Feast of the Assumption. Also called the Assumption into Heaven of the Blessed Virgin Mary or the Theotokos. Commemorates the death of the Virgin Mary, after which she was taken, body and soul, into heaven. A very old Marian feast, and the most intensely popular: this is harvest time in the Northern Hemisphere. In the Eastern Churches, called the Dormition (Falling Asleep) of the Theotokos (the God-Bearer); preceded by a fast, Aug. 1–14. An especially important day in Greece. In Bulgaria, a major day for weddings. An official public holiday in many countries. Orth: Aug. 15 or 28.

HOLIDAYS AND CIVIC DAYS

15

Independence Day in Congo; official public holiday. Commemorates the attainment of independence from France on Aug. 15, 1960.

15

Mother's Day in Costa Rica; official public holiday; on the feast of the Assumption.

15

Constitution Day in Equatorial Guinea; official public holiday. Commemorates the Aug. 15, 1982, Letter of Aconibe, which revised the original constitution of 1968.

15

Independence Day in India; official public holiday. Commemorates Aug. 15, 1947, when the Indian Independence Act went into effect, and independence was attained from the U.K.

15

National Day, the feast of the Assumption, and the Prince's official birthday in Liechtenstein; official public holiday. The previous constitutional monarch, Prince Franz Joseph II, was born Aug. 16, 1905, and his official birthday was celebrated on the Assumption. This joint holiday is unchanged, though the present ruler is Hans-Adam II, born Feb. 14, 1945.

15

Anniversary of the founding of Old Panama City in Panama; local official public holiday. Founded on Aug. 15, 1519. New Panama City was founded on Jan. 21, 1673.

15
Founding of Asunción Day in Paraguay; official public holiday. Celebrates the founding of the capital on Aug. 15, 1536.

15
Liberation Day, and Republic Day, in South Korea; official public holiday. Celebrates Korea's liberation from Japan with that country's formal surrender on Aug. 15, 1945, and the proclamation of the Republic of Korea on Aug. 15, 1948. Celebrated with military parades and ceremonies.

ANNIVERSARIES AND SPECIAL EVENTS DAYS

15
Anniversary of the Battle of Roncevalles, in northern Spain near the French border on Aug. 15, 778. Charlemagne was returning with his army to France following promising peace negotiations in Spain, when his rear guard, led by Roland, was ambushed by Basques and destroyed. This event, immortalized in the *Song of Roland,* caused Charlemagne to seal Christian Europe's border with Moorish Spain.

15
Birthday of Napoleon Bonaparte (Aug. 15, 1769–May 5, 1821). Emperor of France (1804–15), conqueror of most of Europe, and of enduring influence on French institutions. Finally defeated at the Battle of Waterloo. Today is Napoleon's Day in Corsica, his birthplace. Today is also called Chauvin Day, after the French soldier Nicholas Chauvin, who idolized Napoleon to an extreme; his arrogant boastfulness engendered the term "chauvinism."

15
Birthday of T. E. (Thomas Edward) Lawrence (Aug. 15, 1888–May 19, 1935). British soldier of World War I known as Lawrence of Arabia; adventurer; author of *The Seven Pillars of Wisdom.*

15
Birthday of Sir Walter Scott (Aug. 15, 1771–Sept. 21, 1832). Scottish novelist and poet, famous for such books as *Ivanhoe* and *Rob Roy.*

15
Acadian Day in New Brunswick, Canada. Also called Cajun Day; national day for the Acadian people since 1884. Celebrated especially at the Acadian Festival of Caraquet (lasting at least the 8 days, Sunday–Sunday, that include Aug. 15). At-

tended by people from the whole coast; features the blessing of the fishing fleet, on whichever Sunday has decent weather. The festival is a famous showcase for local artistic talent.

15
Cricket Festival (*Festa del Grillo*) in Florence, Italy. Crickets in tiny cages are sold; for good luck, they must be released by nightfall.

15
Ferragosto in Italy. Italy's vacation season, beginning Aug. 15 (Assumption); official public holiday. A time of traditional festivals all over Italy.

HOLIDAYS AND CIVIC DAYS

16
Restoration Day in the Dominican Republic; official public holiday. Celebrates the declaration of independence from Spain on Aug. 16, 1863, after a brief relapse into colonial status (1861–63); independence was attained in 1865, following a bitter war.

16
Battle of Bennington Day in Vt.; official public holiday. Honors the important Revolutionary War victory of N.H. Minutemen, led by John Stark, and the Green Mountain Boys, led by Seth Warner, over the British on Aug. 16, 1777; American morale was much heartened.

ANNIVERSARIES AND SPECIAL EVENTS DAYS

16
Death anniversary of Duncan Phyfe (1768–Aug. 16, 1854). American cabinetmaker famous for fine furniture; honored in museum collections.

16
Death anniversary of the rock-and-roll musician Elvis Presley (Jan. 8, 1935–Aug. 16, 1977). Fans note the day; and at Graceland, his home in Memphis, Tenn., there is a week or more of events (Elvis Week), culminating on the eve of the 16th with a candlelight vigil; very many attend.

HOLIDAYS AND CIVIC DAYS

17
Death anniversary of José San Martín (Feb. 25, 1778–Aug. 17, 1850); official public holiday in Argentina. Hero of the struggle for independence from Spain.

CA. 17

Discovery Day in the Yukon Territory, Canada; Monday nearest Aug. 17; territorial official public holiday. Commemorates the discovery of gold in the Klondike valley on Aug. 16 or 17, 1896, causing a famous gold rush. Celebrated in nearby Dawson on the holiday weekend.

17

Fête Nationale in Gabon; official public holiday, usually for 2 days. Celebrates the attainment of independence from France on Aug. 17, 1960.

17

Independence Day (*Proklamasi Kermerdekaan*) in Indonesia; official public holiday. Commemorates the proclamation of independence from Japan and Holland on Aug. 17, 1945, by the nationalist leaders Sukarno and Hatta. (Independence was attained from Holland on Aug. 17, 1950.) Celebrated nationwide with sports events, puppet and shadow plays, traditional cultural performances, carnivals, and festivals.

ANNIVERSARIES AND SPECIAL EVENTS DAYS

17

Birthday of David "Davy" Crockett (Aug. 17, 1786– Mar. 6, 1836). American frontiersman, congressman from Tenn., adventurer, and soldier. Fought at the Alamo, surrendered, and was executed.

17

Birthday of Marcus Moziah Garvey (Aug. 17, 1887– June 10, 1940). Jamaican leader, author, and orator; lived in New York City for 11 years. Founded the Universal Negro Improvement Association (UNIA, 1914).

17

Atlantic Balloon Day. Anniversary of the first crossing of the Atlantic Ocean by balloon; the journey ended in France on Aug. 17, 1978.

ANNIVERSARIES AND SPECIAL EVENTS DAYS

18

Anniversary of the Sioux Uprising. On Aug. 18, 1862, Little Crow (1810–1863) led the Sioux against settlers and missionaries in an attempt to regain expropriated sacred lands in Minn. On Dec. 26, 1867, 38 Sioux were hanged, the largest mass execution in U.S. history.

18

Birthday of Virginia Dare (Aug. 18, 1587–?). The first child born of English colonists in America, in the Roanoke Colony; all its inhabitants subsequently vanished.

18

Birthday of Meriwether Lewis (Aug. 18, 1774– Oct. 11, 1809). American outdoorsman, soldier, private secretary to President Thomas Jefferson, and explorer; coleader with William Clark of the Lewis and Clark Expedition to the Pacific Northwest.

18

Death anniversary of Genghis Khan (or Chinggis Khan ["Precious Warrior"]; born Temujin; ca. 1162–Aug. 18, 1227). Mongol chieftain who united the Mongols into a nation, and then proceeded to found a huge Eurasian empire. Highly esteemed in Mongolia; invoked at the Naadam Festival; grandfather of Kublai Khan.

HOLIDAYS AND CIVIC DAYS

19

Independence Day in Afghanistan; official public holiday. Commemorates the defeat of British forces on Aug. 19, 1919, and the attainment of effective independence, following 3 Anglo-Afghan wars in the 19th and early-20th centuries.

19

Quezon Day in the Philippines. Celebrates the birth of Manuel Luis Quezon y Molina (Aug. 19, 1878–Aug. 1, 1944; ruled 1935–44); Philippine statesman and first president of the Philippine Commonwealth.

ANNIVERSARIES AND SPECIAL EVENTS DAYS

19

Anniversary of the Battle of Thermopylae in the Persian Wars. On Aug. 19, 480 B.C., Spartan forces under Leonidas died to the last man defending the pass and slowing the Persian advance. The delay allowed Greek forces to rally and saved Greece from conquest by the Persian emperor Xerxes. The battlefield memorial to Leonidas and his Spartans was revered for centuries.

19

Anniversary of the founding of the *New York Times* in its present form. The newspaper's first issue under its new publisher, Adolph S. Ochs, appeared on Aug. 19, 1896. Ochs aimed for the paper to give the news "concisely, clearly, promptly and impartially, without fear or favor," and thereby serve as the nation's journal of record.

19

Baptismal day of Samuel Richardson (baptized Aug. 19, 1689–July 4, 1761). English novelist; founder, with Henry Fielding, of the English novel; wrote *Pamela* and *Clarissa.*

19

Birthday of Bill (William Jefferson) Clinton (born William Jefferson Blythe III; Aug. 19, 1946–). Arkansas governor; 42nd president of the U.S. (1993–2001; Democrat).

19

Birthday of John Flamsteed (Aug. 19, 1646–Dec. 31, 1719). First Astronomer Royal (1675–1719) of the Greenwich Observatory. His comprehensive atlas of star positions (*Historia Coelestis Britannica,* 3 volumes, 1725) was a crucial service to astronomy and navigation.

19

Birthday of Edith Nesbit (Aug. 19, 1858–May 4, 1924). English author; cofounder of the Fabian Society; remembered for her books, such as *The Railway Children,* lively stories of the adventures of the Bastable children.

19

Birthday of Orville Wright (Aug. 19, 1871–Jan. 30, 1948). American aviator and inventor who made the first self-powered airplane flight in history on Dec. 17, 1903. National Aviation Day, on his birthday, honors the Wright brothers and other pioneer aviators; established in 1939 by presidential proclamation. National Aviation Week includes Aug. 19.

19

Death anniversary of Nick Black Elk (1863–Aug. 19, 1950). Native American (Sioux) medicine man; co-author of *Black Elk Speaks.*

19

Buhe in Ethiopia. A celebration for young boys, akin to Halloween in the West. On the eve, bread is baked and bonfires are lit. On the day, troops of boys go house to house, singing songs for bread.

19

Gigantes Festival in Lucban, Philippines. Papier-mâché giants on stilts, made by the community, lead a night of revelry and a solemn morning procession, with the women dressed as mythic figures.

HOLY DAYS AND FEAST DAYS

20

Feast of St. Bernard of Clairvaux (1090–Aug. 20, 1153). French Cistercian monk, the 2nd founder of the order; of enormous religious and political influence; considered by his contemporaries the wisest and holiest man in Europe. Roused Europe to the unsuccessful Second Crusade (1145–47), and gave the Knights Templar their religious rule. Doctor of the church (called the Mellifluous Doctor).

HOLIDAYS AND CIVIC DAYS

20

St. Stephen's Day in Hungary; official public holiday. Honors Stephen (István) I of Hungary, king, saint, and founder of the state (975–Aug. 15, 1038; ruled 977–1038.) His formal coronation was on Aug. 20, 1000. Stephen founded an independent Hungary, and ruled wisely, generously, and to good effect; he is still remembered with reverence.

ANNIVERSARIES AND SPECIAL EVENTS DAYS

20

Anniversary of the birth of Miracle, a female white buffalo, on Aug. 20, 1994, at Janesville, Wis. The birth is seen as the fulfillment of a 19th-century Lakota Sioux prophecy, marking the start of a time of harmony between the first Americans and the immigrants.

20

Birthday of Benjamin Harrison (Aug. 20, 1833–Mar. 13, 1901). His great-grandfather signed the Declaration of Independence, his grandfather (William Henry Harrison) was president, his father was a congressman; Ind. lawyer and Civil War general; 23rd president of the U.S. (1889–93). Buried in Indianapolis, Ind. His administration was marked by financial and antitrust issues.

20

Birthday of Bernardo O'Higgins (Aug. 20, 1778–Oct. 24, 1842). Chilean independence hero, general, and statesman; liberator of Chile; San Martín's second in command; subsequently dictator of Chile, 1817–23.

20

Birthday of Oliver Hazard Perry (Aug. 20, 1785–Aug. 23, 1819). American naval officer famous for the statement "We have met the enemy and they are ours," following the Battle of Lake Erie in the War of 1812.

20
Birthday of (Gottlieb) Eleil Saarinen (Aug. 20, 1873–July 1, 1950). Renowned Finnish architect.

ANNIVERSARIES AND SPECIAL EVENTS DAYS

21
Anniversary of the establishment of the American Bar Association on Aug. 21, 1878, at Saratoga, N.Y.

21
Anniversary of the Lincoln-Douglas debates of Aug. 21–Oct. 15, 1858, a major U.S. political event of the 19th century.

21
Birthday of Ozma, the queen of the fictional kingdom of Oz, from the L. Frank Baum books.

21
Death anniversary of Benigno S. Aquino Jr. (Nov. 27, 1932–Aug. 21, 1983). Filipino politician, assassinated by agents of the dictator Ferdinand Marcos. His murder led to the downfall of the Marcos regime and the subsequent election (Feb. 7, 1986) as president of his wife, Corazon C. Aquino (Jan. 25, 1923– ; ruled 1986–92).

21
Czechoslovakia Invasion Day. Anniversary of the Russian invasion of Czechoslovakia on Aug. 20–21, 1968, in response to Prague Spring, which intended to produce "communism with a human face." Was popularly observed on Aug. 21; now less important, though not forgotten.

HOLY DAYS AND FEAST DAYS

22
Feast of the Queenship of Mary, on the octave of the Assumption. Also called the feast of Mary, Queen of Heaven. Honors Mary as the queen of heaven, angels, all humanity, and Earth. Officially initiated on May 31, 1954.

ANNIVERSARIES AND SPECIAL EVENTS DAYS

CA. 22
Awa Odori Dance Festival ("Fools' Dance") in Tokushima, Japan; Aug. 22–25. Famous dance

festival of great vigor and charm. With many dance troupes and all-night street dancing.

22
King Richard III Day. Anniversary of the death of Richard III of England (Oct. 2, 1452–Aug. 22, 1485; ruled 1483–85); slain in battle; the last of the Plantagenets. Observed by Richard III societies in England and the U.S.

ANNIVERSARIES AND SPECIAL EVENTS DAYS

23
Anniversary of the execution of Nicola Sacco and Bartolomeo Vanzetti on Aug. 23, 1927. Circumstances of their trial aroused worldwide protest against the convictions and a proclamation of vindication from the governor of Mass. on July 19, 1977.

23
Anniversary of the founding of the World Council of Churches on Aug. 23, 1948, in Amsterdam, Holland.

23
Death anniversary of Sir William Wallace (ca. 1270–Aug. 23, 1305). One of Scotland's national heroes; leader of the Scottish resistance forces during the first years of the long, and ultimately successful, struggle to free Scotland from English rule. In 1306 Robert the Bruce raised the rebellion that eventually won independence from England.

HOLY DAYS AND FEAST DAYS

24
Feast of St. Bartholomew (1st century). One of the 12 Apostles; reputedly preached in India and Greater Armenia. Orth.: Bartholomew and Barnabas, June 11 or 24.

HOLIDAYS AND CIVIC DAYS

24
Flag Day in Liberia; official public holiday. Honors the flag and the 1847 convention that approved the flag design.

24
Independence Day in Ukraine; official public holiday. Commemorates the official declaration of independence from the USSR on Aug. 24, 1991.

Independence was formally attained with the dissolution of the Soviet Union on Dec. 26, 1991.

ANNIVERSARIES AND SPECIAL EVENTS DAYS

24

Anniversary of the Battle of Sakarya River in Turkey. On Aug. 24, 1921, Turkish forces decisively defeated Greek forces, leading to a headlong Greek retreat, the Turkish occupation of Izmir (or Smyrna; Sept. 9, 1922) with a massacre of the Greek population, and the assurance of Turkey's subsequent creation.

24

Anniversary of the fall of Rome. On Aug. 24, 410, Rome surrendered to Alaric (ca. 370–410) and his army of Ostrogoths, the city's first surrender to a foreign army in 800 years; though the lineage of Roman emperors continued for another half-century, this was Rome's true fall.

24

Anniversary of the St. Bartholomew's Day Massacre of French Huguenot Protestants. Instigated by King Charles IX and his mother, Catherine de Medicis, on Aug. 24, 1572, Paris mobs began to slaughter Huguenots; the violence spread widely through France; many thousands were killed in 2 days.

24

Birthday of Max Beerbohm (Aug. 24, 1872–May 20, 1956). English caricaturist and critic; best known for his caricature portraits of literary and political figures.

24

Birthday of William Wilberforce (Aug. 24, 1759–July 29, 1833). English crusader against oppression and slavery in the British Empire. Wilberforce College in Ohio is named for him.

24

Festival of St. Bartholomew (St.Barthélemy) in St. Barthélemy, French West Indies; on the feast day of the island's patron saint. Resembles a French country fair, with a blessing of boats, a regatta, booths, fireworks, a public ball, and much food.

24

Vesuvius Day. Anniversary of the volcanic eruption of Mt. Vesuvius, Italy, on Aug. 24, A.D. 79, burying the cities of Pompeii and Herculaneum under ash that preserved the artifacts of the period for study and observation by later generations.

HOLY DAYS AND FEAST DAYS

25

Feast of St. Louis (King Louis IX of France; Apr. 5, 1214–Aug. 25, 1270; ruled 1234–70). Founder of the Sorbonne, a Crusader, a man of great charity and piety, and responsible for the building of some of the most beautiful cathedrals in France.

HOLIDAYS AND CIVIC DAYS

25

Liberation Day in France. Celebrates the end of German occupation of Paris with the arrival of Free French and Allied forces on Aug. 25, 1944; observed with special ceremonials in Paris.

25

Independence Day in Uruguay; official public holiday. Celebrates the declaration of independence from Brazil on Aug. 25, 1825. Independence was attained at the signing of a multinational treaty on Oct. 4, 1828.

ANNIVERSARIES AND SPECIAL EVENTS DAYS

25

Anniversary of the establishment of the U.S. National Park Service on Aug. 25, 1916.

25

Birthday of Bret (Francis Brett) Harte (Aug. 25, 1836–May 5, 1902). American poet and novelist, best known for his short stories "The Luck of Roaring Camp" and "The Outcasts of Poker Flat."

25

Birthday of Walt (Walter Crawford) Kelly (Aug. 25, 1913–Oct. 18, 1973). American cartoonist; creator of the comic strip *Pogo*.

HOLIDAYS AND CIVIC DAYS

26

Heroes' Day in Namibia; official public holiday. Commemorates the beginning of the armed struggle for independence on Aug. 26, 1966.

26

Women's Equality Day; designated by presidential proclamation. Also called Susan B. Anthony Day in Mass. Anniversary of the proclamation of final approval of the 19th Amendment to the U.S. Constitution, on Aug. 26, 1920, which gave voting rights to women.

ANNIVERSARIES AND SPECIAL EVENTS DAYS

26
Anniversary of the volcanic eruption of Krakatoa in the Netherlands Indies (now Indonesia) on Aug. 26–28, 1883. Destruction was enormous, and the world's oceanic and atmospheric currents were affected for years.

26
Birthday of Sir John Buchan (Aug. 26, 1875–Feb. 11, 1940). Scottish statesman; governor-general of Canada; author of *Oliver Cromwell* and such adventure novels as *The Thirty-Nine Steps* and *John Macnab*.

26
Birthday of Lee De Forest (Aug. 26, 1873–June 30, 1961). American inventor; known as the Father of Radio for his 1906 invention of the 3-electrode vacuum tube; pioneer in talking cinema and television.

26
Birthday of James Harlan (Aug. 26, 1820–Oct. 5, 1899). American congressman and secretary of the interior. Represents Iowa in Statuary Hall.

26
Birthday of Antoine Laurent Lavoisier (Aug. 26, 1743–May 8, 1794). Influential French chemist; guillotined in the revolutionary furor because he was once a tax collector.

26
Izmir International Trade Fair in Izmir, Turkey; Aug. 26–Sept. 17. A cultural and entrepreneurial extravaganza on the Aegean, in Turkey's most cosmopolitan city; held since ca. 1930.

CA. 26
Maherero Days in Okahandja, Namibia; on the weekend before or after Aug. 26. The Red Flag Herero honor their ancestors with drill teams, poems to heroes, and processions of horsemen and of women in Victorian dresses to the graveyard of their great leaders, particularly Chief Samuel Maherero (ca. 1820–Oct. 7, 1890), whose remains were brought there from exile in 1923. The Mbanderu (Green Flag) Herero celebrate at Okahanjda on the weekend on or before June 11.

The White Flag Herero celebrate on the weekend on or before Oct. 10, at Omaruru.

HOLY DAYS AND FEAST DAYS

27
Feast of St. Monica (ca. 331–387). Mother of St. Augustine; patron saint of mothers and married women.

HOLIDAYS AND CIVIC DAYS

27
Independence Day in Moldova; official public holiday. Celebrates the declaration of independence from the USSR on Aug. 27, 1991. Independence was formally attained with the dissolution of the Soviet Union on Dec. 26, 1991.

27
Birthday of Lyndon Baines Johnson (Aug. 27, 1908–Jan. 22, 1973); official public holiday in Tex., as LBJ Day. Tex. congressman and senator; as vice president, succeeded President John F. Kennedy upon his assassination; 36th president of the U.S. (1963–69; Democrat). Buried at the Johnson ranch near Johnson City, Tex. His administration was notable for its Great Society social legislation, but was overshadowed by the intense U.S. involvement in the Vietnam War.

ANNIVERSARIES AND SPECIAL EVENTS DAYS

27
Anniversary of the drilling of the first commercial oil well on Aug. 27, 1859, in western Pa.

27
Birthday of Theodore Herman Dreiser (Aug. 27, 1871–Dec. 28, 1945). American author who made his reputation with such naturalistic novels as *Sister Carrie* and *An American Tragedy;* awarded the Merit Medal of the American Academy of Arts and Letters.

27
Birthday of Hannibal Hamlin (Aug. 27, 1809–July 4, 1891). American statesman; vice president in Lincoln's first administration; U.S. minister to Spain. Represents Maine in Statuary Hall.

27
Death anniversary of Lord Montbatten (Louis Francis Albert Victor Nicholas Montbatten; June

25, 1900–Aug. 27, 1979). British World War II hero and the last viceroy of India; assassinated in Donegal Bay by the Provisional Irish Republican Army (Provisional IRA).

27
Death anniversary of Titian (born Tiziano Vecellio; ca. 1488–Aug. 27, 1576). Italian painter famous for the altarpiece *The Assumption of the Virgin* and other religious paintings; recognized as one of the master painters of any period.

HOLY DAYS AND FEAST DAYS

28
Feast of St. Augustine of Hippo (354–Aug. 28, 430). North African philosopher and theologian; a dominant influence in church history for the next millennium; his *Confessions* is a spiritual classic, and one of the first autobiographies.

ANNIVERSARIES AND SPECIAL EVENTS DAYS

28
Anniversary of the Spanish sighting and naming of St. Augustine, Fla. On Aug. 28, 1565 (St. Augustine of Hippo's Day), Spanish explorers arrived at the site of what would become the first permanent European settlement in the future U.S.

28
Anniversary of the beginning of the Trail of Tears. When gold was discovered on Cherokee land in Ga., local tribe members were forced to cede their land and cross the Mississippi River on Dec. 20, 1835. The remaining Cherokee in the South were forcibly marched to Okla. in the movement known as the Trail of Tears, which began on Aug. 28, 1838; the last of 13 parties arrived on Mar. 25, 1839; over 14,000 were forced west.

28
Birthday of (William) Robertson Davies (Aug. 28, 1913–Dec. 2, 1995). Canadian novelist and playwright; best known for The Deptford Trilogy and The Cornish Trilogy.

28
Birthday of Johann Wolfgang Goethe (Aug. 28, 1749–Mar. 22, 1832). German poet, dramatist, novelist, philosopher, statesman, and scientist. His poetic play *Faust* is considered a masterpiece.

28
Birthday of Roger Tory Peterson (Aug. 28, 1908–July 28, 1996). American naturalist whose famous *Field Guide to the Birds* (1934) was the first real bird guide, and inspired many others.

HOLIDAYS AND CIVIC DAYS

29
Slovak National Uprising Day in the Slovak Republic; official public holiday. Commemorates the anniversary of the beginning, on Aug. 29, 1944, of Slovak resistance to Nazi occupation.

ANNIVERSARIES AND SPECIAL EVENTS DAYS

29
Birthday of Henry Bergh (Aug. 29, 1811–Mar. 12, 1888). American philanthropist; founder and first president of the American Society for Prevention of Cruelty to Animals (ASPCA); commemorated through the observance of Humane Days. He also organized the Society for Prevention of Cruelty to Children.

29
Birthday of Ingrid Bergman (Aug. 29, 1915–Aug. 29, 1982). Notable Swedish film actress; won 3 Academy Awards; best-known films include *Casablanca, Gaslight,* and *Anastasia.*

29
Birthday of Oliver Wendell Holmes Sr. (Aug. 29, 1809–Oct. 7, 1894). American physician, poet, essayist, and novelist. His best-known poems include "The Chambered Nautilus" and "The Wonderful One-Hoss Shay." Elected to the Hall of Fame for Great Americans.

29
Birthday of John Locke (Aug. 29, 1632–Oct. 28, 1704). English philosopher who wrote *An Essay Concerning Human Understanding.*

29
Birthday of Maurice Maeterlinck (Aug. 29, 1862–May 6, 1949). Belgian dramatist, poet, essayist; wrote the drama *Pelléas et Mélisande,* on which Claude Debussy based an opera, and *L'Oiseau Bleu.* Awarded the 1911 Nobel Prize in literature for his contributions to drama.

29
Death anniversary of Edmond Hoyle (ca. 1672–Aug. 29, 1769). English teacher of card and board games; wrote *Short Treatise on the Game of Whist* (1742), a model of the genre. Hence the phrase "according to Hoyle."

HOLY DAYS AND FEAST DAYS

30

Feast of St. Fiacre (died ca. 670). Irish hermit in France and founder of a hospice for travelers. Patron saint of gardeners and of Paris cabdrivers, because the first coach for hire was located near the Hotel de St. Fiacre and was called a *fiacre.*

30

Traditional feast of St. Rose of Lima (died Aug. 24, 1486); official public holiday throughout Peru. A mystic credited with great holiness, and with protecting Lima from earthquake. The first canonized saint of the Americas (1671). Patron saint of South America, and of the Philippines. Lima holds a major procession in her honor, conveying her rose-bedecked statue from her home church to the cathedral.

HOLIDAYS AND CIVIC DAYS

30

Victory Day in Turkey, official public holiday; also an official public holiday in Cyprus, for Turkish Cypriots (as Zafir Bairam). A tribute to the warriors who died in the 1922 Battle of Dumlupinar, the final battle for Turkish independence.

30

Huey P. Long Day in La. Anniverary of the birth of Huey Pierce Long (Aug. 30, 1893–Sept. 10, 1935). La. politician and lawyer; the state's most articulate U.S. senator; governor and exponent of a share-the-wealth plan; popularly known as the Kingfish. Assassinated.

ANNIVERSARIES AND SPECIAL EVENTS DAYS

30

Birthday of Mary Wollstonecraft Shelley (Aug. 30, 1797–Feb. 1, 1851). Author of the classic novel *Frankenstein, or the Modern Prometheus* (1818), a seminal work of science fiction; wife of the poet Percy Bysshe Shelley.

HOLIDAYS AND CIVIC DAYS

31

Constitution Day in Kazakhstan; official public holiday. Commemorates the constitution of Aug. 31, 1995.

31

Independence Day in Kyrgyzstan; official public holiday. Celebrates the declaration of independence from the USSR on Aug. 31, 1991. Independence was attained with the dissolution of the Soviet Union on Dec. 26, 1991.

31

Merdeka ("Freedom") Day in Malaysia; official public holiday. Also called *Hari Kebanggsaan.* Commemorates Malaya's attainment of independence from the U.K. on Aug. 31, 1957. Subsequently, the Federation of Malaysia was inaugurated on Sept. 16, 1963, containing Malaya, North Borneo, Sarawak, and Singapore. Singapore later withdrew. Merdeka Day is celebrated nationwide with parades, exhibitions, and music.

31

National Language Day in Moldova; official public holiday. Also called Mother Tongue Day (*Limba Noastra*). The anniversary of the 1991 proclamation replacing the Cyrillic with the Latin alphabet.

31

Independence Day in Trinidad and Tobago; official public holiday. Celebrates independence attained from the U.K. on Aug. 31, 1962, with a splendid military parade, the National Awards Ceremony for outstanding citizens, and an ecumenical religious celebration in the Cathedral of the Immaculate Conception.

ANNIVERSARIES AND SPECIAL EVENTS DAYS

31

Anniversary of the chartering of the Agricultural Hall of Fame on Aug. 31, 1960, to honor farm men and women who have contributed to America's greatness.

31

Anniversary of the occurrence of the destructive Charleston, S.C., earthquake of Aug. 31, 1886. The first major earthquake in the recorded history of the eastern U.S., its magnitude was 6.6 on the Richter scale.

31

Anniversary of the formation of the Polish labor union Solidarity (*Solidarność*). Originally formed at the Lenin Shipyards in Gdansk on Aug. 31, 1980, under the leadership of Lech Walesa, to protest food shortages and to assert workers' rights to unionize and strike; Solidarity was crucial in terminating communist rule in Poland and was an inspiration to other Warsaw Pact countries.

31

Birthday of DuBose Heyward (Aug. 31, 1885–June 16, 1940). American novelist whose novel *Porgy* was used as the basis for the opera *Porgy and Bess* by George Gershwin.

31

Birthday of Ramón Magsaysay (Aug. 31, 1907–Mar. 17, 1957; ruled 1953–57). Philippine statesman and president.

31

Birthday of Maria Montessori (Aug. 31, 1870–May 6, 1952). Italian educator, founder of the Montessori method of teaching.

31

Death anniversary of John Bunyan (Nov. 1628–Aug. 31, 1688). English preacher renowned for the allegory *Pilgrim's Progress* (1678).

31

Death anniversary of Diana, Princess of Wales (born Lady Diana Spencer; July 1, 1961–Aug. 31, 1997). English former wife of Charles, Prince of Wales; much loved by the British people. Her death in an automobile accident was nationally traumatic.

MOVABLE DAYS IN AUGUST

HOLIDAYS AND CIVIC DAYS

PICNIC DAY IN NORTHERN TERRITORY, AUSTRALIA; 1st Monday in Aug.; official public holiday. This day is also a bank holiday and an official public holiday in New South Wales.

BRISBANE ROYAL NATIONAL SHOW DAY IN QUEENSLAND, AUSTRALIA; 2nd Wednesday in Aug.; official public holiday in Brisbane.

EMANCIPATION DAY IN THE BAHAMAS; 1st Monday in Aug.; official public holiday. Also Fox Hill Day, 2nd Tuesday in Aug. There's a joyous Emancipation Day celebration in Fox Hill, which consists of several towns founded by Samuel Fox and other ex-slaves, ca. 1840. Traditionally, Fox Hill Day featured visits to open-house churches and lodge halls.

CROP-OVER (MID-JULY) AND KADOOMENT (1ST MONDAY IN AUG.) IN BARBADOS; Kadooment is an offical public holiday. Barbados's main festival, these events celebrate the sugarcane

harvest. Crop-Over begins after the harvest, starting in mid-July, dependent on the weather; a time of parties, parades, craft displays, plantation fairs, and outdoor music. Festivities climax is Kadooment, a day and night of nonstop partying. Costumed bands parade before judges, and then march along a 3-mile course of highway and beach, packed with stalls and celebrants, in a sea of music. Climax is the burning in effigy of Mr. Harding, the archetypal evil overseer, with fireworks.

BERMUDA'S CUP MATCH (THURSDAY BEFORE THE 1ST MONDAY IN AUG.), AND SOMERS DAY (THAT FRIDAY) IN BERMUDA; both are official public holidays. Somers Day commemorates July 29, 1609, when Sir George Somers and his party were shipwrecked on the coast and formed the Plantation of the Somers' Islands, later named Bermuda.

CIVIC HOLIDAY IN MANY CANADIAN PROVINCES; 1st Monday in Aug. Provincial civic (not statutory) official public holiday in Alberta (Heritage Day), British Columbia (British Columbia Day), Manitoba, New Brunswick (New Brunswick Day), Northwest Territories, Nova Scotia (Natal Day), Ontario, and Saskatchewan (Saskatchewan Day).

AUGUST HOLIDAY (VERSLUNARMANNA-HELGI) IN ICELAND; 1st Monday in Aug.; official public holiday. Most businesses close from Friday afternoon through Monday. Celebrates Iceland's constitution of 1874.

AUGUST HOLIDAY IN IRELAND; last Monday in Aug.; official public holiday. Dedicated to merrymaking and parties.

INDEPENDENCE DAY IN JAMAICA; 1st Monday in Aug.; official public holiday. Commemorates independence attained from the U.K. on Aug. 6, 1962.

NATIONAL HEROES' DAY IN THE PHILIPPINES; last Sunday in Aug.; official public holiday. Commemorates the Aug. 26, 1896, start of the Philippine Revolution for independence from Spain.

LABOUR DAY IN SAMOA; 1st Monday in Aug.; official public holiday.

FARMERS' DAYS IN UGANDA; during the 1st week of Aug.; one day (often the 1st Monday) is proclaimed an official public holiday by the president.

SUMMER HOLIDAY, OR AUGUST BANK HOLIDAY, IN THE U.K. AND IRELAND; official public holiday. Observed on the 1st Monday in Aug. in Scotland, on Alderney in the Channel Islands, and in the country of Ireland. Observed on the last Monday in Aug. in England, Wales, the remaining Channel Islands, the Isle of Man, and Gibraltar. Also observed in parts of Australia.

AMERICAN FAMILY DAY; 1st Sunday in Aug.; official public holiday in Ariz. and observed in Mich.

ADMISSION DAY IN HAWAII; 3rd Friday in Aug.; official public holiday. On Aug. 21, 1959, Hawaii was admitted to the Union as the 50th state.

FAMILY DAY IN TENN.; last Sunday in Aug.; proclaimed by the governor.

FARMERS' DAYS IN ZAMBIA; during the 1st week of Aug.; one day (often the 1st Monday) is proclaimed an official public holiday by the president.

ANNIVERSARIES AND SPECIAL EVENTS DAYS

GIANTS PARADE IN BELGIUM; IN HEUSDEN, begins 3rd Sunday in Aug., and in Ath, begins 4th Sunday in Aug. Originated in 1390 as a religious procession; since mid-15th century, a secular parade, notably of the giants Gouyasse (Goliath) and Madame Gouyasse, who wed; thereafter, David challenges and defeats Gouyasse. With much ancillary revelry.

KLONDIKE DAYS IN EDMONTON, CANADA; about 10 days, ending on the weekend of Heritage Day on the 1st Monday in Aug. (official public holiday). Exuberantly recalls the Gold Rush of 1896 (period structures sprout up and all wear costume); includes a race of rafts, houseboats, barrels, and bathtubs.

FOIRE BRAYONNE IN EDMUNDSTON, CANADA; on the weekend (usually Wednesday–Sunday) of New Brunswick Day (1st Monday in Aug.). The largest francophone festival outside of Quebec; presided over by the mayor, who is president of the mythical Republic of Madawaska, inhabited by the Brayons (the nickname for the locals). Lumberjack tradition is a theme; the festival is a noted venue for emerging artistic talent.

ST. JOHN'S REGATTA IN ST. JOHNS, CANADA; 1st Wednesday in Aug. A notable rowing competition, "the oldest sporting event in North America."

FOLKLORAMA IN WINNIPEG, CANADA; begins the Friday before the 1st Monday in Aug., lasts 10 days or more. Celebrates the city's rich ethnic mosaic, with food, music, dance, and performances; held in informal venues throughout the city.

FESTIVAL INTERCELTIQUE IN MORBIHAN, FRANCE; 1st 2 weeks in Aug. A major international festival of Celtic art and tradition.

DRAGONSTAB (DRACHENSTICH) PLAYS IN FURTH IM WALD (ON THE BOHEMIAN BORDER), GERMANY; Friday before the 2nd Sunday in Aug. through the Monday after the 3rd Sunday in Aug. A communal drama in which St. George lances a huge fire-breathing dragon. An allegory against war. Held for over 500 years: Germany's oldest folk theater.

CARNIVAL IN GRENADA; official public holidays on the 2nd Monday in Aug. (Carnival Monday), and that Tuesday (half-day); celebration begins in late July, with main days the extended weekend of Carnival Monday. Grenada's national festival, with steel bands and calypso, dancing, street parties, and a pageant.

ALL-IRELAND MUSIC FESTIVAL (FLEADH CEOIL NAH EIREANN) IN IRELAND, usually in a town in the west; late August. A 3-day festival to promote Irish music, with keen competitions; first held on May 18, 1897, in Dublin.

SHEPHERDS' FAIR (SHUEBERFOUER) IN LUXEMBOURG CITY; begins the penultimate Sunday in Aug., lasts 2 weeks. The city's major fair, with beribboned sheep led by shepherds in folk costume through the old quarters, to traditional music. Originated in 1340 as a shepherds' market.

HORA AT MOUNT PRISLOP (TRANSYLVANIA-MOLDAVA BORDER), ROMANIA; 2nd Sunday in Aug. Dancing festival to symbolize the long friendship among the peoples of the region.

SLÅTTERGILLE IN RASHULT, SWEDEN; 1st Saturday in Aug. Held at the birthplace of Linnaeus, inventor of our modern system of plant and animal classification. Celebrants gather at his home, parade to the Linné-Grotto and the adjoining ripe fields, and listen to fiddlers and drink coffee while the fields are harvested.

FÊTE DES VIGNERONS ("WINE FESTIVAL") IN VEVEY, SWITZERLAND. This festival of medieval origin, held only once a generation, is considered Europe's best. The 1999 festival (July 29–August 15, 1999) was only the 5th of the century, with the previous one held in 1977. Features a parade of vintners and vineyard workers; evocations of Bacchus, the shepherd goddess Pales, and Dionysian mysteries; and medieval mystery plays. Its songs become famous.

BATTLE OF FLOWERS IN JERSEY, CHANNEL ISLANDS (U.K.); climax on 2nd Thursday in Aug. A spectacular floral carnival that began in 1902 as part of the celebration honoring the coronation of Edward VII and Queen Alexandra.

HIGHLAND GAMES IN SCOTLAND; in late Aug.–early Sept., notably Lonach's and Braemar's. The Lonach Highland Gathering and Games in Strathdon are the 4th Saturday in Aug.; an authentic festival, centered on traditional Highland sports. The Braemar Gathering in Braemar is the 1st Saturday in Sept.; very famous, graced by royalty, more glitzy than Lonach's.

EISTEDDFOD (EISTEDDFOD GENEDLAETHOL FRENHINOL CYMRU); 1st week in Aug.; alternately in north and south Wales. Also known as the Royal National Eisteddfod of Wales. An eisteddfod is a Welsh public gathering with contests in music, singing, and poetry. All is in Welsh, with simultaneous translations. The first eisteddfods were held in the 12th century.

W. C. HANDY MUSIC FESTIVAL IN FLORENCE, ALA.; 1st Sunday–Saturday in Aug. Honors W. C. Handy, the Father of the Blues; a week of blues, jazz, and spirituals; climax is a spectacular concert on Saturday.

FESTIVAL IN THE PINES AT FLAGSTAFF, ARIZ.; 1st Friday–Sunday in Aug. A premier regional festival of northern Ariz. Arts and crafts, ethnic food, music, entertainment, barn dancing.

NATIONAL HOBO CONVENTION IN BRITT, IOWA; weekend of the 2nd Sat. in Aug. Residents host hobos at a free camp, where they tell their stories; with a parade and carnival fair.

PRAIRIE DAY IN MINN.; 2nd Saturday in Aug. Day designated to appreciate prairies; scheduled to fall at the most beautiful flowering time. Other prairie states celebrate on other days.

BAT FLIGHT BREAKFAST AT CARLSBAD CAVERNS, N.M.; 2nd Thursday in Aug. Spectators gather before dawn for an outdoor breakfast while observing the return of the bats from a night's hunting. Began in the late 1950s.

GREAT AMERICAN DUCK RACE IN DEMING, N.M.; 4th Friday–Sunday in Aug. Ducks race (waddle) for prizes; with other festivities. Began in 1979.

INTERTRIBAL INDIAN CEREMONIAL AT GALLUP, N.M.; on Wednesday–Saturday of the 2nd weekend in Aug. The oldest and largest all-Native American exposition in the U.S. (begun in 1922); intended to preserve the Native American culture of the Southwest. With an extensive program of dances, food, art exhibitions and sales, a rodeo, a parade, and a half-marathon race.

INDIAN MARKET IN SANTA FE, N.M.; the Friday–Sunday after the 3rd Thursday in Aug. The oldest and most prestigious sale of Native American arts and crafts in the U.S.; held since 1922.

ALL-AMERICAN SOAP BOX DERBY IN AKRON, OHIO; held for 1 week, climax on Saturday of the 1st full week in Aug. in most years. Boys and girls race their hand-made gravity-propelled cars downhill; first held in 1933.

BRATWURST DAYS IN SHEBOYGAN, WIS.; 1st Friday–Saturday in Aug. A spirited celebration of the city's unique and famous version of the bratwurst sausage.

September

September, the 9th month in our calendar, received its name from the Latin numeral *septem,* meaning "7," because it was the 7th month in the old Roman calendar. It became the 9th month when Julius Caesar changed the calendar to make January the first month. The middle of September brings autumn to the Northern Hemisphere and the beginning of spring to the Southern Hemisphere.

September is an important month in 20th-century military history. The official end of World War II occurred on September 2, 1945, when Japan signed the unconditional surrender papers. Battle of Britain Week, which honors the British flyers who drove back the German planes on September 15, 1940, the most decisive air battle of World War II, is observed in September in Britain. September also honors the mothers who lost their sons and daughters in military service with a day called Gold Star Mother's Day, which is observed in late September.

The flowers for September are the morning glory and the aster, and the birthstone is the sapphire.

The harvest moon, which is the full moon nearest the time of the autumnal equinox, usually occurs in September. If September contains a full moon too early in the month to qualify as the harvest moon, it is called the corn moon, after a traditional Algonquin name, and the following full moon is the harvest moon.

HOLY DAYS AND FEAST DAYS

1

The start of the Christian liturgical year in the Byzantine rite, as used by the Orthodox and other Eastern Churches.

HOLIDAYS AND CIVIC DAYS

1

Day of the Revolution in Libya; official public holiday. Libya's national day, commemorating the deposition of the king on Sept. 1, 1969, and the formation of the Socialist People's Libyan Arab Republic. Libya attained independence from France as a constitutional monarchy on Jan. 2, 1952.

1

Presidential Message Day in Mexico. Annual opening of the Mexican congress with the president's state of the union message; Mexico's most important political ritual.

1

Constitution Day in the Slovak Republic; official public holiday. Anniversary of the adoption of the current constitution on Sept. 1, 1992.

1

Independence Day in Uzbekistan; official public holiday. Commemorates the declaration of independence from the USSR on Sept. 1, 1991. Independence was formally attained with the dissolution of the Soviet Union on Dec. 26, 1991.

ANNIVERSARIES AND SPECIAL EVENTS DAYS

1

Birthday of Sir Roger David Casement (Sept. 1, 1864–Aug. 3, 1916). Irish patriot and martyr for independence.

1

Birthday of Elizabeth Harrison (Sept. 1, 1849–Oct. 31, 1927). American educator, leader in the kindergarten movement, and one of the founders of the organization that became the National Congress of Parents and Teachers (today's PTA).

1

Death anniversary of Jacques Cartier (1491–Sept. 1, 1557). French mariner; explored the North American coast and St. Lawrence River (1534, 1535, 1541–42).

HOLIDAYS AND CIVIC DAYS

2

Independence Day in Vietnam; official public holiday. Also called National Day. Commemorates the Sept. 2, 1945, proclamation of independence from France by Ho Chi Minh and others, forming the Democratic Republic of Vietnam.

ANNIVERSARIES AND SPECIAL EVENTS DAYS

2

Birthday of Eugene Field (Sept. 2, 1850–Nov. 4, 1895). American journalist; author of children's verses, the most well known being "Little Boy Blue" and "Wynken, Blynken, and Nod."

2

Birthday of Henry George (Sept. 2, 1839–Oct. 29, 1897). American economist best known for his work *Progress and Poverty*.

2

Birthday of Lydia Kamekeha Liliuokalani (Sept. 2, 1838–Nov. 11, 1917). Queen of the Hawaiian Islands; overthrown in 1893 but remembered as the author of several songs, including "Aloha Oe" ("Farewell to Thee").

2

Calendar Adjustment Day. Anniversary of the end of the Old Style (Julian) calendar in British territory (including the American colonies), and its replacement with the New Style (Gregorian) calendar. According to the British Calendar Act of 1751, Wednesday, Sept. 2, 1752 O.S., was followed by Thursday, Sept. 14, 1752 N.S.; New Year's Day would occur on Jan. 1, 1752 O.S., replacing Mar. 25.

2

Democracy Day of Tibet. The anniversary of the formation of Tibet's formal government-in-exile on Sept. 2, 1960, in India, following the Chinese expropriation of Tibet. Legislators were installed, and a democratic constitution for Tibet was adopted.

2

London Fire Days. Anniversary of the Great Fire of London (Sept. 2–5, 1666), the most destructive fire in London's history; over 13,000 houses were destroyed.

2

Santa Festival (*La Santa du Niolu*) in Casamaccioli, Corsica (France); for 3 days, from Sept. 2. Corsica's most important festival; honors Mary's nativity and Corsica's traditions. First day is religious: the traditional Corsican folk Mass is chanted; followed by a penitential procession, with a coiling dance. Afterward, shepherds compete in poetic improvisation. The festival is exuberant, with traders, handicraft stalls, and foods. An enormous homecoming for expatriate Corsicans.

HOLY DAYS AND FEAST DAYS

3

Feast of St. Gregory the Great (Pope Gregory I; (ca. 540–Mar. 12, 604; ruled Sept. 3, 590–604). A molder of the Roman liturgy and known for the Gregorian chant. The last of the traditional Latin doctors of the church and founder of the medieval papacy; canonized by acclamation upon his death. Orth.: Mar. 12 or 25.

HOLIDAYS AND CIVIC DAYS

3

Independence Day in Qatar; official public holiday. Independence was attained from the U.K. on Sept. 3, 1971.

3

San Marino's Day, and the Foundation of the Republic, in San Marino; official public holiday. Honors the nation's patron saint and commemorates the founding of the country, by tradition in the 4th century, making it the oldest state in Europe.

3

Official death anniversary of Ho Chi Minh; official public holiday in Vietnam. He actually died on Sept. 2, 1969, but his death was not reported until the next day, lest it mar the celebration of Independence Day on Sept. 2.

ANNIVERSARIES AND SPECIAL EVENTS DAYS

3

Anniversary of the beginning of World War II. On Sept. 3, 1939, the U.K. declared war on Germany in response to its invasion of Poland on Sept. 1; France, Canada, Australia, New Zealand, and South Africa quickly did the same.

3

Birthday of Nicolò Amati (Sept. 3, 1596–Aug. 12, 1684). Celebrated Italian violin maker.

3

Birthday of Sarah Orne Jewett (Sept. 3, 1849–June 24, 1909). Maine novelist; wrote *Deephaven* and *The Country of the Pointed Firs.*

3

Birthday of Louis Henri Sullivan (Sept. 3, 1856–Apr. 4, 1924). American architect who established the principle that form should follow function; mentor of Frank Lloyd Wright.

3

Cromwell's Day in England. Commemorates Oliver Cromwell and his victories at the Battle of Dunbar (Sept. 3, 1650) and the Battle of Worcester (Sept. 3, 1651), his summoning of the first Protectorate Parliament (Sept. 3, 1654), and his death (Sept. 3, 1658). On this day the Cromwell Association conducts a service at his statue outside the Houses of Parliament.

3

St. Gregory's Day in Slovenia. On the eve, children in certain Gorenjska towns and villages (Trzic, Kropa, etc.) set afloat hundreds of tiny boats bearing candles.

ANNIVERSARIES AND SPECIAL EVENTS DAYS

4

Birthday of Daniel Hudson Burnham (Sept. 4, 1846–June 1, 1912). American architect; pioneer in fireproof skyscraper construction; developer of the Burnham Plan, which was used for many years as the basis for city planning in Chicago and preserved the city's beautiful lakefront.

4

Birthday of the city of Los Angeles, Calif. Celebrated with a variety of observances, especially on Olvera Street, the oldest street in the city, to honor the Sept. 4, 1781, founding of *El Pueblo de Nuestra Señora La Reina de Los Angeles de Porcuincula.*

4

Birthday of Dadabhai Naoroji (Sept. 4, 1825–June 30, 1917). Indian statesman; first Indian member of the British Parliament.

ANNIVERSARIES AND SPECIAL EVENTS DAYS

5

Death anniversary of Crazy Horse (Ta-sunko-witko or Tashunca-Uitco; 1842–Sept. 5, 1877). Native American (Sioux) holy man and leader of high ability; murdered by soldiers at Ft. Robinson, Nebr.

HOLIDAYS AND CIVIC DAYS

6

Unification Day in Bulgaria; official public holiday. Celebrates the anniversary of the 1885 reunification of the South with the rest of Bulgaria. Ignored under the communists, the observance is again recognized.

6

Bonaire Day in Bonaire, Netherlands Antilles; official public holiday. Also called Day of the Flag. Commemorates the island's sighting by Columbus on Sept. 6, 1499; observed since 1986.

6

Defense of Pakistan Day in Pakistan; official public holiday. Commemorates events of the Indo-Pakistan War of 1965.

6

Somhlolo Day in Swaziland; official public holiday. Commemorates independence attained from Great Britain on Sept. 6, 1968. Somhlolo, also known as Subhuza, was a great Swazi leader of the 19th century.

ANNIVERSARIES AND SPECIAL EVENTS DAYS

6

Birthday of Abdelkader (Sept. 6, 1808–May 26, 1883). Algerian sharif of great charisma and ability, elected to lead resistance against the French; regained and ruled interior Algeria from 1834, defeated in 1846.

6

Birthday of Jane Addams (Sept. 6, 1860–May 21, 1935). American social worker, advocate of international peace, and founder of Hull House in Chicago. She shared the 1931 Nobel Peace Prize with Nicholas Murray Butler. A Jane Addams Children's Book Award, given annually to the children's book that "best combines literary worth with a strong statement of faith in people," is presented by the Women's International League for Peace and Freedom and the Jane Addams Peace Association. Observance of her birthday occurs at Hull House in Chicago and in programs of peace organizations.

6

Birthday of Henry Melchior Mühlenberg (Sept. 6, 1711–Oct. 7, 1787). German-born American clergyman, chief founder of the Lutheran Church in the U.S. Honored on his death anniversary by the Lutheran Church. Father of John Muhlenberg.

6

Lafayette's Birthday. Day of recognition honoring Marie-Joseph-Paul-Yves-Roch-Gilbert du Motier, Marquis de Lafayette (Sept. 6, 1757–May 20, 1834). French general and statesman who served in Washington's army during the American Revolutionary War.

6

Mayflower Day. Anniversary of the Sept. 6, 1620, departure of the Pilgrims from Plymouth, England, bound for the New World in a small vessel called the *Mayflower.*

HOLIDAYS AND CIVIC DAYS

7

Independence Day in Brazil; official public holiday. Anniversary of Dom Pedro I's proclamation of independence from Portugal on Sept. 7, 1822. Celebrated on the Monday nearest Sept. 7.

ANNIVERSARIES AND SPECIAL EVENTS DAYS

7

Anniversary of the Corbett-Sullivan boxing match of Sept. 7, 1892, in New Orleans. In the first major prize fight under the Marquis of Queensberry rules, James J. Corbett was knocked out by John

L. Sullivan in the 21st round. (John Sholto Douglas, 8th Marquis of Queensberry [1844–1900], was a Scottish boxing patron.)

7

Birthday of Ferdinand Vandiveer Hayden (Sept. 7, 1829–Dec. 22, 1887). American geologist who participated in the 1859–86 geological and geographical surveys of the U.S.; a leader in the movement to preserve Yellowstone as a national park.

7

Lantern Festival (*Festa delle rificolone*) in Florence, Italy. On the evening of Sept. 7 (eve of the birth of Mary, the mother of Jesus), children run through the streets with colored paper lanterns. An ancient festival.

HOLY DAYS AND FEAST DAYS

8

Feast of the Nativity of the Virgin Mary. Commemorates Mary's birthday as a Jewish child and as a lineal descendant of the royal family of David. A very old feast of Eastern origin. Orth.: Sept. 8 or 21.

HOLIDAYS AND CIVIC DAYS

8

National Day in Andorra; official public holiday. Anniversary of the signing of the *Pareatges* in 1278, asserting Andorra's separateness, under the joint command and guardianship of the king (now president) of France and the bishop of La Seu d'Urgell in Spain.

8

Independence Day in Macedonia; official public holiday. Celebrates the Sept. 8, 1991, declaration of independence from the Yugoslav Union.

8

Feast of Our Lady of Victories in Malta; official public holiday. On this day the Great Sieges of Malta ended, first in 1565 (by Turks) and again in 1943 (by Axis powers). Malta's most important holiday, with a colorful regatta in the Grand Harbor.

ANNIVERSARIES AND SPECIAL EVENTS DAYS

8

Birthday of Lodovico Ariosto (Sept. 8, 1474–July 6, 1533). Italian poet; author of *Orlando Furioso,* an epic of Roland recognized as a classic example of Renaissance literature.

8

Birthday of Antonín Dvořák (Sept 8, 1841–May 1, 1904). Czech composer famous for the New World Symphony, which was composed in Iowa.

8

Birthday of Claude Denson Pepper (Sept. 8, 1900–May 30, 1989). American statesman, U.S. senator and representative from Florida; an architect of the country's safety net of social programs and champion of senior citizens.

8

Birthday of Peter Sellers (Sept. 8, 1925–July 24, 1980). British comic actor, famous for his multiple roles in the film *Dr. Strangelove*.

8

Birthday of Robert Alphonso Taft (Sept. 8, 1889–July 31, 1953). American congressman; drafter of the Taft-Hartley Labor Act of 1947, enacted to curb strikes; known as Mr. Republican.

CA. 8

Festival of Mary's Nativity in Peru, with Inca aspects. Coincides with the Inca Festival of the Queen (*Koya Raymi*). In Chincheros, where Mary is the local patron saint, there's a big fiesta, centered on the marketplace's Inca ruins. In Cajamarca, it is the biggest fiesta of the year: Native South Americans join in procession to the Inca baths in honor of *Koya Raymi*. In Ayaviri, near Puno, is a weeklong festival that includes costume dancing and a fair featuring local products.

CA. 8

Festival of Piedigrotta in Naples, Italy; Sept. 7–9. Honors Our Lady of Piedigrotta in an area that is probably the site of an old pagan temple. One of the most important and colorful of Neapolitan festivals, with lively parades and the Canzone Napoletana, a music festival.

8

International Literacy Day. Established by the United Nations to foster universal literacy with assistance, materials, and prizes; observed since 1966 by U.N. countries and organizations.

8

Roy Wilkins Day. Honors Roy Wilkins (Aug. 30, 1901–Sept. 8, 1981), long-time executive director of the National Association for the Advancement of Colored People (NAACP); a quiet, effective force in the movement to advance justice and opportunities for minorities in the U.S.

HOLIDAYS AND CIVIC DAYS

9

Independence Day in Tajikistan; official public holiday. Commemorates the declaration of independence from the USSR on Sept. 9, 1991. Independence was formally attained with the dissolution of the Soviet Union on Dec. 26, 1991.

9

Admission Day in Calif.; official public holiday. Commemorates Calif.'s admission to the Union on Sept. 9, 1850, as the 31st state.

ANNIVERSARIES AND SPECIAL EVENTS DAYS

9

Birthday of Armand-Jean du Plessis, cardinal and duc de Richelieu (Sept. 9, 1585–Dec. 4, 1642). Cardinal of the Roman Catholic Church and French statesman of tremendous political power; founder of the French Academy and the Jardin des Plantes.

9

Birthday of Count Lev Nikolayevich Tolstoy (Sept. 9, 1828–Nov. 20, 1910). Russian novelist, moral philosopher, and social reformer, famous for *War and Peace* and *Anna Karenina*.

9

Death anniversary of William I, the Conqueror (ca. 1028–Sept. 9, 1087; ruled 1066–87). King of England and Duke of Normandy; led the successful Norman Invasion of England.

9

Liberation Day in Luxembourg. Ceremonies are held at the statue of the American Soldier at Petang, especially in honor of the American general George Patton Jr. (Nov. 11, 1885–Dec. 21, 1945) and his men of the Third Army, who liberated Luxembourg in 1944.

9

United States Day. Anniversary of Sept. 9, 1776, when the Second Continental Congress ruled that the words *United States* should replace the term *United Colonies* as the official name of the new nation; commemorated in the programs of many civic organizations.

HOLIDAYS AND CIVIC DAYS

10

St. George's Caye Day in Belize; official public holiday. Its national day; commemorates the Sept. 10,

1798, Battle of St. George's Caye, won by a few local Baymen settlers over a superior Spanish force and preserving an English enclave in Spanish Central America.

10
Gibraltar National Day in Gibraltar (U.K.); official public holiday.

ANNIVERSARIES AND SPECIAL EVENTS DAYS

10
Birthday of Sir John Soane (Sept. 10, 1753–Jan. 20, 1837). English architect whose art collection and fortune formed the basis of the Soane Museum in London.

10
Birthday of Franz Werfel (Sept. 10, 1890–Aug. 26, 1945). Austrian novelist, dramatist, and poet whose most popular novel was *The Song of Bernadette.*

HOLIDAYS AND CIVIC DAYS

11
New Year's Day in the Coptic and Ethiopian Orthodox calendars; official public holiday in Ethiopia.

11
Jinnah Day in Pakistan; official public holiday. Commemorates the death anniversary of Mohammed Ali Jinnah (Dec. 25, 1876–Sept. 11, 1948), called *Quaid-i-Azam* ("Great Leader"), founder of Pakistan.

11
Catalan Day *(Diada de Catalunya)* in the Catalonia region of Spain; regional official public holiday. Memorializes Catalonia's original loss of independence to Spain in 1714. *La Diada* is a day of political demonstrations, fireworks, parades with giants and "bigheads," dancing the *sardana,* and rousing choruses of "Els Segadors" ("The Harvesters"), the Catalan national song.

ANNIVERSARIES AND SPECIAL EVENTS DAYS

11
Birthday of O. Henry (born William Sidney Porter; Sept. 11, 1862–June 5, 1910). American short-story writer and journalist; author of some of the most deftly plotted stories in American literature.

11
Birthday of D. H. (David Herbert) Lawrence (Sept. 11, 1885–Mar. 2, 1930). English writer whose most famous novel is *Lady Chatterley's Lover.*

11
Allende Day. Anniversary of the Chilean military coup of Sept. 11, 1973, when the socialist government of President Salvador Allende Gossens (July 26, 1908–Sept. 11, 1973; ruled 1970–73) was overthrown and Allende murdered in a coup d'état led by General Augusto Pinochet. Pinochet's military dictatorship was rejected in a plebiscite of Oct. 5, 1988, and a democratically elected president was installed on Dec. 15, 1989.

HOLIDAYS AND CIVIC DAYS

12
Birthday of Amilcar Cabral (Sept. 12, 1924–Jan. 20, 1973). Hero of Portuguese colonial West Africa. Sept. 12 is an official public holiday in Guinea-Bissau, and a former official public holiday in Cape Verde; in both countries Cabral is regarded as a founding father. He was assassinated in Conakry, Guinea, probably by agents of the Portuguese.

12
Defenders' Day in Md.; official public holiday. Also called National Anthem Day. Commemorates the Sept. 12, 1814, Battle of North Point near Baltimore during the War of 1812; this was followed by the bombardment of Fort McHenry. Defenders' Day is celebrated with many patriotic events.

ANNIVERSARIES AND SPECIAL EVENTS DAYS

12
Birthday of Florence Kelley (Sept. 12, 1859–Feb. 17, 1932). American socialist and social reformer of great effectiveness, especially in labor and social welfare legislation; a founder of the Women's International League for Peace and Freedom (1919).

12
Birthday of H. L. (Henry Louis) Mencken (Sept. 12, 1880–Jan. 29, 1956). American newspaperman, lexicographer, and social critic, noted for his lucid and acerbic wit.

12
Birthday of Jesse Owens (Sept. 12, 1913–Mar. 31, 1980). African American athlete in track and field; winner of 4 gold medals at the 1936 Olympic Games in Berlin, Germany.

12

Steve Biko Day in South Africa. The death anniversary of Bantu Stephen Biko (Dec. 8, 1946–Sept. 12, 1977), charismatic South African organizer against apartheid and leader in the African National Congress, murdered in prison by the government's security apparatus.

ANNIVERSARIES AND SPECIAL EVENTS DAYS

13

Anniversary of the Battle of Quebec. Decisive battle of the French and Indian War, won on the Plains of Abraham near the city of Quebec, Canada, on Sept. 13, 1759. The victory of the British and Americans under Wolfe over the French under Montcalm assured British dominance on the North American continent. Both commanders died of wounds.

13

Birthday of Oscar Arias y Sanchez (Sept. 13, 1941–). Costa Rican president and statesman who received the 1987 Nobel Peace Prize for his mediation of a peace process for the countries of Central America.

13

Birthday of Adolf Meyer (Sept. 13, 1866–Mar. 17, 1950). American psychiatrist and neurologist who, with Clifford Beers, began the mental-hygiene movement.

13

Birthday of John Joseph Pershing (Sept. 13, 1860–July 15, 1948). American general; commander in chief of the American Expeditionary Force in World War I; U.S. Army chief of staff; winner of the 1932 Pulitzer Prize in history for *My Experiences in the World War.*

13

Birthday of Walter Reed (Sept. 13, 1851–Nov. 22, 1902). American physician and military surgeon who made important studies in the causes of typhoid and yellow fever. Elected to the Hall of Fame for Great Americans.

13

Birthday of Arnold Franz Walter Schoenberg (Sept. 13, 1874–July 13, 1951). Austrian-born American composer who had a revolutionary influence on modern music through his use of the 12-tone scale.

13

Commodore John Barry Day. Anniversary of the death of John Barry (1745–Sept. 13, 1803). Irish-born naval hero of the American Revolution, the nation's first commodore; called the Father of the American Navy.

HOLY DAYS AND FEAST DAYS

14

Feast of the Triumph of the Cross. The Roman Catholic Church now combines two feasts on Sept. 14: the Finding of the True Cross (May 3 traditional) and the Exaltation of the True Cross (Sept. 14 traditional). In the Orthodox Church, the Exaltation of the Cross is a very important feast. Generally, Sept. 14 commemorates St. Helena's finding in A.D. 326 of the cross on which Christ was crucified and the dedication on Sept. 14, 335, of the Basilica of the Holy Sepulchre containing part of the relic. Orth.: Sept. 14 or 27.

HOLIDAYS AND CIVIC DAYS

14

San Jacinto Day in Nicaragua; official public holiday. Commemorates the Sept. 14, 1856, Battle of San Jacinto, a defeat of the U.S. invader William Walker.

ANNIVERSARIES AND SPECIAL EVENTS DAYS

14

Anniversary of the lighting of the first lighthouse in the U.S. On Sept. 14, 1716, the lighthouse erected on Beacon Island in Boston harbor was first lit.

14

Birthday of Karl Taylor Compton (Sept. 14, 1887–June 22, 1954). American physicist, atomic-bomb scientist; recipient of many awards, including the French Legion of Honor.

14

Birthday of Jan Garrigue Masaryk (Sept. 14, 1886–Mar. 10, 1948). Czech diplomat and statesman.

14

Birthday of Margaret Sanger (born Margaret Higgins; Sept. 14, 1879–Sept. 6, 1966). American founder and leader of the birth-control movement; first president of both the American Birth Control League and the International Planned Parenthood Federation; her birthday is commemorated by Planned Parenthood associations and groups.

14

Death anniversary of Dante Alighieri (May 1265–Sept. 14, 1321). Considered the greatest of all Italian poets, known throughout the world for his *Divine Comedy,* composed from 1307 and first printed in 1472.

14

National Anthem Day in the U.S., especially in Md. Honors Francis Scott Key and the writing of the verses of the "Star-Spangled Banner" on the morning of Sept. 14, 1814, following the night bombardment of Fort McHenry on Sept. 13–14.

HOLY DAYS AND FEAST DAYS

15

Feast of Our Lady of Sorrows. Also called Our Lady of the Seven Sorrows. Recalls for meditation 7 sorrows experienced by the Virgin Mary.

HOLIDAYS AND CIVIC DAYS

15

Independence Day in Central America; official public holiday in Costa Rica, El Salvador, Guatemala, Honduras, and Nicaragua. Celebrates independence attained by the 5 provinces of Central America from Spain on Sept. 15, 1821.

15

Old People's Day in Japan; official public holiday. Also called Respect for the Aged Day (*Keiro-no-Hi*). A day of honor and ceremonials for the elder generation.

ANNIVERSARIES AND SPECIAL EVENTS DAYS

15

Birthday of Agatha Christie (Sept. 15, 1890–Jan. 12, 1976). Prolific English mystery writer.

15

Birthday of James Fenimore Cooper (Sept. 15, 1789–Sept. 15, 1851). American novelist and social critic; famous for the Leatherstocking Tales, including *The Last of the Mohicans* and *The Deer-*

slayer. Elected to the Hall of Fame for Great Americans.

15

Birthday of François de La Rochefoucauld (Sept. 15, 1613–ca. Mar. 16, 1680). French moralist, famous for his *Maxims.*

15

Birthday of William Howard Taft (Sept. 15, 1857–Mar. 8, 1930). Ohio lawyer; governor of the Philippines (1901–4); secretary of war under Theodore Roosevelt; 27th president of the U.S. (1909–13; Republican); chief justice of the Supreme Court (1921–30). His administration dissolved Standard Oil and established the Department of Labor. Buried in Arlington National Cemetery.

15

Battle of Britain Day in the U.K. Celebrated in honor of Sept. 15, 1940, when British flyers, greatly outnumbered, drove back invading German planes in the most decisive air battle of World War II. (London was bombed for 57 consecutive nights from Sept. 7, and raids continued until the next April. The German failure saved Britain from invasion.) Jersey, in the Channel Islands, celebrates Battle of Britain Week during the week containing Sept. 15. Features a magnificent air display.

15

International Day of Peace. Also called World Peace Day. Sponsored by the Baha'i faith in the U.S. to encourage American leadership toward world peace.

HOLIDAYS AND CIVIC DAYS

CA. 16

Independence Day in Mexico; official public holiday. Anniversary of Mexico's Sept. 16, 1820, declaration of independence from Spain. Celebrations begin on Sept. 15, when at 11 P.M. the president (and local mayors) give the famous *Grito de Delores,* the call to freedom given by Miguel Hidalgo in 1810. The people shout in response and shoot off fireworks. Sept. 16 is celebrated with fireworks, bells, and parades. On this day the winning National Lottery numbers are drawn.

16

Independence Day in Papua New Guinea; official public holiday. Celebrates independence attained from the U.K. on Sept. 16, 1975.

ANNIVERSARIES AND SPECIAL EVENTS DAYS

16

Birthday of Alfred Noyes (Sept. 16, 1880–June 28, 1958). English poet whose work has often been set to music by Edward Elgar and others. Noyes's best-known single poem is "The Highwayman."

16

Birthday of Sir Anthony Panizzi (born Antonio Genesio Maria Panizzi; Sept. 16, 1797–Apr. 8, 1879). Italian-born British librarian and revolutionary activist against Austrian control of northern Italy; fled to England and became principal librarian of the British Museum. Called the Prince of Librarians; the only librarian ever hanged in effigy.

16

Birthday of Francis Parkman (Sept. 16, 1823–Nov. 8, 1893). Distinguished American historian and author; wrote *The Oregon Trail*. Elected to the Hall of Fame for Great Americans.

16

Death anniversary of Anne Bradstreet (born Anne Dudley; ca. 1612–Sept. 16, 1672). American poet, first woman of letters in America; wife of Simon Bradstreet, governor of Mass.

16

Death anniversary of Tomás de Torquemada (1420–Sept. 16, 1498). Spanish Dominican monk and Inquisitor-General of Spain. Persuaded Ferdinand and Isabella to drive the Jews from Spain; responsible for 10,000 persons being burned at the stake.

16

American Legion Charter Day. Anniversary of Congress's chartering on Sept. 16, 1919, of the American Legion, composed of honorably discharged veterans. It was founded in Paris during a caucus of members of the First Expeditionary Force held March 15–17, 1919.

16

Cherokee Strip Day in Okla. Commemorates Sept. 16, 1893, when land runs were organized by the government for prospective homesteaders to claim land. Celebrations in the Cherokee Strip communities last several days as the pioneer spirit of '93 is reenacted with parades, picnics, dances, and pageantry.

16

Mildred Fish Harnack Day in the schools of Wis. Birthday of Mildred Harnack (born Mildred Fish; Sept. 16, 1902–Feb. 16, 1943). American Goethe scholar and Milwaukee native who with her German husband, Arvid Harnack, deliberately moved to Germany to help resist Hitler's Reich as a member of a *Rotte Kapelle* ("Red Orchestra") espionage cell. The only American woman to be tried and executed by the Nazis.

HOLY DAYS AND FEAST DAYS

17

Feast of St. Hildegard of Bingen (1098–Sept 17, 1179). German abbess and musician; outstanding medieval mystic and seer; called the Sibyl of the Rhine. Long venerated but never formally canonized, her feast is celebrated in some German dioceses.

17

Feast of St. Robert Bellarmine (Oct. 4, 1542–Sept. 17, 1621). Italian Jesuit active in the Counter-Reformation; friend of Galileo; authority on church-state relations. Doctor of the church.

HOLIDAYS AND CIVIC DAYS

17

Heroes' Day in Angola; official public holiday. Honors the victims of the anti-Portuguese revolts of 1961–62 and the subsequent civil war from 1975 onward. The U.S. finally recognized the Angolan government on May 19, 1993, allowing the civil war to end.

ANNIVERSARIES AND SPECIAL EVENTS DAYS

17

Birthday of Andrew "Rube" Foster (Sept. 17, 1879–Dec. 9, 1930). Extraordinary African American baseball pitcher and organizer; called the Father of Negro Baseball. Organized the first Negro League (1919) and served as its president until his death.

17

Bloodiest Day in the U.S. Anniversary of the Civil War battle of Antietam Creek, at Sharpsburg, Md., fought on Sept. 17, 1862; noted by historians as America's bloodiest day on its own soil. Confederate General Robert E. Lee's advance into Md. was repulsed by General George McClellan.

17

Citizenship Day in the U.S. Honors new Americans and is a day of special school observance on the rights and duties of citizenship; replaced "I Am an American Day" and Constitution Day in 1952; by annual presidential proclamation; marks the beginning of Constitution Week (Sept. 17–23).

17

Constitution Day in the U.S. Anniversary of the adoption and signing of the U.S. Constitution on Sept. 17, 1787, by the Constitutional Convention. Also commemorated during Constitution Week, Sept. 17–23, which has been declared annually by presidential proclamation since 1955. A day of special school observance in many states, but official emphasis has shifted to Citizenship Day, also on this date.

17

Von Steuben Day in the U.S. Also known as Steuben Day. Commemorates the birth of Baron Friedrich Wilhelm Ludolf Gerhard Augustin von Steuben (Sept. 17, 1730–Nov. 28, 1794). Prussian-born general who volunteered to serve the American Revolution in 1777. Charged with training the Continental forces, he was invaluable in combat, and was given citizenship, a land grant, and a pension. Von Steuben Day has been celebrated since 1919; observed particularly by German-Americans, variously on Sept. 17, on the Saturday following, and on the 4th Sunday in Sept.

HOLIDAYS AND CIVIC DAYS

18

Independence Day in Chile; official public holiday. Commemorates the first declaration of independence from Spain, on Sept. 18, 1810. Following bitter warfare, independence was attained on Feb. 12, 1818.

ANNIVERSARIES AND SPECIAL EVENTS DAYS

18

Birthday of Samuel Johnson (Sept. 18, 1709–Dec. 13, 1784). English poet, essayist, critic, and dictionary maker (1755); author of *Lives of the Most Eminent English Poets* (1781); his birthday is celebrated annually in his hometown of Lichfield, England.

18

Birthday of Joseph Story (Sept. 18, 1779–Sept. 10, 1845). American jurist and associate justice of the Supreme Court (1811–45) whose writings helped form American legal thought. Elected to the Hall of Fame for Great Americans.

18

Birthday of Clark Wissler (Sept. 18, 1870–Aug. 25, 1947). American anthropologist, the first to develop a systematic concept of culture areas, which he used in studying and writing many books about Native Americans.

HOLY DAYS AND FEAST DAYS

19

Feast of St. Januarius (San Gennaro; died ca. 305). Official public holiday in Naples, Italy. By legend, a Neapolitan, bishop of Benevento, martyred under Diocletian. In Naples, a vial reputedly containing his blood liquifies when exposed in the cathedral. Patron saint of Naples and of blood banks. Orth.: Apr. 21 or May 4 and Sept. 19 or Oct. 2.

HOLIDAYS AND CIVIC DAYS

19

Armed Forces Day (*Día del Ejército*) in Chile; official public holiday. Anniversary of the founding of the armed forces on Sept. 19, 1810. Observed as part of the Independence Day celebrations on Sept. 18.

ANNIVERSARIES AND SPECIAL EVENTS DAYS

19

Birthday of Charles Carroll (Sept. 19, 1737–Nov. 14, 1832). American Revolutionary leader; one of the signers of the Declaration of Independence, and the last signer to die. Represents Md. in Statuary Hall.

19

Birthday of Arthur Rackham (Sept. 19, 1867–Sept. 6, 1939). English artist whose illustrations of literary classics, such as *Grimm's Fairy Tales,* have attracted worldwide appreciation.

19

Washington's Farewell Day. Anniversary of the farewell address of George Washington, the first U.S. president, on Sept. 19, 1796; remembered for its warnings against public debt, large military establishments, permanent alliances with foreign powers, and devices of "small, artful, enterprising minority" to control government.

ANNIVERSARIES AND SPECIAL EVENTS DAYS

20
Birthday of Ferdinand Joseph "Jelly Roll" Morton (Sept. 20, 1885–July 10, 1941). American jazz pianist, composer, singer, and orchestra leader.

HOLY DAYS AND FEAST DAYS

21
Feast of St. Matthew (1st century). Publican tax collector; one of the 12 Apostles; also called Levi. Author of the first Gospel; martyred, perhaps in Ethiopia. Patron saint of bankers, bookkeepers, and tax collectors. Orth.: Nov. 16 or 29.

HOLIDAYS AND CIVIC DAYS

21
Independence Day in Armenia; official public holiday. Armenia declared its independence from the USSR on Sept. 21, 1991. Independence was formally attained with the dissolution of the Soviet Union on Dec. 26, 1991.

21
Independence Day in Belize; official public holiday. Commemorates independence amicably attained by Belize (formerly British Honduras) from the U.K. on Sept. 21, 1981.

21
Independence Day in Malta; official public holiday. Celebrates the attainment of independence from the U.K. on Sept. 21, 1964.

ANNIVERSARIES AND SPECIAL EVENTS DAYS

21
Anniversary of the Battle of Marathon, in the Persian Wars. On the morning of Sept. 21, 491 B.C., Athenian and Plataean infantry, led by Miltiades, routed a much larger Persian landing force and probably saved Athens and Attica from defeat by the Persian emperor Darius. The runner Philippides carried the news of the amazing victory to Athens, a distance of 26 miles, 385 yards, the length of the modern marathon race.

21
Birthday of Kwame Nkrumah (Sept. 21, 1909– Apr. 27, 1972). First president of Ghana; the first to lead an African country to independence; author.

21
Birthday of Girolamo Savonarola (Sept. 21, 1452– May 23, 1498). Italian religious reformer.

21
Birthday of H. G. (Herbert George) Wells (Sept. 21, 1866–Aug. 13, 1946). English novelist famous for works of science fiction, sociological writer, and historian whose most important work of nonfiction is *Outline of History.*

21
Death anniversary of Chief Joseph (born In-mut-too-yah-lat-lat; ca. 1840–Sept. 21, 1904). Native American (Nez Percé) chieftain who led his people in a heroic nonviolent retreat of 1,700 miles across Idaho and Mont.; surrendered on Oct. 5, 1877.

HOLIDAYS AND CIVIC DAYS

22
Independence Day in Mali; official public holiday. Celebrates the attainment of independence from France on Sept. 22, 1960.

ANNIVERSARIES AND SPECIAL EVENTS DAYS

22
Anniversary of the world championship boxing match between Jack Dempsey and Gene Tunney, on Sept. 22, 1927, in Chicago. Tunney won, in a disputed decision. Nearly half the U.S. population is believed to have listened to the radio broadcast.

22
Birthday of Michael Faraday (Sept. 22, 1791–Aug. 25, 1867). English scientist who made one of the most important electrical discoveries, the generation of electricity by magnetism.

22
Birthday of Philip Dormer Stanhope, 4th Earl of Chesterfield (Sept. 22, 1694–Mar. 24, 1773). Brilliant politician; famous for his *Letters to His Son;* responsible for the British Calendar Act of 1751, which caused the introduction of the Gregorian calendar within the British Empire.

22
Death anniversary of Snorri Sturluson (1179– Sept. 22, 1241; murdered). Icelandic politician and historian; his *Heimskringla* is of immense scope; he was also a distinguished Lawspeaker at the Althing (Icelandic Parliament).

22

Hobbit Day. Observed in honor of the birthdays of both Frodo and Bilbo Baggins, characters in *The Lord of the Rings* by J. R. R. Tolkien; celebrated by Tolkien societies on earth and by the inhabitants of the trilogy's Middle Earth and its expatriates.

Holidays and Civic Days

23

National Day in Saudi Arabia; official public holiday. Commemorates the unification of the kingdom on Sept. 23, 1932.

Anniversaries and Special Events Days

23

Anniversary of the discovery of the planet Neptune on Sept. 23, 1846, by the English astronomer John Couch Adams.

23

Birthday of Augustus (born Gaius Octavius, then Gaius Julius Caesar; Sept. 23, 63 B.C.–Aug. 19, A.D. 14). Great-nephew and heir of Julius Caesar; considered the first Roman emperor (ruled 27 B.C.–A.D. 14). His birthday was adopted as New Year's Day in many eastern provinces of the Empire.

23

Birthday of Kublai Khan (Sept. 23, 1215–Feb. 18, 1294). Grandson of Genghis Khan; ruler of the Mongol Empire, and particularly of China; visited by Marco Polo.

23

Birthday of John Avery Lomax (Sept. 23, 1870–Jan. 26, 1948). American folklorist; collector of folk songs; founder of the American Folklore Society and its first president.

23

Birthday of William Holmes McGuffey (Sept. 23, 1800–May 4, 1873). American educator; author of the *Eclectic Readers*, which are collector's items.

23

Birthday of John Sevier (Sept. 23, 1745–Sept. 24, 1815). American pioneer and soldier; Tenn.'s first governor. Represents Tenn. in Statuary Hall.

23

Birthday of Victoria Chaflin Woodhull (Sept. 23, 1838–June 10, 1927). American feminist, reformer, and the first female candidate for the presidency.

CA. 23

The autumnal equinox occurs on Sept. 22 or 23. On this day the sun crosses the equator, and day and night are everywhere of equal length. There is another equinox in the spring; *see* Mar. 21.

23

Lewis and Clark Expedition Day. Anniversary of the end, on Sept. 23, 1806, of the 2-year exploration of the American West by Meriwether Lewis and William Clark. The expedition set out from St. Louis, Mo., on May 14, 1804, crossed the Rockies, and reached the Pacific Ocean at the mouth of the Columbia River in Nov. 1805. The Shoshone woman Sacagawea was their principal interpreter.

Holy Days and Feast Days

24

Traditional feast of Our Lady of Mercy. Now officially lapsed, but very alive in Latin countries, where Mercedes is a common name for girls. Notable celebrations occur in Bolivia, Colombia, the Dominican Republic, Ecuador, Peru, Spain, and Italy.

Holidays and Civic Days

24

Constitutional Declaration Day in Cambodia; official public holiday. Celebrates the new constitution of Sept. 24, 1993, assuring power sharing by the two major political parties.

24

Independence Day in Guinea-Bissau; official public holiday. On Sept. 24, 1973, independence was declared from Portugal; independence was attained on Sept. 10, 1974.

24

Armed Forces Day in Mozambique; official public holiday. Also called Revolution Day. Commemorates the beginning of the war for independence on Sept. 24, 1964.

24

Republic Day in Trinidad and Tobago; official public holiday. Commemorates the attainment of full republic status within the British Commonwealth on Sept. 24, 1976, subsequent to independence.

ANNIVERSARIES AND SPECIAL EVENTS DAYS

24

Anniversary of the first television broadcast on Sept. 24, 1961, of *The Bullwinkle Show,* starring Rocky the Flying Squirrel and Bullwinkle the Moose.

24

Birthday of F. Scott (Francis Scott Key) Fitzgerald (Sept. 24, 1896–Dec. 21, 1940). American author, identified with the Lost Generation of post-World War I writers; *The Great Gatsby* is a classic novel.

24

Birthday of John Marshall (Sept. 24, 1755–July 6, 1835). American lawyer, statesman, jurist; 4th chief justice of the Supreme Court (1801–1835); called the Great Chief Justice; founder of the American system of constitutional law. Elected to the Hall of Fame for Great Americans.

24

Death anniversary of Paracelsus (born Philippus Aureolus Theophrastus Bombast von Hohenheim; ca. Nov. 11, 1493–Sept. 24, 1541). Swiss-born German physician and alchemist.

CA. 24

Family Fair in Port of Spain, Trinidad and Tobago; for 10 days, with a parade climax on the Sunday nearest Sept. 24.

CA. 24

Feast of the Ingathering. Also called Harvest Festival. Celebrated in England around Sept. 24 with the decoration of churches with flowers, fruits, and vegetables for special services of harvest thanksgiving.

24

Festival of Our Lady of Mercy (*Verge Mercè*) in Barcelona, Spain. Patron saint of Barcelona. Focus of Barcelona's major festival, lasting 1 week (the *Semana Gran*). With dancing, parades, concerts, and theater; features the *Carrefoc* (a fire-breathing dragon) and devils chasing victims through the streets.

24

Schwenkenfelder Thanksgiving Day. Observed by members of the Schwenkenfelder Society in the Pennsylvania Dutch country in commemoration of the safe arrival of its first members in 1733 and 1734.

HOLIDAYS AND CIVIC DAYS

25

Republic Day in Rwanda; official public holiday. Marks the opening of sessions of the National Assembly and the anniversary of the Sept. 25, 1961, referendum that abolished the monarchy.

ANNIVERSARIES AND SPECIAL EVENTS DAYS

25

Anniversary of the beginning of Greenwich Mean Time. On Sept. 25, 1676 O.S., 2 very accurate clocks were set in motion at Greenwich Observatory in England by John Flamsteed, and Greenwich Mean Time (now called Universal Time) came into use.

25

Baptismal day of Jean-Philippe Rameau (baptized Sept. 25, 1683–Sept. 12, 1764). Considered the greatest French composer of the 18th century.

25

Birthday of William Cuthbert Faulkner (Sept. 25, 1897–July 6, 1962). American novelist; author of the series known as the Yoknapatawpha Cycle; awarded the Nobel Prize in literature in 1955.

25

Birthday of Dmitri Shostakovich (Sept. 25, 1906–Aug. 9, 1975). Soviet composer of symphonies, chamber music, concerti, and film scores.

25

Pacific Ocean Day. Anniversary of the first sighting of the Pacific Ocean by a European, the Spanish explorer Vasco Núñez de Balboa (1475–Jan. 12, 1519), on Sept. 25 or 27, 1513.

25

Sandra Day O'Connor Day. Anniversary of the Sept. 25, 1981, oath-of-office ceremonies for Sandra Day O'Connor (Mar. 26, 1930–), the first woman associate justice of the Supreme Court.

HOLIDAYS AND CIVIC DAYS

26

Bandaranaike Memorial Day in Sri Lanka; official public holiday. Honors Solomon W. R. D. Bandaranaike, assassinated while prime minister, on Sept. 26, 1959.

26

September Revolution in Yemen; official public holiday. Commemorates the Sept. 26, 1962, declaration of the (north) Yemen Arab Republic, and the beginning of the revolt against the royalist government.

ANNIVERSARIES AND SPECIAL EVENTS DAYS

26
Birthday of Edith Abbott (Sept. 26, 1876–July 28, 1957). American social worker; dean of the University of Chicago School of Social Service Administration; authority on public assistance and immigration problems.

26
Birthday of John Chapman (Sept. 26, 1774–Mar. 18, ca. 1845). Known as Johnny Appleseed, planter of apple orchards from Pa. to Ind.; called the Patron Saint of American Orchards; revered by Native Americans as a great medicine man. He is honored at the Johnny Appleseed Festival in Fort Wayne, Ind.

26
Birthday of T. S. (Thomas Stearns) Eliot (Sept. 26, 1888–Jan. 4, 1965). American-born British poet and playwright renowned for *The Waste Land;* awarded the Nobel Prize in literature in 1948.

26
Birthday of George Gershwin (born Jacob Gershvin; Sept. 26, 1898–July 11, 1937). American composer famed for such compositions as *Rhapsody in Blue* and *Porgy and Bess.*

HOLY DAYS AND FEAST DAYS

27
Traditional feast of SS. Cosmas and Damian. By legend, twin brothers and physicians in Arabia, martyred in 303. Patron saints of barbers and, with St. Luke, of physicians. Orth.: July 1 or 14 and Nov. 1 or 14.

27
Feast of St. Vincent de Paul (Apr. 24, ca. 1580–Sept. 27, 1660). French founder of the Vincentians and cofounder of the Sisters of Charity, dedicated to the alleviation of human misery. Patron saint of all charitable organizations.

HOLIDAYS AND CIVIC DAYS

27
Maskal ("Cross") in Ethiopia and Eritrea; official public holiday. Commemorates the finding of the

true cross. Blooming *Maskal* daisies are gathered and burned in bonfires on the eve of *Maskal*. *Maskal* itself is a day of dancing, singing, and feasting, with strangers made welcome.

ANNIVERSARIES AND SPECIAL EVENTS DAYS

27
Birthday of Samuel Adams (Sept. 27, 1722–Oct. 2, 1803). American patriot, signer of the Declaration of Independence, governor of Mass. Represents Mass. in Statuary Hall.

27
Birthday of Grazia Deledda (Sept. 27, 1871–Aug. 15, 1936). Sardinia's most famous novelist and winner of the 1926 Nobel Prize in literature; wrote *Canne al Vento.*

27
Birthday of Sándor Kisfaludy (Sept. 27, 1772–Oct. 28, 1844). Hungarian poet, considered the founder of the Hungarian school of lyric poetry.

27
Birthday of Alfred Thayer Mahan (Sept. 27, 1840–Dec. 1, 1914). American naval officer and historian whose major work is *The Influence of Sea Power upon History.*

27
Birthday of Thomas Nast (Sept. 27, 1840–Dec. 7, 1902). American illustrator and cartoonist whose work greatly influenced politics and public opinion; creator of the donkey and elephant emblems of the Democratic and Republican Parties; inspired many Civil War enlistments; was instrumental in the downfall of New York's William "Boss" Tweed.

HOLY DAYS AND FEAST DAYS

28
Feast of St. Wenceslas (Václav; ca. 903–Sept. 28, 929; ruled ca. 922–929). Bohemian duke revered by the common people as their protector; assassinated by political rivals and promptly venerated as a martyr of the Czech people. A symbol of Czech Christianity and patron saint of the Czech Republic.

HOLIDAYS AND CIVIC DAYS

28
Teacher's Day in Taiwan, and Confucius's Birthday in China; official public holiday in Taiwan. In

China, especially observed at the Confucius Temple in Qufu as part of a 2-week Confucian Culture Festival.

ANNIVERSARIES AND SPECIAL EVENTS DAYS

28

Birthday of Georges Clemenceau (Sept. 28, 1841–Nov. 24, 1919). French editor and statesman who presided at the Versailles Peace Conference following World War I.

28

Birthday of Sir William Jones (Sept. 28, 1746–Apr. 27, 1794). British jurist and orientalist in India; founder of the Asiatic Society of Bengal; propounder of the theory that the Greek, Latin, and Sanskrit languages derive from a common source (subsequently named Indo-European), and one of the earliest practitioners of comparative linguistics.

28

Birthday of Francis Turner Palgrave (Sept. 28, 1824–Oct. 24, 1897). English poet and critic best known for his classic anthology the *Golden Treasury of the Best Songs and Lyrical Poems in the English Language*.

28

Birthday of Kate Douglas Wiggin (Sept. 28, 1856–Aug. 24, 1923). American educator and author; cofounder of the first free kindergarten in the Far West (1878), who started to write books for children in her own school. Remembered for *The Birds' Christmas Carol* and *Rebecca of Sunnybrook Farm*.

28

Birthday of Frances Elizabeth Caroline Willard (Sept. 28, 1839–Feb. 18, 1898). American temperance reformer, editor, author, and president of the Women's Christian Temperance Union. Elected to the Hall of Fame for Great Americans.

HOLY DAYS AND FEAST DAYS

29

Michaelmas, the feast of the archangel Michael and all angels. Captain of the heavenly host, his feast existed in the 6th century in the West, but is now combined with those of the archangels Raphael and Gabriel on Sept. 29. Michael is patron saint of the church militant and of knights and soldiers, police officers, grocers, paratroopers, and radiologists. Orth.: Nov. 8 or 21.

HOLIDAYS AND CIVIC DAYS

29

Boquerón Day in Paraguay; official public holiday. Commemorates the Sept. 29, 1932, Battle of Boquerón during the Chaco War.

ANNIVERSARIES AND SPECIAL EVENTS DAYS

29

Birthday of Enrico Fermi (Sept. 29, 1901–Nov. 28, 1954). Italian physicist, noted for his studies in nuclear physics, his work on the atomic-bomb project, and his teaching at the Institute of Nuclear Studies at the University of Chicago. Awarded the 1938 Nobel Prize in physics.

29

Birthday of Horatio Nelson (Sept. 29, 1758–Oct. 21, 1805). English admiral in the Napoleonic Wars (1803–15) following the French Revolution. Defeated the French at the decisive Battle of Trafalgar, where he was killed. His monument in London's Trafalgar Square is one of the best known in the world.

29

Birthday of Scotland Yard. The first public appearance of Greater London's Metropolitan Police was on Sept. 29, 1829.

29

Payment of Quit Rent in London, England; on Michaelmas. Since 1235, the city of London has on this day paid symbolic rent to the Crown for certain parcels of land, giving horseshoes and nails, a billhook, and a hatchet. Very solemn and ceremonious.

CA. 29

San Miguel Fiesta in San Miguel de Allende, Mexico. A fete beginning on the Saturday following Sept. 28.

HOLY DAYS AND FEAST DAYS

30

Feast of St. Gregory the Enlightener (ca. 257–ca. 332). Also called the Illuminator. Apostle to Armenia and founder of the Armenian Church; patron saint of Armenia. Orth.: Sept. 30 or Oct. 13.

30

Feast of St. Jerome (ca. 342–Sept. 30, 420). Dalmatian scholar and desert ascetic in Palestine. Especially noted for his monumental Vulgate translation of the Bible into Latin. Patron saint of librarians and scholars of Scripture.

HOLIDAYS AND CIVIC DAYS

CA. 30

Botswana Day in Botswana; official public holiday on Sept. 30 and Oct. 1. Commemorates Sept. 30, 1966, when independence was attained from the U.K. and the Bechuanaland Protectorate became the Republic of Botswana.

MOVABLE DAYS IN SEPTEMBER

HOLY DAYS AND FEAST DAYS

SHAWNEE GREEN BEAN CEREMONY IN OKLA. At the full moon of Sept.

HOLIDAYS AND CIVIC DAYS

LABOUR DAY IN BERMUDA; 1st Monday in Sept.; official public holiday.

FEDERAL THANKSGIVING DAY IN SWITZERLAND; 3rd Monday in Sept.; official public holiday in some cantons.

LABOR DAY IN THE U.S. AND CANADA; 1st Monday in Sept.; federal official public holiday. Founded by Peter J. McGuire of New York City, carpenter, labor leader, and co-founder of the American Federation of Labor. A day of tribute to American labor's contributions and achievements. The Sept. date was chosen to give a holiday between July 4 and Thanksgiving. The first Labor Day parade was on Sept. 5, 1882, in New York.

CHEROKEE NATIONAL HOLIDAY IN TAHLEQUAH, OKLA.; Thursday–Sunday before Labor Day. The Cherokee Nation celebrates its establishment in Okla., on the completion of its final constitution on Sept. 6, 1839.

ANNIVERSARIES AND SPECIAL EVENTS DAYS

INTERNATIONAL DAY OF PEACE AND ANNUAL OPENING OF THE UNITED NATIONS GENERAL ASSEMBLY; 3rd Tuesday in Sept. A day to promote the ideals of peace. Observed since 1982.

TORONTO FILM FESTIVAL IN TORONTO, CANADA; begins the Thursday after Labor Day and lasts 10 days. A magnificent film festival, as good as those of Cannes, New York, or Los Angeles.

WINE FESTIVAL IN LEMESOS, CYPRUS; the biggest festival on the island; begins the last Wednesday in Aug., ends the 2nd Sunday in Sept.

SAUSAGE FAIR (WURSTMARKT) IN BAD DURKHEIM, GERMANY; Saturday–Tuesday of the 2nd weekend of Sept. and Friday–Monday of the 3rd weekend in Sept. Germany's largest wine festival, with much sausage consumed. Originated in 1417, when the fair occurred on St. Michael's Day as pilgrims visited a local shrine.

HISTORICAL REGATTA (REGATTA STORICA) IN VENICE, ITALY; 1st Sunday in Sept. Premier gondola event; held since the 13th century. Includes a costumed gondola regatta and races; winners are the year's princes of the city.

SCHOBERMESSE MONDAY IN LUXEMBOURG CITY; begins the 1st Monday in Sept. A fun fair for children and a time for merchants to sell surplus stocks; the city center's streets are closed to traffic. A relict of a major medieval fair, once lasting 3 weeks. Schobermesse Monday and the Shepherds' Fair are part of one extended event.

OFFICIAL OPENING OF PARLIAMENT IN THE HAGUE, NETHERLANDS; 3rd Tuesday in Sept. The queen rides in a golden coach to the Hall of Knights for the annual opening of parliament.

SALTED CURE FESTIVAL AT THE SAHARAN OASIS OF INGAL IN NORTHERN NIGER. Observed by Tuareg nomads; customarily held at the rainy season's end (Sept.–Oct.); exact date depends on the year's weather. An important event: high government officials attend. Ingal is a favorite grazing ground, and the salt in its new grass is healthful for camels and cattle.

BANNED BOOKS WEEK IN THE U.S.; usually starting the last Sunday in Sept. Celebrates the freedom to read and denounces the harm censorship causes our society. Sponsored by the American Library Association and others.

GOLD STAR MOTHERS DAY IN THE U.S.;
last Sunday in Sept. By presidential proclamation
since 1936. To honor the mothers whose sons and
daughters died in line of duty in the Armed Forces
of the U.S.

GRANDPARENTS' DAY IN THE U.S.; Sunday
after Labor Day. Established by presidential
proclamation in 1979.

NATIONAL GOOD NEIGHBOR DAY IN THE
U.S.; 4th Sunday in Sept. To promote understanding, good relationships, and concern for others, beginning with the people next door.

NATIVE AMERICAN DAY (OR AMERICAN
INDIAN DAY, OR INDIAN DAY) IN MANY
STATES OF THE U.S.; on various dates, most
commonly the 4th Friday in Sept. Founded by the
efforts in 1914 of Red Fox James, a Blackfoot. The
first general American Indian Day was celebrated
on the 2nd Saturday in May, 1916. A day to recognize and appreciate the heritage and contributions
of Native Americans.

NAVAJO NATION FAIR AT WINDOW ROCK,
ARIZ., ON THE NAVAJO RESERVATION;
Tuesday–Sunday after Labor Day. Largest Native
American fair; began in 1938. A national party
and gathering, showing the best of Navajo talent
and accomplishments, with a very dense program:
rodeos, contests, election of Miss Navajo Nation, a
baby contest, exhibits and demonstrations, pow-
wows, song and dance, and markets.

NATIONAL FRISBEE DISC FESTIVAL IN
WASHINGTON, D.C.; Saturday before Labor
Day. With exhibitions, workshops, and Frisbee-
catching dogs.

MACKINAC BRIDGE WALK BETWEEN
LOWER MICH. AND ITS UPPER PENIN-
SULA; on Labor Day. By tradition, only on this
day are pedestrians permitted on the 5-mile sus-
pension bridge; the walk is from St. Ignace to
Mackinaw City.

PENDLETON ROUND-UP IN PENDLETON,
OREG.; during the 2nd full week in Sept. Celebrated since pioneer days, and annually since
1910; its purpose is to recall and honor pioneer
and Native American life.

October

October, the 10th month in the Gregorian calendar, received it name from the Latin numeral *octo,* meaning "8," because in the days of the old Roman calendar it was the 8th month.

One of the notable days in October is Columbus Day, October 12, honoring the Italian mapmaker and explorer Christopher Columbus, the first European to explore the Americas. It is celebrated as Discovery Day in Central and South America and was set aside as a holiday in the U.S. in 1892 by President Benjamin Harrison.

October gave its name to a well-known German fall festival, Oktoberfest, which was first celebrated on October 17, 1810, the wedding day of King Ludwig I. It still retains the name, even though the festivities may start in September, with October having only a partial share of the time schedule.

An important October day for the entire world is October 24, United Nations Day, which commemorates the founding of the United Nations on October 24, 1945. It is a holiday for many of the member nations and is generally observed by all nations as a way of publicizing the aims and achievements of the world organization.

The month ends with Halloween, or All Hallows' Eve. It is a religious festival in some countries but a trick-or-treat night in the U.S., when small children in costume roam through their neighborhoods to solicit candy or cookies.

The flowers for October are the calendula and the cosmos. The birthstones are the opal and the tourmaline.

HOLY DAYS AND FEAST DAYS

1

Feast of St. Thérèse de Lisieux (born Marie-Françoise-Thérèse Martin; Jan. 2, 1873–Sept. 30, 1897). French Carmelite nun; called the Little Flower. Author of *The Story of a Soul,* one of the most widely read spiritual biographies. Patron saint of missions, with St. Francis Xavier, and patron saint, with Joan of Arc, of France.

HOLIDAYS AND CIVIC DAYS

1

National Day in China; official public holiday. Commemorates the founding of the People's Republic of China, under the leadership of Chairman Mao Tse-tung, on Oct. 1, 1949. Every 5 years (1999, 2004, . . .) public celebrations are especially elaborate.

1

Independence Day in Cyprus; official public holiday. Commemorates the formal attainment of independence, and full status as a member of the British Commonwealth, on Aug. 16, 1960; the independence agreement was signed by Britain, Greek and Turkish Cypriots, and Greece and Turkey on Feb. 19, 1959.

1

National Day in Nigeria; official public holiday. On this day in 1960, independence was attained from the U.K.; on this day in 1963, the republic was proclaimed; and on this day in 1979, 13 years of military rule ended.

ANNIVERSARIES AND SPECIAL EVENTS DAYS

1

Anniversary of the introduction of the Model T Ford automobile, priced at $850, by Henry Ford on Oct. 1, 1908.

1

Birthday of Annie Besant (born Annie Wood; Oct. 1, 1847–Sept. 20, 1933). English theosophist and philosophical writer who, through long residence in India, was instrumental in acquainting Europeans with Hindu thought.

1

Birthday of Jimmy (James Earl) Carter (Oct. 1, 1925–). Naval officer under Hyman Rickover; peanut processor; Ga. governor; 39th president of the U.S. (1977–81; Democrat). His administration was notable for the Camp David Accord; it was marred by the Iran Embassy crisis and high inflation. As an elder statesman, Carter has devoted himself to the negotiated end to international conflicts.

1

Birthday of Rufus Choate (Oct. 1, 1799–July 13, 1859). American lawyer, author, and statesman; preeminent among American advocates. Elected to the Hall of Fame for Great Americans.

1

Birthday of Vladimir Horowitz (Oct. 1, 1904–Nov. 5, 1989). Russian-born American piano virtuoso, internationally renowned for his interpretations of the works of Rachmaninov, Chopin, Liszt, and other Romantic composers.

1

Birthday of James Lawrence (Oct. 1, 1781–June 1, 1813). Brilliant American naval officer, killed in a naval battle in the War of 1812; his immortal last words were "Don't give up the ship."

1

Birthday of John Peter Gabriel Muhlenberg (Oct. 1, 1746–Oct. 1, 1807). American revolutionary general, Lutheran pastor, and congressman. Son of Heinrich Mühlenberg. Represents Pa. in Statuary Hall.

1

Birthday of Frederic Remington (Oct. 1, 1861–Dec. 26, 1909). American artist and author famous for his on-site drawings and paintings of frontier life, Native Americans, and horses.

1

Agricultural Fair Day. Anniversary of the first agricultural fair held in the U.S., the Berkshire Cattle Show, held at Pittsfield, Mass., on Oct. 1, 1810. Launched with a quotation from George Washington that "the multiplication of useful animals is a common blessing to mankind," it became the forerunner of the state fairs of today.

1

Fireburn Day in the U.S. Virgin Islands. Commemorates the revolt of harshly repressed ex-slaves on Oct. 1, 1878, when men, women, and children, led by "Queen Mary" (Mary Thomas) and others, burned stores and houses in Frederiksted, St. Croix (Danish West Indies).

HOLY DAYS AND FEAST DAYS

2

Feast of the Guardian Angels. Commemorates the angels protecting humanity from physical and spiritual dangers. Orth.: Nov. 8 or 21, for Michael and All Angels.

HOLIDAYS AND CIVIC DAYS

2

National Day in Guinea; official public holiday. Commemorates independence attained from France on Oct. 2, 1958.

2

Gandhi Day (*Gandhi Jayanti*) in India; official public holiday. Celebrates the birth of Mohandas Karamchand Gandhi (Oct. 2, 1869–Jan. 30, 1948; assassinated), called *Mahatma* ("Great Soul"). Indian lawyer, religious figure, healer of divisions, and leader in the Indian independence movement. A brilliant leader in strategies of nonviolent civil disobedience and an inspiration to many others. Today is a time of pilgrimages to his site of cremation in New Delhi.

ANNIVERSARIES AND SPECIAL EVENTS DAYS

2

Anniversary of two significant popular U.S. entertainments: on Oct. 2, 1950, the *Peanuts* comic strip began publication, and on Oct. 2, 1959, *The Twilight Zone* first aired on U.S. TV.

2

Birthday of Cordell Hull (Oct. 2, 1871–July 23, 1955). American statesman, U.S. secretary of state (1933–44), contributor to American good-neighbor policies, and planner of a postwar world organization; called the Father of the United Nations; recipient of the Nobel Peace Prize in 1945.

2

Birthday of Groucho (Julius Henry) Marx (Oct. 2, 1890–Aug. 19, 1977). American comedian, oldest of the famed Marx brothers; the others were Harpo (Adolph Arthur; Nov. 21, 1893–Sept. 28, 1964); Chico (Leonard; Mar. 26, 1891–Oct. 11, 1961); Zeppo (Herbert; Feb. 25, 1901–Nov. 29, 1979); and Gummo (Milton; 1894–Apr. 21, 1977).

2

Birthday of Ruth Bryan Rohde (Oct. 2, 1885–July 26, 1954). American public official; congresswoman; and first woman ever appointed to head a U.S. diplomatic post, serving as minister to Denmark for 3 years.

HOLIDAYS AND CIVIC DAYS

3

Day of German Unity in Germany; official public holiday. Anniversary of the Oct. 3, 1990, reunification of the two Germanies into one country.

3

Morazán Day in Honduras; official public holiday. Honors Francisco Morazán (Oct. 3, 1792–Sept. 15, 1842), Honduran liberal federalist and statesman; founder of the Central American Union (1823–38); executed by conservatives. This is also Soldier's Day for the Honduran army.

3

Foundation Day (Tan'gun Day) in South Korea; official public holiday. Celebrates the founding of the nation by the legendary Tan'gun (or Dan-gun or Hwan-ung) in 2333 B.C. Koreans climb Kanghwa Island's Mani Mountain on this day, and runners carry a torch from the mountain to Seoul to start a day of athletic activities.

ANNIVERSARIES AND SPECIAL EVENTS DAYS

3

Birthday of George Bancroft (Oct. 3, 1800–Jan. 17, 1891). American diplomat, historian, and public official; U.S. minister to Great Britain, Prussia, and the German empire. Author of the 10-volume *History of the United States,* which he treated as an illustration of a divine plan for democracy, freedom, and equality. Elected to the Hall of Fame for Great Americans.

3

Birthday of William Crawford Gorgas (Oct. 3, 1854–July 4, 1920). American sanitarian, surgeon-general of the U.S. Army, famous for his success in controlling yellow fever, which permitted completion of the Panama Canal. Elected to the Hall of Fame for Great Americans.

3

Birthday of John Gorrie (Oct. 3, 1803–June 16, 1855). American physician and inventor; an innovator in artificial cooling for hospitals and mechanical refrigeration. Represents Fla. in Statuary Hall.

3

Birthday of Sir Patrick Manson (Oct. 3, 1844–Apr. 9, 1922). British physician and parasitologist who is known as the Father of Tropical Medicine.

3

Death anniversary of Black Hawk (born Ma-ka-ta-i-me-she-kia-kiak; 1767–Oct. 3, 1838). Native American (Sauk); reluctant but brilliant leader of the Sauk and Fox in the brief Black Hawk War in Ill. and Wis., which ended with his surrender on Aug. 27, 1832.

3

Death anniversary of Myles (or Miles) Standish (ca. 1584–Oct. 3, 1645). English colonist in America whose memory has been perpetuated by Longfellow's narrative poem *The Courtship of Miles Standish.*

HOLY DAYS AND FEAST DAYS

4

Feast of St. Francis of Assisi (ca. 1181–Oct. 3, 1226). Italian mystic and preacher; founder of the Franciscan Order. One of the West's best-loved and most influential saints. Patron saint of animals: farm animals and pets are often brought to church on this day to be blessed. The blessing in St. John the Divine Cathedral, New York City, is especially delightful.

HOLIDAYS AND CIVIC DAYS

4

Independence Day in Lesotho; official public holiday. Celebrates the attainment of independence from the U.K. on Oct. 4, 1966.

ANNIVERSARIES AND SPECIAL EVENTS DAYS

4

Anniversary of the inauguration of the famous Orient Express railroad route. On Oct. 4, 1883, its first train departed Paris for Istanbul. The route was the brainchild of George Nagelmakers of the Compagnie Internationale des Wagon-Lits et Grands Express Européens.

4
Birthday of Rutherford Birchard Hayes (Oct. 4, 1822–Jan. 17, 1893). Ohio lawyer; Civil War general; congressman; governor of Ohio; 19th president of the U.S. (1877–81; Republican). Buried in Fremont, Ohio. He ended Reconstruction, reformed the civil service, and supported "sound money."

4
Peace Day in Mozambique. Anniversary of the General Peace Accords signed in Rome on Oct. 4, 1992, ending 17 years of civil war and destabilization and allowing multiparty elections in 1994.

4
Sputnik Day. Anniversary of the Oct. 4, 1957, launching by the USSR of the world's first earth-orbiting satellite.

4
Ten-Four Day in the U.S. and elsewhere. Observed by truck drivers and other users of citizen band radios on the 10th month's 4th day, in reference to the code 10–4, which signals an affirmative reply.

HOLIDAYS AND CIVIC DAYS

CA. 5
Sports Day in Lesotho; official public holiday; 1st Monday in Oct., but on Oct. 5 if the 1st Monday is Oct. 4 (Independence Day). A day dedicated to youth sports, especially soccer.

5
Republic Day in Portugal; official public holiday. Commemorates the establishment of the republic on Oct. 5, 1910.

ANNIVERSARIES AND SPECIAL EVENTS DAYS

5
Birthday of Chester Alan Arthur (Oct. 5, 1831–Nov. 18, 1886). N.Y. teacher and lawyer; vice president succeeding the assassinated President James Garfield; 21st president of the U.S. (1881–85; Republican). Buried in Albany, New York.

5
Birthday of Jonathan Edwards (Oct. 5, 1703–Mar. 22, 1758). American theologian, philosopher, and

college president who has been called "the greatest mind of the colonial period." Elected to the Hall of Fame for Great Americans.

5
Birthday of Robert Hutchings Goddard (Oct. 5, 1882–Aug. 10, 1945). American rocket pioneer and a practical visionary; called the Father of Space Flight; launched the first liquid-fueled rocket. Derided for his schemes for rocketry and planetary travel.

5
Death anniversary of Tecumseh (Mar. 1768–Oct. 5, 1813). Native American (Shawnee) chief and orator; defender of his people, denouncing as invalid any treaties ceding their land. Defeated and killed at the Battle of the Thames, while fighting on the side of the British in the War of 1812.

ANNIVERSARIES AND SPECIAL EVENTS DAYS

6
Anniversary of the organization of the American Library Association on Oct. 6, 1876, in Philadelphia.

6
Birthday of Albert Jeremiah Beveridge (Oct. 6, 1862–Apr. 27, 1927). American politician and author, best known for *The Life of John Marshall*. An Albert J. Beveridge Award is given by the American Historical Association for an outstanding book in history.

6
Birthday of Thor Heyerdahl (Oct. 6, 1914–). Norse anthropologist, adventurer, and author whose scholarly research and sailing expeditions (including *Kon-Tiki*, 1947, and *Ra,* 1969) demonstrated the possibility of early worldwide cultural diffusion.

6
Birthday of George Westinghouse (Oct. 6, 1846–Mar. 12, 1914). American inventor of the air brake and propagator of the system of alternating current invented by Nikola Tesla.

HOLY DAYS AND FEAST DAYS

7
Feast of Our Lady of the Rosary. Commemorates an apparition of the Virgin Mary to St. Dominic in 1214, during which she gave him the rosary and urged its wide use.

ANNIVERSARIES AND SPECIAL EVENTS DAYS

7

Anniversary of the founding of the American Numismatic Association, on Oct. 7, 1891, at its first convention in Chicago.

7

Birthday of Martha McChesney Berry (Oct. 7, 1866–Feb. 27, 1942). American educator and founder of the Berry schools for children in the mountain districts around Ga.; recipient of many awards; voted in 1931 one of the 12 greatest American women.

7

Birthday of Niels Henrik Bohr (Oct. 7, 1885–Nov. 18, 1962). Danish physicist; the Bohr atomic model was a radical advance in theoretical physics, incorporating quantum mechanics. Awarded the 1922 Nobel Prize in physics.

7

Birthday of Caesar Rodney (Oct. 7, 1728–June 26, 1784). American patriot; tie-breaking signer of the Declaration of Independence; represents Del. in Statuary Hall.

7

Lepanto Day. Anniversary of the Battle of Lepanto, 1571, when Ottoman naval power was decisively humbled by Christendom; remembered in Greece. The victory was subsequently attributed to Our Lady of the Rosary.

7

Riley Day in Ind. Anniversary of the birth of James Whitcomb Riley (Oct. 7, 1849–July 22, 1916). American poet known for his nostalgic dialect verse; called the Hoosier Poet and the Burns of America (after Scottish poet Robert Burns). The Riley Festival has been celebrated since 1911 in his hometown of Greenfield, Ind., for several days on or near Oct. 7, with poetry contests, events in schools, and parades.

7

Rosario in Peru. The feast of Our Lady of the Rosary, with Inca aspects. Occurs during the Quechua month of *Uma Raymi* ("Festival of the Water"), when the rains begin and crops are planted. A time to petition for rain.

7

Traditional Jewish date for the creation of the world, and Day One in the Jewish calendar, on Oct. 7, 3761 B.C.

HOLY DAYS AND FEAST DAYS

8

Russian Orthodox feast of St. Sergius of Radonezh (ca. 1315–Sept. 25, 1392). Russian monk and abbot; revered Russian saint, with immense influence in his lifetime as an advocate for peace and a source of spiritual wisdom. Orth.: Sept. 25 or Oct. 8, and July 5 or 18 for the uncovering of his relics.

ANNIVERSARIES AND SPECIAL EVENTS DAYS

8

Birthday of Richard St. Barbe Baker (Oct. 8, 1889–June 9, 1982). English forester and colonial administrator in Africa; founder of Men of the Trees (now the International Tree Foundation), which first inspired African men and later everyone to plant and protect trees; he was very effective in protecting and extending forests worldwide.

8

Birthday of Eddie (Edward Vernon) Rickenbacker (Oct. 8, 1890–July 23, 1973). American aviator, auto racer, World War I flying ace, and author.

8

Chicago Fire Day. Anniversary of the catastrophic fire of Oct. 8–9, 1871, which killed about 250 persons and destroyed most of Chicago. The Chicago Fire was one inspiration for the establishment of Fire Prevention Day, Oct. 9.

8

Peshtigo Fire Day. Anniversary of the beginning on Oct. 8, 1871, of the forest fire at Peshtigo, Wis., considered one of the most disastrous fires in history; over 1,100 persons died.

CA. 8

Han Lu ("Cold Dew") in the Chinese calendar; the departure of summer.

HOLY DAYS AND FEAST DAYS

9

Feast of St. Denis (died Oct. 9, ca. 258). Italian missionary, first bishop, and martyr in Paris; the apostle and patron saint of France.

9

Feast of St. Louis Bertran (or Bertrand; 1526–Oct. 9, 1581). Spanish Dominican; outstanding preacher and master of novices in Spain; friend of St. Teresa of Ávila; missionary to Colombia and the

Caribbean, and noted for advocacy of the rights of indigenous people. Patron saint of Colombia.

HOLIDAYS AND CIVIC DAYS

9

Guayaquil's Independence Day in Ecuador; official public holiday. Commemorates Oct. 9, 1820, when the city ousted the Spanish authorities and established a revolutionary junta. In Guayaquil, celebrated over several days, with an International Industrial Fair, concerts, regattas, dances, parades, and shows.

9

Day of National Dignity in Peru; official public holiday. Also called Day of National Honor. Commemorates the nationalization of the country's oil fields in 1968.

9

Han'gul Day (Alphabet Day) in South Korea. Celebrates the anniversary of the 1446 proclamation, by King Sejong of the Yi dynasty, of the Korean alphabet, one of the most amazing inventions of antiquity. On this day elaborate memorial services with Yi dynasty court dances are performed at King Sejong's tomb.

9

Independence Day in Uganda; official public holiday. Celebrates independence attained from the U.K. on Oct. 9, 1962.

ANNIVERSARIES AND SPECIAL EVENTS DAYS

9

Birthday of Lewis Cass (Oct. 9, 1782–June 17, 1866). American statesman, soldier, and author. Governor of the Michigan Territory who improved relations with Native Americans. Represents Mich. in Statuary Hall.

9

Birthday of John Lennon (Oct. 9, 1940–Dec. 8, 1980). English leader of the Beatles, one of the most popular and influential musical groups from the 1960s on; assassinated by a fame seeker. The other Beatles were Paul McCartney (June 18, 1942–); George Harrison (Feb. 25, 1943–); Ringo Starr (born Richard Starkey; July 7, 1940–). The Beatles' last public performance was in London on Jan. 30, 1969.

9

Death anniversary of Benjamin Banneker (1736– Oct. 9, 1806). American astronomer, mathematician, clockmaker, surveyor, almanac author; the First Black Man of Science; participated in the original survey of Washington, D.C.

CA. 9

Fire Prevention Day, Fire Prevention Week, National Firefighters Day, Fire Fighters Memorial Sunday, and ceremonies at the Fallen Fire Fighters Memorial in the U.S., with related events in Canada; all on or near the anniversary of the Chicago Fire of Oct. 8–9, 1871. Fire Prevention Day (Oct. 9), first held in 1911, and Fire Prevention Week (the week including Oct. 9 and observed at least since 1922) are devoted to public information and fire-prevention education. National Firefighters Day is Oct. 8; Fire Fighters Memorial Sunday is the 1st Sunday in Oct., and the National Firefighters Memorial ceremony is held at the Fallen Firefighters Memorial on the grounds of the National Fire Academy at Emmitsburg, Md., on the Sunday following Fire Prevention Week.

9

Leif Eriksson Day in the U.S. Day of tribute to the landing of Norsemen in Vinland on the North American continent in about A.D. 1000, led by Leif Eriksson from Greenland; observed with special events and programming in Norwegian-American communities in the U.S., and is a commemorative day in Iceland and Norway.

HOLY DAYS AND FEAST DAYS

10

Feast of St. Francis Borgia (1510–Sept. 30, 1572). Spanish duke and Jesuit; excellent preacher and administrator; father general of the Jesuits; called their Second Founder.

HOLIDAYS AND CIVIC DAYS

10

Beginning of Independence Wars Day in Cuba; official public holiday. Commemorates the start of the Cuban independence struggle against Spain on Oct. 10, 1868.

10

Health and Sports Day (*Taiku-no-Hi*) in Japan; official public holiday. Commemorates the 1964 Tokyo Olympics.

10

Double Tenth Day in Taiwan and among the Chinese diaspora; official public holiday in Taiwan. Commemorates the Oct. 10, 1911, proclamation of the Republic of China by Sun Yat-sen and the subsequent expulsion of the Manchu dynasty. Celebrated in Taiwan with fireworks and special exhibits.

ANNIVERSARIES AND SPECIAL EVENTS DAYS

10

Anniversary of the founding of the U.S. Naval Academy on Oct. 10, 1845, at Annapolis, Md.

10

Birthday of Giuseppe Verdi (Oct. 10, 1813–Jan. 27, 1901). Italian operatic composer famous for *Aïda, Rigoletto, Il Trovtore,* and *La Traviata.*

10

Birthday of Benjamin West (Oct. 10, 1738–Mar. 11, 1820). American-born painter who settled in London and became official history painter to King George III and a founder of the Royal Academy of Arts. One of the first to paint his subjects in contemporary dress rather than in Greek or Roman togas.

10

Aleksis Kivi Day (born Aleksis Stenvall; Oct. 10, 1834–Dec. 31, 1872); school holiday in Finland. Honors the Finnish author of the highly regarded play *Kullervo* and the novel *Seitsemän Veljestä.*

10

Festival of St. Francis Borgia in Yunguyo, Peru; begins on Oct. 10. The main annual festival. Thousands of costumed dancers come from Peru and Bolivia, including devil dancers from Oruro, Bolivia.

10

Kruger Day in South Africa; formerly an official public holiday. Honors (Stephanus Johannes) Paulus Kruger (Oct. 10, 1825–July 14, 1904). South African statesman, president of the South African Republic, and leader of the Boers.

10

Oklahoma Historical Day in Okla. Anniversary of the birth of Major Jean Pierre Chouteau (Oct. 10, 1758–July 10, 1849), half-brother of Auguste Chouteau, fur trader and pioneer, and the Father of Oklahoma who established the area's first permanent non-Native American settlement in 1796 at Salina.

ANNIVERSARIES AND SPECIAL EVENTS DAYS

11

Birthday of Eleanor Roosevelt (born Anna Eleanor Roosevelt; Oct. 11, 1884–Nov. 7, 1962). American humanitarian; official U.S. delegate to the United Nations; wife of President Franklin D. Roosevelt; author of many books.

11

Birthday of Sir George Williams (Oct. 11, 1821–Nov. 6, 1905). English founder of the Young Men's Christian Association (YMCA).

11

Casimir Pulaski Memorial Day in the U.S. Commemorates the death anniversary of the Polish count Casimir Pulaski, hero of the American Revolution. New York City has a large parade on the Sunday nearest Oct. 11.

HOLIDAYS AND CIVIC DAYS

12

Discovery Day in the Bahamas; official public holiday. Commemorates Columbus's first American landfall on Oct. 12, 1492.

12

Independence Day in Equatorial Guinea; official public holiday. Commemorates the attainment of independence from Spain on Oct. 12, 1968.

12

Hispanity Day (*Día de la Hispanidad*) in Spain; official public holiday. Also called (National) Day of Spanish Consciousness. Honors the achievement of Christopher Columbus and of the Spanish conquerors of Latin America.

ANNIVERSARIES AND SPECIAL EVENTS DAYS

12

Anniversary of Christopher Columbus's arrival in the Americas. At 2 A.M. on Oct. 12, 1492, on his first voyage, Columbus sighted land, probably the island of Guanahani in the Bahamas; from this event dates the modern European expeditions to the Americas.

12

Birthday of Helena Modjeska (Oct. 12, 1840–Apr. 9, 1909). Polish-born American actress noted for Shakespearean roles; barred from Poland because of her anti-Russian speeches.

HOLY DAYS AND FEAST DAYS

13

Feast of St. Edward the Confessor (1003–June 5, 1066). Last of the Saxon kings of England; noted for piety, fair rule, and a peaceful reign. Orth.: Sept. 1 or 14.

HOLIDAYS AND CIVIC DAYS

13

Assassination of the Hero of the Nation Day in Burundi; official public holiday. Honors Prince Louis Rwagasore (or Rwangasore), novelist, independence hero, and statesman; assassinated on Oct. 13, 1961, while prime minister-elect.

HOLIDAYS AND CIVIC DAYS

14

October Revolution in Yemen; official public holiday. Commemorates the Oct. 14, 1963, declaration of (south) Yemen's independence from the U.K., leading to independence in 1967 and the formation of the People's Democratic Republic of Yemen.

ANNIVERSARIES AND SPECIAL EVENTS DAYS

14

Birthday of e. e. cummings (born Edward Estlin Cummings; Oct. 14, 1894–Sept. 3, 1962). Innovative American poet.

14

Birthday of Eamon De Valera (Oct. 14, 1882–Aug. 29, 1975). Irish politician and patriot; prime minister numerous times, and thereafter president.

14

Birthday of Joseph Duveen (Oct. 14, 1869–May 25, 1939). English art connoisseur who gave the British Museum the gallery in which the Elgin marbles are housed.

14

Birthday of Dwight David Eisenhower (Oct. 14, 1890–Mar. 28, 1969). West Point graduate, Army officer, World War II general and commander-in-chief of the Normandy Invasion; statesman; Columbia University president; man of letters; 34th president of the U.S. (1953–61; Republican). His administration was domestically moderate, though scarred by the McCarthy hunts for suspected communists; it also saw the rise of the Cold War. His farewell speech is famous. Buried in Abilene, Kans. President Eisenhower's birthday has been designated as National Friendship Day in the U.S.

14

Birthday of William Penn (Oct. 14, 1644–July 30, 1718). Founder of Pa. and famed leader of the Society of Friends (Quakers). Honorary U.S. citizenship was conferred on him and his second wife, Hannah Callowhill Penn, by presidential proclamation in 1984, a very rare honor. Elected to the Hall of Fame for Great Americans.

14

Battle of Hastings Day. Anniversary of the Oct. 14, 1066, victory of the Normans under William the Conqueror over the Saxons under Harold; the first and most decisive battle in the Norman Conquest and one of the most famous days in English history.

14

Peggy Stewart Day in Md. Honors the sinking of the tea-laden brig *Peggy Stewart* in Annapolis harbor on Oct. 14, 1774, a protest against the stamp taxes.

HOLY DAYS AND FEAST DAYS

15

Feast of St. Teresa of Ávila (Mar. 28, 1515–Oct. 4, 1582). Spanish Carmelite nun; one of the great mystic writers; friend of St. John of the Cross; the first woman doctor of the church. A patron saint of Spain. Ávila, Spain, honors her with a week-long festival ending on Oct. 15.

ANNIVERSARIES AND SPECIAL EVENTS DAYS

15

Birthday of Akbar (born Abu-ul-Fath Jalal-ud-Din Muhammad Akbar; Oct. 15, 1542–1605; ruled 1556–1605). The greatest of the Mughal emperors of India; noted for his tolerance, fairness, and active patronage of scholars, artists, and mystics.

15

Birthday of Helen Maria Hunt Jackson (Oct. 15, 1830–Aug. 12, 1885). American author and activist for Native American rights; wrote *A Century of Dishonor* (1881) and the novel *Ramona,* the century's bestseller after *Uncle Tom's Cabin.*

15

Birthday of Friedrich Wilhelm Nietzsche (Oct. 15, 1844–Aug. 25, 1900). German philosopher; author of *Thus Spake Zarathustra.*

15

Birthday of Virgil (Publius Vergilius Maro; Oct. 15, 70 B.C.–19 B.C.). Roman poet; author of the *Aeneid,* the national epic of Rome.

15

Ether Day in the U.S. Commemorates the first public use of ether to deaden pain in a surgical operation, administered in 1846 by Dr. William Morton.

15

Gregorian Calendar Day. Anniversary of the start of the Gregorian calendar on Friday, Oct. 15, 1582; the preceding day was Thursday, Oct. 4, 1582, in the Julian calendar. The reform was proclaimed in a papal bull of Feb. 24, 1582, by Pope Gregory XIII (ruled 1572–85), and adopted as prescribed in most Roman Catholic countries. Protestant and Eastern Orthodox countries adopted the reform much later.

15

National Grouch Day in the U.S.

15

White Cane Safety Day in the U.S. Dedicated to vision-impaired people by presidential proclamation since 1964.

15

World Poetry Day; observed as Poetry Day in Maine and Tex. A day of tribute and appreciation, on Virgil's birthday, to "unite the nations of the world by the invisible ties of poetry."

HOLY DAYS AND FEAST DAYS

16

Feast of St. Gall (died ca. 635). Irish missionary monk, spiritual son of St. Columbanus, and missionary in what is now Switzerland. Apostle and patron saint of Switzerland. On the site of his hermitage arose the great St. Gall monastery.

HOLIDAYS AND CIVIC DAYS

16

Anniversary of the election of Pope John Paul II; official public holiday in Vatican City and the Holy See, and its only nonreligious holiday. Karol Wojtyla (May 18, 1920–) of Poland was elected the 264th pope of the Roman Catholic Church on Oct. 16, 1978, and installed on Oct. 22, taking the name John Paul II; the first non-Italian pope in 456 years; he survived a May 13, 1981, assassination attempt.

ANNIVERSARIES AND SPECIAL EVENTS DAYS

16

Anniversary of the opening of the first birth control clinic in the U.S., on Oct. 16, 1916, in Brooklyn, N.Y.; by Margaret Sanger, Fania Mindell, and Ethel Burne; Sanger believed the poor should be able to control the size of their families.

16

Anniversary of the Oct. 16, 1859, antislavery raid on the U.S. arsenal at Harpers Ferry, in present-day W.Va., led by the abolitionist John Brown.

16

Anniversary of the founding of Yale University on Oct. 16, 1701, as the Collegiate School in Killingsworth, Conn. Founded by Puritans in reaction to the liberalism of Harvard; moved to New Haven, Conn., in 1745, where it became Yale College; became a university in 1887; degrees were first awarded in 1716.

16

Birthday of Michael Collins (Oct. 16, 1890–Aug. 22, 1922). Irish revolutionary who directed guerrilla strategy during the intensified Anglo-Irish War of 1919–21; signed, with Arthur Griffith, the Anglo-Irish Treaty of Dec. 6, 1921, knowing that Irish intransigents would assassinate them for this.

16

Birthday of William Orville Douglas (Oct. 16, 1898–Jan. 19, 1980). Colorful and controversial associate justice of the Supreme Court remembered for his unflagging support of individual liberties and individual freedom; served as justice for 33 years, longer than any other; also a noted conservationist and world traveler.

16

Birthday of Eugene Gladstone O'Neill (Oct. 16, 1886–Dec. 6, 1953). American playwright, the first one to receive the Nobel Prize in literature (1936); a 3-time recipient of the Pulitzer Prize for drama.

16

Birthday of Oscar (Fingal O'Flahertie Wills) Wilde (Oct. 16, 1854–Nov. 30, 1900). Irish writer renowned for his wit and eccentricity; wrote *The Importance of Being Earnest* and "The Ballad of Reading Gaol."

16

Dictionary Day. Anniversary of the birth of Noah Webster (Oct. 16, 1758–May 28, 1843), American lexicographer and teacher, compiler of the earliest American dictionaries of the English language, and whose name became synonymous with dictionary. His *American Dictionary of the English Language* was published Nov. 28, 1828.

16

World Food Day. Anniversary of the founding of the Food and Agriculture Organization on Oct. 16, 1945; a day sponsored by the United Nations to broaden citizen understanding of the problems of hunger, malnutrition, and poverty that exist in all parts of the world.

HOLY DAYS AND FEAST DAYS

17

Feast of St. Ignatius of Antioch (died Dec. 20, ca. 107). Called the God-Bearer (*Theophore*). By legend, appointed bishop of Antioch by St. Peter. He was martyred by lions in the Roman arena. His letters are among the first Christian writings. Orth.: Dec. 20 or Jan. 2.

HOLIDAYS AND CIVIC DAYS

17

Death anniversary of Jean-Jacques Dessalines (ca. 1758–Oct. 17, 1806); official public holiday in Haiti. Revolutionary leader who saw independence attained in 1804 and subsequently ruled as Emperor Jacques I (1804–6).

17

Burgoyne's Surrender Day in the U.S. Anniversary of the Oct. 17, 1777, surrender at Saratoga, N.Y., of the British general Burgoyne; the turning point in the American Revolutionary War; observed in N.Y. State.

ANNIVERSARIES AND SPECIAL EVENTS DAYS

17

Anniversary of the San Francisco earthquake of Oct. 17, 1989. Magnitude was 6.9 on the Richter scale. Damage was widespread, but without sound building codes it would have been worse.

17

Black Poetry Day in the U.S. Honors the contributions of African American poets to American culture, and honors Jupiter Hammon (Oct. 17, 1711–ca. 1790), the first African American in the U.S. to publish his own verse. First observed in 1970.

HOLY DAYS AND FEAST DAYS

18

Feast of St. Luke (1st century). Greek physician, disciple, evangelist, and companion of St. Paul; author of the 3rd Gospel and of the Acts of the Apostles, covering the years A.D. ca. 35–63; died of old age. Patron saint of painters and physicians. His emblem is the ox. Orth.: Oct. 18 or 31.

HOLIDAYS AND CIVIC DAYS

18

National Independence Day in Azerbaijan; official public holiday. Celebrates independence declared from the USSR on Oct. 18, 1991. Independence was formally attained with the dissolution of the Soviet Union on Dec. 26, 1991.

18

Alaska Day in Alaska; official public holiday. Commemorates the formal transfer of Alaska to the U.S. from Russia on Oct. 18, 1867. Observed in a 3-day festival in Sitka, Alaska, where the original ceremony of transfer occurred.

ANNIVERSARIES AND SPECIAL EVENTS DAYS

18

Anniversary of the revocation of the Edict of Nantes by Louis XIV on Oct. 18, 1685. The revocation deprived French Protestants of their limited religious freedom and resulted in the Huguenot migration to Holland and England, and eventually to the U.S.

18

Birthday of Florence Dahl Walrath (Oct. 18, 1877–Nov. 7, 1958). American humanitarian; founder of the Cradle Society, organized in 1923 to prepare children for adoption.

18

Persons Day in Canada. As a consequence of the Persons Case, on Oct. 18, 1929, Canadian women were declared legal "persons" in matters of rights and privileges, a judgment due to the work of 5 women led by Emily Murphy (1868–1933). Since 1979, commemorative awards have been given to those who have improved the quality of life for Canadian women.

HOLY DAYS AND FEAST DAYS

19

Feast of St. Isaac Jogues (1607–Oct. 18, 1646) and of the (Jesuit) Martyrs of North America. French Jesuit and missionary to the Hurons and Iroquois of Quebec and modern N.Y. State. Martyred by the Mohawks on Oct. 18, 1646, as was his fellow Jesuit, Jean de Lalande, on Oct. 19. These and other Jesuits are commemorated on this day.

HOLIDAYS AND CIVIC DAYS

19

Samora Machel Day in Mozambique. Commemorates the country's first president, Samora Machel, who died Oct. 19, 1986, in a mysterious plane crash inside South Africa.

ANNIVERSARIES AND SPECIAL EVENTS DAYS

19

Birthday of John McLoughlin (Oct. 19, 1781–Sept. 3, 1857). American pioneer in the Oregon Territory. Represents Oreg. in Statuary Hall.

HOLY DAYS AND FEAST DAYS

20

Anniversary of the Birth of the Bab, in the Baha'i faith. A holy day, and Baha'is abstain from work. A day of rejoicing in the birth of the Bab, the faith's prophet and first spiritual leader.

HOLIDAYS AND CIVIC DAYS

20

Revolution Day in Guatemala; official public holiday. Commemorates the 1944 overthrow of the dictator Jorge Ubico Castañeda and the establishment of a democracy.

20

Kenyatta Day in Kenya; official public holiday. Honors Jomo Kenyatta (born Kamau Ngengi; ca. 1894–Aug. 22, 1978), Kenya's first prime minister (1963–64), and thereafter its president (1964–78).

ANNIVERSARIES AND SPECIAL EVENTS DAYS

20

Birthday of John Dewey (Oct. 20, 1859–June 1, 1952). American philosopher and influential educational reformer; his watchword was "learning by doing."

20

Birthday of Mickey Mantle (Oct. 20, 1931–Aug. 13, 1995). American baseball player; New York Yankees home-run hitter inducted into the Baseball Hall of Fame in 1974.

20

Birthday of Sir Christopher Wren (Oct. 20, 1632–Feb. 25, 1723). English architect, astronomer, and mathematician, whose great public buildings include Saint Paul's Cathedral; especially active in rebuilding London after its Great Fire of 1666.

HOLY DAYS AND FEAST DAYS

21

Feast of St. Ursula (died ca. 453). By legend, British virgin martyred at Cologne, Germany. Patron saint of the British Virgin Islands (official public holiday); of Palermo, Sicily; and of teachers and young people.

ANNIVERSARIES AND SPECIAL EVENTS DAYS

21

Birthday of Samuel Taylor Coleridge (Oct. 21, 1772–July 25, 1834). English poet, critic, and philosopher.

21

Birthday of Alfred Bernhard Nobel (Oct. 21, 1833–Dec. 10, 1896). Swedish chemist and engineer who invented dynamite and other explosives, and left his fortune for the Nobel Prizes.

21

Apple Day in the U.K., especially in England; on Oct. 21 or the nearest weekend. A new holiday, to honor the 6,000 local varieties of edible apples (most in danger of extinction) and to highlight the threatened extinction of the world's physical, cultural, and genetic diversity.

21

Trafalgar Day in the U.K. Commemorates the Battle of Trafalgar, Oct. 21, 1805, in the Napoleonic Wars. Lord Nelson decisively defeated a French-

Spanish fleet and prevented a French invasion of Britain. Ceremonies include a naval parade from London's Mall to Trafalgar Square, where after a short service wreaths are placed at the foot of Nelson's Column.

ANNIVERSARIES AND SPECIAL EVENTS DAYS

22

Anniversary of the start of the Cuban Missile Crisis, the closest the world has ever come to nuclear war. On Oct. 22, 1962, President John Kennedy declared the intent of the U.S. to remove Soviet offensive missile installations from Cuba. On Oct. 28, the Soviet Union announced it would remove the missiles.

22

Birthday of Franz Liszt (Oct. 22, 1811–July 31, 1886). Hungarian composer and pianist, famous for the *Hungarian Rhapsodies,* symphonic poems for orchestra, and many piano compositions.

22

Death anniversary of Jean Grolier de Servières (1479–Oct. 22, 1565). French bibliophile for whom the Grolier Society in New York is named and who is honored annually by the society on this day.

22

Death anniversary of Charles Martel (ca. 688–Oct. 22, 741). French ruler who halted the Muslim advance into Europe at the Battle of Poitiers (732; a sequence of running engagements). Grandfather of Charlemagne.

CA. 22

Blessing of the Sea at Stes-Maries-de-la-Mer, France; on the Sunday nearest Oct. 22. A pilgrimage in honor of the saints Mary Jacoby and Mary Salome.

22

Festival of the Ages (*Jidai Matsuri*) in Kyoto, Japan. Reviews the main periods of Kyoto's and Japan's histories from the 8th to the 19th centuries. One of Kyoto's major festivals; held since 1895.

HOLY DAYS AND FEAST DAYS

23

Feast of St. Severinus Boethius (born Anicius Manlius Severinus Boethius; ca. 480–524). Roman scholar, translator of the Greek philosophers into Latin, and author of the influential *Consolations of Philosophy.* The first of the scholastic philosophers.

HOLIDAYS AND CIVIC DAYS

23

Cambodia Peace Treaty Day in Cambodia; official public holiday. Celebrates the peace treaty among the warring factions, signed in Paris on Oct. 23, 1991.

23

Memorial Day for the 1956 Revolution and the Declaration of the Republic of Hungary in 1989; official public holiday. Also called the Uprising Day of Remembrance. The anniversary of the Hungarian Revolt: on Oct. 23, 1956, the people of Hungary revolted against Russian domination and communist rule. The new government was crushed by overwhelming Russian force on Nov. 4, but its heroic memory remained an inspiration. Hungary deliberately chose Oct. 23, 1989, as the day to proclaim the new republic. One of Hungary's three national days.

23

Chulalongkorn Day in Thailand; official public holiday. Commemorates the death of King Chulalongkorn the Great, Rama V (Sept. 20, 1853–Oct. 23, 1910; ruled 1873–1910), following a 37-year reign in which he led his kingdom into the modern world and abolished slavery. Special ceremonies with floral tributes are held at his statue in front of the old National Assembly building, Bangkok.

ANNIVERSARIES AND SPECIAL EVENTS DAYS

23

Birthday of Robert Bridges (Oct. 23, 1844–Apr. 21, 1930). Poet laureate of England, remembered especially for *The Testament of Beauty.*

23

Birthday of Pelé (born Edson Arantes do Nascimento; Oct. 23, 1940–). Brazilian soccer player who led his national team to World Cup victories in 1958, 1962, and 1970. During his career, the most famous athlete in the world; Brazilian national hero.

23

Canning Day. Anniversary of the birth of Nicolas Apert (Oct. 23, 1752–June 3, 1841), French chef, chemist, confectioner, inventor, and author; devised the method of heating and sealing food in air-tight containers.

23

Long-accepted date for the creation of the world, on the evening preceding Oct. 23, 4004 B.C., according to James Ussher (1581–1656), Irish prelate.

23

Swallows of Capistrano Day. Traditional day for swallows to leave the San Juan Capistrano Mission in Calif.; occurs on the death anniversary of St. John of Capistrano.

HOLY DAYS AND FEAST DAYS

24

Traditional feast of the archangel Raphael. One of the seven archangels; his name means "God heals." Patron saint of blind people and travelers.

HOLIDAYS AND CIVIC DAYS

24

Independence Day in Zambia; official public holiday. Commemorates independence attained from the U.K. on Oct. 24, 1964.

ANNIVERSARIES AND SPECIAL EVENTS DAYS

24

Birthday of Alban Butler (Oct. 24, 1710–May 15, 1773). English Catholic priest and scholar; author of the classic *Lives of the Saints* (*Lives of the Fathers, Martyrs, and Other Principal Saints,* 4 volumes, 1756–59).

24

Birthday of Sarah Josepha Hale (Oct. 24, 1788–Apr. 30, 1879). American author and groundbreaking female editor of *Godey's Lady's Book.* The Friends of Richards Free Library in Newport, N.H., present an annual award in her name to an individual who has made a lifetime contribution to literature associated with New England.

24

Birthday of Anton van Leeuwenhoek (Oct. 24, 1632–Aug. 26, 1723). Dutch microscopist and biologist; known as the Father of Microscopy and the first biological scientist.

24

United Nations Day. Anniversary of the founding of the United Nations on Oct. 24, 1945. Each member nation observes the day in some manner.

HOLIDAYS AND CIVIC DAYS

25

Thanksgiving Day in Grenada; official public holiday. Anniversary of the U.S. invasion of Grenada, on Oct. 25, 1983, following a political coup there.

25

Independence Day in Kazakhstan; official public holiday. Celebrates the Oct. 25, 1991, declaration of independence from the USSR. Independence was formally attained with the dissolution of the Soviet Union on Dec. 26, 1991.

25

Restoration Day in Taiwan; official public holiday. Celebrates the return of Taiwan to China on Oct. 25, 1945, after 50 years of Japanese occupation.

ANNIVERSARIES AND SPECIAL EVENTS DAYS

25

Birthday of Georges Bizet (Oct. 25, 1838–June 3, 1875). French composer whose most famous work is the opera *Carmen.*

25

Birthday of Richard Evelyn Byrd (Oct. 25, 1888–Mar. 11, 1957). American naval officer and polar explorer who made 5 important expeditions to the Antarctic. Received the Congressional Medal of Honor in 1926.

25

Birthday of Thomas Babington Macaulay (Oct. 25, 1800–Dec. 28, 1859). English essayist, poet, historian, and statesman, famous for *Horatius at the Bridge* and *History of England* (5 volumes, 1849–61).

25

Birthday of Pablo Picasso (Oct. 25, 1881–Apr. 8, 1973). Catalan Spanish painter, sculptor, and engraver, considered by many the greatest artist of the 20th century.

25

Death anniversary of Geoffrey Chaucer (ca. 1342–Oct. 25, 1400). Most influential English poet before Shakespeare; wrote *The Canterbury Tales.*

HOLY DAYS AND FEAST DAYS

26

Orthodox feast of St. Demetrius (Demetrios) the Myrrh-Gusher of Thessalonika (4th century). Patron saint of Salonika, Greece. Orth.: Oct. 26 or Nov. 8.

HOLIDAYS AND CIVIC DAYS

26

National Day in Austria; official public holiday. Also called Flag Day. Celebrates the withdrawal of Soviet troops on Oct. 26, 1955, and the regaining of national freedom.

ANNIVERSARIES AND SPECIAL EVENTS DAYS

26

Anniversary of the opening on Oct. 26, 1825, of the Erie Canal. First major man-made waterway in the U.S., providing a water route from Lake Erie to the Hudson River.

26

Anniversary of the gunfight at the O.K. Corral, in Tombstone, Ariz., on Oct. 26, 1881. The Clanton gang (5 men) fought against Virgil, Wyatt, and Morgan Earp and Doc Holliday. Three of the Clanton gang were killed.

26

Birthday of Joseph Aloysius Hansom (Oct. 26, 1803–June 29, 1882). English architect and inventor; invented the horse-drawn hansom cab (1834), widely used for public transportation.

26

Death anniversary of Alfred the Great (849–Oct. 26, 899; ruled 871–99). English king of the West Saxons; fondly revered.

26

International Red Cross Day. Anniversary of the establishment of the worldwide Red Cross organization at an Oct. 26, 1863, meeting of nations in Geneva, called by Jean-Henri Dunant.

26

Mule Day in the U.S. Mules are said to have been first bred in the U.S. by George Washington from a pair of Spanish jacks, a gift of King Charles III of Spain, delivered in Boston on Oct. 26, 1785.

26

St. Demetrius Day in Greece and Romania. In Greece, the season's first wine is drunk; a day once religious, now secular. Throughout rural Romania, on the eve, youths gather around bonfires, with incantations, continuing a very ancient tradition.

HOLIDAYS AND CIVIC DAYS

27

Thanksgiving and Independence Day in St. Vincent and the Grenadines; official public holiday. The national day, commemorating independence attained from the U.K. on Oct. 27, 1979. Also on this day is the Community Drama Festival.

27

Independence Day in Turkmenistan; official public holiday on Oct. 27–28. Celebrates the Oct. 27, 1991, declaration of independence from the USSR. Independence was formally attained with the dissolution of the Soviet Union on Dec. 26, 1991.

ANNIVERSARIES AND SPECIAL EVENTS DAYS

27

Anniversary of the publication of the Federalist Papers in the U.S. On Oct. 27, 1787, the first of the 85 Federalist Papers appeared; the last was completed Apr. 4, 1788. These essays, arguing for the adoption of the new Constitution and its form of federal government, were written by Alexander Hamilton, James Madison, and John Jay.

27

Anniversary of the opening of the New York City subway on Oct. 27, 1904, the world's first underground and underwater rail system.

27

Birthday of James Cook (Oct. 27, 1728–Feb. 14, 1779). English sea captain and explorer.

27

Birthday of Theodore Roosevelt (Oct. 27, 1858–Jan. 6, 1919). N.Y. assemblyman and governor; volunteer in the Spanish-American War; naturalist, conservationist, explorer, and man of letters; 26th president of the U.S. (1901–09; Republican). Awarded the Nobel Peace Prize in 1906 for his mediation following the Russo-Japanese War (1904–5). His administration was especially notable for its measures against government and business corruption, and against monopoly power. Buried in Oyster Bay, N.Y. Elected to the Hall of Fame for Great Americans.

27

Navy Day in the U.S. Observed on Theodore Roosevelt's birthday since 1922. Now partially eclipsed by Armed Forces Day. The Navy was founded on Mar. 27, 1794, with an Act of Congress signed by President George Washington.

HOLY DAYS AND FEAST DAYS

28

Feast of St. Jude (1st century). Also named Thaddeus. One of the original 12 Apostles and patron saint of desperate causes. Orth.: June 19 or July 2.

28

Feast of St. Simon (Simeon) the Zealot (died ca. 107). One of the original 12 Apostles. Son of Mary Clopas and cousin of Jesus; bishop of Jerusalem after James the Less; predicted the destruction of Jerusalem and led its Christians to refuge. May be the same man as Simeon, kinsman of the Lord. Orth.: May 10 or 23.

HOLIDAYS AND CIVIC DAYS

28

Independence Day in the Czech Republic; official public holiday. Formerly called the Day of the Republic. Celebrates the bloodless declaration and attainment of independence from the Austro-Hungarian Empire, Oct. 28, 1918, and the unification of Czechs and Slovaks in the former Republic of Czechoslovakia.

28

Ochi Day in Greece; official public holiday. Mussolini's troops invaded Oct. 28, 1940, and invited surrender; Greece said *ochi*—"no!" Celebrated with military parades.

ANNIVERSARIES AND SPECIAL EVENTS DAYS

28

Anniversary of the founding of Harvard University, the oldest university in the nation, on Oct. 28, 1636, in Cambridge, Mass. Mass. General Court voted to provide 400 pounds to establish a "schoale or colledge"; named after the clergyman John Harvard on Mar. 13, 1639, in recognition of his large posthumous bequest.

28

Birthday of (Georges-) Auguste Escoffier (Oct. 28, 1846–Feb. 12, 1935). French chef and author of high reputation.

28

Birthday of Jonas Edward Salk (Oct. 28, 1914–June 23, 1995). American physician; developer of the Salk vaccine against poliomyelitis.

28

Statue of Liberty Dedication Day in the U.S. Anniversary of the dedication, on Oct. 28, 1886, of Frédéric Auguste Bartholdi's colossal *Liberty Enlightening the World,* in New York harbor; a monument to Franco-American friendship.

HOLIDAYS AND CIVIC DAYS

29

Republic Day (*Cumhuriyet Bayrami*) in Turkey; official public holiday in Turkey and also for Turkish Cypriots. Commemorates Oct. 29, 1923, when Turkey formally became a republic; the major civil holiday of the year, with parades and speeches.

ANNIVERSARIES AND SPECIAL EVENTS DAYS

29

Anniversary of the founding of the National Organization for Women (NOW), organized on Oct. 29, 1966, "to press for true equality for all women in America."

29

Birthday of James Boswell (Oct. 29, 1740–May 19, 1795). English author, famous as a diarist and as the biographer of Dr. Samuel Johnson. The two met on May 16, 1763, which has been dubbed Biographer's Day.

29

Death anniversary of Sir Walter Raleigh (ca. 1554–Oct. 29, 1618). English writer, adventurer, and military and naval commander of expeditions to North America.

29

Black Tuesday. Anniversary of the Oct. 29, 1929, U.S. stock market crash that brought ruin to the financial world and precipitated the Great Depression of the 1930s.

ANNIVERSARIES AND SPECIAL EVENTS DAYS

30

Birthday of John Adams (Oct. 30, 1735–July 4, 1826). Great grandson of Henry Adams, who immigrated to Braintree, Mass., in 1636. Mass. teacher, lawyer, diarist, and letter writer; signer of the Declaration of Independence; Revolutionary patriot and statesman; vice-president under Washington (1789–97); 2nd president of the U.S. (1797–1801; Federalist). As president, he opposed war with France, which Hamilton and others wanted; supported the infamous Alien and Sedition Acts, which led to his defeat for reelection. Buried in First Unitarian Church at Braintree, Mass. Elected to the Hall of Fame for Great Americans.

30
Birthday of Ezra Loomis Pound (Oct. 30, 1885–Nov. 1, 1972). American poet, critic, and translator; influenced T. S. Eliot, Robert Frost, and W. B. Yeats, among others; exhorted poets to "make it new."

HOLY DAYS AND FEAST DAYS

CA. 31
Reformation Day and Reformation Sunday. Reformation Day is the anniversary of Martin Luther's posting of his 95 theses ("On the Power of Indulgences") on the door of Wittenberg's castle church on Oct. 31, 1517. The theses denounced corruption in the church and asserted that the Bible was the sole font of authority. The official beginning of Protestantism. Called Luther's Theses Day in some German Lutheran churches. Reformation Sunday is observed on the Sunday preceding Oct. 31.

HOLIDAYS AND CIVIC DAYS

31
Birthday of Chiang Kai-shek (born Chiang Chung-cheng; Oct. 31, 1887–Apr. 5, 1975); official public holiday in Taiwan. Chinese Nationalist leader; founder of Taiwan and first president (1948–75).

31
Nevada Day in Nev.; official public holiday. Anniversary of Nev.'s admission to the Union on Oct. 31, 1864, as the 36th state.

ANNIVERSARIES AND SPECIAL EVENTS DAYS

31
Anniversary of the completion of Mt. Rushmore National Memorial in S.Dak. on Oct. 31, 1941. Sculpted by Gutzon Borglum are the heads of Presidents George Washington, Thomas Jefferson, Abraham Lincoln, and Theodore Roosevelt.

31
Birthday of John Keats (Oct. 31, 1795–Feb. 23, 1821). English Romantic poet; trained as a surgeon. "The Eve of St. Agnes" and other poems assure him a permanent place in world literature; he is known as the Poet's Poet.

31
Birthday of Juliette Low (born Juliette Magill Kinzie Gordon; Oct. 31, 1860–Jan. 17, 1927). Founder of the Girl Scouts of America. She organized the first U.S. troop, originally called Girl Guides, in Savannah, Ga., on Mar. 12, 1912.

31
Birthday of Sir George Hubert Wilkins (Oct. 31, 1888–ca. Nov. 30, 1958). Australian polar explorer; the first to fly an airplane in the Antarctic and to fly over both polar regions.

31
Halloween. Also called All Hallows Eve or Beggars Night. Festival for children in the U.S. and elsewhere, when youngsters in costume roam their neighborhoods with open bags for treats and (formerly) with the threat of tricks played on their absent or ungiving neighbors. Originally derived from the Celtic harvest festival of Samhain.

31
Houdini Day. Commemorates the death anniversary of Harry Houdini (born Ehrich Weiss; Mar. 24, 1874–Oct. 31, 1926). Also called National Magic Day. Hungarian-born American magician, illusionist, and writer, famed for his escape techniques and for his exposure of fraudulent mediums. His death anniversary, on Halloween, is the occasion for meetings of amateur and professional magicians, as well as mediumistic attempts at communication.

31
UNICEF Day in the U.S.; by presidential proclamation, honoring the United Nations Children's Emergency Fund; also observed in other countries.

MOVABLE DAYS IN OCTOBER
HOLIDAYS AND CIVIC DAYS

LABOUR DAY, OR EIGHT HOUR DAY, IN THE AUSTRALIAN CAPITAL TERRITORY, NEW SOUTH WALES, AND SOUTH AUSTRALIA; 1st Monday in Oct.; official public holiday. Honors the labor movement's achievement in

1871 of an eight-hour working day for all Australians. Celebrated with parades and rallies, picnics, and sporting events.

THANKSGIVING DAY IN CANADA; 2nd Monday in Oct.; official public holiday. Celebrates bountiful harvests and the blessings of life on Canadian soil.

FIJI DAY IN FIJI; 2nd Monday in Oct.; official public holiday. Celebrates independence attained from the U.K. on Oct. 10, 1970.

HEROES DAY IN JAMAICA; 3rd Monday in Oct.; official public holiday. Honors citizens of heroic stature. Replaces, since 1968, Queen Elizabeth's Official Birthday (though she still receives military honors on her day).

LABOUR DAY IN NEW ZEALAND; 4th Monday in Oct.; official public holiday.

WHITE SUNDAY (LOTU-A-TAMAITI) IN SAMOA; 2nd Sunday in Oct. A big day for children: children in white lead church services and are feted for the day. The next day (Monday) is an official public holiday. An official public holiday also in American Samoa; many people from American Samoa go to Western Samoa to celebrate the holiday.

DAYLIGHT SAVING TIME (DST) ENDS IN THE U.S. AND CANADA at 2 A.M. on the last Sunday in Oct. Clocks are set back 1 hour (they "fall back").

COLUMBUS DAY IN THE U.S.; 2nd Monday Oct.; federal official public holiday. Columbus Day has been observed in the U.S. since 1892, when it was proclaimed a holiday (Discovery Day) by President Benjamin Harrison. The day is observed in many communities and schools; New York City's Columbus Day Parade is notable.

DISCOVERERS' DAY IN HAWAII; 2nd Monday in Oct. Honors Pacific and Polynesian navigators and all other explorers.

NATIVE AMERICANS' DAY IN S.DAK.; 2nd Monday in Oct.; official public holiday. Celebrated in lieu of Columbus Day.

YORKTOWN DAY IN VA.; 2nd Monday in Oct.; official public holiday. In Yorktown, Va., observed on Oct. 19 and on the weekend nearest the day. Anniversary of the Oct. 19, 1781, surrender of British General Cornwallis and his troops to General George Washington and his army and to French troops, marking the effective end of the American Revolutionary War. Special patriotic services are also conducted by the National Park Service at the Yorktown Monument.

COLUMBUS DAY AND PUERTO RICO FRIENDSHIP DAY IN THE U.S. VIRGIN ISLANDS; 2nd Monday in Oct.; official public holiday. Honors both Columbus and a good neighbor. (Columbus reached the Virgin Islands on Nov. 14, 1493, during his 2nd voyage.)

HURRICANE THANKSGIVING DAY IN THE U.S. VIRGIN ISLANDS; 3rd Monday in Oct.; an official public holiday of prayerful thanks, but only if the islands have been spared.

ANNIVERSARIES AND SPECIAL EVENTS DAYS

INTERNATIONAL CREDIT UNION DAY; 3rd Thursday in Oct.

INTERNATIONAL DAY FOR NATURAL DISASTER REDUCTION; 2nd Wednesday in Oct. Sponsored by the General Assembly of the United Nations to foster international cooperation in reducing the death, destruction, and disruption caused by natural disasters.

WORLD HABITAT DAY; 1st Monday in Oct. Sponsored by the United Nations; first observed in 1986, on the 10th anniversary of the first international conference on the subject.

PIRATES WEEK IN THE CAYMAN ISLANDS, BRITISH WEST INDIES; last week in Oct. The islands' elaborate national festival, with costumes, parades, a mock pirate invasion, selection of a Pirate Queen, and food, music, and dancing.

FRANKFURT BOOK FAIR (BUCHMESSE) IN FRANKFURT, GERMANY; in 1st half of Oct., ends on a Monday. The largest and most prestigious book fair in the world, dating from at least 1564.

OKTOBERFEST IN MUNICH, GERMANY; 16 days total, ends 1st Sunday in Oct., begins Saturday, 2 weeks before. Also called *Wies'n* ("Meadow"). One of Germany's most famous festivals, and one of the world's largest. Began on Oct. 17, 1810, the wedding day of King Ludwig I at the meadow site of the event; celebrated ever since with the best beers, foods, and entertainment of the season.

BEGINNING OF THE U.S. SUPREME COURT'S ANNUAL TERM; 1st Monday in Oct.; by tradition.

CHILD HEALTH DAY IN THE U.S.; 1st Monday in Oct.; by presidential proclamation since 1928; formerly on May 1, on present date since 1959.

CHILDREN'S SABBATH IN THE U.S.; 3rd Friday–Sunday in Oct. Religious congregations of many faiths and denominations focus on children and their families, emphasizing children's needs for health and wholeness, and ways to help them. Sponsored by the Children's Defense Fund, since 1992.

MOTHER-IN-LAW DAY IN THE U.S.; 4th Sunday in Oct. Created to honor mothers-in-law for their contribution to the success of families, and for their good humor though the butt of jokes. First celebrated on Mar. 5, 1934, in Amarillo, Tex.; initiated by the editor of the local newspaper.

NATIONAL BUSINESS WOMEN'S WEEK IN THE U.S.; begins 3rd Monday in Oct. By presidential proclamation; honors U.S. women who work in business.

SWEETEST DAY IN THE U.S.; 3rd Saturday in Oct. Began ca. 1950 in Cleveland, Ohio, as a day to give presents to orphans and shut-ins; now promoted as a day to remember anyone with a kind act or gift.

WORLD WRISTWRESTLING CHAMPIONSHIPS IN PETALUMA, CALIF.; 2nd Saturday in Oct. Annually since 1962; began in 1957.

DANIEL BOONE FESTIVAL IN BARBOURVILLE, KY.; 8 days, beginning 1st Saturday in Oct. Honors Daniel Boone; includes the annual re-signing of the Cherokee Cane Treaty, affirming to descendants of those Cherokee who refused to leave their home the right to harvest cane along the Cumberland River; includes many old-fashioned events; held since 1948.

INTERNATIONAL RICE FESTIVAL IN CROWLEY, LA.; climax usually on the 3rd Saturday in Oct. and the preceding Friday. A huge festival in celebration of rice and the community; the population multiplies 10-fold. Held in the traditional postharvest season, with nightly balls, parties, and street dances; a day of children's events; music and cooking contests; the selection of a queen; recognition of good farmers and noble citizens; traditional rice-farming demonstrations; and a grand parade. Began in 1937, one of Louisiana's oldest agriculture festivals; the whole town prepares and participates.

IG NOBEL PRIZE NIGHT IN CAMBRIDGE, MASS.; 2nd Thursday in Oct. A tongue-in-cheek fabrication; in the name of Ignatius Nobel, the inventor of soda pop and brother of Alfred Nobel, awards are presented by *The Annals of Improbable Research* (originating at the Massachusetts Institute of Technology) for scientific research "that cannot, or should not, be reproduced."

ALBUQUERQUE INTERNATIONAL BALLOON FIESTA IN ALBUQUERQUE, N.MEX.; 9 days, begins the 1st Saturday in Oct. The largest balloon event in the world, and extremely colorful; began in 1972.

NATIONAL STORYTELLING FESTIVAL IN JONESBOROUGH, TENN.; 1st Friday–Sunday in Oct. Intended to revive and preserve the ancient art of storytelling; began in 1973; well-attended and influential.

November

November, the 11th month in the Gregorian calendar, received its name from the Latin numeral *novem* because it was the 9th month in the Julian calendar.

The month of November includes the oldest special day to have originated in the U.S. In 1621, Governor William Bradford of Mass. proclaimed a day for feasting, prayer, and thanksgiving. It had its forerunner in the harvest-home celebrations of England, but it was a very special day for the Pilgrims. The idea spread throughout the states but was not universally celebrated until Sarah Josepha Hale, the editor of *Godey's Lady's Book,* persuaded President Abraham Lincoln to issue a general proclamation in 1863. Since then, Thanksgiving Day has been observed as a holiday by all states and territories of the U.S.

November also has a traditional day for revelry. It is Guy Fawkes Day, the anniversary of the November 5, 1605, gunpowder plot to blow up the English Parliament and the king. It is observed throughout England and in many parts of the British Commonwealth. It is a popular festival for children and students. It is said that the undergraduates at Oxford University fill the streets on Guy Fawkes night, lighting fireworks. The students who get into trouble on this night are eligible to join the Bowler Hat Club, whose members vow to promote the use of the bowler hat. In other parts of England, the celebration centers around big bonfires. In Nassau and in the Caribbean, Guy Fawkes parades are accompanied by calypso bands.

The chrysanthemum is the November flower, and the gem is the topaz.

HOLY DAYS AND FEAST DAYS

1

All Saints' Day. Honors Christian saints of all periods and stations, known or unknown; observed universally by all Western churches. The feast dates from the 4th century. Orth.: the Saturday before Cheesefare Sunday and the 1st Sunday after Pentecost.

HOLIDAYS AND CIVIC DAYS

1

Revolution Day in Algeria; official public holiday. Anniversary of the revolution begun by the National Liberation Front on Nov. 1, 1954, against the French administration and its armed forces.

1

Independence Day in Antigua-Barbuda; official public holiday. Commemorates the attainment of independence from the U.K. on Nov. 1, 1981.

1

Liberty Day in the U.S. Virgin Islands; official public holiday. Honors Judge David Hamilton Jackson (Sept. 28, 1884–May 30, 1946), who secured freedom of the press and assembly from King Christian X of Denmark.

ANNIVERSARIES AND SPECIAL EVENTS DAYS

1

Anniversary of the first hydrogen bomb explosion by the U.S. government, on Nov. 1, 1952, at Eniwetok Atoll, Marshall Islands; overseen by the U.S. scientist Edward Teller.

1

Anniversary of the Lisbon earthquake. Lisbon, Portugal, was struck by a powerful earthquake, estimated at 8.75 on the Richter scale, on Nov. 1,

1755, while the people were in church for All Saints' Day; 60,000 deaths resulted.

1

Anniversary of the Teapot Dome scandal. On Nov. 1, 1929, Albert B. Fall was sentenced to one year in prison and a fine of $100,000. Fall, as secretary of the interior under President Warren G. Harding, had in 1922 secretly granted exclusive drilling rights on federal naval oil reserves to 3 oil companies in exchange for bribes.

1

Birthday of Sholem Asch (Nov. 1, 1880–July 10, 1957). Russian-born American novelist famous for novels and plays in English and Yiddish.

1

Birthday of Charles Brantley Aycock (Nov. 1, 1859–Apr. 4, 1912). American politician and educational reformer. Governor of N.C., best known for the establishment of a rural high-school system in that state. Represents N.C. in Statuary Hall.

1

Birthday of Stephen Crane (Nov. 1, 1871–June 5, 1900). American author, famous for the novel *The Red Badge of Courage.*

1

Birthday of Sir Benjamin Lee Guinness (Nov. 1, 1798–May 19, 1868). His father, Arthur (died 1855), founded the Guinness Stout brewery, a family business. Benjamin made it international, and was also the first Lord Mayor of Dublin. *The Guinness Book of World Records* was commissioned to settle pub disputes.

1

Birthday of Crawford Williamson Long (Nov. 1, 1815–June 16, 1878). American surgeon who pioneered the use of ether for anesthesia. Represents Ga. in Statuary Hall.

1

Author's Day in the U.S. Observed since Nov. 1, 1928, by study clubs to honor the work of writers who have developed American literature and to encourage authors "to lend their talents to making a better America."

CA. 1

Kite Festival in Santiago, Guatemala. Children make kites, many of them elaborate or gigantic, and fly them on Nov. 1 and 2 at the cemetery to banish evil spirits.

1

Northern Areas Independence Day (or Uprising Day) and Gilgit Festival (*Jashan-i-Gilgit*) in Gilgit, Pakistan. Commemorates the Oct. 22, 1947, uprising by Muslims against the Hindu Maharajah of Kashmir (India), with partisans from northwest Pakistan. The Gilgit Festival is a notable weeklong polo tournament that starts Nov. 1.

HOLY DAYS AND FEAST DAYS

2

All Souls' Day. Commemorates the faithful departed; a day of prayers for the dead; observance began in the earliest days of Christianity. Orth.: the Saturday before Meatfare Sunday.

2

Day of the Dead (*Día de Muertos*) in Mexico, especially in the Native American portions of central Mexico. A very important day, dating from pre-Conquest times. In popular belief, the souls of the adult dead return on this day (those of children return on Nov. 1). Highly personalized welcoming altars in homes display foods, flowers, and ornaments. People exchange edible skulls of sugar as a symbol of new life and feast at home with their dead as invisible guests. At midnight, all visit the cemetery and adorn the graves with food, drink, presents, flowers, and candles.

HOLIDAYS AND CIVIC DAYS

2

Independence Day in Chechnya. On Nov. 2, 1991, Chechnya declared its independence from the USSR; despite a bloody war of several years, independence is still not attained.

2

Admission Day in N.Dak. On Nov. 2, 1889, N.Dak. was admitted to the Union as the 39th state.

2

Admission Day in S.Dak. On Nov. 2, 1889, S.Dak. was admitted to the Union as the 40th state.

ANNIVERSARIES AND SPECIAL EVENTS DAYS

2

Birthday of Daniel Boone (ca. Nov. 2, 1734–ca. Sept. 26, 1820). American pioneer explorer, settler, and surveyor, subject of many books, honored particularly in Ky. Elected to the Hall of Fame for Great Americans.

2

Birthday of Warren Gamaliel Harding (Nov. 2, 1865–Aug. 2, 1923). Ohio newspaper editor and publisher; senator; 29th president of the U.S. (1921–23; died in office; Republican). His administration stressed a "return to normalcy," opposed U.S. participation in the League of Nations, and suffered the Teapot Dome scandal. Buried in Marion, Ohio.

2

Birthday of James Knox Polk (Nov. 2, 1795–June 15, 1849). Tenn. lawyer; congressman and speaker of the house; governor of Tenn.; 11th president of the U.S. (1845–49; Democrat). An expansionist president: favored annexing all of the Oregon Territory but settled for half, provoked the Mexican War, and annexed Mexico's northern third. Buried in Nashville, Tenn.

2

Balfour Declaration Day. Anniversary of the Nov. 2, 1917, Balfour Declaration, when Arthur J. Balfour, British Secretary of State for Foreign Affairs, wrote to Lord Rothschild indicating Britain's support for the eventual postwar establishment of a Jewish homeland in Palestine.

HOLY DAYS AND FEAST DAYS

3

Feast of St. Hubert (died May 30, 727). Bishop of Maastrict and Liège; patron saint of hunters, dogs, and victims of hydrophobia. Especially honored at the church and pilgrimage center of St. Hubert in Luxembourg, where on this day people of the Ardennes region bring their dogs to be blessed.

3

Feast of St. Martin de Porres (Nov. 9, 1579–Nov. 3, 1639). Peruvian Dominican lay brother beloved for his work among poor people and enslaved people, and famous for his psychic powers. A friend of St. Rose of Lima; patron saint of interracial justice.

HOLIDAYS AND CIVIC DAYS

CA. 3

Independence Day, Discovery Day, Creole Day, and Community Service Day in Dominica. On Nov. 3 is Independence Day (for independence attained from the U.K. on Nov. 3, 1978) and Discovery Day (for the arrival of Columbus on Nov. 3, 1493); official public holiday. On Nov. 4 is Community Service Day; also an official public holiday. And on the

Friday before Nov. 3 is Creole Day, when women wear the national dress to school and work, clerks and radio announcers speak only Creole to the public, and restaurants serve Creole dishes.

3

Cuenca's Independence Day in Ecuador; official public holiday. Commemorates the city's declaration of independence on Nov. 3, 1820. In Cuenca, celebrated with processions, expositions, dances, and cultural events.

3

Culture Day (*Bunka-no-Hi*) in Japan; official public holiday. Established to encourage public interest in freedom and cultural activities; before World War II, this day honored the birthday of Emperor Meiji (Nov. 3, 1852–July 30, 1912; ruled 1867–1912), who led Japan out of feudalism.

3

National Day in the Federated States of Micronesia; official public holiday. Celebrates the Nov. 3, 1980, Compact of Free Association with the U.S. Full independence was attained on Sept. 17, 1991.

3

Independence Day in Panama; official public holiday. Commemorates the declaration of independence from Colombia on Nov. 3, 1903.

ANNIVERSARIES AND SPECIAL EVENTS DAYS

3

Birthday of Stephen Fuller Austin (Nov. 3, 1793–Dec. 27, 1836), and Father of Texas Day, in Tex. American pioneer and Tex. colonizer; represents Tex. in Statuary Hall.

3

Birthday of William Cullen Bryant (Nov. 3, 1794–June 12, 1878). American poet; one of the most influential newspaper editors of the 19th century. His best-known poem is "Thanatopsis," first published in 1817. Elected to the Hall of Fame for Great Americans.

ANNIVERSARIES AND SPECIAL EVENTS DAYS

4

Anniversary of the founding, on Nov. 4, 1946, of the United Nations Educational, Scientific and Cultural Organization (UNESCO), an autonomous organization affiliated with the United Nations to enlist educational, scientific, and cultural institutions in the service of peace and the ennoblement of humanity.

4

Birthday of James Earle Fraser (Nov. 4, 1876–Oct. 11, 1953). American sculptor who designed the Indian head and buffalo on the pre-1938 U.S. five-cent coin and whose sculpture includes statues of Alexander Hamilton, General George Patton Jr., and other famous Americans.

4

Death anniversary of Yitzhak Rabin (Mar. 1, 1922–Nov. 4, 1995; ruled 1992–95; assassinated). Prime minister of Israel, assassinated in Tel Aviv by a right-wing Israeli extremist in protest against the Israeli-Palestinian peace process. Rabin Day, on the corresponding date in the Jewish calendar, is an official public holiday and day of mourning in Israel.

4

Hostage Day. Anniversary of the seizure, on Nov. 4, 1979, of the U.S. Embassy in Tehran, Iran, a crisis that lasted 444 days with 52 Americans held captive by militant Iranian students. The hostages were released on the hour of Ronald Reagan's inauguration as U.S. president.

4

Mischief Night in northern and midland England, also in Australia and New Zealand; the eve of Guy Fawkes' Day. A young people's night dedicated to merriment, pranks, and high-spirited antics.

4

Will Rogers Day in Okla. Observed by proclamation of the governor to honor William Penn Adair Rogers (Nov. 4, 1879–Aug. 15, 1935), Native American (Cherokee) humorist and actor. Represents Okla. in Statuary Hall. His birthday is celebrated with special events at the Will Rogers Memorial in Claremore, Okla.

HOLIDAYS AND CIVIC DAYS

5

Day of the First Shout for Independence (*Día del Primer Grito*) in El Salvador; official public holiday. Commemorates the first Central American battle for independence from Spain, led by Padre José Matías Delgado on Nov. 5, 1811.

5

Guy Fawkes' Day in England and elsewhere in the British Commonwealth, including Newfoundland, Canada. Anniversary of the Nov. 5, 1605, foiling of the Gunpowder Plot of Guy Fawkes and others to

blow up Parliament and the king; celebrated with bonfires, fireworks, and revelries, and at one time a day of national thanksgiving.

ANNIVERSARIES AND SPECIAL EVENTS DAYS

5

Birthday of Rui Barbosa (Nov. 5, 1849–Mar. 1, 1923). Brazilian statesman, jurist, essayist, and strong advocate of human and civil liberties whose private library has become a national shrine.

5

Birthday of Eugene Victor Debs (Nov. 5, 1855– Oct. 20, 1926). American labor leader, socialist, and politician; first president of the American Railway Union, founder of the Social Democratic Party, and 4 times Socialist candidate for president.

5

Birthday of Ida Minerva Tarbell (Nov. 5, 1857–Jan. 6, 1944). American biographer of Abraham Lincoln and author of the influential *History of the Standard Oil Company*.

5

Puno Day and Puno Week (Nov. 1–7) in Puno, on Lake Titicaca, in Peru. A festival of local folklore, with spectacular costumes, music, and dance. A pageant depicts the legend of Mama Oclio and Manco Cápac, supposed to have arisen from the waters of Lake Titicaca, and founders of the Inca Empire at Cuzco. On Nov. 4 are parades; on Nov. 5, a festival of native dances.

ANNIVERSARIES AND SPECIAL EVENTS DAYS

6

Birthday of James Naismith (Nov. 6, 1861–Nov. 28, 1939). Canadian-American educator and physical-education leader who invented the game of basketball as a class assignment in 1891.

6

Birthday of Ignacy Jan Paderewski (Nov. 6, 1860–June 29, 1941). Polish pianist, composer, and statesman.

6

Birthday of Harold Wallace Ross (Nov. 6, 1892–Dec. 6, 1951). Founder and editor of the *New Yorker* magazine, from its first issue on Feb. 21, 1925, until his death.

6

Birthday of John Philip Sousa (Nov. 6, 1854–Mar. 6, 1932). American composer and bandmaster, called the March King; composer of "The Stars and Stripes Forever" and many other marches.

6

Gustavus Adolphus Day (*Gustav Adolfsdagen*) in Sweden. Anniversary of the death of Gustav Adolph, King Gustav II of Sweden (Dec. 9, 1594–Nov. 6, 1632; ruled 1611–32). Swedish hero, the most formidable Protestant general of the Thirty Years' War. In Gothenburg, his natal city, there's a torchlight procession to lay wreaths at his statue.

6

Saxophone Day. Anniversary of the birth of Adolph (Antoine Joseph) Sax (Nov. 6, 1814–Feb. 7, 1894), Belgian-born French musician and inventor of the saxophone (patented, 1846) and other wind instruments.

HOLY DAYS AND FEAST DAYS

7

Feast of St. Willibrord (ca. 658–Nov. 7, 739). English priest; patron saint of Holland and Luxembourg.

HOLIDAYS AND CIVIC DAYS

7

Solidarity Day in Bangladesh; official public holiday. Commemorates a coup of 1975.

7

Anniversary of the October Revolution in Russia; official public holiday in Russia and Belarus. Formerly also called October Socialist Revolution Day. Was one of the Soviet Union's principal civil holidays and an occasion for huge military displays. Commemorates the Bolshevik Revolution of Nov. 7–8, 1917, when the Menshevik government in St. Petersburg was overthrown by a coup, and the Soviet regime began. Now celebrations are muted.

ANNIVERSARIES AND SPECIAL EVENTS DAYS

7

Anniversary of the abolition of the Costa Rican military on Nov. 7, 1949, following the rebel defeat of the army in the civil war of 1948–49; Costa Rica has since enjoyed peace and social harmony.

7

Birthday of Albert Camus (Nov. 7, 1913–Jan. 4, 1960). French existential novelist; best-known works include *The Stranger* and *The Plague*; awarded the 1957 Nobel Prize in literature.

7

Birthday of Marie Curie (born Maria Sklodowska; Nov. 7, 1867–July 4, 1934). Polish-born French chemist and physicist, the only person to twice receive a Nobel Prize.

7

Birthday of Andrew Dickson White (Nov. 7, 1832–Nov. 4, 1918). American educator and diplomat; first president of Cornell University; cofounder and first president of the American Historical Association.

HOLY DAYS AND FEAST DAYS

8

Feast for Anglican Saints and Martyrs in the Anglican and Episcopalian Churches. Especially honors the unnamed saints of Britain.

HOLIDAYS AND CIVIC DAYS

8

Admission Day in Mont. On Nov. 8, 1889, Mont. entered the Union as the 41st state.

ANNIVERSARIES AND SPECIAL EVENTS DAYS

8

Birthday of Edmund Halley (Nov. 8, 1656–Jan. 14, 1742). English astronomer and mathematician who won lasting fame for his studies of comets; the first predictor of the orbit of the comet named for him.

8

Birthday of Margaret Munnerlyn Mitchell (Nov. 8, 1900–Aug. 16, 1949). American novelist, famous for *Gone With the Wind* (1936), which won the 1937 Pulitzer Prize in fiction.

8

St. Demetrius Day in Bulgaria and other Orthodox countries. The close of the active agricultural year (which begins on St. George Day, May 6) and the end of farm laborers' contracts. The pre-Christian start of winter.

HOLY DAYS AND FEAST DAYS

9

Feast of the Dedication of St. John Lateran. Commemorates the first public dedication of a church, the Basilica of the Most Holy Savior in Rome, on Nov. 9, 324; since the 12th century, the basilica has also been called St. John Lateran in honor of St. John the Baptist.

HOLIDAYS AND CIVIC DAYS

9

National Independence Day in Cambodia; official public holiday. Celebrates independence attained from France on Nov. 9, 1953.

9

Birthday of Dr. Alama Mohammed Iqbal (Nov. 9, 1877–Apr. 21, 1938); official public holiday in Pakistan. Philosopher-poet; he was the first to propose a Muslim homeland (1930).

ANNIVERSARIES AND SPECIAL EVENTS DAYS

9

Anniversary of the fall of the Berlin Wall on Nov. 9, 1989. The wall was built on Aug. 13, 1961, to prevent East Germans from fleeing their then-communist country. The fall was an event of high rejoicing that invigorated both halves of the city.

9

Birthday of Elijah Parish Lovejoy (Nov. 9, 1802–Nov. 7, 1837). American newspaper publisher killed in a mob attack on his presses; known as the Martyr Abolitionist of the Civil War period.

9

Crystal Night (*Kristallnacht*). Anniversary of the street riots of Nov. 9–10, 1938, when Nazi storm troopers raided Jewish homes, businesses, and synagogues in Germany; the name came from the shattering of glass in Jewish homes and stores.

HOLY DAYS AND FEAST DAYS

10

Feast of St. Leo the Great (Pope Leo I; died Nov. 10, 461; ruled 440–61). Instrumental in dissuading Attila from sacking Rome (452). Rebuilder of Rome after its plundering by the Vandals; defender of the faith against the heresy of Pelagianism; doctor of the church. Orth.: Feb. 18 or Mar. 3.

HOLIDAYS AND CIVIC DAYS

10

First Shout of Independence (*El Primer Grito*) in Panama; official public holiday. Commemorates Panama's first battle of the revolution for independence from Spain, in Los Santos province, Nov. 10, 1821.

ANNIVERSARIES AND SPECIAL EVENTS DAYS

10

Anniversary of the sinking of the *Edmund Fitzgerald* on Nov. 10, 1975, in a severe early winter storm on Lake Superior. It disappeared from radar and sank in minutes, with no warning; a complete, mysterious, and deeply traumatic disaster. A memorial service has been held each year on this day at Mariners' Church in Detroit, Mich.

10

Birthday of Sir Jacob Epstein (Nov. 10, 1880–Aug. 21, 1959). American-born British sculptor who gained fame with his controversial bronze figures and unidealized portraits.

10

Birthday of (Nicholas) Vachel Lindsay (Nov. 10, 1879–Dec. 5, 1931). Remembered as the vagabond poet who wrote *General William Booth Enters into Heaven* and *The Congo*. He was the first American poet invited to appear at Oxford University.

10

Birthday of Martin Luther (Nov. 10, 1483–Feb. 18, 1546). German religious reformer and translator of the Bible whose stand led to the establishment of the Lutheran Church. Also famous for the writing of hymns, of which "A Mighty Fortress Is Our God" is the most familiar.

10

Birthday of Padraic Pearse (born Patrick Henry Pearse; Nov. 10, 1879–May 3, 1916, executed). Irish nationalist, poet, and educator; commander in chief of the Easter Rising that proclaimed the Irish Republic.

10

Birthday of the U.S. Marine Corps. Celebrated annually by marines to commemorate the founding of the corps on Nov. 10, 1775. It became a unit separate from the Navy on July 11, 1789.

10

Death anniversary of Kemal Atatürk (born Mustafa, later added Kemal; 1881–Nov. 10, 1938). Turkish soldier and statesman; creator of Turkey from the core of the Ottoman Empire and Turkey's leader until his death.

HOLY DAYS AND FEAST DAYS

11

Martinmas, the feast of St. Martin of Tours (ca. 316–Nov. 8, 397). Legionary soldier in France, turned conscientious objector and Christian; formed the first monastic community in Gaul; later was bishop of Tours. One of Gaul's great saints and a pioneer of monasticism in the West. His shrine became a major pilgrimage center. A patron saint of France and of beggars, vine growers, tavern keepers, and drunkards. Orth.: Nov. 11 or 24.

HOLIDAYS AND CIVIC DAYS

11

Independence Day in Angola; official public holiday. Commemorates independence attained from Portugal on Nov. 11, 1985.

CA. 11

Birthday of the 4th king of Bhutan; official public holiday on Nov. 11–13. A 3-day celebration of the birthday of the present king, Druk Gyalpo Jigme Singye Wangchuck (Nov. 11, 1955– ; rule 1972–).

11

Cartagena Independence Day in Colombia; official public holiday. Commemorates the declaration of independence from Spain by the port city of Cartagena on Nov. 11, 1811.

11

Memorial Day in Latvia. Commemorates a 1919 battle in the war of independence, during which invading German forces were repulsed from Riga.

11

Republic Day in Maldives; official public holiday on Nov. 11–12. Commemorates the anniversary of the abolition of the sultanate and the assumption of the name Republic of the Maldives on Nov. 11, 1968.

11

Independence Day in Poland; official public holiday. Celebrates independence declared from Germany, Russia, and Austria on Nov. 11, 1918, following 125 years of partition. Independence was internationally recognized with the Treaty of Versailles on June 28, 1919.

11

Concordia Day in St. Martin; official public holiday on both the French and the Dutch sides. The island's long-standing amity (dating from Nov. 11, 1648, and reaffirmed in 1816) is commemorated with joint ceremonies at the Border Monument obelisk. Also today the Season of Christmastide begins.

11

Veterans' Day in the U.S.; official public holiday. Honors the members of the armed forces who served in World Wars I and II, Korea, Vietnam, and in other wars.

11

Admission Day in Wash. State; official public holiday. On Nov. 11, 1889, Wash. was admitted to the Union as the 42nd state.

ANNIVERSARIES AND SPECIAL EVENTS DAYS

11

Anniversary of the first public performance of "God Bless America," sung by Kate Smith on Nov. 11, 1938, over the radio. Irving Berlin wrote the song specifically for her.

11

Anniversary of the entombment of the Unknown Soldier of World War I in the Tomb of the Unknowns at Arlington, Va., on Nov. 11, 1921. An Unknown Soldier of World War II and one from the Korean conflict were interred in crypts on either side of the Tomb of the Unknown Soldier on Memorial Day, 1958.

11

Birthday of Fyodor Dostoyevsky (Nov. 11, 1821–Feb. 9, 1881). Russian novelist famed for such books as *The Brothers Karamazov* and *Crime and Punishment*.

11

Birthday of Ephraim McDowell (Nov. 11, 1771–June 25, 1830). American surgeon; pioneer in abdominal surgery who performed the first recorded ovariotomy in the U.S. Represents Ky. in Statuary Hall.

11

Armistice Day. Anniversary of the Nov. 11, 1918, signing at 11:00 A.M. of the armistice between the Allied and the Central powers that ended World War I. Observed as Armistice Day, Remembrance Day, or Veterans' Day in many countries. Honors each country's war dead, especially in 20th-century wars.

HOLY DAYS AND FEAST DAYS

12

Anniversary of the Birth of Baha'u'llah (born Mirza Husayn-Ali; Nov. 12, 1817–May 29, 1892). A holy day in the Baha'i faith, and Baha'is abstain from work. Commemorates the birth of the divine messenger Baha'u'llah ("Glory of God"), Persian spiritual leader and founder of the Baha'i faith. His teachings are directed to the unity of mankind and the creation of harmony throughout the universe.

HOLIDAYS AND CIVIC DAYS

12

Republic Day in Austria. On Nov. 12, 1918, Austria declared itself a republic.

12

Birthday of Sun Yat-sen (Nov. 12, 1866–Mar. 12, 1925); official public holiday in Taiwan. Leader of the Chinese Nationalist Party and founder of Asia's first republic, the Republic of China.

ANNIVERSARIES AND SPECIAL EVENTS DAYS

12

Birthday of Elizabeth Cady Stanton (Nov. 12, 1815–Oct. 26, 1902). American reformer and champion of women's suffrage. Her birthday is observed by women's organizations as Elizabeth Cady Stanton Day.

HOLY DAYS AND FEAST DAYS

13

Feast of St. Frances Xavier Cabrini (July 15, 1850–Dec. 22, 1917). Italian-born American nun; founder of the Missionary Sisters of the Sacred Heart, devoted to the education of girls. The first U.S. citizen to become a saint. Patron saint of immigrants and hospital administrators.

13

Orthodox feast of St. John Chrysostom (ca. 347–Sept. 14, 407). Syrian scholar, hermit, and patriarch of Constantinople; brilliant preacher; doctor of the church. Patron saint of preachers. Orth.: Nov. 13 or 26, and Jan. 27 for translation of relics.

ANNIVERSARIES AND SPECIAL EVENTS DAYS

13

Anniversary of the publication on Nov. 13, 1830, of "Old Ironsides" by Oliver Wendell Holmes Sr., which prevented the scrapping of the frigate USS *Constitution,* now a national memorial in Boston. The *Constitution* was launched on Sept. 20, 1797, and served in the war with Tripoli and the War of 1812.

13

Anniversary of the Nov. 13, 1982, dedication of the Vietnam Veterans Memorial in Washington, D.C. On the walls of the memorial are inscribed the names of over 58,000 American military personnel killed or missing in the Vietnam conflict. Maya Ying Lin was the sculptor. The memorial was later supplemented by the statue "Three Servicemen," unveiled on Nov. 9, 1984, and by the Vietnam Women's Memorial, honoring American women who served in Vietnam, dedicated on Nov. 11, 1993.

13

Birthday of Edwin Thomas Booth (Nov. 13, 1833–June 7, 1893). American tragedian famous for his interpretation of *Hamlet.* Founded the Players Club, a famous club for actors, in 1888. Elected to the Hall of Fame for Great Americans.

13

Birthday of Louis Dembitz Brandeis (Nov. 13, 1856–Oct. 5, 1941). American associate justice of the Supreme Court, for whom Brandeis University, inaugurated in 1948, was named.

13

Birthday of James Clerk Maxwell (Nov. 13, 1831–Nov. 5, 1879). Scottish physicist who discovered the laws of electrodynamics. Einstein called his work "the most fruitful that physics has experienced since the time of Newton."

13

Birthday of Robert Louis Stevenson (Nov. 13, 1850–Dec. 3, 1894). Scottish novelist, poet, and essayist famous for *Treasure Island, A Child's Garden of Verses,* and many other books. Known as *Tusitala,* ("Teller of Tales") in Samoa, where he died at Vailema, the destination of a literary pilgrimage for travelers in the area.

13

Pacific Balloon Day. Anniversary of the first crossing of the Pacific Ocean by balloon, completed on Nov. 13, 1981.

HOLIDAYS AND CIVIC DAYS

14

Children's Day in India. Celebrated on the anniversary of the birth of Jawaharlal Nehru (Nov.

14, 1889–May 27, 1964), the first prime minister of independent India (1947–64).

14

Birthday of the Late King Hussein in Jordan; official public holiday. Honors the beloved and long-ruling King Hussein I (Hussein ibn Talul; Nov. 14, 1935–Feb. 7, 1999; ruled Aug. 11, 1952–Feb. 7, 1999).

14

Discovery Day in the U.S. Virgin Islands. Commemorates the arrival of Christopher Columbus on Nov. 14, 1493.

ANNIVERSARIES AND SPECIAL EVENTS DAYS

14

Birthday of Charles, Prince of Wales (Nov. 14, 1948–), son of Elizabeth II and heir apparent to the British throne. Formerly, an official public holiday in many British territories and British Commonwealth countries, but no longer so.

14

Birthday of Robert Fulton (Nov. 14, 1765–Feb. 24, 1815). American artist, civil engineer, and inventor famous for the development of the steamboat. Elected to the Hall of Fame for Great Americans. Represents Pa. in Statuary Hall.

14

Birthday of Claude Monet (Nov. 14, 1840–Dec. 5, 1926). French landscape and still-life painter who applied scientific principles of light to the art of painting; considered one of the greatest of landscape painters.

14

Birthday of Frederick Jackson Turner (Nov. 14, 1861–Mar. 14, 1932). American historian best known for *The Frontier in American History.* His work *The Significance of Sections in American History* received the Pulitzer Prize in 1933.

HOLY DAYS AND FEAST DAYS

15

Feast of St. Albert the Great (or Albertus Magnus; 1260–Nov. 15, 1280). German Dominican priest, scholastic professor at the University of Paris, teacher of St. Thomas Aquinas, and scholar of Aristotle and of Arabic learning. One of the great medieval intellects; doctor of the church, called the Universal Doctor. Patron saint of scholars, students, medical technicians, and scientists.

15

Feast of St. Leopold (1073–1136). Austrian margrave of Klosterneuburg, fondly remembered as the Good. Patron saint of Austria. His feast day, called *Fasslrutschen,* is particularly observed in Vienna and at Klosterneuberg with a wine festival and a pilgrimage to his shrine. Today marks the start of the new wine season throughout Austria. Also called *Gaense Tag* ("Goose Day"), after the day's traditional meal.

15

Nativity Fast begins among Orthodox Christians. A 40-day fast observed in preparation for Christmas.

HOLIDAYS AND CIVIC DAYS

15

Dynasty Day (*Fête de la Dynastie*) in Belgium; official public holiday. Also called Royal Family Day. Held on the feast of St. Albert the Great, the patron saint of the royal family.

CA. 15

Proclamation of the Republic Day and Election Day in Brazil; official public holiday on the Monday nearest Nov. 15. Also called Republic Day. Anniversary of the proclamation of Nov. 15, 1889, which deposed Emperor Dom Pedro II and instituted a republic.

ANNIVERSARIES AND SPECIAL EVENTS DAYS

15

Anniversary of the adoption of the Articles of Confederation and Perpetual Union by the Continental Congress on Nov. 15, 1777, during the American Revolutionary War.

15

Anniversary of the founding on Nov. 15, 1881, of the Federation of Organized Trades and Labor Unions of the U.S. and Canada. It was reorganized on Dec. 8, 1886, as the American Federation of Labor. The AFL and the Congress of Industrial Organizations merged on Dec. 5, 1955, to form the AFL-CIO.

15

Birthday of Sir William Herschel (born Friedrich Wilhelm Herschel; Nov. 15, 1738–Aug. 25, 1822). German-born English astronomer who built his own telescope and discovered the planet Uranus (Mar. 13, 1781); the founder of sidereal astronomy. His work was carried on with distinction by his son, Sir John Frederick William Herschel, and his sister, Caroline Herschel.

15

Birthday of Marianne Craig Moore (Nov. 15, 1887–Feb. 5, 1972). American poet; winner of the Pulitzer Prize in poetry in 1951, the 1952 National Book Award, and the 1953 gold medal of the National Institute of Arts and Letters; decorated by France for her translation of *The Fables of La Fontaine*.

15

Birthday of Georgia O'Keeffe (Nov. 15, 1887–Mar. 6, 1986). American artist best known for her semi-abstract renderings of common objects, such as *Black Iris* and *Cow's Skull: Red, White, and Blue*.

15

Birthday of William Pitt (Nov. 15, 1708–May 11, 1778). British statesman, called the Elder Pitt and, later, the Great Commoner; advocate of a conciliatory policy toward the American colonies; Pittsburg, Pa., is named for him.

15

George Spelvin Day. Anniversary of the first appearance of the fictitious theatrical character George Spelvin, on Nov. 15, 1886. George (or Georgina, etc.) Spelvin is used on American playbills to conceal the appearance by a single actor in multiple roles. Walter Plinge is the counterpart in England.

15

Seven-Five-Three (*Shichi-Go-San*) Festival in Japan; often observed on the nearest Sunday. Parents take all children aged 3, boys aged 5, and girls aged 7 to temples in thanksgiving for their safety.

HOLY DAYS AND FEAST DAYS

16

Feast of St. Margaret, Queen of Scotland (1045–Nov. 16, 1093). Hungarian-born noblewoman, wife of Malcolm III of Scotland; known for her personal piety, work with poor people, and support of the clergy. A patron saint of Scotland.

HOLIDAYS AND CIVIC DAYS

16

Day of National Rebirth in Estonia; official public holiday. Commemorates the 1988 Declaration of Sovereignty. The USSR recognized the independence of all 3 Baltic nations on Sept. 6, 1991.

16

Oklahoma Statehood Day in Okla. On Nov. 16, 1907, Okla. was admitted to the Union as the 46th state.

ANNIVERSARIES AND SPECIAL EVENTS DAYS

16

Birthday of William Christopher Handy (Nov. 16, 1873–Mar. 28, 1958). American composer best known for his *St. Louis Blues* and called the Father of the Blues.

16

Death anniversary of Louis Riel (Oct. 23, 1844–Nov. 16, 1885). French-Canadian and Métis patriot of western Canada and leader of the Northwest Rebellion of 1885 against English-Canadian domination; hanged for treason. An enduring rallying symbol. His trial is reenacted each Wednesday–Friday during Aug. in Regina, Saskatchewan, Canada.

HOLY DAYS AND FEAST DAYS

17

Feast of St. Elizabeth of Hungary (1207–Nov. 17, 1231). Of Hungarian royalty and a well-loved ruler; later a Franciscan tertiary, caring for the sick. Patron saint of nurses.

17

Feast of St. Hilda of Whitby (614–Nov. 17, 680). Saxon abbess of the double monastery of Whitby; renowned for spiritual wisdom and her nunnery's culture. A major light of Celtic Christianity. Convened the Council of Whitby (664) to reconcile Celtic and Roman differences. Patron saint of business and professional women.

ANNIVERSARIES AND SPECIAL EVENTS DAYS

17

Anniversary of the official opening of the Suez Canal for navigation on Nov. 17, 1869.

17

Queen's Day in England. Anniversary of the coronation on Nov. 17, 1558, of Queen Elizabeth I (Sept. 7, 1533–Mar. 24, 1603; ruled 1558–1603). This day was celebrated as an official public holiday in England for over 3 centuries after Elizabeth I's death in 1603.

HOLIDAYS AND CIVIC DAYS

18

Armed Forces Day in Haiti; official public holiday. Also called Vertières Day. Commemorates the Nov. 18, 1803, Haitian victory over the French in the Battle of Vertières during the wars of independence.

18

Independence Day in Latvia; official public holiday. Commemorates the declaration of independence from Russia in 1918. (Latvia again declared its independence from the USSR on Aug. 21, 1991. The USSR recognized the independence of all 3 Baltic nations on Sept. 6, 1991.)

18

Independence Day in Morocco; official public holiday. Commemorates independence attained from France on Nov. 18, 1956.

18

National Days in Oman; official public holiday on Nov. 18–19. Celebrates the birthday of Sultan Qaboos bin Said (Nov. 18, 1942–), who deposed his father on July 23, 1970.

ANNIVERSARIES AND SPECIAL EVENTS DAYS

18

Anniversary of the signing of the Panama Canal Treaty between the U.S. and Panama on Nov. 18, 1903, providing for the construction by the U.S. of the Panama Canal. This followed Colombia's rejection of the treaty on Jan. 22 and Panama's declaration of independence from Colombia on Nov. 3, 1903. The canal officially opened on Aug. 15, 1914.

18

Birthday of Louis-Jacques-Mandé Daguerre (Nov. 18, 1789–July 10, 1851). French inventor famous for the development of a method of producing permanent pictures called the daguerreotype process.

18

Birthday of Clarence Shepard Day (Nov. 18, 1874–Dec. 28, 1935). American author of *Life with Father*. A Clarence Day Award for "outstanding work in encouraging the love of books and reading" was established in 1960 by the American Textbook Publishers Institute and is administered by the American Library Association; the first recipient was Lawrence Powell, librarian, bibliophile, and author.

18

Birthday of Sir William Schwenck Gilbert (Nov. 18, 1836–May 29, 1911; died saving a woman from drowning). English author of librettos for the unique Gilbert and Sullivan operettas.

18

Birthday of Asa Gray (Nov. 18, 1810–Jan. 30, 1888). American botanist, one of the creators of a systematic classification of American flora. Elected to the Hall of Fame for Great Americans.

18

Birthday of the cartoon character Mickey Mouse. Mickey Mouse appeared in *Steamboat Willie*, the first animated talking picture, on Nov. 18, 1928. Cartoon companion Donald Duck was born on June 9, 1934.

HOLIDAYS AND CIVIC DAYS

CA. 19

Garifuna Settlement Day in Belize; official public holiday. Also called Carib Settlement Day. Commemorates the first arrival in 1823 of Black Caribs fleeing slavery in St. Vincent and Rotan.

19

Fête Nationale in Monaco; official public holiday. The prince attends Mass in the cathedral and gives prizes to police and firefighters. All display Monaco's white and red colors. That night, a fireworks display is offered by the winner of a previously held fireworks competition.

19

Discovery of Puerto Rico Day; official public holiday. Commemorates the landing of Columbus on Nov. 19, 1493.

ANNIVERSARIES AND SPECIAL EVENTS DAYS

19

Anniversary of the founding of the Women's Christian Temperance Union on Nov. 19, 1874, in Cleveland, Ohio.

19

Birthday of George Rogers Clark (Nov. 19, 1752–Feb. 13, 1818). American soldier and surveyor; conqueror of the Old Northwest during the Revolutionary War; older brother of William Clark.

19

Birthday of James Abram Garfield (Nov. 19, 1831–Sept. 19, 1881). Ohio educator and congressman;

Civil War general; 20th president of the U.S. (Nov. 1880–Sept. 1881; Republican). Shot on July 2, died lingeringly. Buried in Lake View Cemetery, Cleveland, Ohio. Represents Ohio in Statuary Hall.

19
Birthday of Ferdinand de Lesseps (Nov. 19, 1805–Dec. 7, 1894). French engineer and diplomat remembered as the planner and engineer of the Suez Canal.

19
Death anniversary of Nicolas Poussin (1594–Nov. 19, 1665). Influential French painter of the Baroque period; painted *The Arcadian Shepherds, The Rape of the Sabine Women,* and other works inspired by myths and Scripture.

19
Gettysburg Address Day. Also called Equal Opportunity Day. Anniversary of the Nov. 19, 1863, consecration of the Gettysburg National Cemetery, when President Abraham Lincoln delivered a 270-word message that lives in history as the Gettysburg Address, one of the greatest speeches of all time. Gettysburg Address Day is commemorated at the National Cemetery with ceremonies sponsored by the Sons of Union Veterans and the Lincoln Fellowship of Pennsylvania.

HOLIDAYS AND CIVIC DAYS

20
Anniversary of the Revolution in Mexico; official public holiday. Commemorates the Mexican Revolution of Nov. 20, 1910, when the common people revolted against poverty and the dictatorship of Porfirio Díaz (José de la Cruz Porfirio Díaz; 1830–1915; president 1877–80, 1884–1911). The principal leader was Francisco Indalécio Madero (1873–1913; president 1911–13). The revolution culminated in the Constitution of 1917.

ANNIVERSARIES AND SPECIAL EVENTS DAYS

20
Anniversary of the beginning of the Nuremberg Trials. Starting on Nov. 20, 1945, high-ranking Nazi German government and military officials were tried for crimes against humanity. The trials lasted about 11 months.

20
Birthday of Edwin Powell Hubble (Nov. 20, 1889–Sept. 28, 1953). American astronomer; formulated the concept of the expanding universe, "the

most spectacular astronomical discovery of the 20th century." The Hubble Space Telescope, deployed Apr. 25, 1990, is named in his honor.

20
Birthday of Robert Francis Kennedy (Nov. 20, 1925–June 5, 1968). U.S. attorney general, senator, and politician; aggressive fighter for civil rights and a leading adviser of his brother, President John F. Kennedy. Assassinated while campaigning for the 1968 Democratic presidential nomination.

20
Birthday of Selma Lagerlöf (Nov. 20, 1858–Mar. 16, 1940). Swedish novelist; first woman to receive the Nobel Prize in literature (1909); first woman elected to the Swedish Academy (1914).

20
Birthday of Peregrine White (Nov. 20, 1620–July 22, 1704). First child born in New England of English parents.

20
Rights of the Child Day. Anniversary of the adoption by the United Nations General Assembly of the Declaration of the Rights of the Child on Nov. 20, 1959, and of the Convention on the Rights of the Child on Nov. 20, 1989.

20
Universal Children's Day. Sponsored by the United Nations General Assembly. A day to honor children with special programs to call governments' attention to the needs of children.

HOLY DAYS AND FEAST DAYS

21
Feast of the Presentation. In Eastern Churches, called the Entry of the Theotokos into the Temple. Commemorates the presentation of the young Virgin Mary in the temple to consecrate her to the service of God. Orth.: Nov. 21 or Dec. 4.

HOLIDAYS AND CIVIC DAYS

21
Admission Day in N.C. On Nov. 21, 1789, N.C. ratified the Constitution and entered the Union as the 12th state.

ANNIVERSARIES AND SPECIAL EVENTS DAYS

21
Birthday of Voltaire (born François-Marie Arouet; Nov. 21, 1694–May 30, 1778). French philoso-

pher and author of poetry, plays, essays, novels, and letters. Attacked bigotry, cruelty, and tyranny, and crusaded for political reform. A lightning rod for controversy, he was imprisoned twice and spent much of this life in exile. Best known for the philosophical tale *Candide* and his social-philosophical articles.

21

Death anniversary of Jakob Böhme (1575–Nov. 21, 1624). German philosopher and mystic, of profound influence on later intellectual movements such as idealism and romanticism. Wrote *The Great Mystery* and *On the Election of Grace* (both, 1623).

21

Death anniversary of Henry Purcell (ca. 1659–Nov. 21, 1695). English composer.

HOLY DAYS AND FEAST DAYS

22

Feast of St. Cecilia (died Sept. 16, between 177 and 235). Martyr; patron saint of music, musicians, and organ builders; many musical societies are named for her. Special concerts are presented in Rome on this day.

HOLIDAYS AND CIVIC DAYS

22

Independence Day in Lebanon; official public holiday. Commemorates the declaration of independence from France on Nov. 22, 1943. Lebanon had become independent from the Ottoman Empire on Sept. 1, 1920, and was controlled by France, 1920–41; the last French troops withdrew in 1946.

ANNIVERSARIES AND SPECIAL EVENTS DAYS

22

Birthday of Abigail Adams (born Abigail Smith; Nov. 22, 1744–Oct. 28, 1818). American; wife of President John Adams, and his feminist conscience; prolific letter writer.

22

Birthday of George Eliot (Mary Ann Evans; Nov. 22, 1819–Dec. 22, 1880). Distinguished English novelist, famous for *Silas Marner, The Mill on the Floss,* and *Middlemarch.*

22

Birthday of Charles de Gaulle (Nov. 22, 1890–Nov. 9, 1970). French general, statesman, president, and leader of the Fifth Republic.

22

Death anniversary of John F. Kennedy, president of the U.S. Assassinated in Dallas, Tex., on Nov. 22, 1963. Lee Harvey Oswald is officially regarded as the sole assassin. John F. Kennedy Day is observed in Mass., his home state, on the last Sunday in Nov.; John F. Kennedy Day is observed in Maine schools on Nov. 22.

HOLIDAYS AND CIVIC DAYS

23

Labor Thanksgiving Day (*Kinro Kansha-no-Hi*) in Japan; official public holiday. A young holiday, combining Labor and Thanksgiving Days.

23

Repudiation Day in Frederick County, Md.; local official public holiday. Commemorates the county's Nov. 23, 1765, refusal to observe the Stamp Act of 1765; observed at the courthouse by the Daughters of the American Revolution.

ANNIVERSARIES AND SPECIAL EVENTS DAYS

23

Anniversary of the founding of the Horatio Alger Society on Nov. 23, 1961, to further the Algerian philosophy "strive and succeed."

23

Birthday of José Clemente Orozco (Nov. 23, 1883–Sept. 7, 1949). Mexican painter, a modern master of fresco painting.

23

Birthday of Franklin Pierce (Nov. 23, 1804–Oct. 8, 1869). N.H. lawyer; Jacksonian congressman; general in the Mexican War; 14th president of the U.S. (1853–57; Democrat). As president, left slavery to popular vote in Kans. and Nebr. (called *squatter sovereignty*), signed a reciprocity treaty with Canada, and approved the Gadsden Purchase from Mexico. Buried in Minot Cemetery, Concord, N.H.

ANNIVERSARIES AND SPECIAL EVENTS DAYS

24

Anniversary of the departure of the last U.S. military contingent from extensive U.S. bases in the Philippines on Nov. 24, 1992.

24

Birthday of Friar Junípero Serra (Nov. 24, 1713–Aug. 28, 1784). Spanish missionary priest, founder of the Calif. missions. Represents Calif. in Statuary Hall. Since 1948, a Serra pageant reenacting his arrival at San Diego has been presented annually at the old mission near Carmel, Calif. His feast day is July 1 in the U.S.

24

Birthday of Benedict (Baruch) de Spinoza (Nov. 24, 1632–Feb. 21, 1677). Dutch philosopher, a foremost exponent of 17th-century rationalism.

24

Birthday of Zachary Taylor (Nov. 24, 1784–July 9, 1850). La.-born soldier, fought in the War of 1812 and various Indian wars, known as Old Rough and Ready; 12th president of the U.S. (1849–50; Whig). Died after 16 months in office. As president, resumed the spoils system; though a former slaveholder, worked to have Calif. admitted as a free state. Buried near Louisville, Ky.

24

Death anniversary of John Knox (ca. 1514–Nov. 24, 1572). Scottish preacher and leader in the Protestant Reformation in Scotland.

HOLY DAYS AND FEAST DAYS

25

Feast of St. Catherine of Alexandria (died ca. 310). By legend, martyred on a spiked wheel. Venerated in the East since the 10th century; her body is reputedly at the monastery on Mt. Sinai. One of the 14 Holy Helpers; patron saint of philosophers, maidens, preachers. Orth.: Nov. 24 or Dec. 7.

HOLIDAYS AND CIVIC DAYS

25

National Day in Bosnia and Herzegovina; official public holiday. Commemorates the Nov. 25, 1943, establishment of the Anti-Fascist Council and the declaration of the country's statehood, within the federation of Yugoslavia.

25

Independence Day in Suriname; official public holiday. Celebrates independence attained from the Netherlands on Nov. 25, 1975.

ANNIVERSARIES AND SPECIAL EVENTS DAYS

25

Birthday of Andrew Carnegie (Nov. 11, 1835–Aug. 11, 1919). Scottish-born American industrialist, philanthropist, and notable benefactor of libraries.

25

Birthday of Carry Amelia Nation (Nov. 25, 1846–June 9, 1911). American temperance leader who used a hatchet in her campaign against saloons.

25

Evacuation Day in New York City. Anniversary of the Nov. 25, 1783, withdrawal of British troops from the city and its official occupation by General Washington and officials of the state.

25

International Day against Violence against Women. Observed, especially by Latin American women's groups, on the anniversary of the death of the Mirabal sisters (Patria Mercedes, María Argentina Minerva, and Antonia María Teresa), assassinated on Nov. 25, 1960, in the Dominican Republic under Trujillo, for their grassroots political work.

HOLY DAYS AND FEAST DAYS

26

Day of the Covenant in the Baha'i faith. Holy day commemorating the covenant in Baha'u'llah's last will and testament, which made clear that the establishment of the kingdom of God on earth depends upon the pure and selfless dedication and obedience of the believers.

HOLIDAYS AND CIVIC DAYS

26

Republic Day in Mongolia; official public holiday. Anniversary of the declaration of the Mongolian People's Republic on Nov. 26, 1924; the world's second communist country.

ANNIVERSARIES AND SPECIAL EVENTS DAYS

26

Anniversary of the third coronation in 1477 of the Romanian ruler Vlad Tepes, Vlad III (ca. 1431–ca. Nov. 26, 1477; ruled 1448, 1456–62, 1477). Commonly called Vlad the Impaler or Dracula. Monarch infamous for his sadistic cruelty and the enormous numbers of persons he painfully executed, whose name was appropriated for the main character of Bram Stoker's novel *Dracula*.

26

Constitution Thanksgiving Day in the U.S. Nov. 26, 1789, was proclaimed by George Washington as a day of thanksgiving following the adoption of the Constitution. The first official holiday in the U.S.

26

John Harvard Day. Commemorates the birthday of John Harvard (ca. Nov. 26, 1607–Sept. 24, 1638), English clergyman and scholar; New England colonist; and chief founder of Harvard College, with his posthumous bequest of a library and funds.

26

Sojourner Truth Day. Honors Sojourner Truth (ca. 1790–Nov. 26, 1883), onetime slave and leading African American abolitionist of the 19th century, who adopted the name Sojourner as a symbol of her lecture tours, which espoused abolition and women's rights.

Anniversaries and Special Events Days

27

Birthday of Robert R. Livingstone (Nov. 27, 1746–Feb. 26, 1813). American statesman and jurist; member of the Continental Congress and chancellor of N.Y. State, who administered Washington's first oath of office as president (1789). Represents N.Y. in Statuary Hall.

27

Death anniversary of Horace (Quintus Horatius Flaccus; Dec. 65 B.C.–Nov. 27, 8 B.C.). Roman poet, famous for his *Odes* and other works.

Holy Days and Feast Days

28

Anniversary of the Ascension of 'Abdu'l-Baha in the Baha'i faith. A holy day that commemorates the death on Nov. 28, 1921, of 'Abdu'l-Baha, Baha'u'llah's grandson and successor, the early-20th-century guardian of the faith and a friend of all humanity.

Holidays and Civic Days

28

Independence Day in Albania; official public holiday. The country's national day, celebrating both the Nov. 28, 1912, declaration of independence from the Ottoman Empire and Albania's liberation from the Nazis on Nov. 28, 1945.

28

Republic Day in Chad; official public holiday. Commemorates the proclamation of the republic on Nov. 28, 1958, which made Chad a member state in the French community.

28

Independence Day in East Timor. The Revolutionary Front for Independence of East Timor (FRETILIN) declared the independence of the Democratic Republic of East Timor on Nov. 28, 1975, in the East Timor capital of Dili; Indonesia invaded and occupied the country on July 16, 1976.

28

National Day in Mauritania; official public holiday. Celebrates independence attained from France on Nov. 28, 1960.

28

Independence Day in Panama; official public holiday. Also called Emancipation Day. Commemorates the attainment of independence from Spain on Nov. 28, 1821.

Anniversaries and Special Events Days

28

Anniversary of the formal incorporation of the Royal Society on Nov. 28, 1660. Granted a Royal Charter by Charles II in 1662 as the Royal Society of London for Promoting Natural Knowledge, its purpose was to reform science on the lines laid down by Francis Bacon.

28

Birthday of Henry Bacon (Nov. 28, 1866–Feb. 16, 1924). American architect who specialized in the classic Greek style. One of his most important works is the Lincoln Memorial in Washington, D.C., completed in 1920.

28

Birthday of William Blake (Nov. 28, 1757–Aug. 12, 1827). English poet, artist, and mystic; his *Songs of Innocence* and *Songs of Experience* are original and profound.

28

Birthday of Friedrich Engels (Nov. 28, 1820–Aug. 5, 1895). German socialist philosopher; collaborator with Karl Marx.

28

Birthday of Frances Amelia Yates (Nov. 28, 1899–Sept. 19, 1981). Revered English historian of Renaissance thought in England and Europe, whose adventurous and scrupulous scholarship made the history of European hermetic philosophy a respectable subject. Wrote *The Rosicrucian Enlightenment* and much else.

28

Death anniversary of Matsuo Bashō (born Matsuo Munefusa; 1644–Nov. 28, 1694). Renowned Japanese haiku poet.

ANNIVERSARIES AND SPECIAL EVENTS DAYS

29

Birthday of Louisa May Alcott (Nov. 29, 1832–Mar. 6, 1888). American author of *Little Women* and other books that appeal to many generations of readers.

29

Birthday of Andrés Bello (Nov. 29, 1781–Oct. 15, 1865). Chilean journalist, statesman, and noted poet; a teacher of Simón Bolívar; developed Bello's Code, which ended juridical anarchy in Chile.

29

Nellie Taylor Ross Day in Wyo.; official public holiday. Honors Nellie Taylor Ross (Nov. 29, 1876–Dec. 20, 1977), inaugurated in Wyo. on Jan. 5, 1925, as the first woman governor in the U.S. Ross later served under President Franklin D. Roosevelt as director of the U.S. Mint for 20 years.

HOLY DAYS AND FEAST DAYS

30

Feast of St. Andrew (1st century). The first Apostle and the brother of Simon Peter. Patron saint of Greece, Russia, and Scotland; revered in Lapland, Peru, Poland, Russia, and Ukraine. Orth.: Nov. 30 or Dec. 13.

HOLIDAYS AND CIVIC DAYS

30

Independence Day in Barbados; official public holiday. Commemorates independence attained from the U.K. on Nov. 30, 1966.

30

Bonifacio Day in the Philippines; official public holiday. Also called National Heroes' Day. Honors the hero Andres Bonifacio (Nov. 30, 1863–May 10, 1897; executed), who led the 1896 independence struggle against Spain.

30

Evacuation Day in Yemen; official public holiday. Commemorates (south) Yemen's attainment of full independence from the U.K. on Nov. 30, 1967.

ANNIVERSARIES AND SPECIAL EVENTS DAYS

30

Birthday of Sir Winston Leonard Spencer Churchill (Nov. 30, 1874–Jan. 24, 1965). British statesman; prime minister 1940–45, 1951–55; symbol of the British spirit during World War II; author of *The Second World War.* In the U.S., Churchill Day is on Apr. 9, the date in 1963 that he was made an honorary citizen.

30

Birthday of Andrea Palladio (born Andrea di Pietro della Gondola; Nov. 30, 1508–Aug. 19, 1580). The greatest architect of 16th-century northern Italy. His work and writings made him one of the most influential figures in Western architecture.

30

Birthday of Jonathan Swift (Nov. 30, 1667–Oct. 17, 1745). Irish clergyman, political writer, and satirist remembered particularly for *Gulliver's Travels.*

30

Birthday of Mark Twain (Samuel Langhorne Clemens; Nov. 30, 1835–Apr. 21, 1910). American author, humorist, and lecturer whose most famous books are *Tom Sawyer* and *Huckleberry Finn.* Elected to the Hall of Fame for Great Americans. An annual Nov. 30 birthday party honoring Samuel Clemons is held in the Mark Twain Memorial House in Hartford, Conn., sometimes called the Birthplace of Tom Sawyer.

30

Death anniversary of Patrick Kavanagh (1905–Nov. 30, 1967). Irish poet; wrote *The Great Hunger* (1942).

MOVABLE DAYS IN NOVEMBER
HOLIDAYS AND CIVIC DAYS

RECREATION DAY IN NORTHERN TASMANIA, AUSTRALIA; 1st Monday in Nov.; local official public holiday.

MELBOURNE CUP DAY IN VICTORIA, AUSTRALIA; 1st Tuesday in Nov.; local official public holiday. The only official public holiday in the world dedicated to a horse race. Australia's premier race meeting; 7 races; held since 1867.

THANKSGIVING DAY IN LIBERIA; 1st Thursday in Nov.; official public holiday.

LORD MAYOR'S DAY IN LONDON, ENGLAND; 2nd Saturday in Nov. Dates from 1215; a day of civic pageantry in which the lord mayor of London drives in state to the Guildhall for ceremonies and on to the law courts to take the oath of office.

STATE OPENING OF PARLIAMENT IN LONDON, ENGLAND; early November. A colorful British ritual dating back to Plantagenet times; observed in London after a general election and preceding the beginning of each parliamentary session; involves the queen in traditional royal ceremonies.

ELECTION DAY IN THE U.S.; Tuesday after the 1st Monday in Nov.; official public holiday in many states and localities to encourage voting. In even-numbered years for general elections; in years divisible by 4 for presidential elections. Date was set by Congress in 1845.

THANKSGIVING DAY IN THE U.S.; 4th Thursday in Nov.; official public holiday. The Friday following is also an official public holiday in many states, sometimes as Family Day. Annually proclaimed by the president. A day of thanksgiving and praise; a major holiday for family reunions, with turkey as the traditional dish. The first Thanksgiving Days in the English colonies were in the Berkeley Plantation on the James River, Va., on Dec. 4, 1619, and in the Plymouth Colony in Oct. 1621. The present Thanksgiving was proclaimed by President Lincoln in 1863 for the last Thursday in Nov.; transferred to 4th Thursday in Nov. in 1942.

ANNIVERSARIES AND SPECIAL EVENTS DAYS

FATHER'S DAY IN SWEDEN; 2nd Sunday in Nov. Festivities resemble a birthday celebration.

ONION MARKET DAY (ZIBELEMARIT) IN BERN, SWITZERLAND; 4th Monday in Nov. Bern's major festival, celebrating onions, which are sold in great variety. Commemorates the granting of market privileges to the men of Fribourg for their assistance in rebuilding Bern after the great fire of 1405. A lighthearted time, with disguises and satiric jesters.

NATIONAL CHILDREN'S BOOK WEEK IN THE U.S.; in the week including Thanksgiving, Monday–Sunday. Intended to encourage the enjoyment of reading for children and to call attention to good children's books. Began in 1919.

SADIE HAWKINS DAY IN THE U.S.; usually the 1st Saturday in Nov. A day created by the cartoonist Al Capp (Alfred Gerald Caplin) in his comic strip *Li'l Abner*; introduced on Nov. 9, 1928, as a day when the unmarried women of Dogpatch might rightfully pursue unattached males; observed on occasion by students and social groups.

TELLEBRATION IN CONN. AND ELSEWHERE; Friday before Thanksgiving. A night of storytelling. Began in 1988.

NEW YORK CITY MARATHON; 1st Sunday in Nov. Held since 1970; about 25,000 runners participate.

TERLINGUA CHILI COOKOFF IN TERLINGUA, TEX.; 1st Friday–Sunday in Nov. National contest of chili chefs, held in the desert. Chili is Tex.'s official state dish.

December

December is the 12th and last month in the Gregorian calendar. It was the 10th month in the ancient Roman calendar, and its name comes from the Latin word *decem,* meaning "10."

December is a particularly festive month. It is the month when Christians all over the world celebrate the birth of Christ, and many activities are carried out in preparation for that day. The season of preparation, which is called Advent in the Christian calendar, begins on the 4th Sunday before Christmas in the West; in the Orthodox Churches, the Nativity Fast begins on November 15 (in either the Gregorian or the Julian calendars).

December is a month of happy traditions. Many people maintain customs that have been in their families for generations. They cook special dishes that originated with their forefathers, such as the English plum pudding or the Swedish lutefisk. December is the month for the singing of Christmas carols, the trimming of the tree, the writing of Christmas cards, and the selection of gifts for Christmas giving.

December is the month of Santa Claus in the U.S. and the month of St. Nicholas in the countries of Europe. This saint has a feast on December 6, and on that day he brings fruit and cakes to children if they have been good.

The period from Boxing Day (December 26) through New Year's Day is a time of festivities and carnivals in many Caribbean countries, and is the season of Kwanza in the U.S.

In the Jewish calendar, Hanukkah, the Feast of Lights, falls in December.

The last day of December closes the year. In Japan it is a time to take stock and pay debts. December 31 is called Hogmanay Day in Scotland, a day when adults exchange presents and give cakes to children. It is also called St. Sylvester's Day, which is observed in Germany and Belgium with customs that anticipate the new year. In Belgium, the last child out of bed on the morning of December 31 is a Sylvester, a lazy one who has to pay a tribute to early risers. In the U.S., the last hours of December constitute New Year's Eve, a time of merrymaking and parties.

The poinsettia has come to be the flower that is symbolic of December. Holly and mistletoe are also special December floral decorations.

December has 2 birthstones, the turquoise and the zircon.

HOLY DAYS AND FEAST DAYS

1
Feast of St. Eligius (ca. 590–Dec. 1, ca. 660). Romano-Gaulish craftsman and artist, served as master of the mint and diplomat under Merovingian kings; later a bishop. Patron saint of metalworkers and jewelers.

HOLIDAYS AND CIVIC DAYS

1
Fête Nationale in the Central African Republic; official public holiday. Celebrates the proclamation of the republic on Dec. 1, 1958. Marching parades are held in every part of the country.

1
Independence Day in Portugal; official public holiday. Commemorates the Dec. 1, 1640, restoration of Portuguese independence, following its temporary absorption within the Spanish Empire (1580–1640).

1

National Day in Romania; official public holiday. Commemorates the overthrow of the communist regime of Nicolae Ceausescu during Dec. 1989 and the formation of the modern Romanian state on Dec. 1, 1918. Celebrated since 1990.

ANNIVERSARIES AND SPECIAL EVENTS DAYS

1

Death anniversary of David Ben-Gurion (Oct. 16, 1886–Dec. 1, 1973). Polish-born Israeli; first prime minister of Israel.

1

Rosa Parks Day in the U.S. On Dec. 1, 1955, the African American Rosa McCauley Parks (Feb. 4, 1913–) defied the rules of the Montgomery, Ala., bus system and refused to relinquish her seat to a white man. Her courageous action led to a confirmation by the U.S. Supreme Court of the unconstitutionality of the bus-seating practice, and Rosa Parks came to be known as the Mother of the Civil Rights Movement.

1

World AIDS Day. Instituted to focus world attention on the auto-immune deficiency syndrome.

HOLIDAYS AND CIVIC DAYS

2

Republic Day in Laos; official public holiday. Commemorates the overthrow of the monarchy on Dec. 2, 1975.

2

National Day in the United Arab Emirates; official public holiday; often celebrated through Dec. 3. The U.A.E. came into existence on Dec. 2, 1971, uniting 7 of the former Trucial States, previously under the suzerainty of the U.K.

2

Pan American Health Day in the U.S. By presidential proclamation of 1940; intended to focus on hemispheric cooperation in the field of public health.

ANNIVERSARIES AND SPECIAL EVENTS DAYS

2

Birthday of Henry Thacker Burleigh (Dec. 2, 1866–Sept. 12, 1949). African American composer and choir director widely known for arrangements of

spirituals, notably "Deep River"; awarded the Spingarn Medal in 1916.

2

Birthday of Pedro II of Brazil (Dom Pedro de Alcântara; Dec. 2, 1825–Dec. 5, 1891; ruled 1831–89). 2nd and last emperor of Brazil. Considered Brazil's best ruler; loved and supported throughout his reign and nostalgically remembered. Deposed by a military coup on Nov. 15, 1889.

2

Monroe Doctrine Day in the U.S. Anniversary of the declaration by President James Monroe in his annual message to Congress on Dec. 2, 1823, that established a policy of American opposition to European intervention in the Americas.

2

Walter Plinge Day in England. Honors Walter Plinge, by lore a pub landlord whose generosity to actors led them to use his name on playbills to conceal an actor's appearance in more than one role. George Spelvin is the counterpart in the U.S.

HOLY DAYS AND FEAST DAYS

3

Feast of St. Francis Xavier (Apr. 7, 1506–Dec. 3, 1552). Spanish Basque Jesuit; missionary to the Orient; considered the greatest missionary after St. Paul; known as the Apostle of the Indies and the Apostle of Japan. Patron saint of Borneo, Australia, and China.

HOLIDAYS AND CIVIC DAYS

3

Admission Day in Ill. On Dec. 3, 1818, Ill. entered the Union as the 21st state.

ANNIVERSARIES AND SPECIAL EVENTS DAYS

3

Birthday of Cleveland Abbe (Dec. 3, 1838–Oct. 28, 1916). American meteorologist known as the Father of the Weather Bureau. Initiated the publication of daily weather forecasts and influential in establishing the use of standard time throughout the U.S.

3

Birthday of Joseph Conrad (Józef Teodor Konrad Korzeniowski; Dec. 3, 1857–Aug. 3, 1924). Polish-born English seaman and novelist of world reputation. Author of *Lord Jim* and *Nostromo,* among others.

3

Birthday of Ellen Henrietta Richards (Dec. 3, 1842–Mar. 30, 1911). American chemist; founder of the home-economics movement; first president of the American Home Economics Association.

3

Birthday of Gilbert Charles Stuart (Dec. 3, 1755–July 9, 1828). American portraitist who painted Washington, Jefferson, Madison, and other great Americans. Elected to the Hall of Fame for Great Americans.

3

Sir Rowland Hill Day. Commemorates the birth of Sir Rowland Hill (Dec. 3, 1795–Aug. 27, 1879), English administrator and educator who invented the world's first postage stamp in England in 1840. This day is observed by philatelic societies.

HOLY DAYS AND FEAST DAYS

4

Feast of St. Barbara (4th century). Martyred by her pagan father, who was then killed by lightning. One of the 14 Holy Helpers; patron saint of architects, builders, firefighters, and members of the artillery; invoked against lightning and fire. Probably legendary. Her day is considered the start of the Christmas season in parts of France, Germany, and Syria. Orth.: Dec. 4 or 17.

4

Feast of St. John Damascene (ca. 675–ca. Dec. 5, 749). One of the last of the great Greek fathers, noted for his eloquence. His poems are used in the Greek liturgy. A doctor of the church. Orth.: Dec. 4 or 17.

ANNIVERSARIES AND SPECIAL EVENTS DAYS

4

Birthday of Thomas Carlyle (Dec. 4, 1795–Feb. 5, 1881). Scottish essayist and historian called the Sage of Chelsea. His *French Revolution* established his reputation.

4

Birthday of Edith Louisa Cavell (Dec. 4, 1865–Oct. 12, 1915). English nurse and hero of World War I who was executed by the Germans. A monument to her memory stands in St. Martin's Place, Trafalgar Square, London.

4

Birthday of John Cotton (Dec. 4, 1584–Dec. 23, 1652). American Puritan clergyman who had great influence in the Massachusetts Bay Colony.

4

Birthday of Francisco Franco (Francisco Paulino Hermenegildo Teódulo Franco Bahamonde; Dec. 4, 1892–Nov. 20, 1975). Spanish military officer who revolted against the Spanish Republic on July 18, 1936, initiating the Spanish Civil War, and subsequently ruling as fascist dictator (*El Caudillo,* "the Leader") until his death and the restoration of democracy.

4

Birthday of Rainer Maria Rilke (Dec. 4, 1875–Dec. 29, 1926.) German lyric poet known for his complex, symbolic, and mystical poems. Considered a founding figure of modern literature.

4

Death anniversary of Prince Hall (ca. 1735–Dec. 4, 1807). Free black of Boston, self-employed leatherworker, highly regarded member of Boston's African American community; founder of Prince Hall Freemasonry.

4

St. Barbara's Day in Mexico, Brazil, Cuba, and elsewhere in Latin America. In Mexico, this is the Day of the Artisans, to honor the workers of the nation.

HOLIDAYS AND CIVIC DAYS

5

King's Birthday in Thailand; official public holiday. The country's national day; honors the revered King Bhumibol Adulyadej (Dec. 5, 1927–). Celebrated nationwide with pageantry, magnificent illuminations, and ubiquitous portraits of His Majesty.

ANNIVERSARIES AND SPECIAL EVENTS DAYS

5

Anniversary of the founding of the scholarly fraternity Phi Beta Kappa on Dec. 5, 1776, at the College of William and Mary in Williamsburg, Va.

5

Birthday of Walt (Walter Elias) Disney (Dec. 5, 1901–Dec. 15, 1966). American motion-picture and television producer; pioneer in the creation of animated motion-picture cartoons; creator of such cartoon characters as Mickey Mouse and Donald Duck; organizer of the first Disneyland in 1955.

5
Birthday of Martin Van Buren (Dec. 5, 1782–July 24, 1862). Lawyer; senator; governor of N.Y.; secretary of state and then vice president under Jackson; 8th president of the U.S. (1837–41; Democrat). A consummate politician called the Little Magician; took office during the Panic of 1837 and inaugurated the independent treasury system; opposed annexation of Tex. Buried in Kinderhook, N.Y.

5
Discovery Day in the Dominican Republic and Haiti. Commemorates the arrival of Christopher Columbus, who ran aground on Hispaniola on Dec. 5, 1492.

5
International Volunteer Day for Economic and Social Development. Sponsored by the United Nations since 1985; anniversary of the founding of the United Nations Volunteer Specialist Program on Dec. 5, 1970.

5
Prohibition Repeal Day in the U.S. Anniversary of the ratification on Dec. 5, 1933, of the 21st Amendment to the Constitution; a day when the sale of alcoholic beverages became legal after 13 years of Prohibition.

HOLY DAYS AND FEAST DAYS

6
Feast of St. Nicholas (died ca. 350). Bishop of Myra; noted for his miracles, striking acts of charity, and the freeing of captives. His following is especially strong in Greece and Russia. Patron saint of Greece, Apulia and Sicily (Italy), Lorraine (France), and Russia. Orth.: Dec. 6 or 19.

HOLIDAYS AND CIVIC DAYS

6
Independence Day in Finland; official public holiday. Commemorates the declaration of independence from Russia on Dec. 6, 1917. A solemn day. In Turku, all assemble outside before dawn and follow a torch procession by silent students who bear flags for each year of Finland's independence. At the grave of the great military leader Carl Mannerheim, the national anthem is sung. And in all cemeteries, candles on the graves of Finland's defenders assure that they are not forgotten.

6
Constitution Day in Spain; official public holiday. The country's national day; commemorates the voters' approval of a new constitution in 1978, following the demise of the Franco regime.

ANNIVERSARIES AND SPECIAL EVENTS DAYS

6
Anniversary of the creation of the Environmental Protection Agency (E.P.A.). U.S. government agency established on Dec. 6, 1970, as a direct and speedy consequence of the first Earth Day.

6
Birthday of (Alfred) Joyce Kilmer (Dec. 6, 1886–July 30, 1918). American poet remembered especially for a single poem, "Trees." Killed in action in World War I.

6
Day of Quito in Ecuador. Anniversary of the city's founding as San Francisco de Quito, in 1534. Festivities include a series of special bullfights, with parades, street dances, greasy pole-climbing contests, and the election of the Queen of Quito.

HOLY DAYS AND FEAST DAYS

7
Feast of St. Ambrose (ca. 340–Apr. 4, 397). Roman lawyer, governor, and bishop; a pivotal figure in the rise of Christianity at the end of the Roman Empire. Doctor of the church; patron saint of beekeepers and domestic animals. Orth.: Dec. 7 or 20.

HOLIDAYS AND CIVIC DAYS

7
Commemoration of the Death of the First President Félix Boigny in Côte d'Ivoire; official public holiday. Honors the first and longtime president, Félix Houphouët-Boigny (Oct. 18, 1905–Dec. 7, 1993; ruled Aug. 7, 1960–Dec. 7, 1993). Independence Day, formerly observed on Dec. 7, is now observed on Aug. 7.

7
Delaware Day in Del.; commemorates Del.'s ratification of the U.S. Constitution on Dec. 7, 1787, and its admission as the first state.

7
Earthquake Victims' Memorial Day in Armenia; official public holiday. Mourns the 55,000 Armenians killed by a major earthquake in 1988.

ANNIVERSARIES AND SPECIAL EVENTS DAYS

7
Birthday of Giovanni Lorenzo Bernini (Dec. 7, 1598–Nov. 28, 1680). Italian architect, sculptor, and painter; creator of the Baroque style; one of the architects of St. Peter's Basilica in Rome.

7
Birthday of Matthew Heywood Campbell Broun (Dec. 7, 1873–Apr. 24, 1947). American journalist and first president of the American Newspaper Guild.

7
Birthday of Willa Sibert Cather (Dec. 7, 1873–Apr. 24, 1947). American author considered to be one of the country's outstanding 20th-century writers. Her novels include *My Ántonia* and *Death Comes for the Archbishop. One of Ours* was awarded a Pulitzer Prize.

7
Birthday of (Avram) Noam Chomsky (Dec. 7, 1928–). Leading American linguist, writer, and political activist. His theory of generative grammar revolutionized the scientific study of language.

7
Pearl Harbor Day in the U.S. Anniversary of the Japanese attack on Pearl Harbor, the Philippines, and Guam on Dec. 7, 1941. The U.S. declared war on Japan on Dec. 8, 1941, and on Germany and Italy on Dec. 11, after the latter two countries declared war on the U.S.

HOLY DAYS AND FEAST DAYS

8
Feast of the Immaculate Conception. Commemorates the preservation of the Virgin Mary from original sin from the moment of her conception by St. Ann. Orth.: Dec. 9 or 22.

HOLIDAYS AND CIVIC DAYS

8
Battle of the Falklands Day in the Falkland Islands; official public holiday. Commemorates the 1914 British defeat of German ships in one of the major naval battles of World War I.

8
Feast of the Immaculate Conception in Nicaragua; official public holiday. *La Purísima* ("the Purest One"), or *La Chiquita*, is the national patron saint, and this is the most important day of the year; celebrated on Dec. 7 and 8, and announced by a *gritería* ("shout"); special foods include sweets, sweet lemon, and orange sugar cane.

ANNIVERSARIES AND SPECIAL EVENTS DAYS

8
Birthday of Bjørnstjerne Bjørnson (Dec. 8, 1832–Apr. 26, 1910). Norwegian novelist, dramatist, and ardent patriot; received the 1903 Nobel Prize in literature.

8
Birthday of Padraic Colum (Dec. 8, 1881–Jan. 11, 1972). Irish poet, folklorist, dramatist, and essayist. His *Collected Poems* reveal his deep involvement with the lore and legends of Ireland.

8
Birthday of Jim Morrison (Dec. 8, 1943–July 3, 1971). American musician; lead singer of the Doors and influential rock musician.

8
Birthday of Diego Rivera (Dec. 8, 1886–Nov. 25, 1957). Mexican painter and muralist, especially of his country's indigenous people. His wife, Frida Kahlo (July 6, 1907–July 13, 1954), was also an important painter, best known for her small self-portraits in a style based on native popular art.

8
Birthday of Kenneth Roberts (Dec. 8, 1885–July 21, 1957). American writer of *Northwest Passage* and other historical novels about the Revolutionary War period.

8
Birthday of Jean Sibelius (Dec. 8, 1865–Sept. 20, 1957). Finnish composer famous for *Valse Triste, Finlandia,* and his symphonic music.

8
Birthday of James Grover Thurber (Dec. 8, 1894–Nov. 2, 1961). American humorist and artist known for the sophisticated humor of his writing and the simplicity of his line drawings. Author of "The Secret Life of Walter Mitty."

8
Birthday of Eli Whitney (Dec. 8, 1765–Jan. 8, 1825). American inventor and manufacturer who invented the cotton gin in 1793. Elected to the Hall of Fame for Great Americans.

8

Beach Day in Uruguay. The start of the country's beach season; on the feast of the Immaculate Conception, a day important to fishers and sailors.

CA. 8

Dance of the Seises ("Sixes") in Seville, Spain. Choristers in traditional 17th-century pages' costumes dance a slow minuet in the sacristy of the Cathedral of Our Lady of the Caves every afternoon during the octave of the Immaculate Conception (Dec. 8–15), at Christmas, during the last 3 days of Carnaval (Sunday–Shrove Tuesday), and on Corpus Christi.

HOLIDAYS AND CIVIC DAYS

9

Independence and Republic Day in Tanzania; official public holiday. On Dec. 9, 1961, Tanganyika attained independence from Great Britain; it became a republic within the British Commonwealth on Dec. 9, 1962. Following union with Zanzibar and Pemba, the name was changed to Tanzania. This holiday is observed especially in Dar-es-Salaam, with a day of parades, speeches, youth marches, games and dances, and air force aerobatics.

ANNIVERSARIES AND SPECIAL EVENTS DAYS

9

Birthday of John Milton (Dec. 9, 1608–Nov. 8, 1674). Renowned English poet, often ranked 2nd only to Shakespeare. Especially noted for *Paradise Lost* (1667) and *Samson Agonistes* (1671).

9

Birthday of Thomas Philip "Tip" O'Neill (Dec. 9, 1912–Jan. 5, 1994). American congressman from Mass. and Speaker of the House. A much-admired politician.

HOLIDAYS AND CIVIC DAYS

10

Human Rights Day; official public holiday at the United Nations. Anniversary of the adoption of the Universal Declaration of Human Rights on Dec. 10, 1948. An official public holiday in Cambodia. Observed in the U.S., particularly in Mass., along with Bill of Rights Day.

10

Human Rights Day in Namibia; official public holiday. Commemorates the Dec. 10, 1959, resistance to relocation by residents of the Old Location township; many were killed and the township was demolished.

10

Constitution Day in Thailand; official public holiday. Commemorates the constitution of Dec. 10, 1932, the nation's first. Also at this time is the King's Cup Regatta, a long-distance yacht race.

10

Admission Day in Miss. On Dec. 10, 1932, Miss. entered the Union as the 20th state.

10

Wyoming Day in Wyo. Commemorates the adoption of women's suffrage in the Wyoming Territory on Dec. 10, 1869; the first such action in the U.S.

10

Constitution Day in Uzbekistan; official public holiday. Commemorates the constitution of Dec. 10, 1991.

ANNIVERSARIES AND SPECIAL EVENTS DAYS

10

Anniversary of the issuance of the first paper money in the Western Hemisphere on Dec. 10, 1692, by the Massachusetts Bay Colony, to pay for a military expedition into Canada; the British government was expected to redeem it, but never did.

10

Birthday of Zachariah Chandler (Dec. 10, 1813–Nov. 1, 1879). American merchant and politician who signed the call for the Jackson, Mich., meeting that is said to have founded the Republican Party. Represents Mich. in Statuary Hall.

10

Birthday of Melvil Dewey (Dec. 10, 1851–Dec. 26, 1931). American librarian who devised the Dewey Decimal System of Classification for library cataloging. More than any other individual, he was responsible for the development of library science in the U.S.

10

Birthday of Emily Dickinson (Dec. 10, 1830–May 15, 1886). American poet noted for her use of irregular rhymes and startling imagery.

10

Birthday of Ada Lovelace (born Lady Augusta Ada Byron; Dec. 10, 1815–Nov. 29, 1852). English mathematician and daughter of the poet Lord Byron; the first computer programmer, in collaboration with Charles Babbage.

10

Death anniversary of Red Cloud (1822–Dec. 10, 1909). Native American (Sioux) warrior, leader, and courageous defender of Native American rights.

10

Gallaudet Day. Anniversary of the birth of Thomas Hopkins Gallaudet (Dec. 10, 1787–Sept. 9, 1851), American founder of the first free school for hearing-impaired people in the U.S.; observed by organizations and institutions working with hearing-impaired people.

10

Nobel Prize Presentation Day in Sweden and Norway. On the death anniversary of Alfred Nobel (Oct. 21, 1833–Dec. 10, 1896), the king of Sweden presents awards in literature, physics, chemistry, medicine or physiology, and economics, and the Norwegian Parliament presents the Nobel Peace Prize.

HOLIDAYS AND CIVIC DAYS

11

National Day in Burkina Faso; official public holiday. Commemorates Dec. 11, 1958, when the territorial assembly of Upper Volta (later Burkina Faso) voted to become an autonomous state within the French community.

11

Indiana Day in Ind. Annually proclaimed by the governor to commemorate the Dec. 11, 1816, admission of Ind. to the Union as the 19th state.

ANNIVERSARIES AND SPECIAL EVENTS DAYS

11

Anniversary of the founding of the United Nations International Children's Emergency Fund (UNICEF) on Dec. 11, 1946.

11

Birthday of Hector Berlioz (Dec. 11, 1803–Mar. 8, 1869). French Romantic composer noted for his symphonies and operas, including Symphonie Fantastique and *La Damnation de Faust*.

11

Birthday of Fiorello Henry La Guardia (Dec. 11, 1882–Sept. 20, 1947). American lawyer, mayor of New York City, congressman, and first director of the Federal Office of Civilian Defense.

11

Abdication Day in the U.K. Remembers the abdication of King Edward VIII on Dec. 11, 1936, necessitated by his intent to marry a divorced commoner, the American Wallis Warfield Simpson.

11

Scaling Day (*Escalade*) in Geneva, Switzerland. Honors the night of Dec. 11, 1602, when the citizens routed the Savoyards, who were scaling the walls of their city. Shops sell chocolate bonbons representing the soup pots the women used on that night to throw hot water on the invaders.

HOLY DAYS AND FEAST DAYS

12

Feast of Our Lady of Guadalupe. Commemorates the apparition on Dec. 12, 1531, of the Virgin Mary to the Blessed Juan Diego, a Mexican Native American, near Mexico City, at the site of a temple to the Aztec goddess Tonantzín. Our Lady of Guadalupe is the patron saint of Mexico and the Americas. Her shrine is the second most visited Catholic site in the world, after the Vatican. Celebrated in Mexico with *conchero* dancers, processions, and fireworks. Celebrated also among the Native American population throughout Latin America and in the southwestern U.S., notably on Olvera Street in Los Angeles.

HOLIDAYS AND CIVIC DAYS

12

Jamhuri ("Rejoice in Freedom") Day and Uhuru ("Freedom") Day in Kenya; official public holiday. Celebrates the attainment of independence from the U.K. on Dec. 12, 1963, and the rejection of dominion status on Dec. 12, 1964. Kenya's biggest civil holiday, especially in Nairobi.

12

Constitution Day in Russia. Commemorates the day in 1993 when Russian voters approved a new constitution.

12

Neutrality Day in Turkmenistan; official public holiday. Commemorates the United Nations' recognition of Turkmenistan's neutrality on Dec. 12, 1995.

12

Ratification Day in Pa. On Dec. 12, 1787, Pa. ratified the Constitution and entered the Union as the 2nd state.

ANNIVERSARIES AND SPECIAL EVENTS DAYS

12

Anniversary of the founding of Washington, D.C. On Dec. 12, 1800, Washington was established as the permanent capitol of the U.S.

12

Birthday of Gustave Flaubert (Dec. 12, 1821–May 8, 1880). French writer and novelist of the Realist school, famous for *Madame Bovary.*

12

Birthday of John Jay (Dec. 12, 1745–May 17, 1829). American lawyer, jurist, statesman, and diplomat; co-author of the Federalist Papers with Alexander Hamilton and James Madison; first chief justice of the Supreme Court.

12

Birthday of Frank (Francis Albert) Sinatra (Dec. 12, 1915–May 14, 1998). American singer and film star. A teen idol during World War II, he earned respect for his sophisticated vocal techniques and interpretations. He won an Academy Award for Best Supporting Actor in *From Here to Eternity* and appeared in many other films, including *Guys and Dolls* and *The Manchurian Candidate.*

12

Crossword Puzzle Day. Anniversary of the publication of Arthur Wynne's first crossword puzzle in the *New York World* on Dec. 12, 1913.

12

Poinsettia Day. Commemorates the death anniversary of Joel Roberts Poinsett (Mar. 2, 1799–Dec. 12, 1851), American diplomat who introduced this Central American plant to the U.S.; it is now a favorite Christmas season decoration.

HOLY DAYS AND FEAST DAYS

13

Feast of St. Lucy (or Lucia; died 304). Patron saint invoked against eye trouble and patron saint of writers and lights. Her feast begins the Christmas season in some countries. Orth.: Dec. 13 or 26.

HOLIDAYS AND CIVIC DAYS

13

Republic Day in Malta; official public holiday. Anniversary of the 1974 resolution that declared Malta a republic within the British Commonwealth; celebrations include horse races at Marsa.

13

National Day in St. Lucia; official public holiday. Commemorates the supposed arrival of Christopher Columbus on Dec. 13 (St. Lucia's Day), 1498 or 1502.

ANNIVERSARIES AND SPECIAL EVENTS DAYS

13

Birthday of Phillips Brooks (Dec. 13, 1835–Jan. 23, 1893). American Episcopalian bishop and composer, remembered as the author of the lyrics of the Christmas carol "O Little Town of Bethlehem." Elected to the Hall of Fame for Great Americans.

13

Birthday of Heinrich Heine (Dec. 13, 1797–Feb. 17, 1856). German lyric poet; his *Buch der Lieder* (*Book of Songs,* 1827) has frequently been set to music.

13

Birthday of Clark Mills (Dec. 13, 1810–Jan. 12, 1883). American sculptor and bronze founder who made equestrian statues of Andrew Jackson and George Washington; did the bronze casting of Thomas Crawford's *Freedom,* or *Armed Liberty,* for the dome of the Capitol; and took a life mask of Abraham Lincoln.

CA. 13

Geminid Meteor Showers; Dec. 7–15, main day Dec. 13. Visible toward the east at midnight. Very rich showers, with moderately swift meteors.

13

Lucia Day (*Luciadagen*) in Sweden, Finland, and in Swedish-American communities. Uniquely Swedish celebration honoring St. Lucia, the Queen of Light. In Stockholm the festival includes a candlelight parade through the city; the queen wears a crown of lighted candles and receives the Lucia jewel; coincides with the short daylight season. Local communities hold St. Lucia competitions. In homes, the youngest girl dresses in white with a crown of lighted candles, and in early morning visits the family in their beds, bringing coffee, ginger biscuits, and mulled wine (glogg); often accompanied by girls in white and boys wearing tall conical paper hats and carrying stars.

13
Russian Orthodox feast of St. Andrew. In Ukraine, this is the Feast of Kalyia; on the eve, young people celebrate with traditional games, fortune-telling, and other entertainments.

HOLY DAYS AND FEAST DAYS

14
Feast of St. John of the Cross (born Juan de Yepes y Álvarez; June 24, 1542–Dec. 14, 1592). Spanish Carmelite priest, friend of St. Teresa of Ávila, and founder of the Discalced Carmelites. One of the great mystical writers, noted for *The Dark Night of the Soul* and other works. Doctor of the church; called the Doctor of Mystical Theology.

HOLIDAYS AND CIVIC DAYS

14
Admission Day in Ala. On Dec. 14, 1819, Ala. entered the Union as the 22nd state.

ANNIVERSARIES AND SPECIAL EVENTS DAYS

14
Birthday of Tycho Brahe (Dec. 14, 1546–Oct. 24, 1601). Danish astronomer whose instruments and measurements made possible future discoveries. Johannes Kepler was his assistant and inherited his records, and Kepler's work paved the way for Isaac Newton's.

14
Birthday of John Mercer Langston (Dec. 14, 1829–Nov. 15, 1897). American lawyer and public official, probably the first African American to be elected to public office in the U.S.; served as minister to Haiti and college president.

14
Birthday of Nostradamus (or Michel de Notredame; Dec. 14, 1503–July 2, 1566). French astrologer and court physician to Charles IX of France; the most widely read seer of the Renaissance. His enigmatic prophecies still generate fervent interest.

14
Margaret Chase Smith Day in Maine. Commemorates the birth of Margaret Chase Smith (Dec. 14,

1897–May 29, 1995), the first American woman to be elected to both houses of Congress.

HOLIDAYS AND CIVIC DAYS

15
Antillean Flag Day in the Netherlands Antilles; former official public holiday. Also called Kingdom Day. Commemorates the islands' autonomy within the kingdom, granted on Dec. 15, 1954, with the Charter of Kingdom; the Antillean flag was first unfurled on this day in 1959.

15
Bill of Rights Day in the U.S. Honors the ratification, on Dec. 15, 1791, of the first 10 amendments to the Constitution; by presidential proclamation since 1941. Human Rights Week extends from Dec. 10 (Human Rights Day) through Dec. 17; by presidential proclamation since 1958. In Mass., Civil Rights Week, Dec. 8–15, has been observed since 1952; it commemorates both the Bill of Rights and Mass.'s first code of laws, the Body of Liberties, adopted Dec. 10, 1641.

ANNIVERSARIES AND SPECIAL EVENTS DAYS

15
Birthday of George Romney (Dec. 15, 1734–Nov. 15, 1802). English portrait painter whose celebrated model was Lady Hamilton.

15
Death anniversary of Sitting Bull (ca. 1834–Dec. 15, 1890). Native American (Sioux; Hunkpapa Teton) leader, medicine man, and warrior; killed by Sioux reservation police.

15
Zamenhof Day. Sponsored by the Esperanto League for North America to commemorate the birthday of Ludwik Lejzer Zamenhof (Dec. 15, 1859–Apr. 14, 1917), Russian physician and oculist who created the most important of the international artificial languages, Esperanto. His textbook on the language was published in 1887.

HOLIDAYS AND CIVIC DAYS

16
Victory Day (*Biganj Dibash*) in Bangladesh; official public holiday. Also called Liberation Day. Commemorates the attainment of independence from Pakistan on Dec. 16, 1971, when the Pakistani army surrendered to the Indian army. Observed

with a citizens' pilgrimage to the Mausoleum of the Martyrs to honor those who died for independence.

16

Day of Reconciliation in South Africa; official public holiday. Formerly called Dingaan's day, then Day of the Vow or Day of the Covenant. Originally commemorated the Dec. 16, 1837, Battle of Blood River, in which the Boers, led by Andries Pretorius, were victorious over the Zulus, led by Dingaan. The Boers had vowed to make the day a sabbath if victory was theirs. With the advent of multiracial democracy in 1994, the day was given its current name. Boers celebrate with camp outs and barbecues.

ANNIVERSARIES AND SPECIAL EVENTS DAYS

16

Anniversary of the New Madrid earthquake in the area of New Madrid, Mo. Main quake was on Dec. 16, 1811, with others on Jan. 23 and Feb. 7, 1812; the most powerful earthquake in U.S. history, with a magnitude of 8.7 on the Richter scale.

16

Birthday of Jane Austen (Dec. 16, 1775–July 18, 1817). English writer, remembered for novels of manners and morals, notably, *Persuasion* and *Pride and Prejudice*.

16

Birthday of Ludwig van Beethoven (Dec. 16, 1770–Mar. 26, 1827). German composer considered to be one of the foremost musicians of all time.

16

Birthday of Sir Noël Peirce Coward (Dec. 16, 1899–Mar. 26, 1973). English playwright, director, songwriter, and actor. His plays include *Blithe Spirit, Private Lives,* and *This Happy Breed.* His songs include "Mad Dogs and Englishmen" and "Someday I'll Find You."

16

Birthday of Ralph Adams Cram (Dec. 16, 1863–Sept. 22, 1942). American architect and authority on Gothic architecture whose firm designed the Cathedral of St. John the Divine in New York City.

16

Birthday of Margaret Mead (Dec. 16, 1901–Nov. 15, 1978). Distinguished American anthropologist. Her studies of primitive societies existing in the South Pacific in the 20th century were major contributions to anthropology and to investigations of cultural conditioning in modern society.

16

Birthday of George Santayana (Dec. 16, 1863–Sept. 26, 1952). Spanish-born American historian who said, "Those who cannot remember the past are condemned to repeat it."

16

Boston Tea Party Day. Commemorates the anniversary of Dec. 16, 1773, when colonists boarded a British vessel and dumped a shipload of tea into Boston Harbor, in a prelude to the American Revolution.

16

Misa de Gallo ("Cock-Crow Mass"). Also called *Simbang Gabi.* Denotes the beginning of the Christmas season in Catholic parts of the Philippines; each day begins with church bells breaking the night silence to call people to dawn Mass; the *Misa de Gallo* period concludes with the midnight Mass on Christmas Eve.

16

Novena of Christmas begins, ending after 9 days on Christmas Eve. A time of preparation for the coming of the Christ child. In some countries, marked by creches, special prayers and hymns, and celebration of the Christmas story. Colombia's observances are notable; so are those of Mexico and the Philippines.

16

Posadas (the "Lodgings") in Mexico. Begins on Dec. 16 in cities and villages with a procession that recalls the journey of Mary and Joseph to Bethlehem. *Posadas* lasts 9 days and includes religious ceremonies, festivities, and the popular ceremony of the breaking of the piñata. *Posadas* is also celebrated on Olvera Street in Los Angeles.

ANNIVERSARIES AND SPECIAL EVENTS DAYS

17

Birthday of Joseph Henry (Dec. 17, 1797–May 13, 1878). American physicist noted for research in electromagnetism. Elected to the Hall of Fame for Great Americans.

17

Birthday of Thomas Starr King (Dec. 17, 1824–Mar. 4, 1864). American Unitarian clergyman and author. Represents Calif. in Statuary Hall.

17

Birthday of Willard Frank Libby (Dec. 17, 1908–Sept. 8, 1980). American educator, physicist, atomic scientist; inventor of the radiocarbon (atomic clock) method for dating ancient and pre-historic plant and animal remains; recipient of the 1960 Nobel Prize in chemistry.

17

Birthday of John Greenleaf Whittier (Dec. 17, 1807–Sept. 7, 1892). American poet, abolitionist, and journalist, known as the Quaker Poet. Elected to the Hall of Fame for Great Americans.

CA. 17

Mevlana Commemoration Ceremony in Konya, Turkey; usually Dec. 10–17. Commonly called the Whirling Dervish Festival; commemorates the death anniversary of Jalal ad-Din ar-Rumi (ca. Sept. 30, 1207–Dec. 17, 1273), Muslim saint, out-standing mystic poet and philosopher, founder of the Mevlevi Sufi order. Dervishes dance the *Sema,* a precise dance of ecstatic union with God.

CA. 17

Newport Harbor Christmas Boat Parade at Newport Beach, Calif.; Dec. 17–23. The largest water parade in the U.S., and the inspiration for many others. Hundreds of imaginatively illuminated boats parade nightly.

17

Wright Brothers Day and Pan American Aviation Day in the U.S.; by presidential proclamation. Honors the first powered heavier-than-air flight at 10:35 A.M. on Dec. 17, 1903, at Kitty Hawk, N.C., by Orville and Wilbur Wright. Observed at Kitty Hawk since 1928, also in Washington, D.C., and in Dayton, Ohio. The Man Will Never Fly Society meets at Kitty Hawk on Dec. 16.

HOLIDAYS AND CIVIC DAYS

18

Proclamation of the Republic Day in Niger; official public holiday. Commemorates the declaration of independence from France on Dec. 18, 1958.

18

Ratification Day in N.J. On Dec. 18, 1787, N.J. rat-ified the Constitution and entered the Union as the 3rd state.

ANNIVERSARIES AND SPECIAL EVENTS DAYS

18

Birthday of William Allen (Dec. 18, 1803–July 11, 1879). American politician, congressman, and governor of Ohio. Represents Ohio in Statuary Hall.

18

Birthday of Edward Alexander MacDowell (Dec. 18, 1861–Jan. 24, 1908). American pianist and composer. Elected to the Hall of Fame for Great Americans. An Edward MacDowell Medal is awarded annually by the Edward MacDowell As-sociation to recognize individuals whose work has enriched the arts.

18

Death anniversary of Antonio Stradivari (ca. 1644–Dec. 18, 1737). Skilled Italian violin maker whose violins, violas, and cellos are today highly prized.

18

Feast of the Expectation of the Blessed Virgin Mary in Spain and also of Our Lady of the Lonely in Mexico and elsewhere in Latin America. A Spanish feast (from A.D. 656) honoring the An-nunciation. Transmuted, apparently, in Mexico and throughout Latin America into the Virgin of the Lonely (or the Virgin of Solitude) in sympathy with Mary's grief at the death of Jesus. Observed especially by pilgrims to Oaxaca, Mexico, where she is the patron saint of muleteers and sailors.

ANNIVERSARIES AND SPECIAL EVENTS DAYS

19

Birthday of Henry Clay Frick (Dec. 19, 1849–Dec. 2, 1919). American industrialist who left his priceless art collection and his mansion to the public as a museum, now known as the Frick Col-lection, in New York City.

19

Birthday of Albert Abraham Michelson (Dec. 19, 1852–May 9, 1931). American physicist; awarded the 1907 Nobel Prize in physics for his research in optics and the speed of light; first American to re-ceive a Nobel Prize.

ANNIVERSARIES AND SPECIAL EVENTS DAYS

20
Anniversary of the establishment of the position of poet laureate in the U.S., on Dec. 20, 1985. Robert Penn Warren was named the first poet laureate.

20
Anniversary of the S.C. legislature's vote to secede from the Union on the Dec. 20, 1860. It was the first state to do so.

20
Louisiana Purchase Day. Anniversary of the Dec. 20, 1803, transfer by France to the U.S. of the million-square-mile Louisiana Territory, doubling the size of the U.S.

20
Samuel Slater Day in Mass. Honors Samuel Slater (June 9, 1768–Apr. 21, 1835), English-born founder of the American cotton-textile industry, and of the American industrial revolution generally. Opened the first successful American cotton mill in Pawtucket, R.I., in 1793.

HOLY DAYS AND FEAST DAYS

21
Feast of St. Peter Canisius (May 8, 1521–Dec. 21, 1597). Dutch Jesuit priest, leader in the Counter-Reformation, called the Second Apostle of Germany, and a doctor of the church.

ANNIVERSARIES AND SPECIAL EVENTS DAYS

21
Birthday of Heinrich Böll (Dec. 21, 1917–July 16, 1985). German novelist who interpreted Germany's experiences in World War II; wrote *Billiards at Half-Past Nine*. Received the 1972 Nobel Prize in literature.

21
Birthday of Jean Henri Fabre (Dec. 21, 1823–Oct. 11, 1915). French entomologist who devoted his life to studying and writing about the habits of insects.

21
Birthday of Pyotr Alekseyevich Kropotkin (Dec. 21, 1842–Feb. 8, 1921). Russian geographer, revolutionary, and foremost 19th-century theorist of the anarchist movement.

21
Birthday of Joseph Stalin (born Iosif Vissarionovich Dzhugashvili; Dec. 21, 1879–Mar. 5, 1953). Russian dictator in power from 1929 until his death in 1953; credited with the ruthless development of the USSR as a major world power.

21
Death anniversary of Giovanni Boccaccio (1313–Dec. 21, 1375). Italian writer famous for the *Decameron* (1353). Known as the Father of Classic Italian Prose, he influenced many, including Chaucer and Shakespeare.

CA. 21
Forefathers' Day in the U.S. Also called Compact Day. Observed since 1769; now observed mainly in Plymouth, Mass., and by various New England societies on Dec. 21 or 22. Commemorates the Pilgrims' signing of the Mayflower Compact and their landing in 1620.

ANNIVERSARIES AND SPECIAL EVENTS DAYS

22
Birthday of Luca Della Robbia (born Luca di Simone di Marco; Dec. 22, 1400–Sept. 22, 1482). Italian sculptor who created the famous Della Robbia reliefs in terra cotta.

22
Birthday of James Edward Oglethorpe (Dec. 22, 1696–ca. June 30, 1785). English soldier and founder of the Georgia Colony in the New World.

22
Birthday of Edwin Arlington Robinson (Dec. 22, 1869–Apr. 6, 1935). American poet and 3-time Pulitzer Prize winner; especially remembered for his poems "Richard Cory" and "Miniver Cheevy."

22
Death anniversary of Stephen Day (ca. 1594–Dec. 22, 1668). First printer in the British colonies in America; printed the *Bay Psalm Book* in Cambridge, Mass., in 1640.

22
Death anniversary of John Newbery (1713–Dec. 22, 1767). English publisher who made a specialty of children's books and in whose honor the annual Newbery Medal has been given since 1922 for the most distinguished contribution to children's literature published in the preceding year.

22

Lantern Festivals in the Philippines; Dec. 22–24. Lanterns glow at sunset along the main streets, while people dance to band music and hear carols. Neighborhoods compete to produce the best lanterns and parade them.

CA. 22

Winter solstice in the Northern Hemisphere occurs on Dec. 21 or 22. On this day the sun rises and sets at its southernmost extreme; in the Northern Hemisphere, the period of daylight is at its shortest of the year. (There is also a summer solstice; *see* June 21.) Note that the Northern Hemisphere's winter and summer solstices are the Southern Hemisphere's summer and winter solstices.

CA. 22

Ysyakh in the Jatutsk region of northeast Russia; at winter solstice time. Celebrates midwinter, featuring races of all sorts (runners, horses, sled dogs, reindeer), folk dances, and enthusiastic feasting, especially on boiled beef and fermented mare's milk.

HOLIDAYS AND CIVIC DAYS

23

Emperor's Birthday (*Tenno Tanjo-Bi*) in Japan; official public holiday. Honors Emperor Akihito (Dec. 23, 1933– ; rule 1989–).

ANNIVERSARIES AND SPECIAL EVENTS DAYS

23

Anniversary of the establishment of the U.S. Federal Reserve System on Dec. 23, 1913.

23

Birthday of Martin Opitz (Dec. 23, 1597–Aug. 20, 1639). German poet and critic known as the Father of Modern German Poetry.

23

Birthday of Joseph Smith (Dec. 23, 1805–June 27, 1844). American founder of the Church of Jesus Christ of Latter-Day Saints. His writings and the Bible form the Mormon scriptures. Killed by a mob while jailed.

23

Official anniversary of the invention of the transistor on Dec. 23, 1947, by scientists of the Bell Laboratories in the U.S.

ANNIVERSARIES AND SPECIAL EVENTS DAYS

24

Birthday of I. F. (Isidor Feinstein) Stone (Dec. 24, 1907–June 18, 1989). American political journalist, publisher of the penetrating *I. F. Stone's Weekly*.

24

Blooming of the Glastonbury Thorn (hawthorn) in Glastonbury, England, on Christmas Eve. By tradition, Glastonbury is the cradle of British Christianity, said to have been introduced by St. Joseph of Arimathea, who also brought and planted the tree. Pilgrims visit.

24

Christmas Eve, the Vigil of Christmas. Many Christians attend midnight church services. Some exchange presents this evening, instead of next morning. Commonly, children dream of the coming presents from Santa Claus (or else the Baby Jesus), while parents labor to assemble them. Caroling door to door is popular.

HOLY DAYS AND FEAST DAYS

25

Christmas, the feast of the Nativity of the Lord. Commemorates the birth of Jesus Christ in a manger in Bethlehem; a day of rejoicing, prayer, and praise. Liturgically, the Christmas season extends from Christmas Eve through the feast of the Epiphany (*see* Jan. 6). Orth.: Dec. 25 or Jan. 7.

HOLIDAYS AND CIVIC DAYS

25

Jinnah's Birthday (Anniversary of the Birth of the Quaid-i-Azam) in Pakistan; official public holiday.

25

Constitution Day in Taiwan; official public holiday. Honors the adoption of the constitution on Dec. 25, 1946.

ANNIVERSARIES AND SPECIAL EVENTS DAYS

25

Anniversary of Washington's crossing of the Delaware. On the night of Dec. 25, 1776, George Washington and the Continental Army crossed the Delaware River from Pa. to N.J., and won the important Battle of Trenton (Dec. 26, 1776). The crossing has been reenacted each year since 1953.

25

Birthday of Clara (Clarissa Harlow) Barton (Dec. 25, 1821–Apr. 12, 1912). Active volunteer with the U.S. Sanitary Commission during the Civil War, and thereafter creator and first president of the American Red Cross.

25

Birthday of Humphrey De Forest Bogart (Dec. 25, 1899–Jan. 14, 1957). American stage and screen actor famous for his portrayals of cool, tough anti-heroes in such movies as *Casablanca* and *The African Queen,* for which he won an Academy Award.

25

Birthday of Evangeline Cory Booth (Dec. 25, 1865–July 17, 1950). English; International Salvation Army general who served in London, Canada, and the U.S.; author and composer of Salvation Army songs.

25

Birthday of Anwar el-Sadat (Dec. 25, 1918–Oct. 6, 1981; ruled 1970–81). Egyptian president who shared the 1978 Nobel Peace Prize with the Israeli prime minister Menachem Begin. Assassinated while observing his country's Armed Forces Day parade.

25

Christmas. The most popular Christian festival, celebrated in all Christian countries; a family- and child-centered time. Each country's celebrations contain unique features that draw from ancient and Christian traditions. Typically, a day for families to attend morning religious services, exchange presents, and eat a traditional meal.

25

Dakar Rally begins at Barcelona, Spain. An international automobile and motorcycle rally, from Barcelona to Dakar, Senegal, on a tortuous route. The "Dakar" is the world's most harrowing rally, lasting about 3 weeks and covering over 6,000 miles.

25

Russian Winter Festival especially in Moscow; Dec. 25–Jan. 5. Particularly for children; features circuses, performances of fables, theater, and outdoor parties with folk games, troika rides, and dancing around fir trees.

HOLY DAYS AND FEAST DAYS

26

Orthodox feast of the Synaxis of the Most Holy Mother of God and of St. Joseph, her spouse. A holy day in the Byzantine calendar and celebrated in the Greek Orthodox Church as the Day of the Theotokos.

26

Feast of St. Stephen (died ca. 35). The first martyr (by stoning); patron saint of stonemasons and horses. Orth.: Dec. 27 or Jan. 9.

HOLIDAYS AND CIVIC DAYS

26

Independence Day in Slovenia; official public holiday. Commemorates Dec. 26, 1990, when the results of a plebescite on separation from the Yugoslav Union were formally announced to the nation.

26

Boxing Day in the U.K., the British Commonwealth, and in former British colonies. An official public holiday in many countries. The term is used for the day after Christmas, which may have started with the opening of the church alms box for the poor or with the custom of distributing gratuities to tradespeople, mail carriers, and employees. British-influenced African countries commonly celebrate with all-night dancing.

ANNIVERSARIES AND SPECIAL EVENTS DAYS

26

Anniversary of the formal dissolution of the Union of Soviet Socialist Republics on Dec. 26, 1991. This is the official date of independence attained (rather than declared) for all countries formerly incorporated in the USSR, history's largest empire.

26

Birthday of Charles Babbage (Dec. 26, 1791–Oct. 18, 1871). English inventor of the first automatic computer, during the Victorian steam age; his computer, constructed much later to his design and using the software of Ada Lovelace, worked impeccably.

26

Birthday of Mao Tse-tung (Mao Ze-dong; Dec. 26, 1893–Sept. 9, 1976). Chinese librarian, teacher, and revolutionary. A founder of the People's Republic of China, he became chairman of the Communist Party and of the new country (1949). Unified China and led a great social revolution, but was criticized for his economic failures and revolutionary excesses.

CA. 26

Junkanoo in the Bahamas, Belize, Montserrat, and the British Virgin Islands; begins Dec. 26 (official public holiday in all 5 places) and ends Jan. 1 (also an official public holiday in all 4 places). The Bahamian Carnival, spirited and lighthearted, and a very important religious event. Troupes in elaborate crepe-paper costumes parade in a dancing motion to *Junkanoo* music. A celebration of African origin.

CA. 26

Kwanza begins in the U.S.; Dec. 26–Jan. 1. An African-American spiritual festival created in 1966 and dedicated to the 7 principles of unity, self-determination, collective work and responsibility, cooperative economics, purpose, creativity, and faith. *Kwanza* means "first fruits of the harvest" in Swahili, and is based on African harvest festivals.

CA. 26

Sidney to Hobart Yacht Race in Australia; begins Dec. 26, lasts several days. Distance is 621 miles for this challenging international race.

HOLY DAYS AND FEAST DAYS

27

Feast of St. John the Evangelist and Theologian (ca. 6–ca. 104). The Beloved Disciple to whom Christ on the cross entrusted Mary; traditionally, the author of the fourth Gospel and the Book of Revelations. Orth.: Sept. 26 or Oct. 9 and May 8 or 21.

ANNIVERSARIES AND SPECIAL EVENTS DAYS

27

Anniversary of the Christmas Rebellion, Jamaica's largest slave revolt. Also called the Baptist War. On Dec. 27, 1831, thousands of Jamaican slaves, led by the slave Samuel Sharpe, rose in resistance, demanding wages for their work; the strike swiftly became an armed rebellion. The revolt formally ended on Feb. 5, 1832. Sharpe and many others were hanged in the Kingston square that bears his name. The slaves' bearing caused missionaries who returned to England to argue persuasively for the abolition of slavery.

27

Birthday of Johannes Kepler (Dec. 27, 1571–Nov. 15, 1630). German astronomer who discovered that the earth and other planets travel about the Sun in elliptical orbits, and transformed the old geometrical astronomy into dynamical astronomy.

27

Birthday of Louis Pasteur (Dec. 27, 1822–Sept. 28, 1895). French chemist and founder of microbiological sciences and of preventive medicine. He gave the first successful antirabies inoculation on July 6, 1885.

HOLY DAYS AND FEAST DAYS

CA. 28

Ethiopian Orthodox feast of Gabriel the Archangel at Kullubi, Ethiopia; celebrated on Dec. 28 or Dec. 29. Pilgrims of all religions come to the archangel's church to make vows and pray for boons, particularly pregnancy; lasts 3 days.

28

Feast of the Holy Innocents. Commemorates the infants murdered by Herod's soldiers seeking to kill the child Jesus. Also called Childermas, and in Guadeloupe, Young Saints Day. Orth.: Dec. 29 or Jan. 11.

HOLIDAYS AND CIVIC DAYS

28

Admission Day in Iowa. On Dec. 28, 1846, Iowa entered the Union as the 29th state.

CA. 28

King's Birthday in Nepal; official public holiday. King Birendra Bir Bikram Shah Dev (Dec. 28, 1945–) is revered as an incarnation of the deity Vishnu. The outdoor celebrations in Kathmandu are thronged.

ANNIVERSARIES AND SPECIAL EVENTS DAYS

28

Birthday of Woodrow Wilson (Dec. 28, 1856–Feb. 3, 1924). President of Princeton University; governor of N.J.; statesman; man of letters; advocate of the League of Nations; 28th president of the U.S. (1913–21; Democrat). Secured American participation in World War I. Was influential in attempting a just peace, with his Fourteen Points, emphasis on self-determination, and advocacy for a League of Nations. Awarded the Nobel Peace Prize in 1919. Buried in Washington Cathedral. Elected to the Hall of Fame for Great Americans.

28
Cross Day in Ireland. A folk belief holds that anything begun on Holy Innocents' Day will come to a bad end.

28
Day of the Innocents in various Latin countries, such as Colombia, Ecuador, Mexico, and Nicaragua; also in Belgium. Similar to April Fool's Day in the U.S. A day of masquerades, dancing, and clowns, with tricks and hoaxes. In Guadeloupe, this is Young Saints Day, with parades for costumed children carrying toys.

HOLY DAYS AND FEAST DAYS

29
Feast of St. Thomas à Becket (Dec. 21, 1118–Dec. 29, 1170). English archbishop of Canterbury. Murdered in the cathedral by knights of King Henry II, an act that shocked all Europe. His shrine became a major pilgrimage center.

HOLIDAYS AND CIVIC DAYS

29
Admission Day in Tex. On Dec. 29, 1845, Tex. entered the Union as the 28th state.

ANNIVERSARIES AND SPECIAL EVENTS DAYS

29
Anniversary of the Wounded Knee Massacre in the U.S. On Dec. 29, 1890, at Wounded Knee Creek, S.Dak., U.S. cavalrymen massacred over 200 Sioux in an effort to suppress the Ghost Dance religion.

29
Birthday of Pablo (Pau) Casals (Dec. 29, 1876–Oct. 22, 1973). Spanish Catalan-born musician, conductor, and composer; great cellist of the 20th century. Left Spain after the Civil War and settled first in France and then in Puerto Rico. Received the United Nations Peace Prize for his "Hymn to the United Nations."

29
Birthday of John James Ingalls (Dec. 29, 1833–Aug. 16, 1900). American congressman from Kans. Represents Kans. in Statuary Hall.

29
Birthday of Andrew Johnson (Dec. 29, 1808–July 31, 1875). Tenn. congressman, governor, senator; military governor of Tenn. during the Civil War; elected vice president for Abraham Lincoln's 2nd term, succeeded him upon his assassination; 17th president of the U.S. (1865–69; Democrat). An antisecession Southerner, he favored amnesty of most Confederates if they accepted the 13th Amendment. His postwar struggles with Congress concerning policies in the South led to his impeachment; he was acquitted by one vote on May 26, 1868. Buried in Greenville, Tenn. Elected to the Hall of Fame for Great Americans.

29
Birthday of Christian Jürgensen Thomsen (Dec. 29, 1788–May 21, 1865). Danish archaeologist who proposed the chronological system that divides prehistory into the Stone, Bronze, and Iron Ages.

HOLIDAYS AND CIVIC DAYS

30
Rizal Day in the Philippines; official public holiday. At a wreath-laying ceremony at the National Hero's Monument in Rizal Park, Manila honors Dr. José Protasio Rizal (June 19, 1861–Dec. 30, 1896), the Philippine doctor and author whose books denouncing the Spanish administration were an inspiration to the Philippine nationalist movement.

ANNIVERSARIES AND SPECIAL EVENTS DAYS

30
Birthday of Simon Guggenheim (Dec. 30, 1867–Nov. 2, 1941). American capitalist and philanthropist; founder with his wife of the John Simon Guggenheim Memorial Foundation in 1925, as a memorial to their son.

30
Birthday of Joseph Rudyard Kipling (Dec. 30, 1865–Jan. 18, 1936). English novelist, poet, and short-story writer famous for the Jungle Books, "The Man Who Would Be King," "Recessional," and many other titles. He was awarded the 1907 Nobel Prize in literature.

30
Birthday of Stephen Butler Leacock (Dec. 30, 1869–Mar. 28, 1944). Canadian humorist and man of letters, political scientist, university professor,

and lecturer, who ranked with Mark Twain in popular esteem.

30

Death anniversary of Danilo Dolce (1924–Dec. 30, 1997). Italian intellectual, poet, and social activist; notable for his fruitful work in Sicily, organizing grassroots nonviolent resistance to the Mafia; writings include *Report from Palermo*.

HOLY DAYS AND FEAST DAYS

31

Feast of St. Sylvester (Pope Sylvester I; Jan. 31, 314–335). Roman pope notable for the many churches erected during his pontificate, including St. Peter's Basilica; officiated at the first public consecration of a church (324), the Basilica of the Most Holy Savior (later called St. John Lateran). Orth.: Jan. 2 or 15.

ANNIVERSARIES AND SPECIAL EVENTS DAYS

31

Birthday of George Catlett Marshall (Dec. 31, 1880–Oct. 16, 1959). American soldier and statesman; chairman of the Joint Chiefs of Staff during World War II; designer of the European Recovery Program implemented in 1948 and known as the Marshall Plan.

31

Birthday of Sir John Eric Sidney Thompson (Dec. 31, 1898–Sept. 9, 1975). English Mayanist and ethnographer who deciphered early Mayan glyphs, and thereby discovered that present-day Native American Mexicans preserve many ancestral customs.

31

Death anniversary of John Wycliffe (ca. 1330–Dec. 31, 1384). English religious reformer called the Morning Star of the Reformation; the first person to translate the Bible into English.

31

Comrie Flambeaux at Comrie in the Scottish Highlands. A New Year's Eve procession of torches and fireballs to the cardinal corners of the village, followed by a bonfire, to banish the accumulated evil of the past year.

31

Feast of Our Lady of Seafarers in Salvador, Brazil. On the evening of Dec. 31, her statue is escorted in gaily decorated boats from the Basilica de Con-

ceiçao ("Conception") to the Boa Viagem beach, where sailors and families convey it to the church; next day, Jan. 1, is a festive return; a very happy celebration. The custom dates from 1750 in Portugal.

31

First Night in Boston, Mass., and other cities. A festival of the arts, begun in 1976 as an alternative to the usual parties, and now widely adopted with great success; emphasizes alcohol-free celebrations.

31

Hogmanay. The greatest Scottish holiday; traditionally, Scots gather outdoors and as the bells chime midnight, sing "Auld Lang Syne," pass the whiskey, and then disperse to go first-footing. (*See also* First-Foot Day, Jan. 1.)

31

New Year's Eve; also St. Sylvester's Day; full or partial official public holiday in various countries. In societies living by the Gregorian calendar, a time to welcome in the new year with parties, midnight toasts, and new year's resolutions. In the warmer countries, celebrations may include lavish fireworks or large outdoor parties.

31

Tinkunako Festival in La Rioja, Argentina. Honors the Christ child and St. Nicholas in memory of the 1593 peace between the Diaguita (Native South Americans) and the Spaniards mediated by St. Francis Solano. Includes a procession and historical reenactment.

MOVABLE DAYS IN DECEMBER
ANNIVERSARIES AND SPECIAL EVENTS DAYS

TREE DRESSING DAY IN THE U.K. AND WORLDWIDE; 1st Friday–Sunday in Dec. A time to honor one's favorite trees by decorating them festively and holding celebrations under their branches. A new festival derived from worldwide traditions; began in 1992 in Great Britain and is spreading to other countries.

OLD SAYBROOK TORCHLIGHT PARADE AND MUSTER IN OLD SAYBROOK, CONN.; night of the 2nd Saturday in Dec. A revival, since 1970, of the colonial custom of a Christmas torchlight parade led by the village militia, followed by communal carol singing outdoors.

CHESTER GREENWOOD DAY IN FARMING-TON, MAINE; 1st Saturday in Dec. Honors Chester Greenwood (Dec. 4, 1858–July 5, 1937), the inventor of earmuffs (1877) and the creator of a new industry in Farmington; residents hold a parade, flag-raising ceremony, and Polar Bear Dip.

MOVABLE DAYS BASED ON CHRISTMAS
Holy Days and Feast Days

ADVENT SUNDAY IN THE WESTERN CHRISTIAN CHURCHES; 4th Sunday before Dec. 25. The beginning of the liturgical year; Advent's 4 Sundays precede and prepare for Christmas; length can vary from 22 to 28 days. In the Eastern Orthodox Churches, the Christmas Fast begins on Nov. 15.

FEAST OF THE HOLY FAMILY; Sunday after Christmas. Commemorates the family of Jesus, Mary, and Joseph as the model of domestic society, holiness, and virtue.

SUNDAY OF ORTHODOXY IN ORTHODOX CHURCHES; 4th Sunday before Dec. 25. Celebrates the victory of Orthodoxy over the Iconoclasts and the restoration to churches of their beloved icons in 843.

Anniversaries and Special Events Days

PERCHTENLAUF IN ALTENMARKT AND OTHER RURAL PARTS OF AUSTRIA; 4th Sunday of Advent. A ritual held on the longest night of the year. St. Nicholaus and the Perchten (spirits of spring and fertility) go house to house caroling and acting out their victorious combat with the ogres of winter.

CHILDREN'S CHRISTMAS MARKETS IN GERMANY. Particularly notable are the *Christkindlmarkt* in Nuremberg (Friday before the 1st Sunday of Advent through Christmas Eve) and the *Weinachtsmarkt auf dem Romerberg* in Frankfurt am Main (4 weeks or slightly more, ending Dec. 22). Church bells ring, glockenspiels and trumpets play, Kris Kringle attends, the downtowns are merry, and toys for children are on sale everywhere.

Calendar Systems

Calendars are intellectual devices to understand time and to predict recurrent events.

The day, the year, and the lunar month have exercised enormous fascination over the human mind since at least the Upper Paleolithic period, and the movements of the heavens were surely a great and early spur to the development of abstract thought, notation, writing, record keeping, and scientific hypothesis.

The earliest calendars appear to have been lunar. The study of the changing behavior of the moon is ancient. The varying lengths of the different phases of the moon were known early on, and the lunar month was divided into bright and dark halves. The moon is a very demanding topic because its behavior is so complicated. The moon does not complete its phases in an exact number of days or even in a simple fraction such as 29½ days. Lunar months vary in length, and the moon's path in the heavens is not the same as the sun's.

The study of the moon long ago led to the archaic structure of the 27 or 28 *lunar mansions*, regions of the ecliptic in which the moon "dwells" for approximately a day. The lunar mansions still survive robustly, especially in traditional Hindu (Indian) and Chinese astronomy and astrology.

Solar calendars are easier by comparison, though still complicated. Determining the exact length of a tropical year (typically from one vernal equinox to the next) requires accurate instruments and well-kept records, but it is well within Neolithic capabilities. Unfortunately for the tidy-minded, there are not 360 days in a tropical year, which would

permit 12 months of 30 days. There is not even an exact number of days in a tropical year, so one must introduce occasional leap days. Additionally, the quarters of the year (from one equinox to the next solstice, and so on) are not of equal length. And coordinating the lunar months with the solar year is complicated.

Moreover, one's location affects the experience of time. In the tropics, there is very little variation in day length throughout the year and little differentiation among seasons. In the polar regions, on the other hand, the first dawn after winter darkness lasts for days and even weeks.

Different societies have devised different calendars in response to their needs and preoccupations.

Some calendars ignore season and moon altogether. The Wuku calendar of Bali is an example: a complex meshing of 10 temporal cogwheels in a cycle of 210 days.

Some calendars focus exclusively on the sun and the seasons and have little interest in the moon. The Coptic, Persian, Old Latvian, Julian, and Gregorian calendars are of this sort. The Coptic calendar is a lineal descendant of the civil calendar of pharaonic Egypt, with each month 30 days long and intercalary days at the end of the year. The Persian calendar is also rather old and is shaped so that each quarter (solstice or equinox) starts on the first day of a month. The Old Latvian calendar is similar, though its structure hints that it is of enormous age. The Julian calendar and its improved daughter, the Gregorian calendar, are obsessed with an accurate length for the tropical year. (At the heart is a focus on both the vernal equinox and the moon.)

The solar level of the Hindu calendar deliberately ignores precession, because this calendar is sidereal, not tropical: It is regulated by the sun's position among the stars rather than by the seasons. This is uncommon for an astronomically sophisticated Eurasian society.

Note, though, that various Native American societies seem to have had the same predilections. A number of them seem to have regulated their New Year's Day by the behavior of the Pleiades, noting when they were overhead at midnight and so forth. And one of the calendars of the Mayans and other Mexicans seems to have been based on the behavior of Venus.

Exclusively lunar calendars, with no reference to the sun, are rare; the Islamic calendar is the only one in common use.

Historically, by far the most common type of calendar has been one that combines lunar and solar periods: a lunisolar calendar. Fashioning such a calendar is a difficult problem, and each society approached it in different ways and with varying success.

A lunisolar calendar in its earliest forms would typically combine a "vague" solar year of 365 days with a lunar "year" of 12 lunar months and the insertion of a 13th intercalary month every 2 or 3 years, as needed. The lunar month would generally begin with the first visibility of the crescent new moon (the phasis), and the solar year would begin with the vernal equinox. The calendars of the various Greek city-states were of this sort. (Other quarters were also used to start the year, in Greece and elsewhere. For instance, the Chinese calendar is tied to the winter solstice, as were others.)

Over time, unique variations and refinements developed:

- Some calendars, such as the various Hindu calendars, begin the lunar month with the instant following the true new

and full moons and intercalate lunar months as required, depending on the predicted relative behavior of the sun and moon.

- Some calendars use tables to determine the official (the ideal) new and full moons; if the tables are accurate, the calendar will keep close step with the moon's behavior, but only over time and on average. The Southeast Asian Buddhist calendar and the Jewish calendar are examples.

- Some calendars—the Chinese, for example—begin the month with the day that includes the actual moment of the new moon, but the official full moon is always on the 15th day.

- Some calendars have regular though complex rules of thumb for intercalating the 13th lunar month. The Southeast Asian Buddhist calendar and the Tibetan calendar in its traditional form are of this sort.

Finally, note that different societies start the day and divide the month and year differently. Days may begin at sunrise or thereabouts (in the Hindu, Buddhist, and Tibetan calendars), at sunset or shortly after (Jewish, Islamic, Baha'i, Coptic), or at midnight (Gregorian, Chinese, and most Julian calendars). The feeling that the day begins with the evening before dawn is deeply buried in the Western subconscious; hence the many holidays that actually begin on the eve.

Months, either lunar or solar, may be divided into halves (in the lunar layers of the Chinese and the Hindu and derivative calendars) or weeks (the Gregorian calendar and its ancestors). The solar joints of the Chinese calendar are each ideally 15 days long. The 7-day week, with a celestial body associated with each day, is at least as old as the classical period in the West, and may actually be many centuries older and of more distant provenance.

The Wuku calendar of Bali uses 10 "weeks" of from 1 through 10 days, each running simultaneously. The Baha'i calendar is unique in its months, and it has no week.

The year is commonly divided into seasons and quarters. In the West, we have from antiquity spoken of the quarters of the year, though one could argue that the northern temperate zone has 6 seasons. And the subtropics have 3 seasons (monsoon, cool and dry, hot and dry).

The quarter days of the Western year occur at the periods of the solstices and equinoxes. Traditionally, the quarter days are on the Annunciation (Mar. 25), St. John's Day (June 24), Michaelmas (Sept. 29), and Christmas (Dec. 25). Note that each quarter day occurs a few days later than the average date of the corresponding equinox or solstice.

About midway between the quarters are the cross-quarter days. These are May Day (May 1), Lammas (Aug. 1), All Saints' Day (Nov. 1), and Candlemas (Feb. 2). Some traditions assign the quarter and cross-quarter days to slightly different dates.

All calendars are complicated and admirable instruments, born of foresight, prudence, and diligent concentration, using a science that prohibits direct experiment. The study of calendars engenders enormous respect for our ancestors.

The Gregorian Calendar and Its Antecedents

The Gregorian calendar is easy, accurate, elegant, single-minded, and imperfect. It is concerned only with the solar year and with the date of Easter (a lunisolar event). It irritates planners because New Year's Day is not always on a Sunday, and the months are of unequal lengths.

The Gregorian calendar is now effectively the world's official calendar. It is used in most countries (sometimes with other calendars operating in parallel) and in international affairs. All of this book's dates are given in terms of the Gregorian calendar.

The Gregorian calendar is a refinement of the still-living Julian calendar. The Christian liturgical calendars, both Gregorian and Julian, contain an additional lunar layer. (*See* the essay on the Christian liturgical calendar.)

GREGORIAN CALENDAR BASICS

All anyone has to know about our common Gregorian calendar is that a year has almost 365.25 days. Each common year has 365 days. The new year begins on Jan. 1, and the year's end (New Year's Eve) is Dec. 31. Every 4th year (one divisible by 4, such as 1980) is a leap year and has an extra day (Feb. 29, Leap Year's Day). However, centurial years such as 1800 and 1900 are not leap years unless divisible by 400 (as is 2000).

Days begin at midnight exactly and are 24 hours long. Each hour contains 60 minutes; each minute 60 seconds. These units are now standardized relative to regular atomic processes and thus are measured independently of celestial phenomena.

Months in our common year have varying lengths, in no deliberate pattern. Our folk mnemonic, taught to schoolchildren, is: "30 days have September, April, June, and November. All the rest have 31, except February, which has 28 and in leap years 29."

Years in our common era are labeled A.D. (*anno Domini,* in the year of the Lord); C.E. (of the common era) refers to the same era. The previous era is labeled B.C. (before Christ) or B.C.E. (before the common era). The first day of our common era was Jan. 1, A.D. 1. The last day of the previous era was Dec. 31, 1 B.C. There is no year A.D. 0 (which confuses computers).

The 20th century technically ends with New Year's Eve, Dec. 31, A.D. 2000, but in popular perception it ended on Dec. 31, 1999.

THE GREGORIAN CALENDAR'S PURPOSE

The Gregorian calendar's primary aim is to keep the length of the calendar year in close step with the actual average length of the solar year; hence its periodic leap year adjustment. (The Julian and other solar calendars have similar rules.) Though the new year's day falls on Jan. 1, the traditional pivot point of the Gregorian calendar year is the

221

date of the vernal equinox (around Mar. 21) and the derivative date of Easter.

Our modern Gregorian calendar was put into force in 1582 by Pope Gregory XIII. It replaced the Julian calendar instituted by Julius Caesar in 46 B.C. and thereafter amended, especially at the Council of Nicaea in 325. (This amended Christian calendar is commonly called the Julian calendar.)

THE JULIAN CALENDAR AND ITS DEFECTS

The original Julian calendar was a drastic reformation of the calendar of Republican Rome. The Republican calendar was inherently defective and in 46 B.C. was 90 days later than the seasons. Julius Caesar's calendar, constructed according to principles proposed by the Alexandrian astronomer Sosigenes, was almost entirely new: The only features retained were its purely solar character, its month names, the method of numbering days, and the placement of the leap day in February. This new calendar was essentially the same as what we call the Julian calendar. (The Julian calendar should not be confused with the Julian period.)

The defect in the Julian calendar was twofold: The lunar tables used by the church were slightly defective (in error by one day as of 1582), and the length assigned to the solar year was too great (producing a cumulative error of 10 days by 1582).

The Julian calendar year contains exactly 365.25 days; it has a leap year of 366 days every 4 years (in years divisible by 4: 1992, 1996, . . .). This is too long by approximately 3 days in 4 centuries; hence the Gregorian rule regarding leap years in centurial years. Gregorian leap years occur only in those centurial years divisible by 400: thus, 1600, 2000, . . .

In the period from 325 to 1582, the Julian year drifted seriously out of alignment with the tropical year and thus with the seasons. By the 16th century, the Julian calendar's formal vernal equinox of Mar. 21 was occurring about 10 days later than the true equinox. Easter and other movable feasts occurred too late, as did fixed feasts with a seasonal component, such as Christmas.

THE GREGORIAN CONVERSION OF 1582

Pope Gregory XIII decreed that Thursday, Oct. 4, 1582, would be followed by Friday, Oct. 15, 1582; that henceforth the new year would begin on Jan. 1; and that leap years would not occur in centurial years not divisible by 400. He also published a new official table of epacts for determining the formal date of each month's new and full moons.

ADOPTION OF THE GREGORIAN CALENDAR IN EUROPE

By the end of 1583, the new calendar had been adopted by the Catholic countries—France, Italy, Portugal, Austria-Hungary, and Spain; the Catholic parts of what is now Holland and Belgium; and all of the Catholic German states except Strassburg (1682).

Non-Catholic Europe lagged, but the Protestant German states, most of the Swiss cantons, and Scandinavia had gone Gregorian by 1702; the U.K. by 1752; Sweden and Finland by 1753; and Russia, Eastern Europe, and Greece by 1920. For liturgical purposes, almost all of the Eastern Orthodox churches (and most of the other Eastern churches) continue to use the Julian calendar for Easter-based movable feast days. Some use the Gregorian calendar for fixed feast days.

The U.K. and its colonies (including the future U.S.) did not adopt the Gregorian calendar until 1752. In that year, New Year's Day, hitherto on Mar. 25, occurred on Jan. 1, and Wednesday, Sept. 2, was followed by Thursday, Sept. 14. Most of America's Revolutionary War personalities were born under one calendar and died under another.

For scholars seeking exact dates of events, this difference in countries' calendars is a nuisance, and the period between 1582 and 1752 is especially troublesome because Great Britain and its territories had not yet converted. The helpful English convention is to use the abbreviations O.S. and N.S. (Old Style and New Style) to indicate dates in the Julian and Gregorian calendars, respectively.

The Christian Liturgical Calendar

The Christian liturgical year (the yearly round of communal religious rituals) reflects the mysteries of the faith and commemorates the principal saints. The Blessed Virgin Mary, Mother of God, is especially revered and has many feast days.

Easter is the central celebration of the Christian liturgical year. It is the oldest and most important Christian feast, celebrating the Resurrection of Jesus Christ. The date of Easter determines the dates of all movable feasts except those of Advent. Easter occurs on the Sunday after the first formal new moon on or after the official spring equinox on Mar. 21; it can occur between the Gregorian calendar dates of Mar. 22 and Apr. 25, inclusive, for Western churches and between the Gregorian calendar dates of Apr. 4 and May 8, inclusive, for Eastern churches that use the Julian calendar for the dating of Easter. See the table on page 226 for the dates of Easter and the start of Lent in both calendars.

For the sake of calendrical uniformity, the Council of Nicaea not only agreed on the formula for Easter's date, but also based it on the Julian calendar, adopted a formal table of new moons (the table of epacts), and assigned the formal date of the vernal equinox to Mar. 21. The result was that any priest, using the tables at the front of his church missal, could easily calculate the date of Easter and other movable feasts for any year and be confident that his congregation was in step with the rest of Christendom. Astronomical exactness is less important than uniformity and ease of calculation.

In sum, the Christian liturgical calendar is dominated by the central event in Christianity and is regulated in part by the movement of the sun and the moon. It is an Easter-based lunisolar calendar.

EASTER-BASED HOLY DAYS

Ash Wednesday in the West and Lent Monday in the Orthodox churches are movable feasts that usher in Lent, a period of penance and fasting in preparation for Easter. Lent Monday is 2 days earlier than Ash Wednesday in years when Gregorian and Julian Easter are on the same day. Ash Wednesday derives its name from the ashes used to mark the sign of the cross on the worshipper's forehead.

ASH WEDNESDAY (46 days before Easter) can fall between Feb. 4 and Mar. 10, inclusive; Lent Monday (48 days before Easter) can occur between the Gregorian calendar dates of Feb. 15 and Mar. 21, inclusive. In Latin countries, Ash Wednesday is preceded by Carnival, with the climax usually on Shrove Tuesday, the day before Ash Wednesday. In many countries, Carnival is a time of uninhibited exuberance.

HOLY WEEK, the week before Easter, begins on Palm (or Passion) Sunday and ends on Holy Saturday. It commemorates the last days of Christ's life.

PALM SUNDAY, OR PASSION SUNDAY, the Sunday before Easter, marks the start of Holy Week by recalling Christ's triumphal entry into Jerusalem and his subsequent Passion. It is called Palm Sunday by the Orthodox. In the Catholic liturgy, Palm Sunday was formerly the Sunday before Easter, and Passion Sunday was the second Sunday before Easter; both feasts are now combined as Passion Sunday. Blessed palm fronds are distributed in the West; Orthodox and Catholic churches in Eastern Europe use other greenery.

HOLY THURSDAY, the Thursday before Easter, commemorates the Last Supper and the establishment of the sacrament of the Eucharist. It is called Maundy Thursday in England.

GOOD FRIDAY, the Friday before Easter, commemorates the Passion and death of Jesus Christ. A day of fasting, abstinence, and penance, climaxing from noon to 3:00 P.M., the traditional period of Christ's Crucifixion.

HOLY SATURDAY, the day before Easter, commemorates the time Jesus' body lay in the tomb. Mass is not said.

ASCENSION THURSDAY, 40 days from Easter, commemorates the ascension of Jesus Christ into heaven.

PENTECOST, the Sunday 50 days from Easter, celebrates the descent of the Holy Spirit and is regarded as the birthday of the Christian church. Called Whitsun in England, it and the next day, Whitmonday, are favored times for festivities throughout the Christian world. Pentecost for the Western churches can occur between May 10 and June 13, inclusive, and between the Gregorian calendar dates of May 23 and June 26, inclusive, for Eastern churches using the Julian calendar.

THE FEAST OF THE MOST HOLY TRINITY, or Trinity Sunday, is observed in Western churches on the Sunday after Pentecost. It commemorates the mystery of the three persons of the one God. The Orthodox churches honor the Trinity on Pentecost Sunday.

CORPUS CHRISTI (the Feast of the Most Holy Body of Christ) is observed in the Catholic Church on the Thursday after Trinity Sunday, or in the U.S., on the Sunday after Trinity Sunday. It commemorates the institution of the sacrament of the Eucharist. The liturgy was composed by St. Thomas Aquinas.

CLASSES OF SAINTS AND FEAST DAYS

In the Western Christian churches, particularly the Catholic Church, there are three gradations of sainthood. A person can be canonized as venerable (with the abbreviation Ven. following the name), blessed (with the abbreviation Bl. following the name), or a full saint (with the abbreviation St. preceding the name). All are, strictly speaking, saints and are listed on liturgical calendars.

The Roman Catholic Church recognizes gradations of feast days: solemnities (the most important), feasts, memorials, and optional memorials. Some feast days are holy days of obligation, days when Catholics must attend Mass. All Sundays are holy days of obligation, particularly Easter Sunday, as are the feasts of Christmas (Dec. 25), the Solemnity of Mary (Jan. 1), the Ascension of the Lord (a movable feast), the Assumption of Mary (Aug. 15), All Saints' Day (Nov. 1), and the Immaculate Conception of Mary (Dec. 8).

THE GREGORIAN REFORM

The inaccuracies in the Julian calendar and in the table of epacts led to the introduction of a reformed calendar by Pope Gregory XIII in 1582. The Gregorian calendar became effective immediately throughout the Roman Catholic Church. It was adopted swiftly in all Roman Catholic countries, but it was not accepted immediately by Protestant churches and countries in the West. Not until this century was it adopted by the Eastern churches, and then only partially.

In the Orthodox and other Eastern churches that are not "in communion" with Rome, adoption of the Gregorian calendar has been partial. Almost all continue to compute the date of Easter and Easter-based movable feasts using the Julian calendar and the old table of epacts. But, following a conference at Constantinople in 1923, some adopted the Gregorian calendar for the dates of fixed feast days.

The Gregorian calendar was adopted for fixed feasts in the Orthodox churches of Constantinople, Greece, Cyprus, Finland, Rumania (1924); Georgia (1927); Alexandria (1928); Antioch (1941); Bulgaria (1960s); Estonia (1966); Crete; and possibly some others.

The Finnish Orthodox Church and all of the Armenian churches use the Gregorian calendar exclusively. The rest of the Orthodox, a majority, and the other Eastern churches generally, still use the Julian reckoning exclusively. Thus, Orthodox churches using the Julian calendar exclusively will during the period 1900–2099 celebrate all identically fixed feasts 13 days later than do Orthodox churches using the Gregorian calendar for fixed feast days.

RECENT REFORM OF THE ROMAN CATHOLIC LITURGY

Following the Second Vatican Council of 1962, the Roman Catholic liturgy was reformed (fully effective in 1972). The dates of the principal movable feasts remained unchanged, but many fixed feast days were assigned new dates. Among other changes, the reformers attempted to eliminate saints who were not supported by firm historical proof or at least many centuries of universal acceptance. Moreover, feast days were transferred to

a saint's death day when possible because that is considered the most important day of his or her life. However, tradition stubbornly subverts hierarchy, and many saints are still locally honored on their traditional feast days.

ORTHODOX AND OTHER EASTERN FEAST DAYS

There are significant but secondary differences between the Roman Catholic and Orthodox liturgical years. Moreover, many Orthodox saints' feast days are on different dates than in the Roman rite. To further complicate matters, some Orthodox churches have adopted the Gregorian calendar for dating fixed feasts. Most Orthodox churches have canonized few saints since the Great Schism of 1054, and they do not recognize most Roman Catholic saints canonized since that time. On the other hand, the Eastern churches have many more feast days for Old Testament persons than does the Roman Catholic Church, which honors only the Holy Maccabees and Shadrach, Meshach, and Abednego.

DATES OF EASTER IN THE WESTERN AND EASTERN CHURCHES A.D. 1997–2010

| YEAR | GREGORIAN (N.S.) | | JULIAN (O.S.) | |
	ASH WEDNESDAY	EASTER	LENT MONDAY	EASTER
1997	Feb. 12	Mar. 30	Mar. 10	Apr. 27
1998	Feb. 25	Apr. 12	Mar. 2	Apr. 19
1999	Feb. 17	Apr. 4	Feb. 22	Apr. 11
2000	Mar. 8	Apr. 23	Mar. 13	Apr. 30
2001	Feb. 28	Apr. 15	Feb. 26	Apr. 15
2002	Feb. 13	Mar. 31	Mar. 18	May 5
2003	Mar. 5	Apr. 20	Mar. 10	Apr. 27
2004	Feb. 25	Apr. 11	Feb. 23	Apr. 11
2005	Feb. 9	Mar. 27	Mar. 14	May 1
2006	Mar. 1	Apr. 16	Mar. 6	Apr. 23
2007	Feb. 21	Apr. 8	Feb. 19	Apr. 8
2008	Feb. 6	Mar. 23	Mar. 10	Apr. 27
2009	Feb. 25	Apr. 12	Mar. 2	Apr. 19
2010	Feb. 17	Apr. 4	Feb. 15	Apr. 4

The Jewish Calendar

The Jewish calendar is lunisolar.

The Jewish calendar is accurate: Over a 19-year period (the Metonic cycle), its average year length is in close accord with the length of the mean solar (tropical) year.

The Jewish calendar is straightforward in principle, but its religious adjustments make it complicated in practice. Fortunately, dependable tables for the dates of all holy days are published several decades in advance.

Months are lunar and ideally begin with the mean (not true) new moon. Month lengths are fixed and are not modified by astronomical reality. The months are of either 29 or 30 days (*see* the table of months below). A 13th month, Veadar (Adar II), is intercalated in 7 years out of 19 (in years 3,

6, 8, 11, 14, 17, and 19). Year 1 of the current 19-year period began in 1997. If Veadar is inserted, holy days normally observed during Adar are observed during Veadar. Thus, Purim is always approximately 30 days before the start of Passover.

Various religious rules can affect the occurrence of New Year's Day (Rosh Hashanah), and thus the start of subsequent months, as well as the actual days of particular events. Many, for instance, cannot be observed on the Sabbath; the adjustment is at most 2 days.

The year lengths are 354 days in common years, alternately 353 or 355 days; 384 days in intercalary years, alternately 383 or 385 days.

The religious new year begins in the autumn, with Rosh Hashanah on Tishri 1. In

---

MONTHS IN THE JEWISH CALENDAR

MONTH	NUMBER OF DAYS	START	COMMENT
Tishri	30	Sept. or Oct.	
Heshvan	29 (or 30)	Oct. or Nov.	
Kislev	30 (or 29)	Nov. or Dec.	
Tebet	29	Dec. or Jan.	
Shebet	30	Jan. or Feb.	
Adar	29 (30 in leap years)	Feb. or Mar.	30 days only if followed by Veadar (Adar II), the extra month
Veadar (Adar II)	(29 if used)	Mar.	
Nisan	30	Mar. or Apr.	
Iyar	29	Apr. or May	
Sivan	30	May or June	
Tammuz	29	June or July	
Ab	30	July or Aug.	Ab or Av
Elul	29	Aug. or Sept.	
TOTAL	354 in common years, normal; can be 353, 355. 384 in leap years, normal; can be 383, 385		

---

post-exilic times, the civil new year was transferred to the spring and began on Nisan 1. In the 20th century, Tishri 1 could occur between Sept. 6 and Oct. 5, inclusive. Nisan 1 could occur between Mar. 13 and Apr. 11, inclusive.

The Jewish calendar's Day One corresponds to Oct. 7, 3761 B.C. Rosh Hashanah (New Year's Day) on Sept. 30, A.D. 2000, begins Jewish year A.M. 5761.

The day begins at sunset. By convention, Western calendars assign Jewish (also Islamic, Baha'i, and Coptic/Ethiopian) holy days to the day in which the holy day's daylight occurs. But the holy day actually begins with the preceding sunset. Thus, Yom Kippur is listed on calendars as having occurred on Oct. 11, 1997, but it began at sunset on Oct. 10 and ended at sunset on Oct. 11.

The Sabbath, Saturday, is the day of rest (officially so in Israel). The week has 7 days, ending with the Sabbath.

Israel varies slightly from American Jewry in its dating and observance of holy days.

HOLIDAYS AND HOLY DAYS IN THE JEWISH CALENDAR

TISHRI

CA. 1–2
Rosh Hashanah; official public holiday in Israel. The new year of the Jewish people, which ushers in the Day of Judgment for all mankind; features special synagogue services and blowing of the ram's horn, the *shofar;* the start of 10 days of repentence that end with Yom Kippur.

3
Tzom Gedalya (Fast of Gedalya); official public holiday in Israel. Commemorates the assassination of Gedalya Ben Achikam and the true start of the Babylonian exile of the Jewish people in the 6th century B.C. Fast begins at morning light. The day is moved, if necessary, to avoid the Sabbath.

10
Yom Kippur (Day of Atonement); official public holiday in Israel. The holiest and most solemn day of the Jewish year; a day of fasting, penitence, and prayer. Fasting begins before sunset, followed by daylong synagogue services and special prayers.

CA. 15–21
Sukkot; official public holidays in Israel; the Feast of Tabernacles, or the Feast of Booths. Originally a celebration of the harvesting of summer crops, it has a historical relationship to the Flight from Captivity in Egypt, when the Israelites lived in *sukkots,* or booths. During this joyous festival, all meals must be eaten in a special temporary hut, a *sukkat;* culminates with special services on Tishri 21, Hoshana Rabba.

CA. 22
Shmini Atzeret and Simchat Torah (Rejoicing in the Law); Tishri 22 and 23, respectively; in Israel, Simchat Torah is observed on Tishri 22, an official public holiday. A special 2-day celebration closing the high holy days. The cycle of synagogue biblical readings is completed and then begun again during Simchat Torah.

KISLEV

CA. 25
Chanukah (Hanukkah); Kislev 25–Tevet 3 (through Tevet 4 in Israel), 8 days total (9 in Israel); official public holidays in Israel. The Jewish Feast of Lights, also called the Feast of Dedication, commemorates the Maccabean victories for independence from the Syrians (2nd century B.C.) and the rededication of the Second Temple in Jerusalem; focuses on the relighting of the Temple Eternal Light. Each night, additional candles of the 9-branched menorah are relit.

TEBET

10
Asarah B'Tevet (Fast of the 10th of Tevet); official public holiday in Israel. Commemorates the beginning of the Babylonian seige of Jerusalem (6th century B.C.). Fast begins at morning light.

SHEBAT

15
Tu B'Shvat (New Year of Trees); official public holiday in Israel. The Arbor Day of the Jewish people; celebrates new fruits and the Land of Israel.

ADAR
Note that in years in which Veadar (Adar II) is inserted, Adar's holy days are observed during Veadar; thus, Purim is always approximately 30 days before the start of Passover.

13

Ta'anis Esther (Fast of Esther); official public holiday in Israel. Commemorates the fast endured by Queen Esther (6th century B.C.) in response to the demands of Ahasuerus for the annihilation of her people in ancient Persia and the subsequent victory of the Jewish people over their enemies. The story is the origin of the feast of Purim. Fast begins at morning light. Observed on Adar 11 when Adar 13 is a Sabbath.

CA. 14

Purim (Feast of Lots); Adar 14–15 are official public holidays in Israel. Celebrates the deliverance of the Jews in Persia from the machinations of Haman. Celebrated with feasts, the sending of gifts, charity, and readings from the Book of Esther. In Jerusalem and other walled cities, the next day, Adar 15 (Shusan Purim), is also observed.

NISAN

CA. 15

Pesach (Passover); Nisan 15–21; official public holidays in Israel. The Feast of Unleavened Bread, instituted in commemoration of the Exodus of the Jews from ancient Egypt. A special home ritual (a *seder*) is conducted on the 1st 2 evenings.

22

Maimona; observed by Jews in North Africa on the day after Passover ends. Commemorates the death anniversary of Maimonides; news of his death reached North African Jews during Passover, so the mourning ceremony was held on the 1st free day.

27

Yom Hashoa (Holocaust Remembrance Day); official public holiday in Israel. Anniversary of the 1945 liberation of the Buchenwald concentration camp on Nisan 27, Jewish year 5705; a memorial to the 6 million Jews slaughtered by the Nazis between 1933 and 1945; observed by many non-Jews around the world. The day is moved, if necessary, to avoid the Sabbath.

IYAR

4

Yom ha-Zikkaron (Memorial Day, or Day of Remembrance) in Israel; official public holiday. Commemorates those who died fighting to establish and preserve the state of Israel. Followed by Independence Day.

5

Yom ha-Atzma'ut (Independence Day) in Israel; official public holiday. Celebrates May 14, 1948, when Israel was declared an independent state.

18

Lag B'Omer, the 33rd of the 49 days between Passover and Shavuot; official public holiday in Israel. The 49 days are a mourning period for the deaths by plague among the student body of Akiva, a rabbinic sage in the 2nd century A.D.; Lag B'Omer is a pause in this period, and the only day in the period when weddings are permitted. A semiholiday celebrated in Israel with bonfires and dancing; Jewish communities in other nations plan programs for Lag B'Omer to express love of the Holy Land.

28

Jerusalem Day, or Jerusalem Liberation Day; official public holiday in Israel. Commemorates Israel's capture and the reunification of Jerusalem during the Six-Day War on June 7, 1967. A recent addition to the Jewish calendar. The mourning period between Passover and Shavuot is suspended on this day.

SIVAN

6–7

Shavuot (Feast of Weeks); official public holiday in Israel. Marks the completion of 7 weeks from the 2nd day of Passover; celebrates the presentation of the Ten Commandments to Israel on Mount Sinai and the offering of the first fruits of the harvest at the Temple in Jerusalem.

TAMMUZ

17

Shiva Asar B'Tammuz; official public holiday in Israel. Remembers the breaching of Jerusalem's walls by the besieging Romans (A.D. 70); the start of a 3-week period of mourning for the Temple (see Tisha B'Av) during which weddings and celebrations are forbidden. The day is moved, if necessary, to avoid the Sabbath.

AV

9

Tisha B'Av (Fast of the 9th of Av); official public holiday in Israel. A day of fasting and mourning for the destruction of the First and Second Temples in Jerusalem and other Jewish tragedies; the climax of a 3-week mourning period (see Shiva Asar B'Tammuz). The day is moved, if necessary, to avoid the Sabbath.

JEWISH HOLY DAYS IN THE U.S., A.D. 1997–2010

HOLY DAY	1997 (5757–58)	1998 (5758–59)	1999 (5759–60)	2000 (5760–61)	2001 (5761–62)	2002 (5762–63)	2003 (5763–64)
Tu B'Shvat	Thurs. Jan. 23	Wed. Feb. 11	Mon. Feb. 1	Sat. Jan. 22	Thurs. Feb. 8	Mon. Jan. 28	Sat. Jan. 18
Ta'anis Esther	Thurs. Mar. 20	Wed. Mar. 11	Mon. Mar. 1	Mon. Mar. 20	Thurs. Mar. 8	Mon. Feb. 25	Mon. Mar. 17
Purim	Sun. Mar. 23	Thurs. Mar. 12	Tues. Mar. 2	Tues. Mar. 21	Fri. Mar. 9	Tues. Feb. 26	Tues. Mar. 18
Pesach (Passover)	Tues.–Tues. Apr. 22–29	Sat.–Sat. Apr. 11–18	Thurs.–Thurs. Apr. 1–8	Thurs.–Thurs. Apr. 20–27	Sun.–Sun. Apr. 8–15	Thurs.–Thurs. Mar. 28–Apr. 4	Thurs.–Thurs. Apr. 17–24
Lag B'Omer	Sun. May 25	Thurs. May 14	Tues. May 4	Tues. May 23	Fri. May 11	Tues. Apr. 30	Tues. May 20
Shavuot	Wed.–Thurs. June 11–12	Sun.–Mon. May 31–June 1	Fri.–Sat. May 21–22	Fri.–Sat. June 9–10	Mon.–Tues. May 28–29	Fri.–Sat. May 17–18	Fri.–Sat. June 6–7
Shiva Asar B'Tammuz	Tues. July 22	Sun. July 12	Thurs. July 1	Thurs. July 20	Sun. July 8	Thurs. June 27	Thurs. July 17
Tisha B'Av	Tues. Aug. 12	Sun. Aug. 2	Thurs. July 22	Thurs. Aug. 10	Sun. July 29	Thurs. July 18	Thurs. Aug. 7
Rosh Hashanah (Jewish New Year)	Thurs.–Fri. Oct. 2–3	Mon.–Tues. Sept. 21–22	Sat.–Sun. Sept. 11–12	Sat.–Sun. Sept. 30–Oct. 1	Tues.–Wed. Sept. 18–19	Sat.–Sun. Sept. 7–8	Sat.–Sun. Sept. 27–28
Tzom Gedalya	Sun. Oct. 5	Wed. Sept. 23	Mon. Sept. 13	Mon. Oct. 2	Thurs. Sept. 20	Mon. Sept. 9	Mon. Sept. 29
Yom Kippur	Sat. Oct. 11	Wed. Sept. 30	Mon. Sept. 20	Mon. Oct. 9	Thurs. Sept. 27	Mon. Sept. 16	Mon. Oct. 6
Sukkot–Hoshana Rabba	Thurs.–Wed. Oct. 16–22	Mon.–Sun. Oct. 5–11	Sat.–Fri. Sept. 25–Oct. 1	Sat.–Fri. Oct. 14–20	Tues.–Mon. Oct. 2–8	Sat.–Fri. Sept. 21–27	Sat.–Fri. Oct. 11–17
Shmini Atzeret / Simchat Torah	Thurs.–Fri. Oct. 23–24	Mon.–Tues. Oct. 12–13	Sat.–Sun. Oct. 2–3	Sat.–Sun. Oct. 21–22	Tues.–Wed. Oct. 9–10	Sat.–Sun. Sept. 28–29	Sat.–Sun. Oct. 18–19
Chanukah	Wed.–Wed. Dec. 24–31	Mon.–Mon. Dec. 14–21	Sat.–Sat. Dec. 4–11	Fri.–Fri. Dec. 22–29	Mon.–Mon. Dec. 10–17	Sat.–Sat. Nov. 30–Dec. 7	Sat.–Sat. Dec. 20–27
Asarah B'Tevet	Thurs. Jan. 8, 1998	Tues. Dec. 29	Sun. Dec. 19	Fri. Jan. 5, 2001	Tues. Dec. 25	Sun. Jan. 15, 2003	Sun. Jan. 4, 2004

HOLY DAY	2004 (5764–65)	2005 (5765–66)	2006 (5766–68)	2007 (5767–68)	2008 (5768–69)	2009 (5769–70)	2010 (5770–71)
Tu B'Shvat	Sat. Feb. 7	Tues. Jan. 25	Mon. Feb. 13	Sat. Feb. 3	Tues. Jan. 22	Mon. Feb. 9	Sat Jan. 30
Ta'anis Esther	Thurs. Mar. 4	Thurs. Mar. 24	Mon. Mar. 13	Sat. Mar. 3	Thurs. Mar. 20	Mon. Mar. 9	Sat. Feb. 27
Purim	Sun. Mar. 7	Fri. Mar. 25	Tues. Mar. 14	Sun. Mar. 4	Fri. Mar. 21	Tues. Mar. 10	Sun. Feb. 28
Pesach (Passover)	Tues.–Tues. Apr. 6–13	Sun.–Sun. Apr. 24–May 1	Thurs.–Thurs. Apr. 13–20	Tues.–Tues. Apr. 3–10	Sun.–Sun. Apr. 20–27	Thurs.–Thurs. Apr. 9–16	Tues.–Tues. Mar. 30–Apr. 6
Lag B'Omer	Sun. May 9	Fri. May 27	Tues. May 16	Sun. May 6	Fri. May 23	Tues. May 12	Sun. May 2
Shavuot	Wed.–Thurs. May 26–27	Mon.–Tues. June 13–14	Fri.–Sat. June 2–3	Wed.–Thurs. May 23–24	Mon.–Tues. June 9–10	Fri.–Sat. May 29–30	Wed.–Thurs. May 19–20
Shiva Asar B'Tammuz	Tues. July 6	Sun. July 24	Thurs. July 13	Tues. July 23	Sun. July 20	Thurs. July 9	Tues. June 29
Tisha B'Av	Tues. July 27	Sun. Aug. 14	Thurs. Aug. 3	Tues. July 24	Sun. Aug. 10	Thurs. July 30	Tues. July 20
Rosh Hashanah (Jewish New Year)	Thurs.–Fri. Sept. 16–17	Tues.–Wed. Oct. 4–5	Sat.–Sun. Sept. 23–24	Thurs.–Fri. Sept. 13–14	Tues.–Wed. Sept. 30–Oct. 1	Sat.–Sun. Sept. 19–20	Thurs.–Fri. Sept. 9–10
Tzom Gedalya	Sun. Sept. 19	Thurs. Oct. 6	Mon. Sept. 25	Sun. Sept. 16	Thurs. Oct. 2	Mon. Sept. 21	Sun Sept. 12
Yom Kippur	Sat. Sept. 25	Thurs. Oct. 13	Mon. Oct. 2	Sat. Sept. 22	Thurs. Oct. 9	Mon. Sept. 28	Sat. Sept. 18
Sukkot–Hoshana Rabba	Thurs.–Wed. Sept. 30–Oct. 6	Tues.–Mon. Oct. 18–24	Sat.–Fri. Oct. 7–13	Thurs.–Wed. Sept. 27–Oct. 3	Tues.–Mon. Oct. 14–20	Sat.–Fri. Oct. 3–9	Thurs.–Wed. Sept. 23–29
Shmini Atzeret Simchat Torah	Thurs.–Fri. Oct. 7–8	Tues.–Wed. Oct. 25–26	Sat.–Sun. Oct. 14–15	Thurs.–Fri. Oct. 4–5	Tues.–Wed. Oct. 21–22	Sat.–Sun. Oct. 10–11	Thurs.–Fri. Sept. 30–Oct. 1
Chanukah	Wed.–Wed. Dec. 8–15	Mon.–Mon. Dec. 26–Jan. 2, 2006	Sat.–Sat. Dec. 16–23	Wed.–Wed. Dec. 5–12	Mon.–Mon. Dec. 22–29	Sat.–Sat. Dec. 12–19	Thurs.–Thurs. Dec. 2–9
Asarah B'Tevet	Wed. Dec. 22	Tues. Jan. 10, 2006	Sun. Dec. 31	Wed. Dec. 19	Tues. Jan. 6, 2009	Sun. Dec. 27	Fri. Dec. 17

231

The Islamic Calendar

The Islamic calendar in its present form was promulgated by Caliph Umar in the year A.H. 17. The Islamic calendar is strictly lunar; it ignores the seasons and stars.

The Islamic year contains 12 lunar months, as postulated in the Koran, and each month begins shortly after the new moon. Relative to the Gregorian calendar, the start of the Islamic year moves backwards approximately 10 or 11 days each year. For example, Islamic New Year's Day fell on or about Apr. 28, A.D. 1998, and Apr. 17, A.D. 1999.

The Islamic day begins after sunset at dusk, when a white thread can no longer be distinguished from a black thread. Daylight fasting (for example, during the month of Ramadan) begins just before sunrise, when those threads become distinguishable.

The Islamic week has 7 days and begins with Friday (actually, with the dusk of Thursday); Friday is the day of rest in Muslim countries. It is called al-Jumu'ah. *Jumu'ah* means "congregational prayers"; these are usually held on Friday afternoon. Among observant Muslims, Thursday's daylight is a time of fasting.

The Islamic month begins shortly after the new moon. It begins when the first observable crescent of the new moon is already visible at the start of the day (shortly after sunset). Under ideal conditions, the moon can first become visible approximately 15 hours after local true new moon, following a separation of at least 9.5°. The dusk that contains this visibility of the crescent new moon begins the 1st day of the month. The 1st day of the month can begin on either the 1st or 2nd day after the day of the true new moon. All subsequent days in the Islamic month are reckoned from this 1st day of the month. According to most Islamic jurists, no month can have more than 30 days.

The Islamic year begins with the 1st day of the month Muharram.

The Islamic era begins with the Hegira (Migration) of Muhammad from Mecca to Medina; he departed Mecca at sunset in the evening preceding July 16, A.D. 622. This moment is the starting point of the Islamic calendar, Muharram 1, A.H. 1 (A.H. stands for anno Hegirae).

By universal convention, an Islamic day is assigned to the Gregorian day during which its daylight occurs (as with dates in the Jewish calendar). Thus, an Islamic holy day beginning with the dusk of May 3 will be assigned to May 4 and will be so listed on most calendars.

Different countries and congregations use different ways of determining the start of a month. Some use formal tables; some use astronomical tables and rules that vary with the country or congregation; some rely on direct observation by a national religious official; and some rely on the official pronouncement by Mecca, which uses direct observation combined with astronomical prediction. There has been some progress toward a set of common rules for the start of each month, and even toward a global calendar.

FORMAL LENGTHS OF THE ISLAMIC MONTHS

MONTH	DAYS
Muharram	30
Safar	29
Rabi al-Awal	30
Rabi al-Akhir	29
Jumuda al-Aula	30
Jumadha al-Ukhra	29
Rajab	30
Shaban	29
Ramadan	30
Shawwal	29
Dhu al-Qada	30
Dhu al-Hijja	29 (or 30)
TOTAL: 354 or 355 days.	

ISLAMIC HOLY DAYS

The principal Islamic holy days are:

- New Year's Day (L.1 1: lunar month 1, 1st day)
- Ashura (L.1 10)
- Muhammad's Birthday (L.3 12; *and see* L.3 17)
- Muhammad's Night Journey to Heaven (L.7 27)
- The entire month of the Ramadan fast (all of L.9), including the Night of Power (L.9 27 or on other days)
- Id al-Fitr, the feast that marks the end of the Ramadan fast (L.10 1)
- The Id al-Adha, the feast of Abraham's sacrifice (L.12 10)

SUNNI AND SHIA

Islam is divided into two doctrinal branches, Sunni and Shia. The schism developed shortly after Muhammad's death, and the formal rupture dates from Oct. 10, A.D. 680, with the death in battle of Husayn, grandson of Muhammad (*see* Ashura, L.1 10, in the following section). The Sunni branch considers itself the orthodox part of Islam, and is pre-dominant in the Arab countries (including Iraq), the Muslim countries of the Mediter-ranean basin, and among Muslims in Africa. The Shia branch was especially appealing in the Persian areas of the Muslim world. It is predominant or very strong in Iran, Afghan-istan, Pakistan, India, Bangladesh, and farther east. Shia Islam has branched into many sects, including the Ismailis (headed by the Aga Khan). Note that Shia Muslims celebrate Muhammad's birth 5 days later than do the Sunnis. (*See* L.3 12 and 17, following).

ISLAMIC HOLIDAYS (RELIGIOUS AND NATIONAL)

Convention: L.1 10 denotes 1st lunar month (Muharram), 10th day.

MUHARRAM (L.1)

1

Muharram is the first month in the Islamic calen-dar. The first 10 days celebrate the beginning of the Muslim new year. L.1 1 is an official public holiday in a number of Islamic countries.

10

Ashura, an official public holiday in countries with a large Shia population. For Sunni Muslims, this day commemorates Noah's leaving the ark on Mount Ararat, but for Shia Muslims, it marks the murder of Muhammad's grandson Husayn by the troops of the Caliph Yazid at the Battle of Karbala, on the Euphrates (Oct 10, A.D. 680). The schism between Sunni and Shia Muslims dates from this event. Ashura is a time of intense mourning, often preceded by many days of prayer and fasting. Pro-cessions on the day itself are often marked by self-mortifications. (*See also* Chhelum, L.2 20.)

SAFAR (L.2)

CA. 14

Death anniversary of Shah Abdul Latif Kazmi, also called Bari Shah Latif or Bari Imam (1689–1752), near Islamabad, Pakistan. Indian Sufi saint, poet, musician, and unofficial patron saint of Islam-abad. Still revered, particularly by the poor and oppressed. Pilgrims celebrate joyously and wel-come non-Muslims.

CA. 18

Death anniversary of Ali Makdum al Hujwiri at Lahore, Pakistan, in 1072 (also called Data Ganj Baksh ["He Who Gives Generously"]). Scholar and author of the oldest Persian text on Sufism, the *Kashf al-mahjub*. One of Pakistan's most popular saints; his tomb is thronged with joyous pilgrims.

20

Chhelum (40th Day of the Martyrdom of Imam Husayn) among Shia Muslims in Iran and Pakistan; an official public holiday in Iran. Another time of mourning for Husayn, but less intense than Ashura (L.1 10). Traditionally, the 40th day after a person's death is a day of mourning.

28

Death Anniversaries of the Prophet Muhammad and of the Second Imam; both observed among Shia Muslims; an official public holiday in Iran.

RABI AL-AWAL (L.3)

1

National Day in Maldives; official public holiday celebrating the liberation of the islands from Portuguese domination.

12

Mulid al-Nabi (the Prophet Muhammad's Birthday); an official public holiday in at least 40 countries. Celebrates the birthday of Abu al-Qasim Muhammad ibn 'Abd Allah ibn 'Abd-al-Muttalib ibn Hashim (ca. 570–June 8, 632). Arab founder and prophet of the religion of Islam, and transmitter of the Koran. Considered by Muslims the last and greatest of the prophets and the intercessor with God for Muslims on Judgment Day. His birthday is especially popular among Sunni Muslims. In India and Pakistan, there are large public processions.

12

Moussem (Death Anniversary) of Moulay Idris, at Zerhoun, Morocco, marked by a 7-day pilgrimage of reverence. Moulay Idris, Morocco's most revered saint, immigrated from Damascus in the late-8th century, following the great Muslim civil war that broke Islam into the Sunni and Shia sects; founded the holy city of Moulay Idris (Zerhoun) in the Middle Atlas. Non-Muslims are unwelcome.

17

Mulid al-Nabi (the Prophet Muhammad's Birthday) among Shia Muslims; an official public holiday in Iran. Shia Muslims observe this event 5 days later than do the Sunni. The week encompassing the two dates (beginning L.3 12) is the Week of Unification in Iran, devoted to reconciliation between the two sects.

19

Muhammad's Naming. Commonly called Maoloud; celebrated among Muslims of West Africa. Official public holiday in Mali. Infants in Mali and The Gambia are named 7 days after birth, with a special ceremony analogous to a christening in the West. The delay was originally due to high infant mortality.

RAJAB (L.7)

13

Ma'ab Ath (Birthday of Ali) among Shia Muslims; an official public holiday in Iran. Ali ibn Abi Talib (600–661) was the cousin and son-in-law of the Prophet Muhammad; revered by Shia Muslims as the first imam and the true successor to Muhammad; regarded by Sunni Muslims as the fourth caliph (ruled 656–661), following the murder of the caliph Uthman.

27

Lailat al-Miraj (Muhammad's Ascent to Heaven). Commemorates the Night Journey (or the Night Flight) by Muhammad to heaven, where he received instructions from Allah on the required number of times for daily prayer. Observed in the evening.

SHABAN (L.8)

The mawlid season among Egyptian Muslims occurs all during the Islamic month of Shaban (L.8). A *mawlid* ("birthday") is a religious festival that honors a saint revered for his great wisdom or miraculous power. The mawlid occurs on the saint's putative birthday. Most saints were Sufis.

15

Lailat al-Bara'ah (Night of Forgiveness). A night for Muslims to ask Allah to forgive their deceased friends and relatives. An intense time, in preparation for Ramadan (L.9 1). On this night, Allah fixes destinies for the coming year

RAMADAN (L.9)

1

Start of the Ramadan fast, all of L.9 (Ramadan). The month of Ramadan commemorates the period during which Muhammad received divine revelations (*see* Lailat al-Qadr, L.9 27). Special observance of this month is one of the five tenets of

Islam and is marked by a strict fast from sunrise to sundown.

21

Martyrdom of Ali, the first imam, in Shia Islam; an official public holiday in Iran. Honors Ali, the son-in-law of the Prophet Muhammad.

CA. 27

Lailat al-Qadr (Night of Power). Commemorates the night in A.D. 610 when the Koran descended, in its entirety, into the soul of the Prophet Muhammad. Observed on one of the last 10 nights of Ramadan, most commonly on the 27th, less widely on the 21st, but also on other nights.

SHAWWAL (L.10)

1

Id al-Fitr (Feast of the Breaking of the Fast); begins L.10 1 and lasts 3 days in most places; an official public holiday of 1 or more days in 62 countries. A celebration of the end of the Ramadan fast. One of the two canonical Muslim festivals (as is the Id al-Adha, L.12 10). Customarily, all gather in festive clothes for morning prayer; then they feast, visit with friends, and give alms to the poor. A time of goodwill to all, much like Christmas in Christian countries.

DHU AL-QADA (L.11)

10–12

Magal Pilgrimage to Touba, Senegal. The great annual pilgrimage of the Mouride brotherhood, the largest order of Sufis in the country. Magal (Return Voyage) celebrates the symbolic return of the order's founder, Cheikh Amadou Bamba, to the city he founded in the 1880s and from which the French later exiled him for his implacable resistance. All commercial activity in the country stops.

DHU AL-HIJJA (L.12)

10

Id al-Adha (Feast of the Sacrifice); commonly lasts 3 days; an official public holiday for 1 or more days in at least 60 countries. The end of the pilgrimage to Mecca, when animals are sacrificed; Muslims everywhere do the same, in commemoration of Abraham's sacrifice. A time of celebration and visits to graves and family. A time of goodwill to all. Meats are exchanged, and alms are given to the poor.

18

Id ul-Ghadir al-Khumm (Feast of Ghadir) among Shia Muslims; an official public holiday in Iran. Commemorates Muhammad's pronouncement of his son-in-law Ali as his successor, at Ghadir, between Mecca and Medina, in the last year of Muhammad's life. Ali is revered as the first imam among Shia Muslims.

29

New Year's Eve in Islam; a day and night for remembrance of the dead. A sacred night, when alms and sweets are given to the poor.

The Chinese Calendar

The Chinese calendar is most obviously lunar, but it has a solar component. The start of the lunar new year is dated from the winter solstice. The lunar calendar was reformed in 104 B.C. and, with brief exceptions, has remained essentially unchanged. The system for dating the solar joints was last reformed in 1645 but has also remained unchanged ever since. Since 1645, the Chinese calendar has been based on current astronomical knowledge in dating both lunar and solar events. True, not mean, celestial motion is used.

The Chinese calendar is used for dating traditional and religious holidays in China, Taiwan, and among the Chinese diaspora. South Korea and Vietnam have lunar calendars that use the same principles as the Chinese calendar, though based on local centers of calculation. Japan's traditional lunar calendar is very similar to the Chinese calendar (but also with its own center of calculation), though it is now little used except for dating certain Shinto events. The Chinese calendar has influenced the Tibetan calendar.

THE GEOGRAPHIC CENTER OF CALCULATION

The Chinese calendar is based on China's official civil time and is not location-dependent. It is not adjusted for events' local times in the user's country (as a strict Muslim would do). Thus, lunar New Year's Day, for example, is observed by all Chinese on the same date worldwide.

The geographic center for Chinese calendar calculations is Beijing, the counterpart of Greenwich for the Gregorian calendar. Civil time throughout both China (including Tibet) and Taiwan is 8 hours earlier than Universal time (U.T.); thus, noon at Greenwich, England, is 8 P.M. in China (U.T. + 8 hours).

South Korea's official civil time is U.T. + 9 hours. Vietnam's is U.T. + 7 hours. Japan's is U.T. + 9 hours.

THE ERA NUMBER

Chinese year 4694 began in A.D. 1996; 4698 begins in A.D. 2000. The era number is a pious convention because there are no reliable records before 841 B.C. However, tradition holds that the Yellow Emperor began his reign in 2698 B.C.

THE CYCLE OF 60 YEARS

Years are named in a cycle of 12 animals. These are combined with a cycle of 10 celestial signs or, in a different system, with a cycle of 5 elements. Each system yields a (different) full cycle of 60 years. Each animal has particular qualities that those born or conceived in the year are believed to share. The year of the dragon (A.D. 1988, 2000, . . .) is considered a very auspicious year in which to conceive a child.

The 12 animals and their corresponding Western years are:

Rat	1996, 2008
Ox	1997, 2009
Tiger	1998, 2010
Hare	1999, 2011
Dragon	2000
Snake	2001
Horse	2002
Sheep	2003
Monkey	2004
Rooster	2005
Dog	2006
Pig	2007

THE SOLAR LAYER

The winter solstice is central for determining the new year and as a reckoning point from which to mark seasonal changes. The actual start of the lunar new year (the first new moon of the year) has varied to reflect political changes. The winter solstice has occurred in the 11th lunar month since at least A.D. 1645.

THE JOINTS

The solar year is divided into 24 fortnightly periods called *joints;* each is approximately 15 days long and corresponds to 15 of longitudinal motion of the Sun on the ecliptic. The odd-numbered joints are called *chhi*-nodes (*chieh chhi,* also spelled *jiequi*) and the even-numbered ones *chhi*-centers (*chung chhi,* also spelled *dongzhi*). The analogy is from the bamboo. Although the numbering system does not indicate this, the joints, like the lunar months, are reckoned from the winter solstice. The system of joints is very ancient, but their present varying durations date only from A.D. 570, and since 1645, the best current astronomical data has been used to date the joints.

The joints are very important. Chinese peasants use this solar calendar to schedule agricultural activities. And a number of Chinese holidays are solar, not lunar, and occur on the day of a joint (for instance, Ching Ming,

Clear and Bright, around Apr. 5). There is, however, an alternative lunar date on which each of these events may also be celebrated.

Moreover, the even-numbered center joints determine the intercalation of lunar months, discussed later.

THE DAY

The traditional Chinese day, both solar and lunar, extends from midnight to midnight, Chinese civil time (U.T. + 8).

THE LUNAR LAYER

Almost every Chinese calendar event is dated as a day in a particular lunar month. If one has this data, knows the new moon of lunar New Year's Day, and has a table of new moons for the year, he or she can date most events readily and accurately, assuming no intercalary month intervenes.

THE LUNAR NEW YEAR

The winter solstice invariably occurs in the 11th lunar month. In general, the lunar new year begins on the day of the 2nd new moon following the winter solstice. It will normally fall between Jan. 21 and Feb. 20, inclusive. This is the case for all years from 1997 through 2036.

THE LUNAR MONTHS

There are 12 lunar months in a common year, with an additional month intercalated every 2nd or 3rd year (never twice in 2 years). Months are intercalated depending on when they actually occur, not by a formal table.

A lunar month has 29 or 30 solar days. Again, the number of days in a lunar month is determined by the actual number of days from one new moon to the next, not by a formal table.

The month begins on the day (midnight to midnight) in China during which the instant of new moon occurs. But note that the 15th day of the month is formally the full moon day, whether or not the astronomical full moon actually occurs on that day.

The lunar months are numbered. Some are tied to solar events.

Month	Begins with
1	2nd new moon after winter solstice (usually)
2	New moon preceding vernal equinox
5	New moon preceding summer solstice
8	New moon preceding autumnal equinox
11	New moon preceding winter solstice
12	1st new moon after winter solstice (usually)

Fractions of a day are irrelevant. Both lunar and solar events are assigned to whole days.

INTERCALATION OF LUNAR MONTHS

If there are 12 new moons between one winter solstice and the next, there will not be an extra month in that period. But if there are 13 new moons between one winter solstice and the next, a month will have to be intercalated somewhere. A month (new moon to new moon) will be intercalated as an extra month if there is no even-numbered center-joint within the period from new moon to new moon. The additional new moon marks the start of the intercalated month.

The intercalated month repeats the number of the true month it follows; all holidays occur in the true month. Thus, in 1998, month 5 was repeated; the Dragon Boat Festival on L.5 5 (5th lunar month, 5th day) was held in the 1st of those 2 months, on May 30.)

HOLIDAYS IN THE CHINESE CALENDAR

Conventions: L.1 2 = 1st lunar month, 2nd day.

THE JOINTS

FEBRUARY

CA. 3

Li Chhun (Spring is Here); Joint 1; the traditional beginning of spring; an important date in the farming year.

MARCH

CA. 5

The Waking of Creatures, or the Festival of Excited Insects; Joint 3; called Ching Che (or Jingzhe) in China, Kyongchip in Korea. Marks the true beginning of spring, when insects and other creatures awake from their winter dormancy.

CA. 21

Vernal Equinox Day; Joint 4. Among other events on this day, ancient Confucian rites honoring Korean and Chinese sages are held at the Confucian Shrine at Sungkyunkwan University, north of Seoul, South Korea. The same ceremony recurs on Autumnal Equinox Day, Joint 16, ca. Sept. 23.

APRIL

CA. 4

Ching Ming, Qing Ming, or Cheng Beng (Clear and Bright); Joint 5; alternatively on L.2 16; official public holiday in Hong Kong and Macau; important among all Chinese. A day to honor one's dead; families visit and repair graves, offer food, and picnic. Formerly, no fires were lit on this day. In South Korea, observed as Hanshik (Cold Food Day) or Grave Visiting Day. In Vietnam, observed on L.3 5.

JUNE

CA. 21

Hsia Chih (the summer solstice); Joint 10; alternative lunar date L.5 5. Called Doan-Ngu in Vietnam, where this is regarded as an unhealthy time of epidemics and the God of Death is appeased.

OCTOBER

CA. 8

Han Lu (Cold Dew); Joint 17; alternative lunar date L.9 11. The departure of summer.

LUNAR HOLIDAYS

(Note that approximate Gregorian dates apply in years when the previous month is not duplicated.)

FIRST LUNAR MONTH

1

Chinese lunar New Year's Day; official public holiday in many countries (celebrated for 1 day, or, in some places, for up to 7 days). The most important holiday in the year for Chinese and Vietnamese, and important for Koreans. Welcomed by Chinese with noise, illumination, and the color red. A day to honor elders and give gifts of money to children. In Korea, called Sulnal; a family day with special foods, kite flying for boys, and see-saws for girls. In Vietnam, called Tet (Tet Nguyen Dan); L.1 1–7; observed throughout Southeast Asia.

SECOND LUNAR MONTH

6

Hai Ba Trung Day in Vietnam; Chinese calendar, L.2 6; between late Feb. and late Mar.; official public holiday in Vietnam. Commemorates the death of the Trung sisters, leaders of the Vietnamese revolt against China in A.D. 41, which briefly established independence. When China recaptured Vietnam 3 years later, the sisters drowned themselves in grief.

THIRD LUNAR MONTH

23

Ma-Tsu's Birthday among coastal Chinese; between mid-Apr. and mid-May. She is called Tin Hau in Hong Kong, A-Ma in Macau, and Ma Cho Po in Malaysia. The goddess of the sea and of sailors, and the patron deity of Taiwan. All regions have legends asserting she was a local girl, subsequently deified.

FOURTH LUNAR MONTH

8

The Buddha's Birthday, particularly in South Korea, Vietnam, and China; between very late Apr. and very late May; official public holiday in South Korea. Korea celebrates with solemnly elaborate ceremonies in Buddhist temples, followed by evening lantern parades.

FIFTH LUNAR MONTH

5

Dragon Boat Festival; between very late May and very late June; official public holiday in Macau, Taiwan, and Hong Kong; also observed in China, Singapore, and Malaysia. One of the most important Chinese holidays. Honors the famous Chinese poet and statesman Ch'u Yuan, who committed suicide in Tungting Lake (288 B.C.) in protest against corrupt government. The colorful dragon-boat races re-create the search for his body. Also called Poet's Day. Ma-Tsu is also honored on this day.

CA. 5

Tano (Swing Day) in South Korea; usually L.5 3–8; between very late May and very late June. A day to offer ancestors summer food at household shrines. Girls and women, in their best clothes, have swinging matches after winter's confinement. As important as lunar New Year's Day and Chusok.

SIXTH LUNAR MONTH

13

Birthday of Lu Pan; between very early July and very early Aug. Honors the Chinese architect, engineer, and inventor, born 507 B.C. Considered the Chinese Leonardo da Vinci, Lu Pan is credited with the invention of numerous carpentry tools. He is the Taoist patron of carpenters and builders, invoked at the start of construction projects.

SEVENTH LUNAR MONTH

CA. 15

Feed the Hungry Ghosts; between very early Aug. and very early Sept. Observed by Chinese everywhere. A day to pray for and comfort the dead. Souls of the dead return for a day, and are feted with food and entertainment. A major holiday. Called Yulan in Malaysia and Trung Nguyen in Vietnam.

7

Ch'ilsok (Festival of the Celestial Lovers) in South Korea; between late July and late Aug. Called Tanabata in Japan. Also observed in China, Malaysia, Taiwan, and Hong Kong. At night, maidens honor the Weaving Girl and the Herdsboy, two love stars who by lore are united only on this night by a bird bridge across the Milky Way.

EIGHTH LUNAR MONTH

15

The Mid-Autumn Festival, or Moon Cake Day; between very early Sept. and very early Oct.; official public holiday in Macau, South Korea, Taiwan, Hong Kong, and Vietnam. Honors the moon goddess, and in China also commemorates an uprising against Mongol overlords. A major holiday, with family reunions, visits to family tombs, the eating of moon cakes, and hill climbing to observe the auspicious full moon. In South Korea, Chusok is the year's most important holiday; L. 8 15–17 are official public holidays; main day is L. 8 15. In Vietnam and Malaysia, primarily a children's festival, with lantern parades.

NINTH LUNAR MONTH

CA. 1

The Phuket Vegetarian Festival in Phuket, Thailand; L.9 1–9; between mid-Sept. and mid-Oct. Features enormous quantities of vegetarian food, Chinese opera, and ceremonies at Chinese temples.

CA. 9

Festival of the Nine Emperor (or Imperial) Gods; L.9 1–9; main day is L.9 9; between late Sept. and late Oct. Celebrated in Malaysia and Singapore.

The gods are welcomed for a 9-day visit, with ceremonies in Taoist and Buddhist temples, daily processions, Chinese opera, and a fire-walking ceremony in Kuala Lumpur on the evening of the 9th day.

9

Cheung Yeung, or Chung Yeung; between late Sept. and late Oct. A festival of ancestors, when family tombs are refurbished and offerings made.

28

Confucius's Birthday; between mid-Oct. and mid-Nov. Observed in Confucian temples in Macau, Hong Kong, and Vietnam (official public holiday). In Taiwan and China the observance has been transferred to Sept. 28. Confucius (551–479 B.C.), China's greatest sage, wrote *The Analects* (*Lun Yü*).

PART THREE

RESOURCES

Related to Anniversaries and Holidays

RELIGIOUS DAYS

CHRISTMAS

Anderson, Raymond, and Georgene Anderson. *The Jesse tree: stories and symbols of Advent.* Minneapolis: Fortress, 1990.

> Guide to readings and prayers, to be correlated with symbolism of the Jesse tree during Advent, in preparation for Christmas.

Barth, Edna. *Holly, reindeer, and colored lights: the story of the Christmas symbols.* New York: Houghton Mifflin, 1985.

> Traces the origins and meanings of such Christmas symbols as the tree, Yule log, bells, ornaments, Santa Claus, cards, shepherds, angels, colors, and candles. Indexed.

Buday, George. *The history of the Christmas card.* Detroit: Omnigraphics, 1992.

> Examines its forerunners, the influence of the valentine, and card makers; includes commentary on types of cards and sentiments expressed in verse.

Blahnik, Judith. *Checklist for a perfect Christmas.* New York: Doubleday, 1996.

> A series of to-do lists helps readers organize preparations for the Christmas season. Includes recipes, gift ideas, party planning tips, and instructions for do-it-yourself decorations.

Bolam, Emily (illus.). *The twelve days of Christmas: a song rebus.* New York: Simon and Schuster/Anne Schwartz, 1997.

> Songbook rebus adaptation of the well-known carol features full-size color illustrations on one page and the words to the song with miniature illustrations to prompt singers on the facing page. Written for preschool children and older.

Carlson, Lori Marie, and Ed Martinez (illus.). *Hurray for Three Kings' Day!* New York: Morrow, 1999.

> Traditional Spanish holiday seen through the eyes of a little girl and her brother. Includes a glossary of Spanish terms used in the text and color illustrations. Appropriate for preschool–grade 2.

Cherkerzian, Diane, and Colleen Van Blaricom. *Merry things to make.* Honesdale, Pa.: Boyd's Mills, 1999.

> Ideas for making gift boxes, decorations, and other holiday items. Includes step-by-step instructions with color illustrations. Appropriate for all ages.

Chorao, Kay. *The Christmas story.* New York: Holiday House, 1996.

> Nativity narratives from the Gospels of Matthew and Luke adapted for children. Accompanied by color Renaissance-style artwork by the author. Appropriate for preschool–grade 2.

Christmas in colonial and early America. Chicago: World Book, 1996.

> Describes how Christmas was celebrated in America from the colonial period through the late 19th century. Gives details of various holiday customs, tracing their roots back to Europe, and explains how each succeeding immigrant group brought its own customs to add to the rich mix. Includes recipes and instructions for homemade holiday gifts. Accompanied by historical photographs and artwork. Appropriate for grades 4–7.

Dearmer, Percy (ed.). *Oxford book of carols: music edition with notes.* New York: Oxford University Press, 1985.

Collection of traditional and 20th century carols.

Dewl, Roberts (ed.). *Christmas in Wales.* Dubuque, Iowa: Seren, 1998.

Reminiscences and poems by Welsh authors serve as vehicles for describing their Christmas customs.

Dickens, Charles. *A Christmas carol in prose: being a ghost story of Christmas.* Nashville: Ideals, 1998.

The most famous of all Christmas stories; illustrated.

Dickens, Charles, and Goodrich Carter (illus.). *A Christmas carol.* New York: Morrow, 1996.

Dickens's own 90-minute performance version of the famous tale, accompanied by 21 sepia-colored illustrations. Appropriate for grades 5 and up.

Duncan, Edmonstoune. *The story of the carol.* Detroit: Omnigraphics, 1992.

Standard history of carols, their antecedents, and forms, related to ecclesiastical days and seasonal celebrations.

Gibbons, Gail. *Santa Who?* New York: Morrow, 1999.

Traces Santa Claus from his origins in the real St. Nicholas through his spread across Europe and the Americas; accompanied by color greeting card-style art. Appropriate for kindergarten–grade 2.

Gibson, George M. *The story of the Christian year.* Salem, N.H.: Ayer, 1972.

The evolution of Christian festivals, from the primitive church to the modern era.

The glorious Christmas songbook. San Francisco: Chronicle, 1999.

Collection of traditional carols and popular holiday songs accompanied by reproductions of art ranging from 17th century paintings to turn-of-the-century postcards. Appropriate for grades 3–7.

Greene, Rhonda Gowler, and Susan Gaber (illus.). *The stable where Jesus was born.* New York: Simon and Schuster/Atheneum, 1999.

The nativity story told in rhyme, with color illustrations. Appropriate for preschool–grade 1.

Hickman, Martha Whitmore, and Giuliano Ferri (illus.). *A baby born in Bethlehem.* Morton Grove, Ill.: Albert Whitman, 1999.

Retelling of the nativity narrative from the Gospels of Matthew and Luke; accompanied by watercolor-and-pencil illustrations. Appropriate for kindergarten–grade 4.

Hines, Gary, and Alexandra Wallner (illus.). *A Christmas tree in the White House.* New York: Holt, 1998.

Interesting tale loosely based on the true story of how Theodore Roosevelt's two sons—with a little help from the chief forester—softened his resolve not to allow a Christmas tree in the White House due to his conservation program. Accompanied by a photograph of the Roosevelts and original color illustrations. Appropriate for kindergarten–grade 2.

Hodges, Margaret, and Tim Ladwig (illus.). *Silent Night: the song and its story.* Grand Rapids, Mich.: Eerdmans, 1997.

Account of the facts surrounding the creation of the famous song by Austrians Joseph Mohr and Franz Gruber on Christmas Eve, 1818; accompanied by color illustrations. Appropriate for grades 3–6.

Hottes, Alfred C. *One thousand and one Christmas facts and fancies.* Detroit: Omnigraphics, 1990.

Legends, stories, carols, toasts, superstitions, omens, and customs around the world, with ideas for making Christmas cards, decorating, and cooking.

Hoyt-Goldsmith, Diane. *Las posadas : an Hispanic Christmas celebration.* New York: Holiday House, 1999.

The 400-year-old Spanish custom is brought to life as we follow a girl and her family through the nine-night celebration that commemorates the story of Mary and Joseph's search for shelter in Bethlehem and the birth of Jesus. Accompanied by color photographs, recipes, and songs with Spanish and English text. Appropriate for grades 3–6.

Irving, Washington. *Old Christmas*. Sandwich, Mass.: Chapman Billies, 1996.

Irving's famous stories of Christmas in Old New England.

Isolde, Helen. *How to have a perfect Christmas: practical and inspirational advice to simplify your holiday season*. New York: Dutton, 1996.

Compilation of one-liners and brief thoughts to help maintain sanity through the hectic season.

Kane, Harnett T. *The Southern Christmas book: the full story from earliest times to present: people, customs, conviviality, carols, cooking*. Detroit: Omnigraphics, 1997.

Reviews Christmas customs in the American South, from the first genial season in Virginia to the "Confederate Christmas," a cowboy's Christmas ball, and other festivities. Includes recipes such as Martha Washington's "Great Cake."

Kidger, Mark. *The Star of Bethlehem: an astronomer's view*. Princeton, N.J.: Princeton, 1999.

Evaluates theories that have tried to explain the phenomenon recounted in the nativity narratives. The author argues that the star was the result of a series of rare planetary configurations that preceded a nova in 5 B.C.

Kurelek, William. *A northern Nativity*. Plattsburgh, N.Y.: Tundra Books of Northern New York, 1996.

Extraordinary paintings depicting the Holy Family as humble folk in various Canadian situations; each painting recalls the biblical account of "no room at the inn." The paintings are accompanied by text.

Langstaff, John. *On Christmas day in the morning*. Cambridge, Mass.: Candlewick Press, 1999.

Carol verses from many places in the world supplement the familiar verses of four traditional carols, such as "On Chris-i-mas day in the morning."

Linsley, Leslie. *Leslie Linsley's quick Christmas decorating ideas*. New York: St. Martin's Griffin, 1996.

Ideas for creating easy-to-make Christmas decorations such as seashell wreaths and potato-printed stockings.

McCullough, Bonnie R. *Seventy-six ways to get organized for Christmas*. New York: St. Martin's, 1992.

Yuletide planner's guide to organizing time, making gifts and decorations, preparing food, and carrying out unique traditions.

Meyer, Carolyn. *Christmas crafts: things to make the 24 days before Christmas*. New York: HarperCollins, 1974.

Guide to Advent crafts, with unique projects for each day correlated with customs; illustrated with project drawings and sketches.

Miles, Clement A. *Christmas in ritual and tradition: Christian and pagan*. Detroit: Omnigraphics, 1990.

Standard study of intermingling customs of Christmas and pagan festivals.

Molnar, Michael R. *The Star of Bethlehem: the legacy of the Magi*. New Brunswick, N.J.: Rutgers University Press, 1999.

Astronomer Molnar provides evidence to support the theory that the star seen by the Magi was the result of a lunar occultation of Jupiter in the constellation of Aries. His argument is supported by early Roman and Jewish source material in addition to modern computer calculations.

Moore, Clement C., Cooper Edens, and Harold Darling (eds.). *The night before Christmas*. San Francisco: Chronicle, 1998.

Moore's classic is accompanied by reproductions of illustrations that have appeared in previous editions of the story dating from 1890 to 1928. Appropriate for all ages.

Moore, Clement C., and MaxGrover (illus.). *The night before Christmas: a visit from St. Nicholas*. San Diego: Harcourt/Browndeer, 1999.

Modern retelling of Moore's poem with contemporary color illustrations. Appropriate for preschool–grade 2.

Moore, Clement C., and Bruce Whatley (illus.). *The night before Christmas*. New York: HarperCollins, 1999.

Moore's classic poem accompanied by traditional color illustrations. Appropriate for preschool–grade 2.

Moser, Johann M. (ed.). *O Holy night!: masterworks of Christmas poetry.* Manchester, N.H.: Sophia Institute, 1994.

Collection of works by great authors past and present who have been inspired by the nativity narratives.

Nettell, Stephanie, and Ian Penney (illus.). *A Christmas treasury.* New York: Dutton/Lodestar, 1997.

International collection of holiday poems, essays, and story excerpts from authors such as A.A. Milne, Charles Dickens, and Laura Ingalls Wilder. Accompanied by color illustrations. Appropriate for all ages.

Newland, Mary R. *The year and our children: planning the family activities for Christian feasts and seasons.* San Diego: Firefly Press, 1995.

Christian approach to family participation in activities for Christmas and other important days in the church calendar; ranges from Advent wreath and Jesse tree to preparing for Thanksgiving.

Osborne, Mary Pope. *The life of Jesus in masterpieces of art.* New York: Viking, 1999.

Jesus' life is recounted using selections from the Gospels and reproductions of artwork by Renaissance masters such as Botticelli and Bosch. Appropriate for grades 4–7.

Pacheco, Ferdie, and Luisita S. Pacheco. *Christmas Eve cookbook: with tales of Nochebuena & Chanukah.* Gainesville: University Press of Florida, 1998.

Ferdie Pacheco presents recipes and stories culled from his childhood in an ethnically rich neighborhood in Florida and from his days as the "Fight Doctor." One memorable story concerns his daughter, Tina, and boxer Muhammad Ali. Recipes are arranged by nationality and food type and are accompanied by color illustrations.

Petit, Florence H. *Christmas all around the house: traditional decorations you can make.* New York: HarperCollins Children's Books, 1976.

A handsome and useful guide to constructing Christmas decorations from around the world.

Rahaman, Vashanti and Frane Lessac (illus.). *O Christmas tree.* Honesdale, Pa.: Boyd's Mills, 1996.

Story of how a little boy and his family celebrate Christmas in the Caribbean; accompanied by colorful folk-style artwork. Appropriate for kindergarten–grade 2.

Robinson, Jo. *Unplug the Christmas machine: a complete guide to putting love and joy back into the season.* Rev. ed. New York: Morrow, 1991.

Practical handbook for Yuletide planning, designed to circumvent the pressures that undercut the values of Christmas. Text includes suggestions on entertaining, gift giving, budgeting, and charities.

Roop, Peter, and Connie Roop. *Let's celebrate Christmas.* Brookfield, Conn.: Millbrook, 1997.

History, folklore, jokes, and riddles are used to explain the facts behind Christmas customs and beliefs. Also includes sections on Hanukkah and Kwanzaa. Accompanied by color illustrations. Appropriate for grades 3–5.

Ross, Kathy. *Christmas ornaments kids can make.* Brookfield, Conn.: Millbrook, 1998.

Step-by-step instructions accompanied by color illustrations for 30 Christmas ornament projects for children to make on their own. Appropriate for grades 2–5.

Santiago, Esmeralda, Joie Davidow (eds.), and Jose Ortega (illus.). *Las Christmas: Favorite Latino authors share their holiday memories.* Van Nuys, Calif.: Alfred, 1998.

Christmas memories and sketches focus on how Christmas is celebrated by Latin Americans in Spanish-speaking countries and in the U.S. Looks at a variety of Hispanic Christmas customs.

Schlicke, Paul (ed.). *Oxford reader's companion to Dickens.* New York: Oxford, 1999.

Compilation of readings on the life and times of the author of *A Christmas carol* by noted Dickens experts. Accompanied by illustrations and maps.

Sechrist, Elizabeth H. *Christmas everywhere: a book of Christmas customs of many lands.* Detroit: Omnigraphics, 1997.

> Looks at Christmas customs in various countries and in the U.S.

Seeger, Ruth Crawford. *American folk songs for Chirstmas.* North Haven, Conn.: Shoe String Press, 1999.

> Carols and folk songs tell the Christmas story.

Thurman, Howard. *The mood of Christmas.* Richmond, Ind.: Friends United Press, 1985.

> Book of Christmas meditation explores the quality and spiritual symbolism of the season.

Tudor, Tasha. *The new "take joy."* New York: Little, Brown, 1999.

> Updated version of Tudor's 1966 anthology of Christmas thoughts, stories, poems, carols, and legends. Describes Advent calendars and wreaths, cornucopias, the "animal Christmas," marionette shows, and other traditions of Tudor's family in New England.

Walsh, William Shepard. *The story of Santa Klaus: told for children of all ages from six to sixty.* Detroit: Omnigraphics, 1991.

> Reprint of 1909 edition of the history of the Santa Klaus legend and its relationship to Saint Nicholas, with accounts of Santa Klaus traditions.

Weiser, Francis X. *The Christmas book.* Detroit: Omnigraphics, 1990.

> Interpretation of origins and meaning of customs, ceremonies, and legends of Christmas.

Wernecke, Herbert H. *Christmas customs around the world.* Louisville: Westminister/John Knox, 1979.

> Record of Christmas customs arranged alphabetically by continent and country.

Wernecke, Herbert H. *Celebrating Christmas around the world.* Detroit: Omnigraphics, 1999.

> Collection of material on Christmas customs arranged alphabetically by continent and country.

WEB SITES

Christmas around the world. www.christmas.com/worldview

> Site produced by Christmas Information Services, Inc., that offers brief descriptions of how Christmas is celebrated in more than 200 countries.

Christmas chronicles. www.bconnex.net/~mbuchana/realms/christmas

> Explains the origins of Christmas traditions; includes Christmas stories and jokes, descriptions of Christmas celebrations around the world, coloring pages, and links to other sites.

Christmas eternal. www.members.carol.net/~asmsmsks/xristmas.html

> Detailed treatment of the origins behind the candy cane, the 12 days of Christmas, Santa Claus, and other Christmas customs. Includes a collection of short stories.

A religious Christmas. www.execpc.com/~tmuth/st_john/xmas/Default.htm

> Provides scripture references, music, and a bibliography of meditational literature to help people focus on the religious significance of Advent and Christmas. Includes essays, art, and craft suggestions.

EASTER

Barth, Edna, and Ursula Arndt (illus.). *Lilies, rabbits, & painted eggs: the story of the Easter symbols.* Boston: Houghton Mifflin, 1981.

> Explanation of Easter symbols: sunrise, flowers, fire and fireworks, hot cross buns, eggs, lambs, rabbits, colors, bells, chants, and rituals; includes illustrations. Appropriate for grades 3–6.

Hague, Michael (ed.). *Michael Hague's family Easter treasury.* New York: Holt, 1999.

> Collection of 32 stories, poems, and meditations that revolve around four Easter-related themes: faith, rebirth, celebration, and love; includes color illustrations. Appropriate for grades 3–5.

Harp, Sybil (ed.). *Egg craft.* Newton, N.J.: Carstens Publications, 1974.

Instructions and diagrams for unique decorations, plus advice on materials and sources for supplies; includes illustrations. Part of the Creative Crafts Library series.

Hopkins, Lee B., and Tomie De Paola (illus.). *Easter buds are springing.* Honesdale, Pa.: Boyd's Mills Press, 1993.

Short poems about Easter by 14 authors. Includes illustrations.

Kimmel, Eric A., and Katya Krenina (illus.). *The bird's gift: a Ukrainian Easter story.* New York: Holiday House, 1999.

Folktale explains the origins of the beautifully decorated Ukrainian Easter eggs called *pysansky;* includes color illustrations. Appropriate for preschool–grade 3.

Newall, Venetia. *An egg at Easter: a folklore study.* Bloomington: Indiana University Press, 1989.

Study of folklore and symbolism of decorated eggs and concepts of their use.

Spirin, Gennady. *The Easter story: According to the Gospels of Matthew, Luke & John.* New York: Holt, 1999.

Selections from the King James Version of the passion narratives of Matthew, Luke, and John are illustrated with the beautiful Eastern Orthodox-style artwork of Gennady Spirin. Appropriate for all ages.

WEB SITES

Easter eternal. www.members.carol.net/~asmsmsks/easter.htm

Detailed treatment of the history of Lent, Easter, and customs associated with their celebration; includes links to related sites.

Easter: Its origins and meanings. www.religioustolerance.org/easter.htm

Explains the origins and customs of Holy Week and Easter Day; includes bibliographical sources.

The Easter page: Traditions, history, and dates. www.wilstar.com/holidays/easter.htm

Explains the meaning of Easter, the Cross, Easter eggs, and the Easter Bunny; includes

links to Easter-related games and crafts. Geared toward children

JEWISH HOLIDAYS

Adler, David A. *The kids' catalog of Jewish holidays.* Philadelphia: Jewish Publication Society, 1996.

Brief essays on the history and customs associated with 13 major holidays and several days of prayer. Each section includes instructions for games, craft projects, and multinational recipes as well as a bibliography and songs (lyrics and music) for each holiday. Accompanied by photographs, drawings, and color illustrations. Appropriate for grades 4–7.

Adler, David A. *A picture book of Jewish holidays.* New York: Holiday House, 1981.

Picture book with words and drawings that evoke the "warmth of the Sabbath, the solemnity of Yom Kippur, the joy of Purim, the awe of Shavuot, and more." Includes a glossary and a chart that clarifies time relationships between Jewish and Julian calendars.

Berger, Gilda. *Celebrate! Stories for the Jewish holidays.* New York: Scholastic, 1998.

Text covers seven holidays: Rosh Hashanah, Yom Kippur, Sukkoth, Hanukkah, Purim, Pesach, and Shavuot, plus Shabbat. A chapter on each holiday explains the underlying biblical story, presents a time line that shows where the holiday falls in Jewish history, reviews holiday customs, and suggests activities, and recipes. Each chapter includes a color illustration depicting the biblical events surrounding the holiday. Appropriate for grades 3–5.

Bloch, Abraham P. *The biblical and historical background of Jewish customs and ceremonies.* Hoboken, N.J.: Ktav, 1980.

Detailed study of the origins of Jewish customs and ceremonies in terms of religious writings and historical records. Text provides full explanations of ceremonies of major Jewish holidays and brief commentaries on minor holidays.

Bloch, Abraham P. *The biblical and historical background of the Jewish holy days.* New York: Ktav, 1978.

Thoughtful, readable study of socioreligious base for the Sabbath and historical background of the holy days as evidenced by sacred literary traditions, rituals, and customs.

Burns, Marilyn. *The Hanukkah book*. New York: Avon, 1991.

> Explains the traditions of Hanukkah, including effect of Christmas on Jewish children, and suggests ways to interpret and share the two holidays. Includes craft ideas.

Cashman, Greer F. *Jewish days & holidays*. New York: Adama Books, 1996.

> Colorful introduction for children to meaning of Rosh Hashanah, Yom Kippur, Sukkot, Simchat Torah, Chanukah, Purim, Pesach, Yom Ha-Atzmaut, Shavuot, Tisha B'Av, and the Sabbath.

Chaikin, Miriam. *Light another candle: the story and meaning of Hanukkah*. New York: Houghton Mifflin, 1981.

> Attractive book on background of the 2,000-year-old holiday. Touches on universal and national Hanukkah customs and describes carrying the Torch of Freedom from Modin to the Western Wall in Jerusalem. Includes glossary and index.

Chiel, Kinneret. *Complete book of Hanukkah*. Hoboken, N.J.: Ktav, 1976.

> Anthology includes history, traditions, legends, stories, songs, prayers, and recipes.

Donin, Hayim H. *To pray as a Jew: a guide to the prayer book & the synagogue service*. New York: Basic Books, 1991.

> Guide to the Siddur, the Jewish prayer book, which includes prayers for the Sabbath, holy days, and personal spiritual needs. Of interest to people of all faiths.

Fishman, Cathy Goldberg, and Melanie W. Hall (illus.). *On Rosh Hashanah and Yom Kippur*. New York: Simon and Schuster/Atheneum, 1997.

> Describes the history, customs, and liturgical practices associated with these two high holidays. Accompanied by color illustrations and a glossary with pronunciation guide. Appropriate for preschool–grade 3.

Gaster, Theodor Herzl. *Passover: its history and traditions*. Westport, Conn.: Greenwood, 1984.

> Explains the history, ceremonials, and significance of Passover in terms of tradition and 20th century research; includes seder and Passover songs.

Glatzer, Nahum N. *Passover Haggadah*. New York: Schocken, 1989.

> Guide to understanding a traditional seder, the feast commemorating Exodus from Egypt, with suggestions for adaptation of historical and liturgical material to contemporary use.

Goodman, Philip (ed.). *Hanukkah anthology*. Philadelphia: Jewish Publication Society, 1992.

> Collection of writings on history and significance of Hanukkah: includes stories, plays, and poems, with material on customs and activities. Part of the Holiday Anthologies Series.

Goodman, Philip (ed.). *Passover anthology*. Philadelphia: Jewish Publication Society, 1993.

> Besides accounts of its origins and history of observance in many lands, the book contains chapters on Passover in literature, art, and music; ideas for programs and projects; and section on ceremonies of observance. Part of the Holiday Anthologies Series.

Goodman, Philip (ed.). *Purim anthology*. Philadelphia: Jewish Publication Society, 1988.

> Tells of Purim origin; identifies special Purims and observances by nations; considers Purim in literature, art, music, and Jewish law; and describes customs of commemoration; with supplement of appropriate music. Part of the Holiday Anthologies Series.

Goodman, Philip (ed.). *Rosh Hashanah anthology*. Philadelphia: Jewish Publication Society, 1992.

> Material on the solemn Jewish New Year from biblical and postbiblical writings, medieval literature, and modern periods; covers law, music, culinary arts, and special programming for cycle known as Days of Awe. Part of the Holiday Anthologies Series.

Goodman, Philip (ed.). *Shavuot anthology*. Philadelphia: Jewish Publication Society, 1992.

> Collection of texts concerning Shavuot, the feast that commemorates the presentation of the Ten Commandments to Moses on Mount Sinai. Includes writings from biblical, postbiblical,

medieval, and modern periods. Part of the Holiday Anthologies Series.

Goodman, Philip (ed.). *Sukkot-Simhat Torah anthology*. Philadelphia: Jewish Publication Society, 1992.

Material on the celebrations of Sukkot and Simhat Torah. Includes a variety of writings from biblical, postbiblical, medieval, and modern periods as well as descriptions of how these holidays are celebrated around the world. Part of the Holiday Anthologies Series.

Goodman, Philip (ed.). *Yom Kippur anthology*. Philadelphia: Jewish Publication Society, 1992.

Demonstrates meaning of Yom Kippur through interpretations of biblical, talmudic, and midrashic selections; inspirational essays, prayers, modern literature, art, and music. Part of the Holiday Anthologies Series.

Hirsh, Marilyn. *Potato pancakes all around: a Hanukkah tale*. Philadelphia: Jewish Publication Society, 1982.

Story of a peddler and his way of making potato pancakes from a crust of bread to celebrate the first day of Hanukkah; combines an amusing person with a recipe in a traditional setting.

Hoyt-Goldsmith, Diane, and Laurence Migdale (illus.). *Celebrating Hanukkah*. New York: Holiday House, 1996.

Follow Leora and her family as they celebrate Hanukkah. Photographs of the family engaged in holiday activities at home, school, and the synagogue accompany the text. Includes detailed information on the history of Hanukkah, directions for playing dreidels, and recipes for latkes. Appropriate for grades 3–6.

Kitov, Eliyahu, and Nathan Bulman (translator). *The book of our heritage*. Spring Valley, N.Y.: Feldheim, 1978.

Comprehensive study of the Jewish year, with interpretations of celebratory cycles and descriptions of rituals.

Lubavitch Women's Organization and Staff. *The spice & spirit of Kosher-Jewish cooking*. Brooklyn: Lubavitch Women's Organization, 1977.

Collection of essays on Jewish culture and dietary laws with interesting menus for festive and family occasions.

McDonough, Yona Zeldis, and Malcah Zeldis (illus.). *Anne Frank*. New York: Holt, 1997.

Picture-book biography of the life of Anne Frank introduces young children to the Holocaust. Appropriate for grades 1–4.

Musleah, Rahel, and Michael Klayman. *Sharing blessings: children's stories for exploring the spirit of the Jewish holidays*. Woodstock, Vt.: Jewish Lights, 1997.

Follows a young family through an entire year of holidays and uses short stories to relate the meaning of each holiday to everyday family life; accompanied by color illustrations. Appropriate for grades 3–5.

Pearl, Sydelle. *Elijah's tears: stories for the Jewish holidays*. New York: Holt, 1996.

Five original stories about the important role of Elijah in Jewish history and folklore are used to explain the spirit of Jewish holidays. There are two stories for Passover and one each for Succot, Hanukkah, and Yom Kippur. Text is accompanied by color illustrations and a glossary. Appropriate for grades 3–5.

Raphael, Chaim. *A feast of history: the drama of Passover*. Rev. ed. Washington, D.C.: B'nai B'rith International Commission on Continuing Jewish Education, 1993.

History of Passover; its rituals, prayers, and songs, with contemporary translation of the Haggadah read at seder meals in commemoration of the Exodus from Egypt. Section on preparations for seder.

Ross, Kathy. *Crafts for Hanukkah*. Brookfield, Conn.: Millbrook, 1996.

Provides instructions for Hanukkah crafts and games, with color illustrations for some of the steps. Also focuses on general themes and symbols such as the yarmulke and the Star of David. Appropriate for grades 2–4.

Scharfstein, Edythe. *Book of Chanukah*. Hoboken, N.J.: Ktav, 1959.

Short introduction to Hanukkah with poems, riddles, stories, songs, and things to do.

Silverman, Morris (ed.). *Passover Haggadah*. New York: Hartmore House, 1999

> Designed for adult study groups, Passover institutes, and home use; explanations and comments are interpolated in text.

Simon, Norma. *The story of Hanukkah*. Rev. ed. New York: HarperCollins, 1997.

> Simple interpretation of history, customs, and significance of Hanukkah as the Festival of Lights, a symbol of religious freedom.

Solomon, Norman. *Historical dictionary of Judaism*. Metuchen, N.J.: Scarecrow, 1998.

> Focuses on the Jewish religion as opposed to the history of the Jewish people or of the Bible. Entries on important personalities, concepts, and beliefs range from a few sentences in length to several pages. Includes a bibliography and a list of the 613 commandments (mitzvot).

Sorosky, Marlene. *Fast & festive meals for the Jewish holidays: complete menus, rituals, and party-planning ideas for every holiday of the year*. New York: Morrow, 1997.

> More than 150 recipes centered around 12 holidays form the nucleus of this cookbook. Author attempts to make recipes healthy by reducing or eliminating high-fat ingredients. Also includes a brief description of each holiday, tips on party planning, and suggestions for table decorations.

Tolen, Jane, and Louise August (illus.). *Milk and honey: a year of Jewish holidays*. New York: Putnam, 1996.

> Describes eight major Jewish holidays, using poems, vignettes, plays, and folktales to provide a more in-depth look at each. Includes music for piano and guitar and black-and-white illustrations to complement the text. Appropriate for grades 4–6.

Zalben, Jane Breskin. *Beni's family cookbook: for the Jewish holidays*. New York: Holt, 1996.

> Beni the bear and his family present a collection of recipes organized around the Jewish holidays; color illustrations are interspersed throughout the text. Appropriate for grades 4 and up.

Zalben, Jane Breskin. *Pearl's eight days of Chanukah*. New York: Simon and Schuster, 1998.

> As Pearl and her family celebrate Hanukkah, they provide recipes for jelly doughnuts and latkes, share songs, and give instructions for a variety of craft projects, including the construction of dreidels and menorahs. Accompanied by color illustrations. Appropriate for preschool–grade 4.

WEB SITES

JCN's award-winning Hanukkah page. www. jcn18.com/scriptsjcn18/paper/Article.asp?ArticleID=703

> Explains the history of Hanukkah and its customs and includes suggestions for celebrating the holiday, songs, recipes, and links to other sites.

General index on Pesach. www.jajz-ed.org.il/festivals/pesach/index.html

> A detailed site, produced by the education department of the Jewish Agency for Israel, that delivers five teaching units that explain concepts related to the festival. Provides activities to reinforce each unit and a list of links to other Passover-related sites.

RELIGIOUS AND SPIRITUAL FESTIVALS

Asad, Muhammad. *Message of the Qu'ran*. Chicago: Kazi, 1996.

> English translation of the Koran, the holy book of Islam, with explanatory prefaces and appendixes.

Bellenir, Karen (ed.). *Religious holidays and calendars: an encyclopedic handbook*. 2nd ed. Detroit: Omnigraphics, 1998.

> Explains the relationship between the religious calendars and holidays of more than 450 religions. Describes the origin, development, and operation of each calendar and provides background on the origins and traditions of each holiday. Bah'ai, Buddhism, Christianity, Hinduism, Islam, Judaism, and Native American religions are covered.

Breuilly, Elizabeth, et al. *Religions of the world: the illustrated guide to origins, beliefs, traditions & festivals*. New York: Facts on File, 1997.

Covers belief systems, customs, festivals, major writings, and history of the world's major religions; accompanied by color photographs. Appropriate for grades 7–12.

Crum, Keith, Roger A. Ballard, and Larry D. Shin (eds.). *Abingdon dictionary of living religions.* Nashville: Abingdon, 1981.

Comprehensive guide to religions of the 20th century; broad in scope, with information on historical developments, beliefs, important religious leaders, traditions, and practices of active religions in every part of the world; topics arranged alphabetically, with excellent cross-references.

Ford, Juwanda G., and Ken Wilson-Max (illus.). *K is for Kwanzaa: a Kwanzaa alphabet book.* New York: Scholastic, 1997.

Uses the ABCs to highlight objects and symbols associated with Kwanza; accompanied by color illustrations. Appropriate for kindergarten–grade 4.

Foy, Felician A. (ed.). *Catholic almanac.* Huntington, Ind.: Our Sunday Visitor, annual.

Handbook of current information on Roman Catholic church. Includes liturgical calendar; significant dates in U.S. Catholic chronology; list of saints, bishops, cardinals, popes, and other church dignitaries; summaries of church doctrine, news events, and reports.

Gulevich, Tanya (ed.). *World history, festival, and calendar books.* Detroit: Omnigraphics, 1998.

Annotated bibliography of more than 1,000 sources of information on holidays worldwide. Sources divided into four categories: religious holidays, ethnic and national holidays, world holidays, and calendars and time reckoning systems.

Henderson, Helene, and Barry Puckett (eds.). *Holidays and festivals index: A descriptive guide to information on more than 3,000 holidays, festivals, fairs, rituals, celebrations, commemorations, holy days and saints' days, feasts and fasts, and other observances, including ethnic, seasonal, art, music, dance, theater, folk, historic, national, and ancient events from all parts of the world, as found in standard reference works. Includes location, date, alternative names, cross-references, and indexes by ethnic group and geographical location, personal name, religion, and calendar.* Detroit: Omnigraphics, 1995.

The title says it all!

Johnson, Dolores. *The children's book of Kwanzaa: a guide to celebrating the holiday.* New York: Simon and Schuster/Atheneum, 1996.

A history of the origins, symbols, and principles surrounding Kwanza. Includes ideas for celebrating the festival and directions for making gifts, decorations, and holiday foods. Accompanied by wood-block print illustrations. Appropriate for all ages.

Kettelkamp, Larry. *Religions, East and West.* New York: Morrow, 1972.

Explores similarities and differences in the beliefs of Hinduism, Buddhism, Taoism, Confucianism, Zoroastrianism, Judaism, Christianity, and Islam.

King, Noel Q. *Religions of Africa: A pilgrimage into traditional religions.* New York: Harper, 1970.

Interprets the religious life of tribal groups in equatorial and tropical Africa; examines the roles of leaders and sacred persons.

Koller, John M. *Asian philosophies.* 3rd ed. New York: Macmillan, 1997.

Introduction to dominant characteristics and philosophies of Hinduism, Buddhism, Confucianism, Taoism, and neo-Confucianism.

McNair, Marcia Odle. *Kwanzaa crafts: gifts and decorations for a meaningful and festive celebration.* New York: Sterling, 1999.

An explanation of each day of the seven-day festival is accompanied by its corresponding principle, symbol, color, and an essay or poem. Also included are easy-to-make craft and recipe ideas with step-by-step color photographs and instructions.

Parrinder, Geoffrey (ed.). *A dictionary of non-Christian religions.* New York: Facts on File, 1985.

Concise compilation of data on modern non-Christian faiths; includes religions of ancient Persia, Mesopotamia, Egypt, Greece, and Rome; faiths of ancient Maya, Aztec, and Inca cultures; and beliefs and customs of Australasia and Africa.

Seeger, Elizabeth. *Eastern religions.* New York: HarperCollins/Crowell, 1973.

Explanation of Buddhism, Confucianism, Hinduism, Shinto, and Taoism; interprets rituals, holidays, and legends; discusses concepts, founders, and development of each faith.

Thompson, Sue Ellen (ed.). *Holiday symbols.* Detroit: Omnigraphics, 1998.

Sourcebook of information on symbols associated with 200 of the most popular holidays in the U.S. and abroad. Each entry provides the meaning, origin, development, traditions, lore, food, colors, customs, and animals connected with that symbol.

Walsh, Michael J. *An illustrated history of the popes: Saint Peter to John Paul II.* New York: St. Martin's, 1980.

A history of the popes, with personal data and commentary on the policies of each pope; explains papal tradition in the context of church and world history.

WEB SITES

Encyclopedia of days. www.shagtown.com/days

Delivers descriptions and links to festivals celebrated worldwide. Also provides information on the holidays of major world religions and a bibliography.

Essentials of Ramadan, the fasting month. www.usc.edu/dept/MSA/fundam...llars/fasting/tajuddin/fast_l.html

Detailed site that discusses the meaning of Ramadan, the purpose of the fast, and the essentials of fasting.

NATIONAL HOLIDAYS AND CIVIC DAYS

INDEPENDENCE DAY (U.S.)

Brand, Oscar, and Ad Young (illus.). *Songs of seventy-six: a folksinger's history of the Revolution.* New York: Evans, 1972.

Words and music to Tory and rebel songs of American Revolution, with commentary on historical and social background of each song.

Ferris, Robert G., and Richard E. Morris. *The signers of the Declaration of Independence.* Flagstaff: Interpretative Publications, 1982.

History of the Declaration of Independence, with biographical sketches of signers, list of sites and homes associated with signers, and text of the document.

King, David C. *Colonial days: discover the past with fun projects, games, activities, and recipes.* New York: Wiley, 1998.

The fictional Mayhew family of Massachusetts provides a vehicle through which students learn of life in colonial America. Projects include candle making, yarn dying, and cooking. Pen-and-ink illustrations, detailed instructions, and an extensive glossary complete this work. Appropriate for grades 3–6.

Murray, Stuart. *America's song.* Bennington, Vt.: Images from the Past, 1999.

Fascinating study traces the history of the song "Yankee Doodle" from its Dutch origins to the Civil War era. Profusely illustrated.

St. George, Judith, and Sasha Meret (illus.). *Betsy Ross: patriot of Philadelphia.* New York: Holt, 1997.

Engaging biography of Betsy Ross explores her life from her early Quaker upbringing in Philadelphia to the famed meeting with George Washington that resulted in the construction of the first American flag. Black-and-white illustrations accompany the text. Appropriate for grades 3–6.

Travers, Len. *Celebrating the Fourth: Independence Day and the rites of nationalism in the early republic.* Amherst: University of Massachusetts Press, 1997.

Study of the origins, history, development, customs, and symbols associated with the Fourth of July. Focuses on the period between 1777 and 1826.

Van Leeuwen, Jean, and Henri Sorenson (illus.). *A Fourth of July on the plains.* New York: Dial, 1997.

In this story based on an 1852 diary entry from a member of the Oregon Trail party, a young boy and his friends devise a unique plan to participate in the Fourth of July celebration. Color artwork highlights the text. Appropriate for grades 1–4.

RESOURCES

WEB SITES

Betsy Ross homepage. www.libertynet.org/iha/betsy/index.html

> Focuses on the history of the first American flag and Betsy Ross's contributions to its creation. Includes a virtual tour of the Betsy Ross house, a biography of Ross, information on flag etiquette and trivia, frequently asked questions about flags, and links to other American history sites.

Colonial Hall: biographies of America's founding fathers. www.colonialhall.com/index.asp

> Features biographies and trivia on 103 founding fathers, including the signers of the Declaration of Independence, the Articles of Confederation, and the Constitution.

The Declaration of Independence. www.nara.gov/exhall/charters/declaration/decmain.html

> Web site produced by the National Archives that provides links to a high-resolution image of the Declaration of Independence, a transcription of the text of the Declaration, and links to sources that provide more detailed information on the history of the Declaration, the language and script of the document, and documents that were influential in the development of the country such as the Articles of Confederation and the Constitution.

Fourth of July celebration database. gurnkel.american.edu/meintze/fourth.htm

> Unique and well-researched site produced by James Heintze, a librarian at American University, containing excerpts from various sources that present an overview of Fourth of July celebrations from 1776 to 1999.

LABOR DAY

Craft, Donna, and Terrance W. Peck (eds.). *Profiles of American labor unions.* 2nd ed. Detroit: Gale, 1998.

> Directory of basic information on 280 unions, 33,000 locals, and 1,200 independent unions in the U.S. Also includes biographies of 170 influential union leaders of the past and present.

Jones, Jacqueline. *American work: black and white labor since 1600.* New York: Norton, 1998.

> Scholarly study of labor, its uses, and its abuses in America from colonial times to the present. Also treats the evolving relationships between black, white, and immigrant workers throughout the country's history. Includes illustrations.

Laughlin, Rosemary. *The Pullman strike of 1894: American labor comes of age.* Greensboro, N.C.: Morgan Reynolds, 1999.

> Covers the rise and professional success of George Pullman and his railway coach business, the founding of Pullman's model city, and the rise and fall of both the city and the business—culminating in the famous strike. Black-and-white photographs, a time line, and a glossary enhance this work. Appropriate for grades 7–12.

Mantsios, Gregory (ed.). *A new labor movement for the new century.* New York: Monthly Review, 1998.

> Twenty-one essays explore the need for labor unions to adapt to changes in today's workforce and environment in order to survive. Covers topics such as democracy and labor unions, ideology, diversity, and "organizing the unorganized."

Murray, Emmett R. *The lexicon of labor.* New York: New Press, 1998.

> Encyclopedia covers labor terms and concepts, labor leaders, legislation, and historical events.

Rothenberg, Daniel. *With these hands: the hidden world of migrant farm workers today.* San Diego: Harcourt, 1998.

> Inspiring account of the plight of migrant farm workers. Interviews from more than 250 sources, including farm workers, growers, lobbyists, and labor organizers, construct a picture of the hardships faced by migrant workers today.

Scott, Geoffrey, and Cherie R. Wyman (illus.). *Labor Day.* Minneapolis: Lerner, 1982.

> Tells of planning for and celebrating the "monster labor festival" on September 5, 1882, in New York City, which sparked the movement to establish Labor Day as a national holiday honoring American workers. Appropriate for kindergarten–grade 3.

Streissguth, Thomas. *Legendary labor leaders*. Hollywood, Calif.: Oliver, 1998.

> Profiles of eight key labor figures from the 19th and 20th centuries, including Cesar Chavez, A. Philip Randolph, Samuel Gompers, Mother Jones, and Jimmy Hoffa. Black-and-white photographs and a glossary accompany the text. Appropriate for grades 7–12.

WEB SITES

An eclectic list of events in U.S. labor history. www.hempwine.com/alleycat/labor.html

> Presents a chronology of labor-related events in U.S. history from 1806 to the present. Includes a short list of links to other labor-related sites.

The history of Labor Day. www.dol/gov/dol/opa/public/aboutdol/laborday.htm

> Department of Labor site explains the history of Labor Day and offers links to other Labor Day resources.

MARTIN LUTHER KING DAY

Abernathy, Donzaleigh. *Partners to history: Martin Luther King, Jr. and Ralph David Abernathy, and the civil rights movement*. Santa Monica, Calif.: General Publishing Group, 1998.

> Collection of photographs compiled by the daughter of the late civil rights leader Ralph Abernathy culled from numerous sources. Presents scenes of King and Abernathy participating in demonstrations, relaxing at home, preaching in church, and being released from jail. The photographs are accompanied by commentary by Ms. Abernathy.

Bray, Rosemary L., and Malcah Zeldis (illus.). *Martin Luther King*. Reprint, New York: Mulberry Books, 1997.

> Pictorial biography of Martin Luther King, Jr.; focuses on his work in the civil rights movement. Large, colorful illustrations enhance the text. Appropriate for grades 2–4.

Carson, Clayborne (ed.). *The autobiography of Martin Luther King, Jr*. New York: Warner, 1998.

> Inviting "autobiography" of Dr. King constructed by Clayton Carson, director of the Martin Luther King, Jr. Papers Project. Carson blends excerpts from King's personal papers into a narrative that traces his path becoming one of the leaders of the civil rights movement. Includes thoughts on his early attraction to the writings of Thoreau, his discovery of Gandhi's nonviolent principles, and his impression of important figures of the period such as Rosa Parks, John F. Kennedy, Lyndon Johnson, and Malcom X.

Carson, Clayborne, and Peter Holloran (eds.). *A knock at midnight: inspiration from the great sermons of Reverend Martin Luther King, Jr*. New York: Warner, 1998.

> Compilation of some of Dr. King's most popular sermons culled from transcriptions of recordings. Most of the sermons are introduced by a minister who knew Dr. King.

Colbert, Jan, and Ann Macmillan Harms (eds.). *Dear Dr. King: letters from today's children to Dr. Martin Luther King, Jr*. New York: Hyperion, 1998.

> Inspiring collection of letters written by Memphis school children of all racial backgrounds to Dr. King. The letters describe the children's personal lives and their thoughts on both the changes that have occurred as well as on the progress that remains to be made since Dr. King's death. Accompanied by photographs of contemporary children interwoven with photographs from the civil rights era.

King, Coretta Scott. *My life with Martin Luther King, Jr*. Rev. ed. New York: Holt; Penguin/Puffin, 1993.

> Biography of Dr. King based on Coretta Scott King's personal memoirs. This edition is an abridgement of an earlier version written for adults. Appropriate for grades 9–12.

King, Martin Luther, Jr. *Strength to love*. Reprint, Minneapolis: Augsburg, 1981.

> Collection of King's sermons, concluding with his personal credo which explains his understanding of Christian faith and way of life.

Posner, Gerald. *Killing the dream: James Earl Ray and the assassination of Martin Luther King, Jr*. New York: Random House, 1998.

> Explores the government complicity and cover-up theories put forth by parties as diverse as Dr. King's family and James Earl Ray and his lawyers.

Smith, Kenneth L., and Ira G. Zepp Jr. *Search for the beloved community: the thinking of Martin Luther King Jr.* Valley Forge: Judson, 1998

> Examination of King's concepts of social justice and nonviolence, based on theology and ethics of his Christian faith.

WEB SITES

Martin Luther King, Jr. scavenger hunt. users.massed.net/~tstrong/Martin.htm

> A clever site that helps children understand the life and times of the slain civil rights leader with links and images that are used as clues in answering questions about Dr. King, his life, and the establishment of the Martin Luther King Jr. holiday.

Seattle Times: MLK, the holiday. www.seattletimes.com/mlk/holiday/index.html

> Focuses on the formation of the Martin Luther King Jr. holiday and ways in which it is celebrated. Includes links to biographical information on Dr. King and the civil rights movement.

MEMORIAL DAY

Ashabranner, Brent, and Jennifer Ashabranner (illus.). *Their names to live: what the Vietnam Veterans Memorial means to America.* Breckenridge, Colo.: Twenty-First Century, 1998.

> Explores the significance of the memorial not just to veterans, but to America as a whole. The authors believe that the power of the memorial lies in the names on the wall and the people behind those names. To highlight this concept, they include illustrated biographies of four of the men whose names appear on the memorial. Appropriate for grades 4–7.

Bennett, Amanda, and Terence Foley. *In memoriam: a practical guide to planning a memorial service.* New York: Simon and Schuster/Fireside, 1997.

> Presents real-life examples of different memorial services to consider when organizing a funeral. Discusses writing eulogies and obituaries, ordering flowers, choosing between burial and cremation, and selecting a funeral home. Includes an appendix of poems, readings, and music.

Gutman, Israel (ed.). *Encyclopedia of the Holocaust.* New York: Macmillan, 1990.

> Four-volume set contains more than 1,000 entries on the Holocaust as reflected in the arts, theology, and politics. Also lists concentration camp sites and documentary centers.

Harris, Jill Werman. *Remembrances and celebrations: a book of eulogies, elegies, letters of condolence, and epitaphs.* New York: Pantheon, 1999.

> Presents a wide range of selections dating from the 17th century to the present. Many entries were written by well-known figures, such as Lillian Hellman's tribute to Dashiell Hammett and Rev. Jesse Jackson's tribute to Jackie Robinson.

Kagan, Berl (ed.). *Luboml: the memorial book of a vanished shtetl.* Hoboken, N.J.: Ktav, 1997.

> Luboml, a Polish town dating back to the 14th century had a Jewish population of 4,000 at the outbreak of World War II. In October 1942, all 4,000 inhabitants were shot to death after digging their own graves. This book, a memorial to those killed, was produced with the assistance of Luboml residents who left the town before the massacre. Details of daily life, social, cultural, educational, religious, and political activities are brought to life in black-and-white photographs.

Klarsfeld, Serge, Glorianne Depondt, and Howard M. Epstein (translators). *French children of the Holocaust: a memorial.* New York: New York University Press, 1996.

> This nearly 2,000-page reference work is a sobering memorial to the 11,400 Jewish toddlers, children, and teenagers deported from France and killed in the gas chambers of concentration camps during World War II. All their names are in the book, along with each child's birth date, age, address, and deportation convoy number. Some entries include photographs and excerpts from diaries and letters. Klarsfeld, who was hunted as a child by the Nazis, wants the proceeds from the book to be used to provide a collective gravestone for those who were killed.

Scott, Geoffrey, and E. Peter Hanson (illus.). *Memorial Day.* Minneapolis: Carolrhoda Books, 1983.

Provides background on the origins and development of Memorial Day as well as a glimpse of how the holiday was celebrated in 1871; includes illustrations. Appropriate for grades 1–4.

Schauffler, Robert Haven. *Memorial Day (Decoration Day): its celebration, spirit, and significance as related in prose and verse, with a non-sectional anthology of the Civil War.* 1930. Reprint, Detroit: Omnigraphics, 1990.

Collection of articles, essays, poems, and speeches about Memorial Day.

Theroux, Phyllis (ed.). *The book of eulogies: a collection of memorials, tributes, poetry, essays, and letters of condolence.* New York: Scribner, 1997.

Contains more than 100 eulogies gathered from editorials, spoken tributes, letters of condolence, essays, and poetry. Many of the contributions are from well-known personalities, such as Robert F. Kennedy's tribute to Martin Luther King, Jr., and tributes to Thomas Merton and Flannery O'Connor. The author provides helpful commentaries for many entries.

WEB SITE

Memorial Day. www.geocities.com/~cybergrandma/memday.htm

A brief introduction to the history of Memorial Day, with links to related resources under the following headings: memorials and casualty files, MIA/POW, Memorial Day messages, Memorial Day pages, and wars.

PRESIDENTS' DAY

Abbot, James A., and Elaine M. Rice. *Designing Camelot: the Kennedy White House restoration.* New York: Van Nostrand Reinhold, 1997.

Interesting account of how Jacqueline Kennedy, with the help of noted architects and interior designers, transformed the White House interior during her time as first lady. Includes a room-by-room description of the furnishings and decorations of the public and private rooms of the White House.

DeGregorio, William A. *The complete book of U.S. presidents.* 4th ed. New York: Barricade Books, 1993.

Collection of chapter-length biographies on every president from Washington to Clinton. Focuses on the personal side of the presidents and on important individuals in their lives.

Hampton, Wilborn. *Kennedy assassinated! the world mourns: A reporter's story.* Cambridge, Mass.: Candlewick, 1997.

Succinct firsthand account by a veteran reporter provides a compelling recreation of the events surrounding the Kennedy assassination. Includes archival photographs. Appropriate for grades 5–10.

Kane, Joseph Nathan. *Facts about the presidents.* 6th ed. Bronx, N.Y.: W. H. Wilson, 1993.

Includes family histories, Supreme Court appointees, portraits, autographs, and comparative data on each president and on his administration.

Kunhardt et al. *The American president.* New York: Putnam/Riverhead, 1999.

Pictorial overview of the presidency arranged thematically under epithets that are descriptive of each president's administration. The accompanying text focuses on the presidents' private lives.

Leiner, Katherine, and Katie Keller (illus.). *First children: growing up in the White House.* New York: Morrow/Tambourine, 1996.

Anecdotes describe life in the White House from the perspective of the children who have lived there. The children profiled range from very young to adult, and a woodcut-style portrait accompanies each history. Includes archival photographs. Appropriate for grades 4–8.

Nelson, Michael (ed.). *Congressional Quarterly's guide to the presidency.* 2nd ed. Washington, D.C.: Congressional Quarterly, 1996.

Two-volume publication covers the origins and development of the presidency. Includes brief biographies of all presidents and vice presidents through the Clinton administration and appendixes that provide electoral college votes, popular votes, Gallup Poll ratings for all administrations from Truman to Reagan, and a list of cabinet members for each administration.

Plissner, Martin. *The control room: how television calls the shots in presidential elections.* Riverside, N.J.: Free Press, 1999.

> Former CBS news coordinator's inside account of the relationship between presidential campaigns and television. Explores how aspects of a political campaign are often restructured to suit the needs of television.

Quiri, Patricia Ryon. *The White House.* New York: Watts, 1996.

> A history of the White House from its earliest days to 1995. Describes all the tour rooms and includes color photographs and archival reproductions to enhance the text. Appropriate for grades 4–8.

Reinhart, Mark S. *Abraham Lincoln on screen: a filmography of dramas and documentaries including television, 1903–1998.* Jefferson, N.C.: McFarland, 1999.

> An annotated listing of all film and television productions that deal with Abraham Lincoln or Lincoln-related events.

Seale, William, and Erik Kvalsvik (photog.). *The White House garden.* Washington D.C.: White House Historical Association, 1996.

> Fascinating history of the White House gardens, established in 1791. Explores how the gardens have changed to reflect the tastes of each first family. Color photographs accompany the text.

Smith, Curt. *Windows on the White House: the story of presidential libraries.* South Bend, Ind.: Diamond Communications, 1997.

> Guide to the libraries of 12 presidents, from Hayes to Bush. Each entry includes a short biography of the president, a history and description of the library and its holdings, contact information, and hours of operation. Photographs of the presidents, the libraries, and objects from the collections accompany the text.

Sobel, Robert (ed.). *Biographical directory of the United States executive branch, 1774–1989.* 3rd ed. Westport, Conn.: Greenwood, 1990.

> Biographical sketches of presidents, vice presidents, and cabinet members.

Southwick, Leslie H (comp). *Presidential also-rans and running mates, 1788–1980.* Jefferson, N.C.: McFarland, 1984.

> Interesting compilation of data on losing presidential candidates. Provides names and brief biographies of the candidates and their running mates, election results, and analyses of each candidate's qualifications.

Taylor, John M. *From the White House inkwell: American presidential autographs.* 2nd ed. Santa Monica: Modoc, 1989.

> Reproductions of letters and documents signed by presidents.

Wallace, Anthony F.C. *Jefferson and the Indians: the tragic fate of the first Americans.* Cambridge: Harvard, 1999.

> Scholarly account of Jefferson's policies toward Native Americans explores personal and public documentation that led to the infamous "removal policy" that nearly annihilated Native American culture in this country.

WEB SITES

The American experience: The presidents. www.pbs.org/wgbh/amex/presidents/indexjs.html

> Companion site to the PBS television series *The American Experience: The Presidents* that provides background on the presidents, a teacher's guide, and links to related resources, including a virtual tour of the Ronald Reagan Presidential Library.

Presidents Day. familyeducati.../topic/front/0,1156,1-4983,00.html

> Site sponsored by the Family Education Network that helps parents teach their children about Presidents' Day. Includes quizzes, background articles, and lists of related resources.

REVOLUTIONS

Burr et al. *Cinco de Mayo: yesterday and today.* New York: Douglas and McIntyre/Groundwood, 1999.

> Explains the Mexican national celebration that commemorates the Battle of Puebla. Contains historical illustrations and photographs of a reenactment of the battle. Appropriate for grades 3–5.

Cobb, Richard. *The French and their revolution: selected writings*. New York: New Press, 1999.

> Essays by the late British historian examine the social origins of the French revolution and its repercussions on French society.

French, Patrick. *Liberty or death: India's journey to independence and division*. North Pomfret, Vt.: Trafalgar Square, 1999.

> Analyzes the events and personalities that played a role in securing India's independence from Great Britain. Includes detailed biographical information on Gandhi, Jinnah, Lord Mountbatten, and other leaders.

Goldstone, Jack A. (ed.). *The encyclopedia of political revolutions*. Washington, D.C.: Congressional Quarterly, 1998.

> Three hundred articles examine the history of political revolutions since A.D. 1500. Using a broad definition of the term "revolution" allows the contributors to cover the civil rights movement of the 1960s and the women's rights movement as well as the American and French revolutions. Also includes biographies of key personalities such as Robespierre, Susan B. Anthony, and Martin Luther King, Jr.

Moses, Catherine. *Real life in Castro's Cuba*. Wilmington: Scholarly Resources, 1999.

> This account of life in Cuba 40 years after the revolution covers topics such as education, the availability of food and other staples, recreation and leisure, and freedom of speech. Includes interviews with political officials and ordinary people.

Ott, Thomas O. *The Haitian revolution, 1789–1804*. Knoxville: University of Tennessee Press, 1973.

> Concise history of the Haitian revolution and its consequences for the nation.

Perez-Stable, Marifeli. *The Cuban revolution: origins, course, and legacy*. New York: Oxford, 1993.

> Examines the social, political, and economic policies that led to the revolution and compares changes in those areas. Includes tables that trace changes in the sugar and tourism industries and the role of the female workforce since 1970.

Press, Robert M., and Betty Press. *The new Africa: dispatches from a changing continent*. Gainesville: University of Florida Press, 1999.

> *Christian Science Monitor* reporter with eight years of experience in Africa examines the political upheavals and freedom movements shaping African nations such as Somalia, Rwanda, and Nigeria.

WEB SITES

Cinco de Mayo. www.worldbook.com/fun/cinco/html/cinco.htm

> Introduces children to the significance of Cinco de Mayo and Mexican culture. Contains instructional resources for parents and teachers.

Mexican holidays: Cinco de Mayo. www.mexonline.com/cinco.htm

> Provides background on the history of Cinco de Mayo and information on past and present holiday celebrations.

THANKSGIVING

Agel, Jerome, Melinda Corey, and Jason Shulman. *The Thanksgiving book: an illustrated treasury of love, tales, poems, prayers, and the best in holiday feasting*. New York: Dell, 1987.

> Traces the origins, customs, and traditions of Thanksgiving Day; includes recipes, stories, and games.

Appelbaum, Diana Karter. *Thanksgiving: an American holiday, an American history*. New York: Facts on File, 1984.

> Describes the history of Thanksgiving and Thanksgiving Day recipes. Traces changes and developments in traditions and customs. Accompanied by illustrations.

Barth, Edna, and Ursula Arndt. *Turkeys, Pilgrims, & Indian corn: the story of the Thanksgiving symbols*. Boston: Houghton Mifflin, 1981.

> History of American Thanksgiving, beginning with the Pilgrims and their 1621 harvest festival. Easy text features the symbols of the day: turkey, corn, beans, pumpkins, the crane berry (which became the cranberry), and the cornucopia. Includes illustrations. Appropriate for grades 3–6.

Bauer, Caroline Feller, and Nadine Bernard Westcott (illus.). *Thanksgiving: stories and poems*. New York: HarperCollins, 1994.

Stories, songs, recipes, and poems develop common Thanksgiving Day themes: family, friendship, sharing, food, and thankfulness. Black-and-white illustrations enhance the text. Appropriate for grades 2–4.

Borden, Louise, and Steve Bjorkman (illus.). *Thanksgiving is . . .* New York: Scholastic, 1997.

An introduction to Thanksgiving Day for young readers. Recounts the history of the holiday and develops the connection between the first Thanksgiving and our contemporary celebration. Color illustrations reinforce the message. Appropriate for grades 1–2.

Garrison, Holly. *The Thanksgiving cookbook*. New York: Macmillan, 1991.

Presents some 350 Thanksgiving Day recipes, both traditional offerings and updated variations of old favorites. Includes recipes for each course of the meal and separate chapters for relishes, stuffing, gravy, and leftovers. Color photographs accompany the recipes.

Greenwood, Barbara, and Heather Collins (illus.). *A pioneer Thanksgiving: a story of harvest celebrations in 1841*. Buffalo, N.Y.: Kids Can Press, 1999.

The Robertson family's 1841 Thanksgiving Day preparations set the stage for the presentation of recipes, craft projects, and period games. Commentary and charcoal-and-sepia illustrations enhance the text. Appropriate for grades 3–6.

Hintz, Martin, and Kate Hintz. *Thanksgiving: why we celebrate it the way we do*. Mankato, Minn.: Capstone Press, 1996.

Examines the meaning of the holiday and the ways we celebrate it. Gives recipes and craft ideas. Accompanied by illustrations. Appropriate for grades 1–4.

Metaxas, Eric, and Sharon Stirnweis (illus.). *Squanto and the miracle of Thanksgiving*. Nashville: Thomas Nelson, 1999.

Traces the life of Squanto, the Patuxet Indian who was kidnapped into slavery by the Spanish in 1608, converted to Christianity, transferred to England, and eventually returned to his village in America. Describes his pivotal role in helping Governor Bradford and the English settlers of Plymouth survive their first winter and thus begin the tradition of Thanksgiving. Color illustrations accompany the text. Appropriate for kindergarten–grade 5.

Raphael, Elaine, and Don Bolognese. *Drawing America: the story of the first Thanksgiving*. New York: Scholastic, 1991.

Recounts the story of the Pilgrims' first Thanksgiving with an unusual twist: at the end of the story, readers are invited to make their own drawings depicting the Pilgrims' experiences. Includes patterns and instructions for creating the characters in the story. Appropriate for grades 2–4.

Rodgers, Rick. *Thanksgiving 101: celebrate America's favorite holiday with America's Thanksgiving expert*. Alameda, Calif.: Broadway Books, 1998.

Rodgers, a cooking teacher and spokesman for Perdue Farms, one of the nation's largest turkey producers, has written the definitive book on preparing for Thanksgiving. He covers all aspects of turkey preparation, from buying and thawing the bird to prepping, roasting, basting, and carving. Also includes 100 recipes for appetizers, side dishes, breads, desserts, beverages, and leftovers.

Roop, Peter, Connie Roop, and Gwen Connelly (illus.). *Let's celebrate Thanksgiving*. Brookfield, Conn.: Millbrook, 1999.

Presents the basic history of Thanksgiving Day, explaining what life was like for the Pilgrims and how the first Thanksgiving celebration developed from their experiences and evolved into our modern celebration. Includes a selection of Thanksgiving Day jokes, riddles, and craft projects. Color illustrations accompany the text. Appropriate for grades 1–4.

Sechrist, Elizabeth Hough, Janette Woolsey, and Guy Fry (illus.). *It's time for Thanksgiving*. Detroit: Omnigraphics, 1999.

Stories, poems, plays, recipes, and games for Thanksgiving, plus a history of the holiday.

Umnik, Sharon Dunn (ed.). *175 easy-to-do Thanksgiving crafts*. Honesdale, Pa.: Boyd's Mills, 1996.

Includes instructions for making turkeys, pilgrims, cornucopias, and other holiday decorations. Appropriate for grades 1–6.

WEB SITES

The first Thanksgiving. www.plimoth.org/Library/Thanksgiving/firstT.htm_

Site produced by Plimoth Plantation, "the living history museum of 17th century Plymouth," that provides information on the first Thanksgiving celebration, ways in which the celebration has changed through the years, and facts and myths surrounding the holiday.

The first Thanksgiving proclamation: June 20, 1676. www.night.net/thanksgiving/First-proc.html

Site prepared by Gerald Murphy that provides background on the first Thanksgiving and a transcript of the first Thanksgiving proclamation, which was issued by the governing council of Charlestown, Massachusetts on June 20, 1676.

Thanksgiving celebrations at the Holiday Spot! www.theholidayspot.com/thanksgiving/index.htm

A compilation of Thanksgiving-related resources, including links to music, crafts, books, and recipes.

VETERANS DAY

Ansary, Mir Tamim. *Veterans Day.* Portsmouth, N.H.: Heinemann, 1998.

Introduction to the history of Veterans Day for children. Focuses on World Wars I and II; Vietnam is not mentioned. Black-and-white photographs accompany the text. Appropriate for grades 2–3.

Blanco, Richard L. (ed.). *The American Revolution, 1775–1783: an encyclopedia.* New York: Garland, 1993.

Two-volume work focuses on the military history of the American Revolution and gives details on major battles and personalities of the period.

Fowler, Arlen, and William H. Leckie. *The Black infantry in the West, 1869–1891.* Norman, Okla.: University of Oklahoma Press, 1996.

This scholarly study provides an overview of African Americans in the U.S. infantry during the years of western expansion.

Hallock, Daniel William. *Hell, healing, and resistance: veterans speak out.* Farmington, Pa.: Plough, 1998.

Veterans from World War II and the Korean, Vietnam, and Gulf Wars explore the emotional and physical issues that have impacted their lives since returning home and their attempts to resolve those issues.

Lanning, Michael Lee. *African-American soldiers: from Crispus Attucks to Colin Powell.* New York: Birch Lane, 1998.

Chronicles the history of African American soldiers, sailors, and pilots from the earliest days of the nation to the present. Describes their contributions as well as the discrimination and lack of recognition many of them suffered. Also treats failures and successes in the integration of military units.

Livesey, Anthony. *Historical atlas of World War I.* New York: Holt, 1994.

Opens with an overview of the war, followed by chapters that document the war year by year. Includes month-by-month time lines in each chapter and detailed maps.

Macdonald, Lyn. *To the last man: spring 1918.* Carroll and Graf, 1999.

Oral testimonies of frontline soldiers during World War I give a personalized account of the horrors of war. Focuses on the campaigns of spring 1918; includes photographs.

McPherson, James (ed.). *Atlas of the Civil War.* New York: Macmillan, 1994.

Color maps, time lines, and photographs combine with personal narratives to provide an overview of the Civil War.

McNamara et al. *Argument without end: in search of answers to the Vietnam tragedy.* Washington, D.C.: Public Affairs, 1999.

Former Secretary of Defense McNamara explores why opportunities to avoid the war in Vietnam, to prevent its escalation, or to terminate it sooner were not pursued. Approaches the issues from both a U.S. and a Vietnamese perspective.

Miller, Grace Porter. *Call of Duty: a Montana girl in World War II*. Baton Rouge: Louisiana State University, 1999.

Miller, the daughter of a farmer in Montana, recounts her experiences as cryptographer during World War II.

Neagles, James C. *U.S. military records*. Salt Lake City: Ancestry, 1994.

Helpful guide to using federal, state, and local military records for fact-finding or genealogy-related pursuits.

Norwalk, Rosemary. *Dearest ones: a true WWII love story*. New York: Wiley, 1999.

The memoirs of an American Red Cross volunteer worker in World War II England are presented through selections from her private letters to family and friends, diary entries, and photographs.

Palmer, Alan. *Victory, 1918*. New York: Atlantic Monthly Press, 2000.

In-depth overview of World War I as it was fought on all fronts: Europe, Mesopotamia, and Egypt. Treats not just the great battles, but also those that were far removed from the well-documented western front.

Paulsen, Gary. *Soldier's heart*. New York: Delacorte, 1999.

Narrative based on the true story of a 15-year-old Union soldier describes the Civil War through his experiences on and off the battlefield. Appropriate for grades 5–8.

Pimlott, John. *Historical atlas of World War II*. New York: Holt, 1994.

Opens with an overview of the war, followed by chapters that document the war year by year. Includes more than 100 maps and a chronology.

Sorel, Nancy Caldwell. *The women who wrote the war*. New York: Arcade, 1999.

Discusses the fate of female war correspondents during World War II, centering on the personal and professional struggles they encountered in a male-dominated profession. Includes photographs.

Summers, Harry G., Jr. *Vietnam War almanac*. New York: Facts on File, 1985.

The historical background of the Vietnam War and the geography of the country are broadly covered in the first two chapters. The remainder of the almanac comprises 500 entries that describe the equipment, events, and social aspects of the war.

Zentner, Christian, and Bedurftig Friedemann (eds.). *Encyclopedia of the Third Reich*. New York: Macmillan, 1991.

Two-volume work examines the history of Hitler's Third Reich. Includes 27 in-depth articles, 3,000 shorter entries, maps, and illustrations.

WEB SITE

Veterans Day. www.computingcorner.com/holidays/vets/veterans.html

Teaches children the history behind Veterans Day. Discusses the origins of the holiday, the history of "Taps," and war statistics; includes coloring pages.

Veterans Day homepage. www.va.gov/pubaff/vetsday/index.htm

Web site produced by the Department of Veterans Affairs offers resources to help teachers plan Veterans Day activities, a discussion of the history of the holiday, and links to other sites.

WASHINGTON'S BIRTHDAY

Dalzell, Robert F., and Lee Baldwin Dalzell. *George Washington's Mount Vernon: at home in Revolutionary America*. New York: Oxford, 1998.

Traces parallels between the evolution of Washington's Mount Vernon estate and his rise from local politician to the first president of the new nation; includes illustrations.

Ferrie, Richard. *The world turned upside down: George Washington and the Battle of Yorktown*. New York: Holiday House, 1999.

Detailed account of the pivotal battle at Yorktown. Provides a time line of events and in-depth information on participants, military strategies, weaponry, battle conditions, and uniforms. Illustrated with reproductions of period engravings and maps. Appropriate for grades 5–9.

Greenberg, Allan. *George Washington, architect.* Woodbridge, Suffolk, Eng.: Andreas Papadakis, 1999.

> Explores the intricate relationship between politics and city planning that Washington sought to exploit in the design of the young nation's capital. Also gives detailed information on Washington's work at Mount Vernon and how that influenced his ideas for the new capital. The closing chapter delves into Washington's complex relationship with Pierre L'Enfant, the gifted, army-trained French engineer who developed the original plan for the capital. Profusely illustrated with color photographs, plans, maps, and facsimiles.

Murray, Stuart. *Washington's farewell to his officers after victory in the Revolution.* Images from the Past, 1999.

> Narrative of Washington's farewell address to his officers at the Fraunces Tavern in New York, 1783. Interweaves biographical sketches of key Washington confidantes with descriptions of important events of the time such as the British withdrawal from New York. Accompanied by illustrations.

Old, Wendie. *George Washington.* Hillside, N.J.: Enslow, 1997.

> Biography follows George Washington from his childhood in Virginia to his role as the first president of the U.S. Debunks the myths that have surrounded him, thus presenting a more human, and more accessible, portrait of the first president. Appropriate for grades 5–8.

Rhodehamel, John. *The great experiment: George Washington and the American republic.* New Haven: Yale University Press, 1998.

> Biography recounts the failures, successes, and personal qualities that led Washington to become the nation's first president; includes illustrations.

WEB SITES

George Washington's Mount Vernon estate and gardens. www.mountvernon.org

> Provides a virtual tour of the Mount Vernon estate, descriptions of pioneer farming, links to the Mount Vernon Library and collections, up-

dates on archeological findings, and a virtual reenactment of Washington's funeral.

George Washington Papers at the Library of Congress: 1741–1799. memory.loc.gov/ammem/gwhtml

> Site produced by the Manuscript Division of the Library of Congress that makes available for viewing on-line approximately 65,000 documents from the George Washington Papers, including correspondence, journals, diaries, and military reports from 1741 to 1799.

DAYS OF OBSERVANCE

ARBOR DAY

Cassie, Brian. *National Audubon Society first field guide to trees.* New York: Scholastic, 1999.

> Guide to major North American trees. Each entry presents a common tree categorized by leaf shape and describes its major characteristics. Color photographs accompany the text.

Grove, Doris, and Marilyn H. Mallory. *My mother talks to trees.* Atlanta: Peachtree, 1999.

> Entertaining story of a young girl whose mother talks to trees while she walks her embarrassed daughter home from school each day. Botanical facts are cleverly woven into the plot so that by the end of the story readers have been introduced to 11 varieties of trees common in the southern U.S. Color illustrations and a glossary complement the text. Appropriate for grades 1–4.

Hickman, Pamela. *Tree book.* Buffalo, N.Y.: Kids Can Press, 1999.

> Presents a broad overview of the biology and function of trees. Includes sidebars with interesting trivia, experiments, activities, and color illustrations. Appropriate for grades 3–5.

Dirr, Michael A. *Dirr's handy trees and shrubs: an illustrated encyclopedia.* Portland, Oreg.: Timber Press, 1998.

> Encyclopedia and guidebook provides information on 500 species of trees based on their suitability for zones 3–8 of the U.S. Department of Agriculture's Hardiness Zone Map. Alphabetically arranged entries provide facts such as the habitat, foliage, flower, fruit, and landscape use

of trees. Accompanied by 1,600 color photographs and the USDA Hardiness Zone Map.

WEB SITES

The Committee for National Arbor Day. www.nationalarborday.org

Official site of the National Arbor Day Committee. Presents the history of Arbor Day, information on tree-planting programs, and links to Arbor Day resources.

The National Arbor Day Foundation. www.arborday.org

Site of the National Arbor Day Foundation. Presents the history of Arbor Day, resources for teaching children about trees, tips for planting and caring for trees, and links to conferences and workshops.

ARMED FORCES DAY

Beckett, Ian F.W. *Encyclopedia of guerilla warfare.* Santa Barbara, Calif.: ABC-CLIO, 1999.

A thorough source that traces the history of guerilla warfare from the American Revolution to the present. Describes guerilla campaigns and individuals who are associated with guerilla warfare as practitioners or theorists.

Clancy, Tom. *Marine: a guided tour of a Marine expeditionary unit.* New York: Berkley, 1996.

The book's opening chapter covers the history, beliefs, weapons, and ethics of the Marine Corps. The rest of the book focuses on the Marine Expeditionary Unit—unique emergency response teams that respond to special situations. Includes photographs.

Current, Richard N., and Paul D. Escott. *Encyclopedia of the Confederacy.* New York: Simon and Schuster, 1994.

More than a thousand articles cover all aspects of confederate life, from politics and warfare to medicine and entertainment. Four-volume encyclopedia includes illustrations and maps.

Dictionary of military terms. Rev. ed. Mechanicsburg, Pa.: Stackpole, 1999.

Defines more than 6,000 military terms that have been approved by the Joint Chiefs of Staff.

Includes 3,000 NATO-approved acronyms and abbreviations.

Eggenberger, David. *An encyclopedia of battles: accounts of over 1560 battles from 1479 B.C. to the present.* Rev. ed. New York: Dover, 1985.

More than a thousand battles waged between 1479 B.C. and 1985 are described in brief entries that place the battles within their political and historical contexts. Includes illustrations.

Kohn, George Childs. *The dictionary of wars.* Rev. ed. New York: Facts on File, 1999.

Presents 1,800 articles that cover the past 4,000 years of warfare within and between nations. Conflicts are arranged alphabetically, and entries include the dates, background, and outcome of each conflict.

Rendall, Ivan. *Rolling thunder: the story of jet combat from World War II to the Gulf War.* New York: Free Press, 1999.

International in scope, the book covers wars fought by countries besides the U.S., such as the various Middle East conflicts and the war over the Falklands. The author explains the role of air combat in each campaign and describes the tactics and technology involved.

Robertshaw, Andrew. *A soldier's life: a visual history of soldiers through the ages.* New York: Lodestar, 1997.

Features sharp, detailed, color photographs of authentic uniforms, equipment, weapons, and supplies used by soldiers from the Roman legions of A.D. 50 through World War II. An informative text about the life of a soldier accompanies the visuals. Includes a listing of forts, military museums, and parks. Appropriate for grades 4–8.

Robotti, Frances Diane, and James Vescovi. *The USS Essex and the birth of the American Navy.* Holbrook, Mass.: Adams Media, 1999.

Chronicles the history of the USS *Essex*, the first American warship. Describes the frigate's service at sea, beginning with its construction in 1801 and ending with its last battle during the War of 1812; includes illustrations.

The visual dictionary of military uniforms. New York: Dorling Kindersley, 1992.

An excellent guide to military uniforms and gear from the time of the Roman legions to Desert Storm. Each uniform is presented in full color and labeled for easy identification of the components.

WEB SITES

DefenseLINK. www.defenselink.mil.

U.S. Department of Defense site that offers military-related news stories, biographies of military leaders, links to armed forces sites, an introduction to the inner workings of the Department of Defense, and a virtual tour of the Pentagon.

Jane's. www.janes.com

Site produced by Jane's, the British publisher of military and geopolitical resource materials, that includes highlights from Jane's publications, links to weapons sites, and information about upcoming conferences.

United States Armed Forces uniform reference. www.mav.net/wguynes/military

Provides information on ensignia for all branches of the armed forces; includes detailed photographs.

AVIATION DAY

Baker, David. *Flight and flying: a chronology.* New York: Facts on File, 1993.

Reviews the history of flight, from the earliest attempts to 1991. Includes information on important figures in the field of aviation and descriptions of the military and commercial airline industries.

Berliner, Don. *Aviation: reaching for the sky.* Minneapolis: Oliver Press, 1997.

This interesting study of man's quest to fly opens with an overview of aeronautic history. Chapter-length biographies of innovators such as the Montgolfier brothers, the Wright brothers, Otto Lilienthal, and Igor Sikorsky complete the work. Archival photographs and lithographs complement the text. Appropriate for grades 5–8.

Cassutt, Michael. *Who's who in space: The international space station edition.* New York: Macmillan, 1998.

Biographical sketches of key figures in space exploration. Also recounts important technical and historical developments in the field. Color illustrations accompany the text.

Gatland, Kenneth, et al. *The illustrated encyclopedia of space technology: a comprehensive history of space exploration.* New York: Crown, 1989.

This chronology of space flight provides data on space pioneers, satellites, communications, shuttles, and more. Includes an in-depth look at the space science developments of the 1980s. Contains numerous color illustrations.

Giblin, James. *Charles A. Lindbergh: a human hero.* New York: Clarion, 1997.

A balanced account of Lindbergh's achievements and faults. It recounts the aviator's historic transatlantic flight and the subsequent kidnapping of his child, but it also deals plainly with Lindbergh's Nazi affiliations and anti-Semitism. Archival photographs accompany the text. Appropriate for grades 4–10.

Harris, Jacqueline L. *The Tuskegee airmen: black heroes of World War II.* Denver: Dillon, 1996.

Recounts the struggles of African Americans in the air force, focusing on the formation of the 99th Fighter Squadron, which trained near the Tuskegee Institute in Alabama. Describes the squadron's military successes, battles against racism, and postwar efforts to form an integrated air force. Also contains personal accounts from former members of the squadron and illustrations. Appropriate for grades 6–9.

Jane's space directory. U.K.: Jane's Information Group, 1997–98.

An annual directory of space programs worldwide. Topics cover international space projects, the military space industry, and space centers. Includes a wealth of illustrations.

Kelly, Emery J. *Paper airplanes: models to build and fly.* Minneapolis: Lerner, 1997.

After explaining the basics of aerodynamics, the author gives patterns and diagrammed step-by-step instructions for 12 paper airplane models. Includes a list of materials needed and color photographs of the finished products.

Pisano, Dominick A., and Cathleen S. Lewis. *Air and space history: an annotated bibliography*. New York: Garland, 1988.

> Annotated bibliography of some 1,800 sources on air and space flight prepared by the curatorial staff of the National Air and Space Museum at the Smithsonian Institution.

Reithmaier, Larry. *The aviation/space dictionary*. 7th ed. Blue Ridge Summit, Pa.: Aero, 1990.

> Defines more than 6,000 air and space terms, with diagrams and photographs. A perennial favorite, this title has been in print since 1939.

Stille, Darlene. *Airplanes*. San Francisco: Children's Press, 1997.

> Small but thorough book introduces children to the history of flight, the mechanics of airplanes, different types of airplanes, and the people involved in the world of air transport. Includes photographs, illustrations, and a list of related Web sites. Appropriate for grades 2–4.

WEB SITES

Aerospace World-wide Web Virtual Library. www.db.erau.edu/www_virtual_lib/aerospace.html

> Site produced by Embry-Riddle Aeronautical University is a gateway to a variety of flight-related resources such as links to university research in flight, images of airplanes and spacecraft, links to aeronautical publications, and links to commercial, government, and international aviation sites.

The International Women's Air & Space Museum, Inc. www.iwasm.org

> Site sponsored by the International Women's Air & Space Museum, located in Cleveland, Ohio, which is dedicated to preserving the history of women in aviation. Provides an assortment of interesting biographies and links to research resources and upcoming events.

BIRD DAY

Attenborough, David. *The life of birds*. Pennington, N.J.: Princeton, 1998.

> Interesting introduction to the history of birds. Covers the development of flight among birds, the mechanics of flight, feeding requirements to sustain flight, mating habits, adaptations to new environments, and the recent extinction of many species. Serves as an accompaniment to Attenborough's PBS series.

Dillon, Mike. *The great birdhouse book: fun, fabulous designs you can build*. New York: Sterling/Chapelle, 1999.

> Presents detailed instructions for building an array of birdhouses and suggestions for adapting each style to suit 20 different species of birds. Includes diagrams, a list of materials needed, and color photographs for each design.

Forshaw, Joseph (ed.). *Encyclopedia of birds*. 2nd ed. San Diego: Academic, 1998.

> A historical overview of birds is followed by an explanation of the classification system used by ornithologists, a description of common habitats, details of basic bird habits, information on endangered species, and conversation suggestions. The main portion of the encyclopedia presents international coverage of bird species and descriptions of each. More than 200 color photographs, 150 paintings, and a selection of maps and diagrams support the text.

Kress, Stephen W. (ed.). *Welcoming wild birds to your yard*. Brooklyn: Brooklyn Botanic Garden, 1998.

> Guide to help homeowners design gardens that will attract various species of birds. After exploring the link between bird biology and plants, the guide offers tips on selecting plants for each region of the U.S. and explains which birds will be attracted to particular plant types and how the birds will use the plants. Includes lists of birds, nurseries, and source materials.

Sonder, Ben. *Hummingbirds: a celebration of nature's most dazzling creatures*. Running/Courage, 1999.

> Text describing the hummingbird's history, physical characteristics, mating, and breeding habits is supported by 100 color photographs of these brilliantly hued creatures. Includes suggestions on choosing feeders to attract hummingbirds for closer observation.

Spaulding, Dean T. *Housing our feathered friends*. Minneapolis: Lerner, 1997.

> After examining why, how, and where birds construct their nests, the author gives detailed

instructions for building a variety of bird-houses; includes color photographs. Appropriate for grades 4–6.

Swinburne, Stephen R. *In good hands: behind the scenes at the Center for Orphaned and Injured Birds.* San Francisco: Sierra Club, 1998.

Get a behind-the-scenes look at the work of the Vermont Raptor Center, which cares for injured and abandoned birds. Color photographs follow a group of school children as they tour the facility and watch their guide demonstrate the proper handling, care, and feeding of birds. The photographs are accompanied by text of the questions and answers that arose during the tour. Sidebars offer additional information on birds. Appropriate for grades 3–6.

Taylor, Ann. *Watching birds: reflections on the wing.* New York: McGraw-Hill, 1999.

Essays by a professor of literature combine the joys of bird watching with the love of books. Taylor weaves bird-related allusions from authors such as Tennyson and Dante with her own observations on bird watching into a collection of engaging writings.

Weidensaul, Scott. *Living on the wind: across the globe with migratory birds.* New York: Farrar/North Point, 1999.

The author follows a group of birds from a wildlife refuge in Alaska to their wintering spots in the southern hemisphere and then back again to the north. Describes how birds navigate by the sun, stars, and the earth's magnetic field. Also discusses how birds are being harmed by environmental degradation.

Weidensaul, Scott. *National Audubon Society first field guide to birds.* New York: Scholastic, 1998.

Handy guidebook with color illustrations of 50 common North American birds, plus descriptions of each bird, information on feeding habits, hints on how to recognize different birds, and similarly useful material. Appropriate for grades 4–6.

Williams, Nick. *How birds fly.* San Marino, Calif.: Benchmark Books, 1997.

Focuses on a bird's unique anatomy, with color illustrations and photographs depicting musculature and bone structure to enhance the text. Also explores the mechanics of flight—takeoffs, landings, gliding, and hovering. Appropriate for grades 5–12.

WEB SITES

Electronic Resources on Ornithology. www.chebucto.ns.ca/Environment/NHR/bird.html

Comprehensive site devoted to ornithology and maintained by Empty Mirrors Press and Christopher Majka, an author of publications on birds. Contains links to numerous associations, organizations, online publications, and commercial enterprises. Sites are divided into the following categories: General, Canada, U.S., New Zealand, Far East, Africa, and Commercial.

O.W.L.: The Ornithological Web Library. aves.net/the-owl

Site maintained by Aves.Net Productions that features over 1,200 links to Web pages focusing on wild birds. Categories include endangered birds: programs and species; bibliographies/discussion groups/online publications; sound and image libraries; living bird taxa; bird travel services and trip reports; population and migration monitoring; and rare bird alerts and digests.

Birding on the Web. www.birder.com

Site devoted to bird watching that provides links in the following categories: global bird checklists, birding hot spots, bird-alert telephone numbers, and suggestions on attracting birds. Also includes bird quizzes and an online nature store that markets bird books, binoculars, and other essentials for quality bird watching.

Bird Watch. www.pbs.org/birdwatch

Companion site to the PBS series of the same name hosted by Craig Tufts and Dick Hutto. Provides links to summaries of past episodes, show times, video purchases, viewer comments and questions, and general bird-watching resources.

World Twitch: Finding Rare Birds around the World. worldtwitch.virtualave.net

Site created by John Hall, an author of bird guidebooks, that provides geographically arranged links to bird-focused discussion groups, bird-watching tours, bird-sound libraries, bird publications, conservation groups, and comprehensive reports on bird-related topics.

Audubon Online. www.audubon.org

Official site of the National Audubon Society. Provides links to information about the society; membership and support; publications—including *Audubon*, the society's journal; and biographical information about the society's namesake, John James Audubon. Also features links to a variety of bird sites, travel-information sites, bird-news sites, conservation and research sites, and K–12 educational resource sites.

Artcyclopedia: John James Audubon—Works Viewable on the Internet. www.artcyclopedia. com/artists/audubon_john_james.html

Features links to on-line exhibits of Audubon's work found at major galleries and museums in the U.S. and England, such as the National Gallery of Art in Washington, D.C.; Chatsworth House in England, and the Wehle Gallery of Sporting Art in New York. Also offers selected links to Audubon image archives, commercial galleries, publications, and general bird-related sites.

HALLOWEEN

Barth, Edna, and Ursula Arndt (illus.). *Witches, pumpkins, & grinning ghosts: the story of the Halloween symbols*. Boston: Houghton Mifflin, 1981.

Symbols of Halloween from ancient Britain to modern times; includes illustrations. Appropriate for grades 3–6.

Christopher, Milbourne. *Houdini: the untold story*. Mattituck, N.Y.: Amereon, 1988.

Character, personality, and career of the celebrated magician whose birthday is observed on Halloween.

Christopher, Milbourne, Maurine Christopher (contributor), and David Copperfield (foreword). *Illustrated history of magic*. Portsmouth, N.H.: Heinemann, 1996.

Comprehensive history of magic from the time of Egyptian sorcerer-priests to Houdini, Blackstone, Dunninger, Doug Henning, David Cop-

perfield, and Melinda. Includes the secrets behind the Indian Rope Trick, the Vanishing Elephant, and other great feats of magic.

Doran, Laura Dover. *The big book of Halloween: creative and creepy projects for revellers of all ages*. Asheville, N.C.: Lark, 1998.

After a brief overview of the history of the holiday, this sourcebook focuses on ways of celebrating Halloween today. Ideas for celebrating the holiday are divided into five sections: "Devilish decorations," "Spooky lighting," "Eerie edibles," "Clever costumes," and "Frightening fun." Each project or recipe provides detailed instructions and photographs. Halloween fun facts and trivia are scattered throughout the text. The book closes with a selection of scary stories and folktales.

Hintz, Martin, and Kate Hintz. *Halloween: why we celebrate it the way we do*. Mankato, Minn.: Capstone Press, 1996.

Describes origins, history, development, and symbols of Halloween, with suggestions for crafts and activities; includes color illustrations. Appropriate for kindergarten–grade 3.

Irving, Washington, and Russ Flint (illus.). *The legend of Sleepy Hollow; found among the papers of the late Diedrich Knickerbocker*. Nashville: Ideals/Candy Cane, 1999.

This 150-year-old Halloween favorite is given new life by Russ Flint's rich oil paintings complementing Irving's original text.

Pratt Bannatyne, Lesley. *Halloween: an American holiday*. Gretna, La.: Pelican, 1998.

In-depth treatment of the history of Halloween and its origins. Provides useful information on traditions, customs, connections with various religions and ethnic groups, legends, and folklore.

Roop, Peter, and Connie Roop. *Let's celebrate Halloween*. Brookfield, Conn.: Millbrook, 1997.

A basic historical overview of Halloween, with information on folklore, customs, symbols, and instructions for making caramel apples, paper bag masks, and other craft projects. Color illustrations accompany the text. Appropriate for grades 3–5.

Santino, Jack (ed.). *Halloween and other festivals of life and death.* Knoxville: University of Tennessee Press, 1994.

> Collection of writings focus on modern-day celebrations of Halloween, changing patterns of celebration, and the influence of related celebrations such as the Mexican tradition of the Day of the Dead.

Silverman, Kenneth. *Houdini!!: The career of Ehrich Weiss.* New York: HarperCollins, 1996.

> Chronicles the life of the great magician and escape artist from his childhood in Wisconsin to his early days in vaudeville and eventual fame in New York. Includes detailed accounts of his friendship and falling-out with Sir Arthur Conan-Doyle, his attempts to expose fraudulent spiritualists, and his often-divergent personality.

WEB SITES

Everything Halloween. www.everythinghalloween. com/home/start.asp

> Provides Halloween celebration suggestions, ideas for costumes and treats, lists of horror videos and television programs, safety tips, and a brief history of the holiday.

Halloween: Facts and misinformation. www. religioustolerance.org/hallowee.htm

> Explains the history of Halloween as it is viewed by neopagans, Christians, and the public. Includes articles on customs, traditions, and myths as well as links to other sites.

MOTHER'S DAY

Anderson, Laurie Halse, and Dorothy Donohue (illus.). *No time for mother's day.* Albert Whitman, 1999.

> Story of how Charity Chatfield devises a plan to give her busy mom the one thing she desperately needs for mother's day: peace and quiet; accompanied by color illustrations. Appropriate for kindergarten–grade 3.

Beard, Patricia. *Good daughters: loving our mothers as they age.* New York: Warner, 1999.

> Interviews, statistics, and anecdotes trace the relationships between female adult baby boomers and their mothers.

Brown, Keith Michael. *Sacred bond: black men and their mothers.* New York: Little, Brown, 1998.

> Interviews and profiles explore the relationship between African American males and their mothers. Handles topics such as raising biracial children, teaching about racism, dealing with sexual issues, and caring for aging parents.

Ford, Judy, and Amanda Ford. *Between mother & daughter: a teenager and her mom share the secrets of a strong relationship.* Emeryville, Calif.: Conari, 1999.

> A how-to manual for facilitating communication between mothers and teenage daughters, written by a family therapist and her daughter. Covers a wide range of issues from both the mother's and the daughter's perspective. Includes suggestions for jump-starting conversations on difficult topics.

Golden, Marita. *A miracle every day: triumph and transformation in the lives of single mothers.* New York: Doubleday, 1999.

> Collection of thoughts from a former single mother regarding the difficulties and unsuspected rewards of single motherhood, with special focus on the need for both the parent and the child to be adaptable and resilient in the face of often desperate circumstances.

Kearns, Caledonia. *Motherland: writings by Irish American women about mothers and mothering.* New York: Morrow, 1999.

> Essays and anecdotes from 19th and 20th century female Irish American authors reflect on the mother-child relationship. Includes writings from authors such as Maureen Howard, Mother Jones, and Anna Quindlen.

Shough, Carol Gandee. *All the mamas: a true love story for mothers and daughters.* Columbia, S.C.: Summerhouse, 1998.

> In this delightful autobiographical poem, the author comments on the mother-daughter relationship for each preceding generation of her family, going back two centuries. For each mother-daughter generation, the relationship is linked to some historic event pertinent to that time. Color illustrations accompany the text. Appropriate for preschool–grade 3.

Wong, Janet S. *The rainbow hand: poems about mothers and children*. New York: Simon and Schuster, 1999.

> Eighteen short poems reflect on the mother-child relationship from both perspectives, each beautifully illustrated with original color artwork. Appropriate for grades 5–8.

WEB SITE

Mother's Day: 100 Moms. www.biography.com/features/mother/main.html

> This site, produced to accompany A&E Television's popular series "Biography," looks at the origins of Mother's Day and provides links to biographies of 100 famous moms, "from TV mom Mrs. Brady to supermom Bobbie McCaughey, mother of septuplets."

NATIVE AMERICAN DAYS

Davis, Mary B. (ed.). *Native America in the twentieth century: an encyclopedia*. New York: Garland, 1994.

> A collection of articles that focus on issues currently facing Native Americans in the U.S. Topics include gaming, land controversies, arts, and education.

Erdoes, Richard, and Alfonso Ortiz (eds.). *American Indian trickster tales*. New York: Viking, 1998.

> Anthology of 106 tales dealing with the theme of the trickster from a Native American perspective. Includes characters such as Coyote, Iktomi the Spiderman, and Rabbit. Each tale is identified with its tribe of origin, and many are accompanied by illustrations.

Malinowski, Sharon. *Notable Native Americans*. Detroit: Gale, 1995.

> Essays recount the accomplishments of 265 prominent Native Americans, both historical and contemporary. Entries encompass law, sports, media, the arts, and journalism; many are accompanied by photographs.

Malinowski, Sharon, and Anna Sheets (eds.). *Gale encyclopedia of Native American tribes*. Detroit: Gale, 1998.

> Four-volume work profiles Native American tribes of the U.S. Each volume corresponds to a region of the country, with tribes listed in alphabetical order. Includes discussion of significant events in tribal history, tribal culture, and current issues facing the tribes. There are some 200 biographical sketches, 600 photographs and illustrations, and a glossary.

Matuz, Roger (ed.). *St. James guide to Native North American artists*. Detroit: St. James, 1997.

> Overview of 400 Native American artists of the 20th century. Entries are arranged alphabetically by genres: painting, textile arts, sculpture, jewelry, photography, carving, pottery, basketry, prints, architecture, performance art, mixed media arts, and drawing. Each entry contains biographical information, tribal affiliation, exhibition history, galleries that house or sell the artist's work, and a bibliography.

Miller, Dorcas S. *Stars of the first people: Native American star myths and constellations*. Boulder, Colo.: Pruett, 1997.

> Combines a Native American perspective on astronomy with "celestial myths" that explain the origins of the constellations. This interesting collection of stories gathered from oral and written sources also provides details of Native American rituals, customs, and beliefs.

Miller, Jay. *American Indian festivals*. Chicago: Children's Press, 1996.

> Explores the cultural and spiritual significance of many Native American celebrations, with details on foods, customs and rituals associated with each; includes color illustrations and a map. Appropriate for grades 3–5.

Miller, Jay. *American Indian foods*. Chicago: Children's Press, 1996.

> Focuses on Native American foods and food-related activities such as hunting, harvesting, and preparation. Each food type is linked with its tribal affiliation. Includes color illustrations and a map. Appropriate for grades 3–5.

Ruoff, A. LaVonne Brown. *American Indian literatures: an introduction, bibliographic review, and selected bibliography*. New York: Modern Language Association, 1990.

> Lists anthologies, essays, and critical works by or about Native Americans. If the author is Native American, his or her tribal affiliation is

indicated in parentheses. Covers both oral and written works.

St. George, Judith. *Sacagawea*. New York: Putnam, 1997.

Biography of the Shoshoni girl who guided the Lewis and Clark expedition. Journal entries from the explorers provide details of Native American daily life in the early 1800s. Appropriate for grades 4–6.

WEB SITE

Native Americans: Internet resources. falcon.jmu.edu/~ramseyil/native.htm

This wonderful site, produced by the Internet School Library Media Center of James Madison University, offers a comprehensive list of links to resources on Native American culture. Includes links to bibliographies, directories, online documents and e-texts, study and teaching resources, museum and history links, and links to Native American periodicals.

PEARL HARBOR DAY

Goldstein, Donald M., and Katherine V. Dillon (eds.). *The Pearl Harbor papers: inside the Japanese plans*. Herndon, Va.: Brassey's, 1999.

Historical documents provide a behind-the-scenes look at the plans for the bombing of Pearl Harbor. Details the air attack from the Japanese perspective.

Lord, Walter. *Day of infamy*. 1957. Reprint, Fredericksburg, Tex.: Admiral Nimitz Foundation, 1991.

Detailed account of the action and human drama in the attack on Pearl Harbor, Sunday, December 7, 1941.

Nicholson, Dorinda Makanaonalani Stagner. *Pearl Harbor child: a child's view of Pearl Harbor—from attack to peace*. Kansas City: Woodson House, 1998.

Fact-based story of the attack on Pearl Harbor from a child's perspective. Nicholson delivers a firsthand account of the confusion, mistakes, fear, and even excitement that she experienced during the attack and throughout the war years. Family photographs, official documents, and newspaper clippings support the narrative. Appropriate for grades 5–8.

Stein, R. Conrad. *World War II in the Pacific: "Remember Pearl Harbor."* Springfield, N.J.: Enslow, 1994.

Thorough account of the war in the Pacific, from the bombing of Pearl Harbor to the Japanese surrender on the USS *Missouri*. Text is enhanced by archival photographs and maps. Appropriate for grades 7 and higher.

Worth, Richard H., Jr. *Pearl Harbor: selected testimonies, fully indexed, from the Congressional hearings (1945–1946) and prior investigations to the events leading up to the attack*. Jefferson, N.C.: McFarland, 1993.

Historic and archival documents deliver a detailed look at previously unexplored American and Japanese activities prior to the Pearl Harbor attack, such as code breaking, espionage, the American radar fiasco, and sabotage.

WEB SITES

Pearl Harbor: Mother of all conspiracies. www.geocities.com/Pentagon/6315/pearl.htm

In-depth report discusses the possibility of a U.S. cover-up and complicity in the attack on Pearl Harbor.

U.S.S. Arizona and Pearl Harbor remembered. members.aol.com/Buckeye34/pearl.htm

Photo-essay relives the attack on Pearl Harbor by focusing on images of the salvaged USS *Arizona*. Captions accompany illustrations.

ST. PATRICK'S DAY

Barth, Edna and Ursula Arndt (illus.). *Shamrocks, harps, & shillelaghs: the story of the St. Patrick's Day symbols*. Boston: Houghton Mifflin, 1982.

Account of Saint Patrick (once called Old Shaved Head) and history of symbols of the day celebrated in his honor. Excellent material on shamrocks, shillelagh, leprechauns, Irish harps, food, parades, and the singing of "Saint Patrick's Breastplate." Illustrations accompany the text. Appropriate for grades 3–6.

Bury, John B. *The life of Saint Patrick and his place in history*. New York: Dover, 1998.

Story of the birth and growth of the Irish church and Saint Patrick's role in its development. Attempts to present a picture of the "real" Saint Patrick by separating legend from reality.

Driscoll, Chris. *And God blessed the Irish: the story of Saint Patrick.* Hempstead, N.Y.: Ambassador Books, 1997.

Delightful biography of the life of Saint Patrick. Includes his real history, as well as the legends and lore that have sprung up around him. Accompanied by black and white illustrations. Appropriate for grades 4–6.

Gribben, Arthur (ed.). *The great famine and the Irish Diaspora in America.* Amherst: University of Massachusetts Press, 1999.

Multidisciplinary collection of essays from the fields of literature, linguistics, folklore, history, journalism, and music provide insights on the great famine of 1845–55. Recounts reactions in the press, experiences of immigrants fleeing famine, the famine's impact on the arts in Ireland, and its continuing impact on Irish and Irish American culture today.

Hippocrene children's illustrated Irish dictionary. New York: Hippocrene, 1999.

Picture dictionary with English/Gaelic translations and pronunciation guide. Useful for introducing adults and children, to a new language.

Hennessey, Thomas. *A history of Northern Ireland, 1920–1996.* New York: St. Martin's, 1998.

Balanced history of troubled Northern Ireland as viewed from both the unionist and nationalist perspectives, with a focus on 1976–96, the "Long War" era.

Howlett, D.R. (ed.) and Lawrence Cunningham (introduction). *The confession of Saint Patrick.* Chicago: Triumph, 1996.

The life of Saint Patrick in his own words. The result is an intriguing picture of a real man, painfully conscious of his flaws but dedicated to his life's mission and burning with love for Christ, the Gospel, and the Irish.

The Irish in America: a history. New York: Hyperion, 1997.

A beautifully illustrated history of the Irish in America from the 1840s to the present. Topics include assimilation and the struggle for accep-

tance, the resurgence of the Irish identity, religion, politics, employment, and entertainment.

Johnson, Margaret M. *The Irish heritage cookbook.* San Francisco: Chronicle, 1999.

The more than 200 recipes in this collection, culled from Irish and Irish American chefs and home cooks, range from the rustic to the extravagant. Sidebars present anecdotes and facts about Irish cuisine.

Laxton, Edward. *The famine ships: the Irish exodus to America.* New York: Holt, 1997.

The flight of nearly one million Irish to the U.S. during the Potato Blight of the 1840s forms the backdrop for this collection of personal narratives, anecdotes, and family histories that focuses on the plight of immigrants aboard the vessels known as "famine ships."

Levy, Una, and Susan Field (illus.). *Irish fairy tales and legends.* Niwot, Colo.: Robert Rinehart, 1997.

Ten Irish tales, from 200 to 2,000 years old, vibrantly retold by Una Levy. Color artwork, background notes, and a glossary with pronunciation guide complete this work. Appropriate for grades 4–8.

Swinnea, Stephanie Lavenia. *"I, Patrick, a sinner . . .": A tale worth telling.* Terlton, Okla.: Aaron Algood Books, 1999.

The life and theology of Saint Patrick is recounted in this fascinating novel that follows the young British noble, Patricus Magonus Sucatas, from his carefree days of reckless ease to his enslavement by the Irish, conversion, release from slavery, and ultimate decision to return and share the gospel of Christ with the very people who enslaved him.

WEB SITES

The Confession of St. Patrick. ccel.wheaton.edu/patrick/confession/confession.html

English translation of the complete Latin text of St. Patrick's autobiographical "Confession." Includes links to related sites.

St. Patrick's Day: Customs and history. www.wilstar.com/holidays/partick.htm

Includes a brief biography of St. Patrick, a history of the holiday, and links to related sites.

VALENTINE'S DAY

Barth, Edna. *Hearts, cupids and red roses: the story of the Valentine symbols.* Boston: Houghton Mifflin/Clarion, 1982.

> Discusses the origin, development, symbols, and customs of the world's most sentimental holiday, which dates back to the Roman festival of Lupercalia; includes illustrations. Appropriate for grades 3–6.

Bulla, Clyde Robert, and Susan Estelle Kwas (illus.). *The story of Valentine's Day.* New York: HarperCollins, 1999.

> Explores the origins of Valentine's Day and explains the symbols and customs connected with our modern-day celebration. Also includes instructions for making Valentine's Day cards and heart-shaped sugar cookies. Color illustrations accompany the text. Appropriate for grades 3–5.

Brenner, Robert. *Valentine treasury: a century of Valentine cards.* Atglen, Pa.: Schiffer, 1997.

> Provides a decade-by-decade account of changes in the 20th century American Valentine card's style, production techniques, and format. Includes a price guide for collectors and a wealth of color illustrations.

Godek, Gregory J.P., and Mark Victor Hansen. *1001 ways to be romantic.* Weymouth, Mass.: Casablanca Press, 1995.

> This guide to romance presents creative and clever ideas to help put "spark" into a relationship. Suggestions range from simple and inexpensive to elaborate and costly.

101 classic love poems. Lincolnwood, Ill.: NTC, 1988.

> Anthology includes standards such as "Sonnets from the Portuguese" by Browning and "A red, red rose" by Burns as well as lesser-known works and ones that are not normally included in anthologies of love poems such as the "Song of Solomon."

Ripple, Wilhelminia. *Valentine school parties: what do I do?* Littleton, Colo.: Oakbrook, 1999.

> Sourcebook for teachers charged with organizing a Valentine's Day party for kindergarten through 6th-grade students. Offers suggestions for refreshments, games, craft projects, and other activities. Includes black-and-white illustrations, patterns for craft projects, and complete instructions.

Roop, Peter, Connie Roop, and Kathy Keck Arnsteen (illus.). *Let's celebrate Valentine's Day.* Brookfield, Conn.: Millbrook, 1999.

> Provides information on the origins, history, and development of Valentine's Day. Includes jokes, riddles, and craft projects. Color illustrations accompany the text. Appropriate for grades 2–4.

WEB SITES

"I love you" in various languages. www.dina.kvl.dk/~fischer/alt.romance/language.html

> Guide to how to say "I love you" in 56 languages.

The history of Valentine's Day. www.historychannel.com/exhibits/valentine

> Site produced by the History Channel that provides background on the origin of the holiday and how it has been celebrated through the years.

St. Valentine. www.newadvent.org/cathen/15254a.htm

> Transcription of an article from the on-line version of the *Catholic Encyclopedia* provides brief biographies of three different individuals identified as St. Valentine and a summary of the origins of the holiday.

HISTORIC EVENTS DAYS

The American scene. Bethel, Conn.: Grolier, 1999.

> Portrays U.S. history through time lines of key events. Appropriate for grades 2–6.

Baron, Robert C. (ed.), and Samuel Scinta. *20th century America: key events in history: Millennium 2000.* Golden, Colo.: Fulcrum Books, 1996.

> Describes significant events of the 20th century that shaped the nation. Entries range from a single paragraph to a full essay and cover topics such as Ford's Model T, the Wright Brothers' first flight, the 1929 stock market crash, and the Cuban missile crisis.

Bunson, Matthew. *Encyclopedia of the Middle Ages.* New York: Facts on File, 1995.

Nearly 2,000 entries explore the key events, personalities, and places that shaped the Middle Ages. Includes chronologies, maps, and genealogies.

Burner, David. *Making peace with the 60s.* Princeton, N.J.: Princeton University Press, 1996.

A critical reconstruction of the key events, philosophies, social concerns, and political issues that defined the period from 1961 to 1974, with a focus on the U.S.

The Cambridge history of American foreign relations. New York: Cambridge University Press, 1993.

Four-volume set interprets key events in U.S. diplomatic history. Each volume covers a particular period, providing details and analyses of major figures and happenings.

Cook, Chris, and Diccon Bewes. *What happened where: a guide to places and events in 20th century history.* New York: St. Martin's, 1997.

Dictionary focuses on sites of important events in the 20th century. Each entry tells where the site is located, explains why it is important, and describes the events that occurred there.

Curtis, A. Kenneth, Stephen J. Lang, and Randy Peterson. *The 100 most important events in Christian history.* Grand Rapids, Mich.: Revell, 1999.

An overview of 100 events that shaped Christianity, beginning with the great fire in Rome in 64 A.D. Each entry summarizes the event, its significance, and the main personalities involved. Sample events include Jerome's Vulgate translation of the Bible in 405 A.D., Gutenberg's first printed Bible in 1456, and the Second Vatican Council in 1962.

Dayan, Daniel, and Elihu Katz. *Media events.* Cambridge, Mass.: Harvard University Press, 1992.

The impact of broadcast journalism, particularly television journalism, is explored in this though-provoking analysis of how major social and political events have been packaged and presented to viewers for consumption.

Events that changed the world in the nineteenth century. Westport, Conn.: Greenwood, 1996.

Events that changed the world in the twentieth century. Westport, Conn.: Greenwood, 1995.

These easy-to-read yet in-depth essays describe world events that shaped the 19th and 20th centuries and provide valuable background information and analysis.

Garner, Joe. *We interrupt this broadcast: relive the events that stopped our lives, from the Hindenburg to the death of Princess Diana.* Naperville, Ill.: Sourcebooks, 1998.

Recounts 38 of the century's most important events, using material from actual broadcasts that covered each happening.

Great events. Hackensack, N.J.: Salem Press, 1992.

Covers a wide range of important events in 20th century world history. Appropriate for grades 7–10.

Hunt, Alfred. *A turbulent time.* Bloomington: Indiana University Press, 1998.

Nine essays by scholars in the field of Caribbean studies chronicle Spanish and French colonization of the area and trace the Caribbean's importance in the development of the U.S.

Kroll, Steven. *The Boston Tea Party.* New York: Holiday House, 1998.

Recounts key events leading up to the Boston Tea Party. Appropriate for grades 2–6.

Levison, Nancy Smiler. *Turn of the century.* Hydesville, Calif.: Lodestar, 1994.

Traces key events in U.S. social and political history; includes black-and-white illustrations and a reading list. Appropriate for grades 2–6.

Life Millennium: The 100 most important events and people of the past 1,000 years. New York: Time-Life Books, 1998.

Explores 100 events that shaped the past 1,000 years. Events range from the discovery of the potato to more spectacular feats such as man's landing on the moon. The work is abundantly illustrated with photographs from the Time-Life image archive.

National Geographic eyewitness to the 20th century. Washington, D.C.: National Geographic Society, 1999.

Time lines, chronologies, and essays by noted scholars deliver an interesting overview of events that shaped the 20th century. The text maintains a balance between historic events such as Watson and Crick's discovery of DNA and pop culture events such as the Woodstock music festival. The work is lavishly illustrated with photographs from the National Geographic image archive.

The Oxford encyclopedia of world history. New York: Oxford University Press, 1998.

Nearly 4,000 entries, alphabetically arranged, cover key world events from prehistory to the present. Entries include information on discoveries, inventions, and personalities. Includes a 27-page chronology of world events.

Rice, Earle. *The final solution.* San Diego: Lucent Books, 1998.

This collection of testimonies, opinions, and essays by researchers and Holocaust survivors presents a vivid history of the events that shaped the world from 1933–45. Includes photographs. Appropriate for grades 7–10.

Schudson, Michael. *Watergate in American memory.* New York: Basic Books, 1992.

Explores the Watergate scandal and its impact on American society, blending the events of 1972–74 with a discussion of societal changes that ensued.

Schwartz, Richard Alan. *The Cold War reference guide: a general history and annotated chronology with selected biographies.* Jefferson, N.C.: McFarland, 1997.

An overview of the general history and causes of the Cold War years, followed by an annotated chronology of major events of the period. Includes biographical sketches of key figures.

Silverman, Maida. *Israel.* Pittsburgh: Dial, 1998.

The history of Israel from biblical times to the present is recounted for children. Includes a time line of major events in the nation's history. Appropriate for grades 2–6.

Simon, Reeva S., Philip Mattar, and Richard W. Bulliet (eds.). *Encyclopedia of the modern Middle East.* New York: Macmillan, 1996.

Approximately 4,000 entries describe key events and personalities that have shaped the Middle East over the past two centuries.

Somerset Fry, Plantagenet. *The Dorling Kindersley history of the world.* New York: Dorling Kindersley, 1994.

Illustrated overview of world history from the dawn of civilization to the early 1990s. Describes wars, societal advances, political and diplomatic happenings, and inventions. A synoptic table portrays events that occurred on five continents, and a time line at the bottom of each page highlights the era under discussion. Appropriate for grades 2–6.

Wakin, Edward. *How TV changed America's mind.* Redmond, Wash.: Shepard Books, 1996.

Explores the social impact of television through historical events as portrayed by the media. Includes black-and-white photographs. Appropriate for grades 7–10.

Wilson, Ellen Judy. *Encyclopedia of the Enlightenment.* New York: Facts on File, 1996.

Examines key philosophies, writings, and personalities from 1674–1814. Includes a chronology of key events and illustrations.

WEB SITES

WebChron: The web chronology project. campus.northpark.edu/history//WebChron/index.html

A compilation of chronologies and articles of important events in world history prepared and maintained by the instructors and students of North Park College. The chronologies are divided into two regional and cross-cultural chronologies. The hypertext nature of the Web allows viewers to see the relations between events in different chronologies, making this an ideal site for those interested in the causal relationships between world events.

Internet modern history sourcebook. www.fordham.edu/halsall/mod/modsbook.html

Site sponsored by Fordham University that presents a vast collection of history-related primary source materials available on the Internet in full text. The materials vary in length and are divided into 32 sections that cover European and American history as well as cultural, legal, and political themes.

PEOPLE RELATED TO THE CALENDAR

Beacham, Walton (ed.). *Research guide to American historical biography.* Osprey, Fla: Beacham, 1991.

Five-volume set explores the lives of notable men and women from American history. Includes essays on each individual's major accomplishments, a chronology of important events, a listing of biographies published about each subject, and a cumulative index.

Bendiner, Jessica, and Elmer Bendiner. *Biographical dictionary of medicine.* New York: Facts on File, 1991.

Contains basic biographical details and career highlights of notable individuals in the medical field. Some entries list resources for further research.

Biel, Steven. *Independent intellectuals in the United States, 1910–1945.* New York: New York University Press, 1992.

Chronicles the lives of notable male and female intellectuals and their contributions to American society.

Champagne, Duane (ed.). *Chronology of Native North American history: from pre-Columbian time to the present.* Detroit: Gale, 1994.

Brief sketches explore the lives of important Native Americans and key events in three time periods: 50,000 B.C.–A.D. 1492; 1500–1959; and 1960–94. A time line on each page charts historical world events of each period.

Garraty, John A., and Mark C. Carnes (eds.). *American national biography.* New York: Oxford University Press, 1999.

Multivolume set provides biographical sketches for 17,450 important American men and women. The essays range in length from 750 words to 7,500 words and include bibliographies. Entries are indexed by name, occupation, and place of birth.

Greenspan, Karen. *The timetables of women's history: a chronology of the most important people and events in women's history.* New York: Simon and Schuster, 1995.

Brief biographical sketches of important figures in women's history are arranged in categories such as humanities/fine arts, science/technology/discovery, and statecraft/military.

Gribetz, Judah, Edward L. Greenstein, and Regina Stein. *The timetables of Jewish history: a chronology of the most important people and events in Jewish history.* New York: Simon and Schuster, 1993.

Presents brief biographical sketches of important Jewish figures from prehistory to the present. Each historical period is subdivided into three categories: general history, Jewish history, and Jewish culture.

Hamilton, Neil A. *Founders of modern nations: a biographical dictionary.* Santa Barbara: ABC-CLIO, 1995.

Presents biographical sketches of more than 300 men and women who were instrumental in the founding of their nations. Each entry includes a brief biography. Includes profiles of each country discussed in the work, chronologies, maps, and an index.

Harley, Sharon. *The timetables of African-American history: a chronology of the most important people and events in African-American history.* New York: Simon and Schuster, 1995.

Presents brief biographical sketches of important figures in African American history from 1492 to 1992. The work is arranged by year and subdivided into categories such as art, law, education, religion, and technology.

Hodgson, Godfrey, and P. Smith (eds.). *People's century: the ordinary men and women who made the twentieth century.* New York: Time-Life Books, 1998.

A companion to the 20-part PBS series "People's Century," which chronicled major events of the century through the eyes of ordinary people. This volume continues that theme through a combination of historical essays and personal narratives of ordinary people who lived out those events.

Marzollo, Jean, and Irene Trivas (illus.). *My first book of biographies: great men and women every child should know.* New York: Scholastic, 1994.

Biographical sketches of 36 famous personalities from all periods and cultures form the nucleus of this work. Each entry is accompanied by a full-page illustration. Appropriate for grades 2–4.

McRedmond, Louis (ed.). *Modern Irish lives: dictionary of 20th century Irish biography.* New York: St. Martin's, 1996.

Biographical sketches ranging in length from one paragraph to one and one-half pages provide an overview of more than 1,400 famous figures in 20th century Irish history.

Morey, Janet, and Wendy Dunn. *Famous Mexican-Americans.* Cobblehill Books, 1989.

Presents biographical sketches of 14 prominent Mexican-Americans from fields such as law, business, sports, and entertainment. Appropriate for grades 2–6.

Notable Black American men. Detroit: Gale, 1999.

Focuses on the lives of lesser-known African American males who have made their mark in public service, education, and science. Serves as a companion volume to a previously published Gale work: *Notable African-American women.*

1,000 Makers of the Millennium: the men and women who have shaped the last 1,000 years. New York: Dorling Kindersley, 1994.

Profiles 1,000 of the millennium's most famous, and infamous, personalities from all fields of endeavor. Entries are arranged chronologically and provide name, birth/death dates, accomplishments, and biographical sketches. A running time line at the bottom of each page helps to set the historical stage, and information boxes give highlights of the era. Lavish color illustrations complete the work.

Opfell, Olga S. *Queens, empresses, grand duchesses, and regents: women rulers of Europe A.D. 1328–1989.* Jefferson, N.C.: McFarland, 1989.

Profiles 39 female European rulers, with essays highlighting each subject's major achievements; includes a bibliography.

Research guide to European historical biography, 1450–present. Osprey, Fla.: Beacham, 1992.

Four-volume set explores the lives of notable European figures through chronologies, time lines, and essays that provide an overview of each subject's achievements. Each entry lists biographical sources for further research.

Riley, Sam G. *Biographical dictionary of American newspaper columnists.* Westport, Conn.: Greenwood, 1995.

Profiles more than 600 newspaper columnists from the Civil War to the present.

Scarre, Christopher. *Chronicle of the Roman emperors.* New York: Thames and Hudson, 1995.

Biographies of the rulers of the Roman Empire from 31 B.C.–A.D. 467 are presented in this readable work. A balance is maintained between commentary from the emperors' contemporaries and commentary from modern scholars. Includes illustrations.

Simons, Doris A. (ed.). *Scientists, mathematicians, and inventors: lives and legacies, an encyclopedia of people who changed the world.* Phoenix: Oryx, 1999.

Presents 200 biographical sketches of people who were influential in science, math, and technology. Entries include time lines and reading lists.

Volkgonov, Dimitrii Antonovich, and Harold Shukman (translator and ed.). *Autopsy for an empire: the seven leaders who built the Soviet regime.* Monroe, LA: Free Press, 1998.

Examines the lives, careers, and personalities of Lenin, Trotsky, Stalin, and four of their successors.

Wakin, Edward. *Contemporary political leaders of the Middle East.* New York: Facts on File, 1996.

Profiles eight Arab and Israeli leaders who helped to shape the Middle East. Appropriate for grades 7–10.

WEB SITES

Time 100: The 100 most important people of the 20th century. www.time.com/time100/index.html

Compilation of the 100 people who most influenced our world in the 20th century. The profiles are divided into six categories: leaders and revolutionaries, artists and entertainers, builders and titans, scientists and thinkers, heroes and icons, and person of the century.

Life's "100 people who made the millennium." www.mind.net/dlmark/pages/handlife.htm

Yet another listing of history's most important personalities, this time based on the opinion of the *Life* magazine editorial staff. The names are listed from most to least influential. Each link leads to Web sites that have biographical material on the figures.

BACKGROUND READINGS

Awards, honors, and prizes. 15th ed. Detroit: Gale, 1998.

Compilation of awards in all fields, from academic honors to sports prizes. Vol. 1 covers awards in the U.S. and Canada; vol. 2 describes awards, honors, and prizes in other parts of world.

Biography almanac. 2nd ed. Detroit: Gale, 1983.

Guide to more than 20,000 people who have left an imprint on history, from biblical times to the 20th century. Entries list complete names, places of birth and death, nationalities, occupations, and achievements. Listings include citations to biographical material.

Book of the states. Lexington, Ky.: Council of State Governments, 1998.

Authoritative information on government of individual states. Historical data on each state, such as source of state lands, date admitted to Union, nickname, motto, flower, bird, and song.

Bowker, John (ed.). *Oxford dictionary of world religions.* New York: Oxford University Press, 1997.

Provides concise, in-depth information on the world's major religions.

Breuilly, Elizabeth, et al. *Religions of the world: the illustrated guide to origins, beliefs, traditions & festivals.* New York: Facts on File, 1997.

Covers belief systems, customs, festivals, major writings, and history of the world's major religions; accompanied by color photographs. Appropriate for grades 7–12.

Brown, Raymond E., et al. (eds.). *The new Jerome biblical commentary.* Englewood Cliffs, N.J.: Prentice-Hall, 1990.

A line-by-line commentary on the Old and New Testaments from a Roman Catholic perspective. Also provides topical articles and updated information on recent archaeological and manuscript discoveries.

Bruce, F.F. (ed.). *The international Bible commentary.* Grand Rapids, Mich.: Zondervan, 1986.

Literary analysis of the Old and New Testaments from a Protestant evangelical viewpoint. Based on the New International Version Bible.

Clevannes, Barry. *Rastafari roots and ideology.* Syracuse, N.Y.: Syracuse University Press, 1994.

Explores the history, doctrine, customs, and sects of the Rastafari religion.

Delaney, John J. *Dictionary of saints.* New York: Doubleday, 1980.

Details the lives of 5,000 saints of the Christian church. Includes appendixes that provide symbols associated with saints, lists of patron saints, and chronological tables.

Doyra, Ramesh Chander and Gobind Singh Mansukhani. *Encyclopedia of the Sikh religion and culture.* Flushing, N.Y.: Vikas, 1995.

Covers major aspects of the Sikh religion, including beliefs, customs, castes, festivals, and history.

Eerdmans' handbook to the world's religions. Rev. ed. Grand Rapids, Mich.: Eerdmans, 1994.

Focuses on the cultural aspects of the world's major religions from ancient to modern times. Photographs, charts, and graphs accompany the text.

Eliade, Mircea (ed.). *The encyclopedia of religion.* New York: Macmillian, 1986.

Sixteen-volume encyclopedia covers the beliefs, practices, symbols, and important personalities of the world's religions.

Glasse, April. *The concise encyclopedia of Islam.* New York: Harper, 1989.

Topically arranged entries explain the basic tenets, customs, and traditions of Islam. Also provides information on important figures in Islam.

Hatch, Jane M. *The American book of days*. 3rd. ed. New York: Wilson, 1978.

Expanded and revised edition of Douglas's American book of days. Comprehensive collection provides background material and current information on significant events associated with every day of the year. Excellent material on American national and civic holidays. Arranged by calendar year.

Kane, Joseph Nathan. *Famous first facts*. 5th rev. ed. New York: Wilson, 1998.

Comprehensive record of more than 9,000 American firsts; major source for confirmation of facts about first happenings, discoveries, inventions, and memorable achievements or occasions in American history. Arranged alphabetically by subject. Quick access to data through four indexes: years, days of month, personal names, geographic location.

Murphy, Larry G. (ed.). *Encyclopedia of African American religions*. New York: Garland, 1993.

Topical look at the cultural background and practices of religion among African Americans.

Myers, Robert J., et al. *Celebrations: the complete book of American holidays*. Garden City, N.Y.: Doubleday, 1972.

History, symbols, and special features of 42 days celebrated in the U.S. Includes selected state holidays, commentary on origins and observances, holy days of major American faiths, federal legal holidays, and local or regional events.

Nanji, Azim A. (ed.). *The Muslim almanac: a reference work on the history, faith, culture, and peoples of Islam*. Detroit: Gale, 1996.

Detailed reference work covers the history, beliefs, and cultures of Islam. Also deals with contemporary issues such as the changing role of women in Islamic society.

New Interpreter's Bible. Nashville: Abingdon, 1994.

This 12-volume set provides exposition and exegesis of Old and New Testaments. Based on the New Revised and New International Versions.

Parise, Frank (ed.). *The book of calendars*. New York: Facts on File, 1982.

Includes historical data on world calendars from ancient times and conversion tables relating calendars to the Julian or the Gregorian.

Plaut, Gunther W. and Bamberger, Bernard J. (eds.). *The Torah: a modern commentary*. New York: Union of American Hebrew Congregations, 1981.

Commentary on the Pentateuch and Haftorot (readings from the prophetic books) in Hebrew, with English translation.

Reid, Daniel G. *Dictionary of Christianity in America: a comprehensive resource on the religious impulse that shaped a continent*. Downers Grove, Ill.: InterVarsity, 1990.

Covers the history of Christianity in the U.S., with information on major movements, sects, and personalities.

Shakir, M.H. (eds.). *Holy Qur'an = al-Qur'an al-hakim*. 5th U.S. ed. Flushing, N.Y.: Tahrike Tarsile Qur'an, 1988.

Arabic/English translation of the Qur'an. Contains commentary.

Snelling, John. *The Buddhist handbook: a complete guide to Buddhist schools, teaching, practice, and history*. Rochester, Vt.: Inner Traditions, 1991.

Thorough overview of Buddhist concepts, beliefs, customs, and history.

The stateman's yearbook, 1999–2000. New York: St. Martin's, 1999.

Major source for confirmation of key dates in the history of nations throughout the world, such as achievement of independence and adoption of a constitution. Contains information on national flags, anthems, populations, and government statistics. Arranged alphabetically by country.

Tanakh: a new translation of the Holy Scriptures according to the traditional Hebrew text. Philadelphia: Jewish Publication Society, 1988.

English translation of the Old Testament from the tenth century Hebrew masoretic text.

Trepp, Leo. *The complete book of Jewish observance.* West Orange, N.J.: Behrman House/Summit Books, 1981.

> Guide to Jewish ceremonial practices, synagogue etiquette, holidays, and prayers.

Unterman, Alan. *Dictionary of Jewish lore and legend.* New York: Thames and Hudson, 1991.

> Explores folklore and traditions of the Sephardic and Ashkenazic cultures. Also covers customs, festivals, and home life.

Walker, Benjamin. *The Hindu world: an encyclopedic survey of Hinduism.* Philadelphia: Coronet Books, 1983.

> Overview of Hinduism's beliefs, practices, and gods.

Wasserman, Paul, and Esther Herman (eds.). *Festivals sourcebook.* Detroit: Gale, 1977.

> Information on some 3,800 events celebrated throughout North America. Entries include location, official names, schedules, description, and year of origin. Celebrations range from agricultural to cultural and historical events (excluding traditional holidays and religious festivals).

Who's who of religion. New York: Penguin, 1996.

> Contains biographical information on leading personalities in various religions from ancient times to the present.

World holiday and time guide. New York: Morgan Guaranty Trust Co. Annual.

> Lists holidays observed by world's principal countries and the 50 American states. Notes provide data on half-day observances and regional or local exceptions.

WEB SITES

GENERAL

Holidays around the World for K–12. falcon.jmu.edu/~ramseyil/holidays.htm

> Site administered by Inez Ramsey, at James Madison University, that contains an extensive listing of sites that provide holiday-related resources for teachers. Includes sites for all major U.S. holidays, international holidays, and holidays from the Islamic calendar.

Through the Year: Holidays and Celebrations. www.noblenet.org/year.htm

> Site maintained by NOBLE, the North Boston Library Exchange, that features links to Web sites for major U.S. and international holidays arranged by month.

Holidays on the Net: Holiday Web Directory. www.holidays.net/cgi-bin/linkmat.cgi

> Site produced by Holidays on the Net that offers a vast database of holiday-related Web sites that can be accessed in one of three ways: by keyword search, by browsing categories, or by accessing a list of sites that have been added to the database within the last 30 days.

The Earth Calendar. www.earthcalendar.net

> Calendar and electronic "daybook of holidays and celebrations around the world" that features a vast listing of global cultural events that can be accessed by date, country, religion, lunar calculations, or keyword search. Each entry shows the name and date of the celebration and the country in which the celebration is observed.

European Festivals and Traditions. festivals.projects.eun.org

> Site composed by a consortium of students from schools in France, Germany, Scotland, and Spain that allows users to access brief histories about European holidays from various countries. Content for each country varies according to the wishes of the students who designed the site. Among the inclusions are seasonal recipes, crafts, explanations of related traditions, illustrations, and links to the schools that created the sites.

Yahoo: Holidays and Observances. dir.yahoo.com/Society_and_Culture/Holidays_and_Observances

> This is Yahoo's master site for accessing information related to holidays, celebrations, and observances of every type and for every region of the globe. Also included are sections that contain holiday-related clip art, recipes, music, screen savers, and electronic greeting cards.

CHINESE CALENDAR

Chinese Calendar. www.saxakali.com/color_asp/chinese.htm

Site sponsored by the nonprofit organization Saxakali, which provides a basic history of the Chinese calendar, an explanation of the 60-year and 60-day cycles found within the calendar, and the signs related to the Chinese constellations and Chinese zodiac.

The Daily Globe: Chinese Calendar. www.dailyglobe.com/china.html

Site maintained by the *Daily Globe* newspaper, based in Berkeley, California, which provides a brief explanation of the Chinese calendar, presents a table of Chinese calendar months with their English equivalents and approximate Gregorian calendar dates, and the length of each month. Also includes links to explanations of the Buddhist calendar, the Chinese 60-year cycle, the Chinese solar calendar, and Chinese holidays.

Chinese Astrology Lunar Fortune Almanac and Astronomical Perpetual Calendar. www.chinesefortunecalendar.com

Provides basic information about the traditional Chinese calendar and links to the Chinese fortune-telling calendar, the Chinese farmer's almanac, Chinese festivals, and a listing of Chinese new year days and related animal names.

China the Beautiful—Chinese Art and Literature. www.chinapage.com/china.html

Page created by Dr. Ming L. Pei, professor emeritus, which presents a wonderful compilation of cultural sites related to classical Chinese art, calligraphy, history, literature, philosophy, and the Chinese lunar calendar and new year.

ISLAMIC CALENDAR

The Islamic Calendar. www.sabr.com/dawah/calendar.htm

Site produced by the Sabr Foundation that provides a brief history of the Islamic calendar and links to other sites related to the calendar, including one that allows users to convert between Gregorian and Islamic calendar dates.

The Islamic Calendar. www.ummah.org.uk/ildl/index.html

Site produced by Dr. Monzar Ahmed that delivers an in-depth look at how the Islamic cal-

endar is calculated based on predicted lunar visibility cycles. Offers a link that allows users to download a program created by Dr. Ahmed that can be used in predicting crescent visibility. Also includes examples of maps created by Dr. Ahmed that were used to predict crescent visibility from April 1999 to April 2000.

What Is the Islamic Calendar? moonsighting.com/calendar.html

Site produced by S. Khalid Shaukat that provides a brief historical introduction to the Islamic calendar and background on its significance. Also contains a listing of major Islamic holidays and festivals.

JEWISH CALENDAR

Hebcal Interactive Jewish Calendar. www.radwin.org/hebcal

Site maintained by Michael J. Radwin, which allows users to compile a list of dates for Jewish holidays for any year. Also calculates candle-lighting times based on latitude and longitude calculated from ZIP codes.

The Eternal's Calendar. www.frontiernet.net/~labomb32/calendar.html

Web version of Ivan L. Labombarbe's book *A Calendar from the Hebrew Scriptures*. Provides an in-depth study of the origins of the Hebrew calendar, its structure, and Scripture references. Also includes a bibliography, a glossary, and several charts and diagrams.

The Ultimate Jewish Calendar Page. ourworld.compuserve.com/homepages/jweizman

Site developed by Jonathan Weizman that permits users to convert Gregorian calendar dates to Hebrew calendar dates.

Virtual Jerusalem: Torah & Tradition Channel—The Jewish Year. www.vjholidays.com/vjholidaysindex.htm

Site sponsored by Virtual Communities, Inc., that provides dates for 21 important Jewish holidays and festivals, historical information about each holiday, customs associated with the holidays, and links to other sites related to the holiday.

References

Much of the information in this book is based on or confirmed by primary sources. However, by their nature, primary sources are rarely printed and published widely, and are thus difficult for the general reader to obtain. Accordingly, it was decided not to enumerate them individually.

My primary sources consisted of (1) countries' embassies, permanent missions to the United Nations, and official cultural and information services; (2) countries' official tourism bureaus; (3) the organizers of events; (4) organizations and institutions; and (5) scholars and other knowledgeable persons. Such sources are not infallible and must be compared with data from other sources.

EMBASSIES, UNITED NATIONS MISSIONS, AND OFFICIAL INFORMATION SERVICES

I was assisted by persons representing 162 countries. Several countries maintain separate institutions dedicated to educating Americans about the home country (notably Germany, Mexico, South Korea, and Sweden). In many cases the person who helped me (usually the embassy's cultural attaché) was informed and helpful, delighted to assist an interested student of his or her country, providing lists of official public holidays, the date-formulae of movable events, the historical significance of particular dates, and information on festivals. Some introduced me to persons with specialized knowledge, some lent or photocopied extensive documentation, and some obtained recondite informa-tion from the home country, which occasionally required diligent persistence.

Embassies are located in Washington, D.C. and United Nations missions are located in New York City. The *World Almanac* lists embassy addresses and phone numbers. Embassies and United Nations missions from the following countries provided valuable information: Afghanistan, Albania, Algeria, Angola, Argentina, Armenia, Australia, Austria, Azerbaijan, Bahrain, Bangladesh, Belarus, Belgium, Belize, Benin, Bhutan, Bolivia, Bosnia and Herzegovina, Botswana, Brazil, Brunei, Bulgaria, Burkina Faso, Burundi, Cambodia, Cameroon, Cape Verde, the Central African Republic, Chad, Chile, China, Colombia, Congo, Costa Rica, Côte d'Ivoire, Croatia, Cuba, Cyprus, the Czech Republic, Denmark, Djibouti, Dominica, the Dominican Republic, Ecuador, Egypt, El Salvador, Equatorial Guinea, Eritrea, Estonia, Ethiopia, Fiji, France, Gabon, the Gambia, Georgia, Germany, Ghana, Greece, Grenada, Guatemala, Guinea, Guinea-Bissau, Guyana, Haiti, Honduras, Hungary, Iceland, Iran, Iraq, Israel, Jamaica, Japan, Jordon, Kazakhastan, Kenya, Kuwait, Kyrgyzstan, Laos, Latvia, Lebanon, Lesotho, Liberia, Libya, Liechtenstein, Lithuania, Luxembourg, Macedonia, Madagascar, Malawi, Malaysia, Maldives, Mali, the Sovereign Military Order of Malta, the Marshall Islands, Mauritania, Mauritius, Mexico, Micronesia, Moldova, Mongolia, Morocco, Myanmar (Burma), Namibia, Nepal, the Netherlands, New Zealand, Nicaragua, Niger, Nigeria, Norway, Oman, Pakistan, Palau, Panama, Papua New Guinea,

Paraguay, Peru, the Philippines, Poland, Qatar, Romania, Russia, Rwanda, San Marino, São Tomé and Principe, Saudi Arabia, Senegal, the Seychelles, Sierra Leone, Singapore, the Slovak Republic, Slovenia, Solomon Islands, Somalia, South Africa, South Korea, Spain, Sri Lanka, St. Lucia, Sudan, Suriname, Swaziland, Switzerland, Syria, Taiwan, Tajikistan, Tanzania, Thailand, Tibet (government in exile), Togo, Tunisia, Turkmenistan, Uganda, Ukraine, the United Kingdom, Uruguay, Uzbekistan, Vatican City, Venezuela, Vietnam, Western Samoa, Yemen, Zambia, and Zimbabwe.

In some cases, I had to communicate directly with a government department of tourism. This was so for Andorra, Gibraltar (U.K.), Man (U.K.), and Turks and Caicos (U.K.).

And, for the U.S., I was assisted by the congressional representatives of American Samoa and Puerto Rico, and the clerks of several counties, parishes, and cities in Florida and Louisiana.

OFFICIAL TOURISM BUREAUS

Many countries maintain an official tourism bureau in the U.S. In some cases, the tourism bureau is better equipped than the embassy to provide detailed information. I received help from 52 of these, representing the following places: Antigua-Barbuda, the Bahamas, Bermuda, Canada (tourism bureaus for the 12 provinces and territories), Cyprus, Egypt, the French West Indies (France), Germany, India, Indonesia, Ireland, Maldives, Malta, Mexico, Monaco, all 6 islands of the Netherlands Antilles, Portugal (including Madeira and the Azores), South Korea, Spain (including the Canary Islands), St. Kitts, St. Vincent and Grenadines, Sweden, Thailand, Trinidad and Tobago, Turkey, and the U.K. (specifically those for Anguilla, the Cayman Islands, Montserrat, Northern Ireland, Scotland, and the British Virgin Islands).

And, for U.S. territories, these: Guam, Puerto Rico, and the U.S. Virgin Islands.

Additionally, all states and many cities maintain departments of tourism, and some were quite helpful, especially those for Fla., Tex., and Memphis, Tenn.

ORGANIZERS OF EVENTS

The organizers of the following events provided detailed information: Acadian Day, the Albuquerque Balloon Fiesta, Astronomy Day, the Birkebeiner, the Boston Marathon, Carnaval Miami, Carnival Memphis, Charro Days, the Cherry Blossom Festival (Washington, D.C.), Chester Greenwood Day, the Concrete Canoe Race, Credit Union Day, the Emmett Kelly Clown Festival, Foire Brayonne, Folklorama, the Gasparilla Pirate Festival, the Gathering of the Clans, International Migratory Bird Day, the International Rice Festival, the Ig Nobel Prize Awards, the Illuminated Night Parade, the Izmir Trade Fair, Jamestown Day, Just for Laughs, Loyalist Days, Memphis in May, the Portland (Wash.) Rose Festival, Professional Secretary's Day, Take Our Daughters to Work Day, and Tulip Time.

ORGANIZATIONS

These following organizations provided information about events and anniversaries:

The Abode of the Message (New Lebanon, N.Y.), the American Federation of Labor and Congress of Industrial Organizations (AFL-CIO), the American Red Cross, the All England Lawn Tennis and Croquet Club, the American Automobile Association (AAA), the American Library Association, the American Numismatic Association, the Arbor Day Council of Canada, the Arbor Lodge State Park (Nebraska City, Neb.), the Associated Press (International Desk), the Associated Press (Jakarta Bureau), Binion's Horseshoe casino (Las Vegas, Nev.), the Boston Athenaeum, the Boston Public Library Reference Desk (Mass.), the Boy Scouts of America, the Cherokee Nation, the Children's Book Council, the Children's Defense Fund, the

Cincinnati Reds baseball team, Common Ground (England), the Cowes Combined Clubs (England), the Daughters of the American Revolution, the Democratic National Committee, the *Encyclopaedia Britannica,* the Experimental Aircraft Association, Graceland (Nashville, Tenn.), the Holocaust Museum, the Inventors Hall of Fame, the International Tree Foundation (U.K.), the Jack Daniel Distillery, the Levi Strauss Company, Lamborn Florists (Alliance, Ohio), the Robert/Bob Marley Foundation (Jamaica), the Madison Public Library Reference Desk (Wis.), the Mustard Museum (Wis.), the National Arbor Day Foundation, the National Association for the Advancement of Colored People (NAACP), the National Conference of Christians and Jews, the National Institute of Arts and Letters, the National Olympic Committee, the National Youth Hostel Association, administrators of the New Orleans school systems, the *Oxford English Dictionary,* Oxford University, Penguin USA, the Peshtigo Historical Museum, the Phi Beta Kappa fraternity, the Police Hall of Fame, the Pulitzer Prize Committee, the household of Her Majesty the Queen (Buckingham Palace, London), the Royal Horticultural Society, the Shrine of the Immaculate Conception (Washington, D.C.), St. Andrews University (Scotland), State of Mass. Legislature Service Bureau, State of Minn. Department of Natural Resources, State of Wis. Department of Natural Resources, Tex. A & M University Student Government Office, the Truman Library, Volunteers of America, Wayne State University, and the Wis. Democratic and Republican Parties.

I was helped by the following agencies of the U.S. government: the Department of Agriculture, the Environmental Protection Agency, the Federal Emergency and Management Authority, the National Park Service, the U.S. Patent Office, the Peace Corps, and West Point Military Academy (U.S. Army).

I was helped by four organizations serving Vietnam War veterans: the Dane County (Wis.) Veterans Service Office, Vietnam Veterans Against the War, Vietnam Veterans of America, and the staff of the Vietnam Veterans Memorial.

SCHOLARS AND OTHER INFORMED PERSONS

The following persons were exceptionally helpful:

For Christian matters: the Bollandists (Brussels), the Armenian Catholic Exarchate of the U.S. and Canada, various liturgical scholars and church officials (about two dozen) in the U.S. and abroad, and a Carmelite monk in Puerto Rico.

Michelle Tafreshi and Yassaman Djalali, librarians, for information about the Persian calendar; the Spertus Library (Chicago), for information about the Jewish calendar; David Wyatt (Cornell University) and two Thai Buddhist monks, for information about the Southeast Asian Buddhist calendar; and Professor Cheng, Tsai-sa (University of Wis.–Madison, East Asian Department) for information regarding the Chinese calendar.

Lawrence Baldassaro (University of Wis.–Milwaukee, Department of French, Italian, and Comparative Literature); Stewart Brand, of the *Whole Earth Catalog;* Cyclone Covey (Wake Forest University); Gaylord Nelson at the Wilderness Society; Harold Scheub (University of Wis.–Madison, African Studies Department); Mark Thiel (University of Wis.–Milwaukee); a scholar of Mildred Fish Harnack; the creator of Master Gardener Day; a midwife, concerning International Midwifery Day; an amateur historian of Freemasonry, concerning Albert Pike; a historian specializing in the history of St. Augustine, Fla.

Many Native American informants from numerous nations (particularly Cherokee, Iroquois, and Hochunk/Winnebago); a raft of serving or returned Peace Corps Volunteers; and a host of informed citizens of various countries.

Several fellow calendar makers, particularly Phoenix, of Phoenix and Arabeth (Ukiah, Calif.).

CHRISTIAN

"The Calendar of the Church Year," in *The Book of Common Prayer, According to the Use in the Episcopal Church.* New York: The Church Hymnal Corporation and Seabury Pr., 1977.

Bugnini, Annibale. *The Reform of the Liturgy, 1948–1975.* Trans. Matthew J. O'Connell. Collegeville, Minn.: Liturgical Pr., 1990.

Butler, Alban. *Lives of the Saints.* 1956. Rev. ed.: Herbert Thurston. 4 vols. Westminster, Md.: Christian Classics, 1981.

Church Calendar and Typicon (1989). Liberty, Tenn.: St. John of Kronstadt Pr., 1988.

> Authoritative Russian Orthodox annual; also includes feasts unique to the Greek Orthodox Church.

Churchman's Ordo Kalendar for 1994. Erie, Pa.: Ashby, 1993.

> Source of dates for the Episcopalian liturgical year.

Delaney, John J. *Dictionary of Saints.* Garden City, N.Y.: Doubleday, 1980.

> Ample descriptions of saints' lives. Also lists saints as patrons of places and as intercessors for particular circumstances.

Foy, Felician A., O.F.M. ed., and Rose M. Avato, associate ed. *Catholic Almanac.* Huntington, Ind.: Our Sunday Visitor, 1992.

> Annual list of modern feast days.

Interlutheran Worship Comm. *Lutheran Book of Worship.* Minneapolis, Minn.: Augsburg, 1978.

Montes, Marcos J. "The Date of Orthodox Easter, 1875 to 2124." Apr. 12, 1997. Published on the www.marcos@cssa.stanford.edu

The New Catholic Encyclopedia. 15 vol. Catholic Univ. of America. New York: McGraw-Hill, 1967.

Tamoush, Philip. *Directory of Orthodox Parishes and Institutions in North America, 1994 Edition.* Torrance, Calif.: Orthodox People Together, and Oakwood, 1994.

GENERAL

The Astronomical Almanac for the Year 1995. United States Naval Observatory. Washington, D.C.: U.S. GPO, 1994.

Bair, Frank E., ed. *Countries of the World and Their Leaders Yearbook 1993.* 2 vols., with Supplement. Detroit: Gale, 1993.

Barraclough, Geoffrey, ed. *The Times Atlas of World History.* Maplewood, N.J.: Hammond, 1978.

> A joy to anyone who loves maps. Its listings of years for battles and political realignments are very helpful.

Belanger, Michael, ed. *Merriam-Webster's Pocket Biographical Dictionary.* Springfield, Mass.: Merriam-Webster, 1996.

> An updated version of the "Biographical Names" section of the superb *Merriam-Webster's Collegiate Dictionary* (10th edition).

Central Intelligence Agency. *The World Fact Book, 1988.* Washington, D.C.: U.S. GPO, 1987.

Chase's Annual Events, the Day-by-Day Directory to 1994. Chicago: Contemporary, 1993.

> Lists a huge variety of events and anniversaries, arranged chronologically for the current year. Its particular strengths are U.S. events (both hoary and upstart), historical and biographical anniversaries from all countries, and current presidential proclamations. Includes the information source for a festival, with address and phone number.

Chase's Sports Calendar of Events, 1997. Chicago: NTC/Contemporary, 1996.

Famighetti, Robert, ed. *The World Almanac and Book of Facts, 1994; 1996, 1998.* Mahwah, N.J.: World Almanac, 1993; 1995; 1997.

> Lists addresses and phone numbers of countries' embassies to the U.S.; gives precise dates of independence and of other events. Includes a perpetual calendar for all years of the Gregorian and Julian calendars.

Grun, Bernard. *The Timetables of History: A Horizontal Linkage of People and Events.* New York: Simon and Schuster, 1963, 1975.

REFERENCES

Hunter, Brian, ed. *The Statesman's Year-Book: Statistical and Historical Annual of the States of the World, for the Year 1993–1994*. New York: St. Martin's, 1993.

Long, Kim. *The Moon Book*. Boulder, Colo.: Johnson, 1988.

Lye, Keith. *The Portable World Factbook*. 2nd ed. New York: Avon, 1997.

MacDonald, Margaret R. *Folklore of World Holidays*. Detroit: Gale, 1992.

Meeus, Jean. *Astronomical Tables of the Sun, Moon and Planets*. Richmond, Va.: Willmann-Bell, 1983; 2nd ed., 1995.

> Gives data through A.D. 2025 for some events, and through A.D. 6000 for others; also gives data well back into the past. Includes tables for lunar phases, solstices, equinoxes, perihelion/aphelion, etc.

Planetary and Lunar Coordinates for the Years 1984–2000. Prepared by H.M. Stationary Office, Nautical Almanac Office, and the U.S. Naval Observatory, Nautical Almanac Office, London and Washington, D.C.: U.S. GPO, 1983.

> Essential for anyone working with lunar calendars; includes data on lunar phases, equinoxes, solstices, apsides, and eclipses. A new edition will not be issued; however, for full solar system data, the observatory's astronomers recommend the excellent tables by Jean Meeus.

Schmidt, Richard. *Phases of the Moon 2000–2049*. U.S. Naval Observatory, Circular No. 169. Washington, D.C. Nov. 4, 1986.

Spicer, Dorothy G. *The Book of Festivals*. 1937. Reprint: Detroit: Gale, 1969.

Thompson, Sue Ellen, and Barbara W. Carlson. *Holidays, Festivals, and Celebrations of the World Dictionary*. Detroit: Omnigraphics, 1994.

> A wonderful book, giving deep detail about a selected collection of notable festivals and observances. It lets each festival come alive in the reader's mind.

Urdang, Laurence, and Christine Donohue. *Holidays and Anniversaries around the World*. Detroit; Gale, 1983.

CALENDAR SYSTEMS AND HOLIDAYS IN NON-GREGORIAN CALENDARS

GENERAL

Dershowitz, Nachum, and Edward M. Reingold. *Calendrical Calculations*. New York: Cambridge Univ. Press, 1997.

> Explains the structure of 14 calendars and provides algorithmic formulas for computing dates in them. Discusses the Gregorian, Julian, Coptic and Ethiopian, Islamic, Persian, Bahá'i, Hebrew, Mayan, Chinese, and Hindu calendars. Readers of the book may also acquire a copy of the authors' computer program for use in calculating Gregorian dates in those calendars. See the book's and authors' home page on the World Wide Web: http://emr.cs.uiuc.edu/home/reingold/calendar-book/index.html.

Gleadow, Rupert. *The Origin of the Zodiac*. New York: Castle, 1968.

> Fascinating discussion of ancient astronomy and calendar systems, by a well-grounded astrologer. Contains precise dates of various ancient events.

Harvey, O. L. *Calendar Conversions by Way of the Julian Day Number*. Philadelphia: American Philosophical Society, 1983.

Marshack, Alexander. *The Roots of Civilization: the Cognitive Beginnings of Man's First Art, Symbol, and Notation*. 1st ed. New York: McGraw-Hill, 1971.

CHINESE

Bodde, Derk. *Annual Customs and Festivals in Peking, As Recorded in the Yen-ching Shi-shih-chi by Tun, Li-Ch'en*. 2nd ed. Trans. and anno. Derk Bodde. Hong Kong: Hong Kong Univ. Press, 1965.

Bredon, Juliet, and Igor Mitrofanov. *The Moon Year: A Record of Chinese Customs and Festivals*, 1927. New York: Paragon Reprint, 1966.

> Contains many interesting details.

Hsu, His-Chi. *Newly Compiled Chinese 3000–Year Calendar Indexing Table* (Hsin pien Chung-kuo san chien nien li jih chien so piao). Beijing, China: People's Educational Publication Society. 1992.

Contains tables listing the first day of each lunar month of the Chinese calendar, over 3000 years.

ISLAMIC

Ahmad, Imad-ad-Dean. *A Uniform Islamic Calendar for the Western Hemisphere (1411 A.H.–1413 A.H.).* Imad-ad-Dean, Inc., 4323 Rosedale Ave., Bethesda MD 20814. 40 pp.

Summarizes several current methods of determining the start of the Islamic month (Malaysian, Egyptian, and Saudi) and proposes an Islamic calendar uniform for the entire world. Note that even since this pamphlet's publication, the Islamic calendar's rules for determining the start of the month have evolved. Mr. Ahmad also answered crucial questions and saved me from error in an important matter.

Esposito, John L., ed. *The Oxford Encyclopedia of the Modern Islamic World.* N.Y.: Oxford Univ. Press, 1995.

Freeman-Grenville, G.S.P. *The Muslim and Christian Calendars, Being Tables for the Conversion of Muslim and Christian Dates from the Hijra to the Year A.D. 2000.* 2d ed. London: Rex Collings, 1977.

Very useful explanation of the system, with formal tables for converting Islamic to Gregorian dates.

Glasse, Cyril. *The Concise Encyclopedia of Islam.* San Francisco: Harper, 1989.

JEWISH

Encyclopedia Judaica. New York: Macmillan, 1971.

Jewish Holiday Calendar 1979–1999. Union of Orthodox Jewish Congregations of America. 116 E. 27th St., New York, NY 10001. 212/563-4000.

Jewish Holiday Calendar 1993–2010. Union of Orthodox Jewish Congregations of America. 116 E. 27th St., New York, NY 10001. 212/563-4000.

REGIONS AND COUNTRIES

As discussed in "Primary Sources," embassies and official tourism bureaus are excellent sources of information. Two series of travel books are also especially helpful. Books in the "Insight Guides" series are culturally sophisticated and offer a deeper "second look" at the country. They are a joy to read. The information on places, festivals, public holidays, historical events, and persons is illuminating. Books in the "Lonely Planet" series are grassroots books, compendious and packed with loving detail. Festivals and other observances described nowhere else are found here.

THE UNITED NATIONS

Department of Public Information, Public Inquiries Unit. 212/963-4475.

A font of helpful information on the United Nations days of special observance and all other United Nations matters.

THE EUROPEAN UNION

Permanent United Nations Mission of the European Union.

UNITED STATES

Special Days and Weeks for Planning the School Calendar (annual publication). Educational Research Service. 2000 Clarendon Blvd., Arlington, VA 22201. 703/243-2100.

A major resource. Reproduces each state's actual statutes regarding official public holidays and school holidays. Also includes an extensive list of important anniversaries and holidays for teachers to keep in mind.

STATE HANDBOOKS

Most states publish a handbook, manual, directory, almanac, or blue book that lists state holidays and other events.

Index

BERNARD TRAWICKY is a calendar maker and text editor for the highly regarded *International Calendar,* published annually since 1987 by the Returned Peace Corps Volunteers of Wisconsin/Madison. He enjoys seeking out holidays and festivals from around the world and, in the process, has mastered the intricacies of many calendar systems.